THIRD EDITION

STATISTICS FOR CRIMINAL JUSTICE AND CRIMINOLOGY

THIRD EDITION

STATISTICS FOR CRIMINAL JUSTICE AND CRIMINOLOGY

Dean John Champion

Texas A & M International University

Richard D. Hartley

University of Texas at San Antonio

Prentice Hall
Upper Saddle River, New Jersey
Columbus, Ohio

Library of Congress Cataloging-in-Publication Data

Champion, Dean J.
    Statistics for criminal justice and criminology / Dean John Champion, Richard D. Hartley. — 3rd ed.
        p. cm.
Includes bibliographical references and index.
ISBN-13: 978-0-13-613585-2 (alk. paper)
ISBN-10: 0-13-613585-4 (alk. paper)
1. Criminal justice, Administration of—Research—Methodology.   2. Criminology—Research—Methodology.
    I. Hartley, Richard D.   II. Title.
HV7419.5.C43 2010
519.5024'364—dc22

2008045133

Senior Acquisitions Editor: Tim Peyton
Editorial Assistant: Alicia Kelly
Media Project Manager: Karen Bretz
Director of Marketing: David Gesell
Marketing Manager: Adam Kloza
Marketing Coordinator: Alicia Dysert
Production Manager: Wanda Rockwell
Creative Director: Jayne Conte
Cover Design: Bruce Kenselaar

Credits and acknowledgments borrowed from other sources and reproduced, with permission, in this textbook appear on appropriate page within text.

Pearson Education Ltd., London
Pearson Education Singapore, Pte. Ltd
Pearson Education, Canada, Ltd
Pearson Education–Japan
Pearson Education Australia PTY, Limited

Pearson Education North Asia, Ltd., Hong Kong
Pearson Educación de Mexico, S.A. de C.V.
Pearson Education Malaysia, Pte. Ltd
Pearson Education Upper Saddle River,
    New Jersey

Prentice Hall
is an imprint of

PEARSON

www.pearsonhighered.com

ISBN-13: 978-0-13-613585-2
ISBN-10:   0-13-613585-4

To the memory of Chablis, one of my best friends.

Dean John Champion

*To the memory of Dr. Dennis W. Roncek, a true mentor
in every sense of the word.*

Richard David Hartley

PREFACE

Statistics for Criminal Justice and Criminology, 3/e, is about how to apply statistical procedures, both descriptive and inferential, to collected data. The book is designed with students in mind, to assist them in acquiring a reasonable appreciation and understanding for why statistical procedures are used in criminological investigations. Within the social sciences, a broad range of research techniques, data-collection strategies, and analytical tools exists that serves the needs of most professionals who conduct independent research investigations. Although certain research procedures and statistical techniques may be relevant only for certain specialized types of investigations, there are numerous techniques and procedures that may be generalizable and applicable to most fields, including criminology and criminal justice.

Much of the technical language and symbolic notation used to describe statistical strategies in this book has been simplified. At the same time, consideration has been given to those who may wish to use this book as a reference or guide in their future statistical work. Thus, several topics have been included that are often given extended coverage in more advanced texts. A key objective is to describe and explain some of the more complex statistical procedures in the most simple fashion. Extensive use of examples drawn from the criminological and criminal justice literature is our effort to make this book user-friendly, to enable criminal justice and criminology students, together with other social science majors, the best opportunity to relate statistical tests to practical problems they will confront when doing research or reading research conducted by others.

THE ORGANIZATION OF THIS BOOK

The plan of this book is to provide a set of statistical tools for use by undergraduate students who wish to read current criminological and social scientific literature and understand what they are reading. There is a dual emphasis here. One emphasis is upon "doing statistics." This means that nuts-and-bolts procedural explanations will be provided so that students will know how to apply particular statistical tests and techniques in practical research situations. The second emphasis is upon "understanding statistics." This means that we are concerned with your understanding of whatever statistical techniques you apply when collected research is being analyzed. Both doing and understanding are emphasized here.

There is also a dual level of statistical coverage. The first level of statistical coverage consists of simpler tests and techniques, especially those catering to undergraduates, most of whom will likely never do social research of any kind. These tests and techniques will be fully explained so that they may be applied and understood in social research read by these students. If some students decide to go the extra mile and do some research on their own, they will have adequate statistical tools to accomplish elementary tasks.

The second level of statistical coverage is directly relevant for students who will take on more significant research projects, such as doctoral dissertations, master's theses, and other types of research. More advanced statistical techniques are presented in later chapters which will be of use to them. Thus, the book is useful at both the undergraduate and graduate levels, inasmuch as a broad range of statistical techniques is covered and discussed. Individual professors with different interests in how the subject matter of this course ought to be taught have the pleasant flexibility of choosing which tests to include in their lectures and examinations and which ones they will exclude, therefore. This is considered to be a flexibility option available to anyone using this book in their particular course. Most professors aren't going to have the time to teach the whole book to students anyway. Different sections of chapters may be skipped, therefore, if professors only want to convey simpler material and provide an overview of what statistics is and what it can do. This pertains to more specialized chapters later in the book dealing with statistical inference, tests of significance of difference, and correlational procedures. We have attempted to provide a reasonably comprehensive set of tools for these respective purposes. It is certainly not expected that all material will be covered in a single semester, therefore. This is why picking and choosing is best left up to individual instructors. Some statistical tests and correlational procedures have deliberately been excluded from some chapters, because they are somewhat redundant. What is presented, however, is considered essential to one's growth and understanding of statistical principles and how they may be applied in the social research process.

Chapter 1 begins with an explanation of how statistics relates to social research. Statistics is actually a supporting player in the overall research process. It is useful for describing gathered data as well as making decisions about it. Chapter 1 presents the research process in a general way, where research problems and problem formulation are described. Once a research problem has been identified, then an investigation of that problem occurs. At some point, data are gathered by various means. It is beyond the scope of this book to include all research methods used for data-gathering purposes, such as questionnaire construction, interview construction and administration, observational techniques, analysis of secondary sources, and other data-gathering options. However, sufficient information is presented to show where statistics fits into this process. There is a circularity associated with the research process. This means that once the research cycle is completed, it may be repeated by other investigators. This process reflects the cumulative nature of scientific inquiry and how we raise our certainty level about why different events happen and how best they can be explained.

Variables are described, both as discrete/continuous and independent/dependent in their respective functions. Variables are a fundamental feature of the research process, and we must understand them and how they are conceptualized in order to manipulate them statistically. Our notation system is briefly described. Quite frankly, most pure statistics books that do not cater to the social sciences contain far more notation than is necessary to perform elementary statistical functions. Our intent is to simplify such notation by reducing it to the minimal notation needed to perform basic statistical functions. Much of the symbolic notation that *could* be used in elaborating statistical formulae are eliminated, therefore. It is easier on the eyes, and far less intimidating, to view more simplified formulae than more complex formulae with superfluous, unnecessary notation.

The functions of statistical procedures are explained. These functions include describing data, making decisions about hypothesis tests, and making inferences about population values from statistics collected from samples of persons. All statistical procedures in this book are designed for samples of persons rather than analyses of entire populations of them. Therefore, several principles of statistical inference are illustrated and explained in some detail. It is also the case that every statistical procedure requires that one or more assumptions should be met before these procedures can be applied in social research properly. Several of these assumptions are discussed and explained. Failure to meet one or more assumptions when applying statistical procedures for any practical purpose jeopardizes the meaning associated with one's results or outcomes. The overall integrity of one's research is called into question as a result. Some of these assumptions include randomness, the level of measurement, sample size, and whether samples are independent or related. Other assumptions are mentioned.

Chapter 2 is a specialized piece dealing with the potential application of *SPSS*, or the *Statistical Package for the Social Sciences*. This is one of several software programs available to researchers to enable them to process their numerical data quickly and easily. Many statistical functions are performed rapidly, once appropriate data have been entered. The general nature of *SPSS* is described. Explained is what *SPSS* does and does not do, and how sometimes we are lulled into a sense that computers can do everything for us. Unfortunately, they cannot. Human intervention is always required to interpret research findings. *SPSS* doesn't interpret one's research work for them, therefore. Several myths associated with *SPSS* are discussed and explained. Often it is simpler to perform certain statistical procedures by hand, using a hand calculator, than it is to enter information into an *SPSS* software program and carry out similar functions. In early chapters dealing with measures of central tendency and dispersion, inspection is often required to yield accurate results about one's collected data. *SPSS* programming is not needed at all. Chapter 2 is not a pitch to use *SPSS*. Rather, it is provided only for those who have access either to a student version of it or the more comprehensive *SPSS* components, which are described. At various points throughout the book, highlighted sections will feature *SPSS* applications as alternatives to manual calculations of formulae where appropriate. Some descriptive, inferential, and other statistical procedures cannot be completed easily through the application of *SPSS*. In any event, instructors who do not have *SPSS* or don't desire to use it may skip Chapter 2 without affecting students' comprehension of statistics, what they can do, and how they can be understood most effectively.

Chapter 3 is a discussion of different graphic devices for describing one's collected data. These include pie charts, bar graphs, frequency polygons, histograms, and other graphic aids to describe one's findings. Additionally, frequency distributions will be discussed. Included in this discussion will be strategies for constructing frequency distributions, understanding intervals and their properties, and graphically portraying such distributions. Percentages, proportions, ratios, and rate computations will also be presented and discussed.

Chapters 4 and 5 respectively cover several important descriptive procedures used to depict values of central tendency and dispersion in arrays of scores. Chapter 4 examines three measures of central tendency: the mode, median, and mean. Each of these measures depicts how scores in a distribution tend to focus around. Each has their weaknesses and strengths given the type of data collected. Applications of these measures are discussed. Chapter 5 examines various measures of variability. These measures depict how scores focus around certain points in a distribution. Thus, both the points around which scores focus and how they are distributed around these points are the subject matter of these chapters.

Chapter 6 examines the normal curve or unit normal distribution. This is a critical chapter in that it covers a basic distribution upon which many statistical tests are based. Normal distributions are described in detail, including scores, known as Z scores, which are used to represent different points along the horizontal axis of normal distributions. When scores in an actual distribution of raw scores are approximately normal in form, then generalizations can be made about these raw scores that can also be made about the normal distribution. The normal distribution is also an assumption underlying the legitimate application of various statistical tests and measures. Nonnormal distributions will also be discussed. It will be seen in later chapters that whenever normality cannot be assumed, several statistical tests that do not require this assumption become extremely useful for one's data analyses.

Chapter 7 is also a critical chapter in understanding statistics, particularly their inferential functions. The process of hypothesis testing is described in detail, including research, null, and statistical hypotheses. Statistical inference is explained and illustrated, including point and interval estimation. These applications pertain to estimating population parameters. Confidence interval construction is examined. Expected values of statistics, standard error terms, and Type I and Type II errors are presented and explained as well. All of this information comprises what are known as decision rules that govern statistical decision making. Researchers frequently test hypotheses with tests of significance. There are different kinds of tests of significance. Each will be described and explained. Both directional and nondirectional hypotheses will be illustrated, and these relate closely with one- and two-tailed hypothesis tests.

Chapters 8, 9, and 10 are discussions of various types of tests of significance. These tests of significance are arranged by the level of measurement assumed for their computation. Chapter 8 examines tests of significance for data measured according to an interval scale. Procedures such as the t and Z test will be illustrated for both one- and two-sample applications. Samples may be related, and a two-sample Sandler A statistic will be presented. For k-sample tests, an F test for analysis of variance will be discussed and illustrated. A two-way analysis of variance will also be shown. The focus of these discussions is more upon how these tests can be interpreted rather than actually applying them. Manual methods for applying these tests are provided, as well as a supplemental *SPSS* alternative. Several assumptions underlie the proper application of such tests and these assumptions are illustrated. Some of these assumptions involve statistical tests as well, and several of the many tests available for these purposes will be examined. Two post hoc or postmortem tests will be described. Once it is determined that k samples differ, it is often unknown which of k samples are actually different. These post hoc tests are designed to answer this question in one easy sequence of steps.

Chapter 9 focuses upon nominal-level statistical tests of significance. This chapter, as well as Chapter 10 which examines ordinal- and interval-level nonparametric significance tests, is organized according to single-sample tests, two-independent sample tests, two-related sample tests, k-independent sample tests, and k-related sample tests. These tests are designated as nonparametric, inasmuch as the normal distribution is not a requirement for their appropriate application. Chapters 9 and 10 should not be regarded as unimportant or trivial, simply because they cover less well-known statistical procedures. The fact is that often, traditional parametric tests familiar to most instructors may not be appropriate to apply under certain circumstances. These nonparametric tests are useful alternatives whenever parametric tests are inappropriate. Circumstances of their use will be explained in detail, and comparisons will be made with the tests in these chapters and their parametric counterparts.

Chapters 11 and 12 examine different measures of association. These measures correlate or associate two variables. In Chapter 11, the meaning of association is explained. Several meanings are discussed, with the most important meaning being a proportional-reduction-in-error (PRE) interpretation that may be given to various correlational procedures. Examples of different types of two-variable associations are graphically illustrated. Chapter 11 examines measures of association designed for two nominal-level variables as well as two ordinal-level variables. Chapter 12 extends this discussion by examining several measures of association for data measured according to the interval level of measurement. The chapter further examines two-variable associations where the two variables are measured according to different measurement levels. For instance, procedures for determining associations between a nominal–ordinal combination, a nominal–interval combination, and an ordinal–interval combination will be presented. These specialized tests are not found in *SPSS*, with a few exceptions. But their importance is such that researchers should consider their application anyway, since in earlier decades, the practice among researchers was to reduce data measured according to different levels of measurement to their lowest common denominator, the lowest measurement level. These association procedures avoid this problem and enable investigators to exploit their data fully. Again, if instructors wish to bypass these tests, they may do so. But later, coverage of these tests may be useful for those who plan to do more extensive research at the graduate level or in their professional careers. The chapter concludes by providing a description of choosing the most appropriate correlational procedure under various circumstances.

Chapters 13, 14, and 15 are considered quite advanced chapters, chapters that cater to students doing graduate-level research. Chapter 13 examines multivariate statistics where relations between k variables are explored. Beta coefficients, standardized effects, error, robustness, and parsimony are covered in some detail. Path analysis is presented with examples from criminological literature. Structural equation modeling is discussed.

Chapter 14 looks at multivariate statistics, including an extension of multiple regression. Ordinary least squares regression is treated, together with multicollinearity, collinearity diagnostics, alternative remedies for collinearity, interaction effects, and dummy variables. Analysis of such data, including OLS regression interpretation, is presented.

Chapter 15 concludes with a discussion of multivariate analysis focusing upon multiple regression with limited dependent variables. Logistic regression is treated and explained, including various interaction effects with logistic regression. Poisson and negative binominal regression are covered. Overdispersion and various limitations of count data are discussed. Multicollinearity for logistic regression techniques is examined.

Some pedagogical features of this book include a full set of interpretive tables in Appendix A. Each chapter has problems to solve at chapter ends. These include both short-answer essay questions and numerical problems. Answers for selected numerical problems are presented in Appendix B. Chapters also include, where appropriate, short discussions of *SPSS* alternative applications, which can be used if students have access to *SPSS* software programs. Where students do not have access to this type of software, such alternative explanations and illustrations may conveniently be skipped. The problems at chapter ends have deliberately been kept simple, because again, our focus for the book is upon understanding statistics and how these tests can be applied and interpreted. It is unnecessary to include exotic and elaborate numerical problems to get across the subject matter, which is simply to understand what is being done and why.

Emphasis has also been placed on advantages, disadvantages, and potential applications of these statistical techniques for criminology and criminal justice. It must be remembered that criminal justice is a sociological creation. Therefore, virtually every statistical technique in this book has been derived from some social science source either directly or indirectly relevant to sociology. Criminology examples and illustrations from the criminal justice literature have been used almost exclusively to make the book user-friendly for students majoring in these fields. However, the practicality of these tests is such that *all* social science students can benefit from their usefulness, regardless of the specificity of examples provided. We welcome any comments and criticisms, especially any errors that may be detected in our examples and illustrations. Statistics books are plagued with problems of numerical accuracy. We have attempted to avoid these problems, but no book is perfect in this respect. Any errors found are our responsibility, therefore, and every effort has been made to minimize them.

One final feature of this book is an accompanying Instructor's Manual with suggested tests that instructors may give in their classes. All problems presented in the Instructor's Manual have numerical answers provided. In cases where questions have been asked about why one or more tests are appropriate or inappropriate for particular kinds of data analysis, brief answers have been provided. Our hope is that this book will be well-received and understood according to our original intent. We seek to simplify, not confound.

In retrospect, perhaps the best way to approach studying the problems in this book is to view it as a collection of strategies for problem-solving. Each strategy that might be used in the investigation of particular criminal justice-related or criminological problems has weaknesses and strengths, limitations and benefits. These features must be weighed carefully as they are considered for application in problem-solutions. The problems are research questions, questions about criminological and criminal justice–related phenomena about which we seek information and answers.

Our general intention is to improve our understanding of the events that occur around us. Perhaps our investigations will lead to certain practical policy decisions. However, our investigations may be unrelated to public policy or to anything of practical value other than a simple understanding and appreciation for why certain events occur. Our position is that we should seek a healthy balance between our practical, substantive concerns and our theoretical ones. While some research may have direct relevance for a particular intervention program to be used for parolees in halfway houses to assist in their community reintegration, other research may not easily be adapted to any helping program. This state of affairs is perhaps as it should be, especially in view of the great diversity of interests among criminologists and criminal justice professionals, the problems they select for study, and the ways they choose to investigate these problems.

We would like to acknowledge the work of several persons who were especially helpful in seeing this book through to completion. First, we thank our editor, Tim Peyton, for his confidence and strong support. His assistant, Alicia Kelly, was instrumental in so many ways, facilitating reviews of earlier manuscript versions and the preliminary production process generally. We appreciate her diligence and constant encouragement. There are many others at Pearson Education who work behind the scenes, preparing art, tables, figures, and other materials that have made this book more presentable for students. We also wish to thank our reviewers, past and present. For this edition, we gratefully acknowledge the constructive criticisms and insights of Arvind Verma, Indiana University-Bloomington; Ruohui Zhao, University of Nebraska-Omaha; David M. Baker, University of Toledo; and Brian Johnson, University of Maryland. Their suggestions for improvement were taken seriously, and we owe them much for this book's coverage and presentation. Statistics texts are especially vulnerable to numerical errors. In every way, we have sought to present a student-friendly, error-free book that will enable students to understand the basics of statistical procedures in the research they conduct.

Dean John Champion **and** *Richard D. Hartley*

BRIEF CONTENTS

CONTENTS

ABOUT THE AUTHORS

Dean John Champion

Dean John Champion is Professor of Criminal Justice and Sociology, Texas A&M International University, Laredo, Texas. Dr. Champion has taught at the University of Tennessee-Knoxville, California State University-Long Beach, and Minot State University. He earned his Ph.D. from Purdue University and B.S. and M.A. degrees from Brigham Young University. He also completed several years of law school at the Nashville School of Law. Dr. Champion has written over 40 texts and/or edited works and maintains memberships in 11 professional organizations. He is a lifetime member of the American Society of Criminology and the Academy of Criminal Justice Sciences. He is a former editor of the Academy of Criminal Justice Sciences/Anderson Publishing Company Series on *Issues in Crime and Justice* and the *Journal of Crime and Justice*. He is a contributing author for the *Encarta Encyclopedia 2000* for Microsoft. He was Visiting Scholar at the National Center for Juvenile Justice and is a former president of the Midwestern Criminal Justice Association.

Among his published books for Prentice Hall include *Administration of Criminal Justice: Structure, Function, and Process*; *Research Methods for Criminal Justice and Criminology, 3/e*; *U.S. Supreme Court Cases: Briefs and Key Terms*; *Criminal Courts: Structure, Process, and Issues, 2/e* (w/Richard D. Hartley and Gary A. Rabe); *The Juvenile Justice System: Delinquency, Processing, and the Law, 6/e*; *Corrections in the United States: A Contemporary Perspective, 4/e*; *Probation, Parole, and Community Corrections, 6/e*; *Crime Prevention in America*; *Policing in the Community* (w/George Rush). Works from other publishers include *Sentencing*; *The Sociology of Organizations*; *Research Methods in Social Relations*; *Sociology*; *The U.S. Sentencing Guidelines*; *Juvenile Transfer Hearings* (w/G. Larry Mays); and *Measuring Offender Risk*; *The American Dictionary of Criminal Justice: Key Terms and Leading Supreme Court Cases, 3/e*; *Police Misconduct in America*; and *Criminal Justice in the United States, 2/e*. Dr. Champion's specialty interests include juvenile justice, criminal justice administration, corrections, and statistics/methods.

Richard D. Hartley

Richard D. Hartley is Assistant Professor of Criminal Justice at the University of Texas at San Antonio. He earned his Ph.D. from the University of Nebraska and B.S. and M.S. degrees from Minot State University. Dr. Hartley is the author of *Corporate Crime* and coauthor of *Criminal Courts: Structure, Process, Issues, 2/e*, as well as several peer-reviewed journal articles. His research interests include disparities in sentencing practices, especially at the federal level, prosecutorial and judicial discretion, sentencing for narcotics violations, and quantitative methods. He was recently awarded an American Statistical Association/Bureau of Justice Statistics grant to study interdistrict variation in the receipt of substantial assistance departures.

CHAPTER 1

Statistics in the Research Process

Chapter Outline

Key Terms

Questions for Review

References

Chapter Objectives

After reading this chapter, the following objectives will be realized:

1. understanding the different meanings of statistics;
2. learning about research problems and alternative explanations and solutions;
3. learning the relationships between research and theory and statistics and research;
4. learning about the circularity of the research process;
5. understanding variables and different dimensions of variables;
6. understanding the significance and importance of notation systems;
7. learning about the functions of statistical procedures; and
8. learning about the assumptions underlying statistical procedures and their application.

INTRODUCTION

The following findings have been derived from five research investigations:

- Offenders who are paroled to disadvantaged neighborhoods recidivate at a greater rate than offenders who are paroled to resource rich or affluent communities (Kubrin and Stewart, 2006:165).
- In police–suspect encounters, with all other factors being equal, white police officers are more likely to make arrests of suspects compared with black police officers (Brown and Frank, 2006:116–118).
- Inmates who volunteer to participate in a Life Connections Program in prison have lower recidivism rates than inmates who do not participate in the Program (Camp et al., 2006:545–546).
- Supervised paroled female offenders will have lower recidivism rates compared with unsupervised paroled female offenders (Solomon, 2006:32–33).
- In states with sentencing guideline schemes, larger criminal courts will be more likely to grant downward departures in sentencing offenders compared with smaller criminal courts (Johnson, 2005:768–769).

How can these investigators make such statements? How do we know about their factual accuracy and generalizability? Each of these statements relies on statistics and **statistical evidence** for their truthfulness and validity. Information has been compiled through **research**, and on the basis of **research findings**, various factual statements have been derived. For instance, for each of these statements, information was obtained and conclusions were reached based on research findings. A more detailed account of what these researchers did to discover these results is given below.

- Charles Kubrin and Eric Stewart (2006) studied 5,002 offenders newly exposed to community corrections supervision during the year 2000. They identified several individual-level characteristics (e.g., age; prior record; nature of conviction offense; gender; race-ethnicity) and several neighborhood-level characteristics (e.g., average poverty rate of neighborhood; proportion of persons on public assistance; proportion of persons unemployed; median family income) and used "multilevel modeling techniques" as well as "descriptive statistics and correlations" to analyze the findings from the data they collected.

- Robert Brown and James Frank (2006) studied samples of 82 white and 54 black police officers affiliated with the Cincinnati (Ohio) Police Department (CPD) through observation from April 1997 to April 1998. The CPD had a 996-officer force at that time. Data collected included age, race/ethnicity, apparent mental state of suspects, type of suspect behavior prompting the police–suspect encounter, and gender. "Descriptive statistics" and "multivariate analysis" were used to analyze and interpret collected information.

- Scott Camp et al. (2006) collected information from 999 inmates in five different prisons between August 2004 and May 2005. Of these, 407 inmates participated in the Life Connections Program, while 592 other inmates did not participate. Camp et al. used "descriptive statistics" and a "conditional logistic model" to analyze collected data and determine differences between the two inmate samples relating to their recidivism and other factors.

- Amy Solomon (2006) studied data released by the Bureau of Justice Statistics for 1994, which included 38,624 offenders released on parole at that time. Female parolees made up 7 percent of the parolees studied. Solomon conducted follow-up comparisons of female offenders who were supervised and unsupervised in their respective jurisdictions. He used "descriptive statistics," including "averages" and "percentages" to make comparisons between these offenders and the different recidivism rates they exhibited.

- Brian Johnson (2005) studied convicted offenders sentenced in criminal courts under the Pennsylvania Commission on Sentencing for 1997. Pennsylvania criminal courts are known for their frequent departures from sentencing guidelines, both upward and downward. Johnson's data consisted of 42,325 downward departure cases and 143,102 upward departure cases. Courts were divided into small, medium, and large, and Johnson used "hierarchical linear modeling" procedures to analyze collected criminal sentencing data.

A common theme throughout all of these studies is that data were collected and analyzed in some way. These researchers found information that supported these statements. This doesn't mean that these statements are necessarily true. Rather, the research these investigators conducted was supported by some of the findings they derived, based in part on their application of various statistical tests and procedures. It is possible that different investigators studying the same phenomena and using different samples may arrive at different conclusions, even contradictory ones, over time. For each of these studies, therefore, statistics were used to analyze collected data. Researchers made interpretations of these statistics, and these and other findings were derived and reported.

This book is about statistics and the application of statistical tests and procedures in the analysis of collected data or research information. *The Reader's Digest, Time, Newsweek, U.S. News & World Report* and newspapers are some of the many documents published daily, weekly, or monthly where statistical information is reported. Almost every reading source requires a limited amount of statistical knowledge in order for readers to understand the material presented.

In politics, city, state, and federal elections always include claims and counterclaims by political opponents. Incumbent mayors may say that during their terms, the city's crime rate decreased by 20 percent. The present mayor wants voters to think he/she was responsible for the crime reduction. But opponents will cite their own statistical information which may show that crime actually increased by 30 percent. Disputes follow where each candidate's statistical information is closely scrutinized by citizens and political commentators. Quite often, these different opponents are citing accurate crime figures, although the crimes they talk about may be different ones and at different points in time. Thus, the results seem contradictory but they are not. Each side uses statistical information to its own advantage to earn support from voters. The public is understandably confused by these "contradictory" results.

In economic affairs, the U.S. Food and Drug Administration (FDA) screens, evaluates, and limits the distribution of drugs and other products for public consumption. FDA actions and recommendations have many implications for our personal health. Every FDA recommendation is accompanied by statistical evidence and findings. Statistical results from various scientific investigations are responsible for most FDA assertions and decisions.

These examples are only a few of many that suggest statistics performs a key role in influencing social policies and consumer behavior, as well as public voting patterns in political elections. Statistics are a pervasive and vital part of our lives. Our society is increasingly complex, and it is important for us to know what statistics are and how statistical information can benefit us. A knowledge of statistics assists us in understanding the literature we read, particularly the professional journals published in our respective areas of criminal justice, criminology, and other social sciences. Also, it is important to understand various limitations of statistics. Sometimes, people use statistical information as the basis for largely unsupported claims about what they have found. We need to understand statistics enough to know the difference between responsible and irresponsible statements which have been allegedly supported by statistical results.

WHAT ARE STATISTICS?

Statistics has at least three different meanings.

- Statistics refers to the general body of methods and procedures used to assemble, describe, and infer facts from numerical data. Information we collect about people and their characteristics, including parolee recidivism and recidivism rates, juvenile homicides, jail suicides, juvenile delinquency trends, sentencing patterns, stress and burnout among corrections officers, police misconduct and excessive use of force, victimizations, and evaluations of crime-prevention strategies are all converted to numerical data. These numbers are manipulated and analyzed in different ways. We study these numerical patterns. Based on our studies of these numbers and how they are distributed, we learn much about the phenomena we are studying.

  If we are interested in studying jail suicides and their patterns, how do we know that jail suicides are increasing from one year to the next? If we study the effectiveness of two different community reintegration programs for parolees, how do we know whether one program is better than another? What are the criteria for deciding how much significance ought to be attached to jail suicide patterns or community reintegration program effectiveness? How much labor turnover occurs among probation and parole officers each year and why? How do stress and burnout relate to labor turnover?

- Statistics involves the application of tests and procedures that can be used to analyze and make decisions about collected data or research information. Over many decades, social scientists have created a wide array of tests and procedures to help us to make objective decisions about whatever we observe. These procedures are generally accepted by criminal justice scholars and criminologists and comprise a common core of tools to help us answer our research questions.

- Statistics refers to numerical, graphic, and tabular descriptions of collected data. Descriptive statistics, such as the mode, median, mean, range, and standard deviation are discussed in Chapters 4 and 5. These are different numerical quantities that describe certain characteristics of the people we investigate. Some researchers include graphs, tables, and other visual aides such as those illustrated and discussed in Chapter 3. We might review a research article that has many charts, figures, tables, graphs, and formulas. The article is full of statistics. Much numerical and graphic data are presented to illustrate what the researchers have found.

  Statistics refers to the characteristics of samples of persons about whom we have collected information. This meaning is most relevant when we distinguish between a **population** and a **sample** taken from it. Populations of persons have certain characteristics, such as average ages, educational levels, a gender distribution, and attitudinal traits. Ordinarily, we do not investigate entire populations of persons. Rather, we study samples of these persons and make generalizations about the populations they represent. The characteristics of these samples are called **statistics** in order to distinguish them from population characteristics. These latter characteristics that describe populations are called **parameters**. Most often researchers study sample statistics to learn about population parameters. Inferences are made about populations based on sample information. A large body of statistics is called "inferential statistics." Such inferential statistics and how they are used will be examined in later chapters.

RESEARCH PROBLEMS AND THEIR SOLUTIONS

All social sciences investigate different types of **research problems.** These research problems are not "problems" in the traditional sense. Research problems relating to criminal justice and criminology are questions of a social nature or various events in need of answers. Let's examine briefly three different hypothetical research problems from different areas of criminology and criminal justice.

- For instance, during the 1990s, juvenile justice investigators and state legislatures experimented with developing more effective mechanisms that could be used by juvenile courts to punish youths for their delinquent acts. One of these mechanisms was the creation of blended sentencing statutes. These are statutes enabling juvenile court judges, even criminal court judges, the option of imposing both a juvenile and an adult punishment on a juvenile for a serious offense. Thus, a 12-year-old juvenile might receive from the juvenile court judge a juvenile punishment of confinement to a juvenile industrial school (the equivalent of an adult prison) until he/she turns 21. The same juvenile court judge might also impose an adult sentence of 25 years upon the same juvenile. Such an adult sentence would commence once the juvenile reached his/her age of adulthood.

  One condition accompanying these blended sentences was that within six months of a juvenile becoming an adult, a hearing would be conducted to determine how well the juvenile behaved while institutionalized in the industrial school. If he/she behaved well, then the committee conducting the hearing would be authorized to waive the adult portion of the sentence. The juvenile would be free and not have to serve any more time for his/her earlier crime. But if the juvenile behaved poorly, violated institutional rules, got into fights, was disruptive, or in other ways posed problems for institution administrators, then the committee would be authorized to allow the adult sentence to proceed the juvenile sentence.

One intent of these blended sentencing statutes, therefore, was to encourage compliance with institutional rules. Youths would seek to avoid the adult penalties imposed and they would be law-abiding and cooperative. They would become involved in educational and vocational programs that would prepare them for jobs as adults. They would participate in anger management and receive other types of counseling for possible drug or alcohol dependencies. Therefore, blended sentencing statutes were believed to offer significant incentives to youths to become law-abiding, productive citizens while confined as juveniles. A research problem related to blended sentencing statutes might be whether such statutes induce law-abiding behavior and conformity with institutional rules.

- A second scenario might involve probation and parole officers and their work effectiveness. It is well established that U.S. probation and parole agencies have high rates of labor turnover. Approximately 25 percent of all new probation and parole officers quit their jobs within the first year they are hired. We don't know why they quit. They just quit. This labor turnover costs probation and parole agencies money, because much of the first year of being a probation or parole officer is spent training these persons to be effective in their job performance and understanding their supervisory roles. We know that some of those who are employed by their respective states move to other states where higher salaries are paid for the same work. Also, some of these state officers may seek employment with federal probation, where job benefits and salaries are greater or higher. But many of these officers quit their jobs because of work stress and burnout. They get frustrated with the clients they supervise. Some may feel that their work is too dangerous. A research problem involving probation and parole officer labor turnover, therefore, might be whether such turnover is the result of work stress and burnout.

- A third scenario might involve judicial disparities when sentencing offenders of different ethnicities or races. It has been found, for instance, that black and white offenders with similar criminal histories and who commit similar crimes often receive disparate sentences from judges. White armed robbers in some jurisdictions may receive more lenient sentences compared with black armed robbers in those same jurisdictions from the same judges. The research problem here is why do such sentencing disparities exist. In a perfect world, those who commit the same crimes and have similar criminal histories should receive the same sentences. When disparate sentences are received by these convicted offenders and these disparities appear to be race- or ethnic-based, we want to know why such disparities exist.

In each of the above cases, a problem is specified (e.g., the effect of blended sentencing statutes on juveniles, labor turnover among probation and parole officers, and judicial sentencing disparities potentially attributable to racial or ethnic differences among convicted offenders). Researchers collect data or information relevant to each of these problems. This information will enable them to understand the problems they are investigating and why these problems occur. Researchers will often use statistics (e.g., measures, tests, descriptors) to answer various questions about these problems and conduct analyses of the data they have collected.

Let's summarize the three different hypothetical research problems presented above.

1. Research problem 1 has to do with blended sentencing statutes for juvenile offenders. Do such statutes encourage youth compliance with institutional rules and personal growth and maturity?
2. Research problem 2 has to do with labor turnover among probation and parole officers. Does type of supervision influence probation/parole officer labor turnover?
3. Research problem 3 has to do with judicial sentencing disparities attributable to race or ethnicity. Does one's race or ethnicity influence one's sentence and how?

An infinite number of research problems exist. All of these research problems are simply questions about why certain events occur (e.g., greater law-abiding behavior among institutionalized juveniles possibly resulting from blended sentencing statutes; greater labor turnover among stressed or burned out probation and parole officers; or the influence of race or ethnicity on the sentences judges impose).

THEORY AND RESEARCH

Theory and research are invariably linked. Theory depends on research to verify it, while research needs theory to guide it. Theory explains events, while research tests these explanations in different ways. In any research project, it is common to devise a **theory** or theoretical schemes or explanatory frameworks. A theory is an integrated body of assumptions, propositions, and definitions related in ways that explain and predict relationships between two or more variables. Theories are designed to explain whatever we expect to find. Researchers tell us their research problem. Then they provide one or more explanations for why they believe the problem exists. These rationales are called **frames of reference** or ways of looking at research problems. They are usually based on the researchers' experiences. These explanations are subsequently tested by analyzing collected data and applying statistical tests.

Almost every professional journal in the social sciences contains articles with accompanying theories about relationships between different phenomena studied. These theoretical schemes explain to readers the logical interrelatedness of different variables. We read these theoretical accounts and explanations for why certain variables are or should be related, and then we examine the findings presented. The information collected, analyzed, and interpreted by investigators are called research findings. Depending on the subjective attitudes and experiences of investigators, different researchers often interpret the same research findings differently. One way of making these subjective interpretations of data more objective is to utilize a common core of statistical tests and procedures. Statistical tests and procedures provide us with an array of objective standards which will yield more consistent interpretations of collected information. It is more difficult to challenge the objectivity of numerical standards compared with one's emotional beliefs and personal opinions. However, despite the objective standards provided by statistical tests, arguments over the meaningfulness of one's data and what it means remain unresolved. This book provides students with the necessary tools to analyze data and make decisions about it.

STATISTICS AND RESEARCH

Whenever someone says that they are "doing research," this usually means they are studying a particular research problem. Some of these research problems were mentioned earlier. As we have seen, these problems are usually "problems" because there is disagreement about how best to explain them. Little agreement exists among investigators about which explanation is best for any particular research problem. And so there is a quest among investigators to determine which explanations of events or problems seem to be most productive. Identifying the best explanations for research problems is not necessarily an easy task. As you may imagine, there are many alternative explanations for the same research problems. However, researchers usually evaluate which explanations are best in terms of their **predictive utility**. This means identifying explanations of events that predict them with the highest degree of accuracy. Statistical procedures and tests help us make these kinds of decisions.

Statistical tests and procedures provide support services for our theories and how we can test them. Statistics and statistical tests are aides, not substitutes, for good thinking, however. In more than a few instances, statistical tests perform minor roles in the overall research process. For some types of research, such as **qualitative research**, statistical tests may not be used at all. Observation and interpretations of written materials, such as letters or autobiographies, seldom rely on statistical procedures. In lieu of statistical test applications, qualitative researchers rely on logic and intrinsic meanings of written descriptions of observed events. **Quantitative research** involves converting collected data to numerical form and analyzing it. Both types of research are important in that they provide different interpretations of whatever is found. Some types of research involve an integration of both qualitative and quantitative analysis of collected data.

THE CIRCULARITY OF THE RESEARCH PROCESS

There are many components that make up the research process. Each part of this process can be viewed as a single link in a chain of events. The chain itself is no stronger than its weakest link. Figure 1.1 shows a diagram of the research process. This is a generic diagram, meaning that it is

Definition of a research problem (some social and/or psychological event in need of an explanation) - - - - - - - - - ->	Frame of reference (our way of looking at the problem) - - - - - - - - - ->	Theoretical scheme
Hypotheses (derived from theoretical scheme) - - - - - - - - - - - ->	Sample - - - - - - - - - - - - - - - - - ->	Methodology (Questionnaires and interviews, other data-collection methods)
Data analysis and interpretation (statistical tests, descriptive procedures) - - - - - - - ->	Preliminary findings (tentative conclusions, theoretical and substantive implications)	
Support or lack of support for tested hypotheses - - - - - - - - - - ->	Support or lack of support for our theories - - - - - - - - - - ->	New research is conducted (same or different)

FIGURE 1.1   The Circularity of the Research Process

not the only way research can be conducted. There is a consistent circularity associated with the research process, however, and this circularity is generally represented by Figure 1.1.

The research process begins with a research problem in need of an explanation, such as the problem of delinquency. An explanation for the problem is given, such as the presence and influence of a delinquent peer group. This explanation is a frame of reference and an indicator of how and why we believe delinquency occurred. A theoretical scheme is devised to explain why the presence and influence of a delinquent peer group possibly explains and causes delinquency. Our theoretical scheme explains and predicts relationships between our research problem and our explanation for it. It also generates hypotheses which can be tested. One way of looking at hypotheses is that they are statements of theory in testable form. In the delinquency/peer group relation, for instance, hypotheses are tentative statements about delinquent peer groups and delinquency deduced from our theory. These statements are tested by gathering data, collecting samples of youths who are delinquent and nondelinquent, and analyzing these data. As a part of our data analysis, we may use statistical procedures to describe and make decisions about whatever we have found. We may also apply statistical tests to determine how samples of delinquents and nondelinquents differ from one another according to several variables, such as parental supervision, associations with delinquent peers or different socioeconomic statuses. Whether we decide to use statistics to describe and/or make decisions about what we have found largely depends upon the goals and personal interests of the investigator.

The chain of events in Figure 1.1 shows that each part of the research process involves doing something to find answers for our original research questions. Statistics and statistical tests, as well as descriptive procedures, have been placed in the chain involving data analysis and interpretation. The role of statistical procedures in the research process is to provide numerical descriptions of our collected data as well as objective confirmation of hypotheses we test. **Hypotheses** are statements usually derived from theories of events that are capable of being tested. We test hypotheses in many different ways. Applications of particular statistical tests and procedures to our hypotheses is one method for determining whether our hypotheses have predictive utility. Do these tests support our theories or don't they?

The primary purpose of statistical tests is to help us describe and make decisions about what we have found based on the data we have collected. Statistical results either provide support for or fail to provide support for our theories of why certain events occur and our explanations of these events. Regardless of whether statistical tests provide support for our theories, most researchers conduct additional investigations, often of the same phenomena. Thus, the work of social scientists never ends. The research process in criminal justice and criminology is a continuing process. One reason is that no research project is perfect. It is common to see in published research phrases such as "More research is needed." This is because each research project doesn't prove anything. Rather, more information is added to clarify what is being investigated. It takes a lot of research on any given subject to decide what causes of problems are most likely and which ones are least likely.

For instance, when electronic monitoring was becoming popular as a supervisory tool for probation and parole officers to use with their offender-clients in corrections in the late 1980s, little research existed about it. There were perhaps fewer than 10 articles about electronic monitoring in the criminological literature. However, as electronic monitoring became more popular and spread among the states, being used more frequently, social scientists studied it more often. By the mid-1990s, there were over 50 articles on the subject.

By 2000, there were over 100 articles in the professional literature about electronic monitoring. By 2005, there were over 200 articles written about this subject. Many of these articles are research investigations about how electronic monitoring is used and how successful it is in verifying an offender's whereabouts. But research about electronic monitoring and its uses and effectiveness will continue to be conducted in future years. There will always be research projects investigating this and other topics.

VARIABLES

Variables are any phenomena that can assume more than one value. The research problems we study are variables. The explanations we use to account for research problems are also variables. Theories we create explain and predict relations between two or more variables. Thus, we need to know about variables and how they are involved in the research process. Several variables studied by investigators include gender, socioeconomic status, age, years of education, political affiliation, type of crime, prior record, recidivism, job satisfaction, labor turnover, stress, burnout, professionalism, victimization, fear of crime, urban/rural background, crime rates, delinquency, peer group influence, and electronic monitoring. It is apparent that everything we choose to study is a variable. Obviously it is beyond the scope of this book to list all variables of interest to criminal justicians and criminologists. An inspection of the annual programs of the Academy of Criminal Justice Sciences and American Society of Criminology, for instance, will disclose literally hundreds of topics researched by thousands of investigators. Most of these topics are variables.

Discrete and Continuous Variables

Variables may be either discrete or continuous. **Discrete variables** are those which have a set of fixed values. For instance, political affiliation is a discrete variable, because political affiliation is only classifiable into a set of fixed categories, such as Democrat, Republican, or some other political party. Religion is also a discrete variable, with subcategories fixed according to whether a person is Jewish, Catholic, Protestant, or of some other religious faith. Gender is also discrete, divided according to male and female. For data analysis purposes, numbers are assigned to these discrete categories. For instance, male + 1, female = 2, Catholic = 1, Jewish = 2, Protestant = 3, and so on. In criminal justice, we might designate felony = 1, misdemeanor = 2, infractions = 3. The numbers themselves merely identify different discrete **subclasses** on these variables. Such variables may also be **dichotomous variables**. Dichotomous variables are naturally divisible into discrete categories, such as male/female, Catholic/Protestant, Republican/Democrat, felon/misdemeanant, property crime/violent crime, and prisons/jails.

Continuous variables are any phenomena that can have an infinite or unlimited number of values. Age is a continuous variable, because it can be infinitely divided into years, months, days, hours, minutes, seconds, and so on. Income is another variable that can have unlimited subdivisions or subcategorizations. All attitudes are continuous variables, since they can assume an infinite number of values from high to low (e.g., high anxiety, low anxiety, high job satisfaction, low work motivation, high security, low stress, moderate recidivism, moderately low professionalism). Usually, these degrees of variation for different attitudes are displayed as **raw scores**. Raw scores are generated from **attitudinal scales** we create. As the result of measuring job satisfaction among corrections officers, for example, we might assign numbers to different levels of job satisfaction according to the raw scores we have assigned from a job-satisfaction scale as follows: high job satisfaction = 4, moderately high job satisfaction = 3, moderately low job satisfaction = 2, and low job satisfaction = 1. In this and other instances with other variables, raw scores are usually grouped into different categories from high to low and numbers are assigned. These categories are considered discrete categories, even though they are based on continuous properties underlying their measurement. In effect, any continuous variable can be divided into a sequence of any number of discrete categories for data analysis purposes or even portrayed as dichotomous variables (e.g., young/old). In many instances, the scores themselves are analyzed directly. If two or more groups of persons are being compared, their scores from various scales may be compared in various ways to determine differences between these groups of persons or samples.

Scaling is a topic included in most research methods courses. Attitudinal scales yield raw scores that show whether persons possess certain attitudes to greater or lesser degrees than others. Scales might be created to measure job satisfaction, for instance. Such scales may contain several statements with which we agree or disagree. Responding to these statements in different ways yields raw scores that show how much persons possess job satisfaction. Persons may be grouped according to their raw scores on these scales and compared with one another. The Minnesota Multiphasic Personality Inventory (MMPI), for example, is a popular personality inventory. It has over 500 true–false statements that purportedly measure several personality characteristics. Persons who take the MMPI receive raw scores that can be analyzed and interpreted. The raw scores generated by the MMPI represent how much persons possess certain personality traits or characteristics.

This book is not about the details of measuring attitudes, however, or learning about the detailed aspects of scaling. Rather, we want to know how scores from various scales can be analyzed and interpreted. We want to make sense out of the numerical information we have gathered. We want to describe it and make decisions about it. These decisions are directly related to the hypotheses we are testing that have been derived from theories.

The importance of whether variables are discrete or continuous is that each statistical test or technique is accompanied by various assumptions that must be satisfied in order to apply such tests correctly. One assumption of each statistical test is that the variable being analyzed or tested should be either discrete or continuous. For instance, if we intended to use a particular statistical test that assumed the data should be continuous and if the data we were analyzing were only discrete, this fact may dissuade us from using the statistical test we originally chose. We might wish to choose another statistical test where this particular assumption is satisfied. The good thing is that there is a wide variety of statistical tests. In many cases, two or more tests exist that perform identical functions. But each has different assumptions that must be met in order to be applied correctly. One test may assume that the variable to be analyzed must be discrete, while another test may require that the variable analyzed must be continuous. This is only one assumption of several, however. Most statistical tests have at least three or more assumptions underlying their correct application.

Independent and Dependent Variables

Variables may also be independent or dependent. **Independent** variables are phenomena or quantities that effect or elicit changes in other variables. **Dependent variables** are phenomena or quantities that are affected by or change in response to changes in other variables. Gender is conventionally used as an independent variable. For instance, we might wonder how one's successfulness on probation is affected by gender? Do females do better on probation than males? In this instance, we are using the male–female distinction as subclasses on the independent variable gender. Successful/unsuccessful are subclasses of the dependent variable, "successfulness on probation." Another example of independent variable/dependent variable relations might be "type of offender supervision" and "recidivism." We may believe that intensive offender supervision while on probation or parole will reduce recidivism compared with standard supervision. This particular two-variable relation might be illustrated as follows:

Type of offender supervision---------------->Recidivism
(Independent variable)   (Dependent variable)

This relation illustrates that type of offender supervision, the independent variable, influences (----->) recidivism, the dependent variable.

One reason we distinguish variables as either independent or dependent is that tabular displays of collected data are arranged in certain ways, depending on how each of these variables is labeled. The convention followed in criminological research is to arrange tables so that the independent variable is presented across the top of a table, while the dependent variable is shown down the left-hand side of the table. For instance, in our example of type of offender supervision and recidivism, we would imagine a cross-tabulation of these variables in a table such as the one in Table 1.1.

Notice that in Table 1.1 "type of offender supervision" has been placed across the top of the table, with "intensive" and "standard" as subclasses or subcategories, and "recidivism" has been placed down the left-hand side of the table, with "high" and "low" as subclasses or subcategories. This is a conventional way of portraying data in a table, showing how type of offender supervision and recidivism are cross-tabulated. **Cross-tabulations** of variables are routine in criminological research, and most researchers construct their tables similarly. With data arranged according to this conventional protocol, more systematic interpretations of data can be made and the tabular information is more easily understood.

TABLE 1.1 Hypothetical Cross-tabulation of Type of Offender Supervision and Recidivism

		Type of Offender Supervision	
		Intensive	Standard
Recidivism	High		
	Low		

NOTATION SYSTEMS

Whenever statistical tests and procedures are presented, different **notation systems** are used. These notation systems are simply ways of expressing different terms symbolically. No given notation system is the most popular one. Notation systems vary according to author preferences. However, most authors conform their notation systems to how research findings are presented in research articles in their respective fields. Convention is an important factor in the use of particular notation systems. Convention defines how tabular arrangements of variables should be displayed, and convention governs which notation systems will be used or preferred.

Simplicity of Notation

In this book, the notation for all formulas has been simplified. There are many ways to symbolize statistical formulae. For instance, suppose we observe the following scores:

$$8, 15, 20, 23, 25, 29$$

If we wanted to add or sum these scores and divide this sum by the total number of values, we could express this as a formula as follows:

$$\sum_{i=1}^{N} X_i$$

where X_i = the ith score

N = the total number of scores

$i = 1$ = the first score in the array of scores

This formula seems complex, but it simply says the following: "Sum (Σ) all of the scores, beginning with the ith or first score (X_1) and ending with the last score (N) or X_6 in this case." The symbol, X_i, stands for any particular score. Thus, we would sum these scores as follows (in parentheses are the symbols for the individual scores): (X_1) 8 + (X_2) 15 + (X_3) 20 + (X_4) 23 + (X_5) 25 + (X_6) 29 = 120. It is also important to know what the formula doesn't say. It doesn't say to sum all of the scores, beginning with the second or third score. It doesn't say sum only two or three of the scores. It says to sum *all* of the scores. Almost never in criminology and criminal justice will we sum only a partial number of scores. Almost always we will sum all scores in any array of them. Thus, the formula, while technically correct, may be somewhat intimidating. How much clearer could we make this formula if we delete some of the unnecessary notation? Let's see. If we want to say, "Sum all of the scores," we could use the simplified formula:

$$\Sigma X_i$$

This more simplified expression looks far less intimidating than the first formula. We have eliminated unnecessary notation to give the formula a simpler appearance. The subscript, i, denotes each specific score (X_i). And therefore, we would again sum all of the scores. Our six scores are symbolically expressed as follows: $8 = X_1$; $15 = X_2$; $20 = X_3$; $23 = X_4$; $25 = X_5$; $29 = X_6$. The assumption is that all scores in our distribution will be summed, not just a few of them.

Simplicity of presentation is found in all subsequent chapters. Only basic symbolic notation will be used when describing how certain tests or procedures are applied. No theoretical derivations of formulae will be presented. Our primary objective is to show how and under what circumstances each statistical procedure can be applied and interpreted. Thus, this is a very hands-on, user-friendly book with criminology and criminal justice students in mind. Social scientists in general, including sociologists, political scientists, and psychologists among others, will find these statistical tests and procedures useful as well. All of them form a common core of tests that are shared. In this book, we have used primarily criminology and criminal justice examples to help students relate more easily to data presentations and analyses.

Statistical Symbols

As we have just seen, **statistical symbols** can be used to represent different values. The values above were arranged in an **array.** An array of values is a listing of them from either low to high or high to low (e.g., 8, 15, 20, 23, 25, 29 or 29, 25, 23, 20, 15, 8).

Whenever we discuss values that describe population characteristics, we use Greek letters (e.g., μ, σ). Whenever we describe sample characteristics, we use Roman letters (X, s). Therefore, summarizing our symbolic references to both population values and sample values, we will use the following:

Population mean $= \mu$ Population standard deviation $= \sigma$

Sample mean $= \overline{X}$ Sample standard deviation $= s$

Again, observe that Greek letters are used for indicating population values or characteristics, while Roman letters (either uppercase or lowercase) are used to represent sample values or characteristics.

FUNCTIONS OF STATISTICAL PROCEDURES

The primary functions of statistical procedures are to (1) describe collected data; (2) make decisions about hypothesis tests; and (3) make inferences about population values based on sample characteristics.

Describing Collected Data

A large category of statistical procedures is called **descriptive statistics**. We use descriptive statistics to portray different characteristics of samples we have drawn from larger populations. Or we may describe population characteristics themselves. Chapters 3–5 present and discuss many descriptive statistics and methods used to depict the data we have collected.

Some descriptions of collected data include graphic and tabular presentation, as illustrated in Chapter 3. We will learn about pie charts, bar graphs, histograms, frequency polygons, and cross-tabulations of data into tables of different sizes. These types of descriptive information help us to visualize various dimensions of the information we have collected. A picture is worth a thousand words. Furthermore, looking at how our data are distributed will indicate which descriptive statistics would be best to use in characterizing our collected information.

Descriptive statistics also include **measures of central tendency** and **measures of dispersion or variability**. Chapter 4 examines several descriptive statistics that depict popular or central scores that other scores tend to gather around. Some of these descriptive statistics include the mode, median, and mean. Most of us are familiar with these types of descriptive statistics, because we are bombarded with them every day in the newspapers and television. Baseball fans can readily quote batting averages and runs batted in for their favorite players. Basketball enthusiasts can readily quote scoring averages of their favorite players or their average rebounds per game. Football enthusiasts can talk about quarterbacks and their pass-reception percentages per game. Bowling enthusiasts can compare their bowling averages with others. In more serious areas, we can cite the average number of deaths per month in the Iraq War due to suicide bombers and insurgents. All of these figures cited are descriptive statistics.

In criminal justice and criminology, we might cite murder rates for different cities, the percentage of successful convictions of local prosecutors, recidivism rates of child sexual abusers, or the average labor turnover among correctional officers nationally or in a particular state.

Measures of dispersion or variability are descriptions of how scores tend to focus around central points. These measures are described in Chapter 5. Some common measures of dispersion include the standard deviation and range. Other less well-known measures of variability include the index of qualitative variation and the average deviation. Certain measures of central tendency are presented together with certain measures of dispersion or variability to describe score arrangements for samples of persons we are studying. Both measures provide a more complete view of how scores for samples of persons are distributed. Many researchers will use this information to decide which statistical tests and techniques are best to apply later when they analyze their data.

Making Decisions About Hypothesis Tests

Statistical tests permit investigators to make decisions about tests of hypotheses derived from their theories. Theories explain and predict relations between variables. An event is in need of an explanation, and a frame of reference to view the event is chosen. A rationale is provided for why there should be a link between the problem studied and the explanation proposed by the researcher. One or more hypotheses are derived from these theories and tested. Hypothesis tests either support the theories from which they are derived or they fail to support these theories. Put another way, our explanations for the research problems we study are put to the test, and statistical procedures enable us to make independent judgments about these explanations. Hypotheses are the means whereby we test our theories, and statistical tests are used to make decisions about these hypotheses. Statistical decision making is always couched in probabilistic terms which will be explained in a later chapter. If one or more hypotheses derived from a theory are supported, this is statistical evidence of support for the theory itself. In turn, this support means support for our explanation for the problem or event we are studying. Thus, statistical test applications for hypothesis testing are quite important, since they advance our knowledge and understanding of our research problems.

Making Inferences About Population Values Based on Sample Characteristics

A third function of statistical procedures is to enable us to make inferences about or estimates of population characteristics based on sample characteristics. In criminological research, investigators study samples of persons drawn from larger populations of them. Depending on how these persons are drawn from their respective populations, their sample characteristics may resemble certain population characteristics. If the average age of a sample is 35, it may be inferred that the population average age is also 35, or close to it. Thus, statistics performs inferential or estimation functions. We can infer things or make estimates about population characteristics by studying the characteristics of samples drawn from those populations. However, the quality of these estimates and inferences depends on how our samples were selected initially. There are many ways to sample persons from populations. Only a limited number of these **sampling plans** are useful and productive for statistical inference or estimation functions, however. Statistical inference and estimation are tantamount to generalizing. In effect, we make generalizations about our populations from the samples drawn from them.

Not all sampling plans are created equal, however. Some sampling plans are better than others. Generalizations made about populations based on sample characteristics are considered valid or good generalizations depending on how the samples were drawn initially. Each sampling plan has pros and cons. The best sampling plans favored by criminologists and other social scientists will be highlighted and discussed later in this chapter.

ASSUMPTIONS UNDERLYING STATISTICAL PROCEDURES

All statistics have assumptions associated with their proper application for describing data, making decisions about hypothesis tests, and/or making inferences about populations from sample characteristics. Thus, each statistic presented in this book states these assumptions.

There are at least four assumptions made by researchers when using statistical tests or techniques for descriptive or inferential purposes. These include (1) randomness; (2) the level of measurement; (3) sample size; and (4) independent or related samples. There are several other assumptions as well, depending on the statistical test or technique presented. But understanding their relevance and importance is based on principles that will be discussed in later chapters where appropriate.

Randomness

Randomness refers to how samples are obtained from populations. In statistics, persons are often referred to as **elements.** Thus a sample of 40 persons may be a sample consisting of 40 elements. Randomness is defined as drawing elements from a population in such a way that each element has an equal and an independent chance of being included in the subsequent sample. An equal chance of being drawn, or **equality of draw**, means that all elements in the population have the same chance of being included. This means that we must be able to identify all elements in the population in order to give them an equal chance for inclusion. Therefore, if there are 200 population elements, each element has 1/200th of a chance of being drawn. **Independence of draw** or having an independent chance of being included means that drawing one or more elements for inclusion in a sample will not affect the chances of the remaining population elements of being included. Samples drawn under these conditions are called **random samples**.

The **fishbowl draw** illustrates both equality and independence of drawing sample elements. If we number all population elements, 200 from the above example, from 1 to 200 and place pieces of paper with these different numbers into a fishbowl, the first piece of paper drawn from the bowl is the first element included in our sample. This action leaves 199 pieces of paper in the bowl. If we draw successive elements from the fishbowl, we will leave fewer pieces of paper in the bowl. Thus, the next element drawn will have 1/199th of a chance of being drawn; the next element will have 1/198th of a chance of being drawn, and so on. This is **sampling without replacement**, meaning that the pieces of paper, once drawn, are withheld from the bowl. The chances of the remaining elements in the bowl of being drawn for our sample are slightly increased each time we select one. Thus, independence of draw does not occur under this scenario, since drawing more elements from the fishbowl influences the chances of the remaining elements of being drawn.

A solution to this problem is to replace each piece of paper (or element) once drawn, always leaving 200 pieces of paper in the bowl. Therefore, each time an element is selected, it has 1/200th of a chance of being drawn. This is called **sampling with replacement**. This type of sampling insures equality and independence of draw, satisfying the assumption of randomness.

In actual practice, the fishbowl method of drawing samples is seldom if ever used. It is functional here because it illustrates equality and independence of draw, the basic ingredients of randomness. Better methods for drawing random samples exist. Researchers commonly use a **table of random numbers** or a **computer-determined draw** to select samples from designated populations. By definition, any sample drawn from a table of random numbers or from a computer-determined draw is a random sample. Research methods texts illustrate how tables of random numbers are used and will not be described here. All statistical tests and procedures require randomness.

PROBABILITY SAMPLING PLANS   Four random samples have been described (Champion, 2006). These include (1) simple random sampling; (2) proportionate stratified random sampling; (3) disproportionate stratified random sampling; and (4) cluster, area, or multistage random sampling. These are also referred to as **probability sampling plans** because they entitle investigators to use **probability theory** in their research. The relevance and importance of probability theory will be discussed in later chapters.

Simple random sampling plans are those that define in advance a population from which a certain number of elements will be drawn randomly. The elements are identified and assigned numbers. Their selection is either by computer-determined draw or from a table of random numbers. Any sample drawn in such a manner from a population is a simple random sample and also a probability sample.

Proportionate stratified random sampling plans are those where all elements in the population are identified and divided into subclasses on one or more variables, such as type of conviction offense, gender, or sentence length. Samples of elements are drawn from these variable subclasses. If 30 percent of a population consists of felony offenders and 70 percent consists of misdemeanants, then the resulting sample of whatever size is desired is made up of 30 percent felony offenders and 70 percent misdemeanants. The result is a sample that resembles the population of criminals according to the proportionate distribution of felons and misdemeanants in that population. The sample is said to be a proportionate stratified random sample controlling for type of conviction offense. The sample drawn is also a probability sample, because randomness was used in the selection and inclusion of elements in the sample.

Disproportionate stratified random sampling plans are those where sample elements are drawn that are not proportionate to their existing numbers in the population. The sample may consist of 50 percent felons and 50 percent misdemeanants. This distribution of sample elements would be disproportional to the numbers of felons (30 percent) and misdemeanants (70 percent) that actually exist in the population. Disproportionate stratified random samples, which have been stratified according to conviction offense, are also probability samples since randomness was used in the selection and inclusion of elements.

Cluster, area, or multistage random sampling plans are those usually drawn from large geographical territories or areas. Vertical and horizontal grids are drawn over a portion of a state or country, and different cells are created which are various areas of land. These may include large farming regions in Iowa or parts of cities such as Chicago. A sample of cells or geographical blocks is taken randomly from the total number of them, resulting in second-stage units. In turn, each of these blocks of land is subdivided by horizontal and vertical grid lines, creating numerous smaller blocks of area. Third- and fourth-stage units may be drawn as well. Once researchers have a random sample of smaller clusters or land areas, all families or household heads within those blocks or units are studied. The sum of these or stages or units or blocks or land areas comprises the random sample of blocks and is a probability sample for statistical purposes. Crime mapping may utilize such a sampling method. These four types of samples are probability sampling plans and comprise the most desirable ones for researchers to use. These probability sampling plans permit the use of probability theory. The probabilistic nature of such sampling plans will be discussed in a later chapter.

NONPROBABILITY SAMPLING PLANS   Several sampling plans are **nonprobability sampling plans**. These sampling methods make no pretense of being random. These include (1) accidental or convenience sampling; (2) quota sampling; (3) purposive or judgmental sampling; (4) systematic sampling; (5) saturation sampling; (6) dense sampling; and (7) snowball sampling. These nonprobability sampling plans do not require equality and independence of draw. Probability theory cannot be used whenever these types of sampling plans are used. These plans are described and discussed in detail elsewhere (Champion, 2006).

The Level of Measurement

The **level of measurement** refers to the meanings associated with numbers we assign to collected data. It will be recalled that numbers may be assigned to attitudinal scores, gender, political affiliation, age, and other variables. Quantifying one's collected data makes the data easier to analyze. But numbers have their limitations. For gender, we may assign the following numbers to two gender subclasses: male = 1; female = 2. For job satisfaction, we may assign numbers to persons who share similar raw scores derived from a job satisfaction scale, or high job satisfaction = 1; moderately high job satisfaction = 2; moderately low job satisfaction = 3; and low job satisfaction = 4. Categories of age may also be assigned numbers: 20 or younger = 1; 21–25 = 2; 26–29 = 3; 30 or older = 4.

Each of these assignments of numbers to different variable subclasses results in a particular level of measurement. When we assign numbers to discrete variables such as gender, political affiliation, type of crime, or religious affiliation, the numbers themselves serve only to differentiate one subclass from another. Male = 1 and female = 2 doesn't mean, for instance, that a "1" is higher or lower than a "2." It just means the numbers are different, because they are intended to stand for different discrete subclasses. In the case of job satisfaction, a "1" is higher than a "2" which is higher than a "3" which is higher than a "4." Persons assigned a "1" on job satisfaction have "high job satisfaction," while those assigned a "4" have "low job satisfaction." The meanings of numbers, therefore, are dependent upon whatever they stand for.

For instance, if a bowler bowls three games and gets scores of 150, 200, and 250, we would readily sum the scores and divide by 3, the number of scores, to get his bowling average. In this case $(150 + 200 + 250)/3 = 600/3 = 200$. The person's bowling average for these three games would be 200. This average means something. But what about male = 1 and female = 2? What if we have a classroom with 20 males and 20 females? If we summed the 20 "1" values and the 20 "2" values, we would have 20 and 40. If we sum these values and divide by the total number of males and females, we would have $(20 + 40)/40$ or $60/40 = 1.5$. What does this average mean? Does it make sense to say that the average gender for the class is 1.5? No. This is silly. Averaging gender is a meaningless calculation. The point is that numbers take on different meanings depending upon whatever they stand for.

Four levels of measurement are (1) the nominal level; (2) the ordinal level; (3) the interval level; and (4) the ratio level. These levels of measurement have been arranged from the lowest (nominal) to highest (ratio). The **nominal level of measurement** is the assignment of numbers to subclasses of variables simply to differentiate between them. Catholic = 1, Protestant = 2, and Jewish = 3 is an assignment of numbers to different religious faiths. It is not expected that we will average these numbers. The importance of these numerical assignments is simply to give us a tally of the numbers of Catholics, Protestants, and Jews in a given sample. Averaging is both impermissible and meaningless.

Assigning numbers to varying degrees of job satisfaction or any other attitude usually yields scores according to the **ordinal level of measurement**. We can say not only that "1"s, "2"s, "3"s, and "4"s are different from one another, but they are also higher or lower than each other. The different scores represent graduated or ordered categories where certain persons have higher or lower levels of given attitudes compared with other persons. Assigning numbers to data measured according to an ordinal scale permits researchers to make "greater than" or "less than" distinctions between different scores. However, we cannot know or determine actual distances between scores on such scales. Consider the intensity continuum of police professionalism below:

```
Nonprofessional                                                          Professional
-------/-------/----------------------/---/---------------------------------/------
   15     25                        26  30                                   31
```

Notice that different professionalism scores are depicted along the continuum, but there are variable distances between numbers. We can say, therefore, that a score of 30 is higher than a score of 26, but we can't say how much higher the score is. Almost all attitudinal scales are measured according to the ordinal level of measurement. Technically, such scores should not be averaged, because there must be equal spacing between scores in order for averaging to be meaningful. But in criminology and other social sciences, raw scores on attitudinal scales are averaged frequently. But whenever averaging is done for scores measured according to an ordinal scale, caution should be exercised when interpreting the results of such data analyses and statistical applications.

The next highest level of measurement is the **interval level of measurement**. Data measured according to the interval level of measurement are also assigned numbers. These numbers permit nominal differentiations between values. Further, these numbers permit determinations of "greater than" or "less than." Additionally, these numbers have equal spacing along an intensity continuum, and researchers may say that there are equal distances between units. Consider the continuum below in Figure 1.2 displaying various ages.

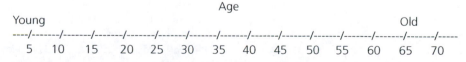

FIGURE 1.2   Hypothetical Continuum of Ages

This hypothetical age continuum is graduated according to five-point intervals. These intervals are considered to be of equal distances from each other. For instance, the distance between 5 and 10 is identical to the distance between 50 and 55. The distance between 10 and 30 would be equal to the distance between 50 and 70. This equal spacing of interval scales is desirable, because it permits us to use statistical procedures and other data analysis techniques that involve arithmetic operations such as averaging and the computation of square roots.

The **ratio level of measurement** is identical to the interval level of measurement with one exception. The ratio level of measurement has an absolute zero. Income is a ratio-level variable, since income may be measured according to a scale having an absolute zero. Persons can have no money. Where an absolute zero is assumed, values may be proportionately related to other values. Therefore, $50 is to $100 as $10,000 is to $20,000. Interval scales lack an absolute zero, and therefore, ratio statements are not permissible with such scales.

However, few procedures discussed in this book require levels of measurement beyond the interval level. For instance, while income is actually measurable according to a ratio scale, it is treated as though it were at the interval level of measurement. Since income has ratio-level properties, it also embraces properties of all other lower levels of measurement, including the interval level, the ordinal level, and the nominal level. Various statistical measures and techniques are associated with different levels of measurement. Therefore, it is important to know how variables are measured initially before we decide which statistical techniques or procedures to apply. Table 1.2 describes various permissible arithmetic actions that can be performed with numbers assigned to different variable subclasses, depending upon the level of measurement assumed and associated with these variables.

Sample Size

Sample size is an important criterion when choosing a particular statistical test or technique for data analyses. Most statistical tests have recommended sample sizes for their optimum application to collected data. Statistical tests are very sensitive to sample size variations. Almost always where statistical tests are described in this book, a reasonable operating range for sample size will be stated. Some statistical tests are designed for applications where large sample sizes have been obtained. Other statistical tests are designed for analyses of small samples. The relation between sample size and its affect on statistical test results will be specified in subsequent chapters as different statistical tests and techniques are discussed.

TABLE 1.2 Levels of Measurement and Statistical Applications

If the measurement level required by our statistical tests is:	Then, we may apply:
1. Nominal	1. Nominal-level statistics and statistical procedures
2. Ordinal	2. Nominal- and ordinal-level statistical procedures
3. Interval	3. Nominal-, ordinal-, and interval-level statistical procedures
4. Ratio	4. Nominal-, ordinal-, interval-, and ratio-level statistical procedures

Independent or Related Samples

When two or more samples of elements are studied or being compared, an assumption is made that the samples are either independent or related. Some statistical tests are designed for applications where two or more samples are related in some way. Other statistical tests are designed for independent samples. **Independent samples** are samples consisting of different elements with no direct connection with one another. A sample of prisoners from the Tennessee State Penitentiary may be compared with a sample of prisoners from the Kentucky State Penitentiary. Two or more samples of probation officers may be compared or contrasted from Illinois, West Virginia, and North Carolina. Samples of police officers from five different cities in Texas may be selected for analysis. In each of these cases, the samples are considered independent of one another. Single samples of persons may be subdivided into males and females or other designations. Therefore, independent samples may be artificially created. It is not necessary to draw separate samples each time we want to analyze independent samples.

Related samples consist of persons related in some way with those in comparison samples. There are at least three ways of creating related samples. The easiest is to use persons as their own controls in before-after experiments. A sample can be studied over time, and in each time period, information about the sample is gathered. A sample of the same persons studied over three different time periods becomes a three-related-sample situation. Each person in each sample is used as his/her own control. The persons in one sample are the same in the other samples, because they are the same elements being studied over time.

A second method is to match persons individually in two or more groups. It is difficult to find persons who match up perfectly with those in a given sample. Usually researchers match elements according to a limited number of variables, such as age, gender, years of education, political affiliation, and several attitudinal characteristics. Matching is extremely difficult to accomplish, although it does serve as a way of creating related samples. It's just that the two samples matched in several respects may not be matched in other, more important, respects.

A third way of obtaining related samples is to engage in frequency distribution control matching or group matching. Group characteristics, such as the average age for a sample, the average years of education, and other aggregate characteristics, are matched with another group with similar traits. This group method of achieving related samples overcomes some of the obstacles encountered by those who wish to match persons according to individual characteristics. Specific statistical tests have been created for related samples, just as specific tests have been created for independent samples. Thus, when two or more samples are being compared, it is important to determine whether the samples being compared are independent or related. Related-sample tests should not be used to analyze differences between independent samples, just like independent-sample tests should not be used to analyze differences between related samples.

Other Assumptions

The assumptions discussed in the previous section are fundamental to and relevant for most statistical test applications. Other assumptions may exist for certain statistical techniques, however. At these times, such assumptions will be explained and illustrated. For instance, there are distributional assumptions underlying the appropriate application of particular statistical tests. Raw scores being examined should be distributed in a certain way. As we will see in a later chapter, one assumption is that an investigator's sample scores should be normally distributed or distributed in a pattern that is bell-shaped. And in later chapters where multivariate statistical techniques are discussed, the normal distribution assumption is a critical requirement in addition to other assumptions that will be specified. Many distributions of raw scores are not shaped in this fashion, and as a result, this distribution assumption is not met. Other statistical procedures require that if two or more samples are being compared, then all distributions of scores being compared should have a similar distribution pattern. When the different distributions of scores lack these distributional similarities, then their application is inappropriate or suspect. Again, these distributional assumptions will be clarified when the appropriate statistical tests involving them are presented and discussed.

PLAN OF THIS BOOK

Criminologists, criminal justice professionals, and social scientists in general are interested in learning about people, either in groups or individually. Whether someone's interest is the study of crime or delinquency, police professionalism, crime trends in a given neighborhood or city, male and female offending patterns, personality systems and sex offenses, or interpersonal relations in work settings, several persistent questions link all such social inquiry.

1. What are the patterns of social and individual behavior?
2. Can these patterns be described in ways that permit predictions about the behaviors observed?
3. What factors tend to increase our understanding of human behavior?
4. In what ways will such factors contribute to our level of understanding?

Every social scientist enters a particular field (e.g., history, sociology, criminal justice, psychology, political science, justice administration) and begins the quest of seeking answers to questions such as those posed above. Most of these scientists will adhere to several basic principles and rules developed in the course of scientific inquiry over many years. These rules and principles are an integral part of the **scientific method**. They set forth particular ways of obtaining information. There are also rules governing how information should be analyzed and how statistical tests and measures should be applied under particular circumstances.

It is beyond the scope of this book to describe the scientific method in detail. This information is usually covered adequately in a research methods course. However, it is important for us to understand that statistical procedures and measures are logical aides for scientific inquiry. These tests and measures assist us in maintaining our objectivity when examining the information we have collected. They also help us to be systematic in data presentation and elaboration. The intent of this book is to minimize bias that might otherwise contaminate our research work and the findings we discover and report. All statistical procedures and measures have assumptions underlying their legitimate application. Also, all statistical procedures and measures have rules. Just as football or basketball games are played according to a set of rules, all statistical procedures and measures are also applied according to a set of rules.

Whenever we follow closely the rules governing the application of particular tests and procedures to the data we have collected in an objective and systematic manner, our test results are the equivalent of a second, independent opinion about any decision we might make. The point is that all of our research activity is governed by rules. Accordingly, statistical tests have requirements that must be met before they can be applied properly. It is important for us to familiarize ourselves with these rules and requirements and follow them closely if we are to be consistent with the canons of scientific inquiry.

The goals of this book are to

1. identify the role statistics plays in the overall research process.
2. describe and discuss an array of descriptive procedures for portraying statistical information in graphic form.
3. describe a variety of useful tests and procedures that can be applied in social scientific data analyses and subsequent hypothesis-testing and decision-making activity.
4. provide real examples of how these tests are or can be applied, their major weaknesses and strengths, and crucial assumptions underlying their proper application.
5. create an awareness of qualitative differences in collectible data that will influence, if not determine, the choice of statistical tests or procedures researchers might use in given instances.
6. provide a set of easy-to-use tables to aid in statistical interpretations.
7. present problems to be solved, to encourage a degree of statistical independence and confidence.
8. give a basic foundation for pursuing more elaborate and advanced statistical methods at a subsequent time.

The organization of this book is as follows. Following this introductory chapter, a description of a useful data analysis software program, *SPSS* or the *Statistical Package for the Social Sciences*, will be presented and discussed briefly in Chapter 2. This is one of several popular software programs that facilitate the processing of numerical information. The usefulness of *SPSS* will be described. Various descriptive statistical techniques will be presented in Chapter 3. This chapter is about graphic presentation. Different types of graphic presentation will be described. Chapters 4 and 5 involve discussions of measures of central tendency and dispersion or variability. These respective descriptive statistics describe the points around which scores focus in any distribution of scores as well as how they are distributed around these points.

Chapter 6 describes the unit or standard normal distribution or bell-shaped curve. Standard scores will be presented and described. This is a very important chapter, because it discusses a very important assumption underlying many statistical tests: normality. Some of our statistical tests require that raw scores should be distributed in such a way that a normal curve or bell-shaped curve is exhibited. Some score distributions fail to exhibit this bell-shaped characteristic, however. Non-normal distributions are discussed as well. But this chapter sets the stage for a general examination of statistical inference and decision making.

Chapter 7 discusses statistical inference and tests of significance. This chapter is followed by Chapter 8 which examines interval-level tests of significance. These tests assume that interval-level data are available for analysis. Tests of significance are designed for hypothesis testing and subsequent theory verification. The chapter organization consists of presenting single-sample tests of significance, two-sample tests for both independent- and related-sample situations, and *k*-sample (more than two samples) tests for both independent- and related-sample situations.

Chapters 9 and 10 respectively examine statistical tests used for hypothesis-test situations involving data measured according to nominal-level and ordinal-level scales. These tests are often useful alternatives to those covered in Chapter 8, since they have fewer restrictive assumptions for their proper application to collected data. At the conclusion of Chapter 10, comparisons will be made for several tests presented in Chapters 8, 9, and 10 where they will be applied to the same data. The application of different tests to answer the same basic research questions will illustrate how data are treated differently by the alternative tests compared and how different outcomes are yielded.

Chapter 11 is a discussion of measures of association for nominal- and ordinal-level variables. One important part of research involves seeking correlations or relationships between pairs of variables. This chapter discusses an array of correlation procedures designed to show how two variables measured according to different levels of measurement can be correlated. A convenient and useful chart will be presented, showing different test groupings according to different levels of measurement.

Chapter 12 examines several measures of association designed for two interval-level variable correlations. This chapter also examines several unique measures of association that take advantage of different combinations of levels of measurement. For instance, a nominal–ordinal level correlation measure will be presented, together with measures of association for nominal–interval and ordinal–interval variable combinations. A *k*-variable measure of association is presented.

Chapter 13 examines multivariate statistics and measures of association for more than two variables. This chapter includes several popular measures applied in criminological research today and it sets the stage for more advanced statistical procedures in later chapters. Chapter 14 focuses upon multivariate analysis and multiple regression. Examined are multivariate statistics, but it includes an examination of multiple regression with limited dependent variables. Chapter 15 extends the discussion of multivariate analysis, including a presentation of multiple regression with limited dependent variables.

Each chapter includes questions for review and problems to solve. Answers to all numerical problems are found in Appendix B. Many of the statistical tests presented in these chapters have interpretive tables in Appendix A. These interpretive tables have headnotes and footnotes indicating how investigators can interpret their numerical test results.

Summary

Statistics are defined as an assemblage of tests and measures designed to describe and make inferences about information we have gathered from samples of elements. Elements are individual units or persons we examine. We study samples of elements drawn from populations of them. Sample characteristics are known as statistics, and these statistics enable us to say things about populations from which they are drawn. Statistics also refers to numerical, graphic, and/or tabular descriptions of collected data.

Statistics are useful aides when investigating particular research problems, which are social scientific questions in need of answers. We collect data and analyze it in different ways. We apply statistical procedures to determine the significance of whatever we have found. There is a close interplay between theory and research. Our statistical techniques and measures may be applied in ways that will help to substantiate or refute theories.

Variables are often used in relation with one another. These variables have different characteristics. Some variables are discrete, while other variables are continuous. Also, variables may be either independent or dependent, depending upon how we choose to use them in our theorizing and research analyses. Independent and dependent variable arrangements in tables frequently rely upon how we have defined these variables relative to one another. In later chapters, conventional tabular arrangements will be illustrated, showing how independent and dependent variables are characterized.

The results of statistical procedures or measures are expressed symbolically. Different notation systems exist to portray aspects or characteristics of information we have collected. Population parameters are expressed symbolically with Greek letters, while sample information is symbolically expressed as uppercase and lowercase Roman letters. Every effort has been made to simplify notation for all statistical tests and measures used in this book.

Several functions of statistical procedures include describing collected data, making decisions about hypothesis tests, and making inferences about population values based on sample characteristics. All statistical procedures have accompanying assumptions. These assumptions include randomness, the level of measurement, sample size, and independent or related samples. Various reasons are given for why it is important to meet these assumptions whenever statistical tests are used for data analyses. Often in criminological and other types of social research, one or more assumptions underlying statistical tests are violated. There are different points of view about what to do whenever this situation occurs. A general admonition is that cautious and conservative interpretations of collected data should be made whenever it is known that one or more assumption violations have occurred with any statistical test application.

Key Terms

array *14*
attitudinal scales *10*
cluster, area, or multistage
   random sampling plans *17*
computer-determined
   draw *17*
continuous variables *10*
cross-tabulation *12*
dependent variables *11*
descriptive statistics *14*
dichotomous variables *10*
discrete variables *10*
disproportionate stratified
   random sampling
   plans *17*
elements *16*
equality of draw *16*
fishbowl draw *16*
frames of reference *7*
hypotheses *9*
independence of draw *16*
independent samples *21*
independent variables *11*
interval level of
   measurement *19*

level of measurement *18*
measures of central
   tendency *14*
measures of dispersion or
   variability *14*
nominal level of
   measurement *19*
nonprobability sampling
   plans *18*
notation systems *13*
ordinal level of
   measurement *19*
parameters *5*
population *5*
predictive utility *8*
probability sampling
   plans *17*
probability theory *17*
proportionate stratified
   random sampling
   plans *17*
qualitative research *8*
quantitative research *8*
randomness *16*
random samples *16*

ratio level of
   measurement *20*
raw scores *10*
related samples *21*
research *2*
research findings *2*
research problems *5*
sample *5*
sample size *20*
sampling plans *16*
sampling with
   replacement *17*
sampling without
   replacement *16*
scaling *11*
scientific method *22*
simple random
   sampling plans *17*
statistical evidence *2*
statistical symbols *2*
statistics *5*
subclasses *10*
table of random numbers *17*
theory *7*
variables *10*

Questions for Review

1. Differentiate between statistics and parameters.
2. What are three meanings associated with statistics?
3. What are frames of reference as we use them in relation to research problems? Think of several frames of reference we might use to explain labor turnover in a company (where employees quit at a fairly high rate over time).
4. What are some qualities that the scientific method encourages as we investigate social scientific phenomena?
5. What types of letters are used to represent population characteristics and sample characteristics?
6. Think of five independent variables and five dependent variables from an area of your interest (e.g., criminal justice, sociology, child development). Show some interrelationships between variables and provide a brief explanation for these interrelations.
7. What are discrete and continuous variables? Give ten examples of each.
8. What are four important assumptions underlying statistical test applications? Why are they important? Explain.
9. Differentiate between independent and related samples. Give an example.
10. What is meant by the level-of-measurement assumption? What are the four levels of measurement? Differentiate between them.
11. What is the significance of sample size as a consideration for applying statistical techniques to collected data? Explain.
12. How important is it to meet statistical test assumptions when applying them to collected data? What can we do if we fail to meet one or more assumptions underlying particular statistical tests?
13. What are notation systems? What are their purposes?

References

Brown, Robert A. and James Frank (2006). "Race and Officer Decision Making: Examining Differences in Arrest Outcomes between Black and White Officers." *Justice Quarterly* **23**:96–126.

Camp, Scott D. et al. (2006). "An Exploration into Participation in a Faith-Based Prison Program." *Criminology and Public Policy* **5**:529–550.

Champion, Dean J. (2006). *Research Methods for Criminal Justice and Criminology, 3/e.* Upper Saddle River, NJ: Pearson/Prentice Hall, 2006.

Johnson, Brian D. (2005). "Contextual Disparities in Guidelines Departures: Courtroom Social Contexts, Guidelines Compliance, and Extralegal Disparities in Criminal Sentencing." *Criminology* **43**:761–796.

Kubrin, Charles E. and Eric A. Stewart (2006). "Predicting Who Reoffends: The Neglected Role of Neighborhood Context in Recidivism Studies." *Criminology* **44**:165–198.

Solomon, Amy L. (2006). "Does Parole Supervision Work? Research Findings and Policy Opportunities." *APPA Perspectives* **30**:26–37.

Using *SPSS* in Social Research

Chapter Outline

Chapter Objectives

After reading this chapter, the following objectives will be realized:

1. understanding *SPSS* and its various functions in the analysis of collected data;

2. learning how to transmit data from questionnaires and other forms of data collection to *SPSS* for analysis through data entry;

3. interpreting output from *SPSS*-generated information;

4. understanding the limitations of software packages such as *SPSS*;

5. understanding that human intervention in the data analysis process is both a necessary and an integral part of the research process; and

6. understanding various myths about data analysis software programs.

INTRODUCTION

Data analysis in criminal justice and criminology has become increasingly complex and sophisticated, although the mechanics of analyzing data have been made easier through the creation of software programs available for **personal computers (PCs)**. Today almost every student has familiarity with different types of PC applications through Internet exploration or word processing for term papers. Useful software exists for virtually every kind of statistical application known. This chapter acquaints students with *SPSS* for Windows and its use for data analysis and computational work. *SPSS* stands for *Statistical Package for the Social Sciences*. While there are several competing types of software for analysis of social science data, the *SPSS* seems to be the most widely known and applied program.

The first part of this chapter examines briefly the increased use of computers and computer software as it pertains to analyses of social data. *SPSS* is explained. Included in this explanation is how data may be entered into *SPSS* software programs so that analyses of data may be rapidly performed. Once data have been analyzed, interpretations must be made of this data. Computers can only do so much analysis. Actual interpretations of data and the significance of it must be performed by investigators and researchers. Thus, the interpretive limitations of *SPSS* and similar software programs will be highlighted.

CALCULATORS AND COMPUTERS

In the 1960s and 1970s, most students relied upon hand calculators in order to calculate statistical formulae and perform simple arithmetic operations, such as adding, subtracting, multiplying, dividing, and calculating squares and square roots. While hand calculators have not been outmoded since their original use in the 1960s and beyond, the invention, proliferation, and use of personal computers and accompanying statistical software packages have done much to change how we think about data analysis and actually carry out data analysis functions.

Computers and computer systems are now an integral part of our lives in many different ways. We have learned to "surf the net" or explore an unlimited number of sites on the Internet. We use computers today for doing some of our research. Databases from both public and private sources can be accessed by computer. We can learn much from different informational sources at Internet sites, which are increasing in number.

In past decades, we often relied upon university computer centers to code and analyze our data sets. We waited patiently, sometimes for a week or longer, while university computers, known as mainframes, were at work, printing numerous tables and charts filled with volumes of data. These individualized operations for special research projects are now a part of our research history. Presently, we have access to our own software programs where we can enter data for analysis and analyze it using complex statistical tools. We have many options available to us, depending upon the statistical software program we choose. We can perform data analyses in a matter of minutes or seconds, and output or products of our data analysis are readily available. We are becoming used to instantaneous data retrieval. Today computer systems are faster, loaded with enormous amounts of memory, and statistical calculations may be performed with blinding speed.

COMPUTER SOFTWARE FOR DATA ANALYSES

From the 1980s to the present, numerous statistical software packages have been created and marketed to simplify social science data analyses. Virtually every known statistical test and measure of association can be computed by using one or more of these existing software programs.

Essentially, data collected from questionnaires or derived from interviews or observation are codified and entered into a specific computer program. This is known as **data entry**. Data entry will be discussed briefly later in this chapter. Once certain variables have been identified and relevant data are entered for *N* research subjects, then relatively simple instructions can be followed to examine different aspects of one's data and perform basic statistical operations and other functions. Data can be tabulated and descriptive statistics can be computed, including the mean, mode, median, range, and standard deviation. Tests of significance, such as the *t* test for differences between means or the *F* test for analysis of variance, can be applied easily by following simple instructions contained in these canned programs. Measures of association can also be computed, depending upon the researcher's needs and the type of data being analyzed. Also available are more complex analytical procedures, including multivariate analysis, path analysis, and different types of regression analysis. Graphics packages are included as well, making it quite easy to generate pie charts, bar graphs, frequency polygons, histograms, and other types of graphic presentation.

THE STATISTICAL PACKAGE FOR THE SOCIAL SCIENCES (*SPSS*)

One of the most popular statistical software programs is the **Statistical Package for the Social Sciences *(SPSS)***. There are different versions of *SPSS* on the market today, depending upon the nature of one's computer system. In the late 1980s, *SPSS*, Inc., in Chicago created *SPSS* for Windows. Almost annually since the advent of *SPSS* software, *SPSS* programming has undergone dramatic transformations, each year with new data analysis features and statistical functions made available to researchers, with each function accessible through a few key strokes on a computer. Each new version is labeled *SPSS 10.0, 14.0, 15.0,* and so forth and because of these frequent changes in *SPSS* versions, we will simply refer them as *SPSS Version X*.

What *SPSS* Does

SPSS for Windows (*SPSS Version X*) is a very comprehensive and flexible statistical analysis and data management system. It can accept data from almost any type of file and use them to generate tabulated reports, charts, and plots of distributions and trends, descriptive statistics, and complex statistical analyses. The capabilities of *SPSS Version X* are such that hundreds of variables and large data sets can be analyzed easily and quickly. Most criminological or criminal justice applications do not involve elaborate analyses of hundreds of variables. Researchers may wish to examine up to 40 or 50 variables in any investigation. Many studies reported in conventional research outlets, such as *Criminology, Justice Quarterly, Journal of Crime and Justice, Journal of Research on Crime and Delinquency,* or *Journal of Criminal Justice,* involve samples of 1,000 or fewer persons. Some research organizations, such as the National Opinion Research Center at the University of Chicago or the Survey Research Center at the

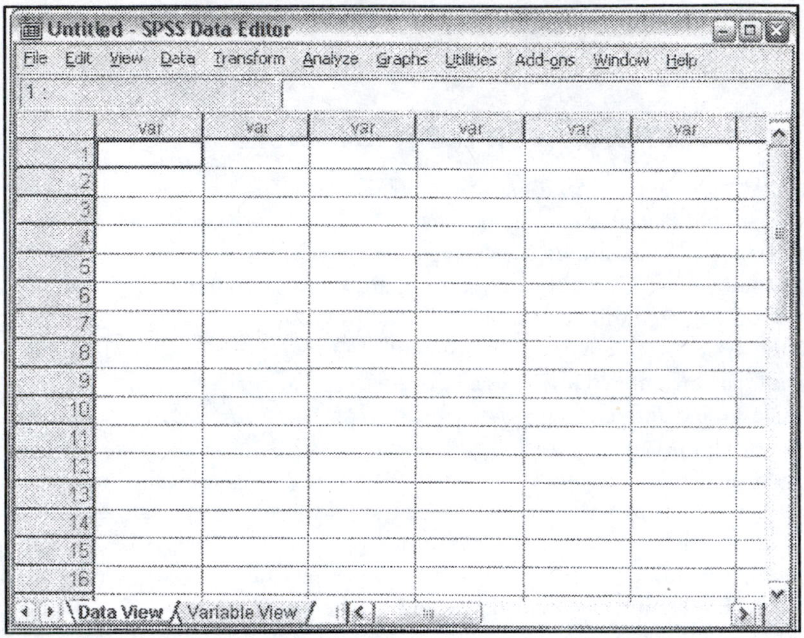

FIGURE 2.1 Data Editor Window for *SPSS*

University of Michigan, frequently investigate opinions and attitudes of 15,000 to 25,000 persons or more. *SPSS Version X* is fully capable of handling such data analyses. Thus, it is difficult to conceive of a project where *SPSS Version X* would not be an appropriate means for data analyses.

SPSS Version X uses easy-to-understand dialog boxes so that statistical commands can be given without reference to or use of complex syntax. Investigators can enter data into a data file and then perform various tests and descriptive procedures by following easy instructions. Figure 2.1 is an example of the "*SPSS* Data Editor" window.

When investigators transfer coded information from a questionnaire or interview schedule to the **Data Editor**, there is a sequence of columns labeled "var" for variable. Researchers may use a **data view**, shown at the bottom of this window, or they may use the **variable view**. It simplifies data entry if investigators give names to variables they wish to use as descriptors for column headings. The variable view is used for naming variables to be studied. The data view shows the actual scores in the different variable columns. While this chapter is not intended to teach students how to use *SPSS*, it is intended to familiarize them with what information might look like if it is displayed in different *SPSS* windows or screens. When *SPSS Version X* is initially launched, the *SPSS* Data Editor window will appear. The variables being investigated by a researcher may be identified merely by clicking on a "var" at the top of a column and typing a short descriptor of the variable. For instance, in the example in Figure 2.2, a Data Editor window is displayed showing several variable column labels, including age, marital (for marital status), address, income, and so forth.

Each of the rows in the Data Editor window represents a particular person and the information the person exhibits for different variables measured. These variables have already been coded and transferred through data entry to the *SPSS* software program or some other

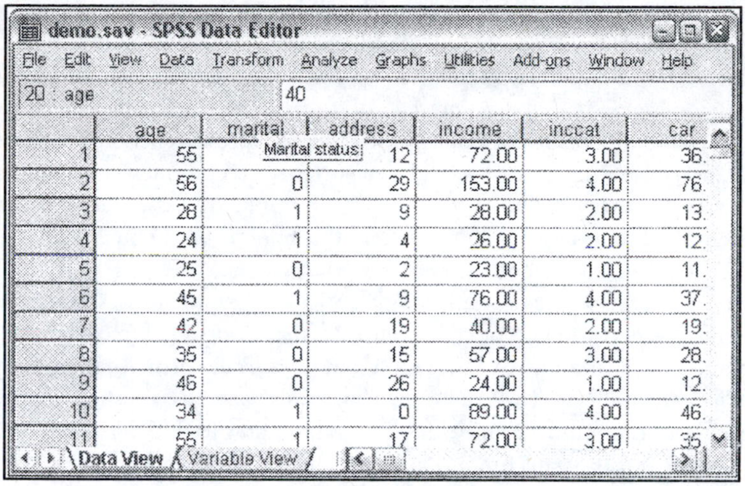

FIGURE 2.2   Data Editor Window Showing Column/Variable Labels

program the researcher may be using. When an investigator starts to use this *SPSS* program, all of these cells are blank. The first step is to define the variables used in the study. If there are 25 variables, these variables will take up 25 columns. If there are 10 variables, 10 columns will be used, and so forth. Column labels are usually abbreviated in relation to a variable. For instance, below is a listing of selected variables and suggested abbreviations for them:

Age	=	age
Gender	=	gend
Years of Education	=	educa
Prior Record	=	priorrec
Drug Abuse	=	drgabuse
Alcohol Abuse	=	alcabuse

Notice in the above listing that three characters are used for "age," while eight characters are used for "alcohol abuse." Using the *SPSS* program, a maximum number of eight characters can be used for variable definitions. Subsequently, when data analyses of different kinds are conducted, the researcher will be asked in various dialog boxes which variables are to be analyzed, tabulated, or manipulated. The variables will be displayed in these dialog boxes according to how they have been abbreviated. Thus, a defined variable listing would be:

age

gend

educa

priorrec

drgabuse

alcabuse

Clicking on each "variable" column in the data view mode will enable the investigator to enter values for age, marital status, income, and other variables contained in the data-collection process through the contents in a questionnaire, material coded from an interview or interview schedule, or identifying numbers from observations. Once all values have been entered for a particular sample collected by the investigator, a **data set** has been created. Note that in Figure 2.2, various values have been entered into the different columns for age, marital status, and income, among others. These values were entered by researchers through the data entry process. Data entry, coding variables, and measurement techniques and issues are generally covered in a basic research methods course and will not be discussed here. It is assumed that all students enrolled in a statistics course where this book is used will already have had some exposure to these research methods.

Once a data set has been created, a wide variety of graphic or descriptive and statistical test analyses may be performed. Notice in Figure 2.2 that across the top of the Data Editor window are included categories such as File, Edit, View, Data, Transform, Analyze, Graphs, Utilities, Add-Ons, Window, and Help. The "Help" function can always be consulted to provide students with instant assistance should they have questions about how to find particular *SPSS* features or functions. The most important functions across the top of the Data Editor window for this course are "Analyze," "Graphs," and "Utilities." Clicking on "Analyze" will list a variety of data analysis functions that may be performed. Clicking on "Graphs" will enable researchers to create a wide variety of illustrative materials constructed from the data they have entered.

SPSS Components

SPSS Version X consists of a Base System. The Base System contains a wide variety of statistical tests and graphic functions. Students can perform the following functions with the Base System:

1. Establish data sets—data entry, specification of variables, and identification of subclasses on variables.
2. Transform data from one form to another—recode data, merge files, and resort cases for selected analyses.
3. Select a random sample for a designated list of elements—assign weights to cases.
4. Create frequency distributions, histograms, frequency polygons, percentiles, and frequency statistics.
5. Cross-tabulate data and calculate percentages.
6. Perform cross tabulation statistics, such as the chi square test.
7. Perform difference-between-means tests, including *t* test, *F* test for analysis of variance, one- and two-way analysis of variance procedures.
8. Measure linear association, partial correlation and multiple linear regression analysis, and curve estimation.
9. Perform numerous nonparametric statistical tests.
10. Create scatter plots and three-dimensional matrices.

Several add-on modules are also available for more advanced and specialized analyses. These modules include:

1. *SPSS* **Professional Statistics:** techniques to measure the similarities and differences in data, data classification, cluster, *k*-means cluster, discriminant, factor, multidimensional scaling, proximity, and reliability.
2. *SPSS* **Advanced Statistics:** loglinear analysis, logistic regression, multivariate analysis of variance, constrained nonlinear regression, probit analysis, Cox regression, Kaplan-Meier and actuarial survival analysis.

3. *SPSS* **Tables:** creates complex stub-and-banner tables and displays multiple-response data; creates a variety of presentation-quality tabular reports.
4. *SPSS* **Trends:** performs comprehensive forecasting and time series analyses with multiple curve-fitting models, smoothing models, and methods for estimating autoregressive functions.
5. *SPSS* **Categories:** performs conjoint analysis and optimal scaling procedures, including correspondence analysis.
6. *SPSS* **CHAID:** simplifies tabular analyses of categorical data, develops predictive models, screens out extraneous predictor variables, and produces easy-to-read tree diagrams that segment a population into subgroups that share similar characteristics.
7. *SPSS* **LISREL:** analyzes linear structural relations and simultaneous equation models (*SPSS*, Inc., 2006).

It is unlikely that most students would ever want to perform statistical functions beyond those contained in the *SPSS* Base System. However, these other modules are available if more complex statistics and analyses are desired. Most larger universities have all of these *SPSS* modules, and some smaller colleges and universities may also have these items. Depending on instructor needs/preferences, students may or may not be required to obtain the latest *SPSS Brief Guide*, which includes a CD with many Base System features. If students do obtain this *SPSS Brief Guide* with the CD, then they may perform most of the functions to yield the statistical results of the tests presented in this book. This book caters to both, whether an *SPSS Brief Guide* CD is possessed, or if it isn't. Thus in subsequent chapters, brief discussions of *SPSS* applications will follow descriptive techniques, inferential procedures, statistical tests of significance, and measures of association between variables. These discussions may be skipped if *SPSS* software is unavailable.

Once all of the data have been entered from whatever sources (e.g., questionnaires, observation notes, or interview records), the data are given a file name which is saved within the *SPSS* program. The investigator labels or gives the file a title and saves it by following simple instructions in the window box. Again, researchers may use up to eight characters for each file name. Thus, several data sets may be saved, containing information for different samples of persons. If the researcher exits from the *SPSS* program, a prompt asks whether the data should be saved, and if so, under which file designation? When the investigator returns to work with the data later, the dialog box will display the saved file under whatever name the investigator chose. Simply placing the cursor on this file and clicking the mouse button will activate the file for subsequent statistical analysis.

One good thing about *SPSS* is that it displays "error" messages whenever data have been entered incorrectly. If you are entering gender information, with two categories (1 = male, 2 = female) and somehow a "3" or an "8" is entered by mistake instead of a "1" or "2," the *SPSS* program will detect this error and question it. Error detections such as these occur if the investigator has defined various subcategories for each variable in advance. Thus the *SPSS* program "knows" whether a "3" or "8" is an error. Investigators can inspect these errors and remedy problems of inaccurate data entry immediately by correcting the proper code for the variable and person being examined. This feature of *SPSS Version X* should give researchers added confidence whenever they transmit raw data to computer files for storage and subsequent analyses.

Analyzing Data from an Established File

Once a file has been created and data entered into it, the data in the file can be analyzed in different ways. For instance, suppose we want to know the ages of persons in each group being investigated (e.g., probation officers, prisoners, and abused spouses). Descriptive information about these different groups can be obtained by clicking on the "Analyze" feature across the top of the window. For instance, if we click on "Analyze," a subheading of different types of analysis will be disclosed. For instance, several menus

> Analyze
>
> Descriptive Statistics
>
> Frequencies

and so on. We can use our computer mouse to click on the appropriate menu which will tabulate and display the different groups, counting the number of persons in each group. The display will also show the means for the different groups, standard deviation, standard error, and other information. This displayed information is dependent upon us identifying a particular variable or two or more variables we wish to describe.

One *SPSS* feature worth noting is that often more information than we want is displayed. This is the nature of *SPSS* and similar competing computer programs. It is simple to identify needed or requested information and ignore other superfluous information provided. The important thing here is to know which information is important for our research interests and which information is unimportant.

Examples of Branches of *SPSS* Analysis Options

It is helpful to understand the array of options available to students using an *SPSS* program for analyses of their data. A display of actual branches from the "Analyze" and "Graphs" features gives us a fair idea of what *SPSS* data analysis options exist. For instance, the full "Analyze" branch of options is as follows:

> Analyze
>
> Reports
>
> Descriptive Statistics
>
> Compare Means
>
> General Linear Model
>
> Correlations
>
> Regression
>
> Classify
>
> Data Reduction
>
> Scale
>
> Nonparametric Tests
>
> Time Series

If we click on the "Reports" subheading above, we will get the following options:

> Reports
>
> OLAP Cubes
>
> Case Summaries

If we click on the "Case Summaries" option under the "Reports" category, we will get the following additional options:

Case Summaries

Mean

Median

Grouped Mean

Standard Error of the Mean

Sum

Minimum

Maximum

Range

First

Last

Standard Deviation

Variance

Kurtosis

Standard Error of Kurtosis

Skewness

Harmonic Mean

Geometric Mean

Percent of Total Sum

Percent of Total N

If we click on "Descriptive Statistics" under the "Analyze" category, we will get the following options:

Descriptive Statistics

Frequencies

Descriptive

Crosstabs

Ratio

If we click on "Compare Means" under the "Analyze" category, we will get the following options:

Compare Means

Means

One-Sample t Test

Independent Samples t Test

Paired-Samples t Test

One-Way ANOVA

The point of displaying these different branches is that usually additional branches are disclosed, gradually narrowing our search for exactly what it is we want to do with the data we have collected. We will be given further instructions, enabling us to identify which variables we want to analyze. The *SPSS* program is very self-explanatory, once we identify particular branching functions.

In Chapter 3, for instance, different types of graphic presentation will be illustrated. The chapter describes what these graphs are and how they depict different types of information we have collected and are analyzing. The *SPSS* program enables us to accomplish rapid graphic portrayals of the data we have collected. Thus, if we click on the "Graphs" designation across the top of the Data Editor screen, we will find the following subheadings:

Graphs

Chart Builder

Interactive

Bar

3-D Bar

Line

Area

Pie

High-Low

Pareto

Control

Boxplot

Error Bar

Population Pyramid

Scatter/Dot

Histogram

P-P

Q-Q

Sequence

ROC Curve

Time Series

If we click on "Pie," we will get the following subheadings:
"Data in Chart are:

- Summaries for Groups of Cases
- Summaries of Separate Variables
- Values by Individual Cases"

There will also be "Define," "Cancel," and "Help" boxes to check. Thus, we can click on "Summaries for Groups of Cases" and then "Define," and a pie chart will be illustrated for the data we have entered for any given variable. It is apparent from the fairly extensive listing of subtopics that we can create simple bar graphs, histograms, and other graphs that will illustrate our collected data in different ways. It is critical to recognize the "Help" box. If you find yourself in a spot where you don't know how to proceed, usually clicking on the "Help" box will give you much information about how to analyze the information you are examining. Never hesitate to use the "Help" function if you need to use it.

Statistical Computations for Data Sets

Various statistical computations are thus available for any data set created and accessed by the researcher. Many statistical computations are possible, and *SPSS* software can generate large amounts of data. Descriptive procedures enable researchers to describe the data they have collected in different ways. There are numerical descriptions as well as graphic descriptions that can be yielded by *SPSS* and similar software programming.

SPSS Output and What to Do With It

It is readily apparent that *SPSS Version X* can do much for researchers who wish to analyze their data. *SPSS* programs can not only provide tables and statistical summaries of data, but graphic material can also be generated. Bar graphs, pie charts, frequency polygons, and other graphic information can be displayed easily, based on the data files researchers create.

The skill of the researcher is important in distinguishing between needed and unneeded information generated by these computer programs. Once tabular displays have been generated, it is the sign of a seasoned researcher to know how best to use this information in report preparation. Report-writing and discussing study results require some familiarity with statistical tests and their assumptions. Graphic materials can add much to the written word.

CAN COMPUTERS AND SOFTWARE PROGRAMS SUCH AS *SPSS* DO EVERYTHING FOR YOU?

No, computer software programs cannot do everything for you. These programs such as *SPSS* can help us do many things with the data we have collected. Printouts from these programs contain much useful information. This information is sometimes interpreted by the software in the sense that probabilities are provided or statements about statistical significance are indicated. However, it is up to individual researchers to make decisions about the usefulness of the available information and how best to interpret it.

Some people believe that everything printed out by software programs such as *SPSS* must be significant. Otherwise, why would such information be generated? But the fact is that the decision-making capabilities of software programs are severely limited. Software programs lack imagination. These programs perform precisely according to what they are capable of doing. This means that they will literally do whatever they are programmed to do, depending upon the software used and the functions to be performed. Frequently, computers will perform certain functions literally that make absolutely no sense to us. An example of such literal functioning is provided below.

Suppose we enter data into an *SPSS* program. We might enter information that would identify each of our elements. For instance, if we had 200 persons in our sample, we would number each person, beginning with person 001, person 002, person 003, up to person 200. These three-digit identification numbers would be entered merely to identify particular persons. Other than serving to differentiate between these persons, these three-digit ID numbers have no other value. Further suppose that we enter information about one's race/ethnicity, gender, educational level, prior criminal record, six or eight personality characteristics, occupational/professional affiliation, years on the job, job satisfaction, self-concept, religion, socioeconomic status, political affiliation, and ten or so other variables. As we have seen from the above discussion, we would create variable labels and values for each variable subclass. Thus, our data entry would consist of entering numbers into our *SPSS* program that refer to a wide variety of variables, ranging from a person's ID to a person's years of education.

Next, we run certain statistical analysis programs. For example, we might use the *SPSS* program to determine means or averages for all variables. This means that averages will be computed for all variables, including gender and race/ethnicity. If we assign a "1" to male and a "2" to female, what does an average gender of 1.3 mean? Accordingly, if we assign "1" to black, "2" to white, "3" to Hispanic, and "4" to "Other," what would be an average race/ethnicity of 2.4 mean? Is this someone who is somewhere between white and Hispanic? Such calculations are nonsense.

Data analysis software such as *SPSS Version X* doesn't discriminate or know about the columns and column labels and values we have created. The data we have entered are simply numbers. For any software program, numbers are numbers are numbers are numbers. Researchers designate different variables and subclasses for those variables. They assign numerical quantities to these subclasses. Software programs manipulate these numbers. *SPSS* does not "understand" that "1s" and "2s" in some cases refer to males and females and should not be averaged. This and other software programs only understand that they should average all numbers on each variable category, regardless of whatever the numbers represent. Researchers must examine these numbers and interpret them appropriately. As we might suspect, researchers acquire considerably more information than they really want or need from these software programs.

An illustration of meaningless data generation is given by the following hypothetical example. Suppose a researcher, Jane Smith, a criminologist, has some data about job satisfaction and years of education for a sample of correctional officers. These data are shown in Table 2.1. Both variable subclasses have been numbered to show what the computer "sees."

This is the table Smith wanted. But she notices that the software program has printed out a second table, one shown in Table 2.2 Jane notices that the new table generated independently

TABLE 2.1 Job Satisfaction and Years of Education for 100 Correctional Officers

	Years of Education			
Job Satisfaction	**12 or less (1)**	**13–14 (2)**	**15–16 (3)**	**17+ (4)**
Very Satisfied (1)	3	0	5	2
Satisfied (2)	2	0	0	4
Undecided, Probably Satisfied (3)	0	2	0	8
Undecided, Probably Dissatisfied (4)	4	11	0	7
Dissatisfied (5)	0	0	8	5
Very Dissatisfied (6)	11	10	8	9

TABLE 2.2 Collapsed Version of Data in Table 2.1

Job Satisfaction	Years of Education	
	16 or less (1–3)	17 or more (4)
(1) through (5)	35	26
(6)	30	9

by the software program represents a collapsing of the first three education subclasses into one category, while the fourth subclass is in a category by itself. For the job satisfaction variable, the first five subclasses have been combined into one general category, while the sixth subclass is in a category by itself. Jane scratches her head in bewilderment. The computer has just combined apples with oranges. Notice that the new categorization on the job satisfaction variable has combined both "satisfied" and "dissatisfied" subclasses. This is meaningless.

The point of producing Table 2.2 is that while software programs can and will do much for you, they cannot think independently and interpret your findings. You must perform this task. And in order to perform this task intelligently, you need the statistical skills this book intends to provide. It is imperative that you know the statistical test options available to you, the weaknesses and strengths of each, and how each test can be applied in the data analysis process most meaningfully. Once you have mastered this information, you can separate the relevant data from irrelevant or meaningless software output.

The Seductive Powers of Software Output: Garbage In, Garbage Out

The fact that software programs offer so much information to researchers is seductive. We are attracted to the ease with which computations are completed and statistical analyses are conducted. But software output generally varies in quality from very meaningful to very meaningless. The best software programs cannot transform a poorly conceived research project into a good one. If we have unreliable measures of variables, or if there are significant omissions in our research, no statistical program can remedy these problems.

Some persons refer to this problem as "garbage in, garbage out," meaning that no software program can improve on the quality of information it is analyzing. Therefore, if a researcher enters data that are deficient in any respect, these deficiencies cannot be remedied by software manipulation.

More than a few researchers are awed by software output. Complex tables are generated and formulae calculated. Elaborate displays of numerical data seem impressive. The fact is that over the years, some investigators have masked poorly conceived and implemented research designs with overwhelming statistical manipulations and presentations of their data. In some cases, research articles consist almost entirely of graphs, tables, and exotic diagrams intended to portray correlations between variables that are at best weak. Readers should be wary of articles that emphasize complex statistical techniques, such as multivariate analyses and path diagrams. There should be enough substance in these articles to carry them independent of complex diagrams and tables. Statistics play a supporting role in the drama of the research enterprise. We should not be impressed first by the complexity of formulae and methods and second, by the theoretical scheme, sampling plan, and other more important research features. This is why we say that software programs such as *SPSS* are seductive in a sense. The sophistication of software output may lull us into a false sense of security, where we believe we have produced research of greater significance than it really is.

When investigators prepare their research for public consumption, ideally they should make every effort to point out the deficiencies of their studies. This doesn't mean that researchers must dwell only on the negative aspects of their research, but rather, they should balance their coverage by noting instances where problems may have arisen or concepts were not fully conceived or measured. Adhering to an objectivity standard for reporting one's findings will enhance one's reputation among other professionals. No one should disguise the limitations of a study with powerful statistics and impressive-looking tables and graphs.

HUMAN INTELLIGENCE AND SOFTWARE POWERS: A PRODUCTIVE SYNTHESIS

Using any software program, such as *SPSS Version X*, should be a productive synthesis between what the investigator knows and what the computer program can do to simplify data analyses and produce useful results. Before data are analyzed by any computer software program, it is imperative that researchers should familiarize themselves with several analytical options or statistical alternatives. Knowing which tests to apply in advance of applying them saves a lot of time. The researcher should be able to go directly to the *SPSS Version X* program, and following data entry should analyze the data according to preconceived statistical tests or procedures.

It is equally important for investigators to know the advantages and limitations of any statistical procedure or correlation technique. This includes a knowledge of when particular tests or procedures should be applied and under what conditions such applications may be unsuitable. This synthesis between human intelligence and software applications is extremely important. Software programs can do only what they have been instructed to do. Human intervention is essential when interpreting software output.

SEVERAL MYTHS ABOUT DATA ANALYSIS SOFTWARE PROGRAMS

Students who are new to statistics and their application to social scientific data often have unrealistic expectations about the abilities of software programs they use, such as *SPSS*. Below are several myths about such software programs.

Myth 1. Software programs such as *SPSS* contain all statistical tests and procedures thus far created for any type of data analysis. *False.* Many statistical tests, including several more important tests and procedures, have not been programmed into *SPSS* software and similar programming

Myth 2. Software programs such as *SPSS* make all important interpretations of one's data following their statistical calculation. *False.* Researchers must interpret software-generated data. Tabular reports and statistical summaries require a working knowledge of statistical tests, their assumptions, their appropriate applications, and how these procedures ought to be interpreted. Much work is required of researchers when interpreting numerical findings.

Myth 3. If a software program such as *SPSS* generates particular statistical information, it is always significant and relevant. *False.* Much irrelevant and/or trivial information is produced by *SPSS* and other software programs. Researchers must be selective in extracting only the most relevant information for their particular purposes.

Myth 4. Software programs such as *SPSS* never make mathematical mistakes. *False.* Through data entry, programming errors may occur. The validity and reliability of tests may be poor. There are many points in the research process where errors may occur. Mathematical mistakes may be generated that give misleading results and cause investigators to misinterpret their statistical findings.

Myth 5. Every type of data analysis is available and can be performed by software programs such as *SPSS. False.* Some unique types of data analysis require special tabular construction or variable controls that are beyond the scope of *SPSS* software and similar programming. More often than not, investigators perform special analyses of data on their own, using hand calculators and special interpretive tables not ordinarily found in *SPSS* software.

Myth 6. Software output such as data generated by *SPSS* is a substitute for good thinking. *False.* No software output is a substitute for good thinking. When researchers theorize and hypothesize about different variables and how they should be related or differentiated, they must think critically and beyond the pure numerical results generated by software programs such as *SPSS*. *SPSS* does nothing but generate numerical information and probabilities, including graph construction, depending on the data entered into particular files. The human ingredient is critical for interpreting these numerical results and making sense out of them.

Myth 7. The more sophisticated and technical a statistical application, the more important it is in one's research. *False.* Usually, the more sophisticated the statistical test, the more assumptions are associated with its legitimate application. Frequently, one or more of these more stringent assumptions are not met with the data one is analyzing. This problem leads to misinformation about the significance of one's findings or results, and the credibility of the overall research project is jeopardized. It is very important to choose the most appropriate tests for particular types of data analysis. It is simply wrong to rely on the most complex statistical tools, assuming erroneously that complex is better than simple. Often simple solutions to research problems are better and more appropriate than complex solutions.

Myth 8. Software programs such as *SPSS* know all variable values and how they should be manipulated and interpreted. *False.* Software programs such as *SPSS* only manipulate numerical information. They do not "understand" the meaning of the numerical information, or what the numbers represent. Often, meaningless calculations are made for data such as city name, numerical IDs of respondents, and other indicators of who a person is and where they are from. Software programs do not interpret variables and what they mean. They merely process numerical information included within variable categories, some of which may be meaningless. This is the garbage in–garbage out phenomenon.

Myth 9. Tests of significance and measures of association are pretty much the same and have similar assumptions underlying their application. *False.* There are numerous differences between tests of significance and measures of association concerning the assumptions underlying their legitimate application. It is imperative for investigators to learn about each test or technique and their particular applications, weaknesses, and strengths. It is also important to become familiar with the assumptions underlying all statistical procedures one plans to use, inasmuch as meeting or not meeting these assumptions determines whether those applications are meaningful or meaningless. It is easy to choose the wrong test for data analysis, especially if a software program such as *SPSS* delivers more numerical information than you originally request.

Myth 10. If a software program such as *SPSS* produces statistical test outputs and correlations for data you are analyzing beyond the immediate tests you requested, you can assume that all assumptions underlying those tests have been satisfied. *False.* This myth is closely related to Myth 9. Software output such as that generated by *SPSS* doesn't guarantee that the assumptions associated with any particular test have been satisfied by the data collected. There are often five or six assumptions underlying the appropriate application of particular tests and correlation procedures. Failure to meet one or more of these assumptions means that applying these tests and procedures may yield erroneous or misleading information. It is up to individual researchers to know whether particular assumptions underlying statistical test applications or correlation procedures have been satisfied and that these test applications are appropriate.

SPSS and Subsequent Text Applications

It cannot be assumed that all students using this book will have access to *SPSS* software. If such software isn't available or difficult to locate, this software unavailability will not prevent students from learning valuable statistical material in subsequent chapters. However, for those students who do have access to *SPSS* software, frequent step-by-step boxes are presented with different presentations of descriptive measures as well as tests of significance and correlation procedures.

If professors teaching this course choose to do so, they may skip these *SPSS* references and boxed materials, instead relying on practical problem-solving solutions through the use of calculators and reasoning. Thus, the inclusion of a discussion of *SPSS* software is merely to add a dimension of flexibility to this text and facilitate problem calculation and solutions where appropriate.

Summary

Several software programs exist to enable researchers to analyze their data quickly and easily with some elementary computer programming. One of the more popular software programs for analyzing criminological data is *SPSS*, or the *Statistical Package for the Social Sciences*. *SPSS* is selected here because it has such wide application. Furthermore, it contains numerous tests, graphic programs, and correlation procedures of use to criminologists who do basic research.

It is assumed that most students taking this course have had a basic research methods course and are acquainted with the fundamentals of data gathering, coding of questionnaire or interview information, and other mechanics associated with doing elementary research. *SPSS* software facilitates the data analysis process. This *SPSS* software is explained to a limited degree in the chapter. The intent is not to replace more extensive discussions of *SPSS* software published elsewhere. Rather, it is important for students to know that statistical packages and software programs exist to assist them in their research endeavors.

The process of using *SPSS* begins with data entry, where researchers enter values for different variables taken from questionnaires and other research tools. Once data have been entered into the software program, a data set is established. From here, various tests, techniques, and graphic presentation may be performed with the data set to describe and make decisions about one's findings. *SPSS* has a base system which includes most of the software most criminologists will ever need to analyze their data. There are additional modules available through *SPSS*, Inc., that can perform specialized and more advanced tasks if needed.

A brief description of branches of different options available to researchers was presented, showing that when *SPSS* is opened different windows allow for various choices concerning what researchers want to do. An investigator's research objectives guide this analysis process by indicating what tests ought to be conducted and what types of graphic presentation will best portray one's findings.

Some of the major limitations of data analysis software were discussed. Software programs, such as *SPSS*, process numerical information. They do not interpret this information. Rather, it is imperative for investigators to do most of the interpretive work. Thus, merely generating numerical information, although useful, requires human intervention and guidance.

Some investigators rely too heavily on software output in their research, and they do not apply a great deal of thought to the interpretive work they must perform in order to get the most from the data they have collected. There are also software program weaknesses, where data of different types are manipulated in ways so as to render the results meaningless or useless for any practical research purpose.

Several myths associated with data analysis software programs were presented. It is imperative that investigators insinuate themselves into the data analysis process and make important interpretations of the data they have collected. Software programs such as *SPSS* cannot do everything for the researcher. Therefore, researchers must become familiar with different statistical procedures, their appropriate applications, and their weaknesses and strengths. Statistics is an art in some respects, and students must learn to distinguish between different tests and techniques that have similar purposes but quite different assumptions for their legitimate application.

Key Terms

Data Editor *30*	data set *32*	Statistical Package for the
data entry *29*	personal computers	Social Sciences (*SPSS*) *29*
data view *30*	(PCs) *28*	variable view *30*

Questions for Review

1. What is *SPSS* software? What is it designed to do?
2. Can software programs such as *SPSS* do everything for researchers? Why or why not? Explain.
3. Define five myths associated with applying software such as *SPSS*. In what respects are these myths?
4. What is meant by data entry? What is a data set? Why is it important in the data analysis process?
5. Do software programs such as *SPSS* interpret one's data for them? Why or why not?
6. What are some important types of analysis *SPSS* can perform when analyzing criminological data?

7. What types of graphic presentation are possible to conduct using *SPSS* software?
8. Is all information produced by data analysis software meaningful? Why or why not?
9. How important is it to know about the assumptions associated with statistical techniques and tests when applying *SPSS* software?
10. What is meant by the seductive powers of software output? Explain.

References

SPSS, Inc. (2005). *SPSS 14.0 Brief Guide.* Chicago: SPSS, Inc.

SPSS, Inc. (2006). *SPSS 15.0 Brief Guide.* Chicago: SPSS, Inc.

CHAPTER 3

Graphic Presentation and Frequency Distributions

Chapter Outline

Chapter Objectives

After reading this chapter, the following objectives will be realized:

1. understanding how data can be presented in either ungrouped or grouped form;

2. understanding the nature of frequency distributions, their construction, and usefulness;

3. describing the nature of intervals, upper and lower limits, and midpoints of intervals;

4. understanding ogive curves and their usefulness;

5. describing centiles, deciles, and quartiles in frequency distributions;

6. describing graphs, including pie charts, histograms, frequency polygons, and bar graphs;

7. describing the calculation of percentages and proportions; and

8. understanding the computation and usefulness of rates and ratios.

INTRODUCTION

The phrase, "a picture is worth a thousand words," is worth remembering. This chapter presents an array of visual tools that assist criminologists and others in descriptions of their collected data. Researchers may write several pages about the raw scores they have derived from questionnaires administered to various samples of elements. However, the same information may be portrayed by a simple graph or chart, and the meaningfulness and relevance of this graphic presentation will be immediately apparent.

This chapter is intended to illustrate different ways that data can be displayed graphically. When investigators collect information from various samples of elements, they must organize the data in some meaningful way to convey their information to readers. It will become clear that there are many ways data can be displayed. The chapter starts with a presentation of raw scores and ways in which they can be displayed. It is useful for researchers to distinguish between data in ungrouped form and data in grouped form. Sample size is relevant here, because when very small samples of $N \leq 25$ are encountered, it is easiest to deal with these scores without attempting to group them in some fashion. As the number of scores increases, where $N > 25$, attempting to manipulate scores and determine particular statistical values becomes increasingly cumbersome. Therefore, criminologists group their scores into intervals of various sizes. This makes it easier to view how large numbers of scores are distributed, from high to low. Thus, the first part of this chapter will examine how scores are treated either as ungrouped or grouped for data presentation.

Data in either ungrouped or grouped form are often placed into frequency distributions. The construction of frequency distributions of scores will be illustrated, and some of the finer points of determining intervals for these distributions will be explained. Certain conventional rules are in place for making decisions about how best to construct such distributions. It is helpful to be aware of these rules and when they should be applied. These and other rules will be explained throughout the chapter.

Once data have been arranged into frequency distributions, various computations, such as various measures of central tendency and dispersion, can be computed. It must always be remembered that software programs, such as *SPSS*, exist to simplify such computational work. However, there are occasions when investigators may want to do this work on the spot with a hand calculator without going to the trouble of data entry with a computer. Another benefit of having data arranged into a frequency distribution is that a diagram can be made of the distribution. These diagrams are called histograms and frequency polygons, and they will also be illustrated. Thus, we are in a position to see the different shapes of distributions of scores and whether they fit certain patterns that suggest which descriptive statistical measures we will choose from later when describing our data statistically. Several types of distributions will be described, including ogive curves.

Data may also be illustrated through the use of bar graphs and pie charts. These and other graphic portrayals of our data are often useful in understanding the information researchers present. In the world of business, for example, bar graphs and pie charts are useful for portraying stock trends and market shares. Criminologists and those in criminal justice use such graphs to illustrate crime trends, proportions of inmates at different custody levels in prisons, and other factual information. While such information is easily displayed numerically, supplemental graphs give us a visual portrayal of how data of this kind are distributed.

This chapter concludes with a section dealing with percentages and proportions, as well as the determination of rates and ratios. These calculations are useful for understanding what segments of the probationer and parolee population are under intensive supervision, or how many clients there are in relation to the number of officers supervising them in different probation/parole agencies. If we are discussing prison or jail inmates, rates and ratios will be useful to show inmate population growth or how many inmates there are in relation to the number of correctional officers who supervise them. How fast is the prison inmate population growing in relation to the general population? Are female inmates increasing in prisons at a proportionately greater rate than male inmates? Rate and ratio computations will be illustrated so that such types of questions may be answered easily.

DESCRIBING DATA

Data Treated as Ungrouped

In criminology and criminal justice, data are originally gathered through questionnaires, interviews, and observation. When raw scores from different scales are yielded, they may be in disarray. Raw scores are the actual scores persons are assigned that depict their position or classification on some scale, such as an attitudinal measure. Suppose we are studying some police officers and give them a questionnaire that investigates their professionalism and other variables. By using a scaling procedure, such as a Likert-type scale, we might determine the following scores for 20 police officers on police professionalism, with the smaller scores reflecting low professionalism and the higher scores reflecting high professionalism:

20 19 22 16 24 19 20 21 23 15 22 16 19 20 23 17 20 22 18 16

These police professionalism scores are in **disarray**. Disarray means that these scores are not distributed in any orderly pattern, such as from low to high or high to low. Thus, rearranging them into an array would yield the following more orderly arrangement such as the scores shown in Table 3.1.

From this new arrangement, we can see in Table 3.1 that the smallest police professionalism score is 15, while the largest score is 24. Simple statistical procedures are possible once we have our data arranged into an array. Some of these procedures will be discussed

TABLE 3.1 Arrayed Police Professionalism Scores for 20 Police Officers

15 16 16 16 17 18 19 19 19 20 20 20 20 21 22 22 22 23 23 24

TABLE 3.2 A Disarray of Hypothetical Aptitude Test Scores for 104 Police Trainees

742	760	731	732	751	724	800	738	723	761	790	710	739
752	722	741	711	731	840	792	803	792	810	794	805	770
708	780	771	821	772	812	774	822	795	806	843	711	740
796	720	753	807	797	813	777	808	830	809	819	809	835
818	823	781	816	775	712	817	783	744	824	745	703	709
763	784	746	754	747	825	764	755	725	785	826	756	765
839	786	757	836	758	766	786	759	779	767	772	773	771
798	787	777	799	775	767	786	775	766	786	730	771	774

in Chapters 3 and 4. Whenever one's sample size is 25 or less, the data are treated as ungrouped. **Ungrouped data** are simple arrays of numerical or nominal information without categorization into intervals of sizes larger than 1. These statistical procedures will be referred to as descriptive procedures and will indicate various features about scores arranged in arrays such as this one.

Data Treated as Grouped

What if we have lots of raw scores, such as 104 of them? These might be scores on an aptitude test received by a class of police trainees. Such scores might appear as shown in Table 3.2.

It is clear that little sense can be made of such scores presented in this fashion. Again, these raw scores are in disarray. But how should we go about the task of arranging them so that something meaningful can be determined from them? It would be extremely tedious to go to the trouble of arranging these scores from high to low as they are presently distributed. One of two general rules will be followed, depending upon how many scores we are describing. These rules are as follows:

Rule 1: Whenever we have 25 or fewer scores, we will treat the data as ungrouped.

Rule 2: Whenever we have more than 25 scores, we will treat the data as grouped.

FREQUENCY DISTRIBUTIONS

Grouped data are arranged into **intervals** of a specified size. Intervals are numerical categories of different sizes which contain 1 or more values. While it may not seem like much to accomplish, we can arrange the police professionalism scores of 20 officers shown in Table 3.1 into intervals of size 1 and recast them below in Table 3.3 into a **frequency distribution**. A frequency distribution is the simple tally of values or scores for any sample of elements in some organized fashion. Frequency distributions may reflect ungrouped or grouped data. Notice that in Table 3.3 we have summed the frequencies and designated this sum as Σf. Another equivalency is that the $\Sigma f = N$. N is the sample size. In a frequency distribution, we might use either N or Σf to portray our sample size, also known as the sum of frequencies. Table 3.3 is a frequency distribution of hypothetical police professionalism scores for a sample of 20 police officers.

The frequencies shown in Table 3.3 are the actual numbers of officers who received different police professionalism scores ranging from 24 to 15. The data in Table 3.3 have been organized in order to see how these scores are distributed. It is arguable whether Table 3.3 actually improves our understanding of how these professionalism scores are distributed

TABLE 3.3 Police Professionalism Scores of 20 Police Officers Rearranged into a Frequency Distribution

Scores (High to Low)	Tally	f
24	/	1
23	//	2
22	///	3
21	/	1
20	////	4
19	///	3
18	/	1
17	/	1
16	///	3
15	/	1
	Sum of Frequencies $= \Sigma f = 20$	

compared with how they are arranged into the array shown in Table 3.1. But Table 3.3 demonstrated an elementary statistical symbol, Σ, which means "the sum of." Also, f was introduced, which stands for frequencies. We also learned that the $\Sigma f = N$, the number of persons in our sample.

Frequency distributions may be constructed for any measurement level, including nominal, ordinal, interval, or ratio. These distributions might portray different income levels, attitudinal variations from high to low or low to high, socioeconomic status, degree of peer pressure among delinquents, offense seriousness levels, achievement test scores, or any other measurable characteristic.

Constructing Frequency Distributions When $N > 25$

If we have substantially larger numbers of scores in excess of 25, frequency distributions of scores have greater importance for us. Suppose we wished to construct a frequency distribution of the 104 hypothetical aptitude scores of police trainees as shown in Table 3.2. Here's how we would do it:

1. The first step in constructing a frequency distribution is to identify the largest and smallest scores in the distribution. Inspecting Table 3.2, we determine that the largest and smallest aptitude scores are 843 and 703 respectively.
2. Next, we must determine the difference between the largest and smallest scores. Thus, $843 - 703 = 140$. This difference is actually a crude range over which all 104 scores are distributed. It is also a measure of dispersion that will be discussed later in this chapter. For the present, we are interested only in this difference so that we may determine the size of intervals we will use in establishing our frequency distribution for these scores.
3. Next, we must divide this difference of 140 by a desirable number of intervals. What is a desirable number of intervals? Conventional guidelines exist to follow in criminological research. Too many intervals are as unacceptable to researchers as too few intervals. Following convention, somewhere between 10 and 20 intervals over which our scores will be dispersed is a desirable number of intervals. This minimum and maximum number of intervals will enable us to visualize the distribution of scores clearly. The frequency

distribution we construct will exhibit a particular shape. The shape of our distribution will influence our choice of descriptive statistical measures we will use to describe certain characteristics of our distribution of scores.

If we have too few intervals, less than 10, our data will appear cramped or bunched up, and we will be unable to distinguish any meaningful patterns for our distribution of scores. If we have too many intervals, more than 20 of them, our data will be distributed over too broad of an area, again making it difficult to determine meaningful distributional patterns associated with our scores. Therefore, a number of intervals between 10 and 20, such as 15 intervals, is considered desirable. Although this number of intervals, 15, is purely arbitrary, it is useful for determining a proper **interval size**. Thus, we divide 15 into 140, or 140/15 = 9.33. This 9.33 is a possible interval size. But we are not going to use it. Rather, we will use a whole number as the size of the interval.

Again, convention assists us in determining an appropriate interval size. Several conventional interval sizes are used, such as 2, 3, 4, 5, 10, 20, 30 and so forth. Our resulting 9.33 is closer to 10 than it is to 5. Therefore, if we use 10 as our interval size, this will give us somewhere between 10 and 20 intervals.

4. With our interval size of 10, we must determine a starting point for our interval construction. Again, conventionally, we should begin our intervals with a multiple of the interval size and create intervals of size 10. The first interval created should contain our largest score. This score would be 843. Not only should our first interval contain the largest score but it should also begin with a multiple of the interval size of 10. Given the magnitude of aptitude scores shown in Table 3.2, the first interval we will create is 840–849. 840 is a multiple of 10, the interval size, and the interval, 840–849, includes the largest aptitude score. Our next interval will be 830–839; the next will be 820–829, and so on, until we reach the interval containing the smallest score, 703, which would be 700–709. These intervals have been constructed and placed in Table 3.4.

TABLE 3.4 Frequency Distribution for 104 Hypothetical Aptitude Scores for Police Recruits

Interval	Tallies	f
840–849	//	2
830–839	////	4
820–829	///// /	6
810–819	///// //	7
800–809	///// ///	8
790–799	///// ////	9
780–789	///// /////	10
770–779	///// ///// /////	15
760–769	///// ////	9
750–759	///// ////	9
740–749	///// //	7
730–739	///// /	6
720–729	/////	5
710–719	////	4
700–709	///	3
		$\Sigma f = 104$

5. After we have constructed all of our intervals from those containing the smallest scores to those containing the largest scores, we then tally the actual number of scores in each interval. From Table 3.2, we determine that there are 2 scores belonging in the interval, 840–849; 4 scores belonging in the interval, 830–839, and so forth. Both tallies and frequencies have been inserted into Table 3.4 as shown.

Table 3.4 is a frequency distribution for the scores in disarray shown earlier in Table 3.2. Contrasting the two forms in which the data appear, it is apparent that our frequency distribution in Table 3.4 provides a much clearer picture of officer aptitude scores. This is the primary reason for grouping our data into intervals of a specified size.

Several important reasons for using conventional interval sizes and beginning our intervals with multiples of these sizes are: (1) using multiples of a conventional interval size enables us to detect possible errors in our frequency distribution construction; (2) we can easily scan the beginning values in each interval to see that they are multiples of the interval size; and (3) we can make a check on the accuracy of our work in subsequent statistical computations. For instance, had we constructed some of these intervals as follows:

840–849

828–840

820–827

809–819

799–810

Scanning the first values in each interval, 840, 828, 820, 809, and 799, will alert us to possible errors. Closer inspection of our intervals indicates that the interval, 840–849, is acceptable. However, the interval, 828–840, is an incorrect interval size. This interval, 828–840, actually contains 13 possible values instead of 10 (e.g., 828, 829, 830, 831, 832, 833, 834, 835, 836, 837, 838, 839, and 840). Accordingly, the interval, 820–827, contains only 8 possible scores instead of 10 (e.g., 820, 821, 822, 823, 824, 825, 826, and 827).

It is important to keep our intervals the same size throughout the frequency distribution. Later, when we compute various measures of central tendency, such as the mean or median, and various measures of dispersion or variability, such as the standard deviation, these computations use the interval size, i, as a part of the formula. Therefore, if the interval sizes differ from one interval to the next, our computations for these descriptive statistics and others will be inaccurate.

Interval Characteristics: Midpoints, Upper Limits, and Lower Limits

All frequency distributions have interval characteristics. These interval characteristics include **interval midpoints, upper limits of intervals**, and **lower limits of intervals**. First, let's examine some of the intervals from Table 3.4. Specifically, let's examine the interval, 830–839. This interval actually extends from 829.5 to 839.5. These are the lower and upper limits of the interval. By adding .5 to the upper value, 839, we get 839.5, while subtracting .5 from the lower value, 830, we get 829.5. The difference between the upper limit and lower limit of the interval is the interval size, or 10.

Upper and lower limits are useful, particularly if we encounter scores expressed in decimal values. Suppose we had several decimal values, 829.1, 839.9, 829.9, and 839.4. If we were using the intervals in Table 3.4, we might need to consider the lower and upper limits of each interval in order to determine where specific values or scores ought to be placed.

For instance, the score, 829.1 would belong in the interval, 820–829, because the interval actually extends from 819.5 to 829.5. 829.1 is within this interval. The score, 829.5, is problematic, however. Notice that the interval, 830–839, actually extends from 829.5 to 839.5. But the interval, 820–829, actually extends from 819.5 to 829.5. Thus, the upper limit of one interval, 820–829, is actually the lower limit of the other interval, 830–839. Where should 829.5 be placed? A rounding rule applies here. The rounding rule followed in this book is that if we have a choice, we will round in the direction of the nearest even number. Thus, 829.5 can be rounded to either 829 or 830 without the rule, but with the rule in effect, we will round this value to 830. Therefore, we will place this value in the interval, 830–839. Values such as 829.1 belong in the interval, 820–829.

This rounding decision is purely arbitrary. Some textbooks require students to round in the direction of the nearest odd number. There is nothing wrong with this. Authors select one rounding method or the other in order to be systematic in their calculations. In this book, therefore, if you want your answers to be consistent with those for different calculations for this and subsequent chapters, round in the direction of the nearest even number if you are midway between two whole numbers. Some examples of rounding are:

382.3 rounded to 382

496.5 rounded to 496

496.6 rounded to 497

382.6 rounded to 383

382.5 rounded to 382

15.4 rounded to 15

15.6 rounded to 16

15.5 rounded to 16

Interval midpoints are center points that divide the interval into two equal parts. If an interval size is 10, such as in Table 3.4, interval midpoints are determined as follows. First, determine an interval lower limit. The interval, 820–829, is an example. The lower limit of this interval is 819.5. Next, we determine half of the interval size, or 10/2 = 5. Then we add this "5" to the lower limit of the interval, or 819.5 + 5 = 824.5. Thus, the midpoint of the interval, 820–829 is 824.5. The midpoints of all intervals in Table 3.4 are, beginning with the interval containing the largest scores, 844.5, 834.5, 824.5, 814.5, 804.5, 794.5, 784.5, 774.5, 764.5, 754.5, 744.5, 734.5, 724.5, 714.5, and 704.5.

Interval midpoints are important because they represent the average value in each interval. The interval, 800–809, in Table 3.4, for instance, has an interval midpoint of 804.5. It is assumed that all values in the interval are 804.5. It makes no difference whether there are actual scores of 804.5. The fact is that this is what is assumed. It may be that all scores in the interval are 800, or 809. But that doesn't matter. There are 15 scores in the interval, 770–779. The interval midpoint is 774.5. All 15 scores in this interval are therefore assumed to be 774.5, even though no such score exists. When scores are arranged into intervals such as those shown in Table 3.4, there is a trade-off of sorts. We sacrifice accuracy for convenience in displaying these scores in a way that can be easily understood. The accuracy sacrificed is that if all 15 scores in the interval, 770–779, are 779, and if it is assumed that all scores in the interval are the size of the interval midpoint, 774.5, then we are underestimating the actual scores in the interval. But we gain by being able to see the distributional shape of the scores. And our computations of different descriptive statistics are made easier because of this midpoint assumption. Some examples of midpoints and lower and upper limits of intervals are as follows:

Interval	Midpoint	Lower Limit	Upper Limit
920–924	922	919.5	924.5
8–11	9.5	7.5	11.5
.12–.15	.135	.115	.155
250–274	262	249.5	274.5

Cumulative Frequency Distributions: Ogive Curves

Sometimes researchers find it useful to construct **cumulative frequency distributions**. Cumulative frequency distributions are constructed so that frequencies from intervals containing the smallest scores are added to the frequencies of successive intervals containing larger scores. We can use the information from Table 3.4 to illustrate cumulative frequency distributions.

To construct a cumulative frequency distribution, we usually start at the bottom of the frequency distribution with the interval containing the smallest scores. In Table 3.5, we would start with the interval, 700–709. This interval contains 3 frequencies. We record these in a column to the far right labeled *cf*. *cf* stands for cumulative frequencies. The next interval, 710–719, has 4 frequencies in it. These should now be added to those in the previous interval, or 4 + 3 = 7. The cumulative frequencies thus far are 12. We next add the frequencies in the interval, 720–729, 5, to the 7 frequencies in the first two intervals, or 5 + 7 = 12 frequencies, and so on. We continue to add frequencies from each successive interval to the sum of all previous frequencies from lower intervals. Eventually, we will reach the interval containing the largest scores, 840–849. Adding these two frequencies to all previous frequencies will give us 104 frequencies.

TABLE 3.5 Data from Table 3.4 Arranged into a Cumulative Frequency Distribution

Interval	f	cf
840–849	2	104
830–839	4	102
820–829	6	98
810–819	7	92
800–809	8	85
790–799	9	77
780–789	10	68
770–779	15	58
760–769	9	43
750–759	9	34
740–749	7	25
730–739	6	18
720–729	5	12
710–719	4	7
700–709	3	3
	$\Sigma f = 104$	

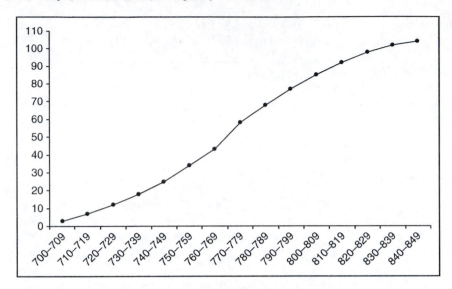

FIGURE 3.1   Ogive Curve for Frequencies in Table 3.5

Cumulative frequency distributions are useful in helping us locate various points such as the approximate center of the distribution. They also depict the rapidity of score increases, from lowest to highest. Figure 3.1 shows an **ogive curve** drawn for the cumulative frequency distribution shown in Table 3.5.

Ogive (pronounced "oh-jive") curves can be used to portray other phenomena as well. The Bureau of Justice Statistics (2007) has presented information about drug use in the United States and specifically discussed the ages at which users or addicts become inactive. For instance, Figures 3.2 and 3.3 two different ways that the Bureau of Justice Statistics has portrayed addict information.

In Figure 3.2, for instance, a hypothetical sample of 40,000 drug users and the peak periods of drug use over time is shown. It appears from Figure 3.2 that drug use peaks during one's 20s and early 30s and then rapidly declines between ages 35 and 45. Very infrequent drug use is shown to continue beyond age 45. Figure 3.3 shows an ogive curve for this same information. This ogive curve shows a cumulative distribution of the ages at which different addicts cease drug use. Thus, ogive curves may represent a wide number of variables and slowly or rapidly they increase or decrease in value.

GRAPHICALLY PORTRAYING FREQUENCY DISTRIBUTIONS

One of the best ways of describing distributions of scores is through the use of **graphs**. Graphs are line drawings that show diagrammatically and pictorially the distribution of scores in any data set. There are different kinds of graphs. One type of graph illustrated in the previous section of this chapter was an ogive curve constructed from a cumulative frequency distribution. Several other types of graphs presented here include (1) bar graphs; (2) trend graphs; (3) pie charts; (4) histograms; and (5) frequency polygons.

Bar Graphs

Bar graphs are charts that use bars consisting of slender horizontal or vertical areas that depict the frequency of occurrence of particular characteristics. All variables have subclasses that can be

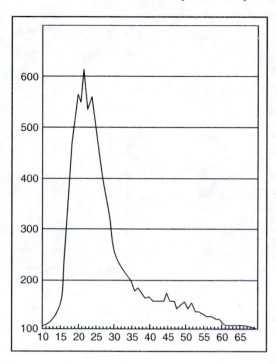

FIGURE 3.2   Incidence of Addicts Becoming Inactive at Given Ages

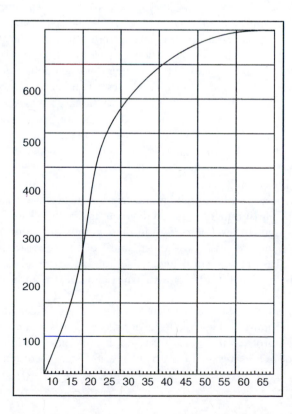

FIGURE 3.3   Cumulative Ogive Curve of Age at which Addicts Become Inactive

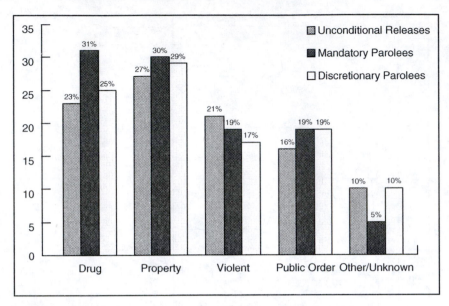

FIGURE 3.4   Bar Graph for Unconditional Mandatory, and Discretionary Releases and Percentage of First Rearrests

portrayed as bar graphs. The bar graph in Figure 3.4, for instance, shows the percentage of first rearrests of state parolees for various types of offenses, including drugs, property crimes, violent crimes, public order crimes, and other/unknown. Amy Solomon (2006) used state figures from the Bureau of Justice Statistics to determine the percentage of rearrests of state parolees for given offenses. The first vertical bar for each crime listed in Figure 3.4 refers to those parolees of unconditional releases. The second vertical bar for each offense category is the percentage of mandatory releases, while the third vertical bar shows the percentage of discretionary releases. This bar graph is informative in that it shows that mandatory releases have higher percentages of first rearrests following parole compared with unconditional or discretionary releases for drug and property offenses. Unconditional releases have the highest percentage of first rearrests for violent offenses. Other interpretations of this information can also be made. The point illustrated is the usefulness of bar graphs for depicting numbers of frequencies or percentages of occurrence of subclasses of variables in criminological research.

Bar graphs are useful for illustrating crime rates, arrest rates, types of incarcerated offenders, and other variables of relevance to criminology and criminal justice. Bar graphs are unrestricted regarding the level of measurement required for their application. They can be constructed for data at any measurement level. Bars used in these graphs can be of various widths to reflect proportions of persons possessing certain attributes or characteristics.

Bar graphs may be horizontal as well as vertical. Figure 3.5 shows a horizontal bar graph of the primary functions of full-time federal officers with arrest and firearm authority for September 2004.

In this instance, horizontal bars have been constructed to depict those officers involved in criminal investigation, police response and patrol, inspections, corrections and detention, court operations, and security and protection. A vertical bar graph could have been used for the same purpose. The method of presenting such bar graphs is at the sole discretion of the researcher (see Box 3.1).

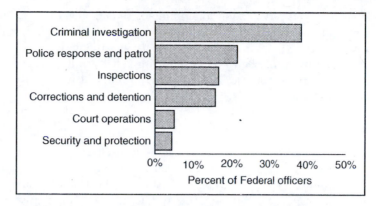

FIGURE 3.5 **Primary Functions of Full-Time Federal Officers with Arrest and Firearm Authority, September 2004**

Source: U.S. Department of Justice, 2006 (public domain), p. 2.

Trend Graphs

Amy Solomon (2006) has also charted state prisoner releases during the years 1980–2000, using Bureau of Justice Statistics information. Using information from Hughes, Wilson, and Beck (2002), Solomon reported **trend information** as shown in Figure 3.6. **Trend data** reflect fluctuations in different variables over time. For instance, in Figure 3.6, it is clear that between 1980 and 2000, the use of discretionary parole declined from approximately 60 percent to about 20 percent, while mandatory parole increased among state parolees from 20 percent to approximately 40 percent. The use of unconditional parole fluctuated the least during this 20-year period, ranging between 10 and 15 percent.

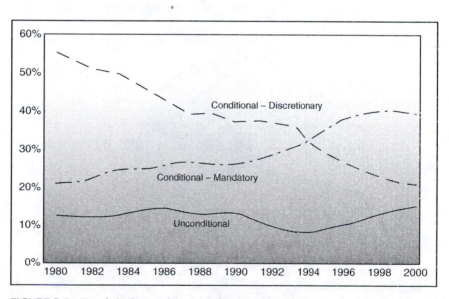

FIGURE 3.6 **Trends in State Prisoners Releases, 1980–2000**

Source: Hughes, Wilson, and Beck, 2002 (public domain).

Trend information is very valuable for criminologists and others. It assists in supporting statements relating to whether certain types of crime are increasing or decreasing over time, and whether certain crime-prevention initiatives are having any effect on crime trends. Other uses of trend information may be to focus on death penalty and murder rates following particular U.S. Supreme Court decisions over a given time interval. Investigators who use such information engage in **trend analysis**.

Pie Charts

Another useful type of graph for illustrating data is a **pie chart**. A pie chart, shaped like a pie, is a circular graph divided into sections that represent segments or portions of the circle or pie. For instance, Figure 3.7 is a pie chart showing the proportionate distribution of felons and misdemeanants according to Class A, B, C, and D felonies, misdemeanors, and "other." This visual portrayal of the distribution of crimes for a given sample of prisoners is useful for determining which crimes are most frequently represented. Such visual portrayals of information are useful supplements to other descriptive information in documents.

Pie charts are useful for illustrating type of prison construction in any given year (e.g., supermax, maximum, medium, or minimum security); proportions of offenders with drug dependencies; proportions of probationers/parolees being supervised intensively; and monetary allocations for different corrections programs. For instance, Figure 3.8 shows correctional services expenditures for fiscal year 2005 for a given state. The pie chart in this case has been portrayed in pie-shaped pieces and set apart from one continuous circle. Custody clearly accounts for a majority of expenditures (56 percent), followed by inmate health care (11 percent). Pie charts shown in Figures 3.7 and 3.8 are simply different ways of presenting information so that readers can readily determine the allocation of expenditures by category.

There is almost no limitation on what pie charts might represent. One recommendation in the construction of pie charts is that they should not be subdivided so extensively that they

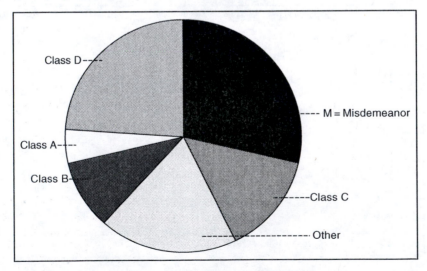

FIGURE 3.7   Pie Chart of a Hypothetical State Distribution of Crimes, by Class A, B, C, and D Felonies, Misdemeanors, and Other

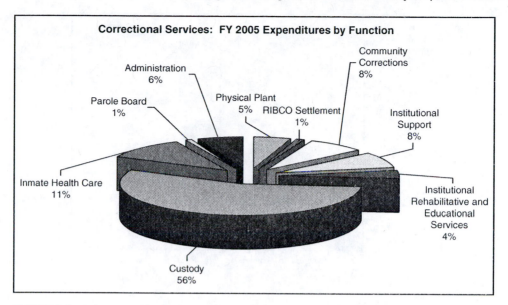

FIGURE 3.8   A Segmented Pie Chart of Correctional Services Expenditures, Fiscal Year 2005 by Function

become cluttered. A good rule of thumb is to limit the number of segments of the pie chart to six. Pie charts with more than six subdivisions may become cluttered and more difficult to interpret. The different sectors of the pie chart may be difficult to label. In the pie chart in Figure 3.7, this chart was divided into five segments. For the pie chart in Figure 3.8, it was divided into 9 segments. While the pie chart in Figure 3.8 exceeds the recommended number of subdivisions, it does not appear cluttered in terms of how it is presented. Usually, guidelines for subdividing pie charts are rules of thumb, and departures from such rules occur occasionally without serious consequences. As long as the pie chart is neatly portrayed and can be interpreted easily, it is useful for researchers who wish to study the phenomena illustrated (see Box 3.1).

Histograms and Frequency Polygons

When investigators have constructed frequency distributions for their data, they may depict these frequency distributions graphically as either **histograms** or **frequency polygons**. Histograms are bar-graph-type portrayals of frequencies in successive intervals. Frequency polygons are line drawings constructed from histograms that link the centers and tops of histogram bars. Figures 3.9 and 3.10 show a histogram and frequency polygon for the data originally presented in a frequency distribution in Table 3.4.

In the case of the histogram in Figure 3.9, this is simply a vertical bar graph, where the bars are centered over interval midpoints of the frequency distribution from Table 3.4. The heights of the bars are determined by the number of frequencies in each interval. Notice in Figure 3.9 that the midpoints of each interval have been indicated, and that the height of each bar reflects the number of frequencies associated with each interval midpoint. A rule of thumb governing the construction of histograms and frequency polygons are that the vertical axes (showing numbers of frequencies in each interval) should be about 2/3rds the length of the horizontal axis, showing interval midpoints.

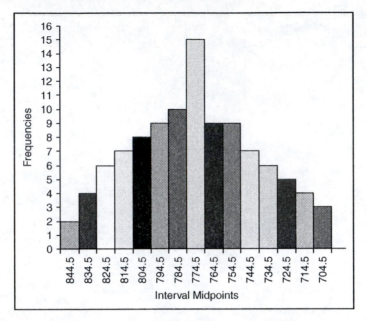

FIGURE 3.9 Histogram Based on Frequencies and Internal Midpoints

Figure 3.10 is a frequency polygon of precisely the same information in Table 3.4, except in this case, where lines have been drawn to connect the tops and centers of the vertical bars that appeared in Figure 3.9. Points have been used to indicate the height (frequencies) and interval midpoint. The bars have been eliminated, leaving nothing more than connected dots showing a pattern of the dispersion of frequencies across the successive intervals. The frequency polygon

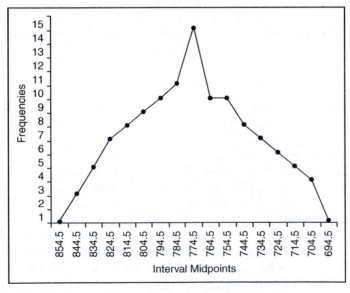

FIGURE 3.10 Frequency Polygon Based on Frequencies and Interval Midpoints

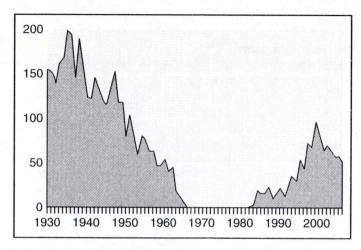

FIGURE 3.11   Executions, 1930–2006

Source: Bureau of Justice Statistics, January 11, 2007.

in Figure 3.10 has been anchored at both ends of the distribution to the next lowest and next highest intervals containing zero frequencies. This means that additional intervals have been added at each end of the distribution, with interval midpoints of 854.5 and 694.5 respectively. These interval midpoints are associated with intervals that have no frequencies in them. Their purpose is simply to tie down or anchor the frequency polygon to the baseline or horizontal axis for closure.

The patterns displayed by these frequency polygons are very important. This is because they denote a particular shape of any distribution of scores. Shapes of distributions of scores are especially important for making decisions about which statistical measures should be chosen and computed later for data analysis purposes. Certain descriptive statistics, such as measures of central tendency and measures of dispersion or variability are chosen largely on the basis of the distribution of a particular set of scores where they will be applied.

Sometimes investigators will fill in or shade the frequency polygons they have constructed for particular kinds of data depicted. For instance, Figure 3.11 illustrates a frequency polygon of executions in the United States from 1930 to 2006.

This frequency polygon has been shaded to make it bolder in presentation. There is a noticeable decline in the death penalty during the period, 1972–1976. This was during a period when the U.S. Supreme Court held that Georgia had been deciding to administer the death penalty on the basis of racial criteria, and thus these criteria, not the death penalty itself, were declared unconstitutional. The death penalty was suspended nationwide for a 4-year period during which time each state administering the death penalty re-examined its procedures in determining its application in capital cases. Eventually, in 1976, the criteria for deciding the death penalty in Georgia were declared constitutional by the U.S. Supreme Court, and Georgia and other states began using the death penalty subsequently in compliance with these new guidelines (see Box 3.1).

BOX 3.1

SPSS Alternative Application

For Pie Chart Construction

1. Code the five categories of "years of service" from 1 to 5, where $1 = 5$ or fewer, $2 = 6-10$, $3 = 11-14$, $4 = 15-19$, and $5 = 20+$. This step need *not* be repeated for each type of graph you decide to create (e.g., pie, bar, and histogram).
2. Activate the *SPSS* program. This opens the *SPSS* Data Editor window. Go to the first "var" on the Data Editor screen and enter 22 scores of 1, 12 scores of 2, 18 scores of 3, 7 scores of 4, and 3 scores of 5. This action will convert "var" to "Var00001." You should see a list of numbers, 22 of which will be "1," 12 will be "2," and so on.
3. Click on the "Graphs" designation across the top of the screen.
4. Click on "Pie." Click on "Summaries for Groups of Cases."
5. Next, check the "Percentage of Cases" circle.
6. Use arrow to "Define Slices by" and VAR00001 will appear in previously blank box. Click "OK."
7. A pie chart will appear, showing unlabeled designations of the proportion of correctional officers in different colored pie slices. If labels are desired for these pie slices, then click "Help" on the screen, and instructions will be provided to assist in labeling these pie parts.

For Bar Graph Construction

1. Click on "Graphs" then "Bar."
2. Click "Simple" then "Define."
3. Click "Summaries for Groups of Cases" under "Data in Chart are."
4. For "Category Axis," use Arrow click. This moves "VAR00001" to window.
5. Click "N of Cases." Click "OK."
6. A bar graph will appear displaying the Ns for each of the five groups of officers according to years of service. No labels are visible for this bar graph. For instructions on labeling these bars, use the "Help" feature.

For Histogram Construction

1. Click on "Graphs" then "Histogram."
2. "VAR00001" appears in box. Click "OK."
3. A histogram appears showing "frequencies" of each group of officers with so many years of service on the vertical axis. The horizontal axis shows the numerical categories 1 through 5 that you created at the point of Data Entry.

For line drawings, such as frequency polygons, these graphs can be similarly displayed by clicking on the different options under "Graphs."

PERCENTAGES, PROPORTIONS, RATES, AND RATIOS

Percentages and Proportions

Whenever investigators discuss their research findings, they frequently use **percentages** and **proportions**. Percentages are expressed by dividing a part of a sum of frequencies by the sum of frequencies and multiplying the result by 100. Proportions are expressed by dividing a part of a sum of frequencies by the sum of frequencies.

TABLE 3.6 Number of Persons Held in State or Federal Prisons or in Local Jails, 1995–2005

Year	Total Inmates in custody	Prisoners in custody on December 31		Inmates held in local jails
		Federal	State	
1995	1,585,586	89,538	989,004	507,044
2000	1,937,482	133,921	1,176,269	621,149
2001	1,961,247	143,337	1,180,155	631,240
2002	2,033,022	151,618	1,209,331	685,475
2003	2,081,580	161,673	1,222,135	691,301
2004	2,135,335	170,535	1,243,745	713,990
2005	2,193,798	179,220	1,259,905	747,529
Percent change, 12/31/04–12/31/05	2.7%	5.1%	1.3%	4.7%
Average annual increase, 12/31/95–12/31/05	3.3%	7.2%	2.5%	4.0%

Source: Harrison, Paige M. and Allan J. Beck. *Prisoners in 2005*. Washington, DC: U.S. Department of Justice, November 2006, p. 2.

An example of calculating proportions and percentages is illustrated by the information shown in Table 3.6. The table shows the number of persons held in state or federal prisons and jails during the years 1995–2005 (Harrison and Beck, 2006:2). The table provides data of total inmates in custody, total state and federal prisoners in custody, and total jail inmates for these years. It also shows average annual increases in inmate growth from 1995 to 2005 as well as percent change from December 31, 2004 to December 31, 2005.

If we wanted to determine the percentage of federal inmates in custody compared with the total number of inmates in custody for 1995, for instance, we would divide the total number of federal inmates, 89,538, by the total number of inmates in custody for that year, or 1,585,586. We would multiply this result by 100. This would give us the following:

$$\text{Percentage of federal inmates in custody for 1995} = \frac{89,536}{1,585,586} \times (100)$$

$$= 0.0564(100) = 5.65\%$$

Thus, 5.65 percent comprised the total number of inmates in custody during 1995. Suppose we wanted to determine the percentage of jail inmates in custody during 2003, we would divide the number of local jail inmates for that year, 691,301, by the total number of inmates in custody that same year, or 2,081,580, and multiply this result by 100. This computation would be:

$$\frac{691,301}{2,081,580} \times (100)$$

$$= 0.332(100) = 33.2\%$$

Therefore, 33.2 percent of all inmates in custody during 2003 were jail inmates.

Had we wanted to compute proportions for these same figures, we would not have multiplied the results by 100. In short, federal inmates in custody for 1995 made up a proportion of .0564, while .332 was the proportion of jail inmates making up the total number of inmates in custody for 2003. Therefore, percentages are the same as proportions, as percentages are computed by multiplying proportions by 100.

Rates: Determining Percentage/Proportion Increases From Year to Year

Suppose we were interested in determining the proportion or percentage increase in the federal inmate population or any other designated inmate population from Table 3.6? Let's suppose we wanted to determine the proportionate increase in the total number of inmates in custody between the years 2000 and 2005? We would accomplish this task by calculating the difference between the two years and dividing the result by the total number of inmates in custody in 2000. These calculations are as follows:

$$\frac{\text{Total Inmates in Custody in 2005} - \text{Total Inmates in Custody in 2000}}{\text{Total Inmates in Custody in 2000}}$$

$$\text{or} \quad \frac{2{,}193{,}798 - 1{,}937{,}482}{1{,}937{,}482}$$

$$\frac{256{,}316}{1{,}937{,}482} = 0.132$$

Thus, there was a .132 proportionate increase in the total number of inmates in custody between the years 2000 and 2005. Converting this value to a percentage would be $(.132)(100) =$ 13.2 percent. There was a 13.2 percent increase in the total number of inmates in custody between the years 2000 and 2005. These are also known as **rates** of growth or **growth rates**.

If we wanted to verify the percentage changes from December 31, 2004 to December 31, 2005 and the average annual increase from December 31, 1995 to December 31, 2005, let's begin with the percent change from December 31, 2004 to December 31, 2005. We would simply perform a function similar to what we have already done, we would only use the 2004 and 2005 figures for this purpose. Thus, taking the total inmates in custody for the years 2004 and 2005, we would have:

$$= \frac{2{,}193{,}798 - 2{,}135{,}335}{2{,}135{,}335}$$

$$= 0.0274$$

Converting this value to a percentage, we would have $(.274)(100) = 2.7$ percent. This is consistent with what is reported in Table 3.6. To calculate the average annual increase from December 31, 1995 to December 31, 2005, as this involves more work, we would have to take each pair of years from 1995 to 2005 and determine the proportion increase each year. Then we would sum these values and divide by the number of values. As shown in Table 3.6, we would calculate percentage growth as follows:

$$1995{-}2000 = (1{,}937{,}482 - 1{,}585{,}586)/1{,}585{,}586 = .221 \,(100) = 22.1\%$$
$$2000{-}2001 = (1{,}961{,}247 - 1{,}937{,}482)/1{,}937{,}482 = .012 \,(100) = 1.2\%$$
$$2001{-}2002 = (2{,}033{,}022 - 1{,}961{,}247)/1{,}961{,}247 = .037 \,(100) = 3.7\%$$

$$2002-2003 = (2,081,580-2,033,022)/2,033,022 = .024\,(100) = 2.4\%$$
$$2003-2004 = (2,135,335-2,081,580)/2,081,580 = .026\,(100) = 2.6\%$$
$$2004-2005 = (2,193,798-2,135,335)/2,135,335 = .027\,(100) = 2.7\%$$

We cannot calculate the average annual rates of increase accurately from these figures. The reason is that information for total inmates in custody is missing for the years 1996, 1997, 1998, and 1999. Had these years been supplied with this table, we would have made similar percentage increase calculations for every year. Evidently this was done for these data, and the average annual increase in total inmates in custody was calculated to be 3.3 percent as shown in the table. Thus there was an average annual growth rate of 3.3 percent per year in the total number of inmates in custody.

Sometimes rates are expressed "per 100,000" or "per 10,000" to give some comparison with other jurisdictions. Different crimes are portrayed in this fashion, as one example. For instance, the murder rates of different cities might yield quite different results if expressed on the basis of per 100,000 or per 10,000. In two cities where the respective populations are 50,000 and 500,000, the number of murders in a given year, such as 2007, might be 25 and 620. If we divide 25 by 50,000, then the murder rate = .0005. For the city of 500,000 and 620 murders, this rate would be 620/500,000 = .0012. If we were to use 100,000 as our comparative standard, we would simply multiply these proportions by 100,000 to get the rate per 100,000, or

$$.0005\,(100,000) = 50 = 50 \text{ per } 100,000 \text{ or } .0005\,(10,000) = 5 = 5 \text{ per } 10,000.$$
$$.0012\,(100,000) = 120 \text{ per } 100,000 \text{ or } .0012\,(10,000) = 12 = 12 \text{ per } 10,000.$$

It is clear from either of these figures that the murder rates for the two cities are distinctly different. There are 50 murders per 100,000 persons (or 5 murders per 10,000) in the first city and 120 murders per 100,000 (or 12 murders per 10,000) in the second city. Bear in mind that the first city size is only 50,000. Therefore, the 100,000 standard is used to standardize these rates for easy comparison. The 10,000 figure as a standard might be a more meaningful comparison for the first city, since it has a population of only 50,000. Regardless of the standard we choose, we would conclude that the second city has twice the murder rate as in the first city. Therefore, if we were interested in a city with a low-murder rate, we might choose the first city over the second. These comparisons are extremes, however. But they do serve as examples of how rates might be calculated.

Ratios

Mark Jones and John Kerbs (2007) studied discretionary decision making and technical/criminal violations of clients supervised by probation and parole officers. They profiled 322 officers, including selected sociodemographic characteristics, job description/title, agency affiliation, caseload, type of caseload, and several other factors. They found, for instance, that in some jurisdictions, officers had average caseloads of 141 offenders, while in other jurisdictions, average caseloads were as high as 4,000. These variations in caseload **ratios** were cited as one reason for why probation and parole officer supervision quality may be adversely affected. A recommendation was made to reduce these caseload sizes in order to enhance the quality of community supervision.

Suppose Jones and Kerbs were studying a probation agency in a large city with 20,400 probationer/clients and a probation officer staff of 12. Further suppose that in a nearby city, another contingent of 42,500 probationer/clients was being supervised by a probation officer staff of 18. Which city probation department would have the lower officer/client ratio? Let's call the first city as City A, while the second city can be called City B. We would have the following information:

	Probation Officer Staff	Probation Clients
City A	12	20,400
City B	18	42,500

The ratio of officers to clients for both cities would be computed as follows:

$$\text{City A: Ratio of officers to clients} = \frac{20,400}{12} = 1,700 \text{ or } 1{:}1700$$

$$\text{City B: Ratio of officers to clients} = \frac{42,500}{18} = 2,361 \text{ or } 1{:}2361$$

City B would clearly have the larger officer/client ratio. In each of these cases, the total number of supervised probationers would be divided by the total number of probation officers. These are considered extremely high officer-to-client ratios by any stretch of the imagination, yet some cities have such high ratios. Compared with intensive supervised probation, where officer-to-client ratios are very low, such as 1:20 or 1:40, a 1:1,700 or 1:2,361 ratio is so large that no individualized attention can be given to any client. It is little wonder that recidivism rates are so high among probationers under situations where officer/client ratios are extremely high. Reducing these ratios would, of course, involve hiring more probation officers and training them. This is a costly affair for states, cities, and counties, and there is always the matter of financing the hiring of new positions. Nevertheless, Jones and Kerbs rightly recommend lowering these high officer/client ratios in the belief that such reductions will have positive benefits for those probationer-clients supervised.

Other applications of ratios might be to prisons, where officers to inmates are often calculated. Maximum-security facilities tend to have lower officer–inmate ratios, while minimum-security institutions may have larger officer–inmate ratios. The reason for these ratio differences is that more dangerous offenders are being supervised in maximum-security prisons, and thus more correctional officers are needed to supervise them closely. In minimum-security prisons, inmates are less inclined to commit violent acts and more inclined to follow institutional rules. Therefore, fewer correctional officers are needed to supervise them and exercise control over them if the need arises.

Summary

Graphic presentation encompasses all ways of illustrating one's collected data apart from statistical calculations such as measures of central tendency or dispersion. Depending on the number of persons studied in one's research, data are usually treated as either ungrouped or grouped. Data are treated as ungrouped if one's sample size is 25 or less. For more than 25 elements, data are grouped into intervals of various sizes.

Raw scores are often arranged into frequency distributions, which are orderly arrangements of intervals of a given size which contain frequencies. Frequencies are the scores elements receive on some variable subclass, such as an attitudinal score, an age, or years of education.

Creating frequency distributions for one's data organizes it in a way that can be viewed by investigators. Establishing intervals of specified sizes to encompass all of the scores in a distribution of them enables investigators to see certain features of them that suggest particular descriptive techniques for subsequent data analysis. Several characteristics of frequency distributions were discussed. Interval midpoints and upper and lower limits of intervals were described.

Actual graphs may be constructed for data arranged into a frequency distribution. Histograms may be constructed. These histograms are usually vertical bars, where the height of each bar represents the number of frequencies in any given interval. Sometimes investigators will construct frequency polygons, which are line drawings of a distribution. The lines in a frequency polygon are the midpoints and tops of vertical bars that are usually constructed first as a histogram. Illustrations of both histograms and frequency polygons were presented. Besides traditional frequency distributions, cumulative frequency distribution construction was described. Histograms constructed from cumulative frequency distributions are called ogive curves and have special purposes.

Such graphic presentation is not limited to raw scores for a sample of elements. Histograms are useful for portraying other information, such as trend information over time. Other forms of graphic presentation include bar graphs and pie charts. Pie charts are designed for representing different portions of a circle, which is designed to portray a population or some whole variable, such as expenditures. Pie charts easily illustrate the largest portions of the "pie" and give a rapid visual appraisal of how subparts of the whole pie chart are divided. Bar graphs look very much like histograms, although they usually represent percentages of persons who have certain characteristics, such as differentiated crime characteristics or other variables. Bar graphs may be either vertical or horizontal, depending on the preferences of the investigator.

The chapter concluded with a discussion of percentages, proportions, rates, and ratios. Percentages are easily computed by dividing a portion of a given population by the population itself. Percentages are also proportions multiplied by 100. Rates, such as growth rates, indicate the percentage increase (or decrease) of a population or subpopulation of elements over different time periods. These growth rates are usually computed by taking different populations for two different years, determining their difference, and dividing by the population of the earlier year. Ratios are also determined by taking two values, such as the number of robberies for 2007 in Atlanta, Georgia, and dividing this number into the total population in Atlanta, Georgia, for 2007. This result is a proportion which can be multiplied by 10,000 or 100,000 or some other figure to yield a rate. Thus, proportions of all crimes in Atlanta, Georgia, for 2007 can be converted to rates when multiplied by some standard figure as indicated above. Reducing these values to a common standard enables researchers to compare rates for different cities according to an infinite number of criteria.

Key Terms

bar graphs *54*
cumulative frequency
   distribution *53*
disarray *47*
frequency distribution *48*
frequency polygons *59*
graphs *54*
grouped data *48*
growth rates *64*

histograms *59*
interval midpoints *51*
intervals *48*
interval size *50*
lower limits of intervals *51*
ogive curve *54*
percentages *62*
pie chart *58*
proportions *62*

rates *64*
ratios *65*
trend analysis *58*
trend data *57*
trend information *57*
ungrouped data *48*
upper limits of
   intervals *51*

Questions for Review

1. What are the guidelines suggested for treating data as either grouped or ungrouped? Explain.
2. What is a frequency distribution? How are intervals determined for frequency distributions?
3. What are upper and lower limits of intervals? Why is it important to know these upper and lower limits? Explain.
4. Differentiate between a histogram and a frequency polygon. What value do these graphs and charts have for illustrating one's data? Discuss.
5. What is a cumulative frequency distribution? What are some of its purposes?
6. What is an ogive curve? What does it depict?
7. What is a pie chart? Are there suggested limitations for creating segments of a pie chart?
8. What is a bar graph? Can it be either vertical or horizontal? What are examples of variables that can be placed into a bar graph?
9. How is a bar graph similar to a histogram?
10. How are percentages and proportions used in criminological research?
11. What are rates and ratios? What are their functions in statistics? Explain.

Exercises

3.1. Given the following:

		Corrections Officers and Prison Size			
		Large	**Medium**	**Small**	**N**
	High	10	22	37	69
Job	Medium	19	21	18	58
Satisfaction	Low	35	22	55	112
	N	64	65	110	239

a. What proportion of corrections officers from large prisons have high job satisfaction?
b. What percentage of correctional officers work in medium prisons?
c. What proportion of correctional officers from small prisons have either medium or low job satisfaction?

3.2. What are the upper and lower limits and midpoints of the following intervals?

Interval Upper limit   Lower limit
Interval Midpoint

a. 575–579
b. 1,000–1,999
c. .236–.238

d. 15–19
e. 160–179

3.3. Given the following frequency distribution:

620–629	12
610–619	15
600–609	13
590–599	9
580–589	12
570–579	15
560–569	12
550–559	11
540–549	10
530–539	3
520–529	14
510–519	17
500–509	8
	N = 151

a. Using graph paper, draw a frequency polygon for the following frequency distribution.
b. Using graph paper, draw a histogram for the same data.
c. What are the upper and lower limits of all intervals?
d. What are interval midpoints?

3.4. Given the following information:

Year	Population
2000	1,849,286
2001	1,956,345
2002	2,353,045
2003	2,849,261
2004	3,945,286
2005	4,125,244
2006	4,852,165
2007	5,215,854

a. What is the rate of population increase from 2000 to 2001?
b. What was the proportion of population increase from 2002 to 2007?
c. What can be said about the overall population increase from 2000 to 2007?

3.5. Below are four prisons, showing numbers of correctional officers and numbers of inmates. Calculate the values requested.

	Number of Inmates	Number of Correctional Officers
Prison A	2,102	16
Prison B	8,252	49
Prison C	822	10
Prison D	1,467	22

a. What are the ratios of correctional officers to inmates for the four prisons?
b. What are the ratios of prisoners to correctional officers for the four prisons combined?
c. Which prison has the lowest officer/inmate ratio?

3.6. Observe the following distribution of correctional officers according to years of service in corrections. Construct (1) a pie chart, (2) a histogram, and (3) a bar graph showing the distribution of these officers by years of service. Use the information from Box 3.1 on page 62 for an *SPSS* application to determine these same graphs.

Correctional Officer Years of Service	Number of Correctional Officers
5 or fewer	22
6–10	12
11–14	18
15–19	7
20+	3

References

Bureau of Justice Statistics (2007). *Drug Use in the United States.* Washington, DC: U.S. Department of Justice, Bureau of Justice Statistics.

Harrison, Paige M. and Allen J. Beck (2006). *Prisoners in 2005.* Washington, DC: U.S. Department of Justice.

Hughes, Timothy A., Doris James Wilson, and Alan J. Beck (2002). "Trends in State Parole: The More Things Change, the More They Stay the Same." *APPA Perspectives* **26**:26–33.

Jones, Mark and John J. Kerbs (2007). "Probation and Parole Officers and Discretionary Decision-Making: Responses to Technical and Criminal Violations." *APPA Perspectives* **31**:35–42.

Solomon, Amy L. (2006). "Does Parole Supervision Work? Research Findings and Policy Opportunities." *APPA Perspectives* **30**:26–37.

U.S. Department of Justice (2006). *Federal Law Enforcement Officers, 2004.* Washington, DC: U.S. Department of Justice.

CHAPTER 4

Measures of Central Tendency

Chapter Outline

Introduction

The Mode, *Mo*
    Ungrouped and Grouped Data Computations of the Mode
    Assumptions, Advantages, and Disadvantages of the Mode

The Median, *Mdn*
    Computing the Median for Ungrouped Data
    Computing the Median for Grouped Data
    Assumptions, Advantages, and Disadvantages of the Median
    Centiles, Deciles, and Quartiles

The Mean, $\overline{X}$
    Computing the Mean for Ungrouped Data
    Computing the Mean for Grouped Data
    Assumptions, Advantages, and Disadvantages of the Mean

The Mode, Median, and Mean Compared

The Mean of Means, $\overline{X}_T$

Summary

Key Terms

Questions for Review

Exercises

References

Chapter Objectives

After reading this chapter, the following objectives will be realized:

1. understanding the meaning of the mode and how it is computed for both ungrouped and grouped data;
2. understanding the assumptions, advantages, and disadvantages of the mode for criminological research;

3. understanding the median and its computation for ungrouped and grouped data;

4. describing the median's assumptions, advantages, and disadvantages for research;

5. understanding the mean and how it is computed for both ungrouped and grouped data;

6. understanding the weaknesses and strengths of the mean, including its assumptions; and

7. understanding the grand mean or mean of means, how it is computed or determined, and some of its applications.

INTRODUCTION

This chapter is about measures of central tendency. **Measures of central tendency** describe points around which the rest of the scores focus. Three measures of central tendency are presented here. These include the mode, median, and mean. Each one of these measures will be presented for both data in ungrouped and grouped form.

The mode is considered the typical or more frequently occurring score in a distribution of scores. It may not occur near the central portion of a distribution, however. Thus, the mode as a measure of central tendency may not be one's first preference. Nevertheless, the mode provides information about a distribution that other measures of central tendency do not provide.

A second measure of central tendency discussed is the median. The median is considered the central score, or that point which divides a distribution into two equal parts, with 50 percent of the distribution on one side of the median and the other 50 percent of it on the other side. The median has some desirable features that the mode does not possess. Furthermore, it, too, describes a particular characteristic of a distribution of scores unlike other measures discussed in this chapter.

The third measure of central tendency presented is the mean. The mean or average is the arithmetic average score of all scores in a set of them. The mean is certainly the most popular of these three measures. Anyone who has ever watched a baseball game, a football game, a basketball game, or any other competitive sport is familiar with batting averages, average passing or rushing yards, average points score per game, and so forth. Most of us grew up calculating various averages, almost before we could do anything else. Since the mean is the most popular measure of central tendency, it is used a lot in criminological research. Sometimes, this is not always a good thing. Using a central tendency measure frequently, simply because it is popular, has led to frequent misuses of it, especially in statistics. But this fact doesn't mean that it should never be used.

Each measure of central tendency has one or more assumptions underlying its proper application in criminological research. It is important to be aware of these assumptions and plan accordingly whether to use one measure of central tendency or another for data analysis purposes. One assumption that we have addressed in an earlier chapter is the level of measurement assumption. This particular assumption is crucial in selecting the best measure of central tendency for data analyses. As each central tendency measure is discussed, its assumptions, advantages, and disadvantages will be illustrated.

Toward the end of the chapter, a grand mean or mean of means will be illustrated. There are some statistical procedures that we will encounter later in the book that feature such a calculation. Thus it is important for us to know about it.

THE MODE, *Mo*

The **mode**, *Mo*, is the score occurring most frequently in a distribution of scores. If more than one score occurs most frequently, each score occurring most frequently is reported as the mode. Conventionally, this definition has a limit of three scores that can occur most frequently. If more than three scores occur most frequently in a distribution, no mode is reported. We say simply that there is no mode under these circumstances.

Ungrouped and Grouped Data Computations of the Mode

Observe the following ungrouped data:

22 23 25 25 26 26 26 27 27 28 29 30 31 32 33 35

An inspection of these scores shows that the score, 26, occurs most frequently. It occurs three times, whereas the scores of 25 and 27 each occur twice. Thus, $M_o = 26$. If we had a slightly different distribution such as the following,

22 23 25 25 25 26 26 26 27 27 27 28 29 30 31 33

then three modes would be reported. These would be 25, 26, and 27 respectively. Each occurs three times. No other score occurs as frequently or more frequently.

Consider a third distribution of scores:

22 22 23 23 24 24 25 25 26 26 27 28 29 30 31 32 33 35 35

In this case, six different values occur most frequently, or twice each. These are the scores of 22, 23, 24, 25, 26, and 35. Since this number of modes exceeds the limit of three scores occurring most frequently, we simply conclude that there is no mode for these data. Nothing more needs to be said.

Mo **FOR GROUPED DATA**   The mode for grouped data is defined as the midpoint of the interval containing the most frequencies. If more than one interval has the most frequencies, these other interval midpoints are reported as modes. Again, conventionally, the maximum number of modes reported for any distribution of scores is three modes. If more than three intervals contain the most scores, then no mode is reported.

EXAMPLE OF MODE DETERMINATION FOR GROUPED DATA   P. Litton (2005) examined the "abuse excuse" in a sample of capital punishment trials in a given state. In the cases Litton studied, defendants charged with capital offenses used the excuse that they had been abused as children, and that this fact affected their later lives when committing capital murder. Suppose Litton had obtained a sample of 70 convicted and sentenced capital criminals who had used such an excuse. Perhaps if the numbers of years each convicted offender was sentenced were determined, we might find a distribution similar to that shown in Table 4.1. Table 4.1 is a hypothetical distribution of years sentenced upon conviction for a capital crime, where the "abuse excuse" was used as a part of the defense's case. We can see from Table 4.1 that no offender received a sentence of less than 20 years, and no offender received a sentence greater than 59 years. Examining the distribution of years in Table 4.1, we see that the 40–44 interval contained the most convicted offenders, 15. No other interval has this many frequencies. The midpoint of this interval, 40–44, is 42. Thus, 42 is the modal number of years these murderers were sentenced. As a reminder of how interval midpoints are calculated, we use the interval

TABLE 4.1 A Hypothetical Sample of Convicted
Murderers Who Used the Abuse Excuse
and Actual Sentence Received (in Years)

Interval (Years Sentenced)	f
55–59	11
50–54	7
45–49	10
40–44	15
35–39	10
30–34	9
25–29	5
20–24	3
	$\Sigma f = 70$

size, 5 (in this case), divide it by 2, or $5/2 = 2.5$, and add this amount to the lower limit of the interval containing the most frequencies, or $39.5 + 2.5 = 42$.

Suppose we had a similar situation such as that shown in Table 4.2 with 77 convicted murderers distributed according to number of years sentenced to prison. Table 4.2 shows a distribution with three intervals containing the most frequencies. These are the intervals 25–29, 40–44, and 50–54. The interval midpoints are 27, 42, and 52 respectively. These are the three modes for the distribution of scores in Table 4.2. This means that the modal years of sentences for these murderers are 27, 42, and 52 respectively. For emphasis, suppose we have a third distribution such as that depicted in Table 4.3.

In Table 4.3, six different intervals contain the most frequencies, or 10 of them each. In this particular case, we state simply that there is no mode.

What should distributions be called when there are one, two, or three modes?

One mode = **unimodal**

Two modes = **bimodal**

Three modes = **trimodal** or **multimodal**

TABLE 4.2 Hypothetical Distribution of Years
of Sentences with Three Modes

Interval	f
50–54	15
45–49	10
40–44	15
35–39	10
30–34	7
25–29	15
20–24	5
	$\Sigma f = 77$

TABLE 4.3 A Hypothetical Distribution of Sentences in Years with No Mode

Interval	f
65–69	10
60–64	8
55–59	10
50–54	9
40–44	10
45–49	10
35–39	9
30–34	10
25–29	3
20–24	10
	$\Sigma f = 89$

BOX 4.1

SPSS Alternative Application

1. These mode problems are easily solved by inspection, especially for ungrouped data. For data in grouped form, such as in Tables 4.1, 4.2, and 4.3, simple inspection of the most frequencies occurring in particular intervals and the computation of an interval midpoint, which can often be done by inspection, is a more rapid way of determining these values rather than taking the time to activate an _SPSS_ software program, go to the _SPSS_ Data Editor, enter data, and then derive descriptive statistics. Alternatively, if you are dealing with a large amount of data, where there are 100 or more scores, and if other descriptive information is desired, it may be worthwhile to simply enter these scores and perform descriptive functions to yield the requested values. _SPSS_ suggestions are made for the median and mean computations in subsequent sections of this chapter which may be applicable here as well.

Assumptions, Advantages, and Disadvantages of the Mode

There are no restrictions on mode computations for data in either ungrouped or grouped form. Any data measured according to the nominal level of measurement or higher are amenable to mode computations. The primary strength of the mode is that it gives the most popular score in a distribution. However, the most popular score may not necessarily be the most central score. For instance, suppose we have a situation such as that shown in Table 4.4.

In the distribution shown in Table 4.4, the mode is 22. However, this mode is certainly not a good portrayal of the distribution's central tendency. Rather, 22 is a value far away from the center of the distribution. By inspection, most scores in the distribution focus around the more central intervals of 45–49 and 50–54. Thus, this example highlights the mode's major weakness.

TABLE 4.4 A Mode Far Away from the Central Tendency of a Distribution

Interval	f
65–69	11
60–64	12
55–59	14
50–54	16
45–49	12
40–44	12
35–39	10
30–34	7
25–29	3
20–24	25
	$\Sigma f = 122$

If we examined a distribution of scores similar to that shown in Table 4.4, the mode would be a poor choice as our preferred measure of central tendency. This quality of the mode is called **instability**. Whenever there are many scores in one particular location at either extreme in a distribution, in the interval containing the largest or the interval containing the smallest scores, these scores are considered **deviant scores** or **outliers**. Deviant scores tend to be located in one extreme or the other of any distribution. In this peculiar situation with the presence of so many deviant scores, we would probably want to select a more stable measure of central tendency. An alternative central tendency measure not susceptible to the presence of extreme scores will be presented in the next section.

Various uses of the mode include determining the most prominent or prevalent nominal characteristics, such as race/ethnicity, type of conviction offense, gender, and/or inmate classifications (e.g., maximum, medium, or minimum security). Other than the possible presence of deviant scores, there are no other restrictive assumptions accompanying the computation of the mode.

THE MEDIAN, *Mdn*

The **median**, *Mdn*, is a point which divides a distribution of scores into two equal parts. This section describes the computation of the median for ungrouped and grouped data.

Computing the Median for Ungrouped Data

Suppose we were to observe the following distribution of scores:

12 15 17

In this distribution of three scores, the median is the central score 15. Technically, the midpoint of the value, 15, is the median. The number, 15, actually extends from 14.5 to 15.5. This is an interval of 1. One half of 1 is 1/2 = .5. Adding .5 to the lower limit of 15 or 14.5 is 14.5 + .5 = 15. Therefore, the median is 15.

Suppose there is an even number of scores such as those in the following example:

12 15 17 19

In this situation, we identify the two central scores of 15 and 17. We can sum these and divide by 2, or $(15 + 17)/2 = 32/2 = 16$. There is no actual score of 16 although this is the median. Thus, the median is a theoretical point dividing a distribution of scores into two equal parts. The median is a stable measure of central tendency. This **stability** is illustrated as follows. Suppose we use three of the four scores in the previous example. But this time, we will change the last score 19 to 100. Thus, our four scores will be:

12 15 17 100

What is the median for this new distribution? The median is still 16. Again, the focus is upon the two central scores. It makes no difference how large the largest score is. There is no effect on the median for these four scores. The only action that will change the median is to create more scores, particularly near the center of the distribution. If we add one additional score, such as 9, we would have:

9 12 15 17 100

In an array of an uneven number of scores, the central score becomes the median. In this case, the central score is 15 and 15 is designated as the median. Or if we had an array such as,

10 35 39 43 55 220 320 480 2,000,000

the median would be 55. Again, the median would leave half of the scores on one side of it and the other half of the scores on the other side of it.

What if we have many of the same scores near the center of the distribution, such as,

9 12 13 15 15 15 15 15 15 17 19 20

In this array of 12 scores, there are several scores of 15 in and around the center of the distribution. The median for this set of scores is 15, determined by simple inspection.

BOX 4.2

SPSS Alternative Application

1. Activate your _SPSS_ program and go to the _SPSS_ Data Editor screen. Enter the scores in the example above, typing in 10, 35, 39, 43, 55, 220, 320, 480, and 2,000,000.
2. Click on "Analyze," then "Reports," then "Case Summaries."
3. This action will bring up a screen with VAR00001 in the left-hand screen. Highlight VAR00001 and move it with the arrow to the "Variable" window.
4. Click the "Statistics" function at the bottom of the screen. This will bring up a list of statistics from which to choose. Highlight "Median" from the left-hand window and move it with the arrow to the window, "Cell Statistics." Click "Continue." Next, Click "OK."
5. This action will display several summary tables. In the table entitled "Case Summaries," scroll down to the bottom of the table to find the median, which is 55 in this case.
6. It is important to remember this sequence of functions, since there are several other measures from which to choose, including the mean, among those in the lengthy list.

Computing the Median for Grouped Data

The median is easily computed for grouped data. The following example is provided. B. Brown, W.R. Benedict, and W.V. Wilkinson (2006) studied public perceptions of police in Mexico. These investigators administered a survey to a sample of law school students in Tampico, Tamaulipas, Mexico and asked them to express their views toward police. Some of their findings disclosed that law school students expressed negative opinions of police. Interestingly, federal police were viewed less negatively than state police, while state police were viewed less negatively than municipal police. Suppose Brown, Benedict, and Wilkinson portrayed the attitudes toward Mexican federal police by 111 law school students and presented their satisfaction scores in Table 4.5? In Table 4.5, let's assume that the law school students expressed their satisfaction scores with federal Mexican police and that these satisfaction scores vary from 115 (the lowest score or low satisfaction) to 179 (the highest score or high satisfaction).

In the example in Table 4.5, there are 111 frequencies. We compute the median for these data by using the following formula:

$$Mdn = LL' + (fn/ff)(i)$$

where

LL' = the lower limit of the interval containing the number of frequencies we need to divide the total number of scores into two equal parts

fn = the frequencies we need in the interval

ff = the frequencies found in the interval

i = the interval size

In order to compute the median for these data, we must first divide the Σf by 2. There are 111 frequencies. This becomes $111/2 = 55.5$. We must find that point leaving 55.5 scores on one

TABLE 4.5 A Hypothetical Distribution of Satisfaction Scores of 111 Law School Students Toward the Mexico Federal Police

Interval	f	cf
175–179	4	111
170–174	6	107
165–169	3	101
160–164	13	98
155–159	8	85
150–154	7	77
145–149	10	70
140–144	9	60
135–139	10	51
130–134	15	41
125–129	11	26
120–124	10	15
115–119	5	5
	$\Sigma f = 111$	

side and 55.5 scores on the other. We add the frequencies from the first interval at the beginning of the distribution where the smallest scores are found, 115–119, to those in successive intervals until we reach 55.5 frequencies. This is similar to what we do when we construct a cumulative frequency distribution. In fact, a cumulative frequency distribution has been constructed as a part of Table 4.5 to assist us with our computational work.

Thus, we sum the following frequencies: $5 + 10 + 11 + 15 + 10 = 51$ frequencies. The next interval, 140–144, contains 9 frequencies. This is too many. We only need 4.5 of them to obtain our 55.5 frequencies. Thus, we use the formula above and substitute the necessary information:

$$Mdn = 139.5 + \frac{4.5}{9} \times 5$$

$$= 139.5 + \frac{22.5}{9}$$

$$= 139.5 + 2.5$$

$$Mdn = 142.$$

The median for these data is 142. We can say that 142 is the point in the distribution that divides the distribution into two equal parts, having 55.5 frequencies below it and 55.5 frequencies above it. The median is a theoretical point here, since there may be no actual score of 142. We might conclude that the median satisfaction score of law school students toward federal Mexican police is 142. If we were to administer our satisfaction scale to other samples of persons, the different median scores yielded could be directly compared with one another.

Assumptions, Advantages, and Disadvantages of the Median

The primary assumption underlying the median is that our data are measured according to an ordinal scale or higher. Rank-ordered information includes attitudinal scores, socioeconomic

---

BOX 4.3

SPSS Alternative Application

1. Activate your *SPSS* software program and go to the *SPSS* Data Editor window. Go to the first "var" column and begin typing in interval midpoints corresponding to those shown in Table 4.5. You need to type in the same number of interval midpoints as are reflected by your frequencies in each interval. For example, type in four (4) interval midpoints of 177 from Table 4.5, since there are 4 frequencies in that interval. Continue typing in interval midpoints in the same "var" column, 6 interval midpoints of 172, 3 interval midpoints of 167, 13 interval midpoints of 162, and so on, until all 111 midpoint values have been entered.
2. Once you have entered these values, click on "Analyze," then "Reports," then "Case Summaries" and repeat the process explained for determining the median for ungrouped data in the last section. Once you have moved "Median" to the "Cell Statistics" window and clicked "Continue," then "OK," you will get the same types of tables generated for ungrouped data. The median value will be shown at the bottom of the "Case Summaries" table. It will show "142" consistent with the manual computation.

status, job satisfaction, and prestige rankings. In sentencing, we might view offense seriousness in guidelines-based sentencing schemes or presumptive sentencing as ordinal-level data amenable to the median computation.

Compared with the mode, the median is a more stable measure of central tendency. Stability in this sense refers to the fact that deviant scores at either end of a distribution may exist and have no effect on the median result. However, modes may occur anywhere in a distribution and not necessarily near the center of it. A modal value may occur in one extreme of the distribution or the other. In this sense, the mode is an unstable measure of central tendency. We cannot always rely upon it to give us an accurate picture of the true central tendency of any distribution of scores. However, the median overcomes this problem and always yields a value that divides distributions of scores into two equal parts. This feature of the median makes it a desirable measure of central tendency.

Centiles, Deciles, and Quartiles

Since we are discussing the median, which divides distributions of scores into two equal parts, it would be appropriate here to describe three other measures which are based on essentially the same procedure for determining the median from grouped data. The median formula can be extended so that **centiles**, **deciles**, and **quartiles** can be computed. Centiles divide distributions of scores into 1 percent units. Deciles divide distributions of scores into 10 percent units. Quartiles divide distributions of scores into 25 percent units.

When computing the median, we were interested in determining the point dividing the distribution into two equal parts. We divided the total number of scores by 2 to obtain one half of all scores in the distribution. From that point, we located the interval containing one half of all scores, entered it with the frequencies we needed, and completed our calculations easily following the median formula.

Centile, decile, and quartile computations are computed similarly. Actually, 50 percent of the scores we sought for the median computation are the numerical equivalent of the 50th centile, the 5th decile, and the 2nd quartile. In the cases of centiles, deciles, and quartiles, these are values in a distribution of scores that define cutting points above and below which certain portions of scores are found. For instance, the 75th centile is that point leaving 75 percent of all scores below it and 25 percent of all scores above it. The 33rd centile is a point leaving 33 percent of all scores below it and 67 percent of all scores above it. The 6th decile is a point leaving 60 percent of all scores in a distribution below it and 40 percent of all scores above it, and so on. Table 4.6 shows various centiles, deciles, and quartiles and proportions of scores above and below these points. This table also shows various equivalencies between certain centile, decile, and quartile points.

In Table 4.6, Q_4 is the same as D_{10}, which is also the same as C_{100}. The value, Q_3, is the same as C_{75}. The value, Q_2, is also the same as D_5, which is also the same as C_{50}, which is also the same as the median. From Table 4.6, we not only know what percentage of scores lies below certain points, but we also know what percentage of scores lies above these scores. For instance, Q_1 leaves 25 percent of the scores below it and 75 percent of the scores above it. This general relation can be applied to all of these points.

Using the data shown in Table 4.5, we can compute various centiles, deciles, and quartiles. Suppose we want to compute the third quartile, or Q_3. This is the point that leaves 75 percent of the scores below it. We need to find 75 percent of 111 scores in order to determine where this point is located. Therefore, we can multiply .75 times 111, or $(.75)(111) = 83.2$. We need

TABLE 4.6 Centile, Decile, and Quartile Points and Proportions of Scores Above and Below These Points

Interval	Quartiles	Deciles	Centiles
Highest Scores			
.	Q_4 =	D_{10} =	C_{100} (point leaving 100% of scores below it)
.		D_9 =	C_{90} (point leaving 90% of scores below it)
.		D_8 =	C_{80} (point leaving 80% of scores below it)
.	Q_3 =		= C_{75} (point leaving 75% of scores below it)
.		D_7 =	C_{70} (point leaving 70% of scores below it)
.		D_6 =	C_{60} (point leaving 60% of scores below it)
.	Q_2 =	D_5 =	C_{50} (point leaving 50% of scores below it)
.		D_4 =	C_{40} (point leaving 40% of scores below it)
.		D_3 =	C_{30} (point leaving 30% of scores below it)
.	Q_1 =		C_{25} (point leaving 25% of scores below it)
.		D_2 =	C_{20} (point leaving 20% of scores below it)
.		D_1 =	C_{10} (point leaving 10% of scores below it)
Lowest Scores			

to find 83.2 scores. In Table 4.5, the cumulative frequency distribution shows that through interval, 150–154, there are 77 frequencies. The following interval, 155–159, has 8 frequencies in it. We don't need all of these frequencies to obtain 83.2 of them. We only need 6.2 more of them. Therefore, we should add the frequencies we need over the frequencies found in the interval and multiply this fraction by the interval size (i), in this case it is 5. The Q_3 is therefore $154.5 + (6.2/8)(5) = 154.5 + 3.9 = 158.4$. The value, 158.4, has 75 percent of the scores below it and 25 percent of the scores above it.

Suppose we wanted to compute the third decile or D_3. What point would leave 30 percent of the scores below it? Again, we multiply our Σf by .30, or $(0.30)(111) = 33.3$. We need 33.3 scores. Beginning at the bottom of the distribution, we count upward until we reach 33.3 scores. In the first three intervals, 115–119, 120–124, and 125–129, there are 26 frequencies. The next interval, 130–134, contains 15 frequencies. We only need 7.3 more frequencies to obtain 33.3 of them. Thus, we want 7.3 out of the 15 frequencies found in the interval. Our D_3 computation becomes $129.5 + (7.3/15)(5) = 129.5 + 2.4 = 131.9$. The point, 131.9, D_3, leaves 30 percent of the scores below it and 70 percent of the scores above it.

If we wanted to compute the 45th centile, or C_{45}, we would multiply the 111 scores by .45, or $(.45)(111) = 50.0$. We need 50 scores. Counting up the distribution to find our 50 scores, we come to the interval, 130–134, which gives us 41 frequencies. We need 9 more frequencies to give us 50 frequencies. However, there are 10 frequencies in the next interval, 135–139. As before, we enter the interval, 135–139, seeking 9 out of the 10 frequencies, or $134.5 + (9/10)(5) = 134.5 + 4.5 = 139$. The point, 139, has 45 percent of the scores below it and 55 percent of the scores above it. Several exercises are provided at the end of this chapter for centile, decile, and quartile practice. Centiles, deciles, and quartiles will have relevance in later chapters, especially when determining different measures of variability. Their inclusion here is useful because of the relevance of the median calculation and the generalizability of this formula to these other measures.

THE MEAN, $\overline{X}$

The **mean**, $\overline{X}$, is the average value in any distribution of scores. It is the most popular measure of central tendency in the sense that almost everyone is familiar with it and how it is determined. The formula for the mean is:

$$\overline{X} = \frac{\Sigma X_i}{N}$$

where

ΣX_i = the sum of the scores

N = the number of scores

Computing the Mean for Ungrouped Data

Suppose we were to observe the following distribution of 21 scores:

18 19 19 20 21 21 22 25 29 32 35 37 37 38 41 41 41 43 47 49 60

$N = 21$

The mean, $\overline{X}$, for the above distribution is calculated by adding and dividing the total number of scores: Thus, $695/21 = 33.1$. The $\overline{X} = 33.1$. By comparison, notice that the median $= 35$. What if we were to change the score of 60 to a score of 600? What difference would this make for our mean computation? Again, we would observe the following 21 scores, but with 600 as the largest score instead of 60:

18 19 19 20 21 21 22 25 29 32 35 37 37 38 41 41 41 43 47 49 600

The mean now becomes $1,235/21 = 58.8$. The extremely large or deviant score of 600 raised the mean substantially. **Extreme scores,** either very large or very small scores, such as a "600" in this distribution, might also be termed outliers because they are so far removed from the rest of the scores that tend to be more similar with one another. Outliers are certainly counted when computing the mean, but their presence gives a distorted or exaggerated impression about the central tendency of most other scores in the distribution. In this hypothetical example, for instance, with one simple score change from 60 to 600, the mean of the distribution increased from 33.1 to 58.8. Thus, the presence of one outlier or extreme score can influence the magnitude of the mean greatly. Under conditions where extreme scores are present, the mean is considered an unstable measure of central tendency. Had the median been computed for these same data, the median value would have been completely unaffected by the score change from 60 to 600. The median in both the first set of scores, with the largest score of 60, and the second set of scores, with the largest score of 600, would still be 35, the central score. Thus, the median is the most stable measure of central tendency whenever there are extreme or outlier scores present.

Computing the Mean for Grouped Data

When we have data in grouped form, the mean computation is more involved. M.A. Dutton et al. (2006) investigated intimate partner violence (IPV). They studied the psychological, biological, neurological, behavioral, and physiological alterations following exposure to IPV, many of which are associated with post-traumatic stress disorder (PTSD). Suppose the investigators wanted to study a sample of women exposed to IPV and who suffered from PTSD. Using hypothetical

TABLE 4.7 Hypothetical Number of Intimate Partner Violence Incidents from Women Suffering from Post-Traumatic Stress Disorder for 2005

Intervals	f	MP	(f)(MP)
57–59	8	58	464
54–56	9	55	495
51–53	3	52	156
48–50	10	49	490
45–47	10	46	460
42–44	8	43	344
39–41	11	40	440
36–37	19	37	703
33–35	12	34	408
30–32	7	31	217
27–29	3	28	84
24–26	8	25	200
21–23	7	22	154
	$\Sigma f = 115$		$(\Sigma f)(MP) = 4{,}615$

data, suppose Dutton et al. had obtained information about the number of IPV episodes during 2005 for a sample of women suffering from PTSD. They might cast their data into a form such as that shown in Table 4.7.

What was the average number of IPV incidents suffered by these 115 women who reported such incidents? In order to determine this average, we need to make several calculations in Table 4.7. First, intervals have been calculated representing the numbers of IPV incidents reported for 2005, ranging from 21 to 59, among these 115 women. The second column represents the number of women in each interval (f). The third column consists of all interval midpoints (MP). The final column is the product of the frequencies in each interval and the interval midpoints, or (f)(MP). The frequencies are summed, or Σf is calculated. Next, the products of frequencies and interval midpoints are calculated and summed $(\Sigma f)(MP) = 4{,}615$. The following formula is used to determine the mean for the data in Table 4.7.

$$\overline{X} = \frac{\Sigma(f)(MP)}{N}$$

$$\overline{X} = \frac{4{,}615}{115} = 40.1$$

The mean IPV incidents reported by these 115 women is 40.1. This value is easily calculated if we were to enter individual IPV incidents for each woman through data entry if we had an *SPSS* program. Performing these calculations with a hand calculator is relatively simple.

These calculations are based on two assumptions. The first is that all intervals are of the same size. The second is that there are no open-ended intervals. An open-ended interval might be "57+." We might have a few women who have IPV incidents in their 70s or 80s, during the year 2005. Under these circumstances, we could still use the formula for computing the mean above, but the midpoint of the open-ended interval would be calculated differently. While open-ended intervals are rare, they do occur occasionally. Researchers generally assume that

BOX 4.4

Alternative Application

1. Activate your *SPSS* software program, if available. Enter your data from Table 4.7 in the Data Editor window as follows. Go to the first column, "var," and begin typing in the midpoint of the interval containing the largest scores, or 58, 8 times, since there are 8 frequencies in this interval. Continue with the next interval, 54–56, and type in 9 midpoints of 55, and so on, until all 115 midpoints are entered.
2. Follow step 2 from Box 4.3. When selecting statistics, click on "Mean" and move it to the "Cell Statistics" window. Click "Continue," then "OK." In the "Case Summaries," the mean will be displayed.

the open-ended interval is the same size as the other intervals (an inaccurate assumption), and this would be done simply to establish closure of the interval and the completion of a mean solution. The other method would involve calculating a midpoint for the open-ended interval where the upper limit of the largest score in the interval would be used. With larger numbers of scores in a frequency distribution, both calculations for determining the mean yield nearly identical mean values. Therefore, it is unnecessary to explore midpoint calculations for open-ended intervals.

Assumptions, Advantages, and Disadvantages of the Mean

The arithmetic average or mean, $\overline{X}$, assumes the interval-level of measurement. Technically, we would not compute means for data at the nominal or ordinal levels of measurement. Means applied to nominal data might yield an average gender of 1.3, an average religious faith of 3.1, an average race of 2.5, and so on. These are meaningless computations. For data at the ordinal level, such as attitudinal information, mean computations are routinely made, even though the interval level of measurement is not attained. However, it has become conventional to use means when determining average attitudinal scores, despite the fact that the most popular attitudinal measures (**Likert scaling** and **Thurstone scaling**) yield only ordinal-level data at best. Means applied to attitudinal information where Likert or Thurstone scaling or other equivalent procedures are used to measure the degree to which certain attitudes exist should always be interpreted cautiously and conservatively.

Besides being the most well-known measure of central tendency, the mean is also the central tendency measure of choice for statistical inference. Sample means are most often used to estimate population μ values. A more extensive discussion of statistical inference is found in Chapter 7. The mean has certain desirable properties that will be described when we discuss statistical inference in a subsequent chapter. One desirable feature of the mean is that it has stability in the sense that if we were to draw numerous means from a given population of elements, there would be less variation among means compared with similar numbers of medians or modes that we might calculate for the samples drawn. This consistency among means is one reason for its popularity and why it is chosen as the best estimate of population means.

Alternatively, the mean is a very sensitive measure of central tendency and can be influenced easily by deviant scores. Deviant scores are extremely large or extremely small scores in a distribution compared with the other scores. Their influence on mean outcomes depends on how large or small these scores happen to be when compared with the rest of the scores in a distribution, and how we choose to deal with these deviant scores. This type of stability is different from that described above, when numerous means are compared.

THE MODE, MEDIAN, AND MEAN COMPARED

Comparing the mode, median, and mean, the mode is the least frequently used measure of central tendency. However, for data measured according to a nominal scale, the mode is most appropriate. The major weakness of the mode is that it may occur far from the center of a distribution of scores rather than near the center of it. The most frequently occurring value in a distribution may not be the most central value. Positively, the mode is probably the easiest central tendency measure to identify and compute compared with the other measures.

Whenever data are measured according to an ordinal scale, the median is preferred. This measure takes advantage of the ordinality of the scores. The median is unaffected by the presence of deviant scores. In this sense, the median is the most stable measure of central tendency.

At the interval level of measurement, the mean is the best measure generally. It is the average value of a distribution of scores. However, a major weakness of the mean is that it is easily influenced by extreme or deviant scores. In this respect, the median is more stable and preferred. Nothing prevents researchers from using all three measures of central tendency simultaneously, however. When presenting one's research, more information about a distribution of scores is generally better than less information. Having a knowledge of these three measures of central tendency can give us a fairly accurate impression of what the distribution looks like and whether the distribution is bell-shaped or normal appearing. The shape of a distribution of scores becomes critical when we consider certain tests of significance to evaluate or make decisions about our observations.

THE MEAN OF MEANS, $\overline{X}_T$

When investigators have sample means for several samples, they may want to compute a **mean of means** or **grand mean**, $\overline{X}_T$. The grand mean is the average of several sample means we may be analyzing. If all of our samples are the same size, the grand mean or mean of means is easy to compute. We would simply sum the means and divide by the number of means. Thus, if we had three means, such as 40, 50, and 60, the grand mean would be $(40 + 50 + 60)/3 = 150/3 = 50$. However, investigators analyzing multiple means cannot always count on having the same sample sizes for each mean examined. If sample sizes vary associated with the different means, then simply summing the means and dividing by the number of means won't work. The problem is that this procedure assumes all sample sizes are equal. If they are not equal, then an alternative procedure must be used. This procedure is explained below. Actually, it may be used for situations where sample means are equal or unequal.

Consider the following example. J. Annison (2006) has studied various intervention criteria used to assist probationers. Several accredited programs have been used in different probation departments for various samples of probationers. Among the criteria assessed by Annison were relevance to offenders and the use of different learning styles. Suppose Annison examined six different probation departments and focused upon the different interventions each used to teach probationers simple skills in coping with society. First, an examination of

TABLE 4.8 Grand Mean Determination for Six Hypothetical Probation Departments and Average Learning Scores for 165 Probationers

Probation Department	Probationers in Program N_i	Average Learning Score $\overline{X}_i$	Weighted Means $(N_i)(\overline{X}_i)$
1	30	25	750
2	40	30	1,200
3	20	50	1,000
4	10	90	900
5	60	5	300
6	5	60	300
	$\Sigma N_i = 165$	$\Sigma \overline{X}_i = 260$	$\Sigma(N_i)(\overline{X}_i) = 4{,}450$

this information discloses that each N_i is different. When the sample sizes differ, we must use the method shown in Table 4.8.

Table 4.8 shows six different probation departments as well as different numbers of probationers. A column labeled "Average Learning Score" has been included and is based on an interval-level measure of skills and vocational abilities hypothetically devised by this researcher. This column contains the average scores on a skills and abilities test administered to these probationers. A final column is calculated, which is the product of the average learning score for each group and the number of probationers in each group. A formula for the grand mean or $\overline{X}_T$ is:

$$\overline{X}_T = \frac{\Sigma(N_i)(\overline{X}_i)}{\Sigma N_i}$$

where

$\Sigma(N_i)(\overline{X}_i)$ = sum of products of sample sizes and sample means

ΣN_i = sum of the sample sizes

Using the information from Table 4.8, the formula becomes:

$$\overline{X}_T = 4{,}450/165 = 27.$$

The grand mean, $\overline{X}_T$, is equal to 27. This is also known as the mean of means for these 6 sample means. This is also the accurate mean of means because we have weighted each sample mean by its respective sample size. Each sample size is considered a **weight**. Had we simply totaled the sample means and divided by 6, the number of means, this computation would have assumed that all of the sample sizes were equal. As we can see from Table 4.8, this is not the case. Had we actually treated each sample as equal, we would have summed the 6 means and dividing by 6, or $(25 + 30 + 50 + 90 + 5 + 60)/6 = 260/6 = 43.3$. This grand mean is misleading in that it gives equal weight to all means averaged. However, the numbers of persons in each sample vary from 5 to 60. An inordinate amount of weight is given to the sample mean of 60 where the sample size is only 5. Also, the sample mean of 5 is greatly underweighted since it is associated with a sample size of 60. The procedure described in Table 4.8 corrects for sample size variations and weights means appropriate to yield accurate grand mean results. The grand mean will be a useful computation later when determining various tests of significance.

Summary

This chapter has examined three measures of central tendency. Measures of central tendency are designed to depict points around which scores in any distribution focus. Some measures of central tendency are better than others. The easiest measure of central tendency to understand and compute is the mode. The mode is the value occurring most frequently in an array of raw scores. If there are larger numbers of scores grouped into a frequency distribution, the mode is the midpoint of the interval containing the most frequencies. While it is unusual to have more than one mode in a distribution, if this situation is encountered, a rule of thumb is to report up to three modal values as the modes for the distribution. However, if more than three intervals contain the most frequencies, no mode is reported. The same principle applies to raw scores in ungrouped form.

While the mode is easy to compute, it is not always the best choice for depicting the central tendency of a distribution. The mode may be far away from the center of a distribution. As such, it may not be a good representative of the centrality of a distribution. This situation can occur if deviant scores are present that are located far away from the center of a distribution, either above or below it. The mode's primary advantage, however, is that it may be used for data at any level of measurement. It is best suited for data measured according to a nominal scale, although researchers may compute modes for any level of measurement.

The median is that point in a distribution that divides the distribution into two equal parts. The median is a theoretical value, since no actual score may exist that equals the median value computed. In a distribution of raw scores, the median is simply the central value. If there is an even number of values, the average of the two central values is defined as the median. The median is unaffected by extreme scores, either very large or very small scores. Their presence will leave the median virtually unaffected. Only changing the number of scores or adding scores near the center of a distribution will change the median's value. Thus, the median is considered to be a very stable measure of central tendency. The median is associated with attitudinal data and is appropriate for use where investigators have data measured according to at least an ordinal-level scale.

The mean, or average, is the most popular measure of central tendency. For ungrouped data, the mean is simply the sum of the scores divided by the number of scores. It is easy to calculate. If the mean is computed for scores grouped into a frequency distribution, an easy method of utilizing interval midpoints exists for easily computing the mean. Most software programs for criminological analyses, such as the *SPSS*, automatically compute the mean as a part of other statistical functions. Because of the popularity of the mean, some researchers have misapplied it. That is, the mean has been applied to data where the interval level of measurement has not been achieved. But such a practice in criminology and other social sciences has become conventional. Cautious interpretation of statistical results under such circumstances is recommended.

Considering the mode, the median, and the mean, the mode is the least stable measure of central tendency. If we were to have multiple modes, medians, and means, the greatest variation from sample to sample would occur among sample modes. The least amount of variation among samples would occur among sample means. Thus, in this sense, where multiple means are examined, there is the least amount of variation among means compared with the mode or median. However, within any given distribution of scores, the median is considered the most stable measure of central tendency. Stability in this sense refers to the fact that the median's value is unaffected by the presence of extremely large or extremely small scores, or deviant scores. In contrast, the mean's value is very sensitive to such deviant scores. If deviant scores are present in a distribution, then the mean probably should not be used. The median would be considered most stable under these circumstances.

It is not unusual for researchers to report all measures of central tendency in their research reports. It is often better to have more information than less information. Also, a knowledge of the mode, median, and mean will give investigators a more complete picture of the shape of a distribution. This will enable them to determine if certain distributional assumptions are satisfied and direct them toward choosing certain tests of significance where distributional assumptions are made and considered important.

Under certain conditions, investigators may have multiple means from several samples.

In this chapter, the grand mean or mean of means was illustrated. If sample sizes are equal throughout all samples the investigator may have, then a simple summation of mean values divided by the number of means will yield the grand mean or mean of means. This situation does not occur too frequently, however. Whenever sample size varies among different means, the different samples become weights that must be factored into any grand mean computation. Weighting each mean by its sample size and then dividing by the total number of samples gives us the most accurate result in terms of a grand mean value. The grand mean will have relevance for several tests of significance encountered in later chapters.

Key Terms

bimodal *73*
centiles *79*
deciles *79*
deviant scores *75*
extreme scores *81*
grand mean, $\overline{X}_T$ *84*
instability *75*
Likert scaling *83*

mean, $\overline{X}$ *81*
mean of means *84*
measures of central
  tendency *71*
median, *Mdn 75*
mode, *Mo 72*
multimodal *73*

outliers *75*
quartiles *79*
stability *76*
Thurstone scaling *83*
trimodal *73*
unimodal *73*
weight *85*

Questions for Review

1. What are measures of central tendency? What are they intended to portray?
2. What is the difference between data in grouped and ungrouped form? Does it make a difference in how measures of central tendency are computed? Why or why not? Explain.
3. What does it mean for a distribution to be multimodal?
4. What measure of central tendency is most susceptible to being influenced by extreme or deviant scores? Why?
5. Which measure of central tendency is most stable and why?
6. What is the mean of means? If the sample sizes are the same, is it important to weight the sample means in order to determine the mean of means? Why or why not? Explain.
7. What is meant by weighting?
8. What factors influence the value of the median?
9. Why is the mean considered the best measure of central tendency for making inferences about population values? Explain.
10. What is a bimodal distribution? Can bimodal distributions have means and medians? Why or why not? Explain.

Exercises

Below are several exercises to test your ability to compute and understand the following measures of central tendency. You may compute the answers manually or use SPSS if you have access to SPSS software. Both sets of answers, manual and SPSS-derived values, are provided in Appendix B for all numerical problems.

4.1. Below is an array of dangerousness scores for a group of 16 prison inmates. Determine the values requested.

11 13 13 15 19 25 29 29 30 31 38 48 81 83 85 90

$$N = 16$$

a. Mean
b. Median
c. Modes

4.2. Below are job-satisfaction scores for a group of 100 probation officers. Determine the requested values.

Interval	f
690–692	8
687–689	3
684–686	9
681–683	7
678–680	9
675–677	11
672–674	13
669–671	12
666–668	10
663–665	10
660–662	8
	$\Sigma f = 100$

a. Mean
b. Mode(s)
c. Median

4.3. What are the upper and lower limits of the following intervals?
a. 575–579
b. 1,000–1,999
c. .236–.238

4.4. Below are achievement scores for 94 at-risk youths. Determine the values requested.

Interval	f
40–41	14
38–39	14
36–37	13
34–35	7
32–33	11
30–31	9
28–29	3
26–27	14
24–25	3
22–23	6
	$\Sigma f = 94$

a. Mean
b. Mode(s)
c. Median

4.5. Below are numbers of acquittals for a sample of 119 public defenders working with misdemeanants for two years. Determine the values requested.

Interval	f
840–842	2
837–839	16
834–836	6
831–833	10
828–830	16
825–827	11
822–824	13
819–821	14
816–818	9
813–815	10
810–812	12
	$\Sigma f = 119$

a. Mean
b. Mode(s)
c. Median

4.6. Below is an array of numbers of convictions for 17 assistant district attorneys working in the Los Angeles County District Attorney's Office for one year. Determine the requested values.

24 24 25 26 26 27 28 29 29 30 30 31 31 31 35
38 50
$N = 17$

a. Mean
b. Median
c. Mode(s)

4.7. Below are several means and sample sizes. Determine the grand mean or mean of means.

$\overline{X}_1 = 32.8, N_1 = 13$
$\overline{X}_2 = 41.6, N_2 = 22$
$\overline{X}_3 = 82.5, N_3 = 48$

a. Grand mean
b. What is the influence of sample size variations on the grand mean?

References

Annison, J. (2006). "Style Over Substance? A Review of the Evidence Base for the Use of Learning Styles in Probation." *Criminal Justice: The International Journal of Policy and Practice* **6:**239–257.

Brown, B., W.R. Benedict, and W.V. Wilkinson (2006). "Public Perceptions of the Police in Mexico: A Case Study." *Policing: An International Journal of Police Strategies and Management* **29:**158–175.

Dutton, M.A. et al. (2006). "Intimate Partner Violence, PTSD, and Adverse Health Outcomes." *Journal of Interpersonal Violence* **21:**955–968.

Litton, P. (2005). "The 'Abuse Excuse' in Capital Sentencing Trials: Is It Relevant to Responsibility, Punishment, or Neither?" *American Criminal Law Review* **42:**1027–1072.

Measures of Variability

Chapter Outline

Chapter Objectives

After reading this chapter, the following objectives will be realized:

1. understanding the concepts of variability and dispersion;
2. understanding the range and its functions;
3. describing deviation scores and their importance;
4. understanding the variance and standard deviation and their respective functions;

5. describing the interplay between measures of central tendency and measures of dispersion or variability for describing distributions; and

6. understanding the importance of the standard deviation for tests of significance.

INTRODUCTION

This chapter describes several measures of variability or dispersion. Scores in a distribution not only focus around certain points or central tendency, but they also focus in particular ways around these central points. In order to understand the full significance of any distribution of scores, we must know about both central tendency and dispersion or variability. It is insufficient to simply identify central tendency points, such as the mode, median, or mean, without providing the rest of the distributional picture.

This chapter is organized as follows. First, several measures of variability are presented to help us understand the concept of how scores are distributed generally. Only one measure of dispersion or variability exists for data measured according to a nominal scale. This is Mueller's and Schuessler's index of qualitative variation. It is both unique and important, because it is one of a very limited number of variation measures that can be applied to nominal categories.

Subsequent measures of dispersion are grouped into ranges as well as deviation scores. Ranges refer to distances over which particular proportions of scores are spread. We are already familiar with the range, inasmuch as it was used for the purpose of determining how large our interval sizes should be when constructing frequency distributions. Other ranges will be presented as well.

Next, deviation scores are presented. Deviation scores are distances of scores from the means of their distributions. Deviation scores introduce us to the idea of deviation generally. If we average all deviation scores in a distribution, an average deviation will be yielded. While average deviations have little importance to criminologists, they do help us to understand the importance of variances and standard deviations. Thus, they are an important means to an end.

The most important measures of dispersion or variability are the variance and standard deviation. The standard deviation or the square root of the variance is critical to understanding many important statistical procedures, particularly those associated with statistical inference and decision making. Programs, such as *SPSS* and other software packages for analyzing data, automatically compute variances and standard deviations based on the collected data we are analyzing. For all of the measures presented in this chapter, the assumptions, advantages, and disadvantages of these measures will be explained.

THE INDEX OF QUALITATIVE VARIATION

Mueller's and Schuessler's **index of qualitative variation (IQV)** is the percentage of actual heterogeneity for a particular attribute according to the expected distribution or maximum heterogeneity of that attribute. It is the only variation measure available for determining the amount of variability among k attributes. An application of the IQV is illustrated by the following example.

S.E. Ullman et al. (2006) studied victim–offender relationships in women's sexual assault (rape) experiences. These investigators wanted to know the nature of the relationship between a sample of female rape victims and their victimizers. Prior research has disclosed that many rapes are committed by strangers, although family members and close friends of victims are also victimizers. Suppose Ullman et al. wanted to study the amount of heterogeneity among rape perpetrators and their relationships with victims. Perhaps a sample of 1,000 rape victims was obtained and the nature of each victim's relationship with their rapist was determined. We might find a pattern such as that in Table 5.1.

In Table 5.1, a hypothetical number of women who were victims of rape are shown. The first column in Table 5.1 shows whether the rapist was a date, a close friend, a family acquaintance, a stranger, or a relative. The second column lists the numbers of rape victims according to their victimizers. The third column, expected rapes, is simply a chance distribution of rapes determined by dividing the total number rapes by the number of relationship categories, or $1,000/5 = 200$. Thus, it might be surmised that if pure chance were operating in this situation, we might expect 200 rapes per relationship category. This third column is also known as maximum variation since each type of relationship between perpetrator and victim is equally distributed. The second column is the actual distribution of how the rape victims were related to their victimizers. We would apply the IQV as follows:

$$IQV = \frac{observed\ heterogeneity}{maximum\ heterogeneity} \times 100$$

where

observed heterogeneity = sum of products of all observed category totals
maximum heterogeneity = sum of products of all expected category totals

The "$\times 100$" converts the resulting proportion to a percentage. There are five categories of relationships. Let's label these as A, B, C, D, and E. If we were to obtain the products of each relationship pair of frequencies (the distribution of observed rapes), we would have (A)(B), (A)(C), (A)(D), (A)(E), (B)(C), (B)(D), (B)(E), (C)(D), (C)(E), and (D)(E). The sum of these products would equal our observed amount of heterogeneity, while the sum of products of the expected frequencies would be the sum of products on the expected frequency

TABLE 5.1 Hypothetical Distribution of 1,000 Rape Victims According to Relationship with Rapist

Relationship of Rapist to Victim	Observed Rapes	Expected Rapes
Date	200	200
Close friend	100	200
Family acquaintance	200	200
Stranger	350	200
Relative	150	200
Total	1000	1000

category, or column 3. Computing an IQV for the information in Table 5.1, we have the following:

$$IQV = \frac{(200)(100) + (200)(200) + (200)(350) + (200)(150)}{(200)(200) + (200)(200) + (200)(200) + (200)(200)}$$

$$\frac{+(100)(200) + (100)(350) + (100)(150) + (200)(350)}{+(200)(200) + (200)(200) + (200)(200) + (200)(200)}$$

$$= \frac{320,500}{400,000(100)} = (0.801)(100) = 80.1\%$$

There is 80.1 percent of maximum heterogeneity, meaning that a high degree of heterogeneity existed among the different types of persons who committed sexual assault against these 1,000 women. Had all perpetrators been dates of their rape victims, then the distribution of relationships would have been 1,000, 0, 0, 0, and 0. The sum of products of observed relationships of rapists would have been 0 and the resulting IQV would have been 0. Zero percent of maximum heterogeneity would mean 100 percent homogeneity, or that all persons committing rape against these 1,000 women came from the same category. Accordingly, had we observed 200 persons in each of the five categories, we would have had 200, 200, 200, 200, and 200, the same as the expected distribution of frequencies. The sum of products would have been 400,000 and the IQV would have been 100 percent, or 100 percent of maximum heterogeneity. This would have meant that there was a completely equitable distribution of rapists among the different relationship categories.

Had Ullman et al. wished to compare female victims of sexual assault according to ethnicity or race, they could have done so easily. These researchers reported, for instance, that stranger assailants are associated with greater victim-perceived life threat, more severe sexual assaults, and ethnic minority victims. Therefore, it is conceivable that they could have studied different IQVs for black or Hispanic sexual assault victims, older or younger victims, or any other variable combination of interest.

For example, if these researchers had obtained samples of sexual assault victims and divided them according to greater or lesser severity of their assault, two IQVs of 40 percent (showing larger numbers of stranger perpetrators) and 60 percent (showing fewer stranger perpetrators) could have assisted them in their data analysis. If the IQV = 40 percent had been computed for 1,000 female Hispanic victims and showed a large number (500 or more) of stranger sexual assaults, this finding would have supported their supposition about stranger assaults and the violence of the sexual assault.

Another example might be a comparison of two state prisons, where state prison inmates are divided into supermax, maximum, medium, and minimum-security inmates. An IQV = 75 percent for the first state prison could show more diversity among inmates according to their classification level, whereas an IQV = 20 percent associated with the second state prison could show a low degree of heterogeneity regarding prison classification status or relatively high homogeneity in this regard. An inspection of the actual numbers of offenders in different classification levels could have led researchers to reach different conclusions about the two prisons being compared and whether one prison was more or less heterogenous than the other regarding offender classification. These are some of the potential applications of the IQV for criminology and criminal justice research problems.

For any distribution of persons, there is a simple formula for determining how many products we should have for any given distribution of attributes. The formula is:

$$\text{Number of Products} = \frac{k(k-1)}{2}$$

where k = the number of subclasses on any given attribute.

Thus, in Table 5.1, there were five categories into which the 1,000 rape victims were divided according to their relationship with their attackers. With this category information, we would have $5(5-1)/2 = 20/2 = 10$ products. This formula enables us to check our work and make sure we have made the necessary number of product calculations.

Assumptions, Advantages, and Disadvantages of the IQV

The IQV is merely an index number reflecting the amount of heterogeneity that exists for any attribute and its subclasses. This index is the only measure of its kind for determining attribute heterogeneity among subclasses on a nominal-level variable. This is its primary strength. IQVs computed for different samples may be compared directly with one another. There are no disadvantages associated with calculating IQVs other than they are cumbersome to compute manually. There is no *SPSS* operation to complete for this particular measure.

THE RANGE, *Rg*

The **range**, *Rg*, is defined as the distance over which 100 percent of the scores in a distribution are spread. For ungrouped data, the range is the distance between the upper limit of the largest score and the lower limit of the smallest score. For instance, suppose we observe the following raw scores:

20 23 25 27 28 30 35 35 35 36 39 40 42 43 44 45 45 45 46 49

The largest score is 49, while the smallest score is 20. The upper limit of the largest score is 49.5, while the lower limit of the smallest score is 19.5. Thus, the $Rg = 49.5 - 19.5 = 30$. We can say that the scores in this distribution are dispersed over 30 points. For ungrouped data, an *SPSS* application would involve substantial time by using the data editor. Simple inspection and a quick manual calculation are sufficient to determine the range for ungrouped data.

For grouped data, the *Rg* may be defined in one of two ways. The first way is to define the range as the distance between the midpoint of the interval containing the largest scores and the midpoint of the interval containing the smallest scores. The second way is to determine the distance between the upper limit of the interval containing the largest scores and the lower limit of the interval containing the smallest scores. Suppose we have a frequency distribution such as that shown in Table 5.2.

Using the first method, we would compute the midpoint of the interval containing the largest scores, 270 – 279 or 274.5, and the midpoint of the interval containing the smallest scores, 160 – 169 or 164.5, and then compute the difference between them. Thus, 274.5 – 164.5 = 110 is the range or the distance over which 100 percent of these scores are spread.

Using the second method, we would determine the upper limit of the interval containing the largest scores, 270 – 279 or 279.5, and the lower limit of the interval containing the smallest scores, 160 – 169 or 159.5, and then determine the difference between them.

TABLE 5.2 A Frequency Distribution Showing Different Points for Range Computations

Interval	f	cf
270–279	2	122
260–269	7	120
250–259	10	113
240–249	12	103
230–239	17	91
220–229	4	74
210–219	17	70
200–209	10	53
190–199	13	43
180–189	12	30
170–179	15	18
160–169	3	3
	$\Sigma f = 122$	

Thus, $279.5 - 159.5 = 120$ is the range for these data, and it is the distance over which 100 percent of the scores is spread. Since there is no agreement in the research literature about which method is preferred, both computations are acceptable representations of the range. Again, an *SPSS* computation for the range would involve more trouble than the time taken to manually calculate it. If researchers are entering large amounts of data for additional statistical analysis purposes, however, the range is a standard feature of any descriptive statistics calculation package.

Assumptions, Advantages, and Disadvantages of the Range

The *Rg* requires data measured according to the interval level of measurement. However, it is conventional to apply the *Rg* for lower levels of measurement, such as the ordinal level. As we have seen in earlier chapters, the *Rg* was useful for us to determine a proper interval size for frequency distribution construction.

The primary disadvantage of the range is that it is a very unstable measure of dispersion. Suppose we observe the following distribution of raw scores:

20 21 21 21 23 23 23 23 23 24 25 25 26 26 27 27 28 29 30 500

If we were to calculate the range for these ungrouped data using the difference between the upper limit of the largest score and the lower limit of the smallest score, we would have $500.5 - 19.5 = 481$. Thus, the true distance over which 100 percent of these scores is spread is 481 points. All of the other scores are dispersed over a distance of only 11 points ($30.5 - 19.5 = 11$). Therefore, the *Rg*, such as the mean, is very sensitive to deviant scores. Whenever deviant scores are present in a distribution, the *Rg* would be a poor choice as a dispersion measure.

THE AVERAGE DEVIATION, *AD*

Another variability measure is the **average deviation (*AD*)**. The average deviation is defined as the average variation of scores from the mean of their distribution. The *AD* is illustrated for ungrouped data as follows. Suppose we observe the following distribution of 11 raw scores in Table 5.3. In Table 5.3, the mean for these 11 scores, $\overline{X} = 25$. With a $\overline{X} = 25$, we determine how far each raw score varies from the mean of 25. How far is 20 from 25? The score of 20 is 5 points from 25 and below it, and therefore, we assign a -5 to the score of 20. This **deviation score** is entered in a column labeled x' as shown in the table. How far is 28 from 25? The score of 28 is 3 points above 25 and thus receives a deviation score of 3. How far is 26 from 25? The score of 26 is 1 point above 25 and thus receives a deviation score of 1. We calculate deviation scores for all 11 scores. The raw score of 25 lies directly at the point where the mean occurs, and thus there is no deviation from the mean associated with a raw score of 25. The deviation score assigned a raw score of 25 where the mean is 25 is 0. Next, we sum all deviation scores. If the mean was calculated correctly, the sum of all deviation scores will always equal 0. If there are minor departures from 0 after summing deviation scores, this is due to rounding error, where the mean may be 25.26 or 24.97. Under these circumstances, deviation scores may not always sum to 0, again because of rounding error.

Next, a final column is created, $|x'|$. This column contains the sum of the absolute deviation scores, where the sign associated with the deviation score has been ignored. The sum of the absolute deviation scores $= 30$ in this case. Dividing this sum by the N, number of scores, 11, will yield the average deviation. The formula is:

$$AD = \frac{\Sigma|x'|}{N}$$

where

$\Sigma|x'|$ = the sum of the absolute deviation scores
N = sample size

TABLE 5.3 The Average Deviation Computation for Ungrouped Data

Score	x'	$|x'|$
20	−5	5
21	−4	4
22	−3	3
23	−2	2
24	−1	1
25	0	0
26	1	+1
27	2	+2
28	3	+3
29	4	+4
30	5	+5
	$\Sigma x' = 0$	$\Sigma|x'| = 30$
$N = 11$		
$\overline{X} = 25$		

With the values from Table 5.3, we can solve for the AD, or

$$AD = \frac{30}{11} = 2.7$$

The 11 scores in this distribution fluctuate around the mean of 25, an average of 2.7 points.

Assumptions, Advantages, and Disadvantages of the Average Deviation

The AD assumes that the interval level of measurement must be attained for the variable under investigation. But convention is powerful and suggests that with less than interval-level data, average deviation scores may be computed for ordinal-level data if interpreted with caution. There are no advantages of the AD for researchers, only disadvantages. Comparisons of ADs from different distributions show that no consistent interpretation can be made. The primary reason for discussing the AD here is that it illustrates the meaning of a **deviation score**. Deviation scores are fundamental to understanding the standard deviation, a topic addressed in the following section. There is no *SPSS* computational procedure for the average deviation.

THE VARIANCE, S^2, AND STANDARD DEVIATION, S

The most important measure of variability or dispersion in this chapter is the standard deviation. Before we examine the standard deviation, however, we must examine another statistic from which it is derived. This statistic is called the variance.

The Variance

The **variance** is the sum of the squared deviation scores divided by N. Another way of defining the variance is the mean of the sum of the squared deviation scores for any distribution of scores. The formula for the variance is:

$$\text{Variance}, s^2 = \frac{\Sigma x^2}{N}$$

where Σx^2 = the sum of the squared deviation scores
N = the sample size

Recalling our computation of the AD for ungrouped data illustrated in Table 5.3, we will reproduce this information and include an additional step in Table 5.4. These scores are presumed measured according to an interval scale. They might be the ages of 11 new jail admissions on a given day, the numbers of citations given for parking violations by 11 meter maids, or years on the job for a sample of prison administrators. In a conventional application where the level-of-measurement rules might be relaxed, these might be 11 scores from some attitudinal scale.

In the original solution for the AD, we summed the absolute deviations of scores from the mean of the distribution and divided by N. For the variance calculation, we must square all deviation scores, or x' values. This has been done for each deviation score in a column to the far right in Table 5.4. These squared deviation scores are then summed to yield the $\Sigma x'^2 = 110$. This value is divided by N to yield the variance, or

$$s^2 = \frac{\Sigma x'^2}{N} = \frac{110}{11} = 10$$

The variance, s^2, for the data in Table 5.4 is 10.

TABLE 5.4 The Variance Computation for Ungrouped Data

Score	x'	$\lvert x' \rvert$	x'^2
20	−5	5	25
21	−4	4	16
22	−3	3	9
23	−2	2	4
24	−1	1	1
25	0	0	0
26	1	+1	1
27	2	+2	4
28	3	+3	9
29	4	+4	16
30	5	+5	25
	$\Sigma x' = 0$	$\Sigma \lvert x' \rvert = 30$	$\Sigma x'^2 = 110$

$N = 11$
$\overline{X} = 25$

The computation of the variance for the scores in Table 5.4 was relatively easy. One reason is the mean was a whole number, and the deviation scores were easily determined by inspection. But if the mean had been 24.89 or 25.02, this method would have involved more difficult computations for deviation score values. An alternative procedure may be used for determining the variance for a set of scores, where $N \leq 25$ using the scores, the squared scores, and the sums of the scores and squared scores.

Below are the 11 scores and the squared scores from Table 5.4. Notice that both columns of values have been summed.

X	X^2
20	400
21	441
22	484
23	529
24	576
25	625
26	676
27	729
28	784
29	841
30	900
$\Sigma X = 275$	$\Sigma X^2 = 6,985$

BOX 5.1

***SPSS* Alternative Application**

1. Activate your *SPSS* program and proceed to the *SPSS* Data Editor screen.
2. Enter the 11 scores as shown in the above problem in the first "var" column. This will create VAR00001.
3. Click on "Analyze," then "Descriptive Statistics," then "Descriptives."
4. This action brings up a screen with two windows. VAR00001 is displayed in the left-hand window. Highlight this variable and use the arrow to move it to the "Variable(s)" window to the right.
5. Next, click "Options" below these windows. Clicking "Options" will give you a lengthy list of statistics with boxes to check. You can check "Mean," "Sum," "Std. Deviation," "Minimum," "Maximum," "Variance," "Range," "Kurtosis," "Skewness," and several other statistics. If you click "Variance," then "Continue," this will bring you back to the page with the two windows. Next, click "OK."
6. Several tables will be produced as output. These tables can be inspected to disclose the variance and other statistics.

In this example, the sum of scores, $\Sigma X = 275$, and the sum of the squared scores, $\Sigma X^2 = 6{,}985$. With these two sums and $N = 11$, we can solve for the variance as follows:

$$\text{Variance, } s^2 = \frac{\Sigma X^2 - \left(\dfrac{(\Sigma X)^2}{N} \right)}{N}$$

where $\Sigma X =$ the sum of the scores
$\Sigma X^2 =$ the sum of the squared scores
$N =$ the sample size

Substituting the values in the above equation, we have:

$$s^2 = \frac{6985 - \left(\dfrac{275^2}{11} \right)}{N} = \frac{(6985 - 6875)}{11} = \frac{110}{11} = 10$$

The numerator in the variance formula is the sum of the squared deviation scores, or Σx^2. In this case, we have dropped the "prime" ($'$) to simplify notation and use x^2 as a squared deviation score. By itself, this numerator expression is:

$$\Sigma x^2 = \Sigma X^2 - \frac{(\Sigma X)^2}{N}$$

The Standard Deviation

The **standard deviation** is the square root of the variance. As previously described, the variance is the average of the sum of the squared deviation scores about the mean of a distribution. Using the information from the discussion of the variance in the previous section, this relationship is illustrated by the following formula.

$$s = \sqrt{s^2} = \sqrt{\frac{\Sigma x^2}{N}} = \sqrt{\frac{110}{11}} = \sqrt{10} = 10$$

where

Σx^2 = the sum of the squared deviation scores

N = the sample size

The standard deviation, s, is the square root of the variance, s^2, or 3.2 as is shown. Most software programs for data analysis such as *SPSS* will calculate these values automatically from supplied scores.

The Standard Deviation Computation for Grouped Data

Computing the variance and standard deviation from grouped data, where $N > 25$, is somewhat more involved. Table 5.5 shows a distribution of intervals and frequencies. Table 5.5 includes the frequencies in each interval; interval midpoints; distances of interval midpoints from the mean of the distribution, 639.2, which are deviation scores expressed in absolute terms; squared deviation scores, x^2; and products of frequencies (f) and squared deviation scores, fx^2. The sum of the products of the frequencies and the squared deviation scores provides weights for these deviation scores such that they can now be summed. The resulting $\Sigma fx^2 = 3,668.2$.

We can now apply the standard deviation formula, using the $\Sigma fx^2 = 3,668.2$ and $N = 100$ to yield the following:

$$\Sigma s = \sqrt{\frac{\Sigma fx^2}{N}} = \sqrt{\frac{3,668.2}{100}} = \sqrt{36.68} = 6.1$$

TABLE 5.5 Frequency Distribution Showing Absolute Deviations from the Mean

Interval	f	Midpoint	$|x'|$	x'^2	fx'^2
652–653	3	652.5	13.3	176.9	530.7
650–651	3	650.5	11.3	127.7	383.1
648–649	5	648.5	9.3	86.5	432.5
646–647	5	646.5	7.3	53.3	266.5
644–645	9	644.5	5.3	28.1	252.9
642–643	15	642.5	3.3	10.9	163.5
640–641	3	640.5	1.3	1.7	5.1
638–639	15	638.5	.7	.5	7.5
636–637	9	636.5	2.7	7.3	65.7
634–635	10	634.5	4.7	22.1	221.0
632–633	13	632.5	6.7	44.9	583.7
630–631	10	630.5	8.7	75.6	756.0
	$\Sigma f = 100$				$\Sigma fx^2 = 3,668.2$
				$\overline{X} = 639.2$	

BOX 5.2

SPSS **Alternative Application**

1. Activate your *SPSS* software program, if available. Go to the Data Editor window and begin entering midpoints of all intervals as shown in Table 5.5.
2. Click on "Analyze," then "Descriptive Statistics," then "Descriptives." This will bring up a screen with several windows. Highlight VAR00001 in the left-hand window and move it with the arrow to the right-hand window, "Variable(s)." Click on "Options" at the bottom of the screen. This will yield several statistical choices, including "Std. Deviation." Check this statistic and then click on "Continue." Now click "OK."
3. A summary table is displayed, showing several values, including the standard deviation, which is 6.08 or 6.1 (rounded). This value is consistent with that computed manually.

The standard deviation for the data in Table 5.5 is 6.1. There are several alternative ways of obtaining the variance and standard deviation from data portrayed in different forms. Slightly different answers may be generated, although these differences are largely due to rounding error.

The Meaning of the Standard Deviation

What does the standard deviation mean? First, it is the most consistent measure of variability or dispersion discussed in this chapter. It has a consistent meaning. In Table 5.5, for instance, the $s = 6.1$ means that within 6.1 points of the mean of 639.2 on either side of it (633.1 and 645.3), a certain proportion of scores will likely be found. If we had another distribution of scores, for instance, where the mean of the distribution were 1,200 and the standard deviation were 200, then between 1,000 and 1,400 (1 standard deviation of 200 on either side of the mean of 1,200), a proportion of scores would be found similar to the proportion found within 1 standard deviation of the mean in the distribution of scores shown in Table 5.5, and so on. To this extent, at least, the standard deviation has more comparative value in relation to other measures of dispersion or variability discussed in this chapter.

The distribution in Table 5.5 is not the most ideal distribution for a standard deviation computation. If the distribution of scores is inspected carefully in Table 5.5, there are large numbers of frequencies in the intervals 642–643, 638–639, 636–637, 634–635, 632–633, and 630–631. These are intervals containing more of the smaller scores in the distribution of 100 scores. All of the intervals from 646–647 through 652–653 have 5 or fewer frequencies in them. Therefore, there are more smaller scores than there are larger scores. This is one reason why the mean is 639.2 toward the end of the distribution containing the smallest scores. Under more ideal conditions, a majority of scores would occur near the center of the distribution, and the remaining scores would be fewer in number, tapering off in both directions toward the ends of the distribution.

Table 5.6 is a more ideal distribution for maximizing the meaning of the standard deviation, using an $N = 100$. The same intervals have been preserved, but the scores are distributed so that most accumulate near the center of the distribution. If a graph of this table were constructed, it would appear bell-shaped, with the highest point at the center of

TABLE 5.6 Hypothetical Distribution of Scores Rearranged from Scores in Table 5.5

Interval	f
652–653	4
650–651	5
648–649	6
646–647	7
644–645	9
642–643	13
640–641	15
638–639	13
636–337	10
634–635	8
632–633	6
630–631	4
	$\Sigma f = 100$

the distribution, in the interval containing 15 scores, 640–641. In Table 5.6, the scores taper off gradually toward the end of the distribution.

Having an ideal distribution of frequencies for a standard deviation computation is important. The ideal distribution sought is bell-shaped and known as a normal distribution. The normal distribution will be discussed at length in Chapter 6.

Assumptions, Advantages, and Disadvantages of the Standard Deviation

An assumption underlying the standard deviation is the interval level of measurement. However, standard deviations are conventionally calculated for variables measured according to ordinal scales in criminology, criminal justice, and other social sciences. A second assumption is that the meaning of a standard deviation is enhanced whenever it is calculated for any distribution of scores resembling normality or a bell-shaped curve.

Generally, when applied to most distributions of raw scores, the standard deviation refers to a given distance on either side of the means of these distributions where a fixed proportion of scores will be found. This fact is the standard deviation's primary importance. For instance, if we had a distribution of scores with a $\overline{X} = 300$ and a $s = 50$, there would be a fixed proportion of scores on either side of the mean and 1 standard deviation above and below it. Thus, between 250 and 350, or 1 standard deviation of 50 below and above the mean of 300, approximately 68 percent of the scores in the distribution would be found.

A second distribution of scores may have a $\overline{X} = 25$ and $s = 3$. Between the scores of 22 and 28, or 1 standard deviation of 3 below and above the mean of 25, we might also find approximately 68 percent of the scores in this distribution. This percentage similarity of the proportions of scores included within 1 standard deviation on either side of the mean of both distributions is no coincidence. These similarities exist because of the resemblance of these distributions to the bell-shaped curve known as the normal distribution. This distribution will be presented and discussed in Chapter 6.

Summary

Measures of variability or dispersion refer to how scores are distributed around central tendency points, such as means, modes, or medians. While most measures of variability have been designed for use with interval-level data, one measure of dispersion is useful for the nominal level of measurement. This is the index of qualitative variation (IQV). The IQV is an expression of the amount of heterogeneity found among the subclasses of a given variable. Nominal-level properties, such as gender, race/ethnicity, gang affiliation, categories of crime and delinquency, or any other classifiable entity are amenable to IQVs. IQVs have no restrictive assumptions and may be compared. IQV information is valuable in that it provides investigators with how certain nominal-level variables are distributed. Different amounts of heterogeneity (or homogeneity) in one variable can assist researchers in explaining variations in other variables. IQVs are inherently intuitive and have considerable explanatory utility.

The range is the distance over which 100 percent of all scores in a distribution are spread. It was used in Chapter 4, for instance, as a way of determining interval sizes for frequency distributions of scores. This feature of the range is quite useful. The range itself as a measure of variability is unstable, however, particularly if there are extreme scores in a distribution. The instability of the range under deviant score conditions was illustrated.

Two additional measures of variability discussed were the variance and standard deviation. The best measure of variability is the standard deviation, largely because of the consistency of its meaning from among different distributions. The standard deviation is the square root of the variance. In later chapters, the variance has relevance as one of the requirements for certain tests of significance. But the standard deviation has the greatest application value as a dispersion measure. In Chapter 6, the standard deviation is used extensively in discussions about the normal distribution and how different scores may be interpreted.

Key Terms

average deviation (*AD*) 96
index of qualitative
   variation (IQV) *91*

deviation score *96*
range *94*

standard deviation *99*
variance *97*

Questions for Review

1. What are measures of variability? What do they measure?
2. Does it make a difference in computing measures of variability whether data are in ungrouped or grouped form? Why or why not? Explain.
3. What is the index of qualitative variation? What are some of its uses?
4. What is the range? What are some of its purposes?
5. What are the weaknesses and strengths of the range? Discuss.
6. What is a deviation score? Why is it important?
7. What are some general weaknesses of the range? Discuss.
8. What is the purpose of presenting a measure such as the average deviation, especially if it isn't used much anymore in statistics or criminological research?
9. What is the standard deviation?
10. Why is the standard deviation important for criminologists and others? Explain.

Exercises

The following exercises are designed to enable students to practice what has been learned in this chapter on actual scores and distributions of frequencies. Answers to all numerical questions are found in Appendix B as a check on your work. Depending on whether you perform requested values manually or through SPSS, slightly different results may be obtained. These will be noted where answers are provided in Appendix B.

5.1. Below are two groups of prisoners, classified according to booking offense. Determine the requested information. Use the IQV to determine your answer.

Trait	Group 1	Group 2
Robbery	50	20
Burglary	30	10
Larceny	70	60
Auto Theft	0	30

a. IQV_1
b. IQV_2
c. Which group is more heterogeneously distributed according to booking offense?

> **SPSS Alternative Application:** There is no IQV computation in *SPSS* software.

5.2. Below is a frequency distribution of social adjustment scores for 116 delinquent boys. Determine the values requested.

Interval	f
325–329	6
320–324	10
315–319	11
310–314	3
305–309	12
300–304	2
295–299	6
290–294	10
285–289	9
280–284	4
275–279	8
270–274	15
265–269	11
260–264	9
	$N = 116$

a. Standard deviation
b. Range
c. Variance

> **SPSS Alternative Application:** If *SPSS* software is available, enter data according to instructions mentioned in Box 5.2 and complete your calculations.

5.3. Below is an array of aggression scores for a sample of 21 prisoners in a supermax prison. Determine the values requested.

18 19 19 20 21 21 22 25 29 32 35 37 37 38
41 41 41 43 47 49 60

$N = 21$

a. Standard deviation
b. Range

> **SPSS Alternative Application:** If *SPSS* software is available, use instructions from Boxes 5.1 and 5.2 to enter data and solve for these values.

5.4. A sample of 151 correctional administrators responded to a measure to evaluate administrative skills. Their scores are shown in the intervals below. Determine the values requested.

Interval	f
620–629	12
610–619	15
600–609	13
590–599	9
580–589	12
570–579	15
560–569	12
550–559	11
540–549	10
530–539	3
520–529	14
510–519	17
500–509	8
	$\Sigma f = 151$

a. Standard deviation

b. Range(s)

SPSS **Alternative Application:** If *SPSS* software is available, use instructions from Boxes 5.1 and 5.2 to enter data and solve for these statistics.

5.5. Below is an array of self-report delinquency incidents for a sample of 18 delinquents. Determine the values requested.

10 15 15 17 17 17 18 18 19 22 25 27

33 35 39 50 75 76

$N = 18$

a. Standard deviation

b. Variance

c. Range

SPSS **Alternative Application:** If *SPSS* software is available, follow the instructions in Boxes 5.1 and 5.2 to enter data and solve for these requested values.

5.6. The average deviation: (A) averages the mean departures of each mean about the grand mean; (B) is an average of all standard deviations in several samples; (C) is the average of all deviation scores about a common mean; (D) None of the above.

5.7. The standard deviation: (A) is the best interval-level measure of central tendency available; (B) is the most frequently overlooked measure of central tendency; (C) has no precise interpretation; (D) has a fairly consistent interpretation from one distribution to the next.

References

Ullman, S.E. et al. (2006). "The Role of Victim–Offender Relationship in Women's Sexual Assault Experiences." *Journal of Interpersonal Violence* 21:798–819.

CHAPTER 6

The Unit Normal Distribution and Standard Scores

Chapter Outline

Chapter Objectives

After reading this chapter, the following objectives will be realized:

1. understanding the unit or standard normal distribution;
2. describing the characteristics of the unit normal distribution as they can be generalized to different distributions of scores;
3. understanding the meaning of Z scores or standard scores;
4. determining proportions of curve area on the unit normal distribution;
5. converting raw scores into Z scores;
6. converting Z scores into raw scores;
7. understanding the process of standardizing different distributions of scores;
8. understanding the usefulness of the unit normal distribution in statistical inference and statistical decision making;
9. understanding the probability function of the unit normal distribution; and
10. understanding skewness and kurtosis and how the unit normal distribution is affected.

INTRODUCTION

In criminological research and various types of statistical analyses conducted by social scientists, much use is made of normal distributions or bell-shaped curves depicting distributions of collected data. This chapter examines the unit normal distribution and its characteristics. This is a theoretical distribution against which various distributions of raw scores are compared. The unit normal distribution has several ideal properties that are generalizable to any distribution of scores that approximates it.

Standard scores, also known as Z scores, are values that depict different points along the horizontal axis of the unit normal distribution and encompass certain portions of it. Different proportions of normal curve area are associated with these Z scores. These proportions of curve area are standardized and do not change among distributions examined. The importance of these constant or standard proportions of curve area will be explained. Ample illustrations are provided showing relationships between different Z scores and curve areas associated with them. Several examples are provided of raw score distributions that approximate the unit normal distribution. Parallels between these distributions are described and explained.

Various types of score conversions may be performed by researchers. Raw scores may be converted into Z scores and Z scores may be converted into raw scores. These different types of score transformations will be illustrated. Several applications of the unit normal distribution will be presented and the usefulness of it for research purposes will be examined.

Researchers can also transform scores from any distribution of raw scores into a standard form with new parameters different from a normal distribution which will permit them to make interdistributional score comparisons. This option is extremely useful for investigators who are examining several distributions of scores with different means and standard deviations. The mean and standard deviation, two important descriptive statistics presented earlier in Chapters 4 and 5, have direct relevance for raw score transformations and the entire standardization process. The various purposes of standardizing scores in distributions will be examined and explained. Various exercises will be presented for determining proportions of curve area on the unit normal distribution lying above, below, or between two Z score points.

Several nonnormal distributions are described. Nonnormal distributions differ markedly from unit normal distribution characteristics. Nonnormal distributions of scores have much skewness and kurtosis. The normal distribution has no skewness or kurtosis. However, actual distributions of raw scores almost always have some skewness and kurtosis. Acceptable levels of these distributional properties will be discussed. *Z* scores have some limited applications even where conspicuous skewness and kurtosis are present. These general and limited applications will be explained.

Finally, the importance of the normal distribution as a probability distribution will be discussed. The assumption of a normal distribution underlies several key tests of significance and correlation procedures. If this normality assumption is violated, one's statistical output and findings are affected in different ways and must be interpreted cautiously. The probability function of the normal distribution is crucial in every hypothesis test involving this assumption.

THE UNIT OR STANDARD NORMAL DISTRIBUTION

Most criminologists and other social scientists are interested in generalizing from their samples to larger populations from which the samples were drawn. Often, sample characteristics approximate the characteristics of their parent populations. A key research goal is to make meaningful inferences about population characteristics from sample characteristics.

Sample statistics, therefore, become estimates of their respective population parameters. For instance, the sample mean, $\overline{X}$, is an estimate of the population μ, the sample standard deviation, s, is an estimate of the population σ, and so on. Population characteristics are most often unknown. It is cheaper and easier to study some persons from the population, a sample, and use this sample information as the basis for estimating unknown population values. Investigators can use the **normal distribution**, also termed as **unit normal distribution** or **standard normal distribution**, for making subsequent inferences about population parameters, therefore. The unit or standard normal distribution, often referred to as the bell-shaped curve, exists only in theory. It has been derived mathematically from the following formula

$$Y = \left(\frac{1}{\sigma\sqrt{2\pi}}\right) e^{-\frac{1}{2}\left(\frac{X-\mu}{\sigma}\right)^2},$$

where
$\pi = 3.1416$
$e = 2.7183$
$\sigma = $ parameter equal to the standard deviation of the distribution
$\mu = $ parameter equal to the mean of the distribution
$X = $ abscissa—measurement or score marked on the horizontal axis
$Y = $ ordinate—height of the curve at a point corresponding to an assigned value of X

Figure 6.1 shows that the normal distribution is bell-shaped and has two parameters, a mean, $\mu = 0$ and a standard deviation, $\sigma = 1$.

Whenever the normal distribution is approximated by any distribution of raw scores we are studying, this condition is **normality**. The properties of the normal distribution are that:

1. The curve of the normal distribution is bell-shaped.
2. The normal distribution is perfectly symmetrical. The highest point of the normal distribution is the center of it.

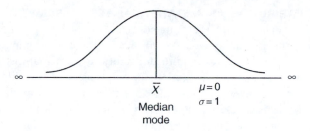

FIGURE 6.1 **Unit or Standard Normal DistributionF**

3. The mean, mode, and median are identical with one another and occur at the center of the normal distribution.
4. The normal distribution has an asymptotic property, where each end of the distribution tapers off toward the baseline of the horizontal axis; these curve lines approach the baseline but never touch it.
5. The ends of the normal distribution extend toward infinity (∞).
6. The mean of the normal distribution is $\mu = 0$ and its standard deviation, $\sigma = 1$. The unit of measurement along the horizontal axis of the normal distribution is in σ units of 1.
7. The total area under the normal curve is equal to 1.0000, and various portions of this curve area are equal to proportions of 1.0000.
8. Because of the perfect symmetry of the normal distribution, the mean of the normal distribution divides it into two equal halves, where each half is equal to .5000.
9. A given distance to the left or right of the mean, $\mu = 0$, cut off by a certain number of σ's of 1 will include identical or equivalent proportions of curve area.

There is only one normal distribution. However, there is an infinite number of normal distributions of raw scores that resemble the normal distribution. Many of the statements that can be made about the normal distribution can also be made about any distribution of raw scores that is normal in form.

Why is the Normal Distribution Important to Criminologists?

THE GENERALIZABILITY FUNCTION   Distributions of raw scores that approximate the normal distribution are said to be normally distributed. If we have a random sample of inmates from the Louisiana State Penitentiary at Angola, and if we have computed prisonization scores for these inmates, there is a presumption that the distribution of prisonization scores is normally distributed. This may or may not be a true assumption, but it is made anyway. Sample scores are used as estimates of the entire inmate population. Another assumption is that these scores probably typify the prisonization scores of all prison inmates. Again, this assumption may or may not be true, but it is made anyway.

THE STATISTICAL INFERENCE FUNCTION   A knowledge of the normal distribution helps us to understand statistical inference. Several types of distributions discussed in later chapters resemble the normal distribution. To the extent these other distributions are normal in form, the characteristics of the normal distribution may also apply to these other distributions. These other distributions are called sampling distributions of statistics and they are different from distributions of sample raw scores. Their meaning and importance will be discussed in Chapter 7.

THE NORMAL DISTRIBUTION AS A STATISTICAL TEST ASSUMPTION Several tests of significance presented in later chapters assume normality for their proper application in research work. Thus, besides the assumptions of level of measurement, randomness, and sample size, some statistical tests and measures require normality or a normal distribution of scores. Normality, therefore, may be one of several assumptions associated with particular statistical tests. If normality is not achieved and the statistical test is applied anyway, then the statistical test results will be unreliable. Each research situation and statistical application must be evaluated on its individual merits, therefore. The nature of any test assumption violation should always be taken into account when interpreting our numerical results in hypothesis tests.

STANDARD SCORES AND THE NORMAL DISTRIBUTION

Much will be learned in this chapter about the normal distribution and what it can do for us. It is essential that we acquire a thorough familiarity with the normal distribution and its properties. Procedures, such as statistical inference, will become less intimidating as we increasingly understand the principles of the normal distribution being applied.

The normal distribution has two parameters: a $\mu = 0$ and a $\sigma = 1$. The unit of measurement along the horizontal axis of the normal distribution is $\sigma = 1$. Thus, movements of so many σ values of 1 to the left or right of the mean, $\mu = 0$, include standardized portions of curve area. There is a basic equivalency between specific σ departures to the left or right of μ along the horizontal axis and **standard scores**. Standard scores or standard values define particular increments of 1 (σ) either to the left or right of $\mu = 0$. Thus, if we were to move 1.50 σ's to the right of the $\mu = 0$, this point would become a standard score $= 1.50$. Any departures of σ's to the left of the μ are negative and indicated by the negative sign ($-$). Thus, moving 2.30 σ's to the left of μ yields a standard score $= -2.30$. The following are examples of different departures of $\sigma = 1$ along the horizontal axis of the normal distribution and equivalent standard scores:

σ departure to left or right of μ	Equivalent standard score
1.96 σ's to left of μ	-1.96
3.18 σ's to right of μ	3.18
0.35 σ's to left of μ	-0.35
2.09 σ's to right of μ	2.09
1.14 σ's to right of μ	1.14

Standard scores or **Z scores** indicate a certain number of σ's either to the left or right of μ on the horizontal axis of the normal distribution. In the above examples, the standard scores of $-1.96, 3.18, -0.35, 2.09,$ and 1.14 are also Z scores of $-1.96, 3.18, -0.35, 2.09,$ and 1.14. If we know a particular Z score, we also know how far it is from μ and in which direction, left or right. Figure 6.2 shows these Z scores at different points along the horizontal axis of the normal distribution in relation to μ.

Every Z score to the left or right of μ on the normal distribution cuts off a certain proportion of it. These proportions have been tabled for easy reference. Table A.2 in Appendix A, p. 445–446, shows proportions of curve area cut off by various Z scores either to the left or right of μ.

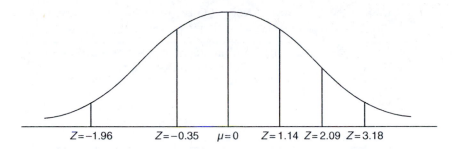

FIGURE 6.2   Different Points Along the Horizontal Axis of the Normal Distribution

Interpreting Table A.2 of Appendix A

Table A.2 contains various proportions of curve area expressed to four places (e.g., .0068, .3413). These proportions are associated with different Z scores ranging from 0.00 to ±3.59. Z scores beyond ±3.59 encompass nearly 50 percent of the normal distribution. As can be seen, ±3.59 encompasses .49999 of curve area. Moving beyond ±3.59 to ±4.60 or ±5.18 would merely extend the number of 9s (e.g., .4999999999999). The tails of the normal distribution always extend toward infinity and thus, 50 percent or .5000 is never reached by any Z score, however large it may be. This is the reason tabled proportions of Z scores extend only to 3.59.

Z scores are always expressed to the nearest hundredth (e.g., 1.66, −.93, 3.22, −2.10). Down the left-hand side of the table are the first two digits of a Z score, ranging from 0.00 to ±3.5. The digit for the hundredth is found across the top of the table, ranging from .00 through ±.09. Thus, if we wanted to look up a Z score = 1.63, we would find 1.6 down the left-hand side and .03 across the top of the table. Where these values intersect identifies the curve area cut off between $\mu = 0$ and a Z score = 1.63. In this case, the proportion of curve area found is .4484. As additional examples, the following Z scores and accompanying proportions of curve area are provided in Table 6.1.

Whenever Z scores are located below or to the left of $\mu = 0$, the proportions of curve area are the same as those to the right of the mean. Table 6.2 shows the same Z scores taken from Table 6.1. However, these same Z scores occur below or to the left of μ and are therefore negative. In each case, the same proportion of curve area is cut off for the negative Z scores in Table 6.2 as would be cut off for the same positive Z scores shown in Table 6.1.

TABLE 6.1 Proportions of Normal Curve Area Cut Off Between Mean and Different Positive Z Scores

Z Score	Cuts off from mean, $\mu = 0$, a proportion of curve area equal to:
1.96	.4750
2.33	.4901
3.69	.4999
0.06	.0239

TABLE 6.2 Proportions of Normal Curve Area Cut Off Between Mean and Different Negative Z Scores

Z Value	Cuts off from mean, $\mu = 0$ a proportion of curve area equal to:
−1.96	.4750
−2.33	.4901
−3.69	.4999
−0.06	.0239

Figure 6.3 shows a normal distribution with identical Z scores of ±1.00 to the left and right of μ. Notice that .3413 of curve area is cut off from each of the Z scores from the mean both to the left and right of it. These curve areas have been shaded.

Figure 6.4 shows another normal distribution where four Z scores are located. Arrows have been drawn from the mean, $\mu = 0$, to each of the points associated with each Z score. The four different Z scores, −2.95, −1.86, .99, and 2.77, cut off different proportions of curve area. Thus, the Z score = −2.95 cuts off .4984 of curve area; the Z score = −1.86 cuts off .4686 of curve area; the Z score = .99 cuts off .3389 of curve area; and the Z score = 2.77 cuts off .4972 of curve area.

Determining Proportions of Curve Area Above and Below Z Scores

If we know a particular Z score, we will also know the proportion of scores found above and below that Z score. Table 6.3 shows 5 Z scores and the proportion of curve area cut off below and above particular Z scores.

Using Table A.2 in Appendix A, we look up each Z score and identify the curve area from the mean, μ, to the particular Z score. Knowing this proportion of curve area allows us to determine how much curve area lies either above or below each Z score we examine. Thus, the first Z score of −1.00 cuts off .3413 of curve area from μ to that particular Z score. Determining the total amount of curve area either above or below any given Z score involves taking what we know about the normal curve area and determining the unknown area. For instance, we know that one half (.5000) of the normal distribution lies to the left and to the right of μ. We also know that a Z score of −1.00 lies to the left of μ and cuts off .3413 of curve area. If we want to know how much curve area occurs below this particular Z value of −1.00, we must subtract from .5000 the known amount of curve area included by a $Z = −1.00$, or $.5000 − .3413 = .1517$. Therefore, .1517 or approximately 15 percent of the curve area lies

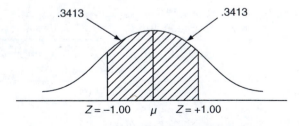

.3413   .3413

Z = −1.00 μ Z = +1.00

FIGURE 6.3 Normal Distribution Showing Identical Proportions of Curve Area Between Identical Z Values to the Left and Right of the Mean

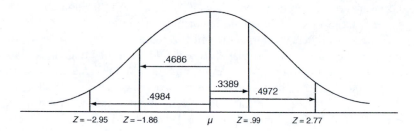

FIGURE 6.4 **Four Different Z Values on the Normal Distribution**

below or to the left of the Z score of −1.00. Other proportions of curve area lying below and above different Z scores are shown in Table 6.3.

Notice the Z score of 5.00. This score is to the far right of μ. Table A.2 includes Z scores only up to ±3.59. Any Z score above ±3.59, such as 5.00, cuts off .4999 of curve area. Thus, we will add the curve area to the left of μ = 0, .5000, to .4999 to yield .5000 + .4999 = .9999. Therefore, 99.99 percent of the curve area lies below a Z score of 5.00, while only .0001 of curve area lies above or to the right of it. The Z score of 0.00 lies directly upon μ, and therefore, one half or .5000 of curve area lies either to the left or right of it. This last calculation was determined by simple inspection.

The Tails of the Normal Distribution

The amount of curve area remaining either to the left of a negative Z score, such as −2.00 or −1.36, or to the right of a positive Z score, such as 2.48 or 0.89, is the amount of curve area remaining in a **tail** of the distribution. Tails of distributions are the areas to the extreme left and extreme right of the mean of the distribution. The normal distribution has two tails, a tail to the left and a tail to the right. These **tails of the distribution** have significance for statistical decision making and will become more relevant for statistical inference work given in Chapter 7. For now, we must become familiar with these tails of curve area and how they are determined.

Determining the amount of curve area either in the left or right tail involves taking a known value and solving for an unknown value (e.g., the area of curve remaining in the tail). If we know that .4500 of curve area is cut off by a given Z score to the left of μ, and if we know that one half or .5000 of the curve area lies to the left of μ, then we simply subtract .4500 from .5000, or .5000 − .4500 = .0500. This result is the amount of curve area remaining in the left tail of the normal distribution, or about 5 percent. If we have a positive Z score that includes

TABLE 6.3 Five Z Scores and Proportions of Curve Area Below and Above These Z Scores

Z Score	Proportion of Curve Area Below Z Score	Proportion of Curve Area Above Z Score
−1.00	.1517	.8413
−2.00	.0228	.9772
5.00	.9999	.0001
−3.00	.0013	.9987
0.00	.5000	.5000

.4750 of curve area from μ to that point, then .5000 $-$ .4750 $=$ .0250 or about 2.5 percent of the curve area remains in the right tail of the normal distribution.

Sometimes researchers want to know which Z score to the left of μ leaves 10 percent of the curve area in the left tail. A particular Z score would be needed that cuts off 40 percent of curve area (.4000) from μ to that point. An examination of Table A.2 shows that the closest proportion to .4000 is .3997. This is a proportion associated with a $Z = -1.28$. Thus, we would use the Z score $= -1.28$ to cut off nearly 40 percent of curve area, leaving approximately 10 percent in the left tail of the normal distribution. If we wanted to know which Z score would leave 15 percent of the curve area in the right tail of the curve, we would search for .3500 in the body of Table A.2. In this instance, we find that there is no exact .3500, only .3485 and .3508. We would choose the closer proportion to .3500 in this case, or .3508, which has a $Z = 1.04$. Therefore, a $Z = 1.04$ cuts off approximately 35 percent of curve area, leaving approximately 15 percent of the normal distribution in the right tail of the curve.

If the precise amount of curve area we are seeking that leaves a particular amount of curve area in a tail is not found, but if there are two proportions that are at the same distance from the curve area we seek, then we decide to use the nearest even Z score associated with that proportion. For instance, if we seek a Z score that leaves 5 percent (.0500) in the right tail of the normal distribution, we cannot find .0500 precisely. However, we do find the proportions of .0495 and .0505. These proportions are associated with $Z = 1.64$ and $Z = 1.65$ respectively. We would choose $Z = 1.64$ because it is the even Z value, and not $Z = 1.65$. This decision is purely arbitrary, but it is the standard used in this book if we are faced with such choices.

Determining Proportions of Curve Area Between Two Z Scores

Another scenario is that we want to know how much of the normal distribution lies between two different Z scores. For example, suppose we want to know the amount of curve area occurring between the Z scores of -1.83 and 2.66. The solution is a three-step process. First, we look up the $Z = -1.83$ in Table A.2 and determine that it cuts off .4664 of curve area. Second, we look up the $Z = 2.66$ and find that it cuts off .4961 of curve area. Third, we simply sum these two proportions, or .4664 + .4961 = .9625. There is .9625 of curve area, or about 96.2 percent, between these two Z scores of -1.83 and 2.66, therefore. Let's refer to this example "A." It is illustrated in Figure 6.5. Suppose we have two identical Z scores, such as $Z = -1.00$ and $Z = 1.00$. From Table A.2, we determine that each cuts off .3413 of curve area from μ to those points. We would

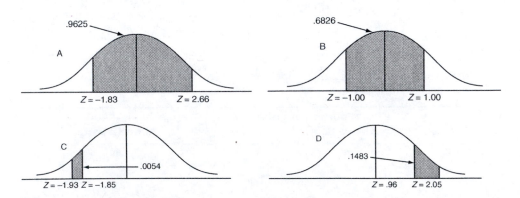

FIGURE 6.5 Four Scenarios Showing Proportions of Curve Area Between Two Different Z Values Either on Both Sides or on the Same Side of the Mean of the Normal Distribution

simply sum these two proportions, or .3413 + .3413 = .6826. Thus, approximately 68.3 percent of normal curve area would be found between these two Z scores. Let's call this example "B," also illustrated in Figure 6.5. What if both Z scores occur on the same side of the μ or the other, such as two Z scores of −1.85 and −1.93 respectively? How do we determine how much curve area lies between these two Z scores? The solution is as follows:

1. Determine the curve area from μ to $Z = -1.85$.
2. Determine the curve area from μ to $Z = -1.93$.
3. Determine the difference between these two proportions.

Using Table A.2, a Z score $= -1.85$ cuts off .4678 of curve area. A $Z = -1.93$ cuts off .4732. The difference between these proportions is .4732 − .4678 = .0054. Therefore, .0054 of curve area lies between the two Z scores. Let's call this example "C." It is the third illustration in Figure 6.5.

What if we want to determine the proportion of curve area between two positive Z scores, such as .96 and 2.05? Again, a three-step process is involved similar to our earlier problem. First, we determine from Table A.2 that a Z score of .96 cuts off .3315 of normal curve area. Second, a Z score of 2.05 cuts off .4798 of curve area. The difference between these two proportions is .4798 − .3315 = .1483. Thus, .1483 or almost 15 percent of curve area lies between the Z scores of .95 and 2.05. Let's call this example "D." It is the fourth illustration shown in Figure 6.5. Figure 6.5 shows shaded areas of the normal distribution where different portions of curve area between different Z values are found.

APPLYING THE NORMAL DISTRIBUTION IN RESEARCH

Converting Raw Scores Into Z Scores

Since Z scores define particular points on the normal distribution where fixed curve areas can be determined, how can this information help us in our research work? How can we relate Z scores to our collected data? One example is provided from the criminological literature.

Faye S. Taxman (2005) has written about various problems parolees face when reentering their communities. One problem is that they often lack educational and vocational skills to be placed in jobs where they can earn enough money to support their families. Correctional officials have found it helpful to assess pre-parolees to determine their educational and vocational needs. Prisons may be able to assist inmates in different ways. One method of determining offender needs is to assess their competencies and determine their strengths and weaknesses. Tailoring programs to their needs would help them become successfully reintegrated into their communities. Suppose Taxman studied a sample of pre-parolees and the results of five different inventories designed to measure verbal, quantitative, analytical, logical, and dexterity abilities and aptitudes. Table 6.4 shows hypothetical scores received by one female pre-parolee undergoing a prison

TABLE 6.4 Hypothetical Pre-Parolee Scores on Several Skills Tests

Assessment Measure	Raw Score
Smith Mathematical Inventory	120
Jones Verbal Aptitude Test	250
Avril Manual Dexterity Test	75
Johnson California Logic Assessment Index	3,000
Redford Analytical Skills Measure	700

assessment. The hypothetical raw scores are for five different tests and inventories designed to measure one's skill levels according to various criteria.

At first glance, anyone examining the scores in Table 6.4 received by the pre-parolee might assume that her best performance was on the Johnson California Logic Assessment Index, with a raw score = 3,000. Her worst performance might appear to be the score of 75 received on the Avril Manual Dexterity Test. However, these are five different inventories, each with different means and standard deviations. If we want to know for sure which of her skills was the best one according to these measures, we must standardize these scores.

Standardization means to reduce each set of raw scores to a common standard, where a given mean and a standard deviation are fixed. Usually this means converting scores to fit the parameters of the normal distribution, with a $\mu = 0$ and $\sigma = 1$. Thus we can **standardize** any distribution of raw scores in various ways. Creating a scale with a common mean and standard deviation will allow us to compare five different scores from five different scales with five different means and standard deviations. Standardization will reveal in which area our pre-parolee performed best, and which area yielded the worst performance. Table 6.5 is a re-creation of Table 6.4 but with different means and standard deviations attached.

From Table 6.5, we are now in a position to determine which skill area was the best and which was the worst. In order to **normalize** or standardize these raw scores, we will use the formula,

$$Z_i = \frac{X_i - \overline{X}_i}{s}$$

where

Z_i = the standard score for a particular raw score

$\overline{X}_i$ = the mean of the distribution of scores

X_i = a particular raw score from the distribution of scores

s_i = the standard deviation from the distribution of scores

For the Smith Mathematical Inventory, we can convert the raw score of 120 to a standard form as follows:

$$Z_1 = \frac{120 - 150}{30}$$
$$= \frac{-30}{30}$$
$$= -1.00$$

TABLE 6.5 Re-Creation of Table 6.4 with Different Means and Standard Deviations

Assessment Measure	Raw Score X_i	Mean $\overline{X}_i$	Standard Deviation s_i
Smith Mathematical Inventory	120	$X_1 = 150$	30
Jones Verbal Aptitude Test	250	$X_2 = 300$	25
Avril Manual Dexterity Test	75	$X_3 = 50$	5
Johnson California Logic Assessment Index	3,000	$X_4 = 6,000$	1,000
Redford Analytical Skills Measure	700	$X_5 = 700$	150

We can convert the pre-parolee's score of 250 on the Jones Verbal Aptitude Test as follows:

$$Z_2 = \frac{250 - 300}{25}$$

$$= \frac{-50}{25}$$

$$= -2.00$$

The score of 75 on the Avril Manual Dexterity Test can be normalized as follows:

$$Z_3 = \frac{75 - 50}{5}$$

$$= \frac{25}{5}$$

$$= 5.00$$

The score of 3,000 on the Johnson California Logic Assessment Index is normalized as follows:

$$Z_4 = \frac{3000 - 6000}{1000}$$

$$= \frac{-3000}{1000}$$

$$= -3.00$$

And finally, we can standardize the score of 700 on the Redford Analytical Skills Measure as follows:

$$Z_5 = \frac{700 - 700}{150}$$

$$= \frac{-0}{150}$$

$$= 0.00$$

We can now assess our female pre-parolee according to these five aptitude measures. This information is shown in Table 6.6.

Table 6.6 shows all Z scores associated with the female pre-parolee's performances on the five inventories. It is clear from these Z scores that her best performance was on the Avril Manual Dexterity Test, with a $Z = 5.00$. The poorest performance was on the Johnson California Logic Assessment Index, with a $Z = -3.00$.

TABLE 6.6 Five Z Scores for Five Different Aptitude Tests

Assessment Measure	Z Score
Smith Mathematical Inventory	−1.00
Jones Verbal Aptitude Test	−2.00
Avril Manual Dexterity Test	5.00
Johnson California Logic Assessment Index	−3.00
Redford Analytical Skills Measure	0.00

If Taxman or prison officials were to use these Z scores to design more meaningful training programs and provide better services to pre-parolees, then the weaknesses in these and other Z scores could be highlighted and addressed. Rarely do officials rely on one set of test results, however. Many factors influence one's test performance. Relative to other pre-parolees who took these tests, we can assume that our pre-parolee has good dexterity skills. The difficulty of each of these tests was unknown, however. The conditions under which the tests were administered may not have been ideal either. There are many unknowns in this example to use these test results alone as the basis for creating specific treatment programs for pre-parolees. But these test results are helpful to some extent at least. We now have a better knowledge of our pre-parolee's skills.

Converting Z Scores Into Raw Scores

What if we wish to convert Z scores back to raw scores? A simple formula exists for this purpose. It is:

$$X_i = \overline{X}_i + (s_i)(Z_i)$$

where

X_i = the original score

$\overline{X}_i$ = the original mean of the distribution where the score is found

s_i = the original standard deviation of the distribution where the score is found

Z_i = the Z score calculated for the original raw score, X_i

If we wanted to use the information from Table 6.6 and convert these five Z scores back into their original form, we would take the following steps with each Z score, again utilizing the original mean and standard deviation from each test or assessment measure. For the Smith Mathematical Inventory, we would begin with the mean of 150, using the standard deviation as well as the Z score we originally determined and solve for the original raw score as follows:

$$\text{Smith Mathematical Inventory} = 150 + (30)(-1.00)$$
$$= 150 + (-30)$$
$$= 150 - 30 = 120$$

The original raw score for our pre-parolee on the Smith Mathematical Inventory is 120. Raw score conversions for the other assessment measures are shown below:

$$\text{Jones Verbal Aptitude Test} = 300 + (25)(-2.00)$$
$$= 300 + (-50)$$
$$= 300 - 50 = 250$$
$$\text{Avril Manual Dexterity Test} = 50 + (5)(5.00)$$
$$= 50 + (25) = 75$$
$$\text{Johnson California Logic Assessment Index} = 6,000 + (1,000)(-3.00)$$
$$= 6,000 + (-3000)$$
$$= 6,000 - 3,000 = 3,000$$
$$\text{Redford Analytical Skills Measure} = 700 - (150)(0.00)$$
$$= 700 - 0 = 700$$

This formula works for all Z score conversions whenever we know three pieces of information:

1. The original Z score associated with the unknown raw score.
2. The original mean, $\overline{X}_i$, for the distribution for the raw score.
3. The original standard deviation, s_i, for the distribution for the raw score.

Transforming Scores to Standard Forms Other Than the Normal Distribution

From time to time, criminologists and others might want to convert raw scores for large numbers of persons to a standard form different from the normal distribution. Why would investigators want to do this? For one thing, the normal distribution has negative Z values as well as positive ones. Sometimes, it is awkward working with negative values, such as $Z = -1.25$ or $Z = -2.21$. Negative values can be eliminated entirely if new standards are established. For instance, we might decide to convert several sets of scores from different assessment measures to a new standard, where the new mean is $= 10,000$ and the new standard deviation $= 500$. This action would probably eliminate any and all negative scores that might otherwise occur if the normal distribution parameters, $\mu = 0$ and $\sigma = 1$ were used.

What information do we need to convert scores to a new standard, such as a distribution with a mean $= 10,000$ and a standard deviation $= 500$? The key is a knowledge of one's original Z score from the inventory measures examined earlier. Using the Taxman example previously discussed, suppose the pre-parolee had received a Z score of 3.20 for her original raw score on one of the inventories. This Z is 3.20 σ's above μ on the normal distribution. But where would this same value occur if the new mean $= 10,000$ and the new standard deviation $= 500$? In order to perform this score conversion, we merely substitute the new mean and standard deviation and use the following formula:

New Raw Score $=$ (New Mean) $+$ (New Standard Deviation) (Original Z Score)

Substituting our new information the original Z score of 3.20 into this formula, we have

Pre-parolee's new score $= 10,000 + (500)(3.20)$
$= 10,000 + 1,600 = 11,600.$

Our pre-parolee's new score for comparison purposes is 11,600, according to our revised standards of a new mean $= 10,000$ and a new standard deviation $= 500$. Actually, the new score of 11,600 is at precisely the same point on that new distribution compared with where a $Z = 3.20$ would be located on the normal distribution.

NONNORMAL DISTRIBUTIONS

When criminologists can assume normality with their collected sample information, means and standard deviations can be used to provide consistent interpretations of raw scores and curve areas among different distributions. This is the valuable comparative function provided by the normal distribution. But what if normality doesn't exist?

Seldom it is the case that perfectly normal distributions of scores occur. Usually, there are minor departures from normality where the mean, mode, and median are slightly different from one another, or where the distribution is not exactly bell-shaped. These slight departures from normality are frequently disregarded. However, where serious distribution skewness and/or kurtosis are present, the normal curve assumption cannot be made. Any distribution that has substantial skewness and/or kurtosis is not normal. **Skewness** is a distributional property occurring whenever scores or curve area accumulate in one end of the distribution or the other. **Kurtosis** refers to curve peakedness. These characteristics of distributions are discussed in the following section.

Skewness

Skewness is illustrated in Figures 6.6 and 6.7. Figure 6.6 shows negative skewness, where the scores in a distribution accumulate toward the left end of the distribution. Figure 6.7 shows positive skewness, where the scores in a distribution accumulate toward the right end of the distribution. A simple way of determining whether a distribution is negatively or positively skewed is to examine the tapering tail of the distribution. In negatively skewed distributions the tail of the curve tapers off toward the left, while in positively skewed distributions the tail tapers off toward the right. These properties are illustrated in Figures 6.6 and 6.7 respectively.

Almost every distribution is skewed to a degree. Skewness, *Sk*, can be measured easily by the formula,

$$\text{Skewness} = \frac{3(\overline{X} - Mdn)}{s}$$

where

$\overline{X}$ = observed mean

Mdn = observed median

s = observed standard deviation

3 = a constant

Thus, if we observed an $\overline{X} = 50$, a $Mdn = 55$, and an $s = 2$, the amount of skewness, *Sk*, would be:

$$Sk = \frac{3 \times (50 - 55)}{2}$$

$$= \frac{(3)(-5)}{2}$$

$$= \frac{-15}{2}$$

$$Sk = -7.5$$

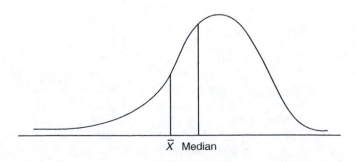

$\overline{X}$ Median

FIGURE 6.6   A Negatively Skewed Distribution

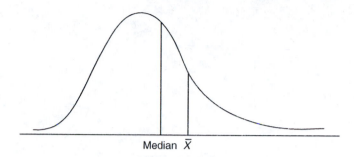

FIGURE 6.7   **A Positively Skewed Distribution**

$Sk = -7.5$, which means that the distribution is (a) negatively skewed and (b) skewed to a great degree. In another scenario, suppose we have an $\overline{X} = 20$, a $Mdn = 18$, and an $s = 4$. Calculating our skewness for this distribution, we would have:

$$Sk = \frac{3 \times (20 - 18)}{4}$$

$$= \frac{6}{4}$$

$$Sk = 1.5$$

$Sk = 1.5$, which means that our distribution is (a) positively skewed and (b) skewed to a small degree.

How much skewness is too much skewness? We have no definitive criteria to judge how much skewness is too much. An arbitrary and conventional rule of thumb used by many researchers is whether Sk exceeds ± 1.00. If we observe ± 1.00 or less in the skewness for any distribution, the distribution is not considered skewed sufficiently to qualify it as normal. However, if our distribution has ± 1.01 or more skewness, then it is skewed too much to be considered normal in form. This interpretive guideline is purely arbitrary, however. Investigators usually exercise their own judgment in determining whether any distribution of scores is too skewed to be normal. *SPSS* tests for skewness are available if researchers are analyzing data with such software programs.

Kurtosis

Kurtosis is the amount of curve peakedness in any distribution. The normal distribution is bell-shaped, as originally shown in Figure 6.1. Sometimes, distributions are more flat-appearing, or more peaked near the center, or have a wavy appearance with bulges. The curves in Figure 6.8 show different kinds of kurtosis.

There are three types of kurtosis. Figure 6.8 shows **platykurtosis**, which is a flat-appearing distribution. Also shown is **mesokurtosis**, which is a bulging distribution without smoothly tapering tails. A third type of kurtosis, **leptokurtosis**, is also illustrated. In leptokurtic distributions, the curve is extremely pointed or peaked near the center of the distribution. None of these distributions is normal. Any distribution which is platykurtic, mesokurtic, or leptokurtic is never normal in form. However, it is possible that some distributions may appear to be platykurtic, mesokurtic, or leptokurtic and yet have normality. Looking at a distribution cannot always tell you whether a distribution has any type of kurtosis. Some distributions of

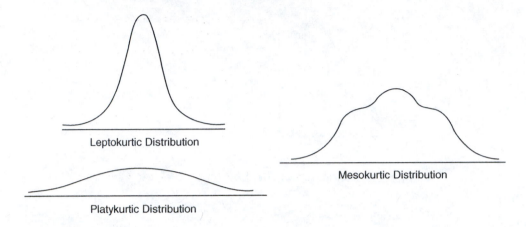

FIGURE 6.8 Different Types of Kurtosis: Platykurtosis, Mesokurtosis, and Leptokurtosis

scores appear to have one type of kurtosis or another, but again, there are no foolproof ways of determining whether kurtosis exists without some type of numerical verification. A formula exists to determine kurtosis, but it is beyond the scope of this book. If investigators are using *SPSS* software, then a kurtosis number is calculated for virtually any data set. Again, no clear-cut rules exist for determining how much kurtosis is too much. This decision is up to individual researchers.

Working With Skewness and Kurtosis

It is assumed throughout this book that most distributions of scores examined are normal in form. Even where there are minor departures from normality, statements made about normal distributions will hold under most conditions. Even if researchers suspect that their distributions of scores may have some substantial kurtosis or skewness, some general statements can be made about these distributions. Such statements are extremely conservative but considering the distorting effects of skewness and kurtosis, this conservatism is justified.

Whenever skewness and/or kurtosis is suspected or apparent, standard deviations for any distribution of scores can be used to estimate proportions of curve area between the mean of the distribution and different standard deviations from the mean. For instance, regardless of the amount of skewness or kurtosis present in any distribution, it may be said that always at least 75 percent of the distribution of scores will be found within 2 standard deviations on either side of the mean. Also, it may be said that always at least 90 percent of the scores in any distribution will be found within 3 standard deviations on either side of the mean. These generalizations are illustrated in Figure 6.9.

The conservative nature of these general statements about how much curve area will always be found within 2 or 3 standard deviations on either side of the mean of any given distribution is that for the normal distribution, the actual area included within $\pm 2\sigma$'s on either side of μ is (2).4772 = .9544, or over 95 percent of the curve area. Within $\pm 3\sigma$'s on either side of μ on the normal distribution would include (2).4987 = .9974, or nearly 100 percent of the entire distribution. Therefore, "always at least 75 percent of the distribution" and "always at least 90 percent of the distribution" of scores being found within 2 and 3 standard deviations on either side of some $\overline{X}$ under extreme skewness or kurtosis are extremely conservative estimates.

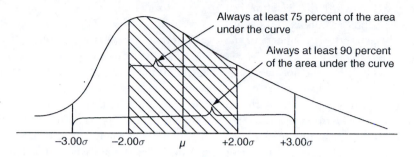

FIGURE 6.9   Areas of Curve Always Found Within 2 and 3 Standard Deviations from the Mean of Any Distribution of Scores

THE PROBABILITY FUNCTION OF THE NORMAL DISTRIBUTION

Besides being useful for comparative purposes in criminological research, the normal distribution also performs a probability function. Proportions of curve area can be equated with or translated into probabilities. For instance, scores that occur within 1σ on either side of μ on the normal distribution are said to have a 68 percent chance of occurring within this general area. Thus, the different proportions of curve area can also be interpreted as probabilities. Scores found in the extremes of the distribution or tails of it, for instance, are less plentiful than those scores that occur in and around the center of the distribution where the mean is located. Therefore, there is a lower likelihood or probability of these scores (either very large ones or very small ones) occurring.

Also, some of the statistical tests discussed in later chapters make the distributional assumption of normality. In order to optimize the use of several of these statistical procedures, researchers must assume that their distributions of scores are normal and that they match closely the characteristics of the bell-shaped curve known as the normal distribution. If they are unable to make this assumption, then the meaningfulness of those statistical tests requiring normality is undermined and their interpretation may be compromised. The normal distribution, therefore, is a critical distributional assumption made by many tests known as parametric tests. Several of these parametric tests and the characteristics of parametric tests will be covered generally in Chapter 8.

Summary

The normal distribution or standard normal distribution is theoretically derived. It has several desirable properties or features of interest to criminologists. The resulting curve is bell-shaped and perfectly symmetrical. One half of the curve area equals precisely the other half of it. Portions of curve area cut off between μ and any given distance of σ's from μ in one direction are equivalent to portions of curve area cut off between μ and the same distance of σ's in the other direction. The normal distribution has a $\mu = 0$ and a $\sigma = 1$. Movements to the left and right along the horizontal axis of the normal distribution are measured in σ units of 1. Points along the horizontal axis of the normal distribution are referred to as Z scores or standard scores. Each Z score or standard score is associated with cutting off a fixed amount of curve area from μ to that point.

The highest point of the normal curve is at the center of it. Thus, the mean, mode, and median of the distribution all occur at the same point. The entire area under the normal distribution is equal to 1.0000, and different portions of normal curve area are equal to different proportions of 1.0000. The tails of the distribution taper off from the center of it in opposite directions toward the baseline but never touch it. The ends or tails extend toward infinity. This is the **asymptotic property of the normal distribution**.

Most statements about the normal distribution can be applied to any distribution of raw scores that approximates it. For some statistical procedures and measures of association, the normal distribution is an assumption associated with their research applications. When this assumption is met by any distribution of scores, then different proportions of curve area are equivalent to those same proportions of curve area on the normal distribution. Areas of the normal distribution are constant and have been tabled for research use. These proportions are also interpretable as probabilities and have significance for statistical inference.

Proportions of curve area lying to the left or right of given distances from μ can be determined easily. Also, the amount of curve area lying between two Z scores can be determined. Any amount of curve area lying between a given Z score and μ also leaves a certain amount of curve area in either tail of the distribution. The areas remaining in the tails of the normal distribution are determined by subtracting the area covered by a Z score from .5000, one half of the normal distribution. Thus, a Z score of ± 1.28 includes .3997 of curve area from μ to each of these points, and $.5000 - .3997 = .1003$ or about 10 percent of the curve area remains in each tail of the distribution. Again, this information is valuable and the relevance of it for statistical inference and statistical decision making will be discussed in the following chapter.

Most applications of the information presented in this chapter are based on the assumption that any distribution of scores is normal or approximately normal in form. However, it is seldom the case that any given distribution of scores is perfectly normal. Scores may not be normally distributed. They may be bunched up in one end of the distribution or the other. This condition is known as skewness. Scores that accumulate in large numbers in the left part of a distribution and taper off toward the right end of it are positively skewed, whereas scores that accumulate in the right end of a distribution and taper off toward the left end of it are negatively skewed. Another nonnormal condition is kurtosis, or curve peakedness. Some distributions may be very flat, or platykurtic, whereas other distributions may sharply rise near the center of the distribution. These are called leptokurtic. Yet other distributions may not taper off evenly in opposite directions but rather exhibit bulging shapes that are referred to as mesokurtic. The proportions of curve area within certain distances of their means in platykurtic, leptokurtic, or mesokurtic distributions are not consistent with the proportionate areas encompassed by those same distances or Z scores on the normal distribution. Minor discrepancies almost always exist between proportions of curve areas covered by common Z scores on raw score distributions and their counterparts on the normal distribution, but dramatic discrepancies suggest that kurtosis exists. Any distribution of scores with too much skewness or kurtosis is not normal in form. Investigators usually make subjective judgments about whether their distributions of scores approximate normality.

Key Terms

Questions for Review

1. What are four important properties of the unit normal distribution? How important is it to know that the mean, mode, and median all occur in the center of the distribution? Explain.

2. What are Z scores? How are they calculated or determined?

3. Are standard scores the same thing as Z scores? What is the usefulness of standard scores?

4. What does it mean to normalize a distribution of raw scores?

5. What are tails of distributions of scores?

6. Can we convert raw scores from one distribution into scores for another distribution with a new mean and a new standard deviation? What advantages are there for doing this?

7. What is the importance of the normal distribution as an assumption underlying statistical tests and measures of association?

8. How is the normal distribution a probability distribution? Explain.

9. Differentiate between skewness and kurtosis? Are distributions that have substantial skewness or kurtosis normal distributions? Why or why not?

10. What is the rule of thumb regarding whether a distribution has too much kurtosis?

11. What are some generalizations that can be made using normal curve proportions and Z scores if we have distributions with too much skewness or kurtosis? Explain.

Exercises

The purpose of these exercises is to familiarize students with the normal curve and areas of the normal curve within given distances from the mean of it. Table A.2 of Appendix A will be used almost exclusively to solve most of these exercises. What is learned here about the normal curve and areas in its tails, between different points along its horizontal axis, and other features of the distribution will subsequently have direct relevance for finding solutions to statistical tests presented in later chapters. Table A.2 contains information pertaining to statistical decision making and hypothesis testing. Therefore, it is imperative that students have a fundamental understanding of the normal distribution and its properties. As you acquire greater familiarity with the normal distribution and its properties, you will have a greater appreciation for several of the more difficult concepts discussed in subsequent chapters, especially Chapter 7.

6.1. For the following Z scores, determine the proportion of curve area from the mean to these points:
   a. 1.16
   b. −.33
   c. 2.88
   d. 2.22
   e. −.19
   f. 2.00

6.2. Determine the raw scores associated with the Z scores below, where $\overline{X} = 100$ and $s = 7$:
   a. 6.00
   b. −2.50
   c. 3.50
   d. 0.00

6.3. Determine the amount of curve area between the following pairs of Z scores:
   a. 2.11 and −.03
   b. 3.00 and 1.00

   c. 1.18 and −1.18
   d. −2.14 and −1.37

6.4. Determine amount of curve area to the right of the following Z values:
   a. 2.10
   b. −3.00
   c. −2.80
   d. 3.00

6.5. What proportion of curve area lies to the right of the following Z values?
   a. −1.32
   b. 1.94
   c. −.18

6.6. What proportion of curve area is included between the following Zs?
   a. 1.94 and −.62
   b. 2.41 and 1.68
   c. −1.20 and −2.99
   d. 2.18 and −1.93

6.7. Transform the following raw scores into standard scores with an $\overline{X} = 150$ and $s = 25$: (Assume $\overline{X} = 35$ and $s = 6$)

a. 42

b. 28

c. 56

6.8. With an $\overline{X} = 60$ and $s = 5$, what proportion of scores lies above the following values?

a. 65

b. 47

c. 55

6.9. Using the same information from problem 6.8 above, what proportion of scores lies between the following values? (Hint: convert each raw score to a Z score)

a. 51 and 75

b. 70 and 86

c. 40 and 46

6.10. Convert the following raw scores to Z scores, where $\overline{X} = 85$ and $s = 6$:

a. 99

b. 85

c. 50

d. 105

6.11. Convert the following Z scores to raw scores, where $\overline{X} = 110$ and $s = 15$:

a. −4.55

b. 8.45

c. 2.88

d. −6.66

6.12. Convert the following raw scores to a standard form with a new $\overline{X} = 5,000$ and a new $s = 1,500$, where the old $\overline{X} = 22$ and old $s = 3$:

a. 28

b. 22

c. 15

d. 19

6.13. Change the following raw scores from old information and transform them to a new form, where old $\overline{X} = 15$, old $s = 2$, new $\overline{X} = 300$, new $s = 25$:

a. 14

b. 22.5

c. 19

d. 3

e. 5.5

f. 33.5

6.14. Determine the skewness associated with the following:

a. Sk_1

b. Sk_2

c. What can be said about the two distributions in terms of skewness?

Characteristics	Distribution 1	Distribution 2
Means	15.2	75.3
Standard deviations	2.2	5.9
Modes	19.0	85
Medians	10.1	97.1

References

Taxman, Faye S. (2005). "Brick Walls Facing Reentering Offenders." *International Journal of* *Comparative and Applied Criminal Justice* 29:5–18.

CHAPTER 7

Statistical Inference and Tests of Significance

Chapter Outline

Chapter Objectives

After reading this chapter, the following objectives will be realized:

1. understanding how hypotheses are formulated;
2. distinguishing between research, null, and statistical hypotheses and their interrelations;
3. understanding decision rules and their relevance in hypothesis testing;
4. learning about sampling distributions of statistics, expected values, and critical regions;
5. distinguishing between point and interval estimation and the concept of confidence intervals;
6. understanding one- and two-tailed tests of significance;
7. distinguishing between Type I and Type II errors in statistical decision making; and
8. learning the power of convention in hypothesis test decision making.

INTRODUCTION

This chapter examines statistical decision making and hypothesis testing. Most criminologists and criminal justice professionals test hypotheses and, indirectly, the theories from which they were derived. This is a decision-making process in hypothesis testing where different statistical tests and measures of association are selected and used. There are many statistical tests available. Some are appropriate for particular kinds of data analysis, while some tests are not appropriate. Some of the criteria for hypothesis testing and statistical applications for this purpose will be examined.

Hypothesis testing and its importance are illustrated. Statistical tests and techniques are tools used in hypothesis testing. Our statistical tests and measures are objective methods for evaluating our theoretical predictions and explanations of criminological phenomena.

Whenever hypotheses are tested, statistical test choices, as well as their outcomes, are governed by rules called decision rules. Three important decision rules described in this chapter are the sampling distribution of a statistic, the level of significance, and critical regions or regions of rejection.

We most often study samples of persons drawn from populations of them. Much of our hypothesis testing is focused upon estimating population characteristics or parameters by examining the characteristics of samples we have collected. Two types of estimation will be described. These are point estimation and interval estimation.

As our research becomes more focused, we may wish to glean more specific details about the persons we are studying. If we are studying two groups of persons, for instance, we might wish to know whether one group possesses some characteristic to a greater degree than another. Therefore, we will focus upon directional differences and whether one group differs from another in a particular way. Is one group more violent or less violent than another? Does one sample of probationers have higher recidivism than another sample of probationers? The types of statistical tests we apply in these cases are considered one-tailed or directional. If two groups simply differ on some measured characteristic, we may conduct two-tailed or nondirectional hypothesis tests. Sometimes it is important for us to know not only that two or more groups differ, but how they differ and in what direction. Thus, both one- and two-tailed tests of hypotheses will be described.

In subsequent chapters, tests of significance and measures of association will be described. These tests and measures enable us to make objective decisions about the samples we study. Therefore, a brief overview of tests of significance will be presented. Whenever samples are studied, some error in sampling occurs. This error is called sampling error and is important in assessing our statistical findings.

When we make predictions about what we expect to find, our predicted outcomes may not occur. Thus there is always some amount of error in our predictions about variables and how they are related. Two types of error are defined and described. These are called Type I error and Type II error. No one likes to make errors. But in statistics, some errors always exist. Type I and Type II errors are relatively easy to understand and will be explained. We will learn that neither type of error can be completely eliminated. Furthermore, these errors influence the decisions we make as well as the accuracy of our predictions of relationships between variables or differences between groups. Although our research and statistical decision making is never error-free, this doesn't prevent us from reducing different types of error in different ways. Strategies for error reduction will be described and explained.

DERIVING HYPOTHESES TO TEST

When a problem or event is chosen for study, investigators have a rationale for why the event is important and how it should be viewed. Theories explain and predict relations between different variables. The results of our theorizing result in deducing various hypotheses that can be tested. Several different types of hypotheses to be illustrated in this section include (1) research hypotheses, (2) null hypotheses, and (3) statistical hypotheses.

Research Hypotheses

Research hypotheses are statements derived directly from our theories. Our theory may seek to relate broken homes with delinquency. We may expect greater delinquency among children from broken homes than from stable home environments. Thus, one research hypothesis might be that delinquency rates will be higher among children from broken homes compared with children from stable homes. If we found higher delinquency rates among children from broken homes compared with children from more stable homes, then this finding might support our research hypothesis. Accordingly, any support for a research hypothesis is also support for the theory from which it was derived. Of course, delinquency is the result of many factors, not just broken homes. But the intent here is to provide an example of where research hypotheses might come from and how they might be tested.

After we have collected information about whatever we are studying, we subject our explanation to an empirical test. An empirical test consists of doing research to see whether our explanation of some variable (such as delinquency) actually explains it or has predictive utility. Several examples of research hypotheses are:

1. *Poorly trained state criminal court judges will have more of their verdicts overturned compared with well-trained state criminal court judges.*
2. *The longer the prison term served by an inmate, the less likely the inmate is to reoffend.*

3. *Greater police officer professionalism will decrease the number of civilian complaints against the police.*
4. *Placement in a halfway house following parole will result in lower recidivism rates compared with parolees who are not placed in halfway houses.*
5. *Conviction rates vary according to whether defense counsel is publicly appointed or private.*

In each of these hypotheses, one variable is explained by another variable. In the first hypothesis, for instance, the amount of training among state criminal court judges (or lack of it) may result in verdict reversals. The second hypothesis suggests that the longer prison term inmates serve, the less likely they will reoffend when released. The third hypothesis suggests that greater police professionalism will decrease numbers of citizen complaints against police officers. The fourth hypothesis suggests that halfway houses are helpful in reducing parolee recidivism. Finally, the fifth hypothesis suggests that convictions of offenders are influenced by whether defendants have public defenders or private counsels to represent them.

Whenever research hypotheses are tested, research findings are generated with different types of significance. These types of significance are (1) substantive or applied, (2) theoretical, and (3) statistical.

Substantive significance or **applied significance** has to do with the practical implications of whatever we observe. Are our findings meaningful? Substantive significance stresses practicality. **Theoretical significance** is theory-driven and implies that our findings are generalizable to other samples. Whenever we conclude that a finding has theoretical significance, this means that it contributes to our understanding of interrelationships between variables. Criminologists are concerned with the theoretical significance of research findings. Persons associated with the criminal justice system are interested in what works to reduce crime or recidivism, or the mechanics of the criminal justice system itself.

Statistical significance is the focus of this chapter. It relies exclusively on quantitative results derived from the application of statistical tests or measures. Statistical significance also relies on probability theory and **probabilities** associated with our numerical results. Numerical results lend greater objectivity and credibility to whatever we study. In sum, substantive significance is concerned with the practical effects of our research. Theoretical significance is concerned with possible interrelationships between variables. Statistical significance is a quantitative assessment of our research findings.

Null Hypotheses

A second type of hypothesis is the **null hypothesis**. Null hypotheses are derived from research hypotheses. Null hypotheses are statements, which, if refuted, will lead to the support of some alternative true research hypothesis.

Given the five research hypotheses presented above, the following null hypotheses are derived from them.

1. *Poorly trained criminal court judges will not differ from well-trained criminal court judges insofar as having their verdicts overturned; or if there is a difference, poorly trained criminal court judges will have fewer of their verdicts overturned.* (If this hypothesis is refuted or demonstrated false, then it must be true that poorly trained criminal court judges have more of their verdicts overturned compared with well-trained criminal court judges.)
2. *The length of prison term served by inmates has no effect on the likelihood that inmates will reoffend; or if there is a difference, inmates serving longer sentences will reoffend more*

frequently than those offenders serving shorter sentences. (If this hypothesis is refuted or demonstrated false, then it must be true that the longer the sentence length, the less the recidivism.)

3. *The amount of police professionalism will have no effect on the number of citizen complaints against police; or if there is a difference, greater police professionalism will yield greater numbers of citizen complaints.* (If this hypothesis is refuted, then it must be true that greater police professionalism will yield fewer civilian complaints against police.)

4. *Placement in a halfway house following parole will have no influence on recidivism rates of parolees compared with those parolees not placed in halfway houses; or if there is a difference, parolees placed in halfway houses will have higher rates of recidivism compared with parolees not placed in halfway houses.* (If this statement is refuted by our data, then it must be true that halfway house placement following parole reduces recidivism rates of parolees compared with parolees not assigned to halfway houses.)

5. *Conviction rates are the same for those represented by publicly appointed counsel and those represented by private counsel.* (If this statement is rejected by our data, then it must be true that conviction rates differ according to the type of counsel representing defendants.)

WHY USE NULL HYPOTHESES?   When testing research hypotheses in criminological research, the use of null hypotheses may seem confusing. The most frequently asked question is, "Why use null hypotheses in the first place?" At least four alternative answers have been given. Arguably, some of these answers are better than others. These answers include:

1. It is easier to prove a hypothesis statement false than it is to prove it true. However, there is no proof to show that either type of hypothesis is easier to support or refute.

2. It is more objective for researchers to test null hypotheses than research hypotheses. This reason has some appeal to criminologists, since it gives the appearance of objectivity to deny the truthfulness of whatever you believe. At least the appearance of greater objectivity exists.

3. It is conventional to use null hypotheses in hypothesis testing. This reason is one of the most compelling ones. Convention is a powerful incentive to follow a protocol established by your colleagues. Investigators use null hypotheses because most other professionals in the field use them.

4. Null hypotheses fit the probability model underlying all hypothesis testing.

Probability theory is always utilized as the means for evaluating and assessing the significance of whatever we observe. All of our decisions about hypothesis tests are made using probability theory. Hypotheses are always supported or not supported in a probabilistic context.

In actual practice in criminological research, there is not much formality associated with hypothesis testing. Either research or null hypotheses may be stated in research articles. Sometimes no hypotheses are stated. But they are there, at least implicitly. Readers will see all forms of hypothesis statements. It is always important to clarify what investigators are hypothesizing.

In this section, several ideal scenarios will be illustrated where both research and null hypotheses have been created. These hypotheses are presented in what are called **hypothesis sets**. Hypothesis sets are used for convenience throughout this text as ideal models for framing all hypothesis tests. Some of the hypotheses used here as illustrations were used in several of the examples presented earlier. For instance, suppose we were to hypothesize that conviction rates vary according to whether defense counsel is publicly appointed or private. It is conventional in criminal justice and criminology to use the symbol, H_o (read: "H sub O") to represent null hypotheses. Also, it is conventional to use the symbol, H_1 (read "H sub 1") to represent our research hypotheses. (Some statistical texts use alternative notation systems for illustrating null and research hypotheses, such as H_1 and H_2) In this book, we will use H_o for null hypotheses and H_1 for research hypotheses. No notation system is the best notation system. It is important only that we agree on how terms should be symbolically portrayed. The hypothesis set for the above hypothesis would read as follows:

H_o: *Conviction rates do not vary according to whether defense counsel are publicly appointed or private.*

H_1: *Conviction rates vary according to whether defense counsel are publicly appointed or private.*

Notice in H_o, the null hypothesis, the statement is framed in such a way so that if it is shown to be false by our collected data, H_1 will be supported.

Another example is the hypothesis about the length of prison terms served by inmates and the likelihood of inmates to reoffend or recidivate. Our H_o and H_1 would be:

H_o: *There is no difference in reoffending among inmates serving different prison term lengths; if there is a difference, the longer the prison term served by inmates, the more likely the inmates are to reoffend.*

H_1: *The longer the prison term served by inmates, the less likely the inmates are to reoffend.*

In this example, we have put together a more elaborate H_o. In this case, the wording of H_o is such that if it is subsequently tested and shown not to be true, then the H_1 accompanying it will be supported.

Three other examples of null and research hypothesis statements are provided below.

H_o: *The average age for group 1 is not equal to 20.*

H_1: *The average age for group 1 is 20.*

H_o: *Two groups of police officers do not differ according to their level of professionalism.*

H_1: *Two groups of police officers differ according to their level of professionalism.*

H_o: *The higher the level of stress among probation officers, labor turnover will either remain the same or decrease.*

H_1: *The higher the level of stress among probation officers, the greater the labor turnover.*

Each of these hypothesis sets illustrates that rejecting or refuting the specific H_o will result in supporting the accompanying H_1. In short, H_os are derived directly from how H_1s are worded.

Therefore, whenever a specific H_o is tested and rejected, a specific H_1 will be supported.

Null hypotheses enable us to conduct indirect tests of our research hypotheses. When null hypotheses are tested, we want to reject them and support our research hypotheses. If we fail to reject or refute a null hypothesis, this does not mean that we accept it or support it. It simply means that we have failed to support our research hypothesis. Some researchers erroneously conclude that failing to refute or reject null hypotheses means that these null hypotheses are supported. They are not. Null hypotheses do not exist but for the existence of research hypotheses derived from a viable theoretical scheme. The following relation exists between null and research hypotheses.

1. If we reject or refute a null hypothesis, then we support the accompanying research hypothesis.
2. If we fail to reject or refute a null hypothesis, then we fail to support the accompanying research hypothesis.
3. Failing to reject or refute null hypotheses does not mean that we accept or support them.

As was indicated earlier, the best reason for using null hypotheses is that they fit the probability model associated with statistical tests and measures. Probability theory is always used with all statistical tests and measures. Therefore, a probability is always assigned to any hypothesis set and to any statistical test used for hypothesis-testing purposes. This probability is expressed symbolically as P. It is common to see the following Ps associated with our hypothesis sets.

H_0: *There is no difference between group 1 and group 2 regarding average age.*

H_1: *There is a difference between group 1 and group 2 regarding average age.*

$P \leq .05$

or

H_0: *X* and *Y* are not related.

H_1: *X* and *Y* are related.

$P \leq .01$

In the first hypothesis set, the notation $P \leq .05$ reads as "the probability is equal to or less than 5 percent." When we test our H_0 and are able to reject it, this action supports the accompanying H_1. We conclude that there is a 5 percent chance of being wrong in rejecting H_0 and supporting H_1. Put another way, if we reject the hypothesis that there is no difference between group 1 and group 2 regarding average age, then we support the hypothesis that there *is* a difference between the two groups regarding average age. And because $P \leq .05$, there is a 5 percent chance we could be wrong in making this decision.

In the second hypothesis set, H_0 says that variables *X* and *Y* are not related. If we reject the H_0 that says these variables are not related, then we support H_1 that says these variables are related. In this instance, there is a 1 percent chance we could be wrong in making this decision. Again this is because our $P \leq .01$. In later chapters when statistical tests are presented, there will always be a hypothesis set given with an accompanying probability or P. This P represents the probability that we could be wrong in rejecting or refuting the null hypothesis and supporting the accompanying research hypothesis. This P is also referred to as the **level of significance, Type I error,** and **alpha (α) error.** We will examine these concepts and describe how they are calculated later in this chapter.

Statistical Hypotheses

The hypothesis sets presented below have spelled out hypothesis statements in some detail. It is customary for investigators to use statistical notation to represent these hypothesis statements. For instance,

Hypothesis set 1:

> H_o: *There is no difference between group 1 and group 2 regarding average age.*
>
> H_1: *There is a difference between group 1 and group 2 regarding average age.*

is statistically represented as

> H_o: $\overline{X}_1 = \overline{X}_2$ (read: X bar sub 1 is equal to X bar sub2).
>
> H_1: $\overline{X}_1 \neq \overline{X}_2$ (read: X bar sub 1 is not equal to X bar sub 2).
>
> $P \leq .05$ (read: Probability is equal to or less than 5 percent or .05).

Hypothesis set 2:

> H_1: *X and Y are related.*
>
> H_o: *X and Y are not related.*
>
> $P \leq .01$

is statistically represented as

> H_o: $r_{xy} = 0$ (read: The relation, r, between variables X and Y, the subscripts, is equal to zero, or no association or correlation).
>
> H_1: $r_{xy} \neq 0$ (read: The relation, r, between variables X and Y, the subscripts, is not equal to zero; zero is no association or correlation).
>
> $P \leq .01$

The probabilities, .05 and .01, are used in these two hypothesis sets because they are conventional probabilities that are most frequently used whenever hypotheses are tested. Also, many of the tables in Appendix A used to interpret statistical test results have statistical values only for the .05 and .01 levels of significance. For the two hypothesis sets above, if we show in hypothesis set 1 that the two groups do not have the same average age, then the average ages must be different. There is a 5 percent chance we could be wrong in making this decision, since the probability level $P \leq .05$ is being used. In hypothesis set 2, if we show that the two variables, X and Y, are not related, then the two variables must be related. In this case, there is a 1 percent chance of being wrong in this decision, since $P \leq .01$ is used for the hypothesis test. Statistical notation greatly simplifies the presentation of our hypothesis statements, and we can avoid lengthy statements that can be abbreviated symbolically.

STATISTICAL INFERENCE: AN OVERVIEW

Statistical inference is making statements about population parameters (population characteristics) based on the sample statistics (sample characteristics) that represent them. Samples of elements are drawn from larger populations. The *population* may be all probation officers in Illinois, all police officers in Detroit, all state criminal court judges in Florida, or all prosecutors in Indiana. If we select a *sample* of probation officers from all probation officers in Illinois, or a sample of police officers from all police officers in Detroit, or a sample of state criminal court judges from all state criminal court judges in Florida, or a sample of prosecutors from all prosecutors in Indiana, we will have different samples of elements for each of these populations.

After drawing these samples, we will describe their characteristics and make inferences about their populations. The samples we obtain may or may not be representative of their populations. But this assumption is made anyway. One assumption made in this book is that all samples presented in examples have been randomly drawn and are representative of their respective populations. Also, no statistical tests described here apply to entire populations of elements. If we have complete population information, then there is no need for statistical tests. We merely describe the population's characteristics.

Statistical inference might mean that if a given sample mean is 20, then the population mean is also 20 or near 20. If the sample median were 35, an inference would be made that the population median is also 35, or close to 35. Furthermore, if two samples of police officers differ in their professionalism, then we might infer that the populations of police officers from which those two samples of officers were drawn are also different in their professionalism.

Any inferences made about populations based on sample information are always framed as probability statements. This is where our P becomes relevant. For example, suppose we selected two samples of 200 police officers, one from Detroit and one from Chicago. Then, suppose we administered a measure of professionalism to all of these police officers from both cities. A comparison of resulting professionalism scores would help us determine whether Detroit police officers differ from Chicago police officers in their professionalism. The P we use in any hypothesis test involving differences in professionalism between these two samples of police officers is directly relevant in evaluating any differences we observe. If we reject an H_o that says the two samples of police officers have the same amount of professionalism, the research hypothesis, H_1, that the two samples of officers are different would be supported. The P used in the hypothesis test would be the amount of error assigned to our test decision. If $P \leq .05$, then there would be a 5 percent chance of being wrong in concluding that the two samples of officers differ in their professionalism. This P can never be eliminated. It can only be increased or decreased.

DECISION RULES

Whenever a statistical test is made of any hypothesis, the result is a numerical expression and its significance is interpreted by the investigator. The result may cause the researcher to reject a null hypothesis and support some alternative research hypothesis. Or the result may be to fail to reject the null hypothesis and fail to support the research hypothesis. Guiding the researcher's decision making regarding the outcomes of hypothesis tests and how such outcomes are interpreted are **decision rules**.

Decision rules are conditions specified in advance of any statistical test application which define how test outcomes should be interpreted. Applying statistical tests without decision rules is like playing a football game without goal lines, yard markers, or time limits. Decision rules are used as impartial arbiters that remove all subjectivity and guesswork from hypothesis testing. Three decision rules are discussed here. They are: (1) the sampling distribution of a statistic; (2) the level of significance; and (3) the critical region or region of rejection.

Sampling Distributions of Statistics

A **sampling distribution of a statistic** is the distribution of all possible values a given statistic may assume for samples of a specified size drawn from a specified population. Every statistic presented in this book has a sampling distribution. This includes the mean, mode, median, and standard deviation. All known statistics have sampling distributions.

If we were to draw all possible samples of size 3 from a population of 10 persons, for instance, the number of samples drawn would be equal to N^n or $(10)^3$, where $N =$ the population size and $n =$ the sample size. In this case, there would be $(10)^3$ or $(10)(10)(10)$ or 1,000 samples of size 3 that could be drawn from a population of 10. How many samples of size 500 could be drawn from a population of 30,000? $30,000^{500}$ or $(30,000)(30,000) \ldots$, until 500 products had been obtained. This number of samples is staggering.

Returning to our smaller-scale example of drawing all possible samples of size 3 from a population of 10, we would be able to draw 1,000 samples. Let's assume that for each sample drawn, we will compute a mean, a median, a standard deviation, and a range. The results of such computations will yield 1,000 means, 1,000 medians, 1,000 standard deviations, and 1,000 ranges. Now, if the researcher arranges all of these means into a frequency distribution of them, the resulting distribution is called a sampling distribution of 1,000 sample means. If the medians are arranged into a frequency distribution as well, the resulting distribution would be called a sampling distribution of 1,000 sample medians, and so on. These expressions are frequently abbreviated so that we have a sampling distribution of the mean, a sampling distribution of the median, a sampling distribution of the standard deviation, and/or a sampling distribution of the range.

In each of these sampling distributions, the researcher has arranged all observed statistical values (e.g., mean, median, standard deviation, and range) into a frequency distribution. This frequency distribution is similar to the ones described in Chapter 3. The sampling distribution of mean is a distribution of all possible values that the mean can assume for samples of a specified size (in this case, 3) drawn from a given population (in this case, 10). And the sampling distribution of standard deviations is a distribution of all possible values that the standard deviation can assume for samples of a specified size (in this case, 3) drawn from a specified population (in this case, 10).

Using a small-scale example as an illustration, a sampling distribution of a statistic, such as the mean, is shown below. Suppose we have a population of seven police officers. Also we have information about the number of citizen complaints filed against these seven officers for a given period, such as six months or a year. We can designate each of these police officers in our population with the letters A, B, C, D, E, F, and G. The number of complaints filed against each officer annually are shown to the right of each letter in Table 7.1.

In Table 7.1, officer A has 10 citizen complaints, officer B has 11 citizen complaints, and so forth. Further suppose that we wish to draw all possible samples of size 2 from this population of 7. The possible number of random samples of $n = 2$ that could be drawn from a

TABLE 7.1 Hypothetical Population of Police Officers and Numbers of Citizen Complaints

Police Officer	Number of Complaints
A	10
B	11
C	12
D	13
E	14
F	15
G	16

population of $N = 7$ would be N^n or $(7)^2 = 49$ possible samples. The possible samples of size 2 that researchers could draw from the population of 7 are shown below with the following letter combinations:

AA	BA	CA	DA	EA	FA	GA
AB	BB	CB	DB	EB	FB	GB
AC	BC	CC	DC	EC	FC	GC
AD	BD	CD	DD	ED	FD	GD
AE	BE	CE	DE	EE	FE	GE
AF	BF	CF	DF	EF	FF	GF

The reason that there are AA, BB, CC, DD, EE, FF, and GG sample combinations is that sampling distributions are created here by using sampling with replacement. This means that once an element is drawn from the population for inclusion in a sample, it can be drawn again. All of the statistical procedures presented in this book assume sampling with replacement. This is a purely theoretical sampling consideration.

Sampling without replacement is not assumed. Sampling without replacement means that once an element has been drawn for a sample, it cannot be drawn again. Thus, the overall population of elements is reduced by one each time an element is drawn. Sampling without replacement simply does not offer the probabilistic benefits of sampling with replacement.

After these 49 samples of size 2 have been drawn, the investigator computes all of the sample means. These means would be symbolically portrayed as $\overline{X}_1, \overline{X}_2, \ldots \overline{X}_{49}$:

$\overline{X}_1$	$\overline{X}_2$	$\overline{X}_3$	$\overline{X}_4$	$\overline{X}_5$	$\overline{X}_6$	$\overline{X}_7$	10.0	10.5	11.0	11.5	12.0	12.5	13.0
$\overline{X}_8$	$\overline{X}_9$	$\overline{X}_{10}$	$\overline{X}_{11}$	$\overline{X}_{12}$	$\overline{X}_{13}$	$\overline{X}_{14}$	10.5	11.0	11.5	12.0	12.5	13.0	13.5
$\overline{X}_{15}$	$\overline{X}_{16}$	$\overline{X}_{17}$	$\overline{X}_{18}$	$\overline{X}_{19}$	$\overline{X}_{20}$	$\overline{X}_{21}$	11.0	11.5	12.0	12.5	13.0	13.5	14.0
$\overline{X}_{22}$	$\overline{X}_{23}$	$\overline{X}_{24}$	$\overline{X}_{25}$	$\overline{X}_{27}$	$\overline{X}_{27}$	$\overline{X}_{28}$	11.5	12.0	12.5	13.0	13.5	14.0	14.5
$\overline{X}_{29}$	$\overline{X}_{30}$	$\overline{X}_{31}$	$\overline{X}_{32}$	$\overline{X}_{33}$	$\overline{X}_{34}$	$\overline{X}_{35}$	12.0	12.5	13.0	13.5	14.0	14.5	15.0
$\overline{X}_{36}$	$\overline{X}_{37}$	$\overline{X}_{38}$	$\overline{X}_{39}$	$\overline{X}_{40}$	$\overline{X}_{41}$	$\overline{X}_{42}$	12.5	13.0	13.5	14.0	14.5	15.0	15.5
$\overline{X}_{43}$	$\overline{X}_{44}$	$\overline{X}_{45}$	$\overline{X}_{46}$	$\overline{X}_{47}$	$\overline{X}_{48}$	$\overline{X}_{49}$	13.0	13.5	14.0	14.5	15.0	15.5	16.0

To the far right of these 49 mean symbols are the actual means calculated for each of these samples. The smallest mean, $\overline{X}_1$, is 10.0 and the largest mean, $\overline{X}_{49}$, is 16.0.

Next, the researcher constructs a frequency distribution of these sample means as shown in Table 7.2. The resulting frequency distribution of these sample means is the sampling distribution of the mean for samples of size 2 drawn from a population of size 7.

The sampling distribution of the mean has several desirable properties. First, the distribution is usually normal in form. This particular distribution appears triangular. This is because a small-scale example is being used to illustrate the sampling distribution of a statistic.

With larger samples drawn from larger populations, theoretically at least, the sampling distribution of means is normal, approximating most of the characteristics of the normal distribution. Figure 7.1 is a smoothed frequency polygon of the distribution of mean values shown in Table 7.2.

The distribution of means shown in Figure 7.1 is approximately bell-shaped, symmetrical, and normal in form. Of all statistics discussed thus far (e.g., the mean, mode, median, standard

TABLE 7.2 Sampling Distribution of X̄s for Samples of Size 2 from a Population of Size 7

Observed X̄$_i$s	f	Proportion	Probability
10.0	x	1/49	.020
10.5	xx	2/49	.041
11.0	xxx	3/49	.061
11.5	xxxx	4/49	.082
12.0	xxxxx	5/49	.102
12.5	xxxxxx	6/49	.122
13.0	xxxxxxx	7/49	.143
13.5	xxxxxx	6/49	.122
14.0	xxxxx	5/49	.102
14.5	xxxx	4/49	.082
15.0	xxx	3/49	.061
15.5	xx	2/49	.041
16.0	x	1/49	.020
			$\Sigma = .999^*$

* Would otherwise sum to 1.00 but .999 occurs because of rounding error.

deviation, range, and average deviation), only the sample mean has a sampling distribution with these normal distribution properties. The sampling distributions of all other statistics examined do not approximate normality.

EXPECTED VALUES OF STATISTICS   Another characteristic of the sampling distribution of the means is that the mean of it (the mean of means or grand mean) is equal to the population mean. If we were to compute the population μ for the numbers of complaints filed against the population of 7 police officers, we would have the sum of the 7 individual complaint totals divided by 7, or

$$\frac{10 + 11 + 12 + 13 + 14 + 15 + 16}{7} = \frac{91}{7} = 13.0.$$

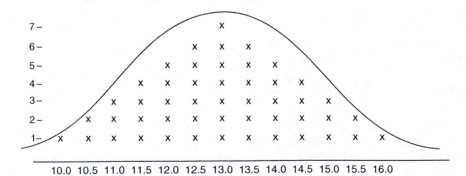

FIGURE 7.1   Smoothed Frequency Polygon of the Distribution of Means Shown in Table 7.2

$13.0 = \mu$, the population mean. If we were to compute the mean for the sampling distribution of means shown in Table 7.2, it would also equal 13.0, or μ, the population mean.

The mean of *any* sampling distribution of *any* statistic is called the **expected value** of that statistic. Therefore, the mean of the sampling distribution of means is called the **expected value of the mean**. The mean of the sampling distribution of sample medians is called the expected value of the median, and so on. In the general case, the expected value of a statistic is the mean of the sampling distribution of that statistic.

Another unique feature of the sampling distribution of means is that the mean of it is equal to the population mean. Whenever a sample statistic equals the population parameter it estimates, that statistic is called an **unbiased estimate** of its population parameter. Thus, the sample mean, $\overline{X}$, equals the population mean, μ, and therefore the sample mean is an unbiased estimate of the population mean. No other statistic in this book is an unbiased estimate of its population parameter. This is because these statistics do not have sampling distributions whose means equal their respective population parameters. This fact gives the sample mean exclusivity regarding its estimation of the population mean. It also explains why the mean is chosen most frequently compared with other measures of central tendency and dispersion for statistical inference purposes.

STANDARD ERROR TERMS In an earlier discussion of frequency distributions in Chapter 3, and subsequently measures of central tendency and dispersion or variability in Chapters 4 and 5, we learned that means and standard deviations can be computed for any frequency distribution of scores. Sampling distributions of the mean also have means and standard deviations and these values can be computed.

We have seen that means of sampling distributions of statistics are called expected values of those statistics. Standard deviations of sampling distributions of statistics are also given a special name. These values are called **standard errors of statistics**. Therefore, instead of referring to the standard deviation of a sampling distribution, we refer to this value as the **standard error of the sampling distribution**. For instance, the standard error of the mean is the standard deviation of the sampling distribution of sample means. The standard error of the sampling distribution of the standard deviation is called the standard error of the sampling distribution of standard deviations, or more simply, the standard error of the standard deviation, and so on. These are collectively referred to as **standard error terms**. All statistics have standard error terms.

Let's examine the sampling distribution of sample means more closely. It has two parameters—a population mean, μ, and a standard error term, the standard error of the mean, or $s_{\overline{x}}$ (read: *s* sub *x* bar), which is calculated as follows:

$$s_{\overline{x}} = \frac{s}{\sqrt{N - 1}}$$

where s = the standard deviation for the sample

N = the sample size

While a distinction was made earlier between n and N as the sample size and the population size respectively for illustrating how many samples of a given size could be drawn from a population of a given size, from here we will use N when referring to sample sizes. In the standard error term shown, $s_{\overline{x}}$, N is the sample size.

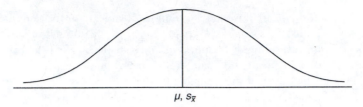

FIGURE 7.2 The Sampling Distribution of the Mean,
Showing μ and $s_{\bar{x}}$

The standard error of the mean functions in relation to the sampling distribution of means in precisely the same way that standard deviations function in relation to a distribution of sample scores. Therefore, if we were to move ± 1.00 $s_{\bar{x}}$'s either to the left (below) or to the right (above) the mean, μ, of the sampling distribution of means, we would cut off a portion of curve area equivalent to that cut off by $\pm 1\sigma$ on the normal distribution, or .3413 in one direction and .3413 in the other. Table A.2 of Appendix A can be used to determine proportions of curve area from μ to any given number of $s_{\bar{x}}$s from μ. Thus, approximately 68 percent (.3413 + .3413 = .6826) of the curve area of the sampling distribution of means would be included within 1 standard error of the mean, $s_{\bar{x}}$, on either side of μ. This means that about 68 percent of all sample means will occur within this area, just like 68 percent of the normal curve area would be found within $\pm 1.00\sigma$s on either side of the mean of the normal distribution. Figure 7.2 illustrates the sampling distribution of the mean, showing its parameters, μ and $s_{\bar{x}}$.

Figure 7.3 shows the sampling distribution of the mean within a portion of curve area shaded. In Figure 7.3, the shaded area is the proportion of curve area included with one standard error from μ measured in $s_{\bar{x}}$ units. For instance, within ± 1 $s_{\bar{x}}$ on either side of μ, 68 percent or .6826 of curve area will be found. This means that approximately 68 percent of all sample means will be found within ± 1 $s_{\bar{x}}$ on either side of μ. Figures 7.4 and 7.5 show amounts of curve area cut off on either side of μ by $\pm 2s_{\bar{x}}$ s and $\pm 3s_{\bar{x}}$ s respectively. In Figure 7.4, approximately 95 percent (.9544) of curve area is cut off. In Figure 7.5, approximately 99.7 percent (.9974) of curve area is cut off. All areas in Figures 7.3, 7.4, and 7.5 have been determined by Z values of ± 1.00, ± 2.00, and ± 3.00 from the Table of Areas of the Normal Curve, Table A.2 of Appendix A, p. 445–446.

The probability function of the sampling distribution of the mean is illustrated by Table 7.2. The probabilities associated with different sample means shown in Table 7.2 illustrate the probability of drawing a particular sample mean. There is a .020 chance of drawing a

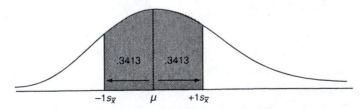

FIGURE 7.3 Curve area on Sampling Distribution of Mean
Showing Amount of Curve area cut off from μ to $\pm 1s_{\bar{x}}$, or
68% (.6826)

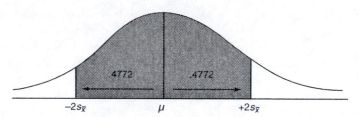

FIGURE 7.4 Curve area on Sampling Distribution of Mean Showing Amount of Curve area cut off from μ to $\pm 2 s_{\bar{x}}$'s, or Approximately 95% (.9544)

random sample with a mean of 10.0, for instance. But there is a 14.3 percent chance or .143 of drawing a sample with a mean of 13.0. This is because there are more sample means of 13.0 than there are samples with means of 10.0.

We can also sum these probabilities shown in Table 7.2. For instance, what is the probability of drawing a sample with a mean of 10.0, 10.5, or 11.0? This would be the sum of the individual probabilities of drawing each of these samples, or .020 + .041 + .061 = .122. Therefore, there is a 12.2 percent or .122 chance of drawing a sample with one of these three means. What is the probability of drawing a sample with a mean of 11.5, 12.0, 12.5, 13.0, or 13.5? This would be the sum of these individual probabilities, or .082 + .102 + .122 + .143 + .122 = .571 or 57.1 percent. Thus, a 57.1 percent chance exists of drawing a sample with a mean of 11.5, 12.0, 12.5, 13.0, or 13.5. This is a fairly high probability because we know that there are more sample means near the center of the distribution than there are in the extremes of it. Notice that the means of 10.0 and 16.0 occur once each, or .020 each. The probability of drawing a sample with either a mean of 10.0 or 16.0 is the sum of the individual probabilities of getting either mean, or .020 + .020 = .040, or a 4 percent chance. It would be extremely unlikely that in a random draw of two elements from this population of 7, we would draw a sample with a mean of either 10.0 or 16.0. This is because these means occur only once each out of 49 sample means. They have a very low likelihood of being included in any particular two-element draw.

Figures 7.3, 7.4, and 7.5 show different proportions of curve area cut off by different standard errors from the mean of the sampling distribution of the mean.

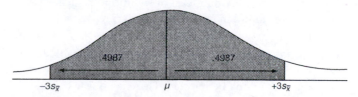

FIGURE 7.5 Curve area on Sampling Distribution of Mean Showing Amount of Curve area cut off from μ to $\pm 3 s_{\bar{x}}$'s or Approximately 99.7% (.9974)

These different proportions encompass a certain proportion of sample means. Thus, if we have a knowledge of the sample size, N, and standard deviation, s, we can calculate a standard error term and then easily determine what percentage of means would fall within given distances of the population mean, μ. In Figure 7.3, for instance, approximately 68 percent of all sample means fall within 1 standard error on either side of μ. In Figure 7.4, approximately 95 percent of all sample means fall within 2 standard errors on either side of μ. And in Figure 7.5, approximately 99.7 percent (almost all) of the sample means fall within 3 standard errors on either side of μ. The standard error of the mean functions the same way as does the sample standard deviation, s, in determining proportions of scores lying within given distances on either side of the sample mean, $\overline{X}$. But when we are discussing the sampling distribution of means, we refer to the proportion of means included within given distances from the population mean instead of proportions of raw scores included within given distances from some sample mean.

The sampling distribution of the mean is a very useful concept and helps to illustrate and understand related concepts, such as levels of significance and critical regions or regions of rejection.

Levels of Significance

The level of significance is the probability or P that we assign to any hypothesis test conducted. The level of significance states the amount of error incurred whenever a null hypothesis is rejected and some alternative research hypothesis is supported. All hypothesis tests are couched in the context of probability theory. There is always a likelihood that we could be wrong when making a decision about any hypothesis tested. Criminologists and other social scientists use convention to guide them in their selection of levels of significance for their hypothesis tests.

Most hypothesis tests are made using the .05 or .01 levels of significance. Interpreting these levels of significance according to probabilities, we would say that when using the .05 level of significance, there is a 5 percent chance we could be wrong if we reject a null hypothesis and support an accompanying research hypothesis. If we were to use the .01 level of significance, then there would be a 1 percent chance of being wrong in rejecting the null hypothesis and supporting the accompanying research hypothesis. This probability of being wrong in our statistical decision making cannot be eliminated. We can only raise it or lower it.

Another important reason .05 and .01 significance levels are chosen and considered conventional is that many of the interpretive tables in Appendix A involving statistical test applications have tabled interpretive values only for the .05 and .01 levels of significance. Thus, even if we wanted to use some other level of significance, such as .03, .08, .19, or .02, such probabilities could not be found in most of these interpretive tables.

TYPE I AND TYPE II ERROR   The level of significance associated with any hypothesis test is also called Type I error or alpha error (α error). Type I error is the error made when a null hypothesis is rejected and it shouldn't be rejected. There is no way to eliminate Type I error. As we have seen, levels of significance are chosen in part because of convention and also because they are considered reasonable probabilities for hypothesis testing. Other factors influencing level of significance selections include one's sample size and the professional standards of researchers.

There are certain risks when particular levels of significance are chosen in hypothesis testing. One risk is to minimize Type I error and make it very small. Some investigators set their levels of significance at .001, or .0005, or even lower, allowing themselves 1 time in a 1,000 of being wrong or 5 times in 10,000 of being wrong if a null hypothesis is rejected. These very low probabilities for making Type I error make it almost impossible to reject null hypotheses when they probably ought to be rejected. Thus, some researchers run the risk of being too rigorous in their standards. At the same time, levels of significance may involve high amounts of risk, thus making it too easy to reject null hypotheses when they shouldn't be rejected. If significance levels are set at .10 or .20, the chances increase of rejecting null hypotheses when they are true and should not be rejected. This is one reason why .05 and .01 are often selected. They are both reasonable and conventional.

Other factors affect Type I error as well. For instance, if investigators are studying small samples less than 50, sometimes greater Type I error is better, such as raising .05 to .10, or .10 to .20. There is nothing wrong with this change in Type I error. Sampling error tends to be greater when the sample size is smaller, and it tends to be smaller as larger samples are studied. Setting significance levels is an art form to a degree. The skill and experience of the researcher does much to influence one's level of significance choices. But as Appendix A illustrates, sometimes we may be locked into particular significance levels simply because they are the only ones available for particular statistical tests we choose to apply.

Raising or lowering Type I error is under the direct control of the investigator. But raising or lowering Type I error has an indirect effect on Type II error. **Type II error (β error)** is failing to reject a null hypothesis when it is false and ought to be rejected. Type II error is influenced by Type I error, sample size, and sampling error, as well as the discrepancy between our observations and what is predicted or expected according to chance. We only indirectly affect Type II error by increasing or decreasing Type I error. For instance, If we raise Type I error from .01 to .05, we do not automatically change Type II error by .04 (the difference between .01 and .05). There is no one-to-one correspondence between these two types of error.

One of the investigator's goals is to reduce *both* Type I and Type II errors. Researchers cannot eliminate either type of error, but both types of errors can be minimized. If random sampling is used, and/or if a sufficiently large sample is selected, these events can decrease Type II error, although each sampling situation is unique. It cannot be predicted with absolute certainty how sample size changes will affect the magnitude of Type II error. We can only discuss this phenomenon in generalities. For instance, we know that usually increasing sample size will reduce sampling error, which will, in turn, decrease Type II error. We also know that increasing Type I error will reduce Type II error. But again, there is no precise formula to follow in order to understand the exact impact of each change we make. All sampling and decision-making situations are different. Following the guidelines recommended for each statistical test's application, as well as applying certain conventional guidelines, including the use of .05 or .01 for Type I or alpha (α) error, will usually optimize conditions for having a reasonable amount of Type II error.

Finally, one of the most important factors that influences Type II error is the statistical test we choose to test our hypotheses. Some statistical tests are more powerful than others. **Power** is the ability of a statistical test to reject a null hypothesis when it is false and ought to be rejected. Power is defined as $1-\beta$, or 1–Type II error. Selecting powerful tests may seem to be a good idea, since we want to reject false null hypotheses. But more powerful tests often have more restrictive assumptions associated with their application. Thus, we may select a more powerful statistical test, but we may fail to meet certain critical assumptions underlying the test. When one or more assumptions of statistical tests are violated, the numerical results produced by such tests may be misleading.

There are many statistical tests with varying degrees of power. Some of these tests are more appropriate for use under certain conditions compared with others. We should be familiar with test power and its importance if we are to make sound statistical test choices when analyzing our data and interpreting numerical results. Table 7.3 summarizes the relation between Type I and Type II errors.

Table 7.3 is premised on the idea that H_o, the null hypothesis, may be either true or false. This possibility always exists. In short, there is always a likelihood that H_o is both true and false. When making our hypothesis tests, we will either reject H_o or we will fail to reject H_o. Those are our only choices. If we choose to reject H_o, it is possible that H_o is true and the decision to reject it would be an incorrect one. That decision would be reflected by Type I error or alpha (α) error. If our decision is to reject H_o and it is indeed false and ought to be rejected, that is a good decision. That's the power of the test or $1-\beta$, as shown in Table 7.3.

If we fail to reject H_o, there is the possibility that H_o is true and shouldn't be rejected. That would also be a good decision. This is the probability known as $1-\alpha$ error. We can also fail to reject H_o when it is false and ought to be rejected. This is Type II error, or β error.

LEVELS OF SIGNIFICANCE AND THE SAMPLING DISTRIBUTION OF THE MEAN When we set levels of significance in making our hypothesis tests, and if those hypothesis tests involve sample means, these levels of significance we choose indicate an area on the sampling distribution of the mean in one or both tails of it. In this discussion, we will simply look at the idea of how levels of significance relate to sampling distributions of means and the areas they indicate.

There are two kinds of tests we can make of hypotheses. We can make either (1) one-tailed or directional tests or (2) two-tailed or nondirectional tests. As we have seen, in one-tailed tests, a directional prediction is made. For instance, we believe our sample mean will be greater or smaller than the population mean. We will predict the sample mean will be greater than the population mean. Or we will predict the sample mean will be smaller than the population mean. These statements become hypotheses, such as

"The sample mean will be greater than μ" or

"The sample mean will be less than μ"

These are directional statements because we are specifying the direction where we expect our sample mean will occur in relation to some hypothesized μ.

TABLE 7.3 Type I and Type II Errors in Statistical Decision-Making Situations

		H_o is	
		True	**False**
	Reject H_o	Type I error, Alpha (α) error	$1-\beta$ error (Power)
Decision is to	Fail to Reject H_o	$1-\alpha$ error	Type II error, β error

For two-tailed, nondirectional hypothesis tests, it doesn't matter whether our sample mean is greater or less than the population μ. We are only interested in whether the sample mean is different from μ. Most of the time, our sample means will indeed differ from some hypothesized μ. Our primary interest is whether there is a significant difference between our observed sample mean and the hypothesized μ.

With a one-tailed, directional prediction scenario, assume that we are predicting that our sample mean will be greater than μ. We provide a level of significance, such as .05 or .01. Suppose the .05 level of significance is chosen, we must hypothesize a value of μ. Suppose we hypothesize that $\mu = 50$, a one-tailed, directional prediction is that the observed sample mean will be greater than 50. Next, using the .05 level of significance, we can identify an area on the sampling distribution of means which leaves .05 in the right tail of the curve. This makes sense, because we are predicting that our sample mean will be to the right of 50, or above it, toward the right tail of the sampling distribution of the mean. Illustrated, this area will look like that shown in Figure 7.6.

In Figure 7.6, a shaded area on the sampling distribution of the mean has been identified to the far right, where .05 of curve area is found. The population mean, $\mu = 50$. We believe that our sample mean will be greater than 50. The .05 level of significance is being used. The question to be answered is what Z value defines the shaded area of the sampling distribution of the mean. What Z value cuts off .4500 and leaves .0500 of curve area in the right tail? Looking up the proportion, .4500, we locate a $Z = 1.64$. Therefore, this Z value is the one we select that cuts off .4500 of the sampling distribution of sample means and leaves .0500 in the right tail of it. So far, so good.

But what if we make a prediction in the opposite direction? What if we predict that our sample mean will be less than 50? And what if we use the .05 level of significance as well in making this prediction? Then we would simply locate an area in the left tail of the sampling distribution of the sample mean. This distribution with the appropriate shaded area would look like the distribution shown in Figure 7.7.

In Figure 7.7, we have made the prediction that our sample mean will be less than 50 or to the left of it. Therefore, using the .05 level of significance, we want to identify an area on the sampling distribution of sample means that will leave .05 of curve area in the left tail of it. This is illustrated as the shaded area in Figure 7.7. What Z value must be obtained that will cut off .4500 of curve area to the left of our predicted $\mu = 50$, leaving .0500 of curve area in the left tail? The Z value is again found in Table A.2 of Appendix A, p. 445. This is the same Z value shown in Figure 7.6. However, in this case, a $Z = -1.64$ is yielded since the left tail of the sampling distribution of the mean is involved. All Z values to the left of μ are negative values.

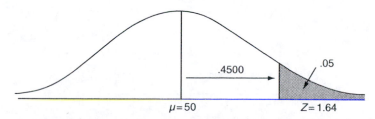

FIGURE 7.6 Sampling Distribution of the Mean with Predicted $\mu = 50$, .05 Level of Significance, Sample Mean is greater than 50

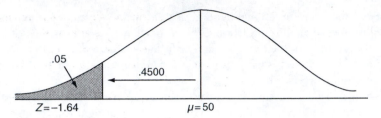

FIGURE 7.7   Sampling Distribution of the Mean with Predicted μ = 50, .05 Level of Significance, Sample Mean is less than 50

Summarizing briefly for one-tailed, directional tests and levels of significance, we set a level of significance such as .05. We hypothesize a μ such as 50 as has been done in Figures 7.6 and 7.7. Next, we use the .05 level of significance to locate Z values for both figures that will leave .05 of curve area in either the right tail (Figure 7.6) or the left tail (Figure 7.7), because of the predicted direction of where our sample mean will occur in relation to the hypothesized μ. We determine Z values for each of these points by referring to curve areas that cut off a certain amount of the sampling distribution of the mean, leaving .05 of curve area in either one tail or the other.

What about two-tailed or nondirectional tests? Let's use the same scenario that was used in Figures 7.6 and 7.7. This time we will make a prediction that our observed mean will simply differ from μ = 50. It is irrelevant whether the observed sample mean is to the right of μ or the left of μ. We are simply predicting that the sample mean will differ from μ in either direction above or below it.

Again, we choose the .05 level of significance. But because a two-tailed, nondirectional test is being made, we must divide the .05 level of significance into two equal parts, or $.05/2 = .025$. This means we will place half of .05 or .025 in the right tail of the sampling distribution of sample means and one half of .05 or .025 in the left tail of it. This will yield a figure such as that shown in Figure 7.8.

Notice in Figure 7.8 that two shaded areas have been created, one to the far left and one to the far right of μ. These areas contain .0250 each of curve area. If we sum these two amounts of curve area, they will equal .0500. Thus, we are identifying two areas on the sampling distribution of the mean that will each leave .025 of curve area in the tails of it. We must find the Z value for each that will cut off .4750 in either direction. From Table A.2 in Appendix A, p. 445–446, this Z value is determined to be ±1.96.

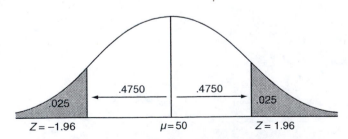

FIGURE 7.8   Sampling Distribution of Means Showing Two-Tails areas for .05 Level of Significance and where μ = 50

If we had chosen the .01 level of significance for our two-tailed, nondirectional test with the same $\mu = 50$, then we would be looking in Table A.2 in Appendix A for Z values that would leave .005 (one half of .01) in each tail, or ± 2.58, and so on. Had we made a one-tailed prediction at .01, depending on whether we forecast the sample mean to be above or below the population $\mu = 50$, we would locate a Z value in either direction that would leave .01 of curve area in the right or left tail, depending on our prediction. This would be the Z value cutting off .4900 of curve area, or ± 2.33, and so on. These areas of the curve or the sampling distribution of the mean that we have just identified are called critical regions or regions of rejection.

The Critical Region or Region of Rejection

Critical regions or **regions of rejection** are areas on sampling distributions of statistics that are defined by levels of significance (Type I error, α error) used in hypothesis testing. They are also defined by whether our hypothesis tests are one-tailed or directional or two-tailed or nondirectional. For instance, the shaded areas in the curve tails of the sampling distributions of means illustrated in Figures 7.6, 7.7, and 7.8 are critical regions or regions of rejection. These critical regions were defined by rules, specifically by the levels of significance we have chosen for our hypothesis tests, our predicted μ values, and whether our hypothesis test predictions were one-tailed or directional or two-tailed or nondirectional.

These critical regions are delineated by specific Z values cutting off fixed portions of curve area. These Z values are associated with various levels of significance, and they cut off portions of curve area that leave desired portions in one tail of these curves, or the other tail, or both tails. These regions are called critical regions or regions of rejection because the Z values identified with these regions are the values we must equal or exceed in our hypothesis tests. If we test a hypothesis that says our sample mean is greater than $\mu = 50$, then in order to reject the null hypothesis that says the sample mean is either the same as or less than 50, we must observe a sample mean that lies on the line of or in the critical regions we have identified in these figures.

Sample means differ from predicted μ values when occurring given distances from μ. We can locate how far a given $\overline{X}$ is from the hypothesized μ according to standard error units. The sampling distribution of means has a standard error term known as the standard error of the mean, or $s_{\overline{x}}$. This standard error term is the unit of measurement along the horizontal axis of the sampling distribution of the mean. We can move from the hypothesized μ to some point above or below it by calculating how many standard errors of the mean cover that distance. If we observe a mean $= 55$, if the hypothesized $\mu = 50$, and if the standard error of the mean is 5.00, then 55 is 1 standard error of 5 above the mean of 50. If our observed mean is 60, then 60 is 2 standard errors of the mean of 5 above 50. If our observed mean is 30, then that point is 4 standard errors of the mean of 5 below 50, and so on. In order to determine how far any given $\overline{X}$ is from the hypothesized μ, we use the formula for Z_{obs},

$$Z_{obs} = \frac{\overline{X}_{obs} - \mu}{s_{\overline{x}}}$$

where $\overline{X}_{obs}$ = the observed mean

μ = the hypothesized population mean

$s_{\overline{x}}$ = the standard error of the mean

Thus, for any observed sample mean, we can determine a Z value associated with it in relation to some hypothesized μ. We just divide the difference between the hypothesized μ and the observed sample mean by the standard error of the mean. The resulting Z value is our observed Z or Z_{obs}.

Our next step is a comparison of our observed Z, Z_{obs}, with the critical value of Z, Z_{cv}, to see whether the Z_{obs} equals or exceeds the Z_{cv}. In all one-tailed hypothesis tests, Z values will be positive or negative, and it is quite important to the final outcome if we have made a directional prediction in the wrong direction. Assuming that a correct directional prediction has been made, the question is whether our observed sample mean is on the line of or in the critical region that we have established by the level of significance chosen and the hypothesized direction of difference. Our observed Z value is in the critical region or region of rejection or it isn't in this region. If our Z_{obs} lies on the line of or in the critical region on the sampling distribution of the mean, then H_o can be rejected and H_1 can be supported at the level of significance we have designated. Thus, if our Z value for the critical region is 1.64, and we observe a $Z = 1.65$ with our observed sample mean in a one-tailed test where we have predicted that our sample mean will be greater than the population μ, then the result is that our Z_{obs} is statistically significant at the level of significance chosen. Even if we have a $Z_{obs} = 1.64$ and the critical value of $Z = 1.64$, this observed Z value lies on the line of the critical region and is thus significant statistically. The $Z_{obs} = 1.64$ is considered the same as being in the critical region even though it is on the line of it. Since we reject the null hypothesis, H_o, as a result, we sometimes call this area the region of rejection. The region of rejection refers to rejecting null hypotheses.

For other sampling distributions, such as the distribution of t, F, or some other statistic, there will be guidelines to follow, critical values to equal or exceed, and rules to follow that will govern hypothesis test outcomes. But for now, it is important to understand how these critical regions or regions of rejection relate to sampling distributions of means. All subsequent hypothesis tests in later chapters will include explicit instructions for statistical decision making and interpreting the numerical results. As a result, we will always be comparing observed values with critical values of different statistics and either rejecting or failing to reject null hypotheses.

In the two-tailed test of the hypothesis made in Figure 7.8, for instance, had we observed a sample mean that had a $Z_{obs} = -2.03$, this Z_{obs} would have occurred in the far left tail of the sampling distribution of the mean, where a $Z_{cv} = -1.96$ was defined from Table A.2, Appendix A. We would have rejected the null hypothesis and concluded that our observed sample mean was significantly different from $\mu = 50$ at the .05 level of significance (two-tailed test). However, if our observed mean had a $Z_{obs} = -1.95$, then we would have failed to reject the null hypothesis at the .05 level of significance. The $Z_{obs} = -1.95$ would not have fallen in the critical region or region of rejection.

ESTIMATING POPULATION PARAMETERS

Besides describing different characteristics of samples, sample statistic information is also used for estimating population parameters. Two methods for estimating population values are (1) point estimation and (2) interval estimation.

Point Estimation

Point estimation is predicting the value of a population parameter and comparing that predicted value with the sample statistic estimating that parameter. For instance, we could predict that some population $\mu = 100$. A sample from the population is drawn and a mean, $\overline{X}$, is computed. A comparison is made between the predicted μ and the observed $\overline{X}$. The difference between $\overline{X}$ and μ will indicate the accuracy of our inference or estimation. Thus, we estimate a point where we believe the population μ occurs, and then we compare the μ with our observed $\overline{X}$ in order to determine the accuracy of our estimate.

Several problems with point estimation are that (1) we must guess the value of the population μ, and (2) unless we know a great deal about the population we are studying, we will have little basis for making this guess. Usually the basis for guessing population μs is previously known information about the population. If no previous information about the population exists, no logical basis for our estimates exists. However, we might use information about the population collected at an earlier point in time, such as one or more years earlier than our present investigation. The problem with this method of estimating is that the population changes over time. Using previous information about the population for making current inferences about μ values is somewhat unreliable. However, it has been argued that some information is better than no information. Thus, prior information is most often used for point estimation work.

AN EXAMPLE OF POINT ESTIMATION   Point estimation is illustrated by the following problem. Suppose investigators studied the influence of new sentencing guidelines on reductions in sentencing disparities that have previously been attributed to gender, race, ethnicity, and socioeconomic factors. An obvious example is sentencing two convicted male robbers, one black and one white, to terms of 10 years and 5 years respectively. Both offenders have similar criminal records, are about the same age, and the circumstances of their instant offense are nearly identical. Yet, the black offender receives a sentence twice as harsh (10 years) compared with the white offender (5 years).

Suppose a jurisdiction is selected where indeterminate sentencing has been used previously to sentence offenders. In the most recent year, suppose this jurisdiction has implemented new sentencing guidelines for punishing convicted offenders. The belief is that the new guidelines will minimize previous sentencing disparities that were considered discriminatory.

Previous information available from this fictitious jurisdiction shows that sentencing disparities according to race averaged about 12 months. Sentences for black offenders convicted of the same crimes as white offenders averaged 12 months longer. Using this previous information as the basis for our current estimate, we obtain a sample of 400 black and white convicted offenders in that jurisdiction and determine their conviction offenses and sentences imposed under the new guidelines. Using point estimation, we predict sentencing disparity as follows:

H_0: $\mu > 12$ months

H_1: $\mu \leq 12$ months

$P \leq .05$ (one-tailed test)

The research hypothesis says that the average sentencing disparity between black and white offenders in this jurisdiction will be equal to or less than 12 months. The null hypothesis is that the average sentencing disparity will be greater than 12 months. A one-tailed hypothesis test is made at the .05 level of significance, since we reasonably expect disparities in sentences between black and white convicted offenders to decrease as the result of implementing the new sentencing guidelines. Based upon current sentencing and racial information, an observed $\overline{X} = 6.5$ months is determined, which is the current amount of sentencing disparity between black and white offenders under the new sentencing guidelines, with a standard error of the mean, $s_{\bar{x}} = 2.00$.

The first action taken in any directional hypothesis test is to examine whether the directional prediction made under H_1 is correct. In the present example, it is. The sentencing disparity predicted is consistent with H_1 and is less than 12 months. White offenders continue to receive shorter sentences compared with black offenders despite the new sentencing guidelines. However, is the 6.5-month disparity significantly different from 12 months statistically?

The following steps enable us to test our hypothesis:

1. Identify the level of significance at which the hypothesis is tested.
2. Determine whether the test is one-tailed or two-tailed (directional or nondirectional).
3. Identify a Z value in Table A.2 of Appendix A which cuts off a portion of normal curve area leaving an amount of curve area in the tail of the distribution as specified by the level of significance and whether the test is directional or nondirectional.
4. Compute a Z value for the difference between our expected μ value and the observed $\overline{X}$ value.
5. Make a decision based on a comparison between the tabled Z value for the level of significance and our observed Z value we computed.

Assume the following information:

$\overline{X}_{obs}$	$= 6.5$ months
μ	$= \leq 12$ months
$s_{\bar{x}}$	$= 2.00$
N	$= 400$
P	$= \leq .05$ (one-tailed, directional test)
Z value	$= -1.64$ (leaves .05 in left tail of normal curve)

From Table A.2, we would calculate our observed Z value as follows:

$$Z = \frac{\overline{X} - \mu}{s_{\bar{x}}} = \frac{\overline{X} - \mu}{\dfrac{s}{\sqrt{N-1}}} = \frac{6.5 - 12}{2.00} = \frac{-5.5}{2.00} = -2.75.$$

Our observed $Z = -2.75$, which is in the predicted direction under H_1 and equals or exceeds the critical value of $Z = -1.64$. Therefore, we reject H_o and support H_1 at the .05 level of significance (one-tailed test). Although disparities in sentencing still exist, these disparities have decreased significantly, at least according to these test results. Also, there is a 5-percent chance we are wrong in making this decision, given the Type I error or level of significance we have chosen. This concludes our point estimate test.

Actually, we have conducted our first test of significance with the Z formula for this problem. The test of significance evaluated the difference between our observed mean and the hypothesized μ. This is a Z test of significance for a single sample and will be discussed at length together with another test, the t test for significance of difference, in Chapter 8.

Another example of point estimation is provided. Suppose we believe that based on previous information, the average length of time between a death sentence in a capital case and the subsequent execution is 13 years. Because of changes in the law, U.S. Supreme Court decisions, and more frequent inmate appeals in later years, we might expect that the actual time between conviction, sentencing, and execution is greater than 13 years now, but to be conservative, we decide to make a simple two-tailed nondirectional test. Therefore, we might hypothesize the following:

$H_o: \mu = 13$ years

$H_1: \mu \neq 13$ years

$P \leq .01$ (two-tailed test)

In this scenario, we are predicting under H_1 that the mean time lapse between conviction, sentencing, and execution is different from 13 years. Therefore, H_o says that the average length of time between sentence and execution is 13 years. Suppose that we have information from 50 executions that have been carried out in various state jurisdictions for 2007 which disclose that the average length of time, in years, between a death sentence and one's execution is 15.3 years. Further, suppose the standard deviation for these 50 executions is 5.6 years. Quickly doing the math, we determine that our $s_{\bar{x}} = .8$. This value is determined by the formula,

$$s_{\bar{x}} = \frac{5.6}{\sqrt{50 - 1}} = \frac{5.6}{7} = .8.$$

where $N = 50$, or the sample of executions for 2007

$\quad s =$ sample standard deviation in years

Carrying out a Z test to determine the difference between our hypothesized μ and observed $\overline{X}$,

$$Z = \frac{15.3 - 13}{.8} = \frac{2.3}{.8} = 2.88.$$

we have a $Z_{obs} = 2.88$. Using a two-tailed test at the .01 level of significance, $Z_{cv} = \pm 2.58$. Does our Z_{obs} of 2.88 equal or exceed $Z_{cv} = \pm 2.58$? Yes. Therefore, H_o is rejected and H_1 is supported at the .01 level of significance. The average length of time between conviction, sentence, and execution is different from 13 years. Of course, in this instance, we could have made an informed prediction of direction based on previous information, where our predicted time lapse between conviction and execution would be greater than 13 years. Had we done so with our research hypothesis, then the Z_{cv} for .01 would have been + 2.33 instead of ± 2.58 (the two-tailed Z_{cv}'s). One-tailed tests, therefore, make it easier to reject H_o's, particularly if we have prior information and a plausible rationale for making a one-tailed directional prediction. There is always a risk involved in making one-tailed directional tests, however. This risk is that we might make an incorrect directional prediction. For instance, the observed mean could have been less than 13 years.

Briefly summarizing, point estimation means that we predict a point where μ occurs. We then compute a mean for the sample we have obtained, and we compare this mean with the hypothesized μ. An objective decision is made based on tabled values of the normal curve, where the sampling distribution of the mean is used. Levels of significance and test directionality determine the critical values of Z used in order to reject H_o's and support H_1's. We can avoid making point estimates altogether if we use another form of estimation, interval estimation.

Interval Estimation and Confidence Intervals

Interval estimation is used to answer the same questions raised in point estimation. Namely, do observed mean values differ significantly from hypothesized μ values? Interval estimation answers this question, but in a different way. The logic of interval estimation is explained below.

If we obtain a sample of elements and compute various statistics for it, there is a strong likelihood our sample statistics approximate their parametric counterparts. For example, a sample $\overline{X}$ is probably close to the population μ rather than being far away from it. On the sampling distribution of sample means, there are more sample means near μ than far away from it in the tails of the distribution.

Because there are more sample means near the center of the sampling distribution of the mean than in the extremes of it, we might call this part of the distribution an area of high probability. Similarly, we may designate the tails of the sampling distribution of means as areas of low probability. Using what we know about the sampling distribution of the mean and its similarity to the normal distribution, about 68 percent of all sample means occur within $\pm 1.00 s_{\overline{x}}$'s on either side of μ. This is because approximately 68 percent of the normal curve area lies between $\pm 1.00\sigma$ on either side of μ of the normal distribution.

In making this statement, we don't need to know the actual value of μ for the sampling distribution of means. We only need to know that the sampling distribution of means is normally distributed. A given distance to the left or to the right of the unknown μ will cut off a certain amount of curve area, which is also equivalent to a proportion of means occurring there. Thus, for any sample we select and study, the probability is greater for obtaining a sample with a $\overline{X}$ near μ than far away from it.

What if we were to create an interval around our observed $\overline{X}$? What if we have an $\overline{X} = 100$ and add and subtract 5 points from it? This will create an interval ranging from 95 to 105 around $\overline{X} = 100$ ($100 \pm 5 = 95 - 105$). This interval we've just created around our observed $\overline{X}$ is a **confidence interval** and is the subject of interval estimation. Confidence intervals are designated distances above and below an observed $\overline{X}$ that have a particular probability of overlapping μ. Confidence intervals are often labeled as 95 percent confidence intervals, 90 percent confidence intervals, or 99 percent confidence intervals, and so forth. These percentage values are probabilities that the confidence intervals we create will overlap μ. The wider the confidence interval, the greater the probability of overlapping μ. The narrower the confidence interval, the less the probability of overlapping μ.

Since the true population mean is always unknown, we never know with absolute certainty that any confidence interval we create around an observed $\overline{X}$ will overlap μ. For an explanation of the logic of confidence intervals, imagine that researchers were to draw all possible samples of size 50 from a population of 2,000. There would be N^n or $2,000^{50}$ samples that could be drawn. Further suppose that means are computed for all of these samples. We would have $2,000^{50}$ sample $\overline{X}$s.

Next, imagine that 95 percent confidence intervals were established around all $2,000^{50}$ of these sample means. Since all of these confidence intervals would be 95 percent confidence intervals, we could say with certainty that 95 percent of these confidence intervals would overlap μ but 5 percent of them would not overlap μ. The primary problem is that we don't know *which* sample means have confidence intervals that overlap μ and which ones don't overlap it.

As an additional example, if we had created 99 percent confidence intervals for all of these $\overline{X}$s, we would have $2,000^{50}$ 99 percent confidence intervals. We could say that 99 percent of them would overlap μ, but 1 percent would not overlap μ. We simply don't know which confidence intervals overlap μ and which ones don't overlap it. But we do have probability or chance working in our favor.

Let's use what we know about the sampling distribution of the mean and see what can be said about any confidence interval we establish around any given $\overline{X}$. One known fact is that larger numbers of sample means occur near μ than far away from it. Thus, whenever we draw a sample, compute a mean, and establish a confidence interval of any size, the probability is in our favor that our particular confidence interval overlaps μ. But there is also a small likelihood that the confidence interval does not overlap μ.

What typically happens in actual research? Investigators are going to draw one sample and compute $\overline{X}$. They will not draw all $2,000^{50}$ samples and create all confidence intervals with the sample $\overline{X}$ computed. A single confidence interval of some magnitude will be established around the $\overline{X}$. A probability is determined (e.g., 99 percent, 90 percent, and 95 percent) for the confidence interval, which is the likelihood that μ will be overlapped by it. But a small probability remains that defines the likelihood that μ will not be overlapped. For instance, 99 percent confidence intervals have a 1 percent likelihood of not overlapping μ. A 95 percent confidence interval has a 5 percent chance of not overlapping μ. An 80 percent confidence interval has 20 percent chance of not overlapping μ, and so forth.

An example of how confidence intervals with a certain probability overlap μ is illustrated in Figure 7.9.

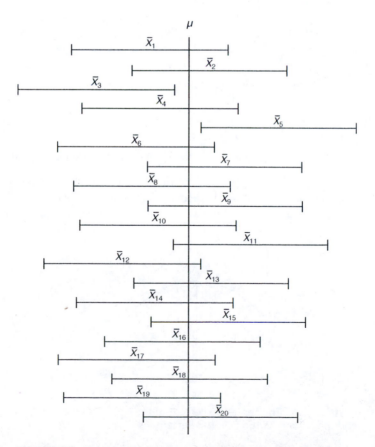

FIGURE 7.9 Twenty Confidence Intervals (90% Confidence Intervals)

In Figure 7.9, 90 percent confidence intervals have been established around a sample of sample means. This is a small-scale example, because an example using the $2,000^{50}$ $\overline{X}$'s would be unwieldy. Suppose we have 20 sample means, $\overline{X}_1$ through $\overline{X}_{20}$ as shown in Figure 7.9. Since these are 90 percent confidence intervals and there are 20 of them, it would be expected that 10 percent or 2 of these $\overline{X}$'s would have confidence intervals that would not overlap μ, but 18 of these confidence intervals would overlap μ. Notice $\overline{X}_3$ and $\overline{X}_5$. These two $\overline{X}$'s do not have confidence intervals that overlap μ. The other 18 sample means would overlap μ at some point, either to the left or right as illustrated.

We might also imagine these means as occurring along the horizontal axis of the sampling distribution of the mean, each confidence interval overlapping the others. Most confidence intervals would overlap μ at some point, but two of these confidence intervals would not overlap μ. Again, the problem is we don't know which confidence intervals overlap or don't overlap μ. But the probability is in our favor that for any $\overline{X}$ we compute, there is a 90 percent chance that the confidence interval created around it overlaps μ. However, there is also a 10 percent chance that the confidence interval doesn't overlap μ.

Constructing Confidence Intervals

Constructing confidence intervals is fairly easy. We need to know several values. First, we need to know a sample $\overline{X}$ and the standard error of the mean. This requires a knowledge of the sample s and N. Both of these values are known as the result of the sample we draw.

With a knowledge of these values, we can construct any confidence interval. Suppose a researcher has drawn a random sample of 226 and has observed $\overline{X} = 25$ and $s = 5$. Further, suppose the researcher wants to construct a 90 percent confidence interval around the $\overline{X}$. The 90 percent confidence interval is constructed as follows:

$$\text{90 percent confidence interval} = \overline{X} \pm (s_{\overline{x}})(Z)$$

where

$\overline{X}$ = the observed sample mean

$s_{\overline{x}}$ = the standard error of the mean

Z = the standard score associated with the 90 percent confidence interval.

The Z score associated with the 90 percent confidence interval is the Z score cutting off the central 90 percent of normal curve area, leaving 10 percent of the curve in the tails of it. If we were to envision this Z score, it would appear on a normal curve as is shown in Figure 7.10.

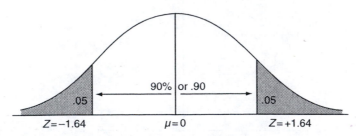

FIGURE 7.10 The Central 90 percent of the Normal Curve Area and the Z Scores Cutting Off this Percentage

Consulting Table A.2 of Appendix A, p. 455–446, we want the Z score that cuts off .4500 of curve area. This is half of .9000 or 90 percent, consistent with the 90 percent confidence interval we are creating. One half of .9000 = .9000/2 = .4500. The Z score cutting off .4500 = ±1.64. The total amount of curve area between − 1.64 and + 1.64 = 90 percent or .9000. This is the Z value used in our confidence interval computation. Using this information, we have:

$$90 \text{ percent confidence interval} = 25 \pm \left(\frac{5}{\dfrac{s}{\sqrt{226 - 1}}} \right)(1.64) = 25 \pm (.33)(1.64)$$

$$= 25 \pm .54$$
$$= 24.46 \text{ to } 25.54.$$

The 90 percent confidence interval around our observed $\overline{X}$ is 24.46 to 25.54. There is a 90 percent chance that μ is overlapped between 24.46 and 25.54, but there is also a 10 percent chance that μ is not overlapped by this confidence interval.

We can expand the width of this confidence interval by using 95 percent or 99 percent or some other percentage larger than 90 percent. If we wanted to create a 95 percent confidence interval around our observed $\overline{X}$, we would seek a Z value cutting off the central 95 percent of normal curve area, a Z value derived again from Table A.2. This Z = ±1.96. A Z = ±1.96 leaves .4750 of curve area from μ to each point. A curve amount of 5 percent or .05 would remain in the tails of the curve. A confidence interval of 99 percent would mean finding a Z value cutting off the central 99 percent of normal curve area, leaving 1 percent of the curve area in the tails. Finding a Z cutting off .4950 of curve area leads to a Z = ±2.58. The respective 95 percent and 99 percent confidence intervals would be displayed as follows:

95 percent confidence interval = $25 \pm (.33)(1.96) = 25 \pm .65 = 24.35$ to 25.65

99 percent confidence interval = $25 \pm (.33)(2.58) = 25 \pm .85 = 24.15$ to 25.85

In each of these confidence intervals created around an observed $\overline{X}$ = 25, we have expanded the interval by increasing the confidence interval percentage.

In the general case, if we want to construct any confidence interval around any observed sample $\overline{X}$, we would use the formula:

$$\% \text{ confidence interval} = \overline{X} \pm (s_{\overline{x}})(Z)$$

where

$\overline{X}$ = the observed mean

$s_{\overline{x}}$ = the standard error of the mean

Z = the standard score associated with cutting off the middle percentage of the normal curve desired

Determining which Z value should be used in this formula means dividing the percent of the confidence interval desired by 2. If we are determining the 90 percent confidence interval, we divide 90 percent by 2 or .90/2 = .4500. If we are computing the 80 percent confidence interval, we would divide 80 percent by 2 or .80/2 = .4000, and so on. Once we have determined these proportions, we can find the appropriate Z value in Table A.2. As an example, the Z value cutting off .4500 (from the mean, μ = 0 to that point) is ±1.64, while the Z value cutting off .4000 (from the μ = 0 to that point) is ±1.28.

What Do Confidence Intervals Mean?

What are confidence intervals? How can they be used in hypothesis testing? The 95 percent confidence interval means that there is a 95 percent chance that μ lies somewhere within the 95 percent confidence interval range around an observed sample $\overline{X}$. The 99 percent confidence interval means that there is a 99 percent chance that the population μ lies somewhere within the 99 percent confidence interval range around some observed $\overline{X}$. The 80 percent confidence interval means that there is an 80 percent chance or likelihood that the population μ lies somewhere within the 80 percent confidence interval range we have created around some observed sample $\overline{X}$.

Confidence intervals expand as the percentage associated with the confidence interval increases. Also, confidence intervals narrow as the percentage of the confidence interval decreases. This reflects an increase or decrease in our confidence that the population mean will be found in any given percent confidence interval established around any given observed sample $\overline{X}$. This is one reason why the term, confidence interval, is used. It provides us with a certain amount of confidence that μ will be overlapped by our confidence interval. There are no guarantees, however. There are always small probabilities existing that μ's will not be overlapped by these confidence interval ranges.

Confidence intervals have a distinct advantage over point estimation in that they provide a range of values within which μ might occur. We begin our estimation with an observed $\overline{X}$ and create an interval around it which likely overlaps μ. This is superior to the method of guessing a population μ in advance, with little or no information, and then comparing a sample mean with our point estimate.

A comparison of point estimation with interval estimation can be illustrated with a problem we have already solved involving forecasts of population μs. Regarding the problem of sentencing disparities discussed earlier under point estimation, we forecast a population μ of 12 months, indicating the disparity in sentence lengths between convicted black and white offenders. Under a new sentencing guidelines scheme, it was anticipated that sentence lengths would be more equitable as disparities due to racial factors diminished. A single one-tailed test was made which predicted that under new guidelines, disparities in sentence lengths between black and white offenders would be less than 12 months.

In the following scenario, let's assume the same information as provided from our original problem, where the predicted μ under H_1 was $\leq$ 12 months, the observed $\overline{X}$ = 6.5 months, and the $s_{\overline{x}}$ = 2.00. However, this time we will establish a two-tailed hypothesis set, where direction of difference is not predicted:

$H_o: \mu = 12$ months

$H_1: \mu \neq 12$ months

$P \leq .05$ (two-tailed test)

H_1 says that the average length of sentencing disparity (measured in months) will be different from 12 months, while H_o says the average disparity will be equal to 12 months. The level of significance, .05, is used. Because the direction of difference is not predicted in this situation, a two-tailed or nondirectional test is made. This means that we must divide the .05 into two equal parts and place each part in the two tails of our sampling distribution of means. This will require that we locate a Z value that cuts off .4750 of curve area in both directions from the mean, leaving .0250 in each tail of the curve as the **rejection regions**. The Z value we seek is ± 1.96 and is designated as our critical value of Z for the .05 level of significance, using a two-tailed test.

Since we already know that our observed mean = 6.5 months and has a $Z_{obs} = -2.75$, we only need to determine whether -2.75 equals or exceeds the $Z_{cv} = \pm 1.96$. Yes, the $Z = -2.75$ is in the rejection region to the far left of -1.96. H_o can be rejected and we may conclude that the sentencing disparity in that jurisdiction is not equal to 12 months. Because the .05 level of significance was used, there is a 5 percent chance of being wrong in making this decision.

Interval estimation can be used to answer the same question about sentencing disparity. But for interval estimation, we will not hypothesize anything. Rather, we will compute our $\overline{X} = 6.5$, the $s_{\overline{x}} = 2.00$, and construct a 95 percent confidence interval around our observed $\overline{X} = 6.5$. A 95 percent confidence interval is chosen because the .05 level of significance was used earlier in our point estimate and hypothesis test. Therefore, we have:

$$95 \text{ percent confidence interval} = 6.5 \pm (2.00)(1.96)$$
$$= 6.5 \pm 3.92$$
$$= 2.58 \text{ to } 10.42.$$

Our 95 percent confidence interval extends around the mean of 6.5 from 2.58 to 10.42. We may now say that the population μ falls within 2.58 to 10.42 with 95 percent confidence. At least this is one way of saying it. Notice that our population $\mu = 12$ months occurs outside of this confidence interval. Any population μ occurring outside of this confidence interval range is considered significantly different from the sample $\overline{X}$. We are answering the same question about differences in sentence lengths, but we are solving the problem using an alternative strategy, the confidence interval, instead of a point estimate.

Note that the Z value selected for our 95 percent confidence interval problem was the same Z used for a two-tailed hypothesis test at the .05 level of significance. This is the general relation between point estimation and interval estimation. Two-tailed point estimation is the functional equivalent of interval estimation, where the same level of significance is used. Several examples illustrate the linkages between levels of significance and confidence interval percentages as follows:

90 percent confidence interval = .10 level of significance, two-tailed test

95 percent confidence interval = .05 level of significance, two-tailed test

80 percent confidence interval = .20 level of significance, two-tailed test

99 percent confidence interval = .01 level of significance, two-tailed test

TESTS OF SIGNIFICANCE AND THEIR FUNCTIONS

All of the decision rules discussed in this chapter have set the stage for a discussion of **tests of significance.** Tests of significance are devices or methods used by researchers for determining the statistical significance of whatever is observed. Almost always, hypothesis testing is conducted with a test of significance. As the result of applying one or more tests of significance, an H_1 is tested and either supported or refuted according to the test results. Tests of significance, therefore, are mathematical tools designed to assess the significance of difference between whatever is observed, such as a sample statistic, and some hypothesized value, such as a population parameter. But this definition only partially explains tests of significance and what they do. Some tests of significance are designed so as to determine whether two or more groups differ significantly on some measured characteristic. Other tests of significance pertain to correlation or association. All tests of significance are couched in a probabilistic context.

That is, a probability is always established when computing a test of significance. Most of the remaining chapters in this book involve tests of significance, and therefore, it is important to learn about them and how they are applied in research work.

In this section, tests of significance are examined according to: (1) tests of significance of point estimation; (2) tests of significance between two and k samples; and (3) tests of significance of measures of association.

Tests of Significance of Point Estimation

Tests of significance of point estimation are mathematical formulae that determine the probability that an hypothesized population parameter differs from an observed sample statistic which is an estimate of that parameter. We have already seen applications of tests of significance of point estimation. The test of significance is either a t or a Z test. This means that a table of values in Appendix A, either Table A.2 or Table A.3, the normal curve table or t distribution, is consulted and a critical value of a statistic is determined. Critical values are determined according to the level of significance selected for hypothesis testing. Appendix A contains tables for many statistical tests of significance, each performing a specific function depending on the types of variables examined and questions asked. Headnotes in each table usually explain how critical values are determined. The result of a test of significance of point estimation is that there is or isn't a difference between what is hypothesized and what is observed. A familiar illustration is provided:

$H_o: \mu = 100$

$H_1: \mu \neq 100$

$P \leq .05$ (two-tailed)

Observed sample $\overline{X} = 95$

The hypothesis set says the following. The research hypothesis is that the population $\mu \neq 100$, while the null hypothesis is that $\mu = 100$. We observe a sample mean $= 95$. The level of significance is .05. We don't care whether the observed mean is greater or less than 100. Our main concern is whether there is a significant difference between the two values at the .05 level of significance.

We test this hypothesis by applying the formula,

$$t, Z = \frac{\overline{X} - \mu}{\dfrac{s}{\sqrt{N - 1}}}$$

The formulae for t and Z are identical for this test of significance for point estimation. This similarity has to do with the similarity between the t and Z (normal) distributions. As sample size increases, both the t and Z distribution have identical critical values for various significance levels. The result of applying the t or Z formula is either a t_{obs} or Z_{obs} which equals or exceeds some t_{cv} or Z_{cv}. If t_{obs} or Z_{obs} equals or exceeds the t_{cv} or Z_{cv} for the level of significance used, the decision is to reject H_o and support H_1. Other significance levels may be chosen besides .05. This decision rule is determined by the researcher.

Tests of Significance of Difference Between Two and k Samples

Tests of significance of difference between two and k samples are mathematical formulae that determine the probability of whether two or more samples differ significantly on some measured characteristic, such as an attitude. Do two samples of police officers differ in their professionalism? Is there a significant difference between a sample of felons and a sample of misdemeanants concerning their recidivism rates? Does a sample of drug addicts change over several different time periods after being exposed to an experiment designed to decrease drug dependency? These and other similar types of questions pertain to the significance of difference between two or more groups. More than two groups is designated as k, although k technically means "2 or more." In this book, because there are specific two-sample tests of significance, k is used to distinguish tests of significance where three or more samples are compared.

Also, are the samples being compared independent or related? Tests of significance of difference between two and k samples may involve independent or related samples. If we have related samples, we will use related-sample tests of significance, not independent sample tests. If we have independent samples being evaluated, we will use independent-sample tests of significance, not related-sample tests.

The level of measurement associated with the variables being evaluated is important as well. In fact, several chapters about tests of significance are divided according to different levels of measurement assumed. As we have seen, levels of measurement include the nominal, ordinal, interval, and ratio levels. For each level of measurement, there are tests of significance of difference that fit these particular measurement levels. An example of a two-sample comparison might be the following:

$$H_o: \overline{X}_1 = \overline{X}_2 = \mu_1 = \mu_2$$
$$H_1: \overline{X}_1 \neq \overline{X}_2 = \mu_1 \neq \mu_2$$
$$P \leq .05 \text{ (two-tailed)}$$

In this illustration, we hypothesize under H_1 that two sample means differ. Under H_o, we hypothesize that the means are equal. The .05 level of significance is selected for this hypothesis test. A test of significance for this mean difference might be a Z test. A special formula is applied. Examples of such tests will follow in later chapters.

Tests of Significance of Measures of Association

Tests of significance of measures of association are mathematical formulae that determine whether any observed coefficient of association is different from no association or 0. Measures of association are discussed in detail in Chapters 11 and 12. However, a brief explanation of specific tests of significance for measures of association will be provided. Are two variables associated? For instance, are inmate prior records correlated with recidivism? Perfect association occurs whenever a correlation coefficient $= \pm 1.00$. No association is 0. Usually, most variables relate with one another somewhere between 0 and ± 1.00. Tests of significance of measures of association determine whether there is a significant difference between the observed coefficient and 0.

ONE- AND TWO-TAILED HYPOTHESIS TESTS

Is a hypothesis test one-tailed or two-tailed? This depends on whether the direction of difference is predicted or not predicted. If the direction of difference is specified, the test is a **one-tailed test.** If it is a nondirectional test, it is considered a **two-tailed test.** Determining whether a test is one- or two-tailed is an investigator's option. We have already seen one- and two-tailed examples, but these were related to point and interval estimation. The distinguishing features of one-tailed tests are the symbols, ">" and "<," where ">" means "greater than," and "<" means "less than."

Variations may be "≤" or "≥." Any time these symbols are a part of any hypothesis set, the test conducted is a one-tailed or directional one. Symbols such as "=" or "≠" are indicative of two-tailed or nondirectional tests. Researchers only have to look at these symbols to make a determination of whether tests conducted are one- or two-tailed.

PARAMETRIC AND NONPARAMETRIC TESTS

A distinction is made in the statistical literature between **parametric tests** and **nonparametric tests** and procedures. The statistical tests discussed in Chapter 8 are parametric tests. Those discussed in Chapters 9 and 10 are called nonparametric tests. What is this distinction and why is it meaningful? Parametric tests refer to statistical tests that estimate population parameters, assume normality, similarity of variation in multiple-mean comparisons, and have larger sample sizes, usually of 100 or greater. Whenever null hypotheses are tested, parametric tests have the greatest likelihood of rejecting these hypotheses when they are false and ought to be rejected. In short, parametric tests are the most powerful tests researchers can use for hypothesis testing. They also involve variables which are measured according to an interval scale.

But because of these rigorous assumptions, parametric tests may not always be the best choices for statistical analyses of data. Not all distributions of scores are normally distributed. Not all variables are measured according to an interval scale. Not all variances in multiple-sample comparisons are equal. Not all sample sizes are 100 or greater. Whenever one or more of these assumptions associated with parametric tests cannot be achieved when statistical analysis is planned, questions may arise later about the meaning associated with one's research results. Can we rely on tests and their numerical outcomes, especially where one or more assumptions of those tests have been violated?

Alternative statistical procedures have been devised to answer the same sorts of questions answered by parametric tests. These are nonparametric statistical tests and measures. Many of the variables studied by social scientists, including criminologists and criminal justicians, are attitudinal and categorical, such as job satisfaction, dangerousness, type of crime committed, gender, race/ethnicity, prosecutorial discretion, sentencing disparity, and punishment leniency. When these and similar variables are studied, parametric tests may not be suitable. Relatively few distributions of these and other variables are normal. Sample sizes may be small. When these situations arise, nonparametric tests have been created to answer questions otherwise answered by parametric tests. Nonparametric tests do not make the assumption that the data analyzed are normally distributed. In fact, there are no special distributional assumptions accompanying most of these procedures. Sometimes they are referred to as **distribution-free statistics.** Also, they do not necessarily assume that data are measured according to an interval scale. Most of these procedures are applicable whenever data are measured according to either nominal or ordinal scales. Therefore, for every parametric statistical test and measure, there exists at least one or more nonparametric statistical tests and measures. Categorically, nonparametric tests are generally less powerful than parametric tests designed to accomplish the same tasks. But this power differential is not especially great. Some nonparametric tests have nearly equivalent power contrasted with their parametric counterparts. A more extensive discussion of nonparametric test power will be presented in Chapter 9.

Even certain measures of association are parametric. A variety of measures of association for different levels of measurement will be presented in Chapters 11 and 12. The chief parametric measure of association is the Pearson *r*. It assumes normality and has several other stringent assumptions about the distribution of variables to be correlated. But numerous nonparametric measures of association have been devised to yield reliable results that can give us a good impression of how closely two or more variables are correlated or related. All nonparametric procedures have assumptions as well, but nonparametric test assumptions are usually far less rigorous compared with their parametric test counterparts.

As we move into the next few chapters, the parametric–nonparametric distinction will become readily apparent. Several examples will be provided to show how these different tests compare with one another, especially when they are applied to the same data being analyzed. The numerical results differ markedly. More will be said about parametric and nonparametric tests as we cover them.

DISCRETION AND CONVENTION: LIVING WITH ERROR

All research has some error associated with it. There is no way that we can totally eliminate any error involved in hypothesis testing and the application of statistical tests. Some Type I and Type II error are always present in any hypothesis test and cannot be eliminated. But as we have seen, there are ways that they can be minimized. Conventional guidelines exist in most research applications, and these guidelines are followed fairly closely by most investigators. Thus, reasonable amounts of error are established and accompany all statistical testing.

Summary

This chapter has described hypotheses and the general practice of testing hypotheses. The hypothesis-testing process involves articulating research hypotheses which are most often derived from theory. These hypotheses are not ordinarily tested directly, however. Much of the time, null hypotheses are created and tested. Thus, if a null hypothesis is rejected later, a particular research hypothesis is supported. Null hypotheses are used in criminological research for a variety of reasons. The most important reasons are that it is conventional to do so and that such hypotheses fit the probability model.

Quantitative expressions of research and null hypotheses are called **statistical hypotheses**. We use statistical hypotheses frequently in criminological research. Governing our decision making in hypothesis testing are several important decision rules. These decision rules include sampling distributions of statistics, levels of significance, and critical regions or regions of rejection. Sampling distributions accompany all known statistics. Some of these sampling distributions have desirable properties of interest to criminologists. For instance, the sampling distribution of the mean is used frequently, because it has a distribution which is normal in form. Most sampling distributions of statistics do not have this desirable feature. The sampling distribution of the mean, for instance, consists of all possible values the mean can assume based on samples of a specified size drawn from a specified population.

Sampling distributions of statistics have means and standard deviations, just like distributions of raw scores. These means and standard deviations are given special names, however. Means of sampling distributions are called expected values, while standard deviations of these distributions are called standard errors. Thus, the sampling distribution of the mean has an expected value of the mean. In this particular sampling distribution, another desirable feature is that the population mean is also the mean of the sampling distribution of the means. Most sampling distributions do not have this property. Standard error terms are units of measurement along the horizontal axes of sampling distributions of statistics. For instance, the unit of measurement along the sampling distribution of sample means is called the standard error of the mean. These standard error terms are fundamental components of various tests of significance that may be applied later.

Levels of significance define Type I or alpha error (α), the probability of being wrong whenever a null hypothesis is rejected and a research hypothesis is supported. Researchers have direct control over Type I error or test significance. Another type of error, Type II or **beta error (β)**, occurs whenever researchers fail to reject null hypotheses when they are untrue and ought to be rejected. Raising or lowering one type of error will influence the other type of error. But there is not a one-to-one relationship in these error changes. Other factors are involved, including sample size, the magnitude between predicted and observed statistical values, and the magnitude of standard error terms.

Critical regions are areas on sampling distributions of statistics. These regions are set by the level of significance or Type I error. Any observed statistic lying on the line of or in the critical region is considered significantly different from the mean of the sampling distribution of that statistic. Since these expected values of sampling distributions are generally unknown, we are never certain that our observed statistics are significantly different from what we hypothesize these expected values to be. But probability is on our side, and there is a greater likelihood of being right in our statistical decision making than being wrong.

Criminologists use both point and interval estimation. These are ways of estimating population parameters and making hypothesis tests involving them. Interval estimation is more popular than point estimation, however. This is because there is too much guesswork associated with point estimation. Interval estimation takes what is known, a sample statistic, and an interval is created around these known values to form confidence intervals of some magnitude. Levels of significance for hypothesis testing are directly relevant in establishing these confidence intervals. Thus, different confidence intervals have a probability of overlapping expected values of their sampling distributions, depending upon the level of significance we choose.

Tests of significance are mathematical formulae applied to differences between what are hypothesized and what are observed. But they are not limited to this definition. Several types of tests of significance include tests of significance of point estimation, tests of significance of difference between two and k sample means, where the samples are independent or related, and tests of significance of measures of association. Also, whenever hypothesis tests are conducted, they may be either one-tailed or two-tailed. One-tailed tests involve directional predictions, whereas two-tailed tests are nondirectional. Thus, if two sample means are being compared, if one mean is predicted to be higher or lower than another, this would be a one-tailed hypothesis test where the direction of difference between means has been predicted. Nondirectional testing would simply predict that a difference between means would exist, regardless of the direction of that difference. Two-tailed tests are considered more conservative than one-tailed tests, since one-tailed tests run the risk of predicting in the wrong direction. It has been established that with all statistical testing, some risk is involved of being wrong. Probabilities have been associated with this risk, and such probabilities cannot be eliminated under any circumstance.

Key Terms

Questions for Review

1. Differentiate between research, null, and statistical hypotheses. Give examples.
2. What are some reasons for why null hypotheses are used in statistics?
3. What is meant by statistical inference?
4. What are decision rules? Identify three decision rules. In each case, specify the importance of each rule.
5. What is the sampling distribution of a statistic? How is sampling with replacement related to sampling distributions of statistics?
6. What is meant by the expected value of a statistic? Explain.
7. What are standard error terms? What relevance do standard error terms have for hypothesis testing? Explain.
8. Differentiate between Type I and Type II error. How does each affect the other? Can we eliminate either one? Why or why not? Explain.
9. Distinguish between point and interval estimation. Which is more popular? Why?
10. What are tests of significance? Describe the functions of tests of significance.
11. What are tests of significance of difference between two and *k* samples? Explain.
12. Does it make a difference in two-sample tests of significance whether the samples are related or independent? Why or why not? Explain.
13. Distinguish between one- and two-tailed hypothesis tests. How can we tell whether a test is one-tailed or two-tailed? Explain.

Exercises

The exercises below consist in part of numerical problems, multiple-choice questions, and short-answer essay questions. All answers to multiple-choice and numerical questions are found in Appendix B. Use provided information in each of the numerical-problem questions and make the necessary computations to determine correct answers.

7.1. The mean of the sampling distribution of range is called: (A) the standard error of the median; (B) the standard deviation of the range; (C) the expected value of the median; (D) the expected value of the range.

7.2. An unbiased estimate is a statistic: (A) which has a sampling distribution whose standard error is equal to the standard error of what it is trying to estimate; (B) whose sampling distribution has a mean equal to the statistic's counterpart (parameter) in the population; (C) a statistic that has a sampling distribution; (D) a statistic that has no sampling distribution.

7.3. With an observed $\overline{X} = 200, s = 20, N = 131$, determine the following confidence intervals: ($s_{\overline{x}} = 1.75$)
   a. 90% confidence interval
   b. 80% confidence interval
   c. 40% confidence interval

7.4. What is the difference between point estimation and interval estimation? Describe the basic logic of each approach.

7.5. Which statistics have sampling distributions?

7.6. Why is the sampling distribution of the mean so valuable to researchers? Give three reasons.

7.7. How many ranges can you compute for all possible samples of 15 taken from a population of 200? (Use a simple formula here)

7.8. Given $s_{\overline{x}} = 2, \mu = 300, \overline{X} = 309$. What is the Z for the observed $\overline{X}$?

7.9. The range is an unbiased estimate of: (A) the population range; (B) the standard error of the estimate of the range; (C) the expected value of the range; (D) none of the above.

7.10. The expected value of the standard deviation is: (A) the mean of the sampling distribution of standard deviations; (B) the mean of the sampling distribution of means; (C) the standard error of the estimate; (D) the standard error of the standard deviation.

7.11. The 95 percent confidence interval means that: (A) the sample mean you select will definitely have a confidence interval that overlaps the population mean; (B) of all possible confidence intervals that can be constructed for all possible means computed from samples of size "n" from a population of size "N", 95 percent of them will overlap the population mean; (C) you are 95 percent confident that your standard error of the estimate will not overlap the population standard deviation; (D) the expected value of the mean will be overlapped by the confidence interval 5 percent of the time.

7.12. Determine confidence intervals for the following, where $s_{\overline{x}} = 2.13 \ N = 56$, and $\overline{X}_{obs} = 92$:
   a. 99% confidence interval
   b. 85% confidence interval
   c. 60% confidence interval

7.13. What Z values define regions on the sampling distribution of the mean under the following circumstances?
   a. .05 (two-tailed test)
   b. .01 (one-tailed test)
   c. .10 (one-tailed test)
   d. .001 (two-tailed test)

References

Alpert, Geoffrey P., Dennis J. Kenney, and Roger Dunham (1997). "Police Pursuits and the Use of Force: Recognizing and Managing 'the Pucker Factor'—A Research Note." *Justice Quarterly* **14**:371–385.

Luginbuhl, James and Michael Burkhead (1995). "Victim Impact Evidence in a Capital Trial: Encouraging Votes for Death." *American Journal of Criminal Justice* **20**:1–16.

Meyer, Jon'a F. (2001). "Strange Science: Subjective Criteria in Parole Decisions." *Journal of Crime and Justice* **24**:43–70.

CHAPTER 8

Interval-Level Tests of Significance

Chapter Outline

Chapter Objectives

After reading this chapter, the following objectives will be realized:

1. understanding single-sample tests of significance for interval-level data;
2. examining two-sample tests of significance when samples are independent;
3. understanding two-related sample tests of significance;

4. understanding *k*-related tests of significance, including the analysis-of-variance *F* test;

5. examining two-way analysis of variance and its applications; and

6. understanding post hoc or postmortem tests, including the Newman–Keuls procedure and the Scheffé procedure.

INTRODUCTION

This chapter examines several tests of significance that may be applied whenever investigators wish to compare two or more samples with one another. It is assumed that researchers have interval-level data at their disposal and that certain restrictive assumptions have been met.

This chapter is organized as follows. For simple, single-sample test situations, the *t* test for significance of difference is described. Examples from the criminological literature are used to illustrate how the *t* test is applied in actual research. The *t* test is perhaps the most powerful test of significance for determining whether two sample means differ. There are limitations of the *t* test, and these will be described. One limitation applies to sample size. The *t* test is designed for smaller sample size applications when one's sample size is 120 or smaller. For larger sample sizes, however, an alternative *Z* test is presented. The *Z* test makes use of the table of areas of the normal curve, Table A.2 in Appendix A. It has no sample size restrictions. Following this presentation, two two-sample tests of significance are presented. Whenever two samples are being compared, the samples may be either independent or related. An extension of the single-sample *t* test is illustrated. This version of the *t* test is applied whenever it is assumed that both samples are independent of one another. In another case where the two samples being compared are related, the Sandler *A* statistic will be illustrated. In all instances, the assumptions, advantages, disadvantages, and potential applications of these tests will be discussed and illustrated.

In a subsequent section, investigators may examine more than two samples of elements. When these situations occur, it is conventional to label these as *k*-sample comparisons. Technically, *k* refers to two or more, but since several specific two-sample tests are discussed exclusively for two-sample situations, in this book *k* designates tests that have applications for more than two samples. One *k*-sample test is presented. This is the *F* test for analysis of variance, frequently used in criminological research. It has several important assumptions underlying its application, and these assumptions will be illustrated. One of these assumptions involves equal variances. While there are numerous tests to determine whether *k*-sample variances are statistically equal, two simple and conservative tests are provided here. One test is the Hartley F_{max} test. It involves an efficient and rapid determination of whether it can be assumed that homogeneity of variance or equal variances exists. Another test for equal variances is the Cochran *C* test. Since sample variances are being compared, it may occur to some investigators that comparing variances, two at a time, might accomplish the same objective as the Hartley F_{max} test or Cochran *C* test. This would be the equivalent of utilizing multiple tests, taking two samples at a time, and determining the significance of difference between each pair of variances. But this process is inefficient and needless, since both the Hartley F_{max} test and Cochran *C* test accomplish this task by comparing all sample variances at once. These different sample variance comparison methods will be discussed.

The chapter concludes with a presentation of an extension of the *k*-sample *F* test of analysis of variance. This is the two-way analysis-of-variance *F* test, which will be illustrated. This test is useful when a third variable is introduced, and its effect upon intergroup variation can be determined. All computational procedures will be explained in detail.

SINGLE-SAMPLE TESTS OF SIGNIFICANCE

Two tests will be featured in this section. These include the *t* test and the *Z* test. Both of these procedures are designed to test hypotheses about population means and whether observed sample means are significantly different from them. However, these tests differ according to the sizes of samples where they may be optimally applied.

These single-sample tests of significance involve predictions by investigators about what population means are for different variables, such as average sentence lengths, average ages, number of years on the job, or any other variable that can be measured according to an interval scale. These predictions made by researchers are sometimes confusing for students to understand. Where do these predictions about population means come from? The answer is that these predictions are often based on previous information and study data analyzed by other investigators. Usually, some prior information exists that enables researchers to make educated guesses about what population values will be. These predictions are sometimes called **point estimates**, since we are estimating particular values which we believe are near their population means. Both tests discussed in this section are about educated guesses of population means, therefore. A sample is selected from some designated population, and then the sample mean we compute is compared with the population mean we have estimated or predicted. The difference between what we have predicted to be the population mean and the actual sample mean observed is evaluated by these two tests. Our conclusion will be that the observed difference between the two means will or will not be significant statistically. A probability level is assigned as a standard for determining the significance of whatever difference we observe.

The *t* Test and *Z* Test

The **t test** is the best and most well-known single-sample test of significance of difference. Both the *t* test and the **Z test** share the same formula,

$$t, Z = \frac{\overline{X} - \mu}{\dfrac{s}{\sqrt{N-1}}}$$

where

$\overline{X}$ = the observed sample mean

μ = hypothesized population mean

$s_{\overline{x}}$ = the standard error of the mean estimated by $\dfrac{s}{\sqrt{N-1}}$

where

s = the sample standard deviation

N = the sample size

One important difference between the *t* test and the *Z* test is that a *t* table of critical values (Appendix A, Table A.3, pps. 446−447) exists for interpreting various observed *t* values, whereas the normal distribution is used for identifying critical *Z* values which may be compared with observed sample *Z* values (Table A.2). For sample sizes less than 120, critical values from the *t* test are generally larger than those derived by the *Z* test applied to the same data. Whenever the sample size exceeds 120, however, both the *t* distribution and *Z* distribution are identical, meaning that the *Z* and *t* critical values for different levels of significance are the same. The meanings of these t and Z values are illustrated by the following example.

Christopher A. Mallett (2006) studied a sample of juvenile court probation–supervised youths in Cuyahoga County, Ohio. Mallett determined that between 1990 and 2003, there was a substantial increase in juvenile delinquency nationally as well as in Cuyahoga County for youths aged 10–17. Focusing particularly on at-risk youths or those with problematic personal histories, fractured families, lower socioeconomic status, lower scholastic scores in schools, and other factors, Mallett found that the average age of all youths who received probation supervision in the county was 15, according to official reports and estimates collected by government agencies. Mallett also found that approximately two-thirds of all youths receiving probation lived with their mothers only, and that this single-parent home environment was closely associated with being considered at-risk. Suppose Mallett believed that most youths who lived with their mothers and who were placed on probation were likely to be less than 15, the probationer average age. Further suppose that Mallett obtained a sample of 61 juvenile probationers who lived with their mothers and examined their ages when probation was initially imposed on each of them. Mallett might have hypothesized the following:

$H_o: \mu \geq 15$

$H_1: \mu < 15$

$P \leq .05$ (one-tailed test)

This hypothesis set says the following. The null hypothesis, H_o, is that the population mean, μ, is equal to or greater than 15, which refers to the average age of all juvenile probationers. The research hypothesis is that the population mean, μ, will be less than 15. Thus, this hypothesis set shows that a directional or one-tailed prediction is being made under H_1 that for an observed sample of 61 juvenile probationers who live with their mothers, their average age will be less than 15. The level of significance, the probability level at which the hypothesis is being tested, is .05. Mallett would predict H_1 if he believed that youths who live with their mothers had an average age less than 15. A significant difference in average age in the predicted direction under the research hypothesis will support Mallett's belief. A t test can determine whether a significant difference exists between the hypothesized mean and the observed sample mean. Suppose the following hypothetical information has been obtained, based upon a sample of 61 juvenile probationers: $\overline{X}_{obs} = 14.3$, $s = 2.7$, and $N = 61$.

A t test is conducted, yielding the following t_{obs}:

$$t_{obs} = \frac{14.3 - 15}{\dfrac{2.7}{\sqrt{61 - 1}}}$$

$$t_{obs} = \frac{-.7}{.38}$$

$$t_{obs} = -1.84$$

The $t_{obs} = -1.84$ in this case. What does this t_{obs} mean? First, is Mallett's prediction in the correct direction? Is the observed mean less than the population mean? Yes. Therefore, Mallett must determine whether the difference in average ages is significant at $P \leq .05$. We must turn to Table A.3 of Appendix A, p. 446–447, the distribution of t. This table contains **critical values** of the t statistic which must be equaled or exceeded by our t_{obs} to be significant at the appropriate level of significance shown across the top of the table. These critical values may be either positive or negative, depending upon whether one-tailed (directional) or two-tailed (nondirectional) tests are being made. Table A.3 displays both one- and two-tailed probabilities. Since our hypothesis test is being made at the .05 level of significance for a directional or one-tailed test, we locate the .05 one-tailed probability across the top of the table. Next, we must determine **degrees of freedom**. Degrees of freedom (*df*) are the number of values in a set which are free to vary. For single-sample tests of significance, *df* are defined as $N - 1$. In this case, since there are 61 juveniles in Mallett's hypothetical sample, $df = 61 - 1 = 60$.

In Table A.3, *df* are located down the left-hand side of the table. We simply locate $df = 60$ and the .05 level of significance for a one-tailed test across the top of the table and where they intersect, a critical value of *t* is identified. In this case, the critical value of $t = -1.671$. Does our $t_{obs} = -1.84$ equal or exceed the critical value of $t = -1.671$? Yes. Therefore, we may reject H_o and conclude that the sample mean, 14.3, is smaller and significantly different from the hypothesized population mean of 15. For Mallett's sample of youths, those who live with their mothers are significantly lower than age 15 when placed on probation. Because the level of significance $= .05$, there is a 5 percent chance we could be wrong in rejecting H_o, however. But there is also a 95 percent chance our decision to reject H_o is the right one. Further study would be necessary for more generalized conclusions about youths who live with their mothers when initially placed on probation.

Had the *Z* test been applied to this same problem, we would have used Table A.2 in Appendix A, pps. 445–446. We would need to define a critical value of *Z* in order to interpret the $Z = -1.84$ (both *t* and *Z* values are the same, since the same formula is used in their derivation). Since the .05 level of significance is being used in this one-tailed hypothesis test, a *Z* value cutting off 45 percent of the curve area in a specific direction would be used. Under the research hypothesis from the hypothesis set above, the left tail of the normal distribution would contain the critical region. The critical value of *Z* would be -1.64. This is the *Z* value cutting off 45 percent of the curve area between μ and the *Z* value. If our observed *Z* equals or exceeds the critical *Z* value of -1.64, we may reject the null hypothesis and conclude H_1. In this case, an observed $Z = -1.84$ equals or exceeds the critical value of $Z = -1.64$. Conventional levels of significance and critical values for *t* and *Z* are shown in Table 8.1.

While a headnote in Table A.3 explains what to do when the precise *df* cannot be found down the left-hand side of the table, it is helpful to indicate here how this problem can be resolved. In Table A.3, specific *df* between points 30 and 40, 40 and 60, and 60 and 120 are not provided. If we do not have the exact *df* as shown in the table, our recommendation is to always choose the smaller *df* value in the table rather than the larger one. This is a conservative step and yields a slightly larger critical *t* value to equal or exceed. It is slightly more difficult to reject null hypotheses when we make this conservative choice.

TABLE 8.1 Conventional .05 and .01 Levels of Significance and Critical Values of Z or tᵃ

	Levels of Significance	
	.05	.01
One-tailed Z or t values =	1.64	1.96
Two-tailed Z or t values =	2.33	2.58

ᵃWhen $N \geq 120$, critical values of *t* and *Z* are identical.

A brief example illustrating such a conservative choice is if we were to observe a $t = 1.690$, with 35 degrees of freedom for the .05 level of significance (one-tailed test). An inspection of df values in Table A.3 shows that there are no $df = 35$. One must choose between $df = 30$ and $df = 40$. If $df = 40$ is chosen, then the critical value of t which must be equaled or exceeded is 1.684. If $df = 30$ is chosen, the critical value of t is 1.697. H_o will be rejected using the first critical value, 1.684 ($df = 40$), but not under the second critical value, 1.697 ($df = 30$).

Like the normal distribution, the t distribution is perfectly symmetrical. It also has a $\mu = 0$, with one side of the distribution identical to the other side of it. Therefore, only one side of the table

---

BOX 8.1

SPSS Alternative Application

Since Mallett's problem used to illustrate the t and Z tests was completed above with hypothetical values, there were no original raw scores upon which to base t or Z computations. We have attempted to simulate a data set that might generate figures similar to those shown in the above example. The following is an explanation of how our data set was artificially created and the t test was calculated, generating very similar values to those leading to the original hypothesis test result and decision.

1. Activate your *SPSS* software and go the Data Editor window. Go to the first "var" column and type in 8 "10" values; 3 "11" values; 8 "12" values; 3 "13" values; 10 "14" values; 5 "15" values; 4 "16" values; 15 "17" values; 2 "18" values; and 3 "19" values. This will create a VAR00001 column. This column can be labeled "Age" using the "Variable View" at the bottom of the Data Editor window and typing in "age." This will change the variable from VAR00001 to "Age."

2. Next, click on "Analyze," then "Compare Means," then "One-Sample T Test." This action brings up a screen with three windows. The left-hand window shows "Age." Highlight "Age" and move it with the arrow to the right-hand window.

3. A small window underneath these larger windows is labeled "Test Value." The Test Value is what-ever value hypothesized as μ. Type in "15" since 15 is the hypothesized μ according to the hypothesis set used as the example in Mallett's research. Click "Options."

4. This brings up a screen that shows a window, "Confidence Interval." The hypothesis set in Mallett's example was a one-tailed test at the .05 level of significance. This probability level would approximate a 90 percent confidence interval. Type in "90." Then click "Continue."

5. Click "OK." This action produces four tables of varying sizes. This output is shown below within this box. The first table is small and shows N, which is 61. This confirms that you are analyzing 61 youths. A second table is labeled "age" and shows a distribution of ages. A third table shows age with the N, mean, standard deviation, and standard error of the mean. The fourth table shows the t value of -1.879, $df = 60$, .065 (two-tailed significance), the mean difference between 14.3 and $15 = -.65$, and the 95 percent confidence interval of the difference. Our interest is the $t_{obs} = -1.879$.

6. The same procedure is used for entering Table A.3 of Appendix A, with $df = 60$ and the .05 level of significance for a one-tailed test. The critical value of $t = -1.671$ in this case. Our observed $t = -1.879$ equals or exceeds this value and therefore H_o may be rejected at the .05 level. It should be noted that the last table generated showed two-tailed significance of .065. We would halve this two-tailed value, or $.065/2 = .0325$ for a one-tailed interpretation. This one-tailed probability is clearly equal to or less than .05.

7. The fact that we had to create fictitious ages for this example yielded a slightly smaller standard error of the mean of .35 instead of .38. This smaller standard error term yielded a slightly larger observed t value $= -1.879$ instead of -1.84 in the manually computed example. However, there are sufficient similarities between the two examples to show how this problem might be resolved if we were to use an *SPSS* program for actual data.

(continued)

(*continued*)

Frequencies
(DataSet0)

Statistics

age

N	Valid	61
	Missing	0

age

		Frequency	Percent	Valid Percent	Cumulative Percent
Valid	10.00	8	13.1	13.1	13.1
	11.00	3	4.9	4.9	18.0
	12.00	8	13.1	13.1	31.1
	13.00	3	4.9	4.9	36.1
	14.00	10	16.4	16.4	52.5
	15.00	5	8.2	8.2	60.7
	16.00	4	6.6	6.6	67.2
	17.00	15	24.6	24.6	91.8
	18.00	2	3.3	3.3	95.1
	19.00	3	4.9	4.9	100.0
	Total	61	100.0	100.0	

T–Test
(DataSet0)

One-Sample Statistics

	N	Mean	Std. Deviation	Std. Error Mean
age	61	14.3443	2.72571	.34899

One-Sample Test

	Test value = 15					
					95% Confident Interval of the Difference	
	t	*df*	Sig.(2-tailed)	Mean Difference	lower	upper
age	−1.879	60	.065	−.65574	−1.3538	.0423

is needed for interpretive purposes. ± signs may be assigned to these critical *t* values, depending on whether one-tailed (directional) or two-tailed (nondirectional) tests of hypotheses are being made.

COMING OR NOT COMING FROM THE SAME POPULATIONS   Sometimes, interpretations of statistical test results are phrased in seemingly unusual language. This phraseology might go something like this: "We reject the null hypothesis and conclude that our sample comes from a different population." Another way of saying this is that "The two means (i.e., $\overline{X}$ and μ) come from the same (or different) populations." Both of these phrases are confusing to students. Remember that statistical inference is the process of saying something about a population of elements based upon a sample drawn from that population. The sample mean, $\overline{X}$, is considered the best estimate of the hypothesized population mean, μ. When we conduct t or Z tests and find that the two mean values differ from one another, saying that one mean does not come from the same population as the other mean is the same as saying the two means differ in a statistically significant sense.

ASSUMPTIONS, ADVANTAGES, AND DISADVANTAGES OF THE t TEST AND Z TEST   The assumptions of the t and Z tests include (1) randomness; (2) the interval level of measurement underlying the characteristic measured; and (3) an approximately normal distribution associated with the observed scores.

The primary advantages of the t and Z tests are: (1) they are easy to use; (2) tables of critical t and Z values exist for convenient interpretations of observed t and Z values; (3) there are no sample size restrictions; (4) these tests are well known and conventionally applied in social scientific work; and (5) these tests have high power for rejecting false null hypotheses. Several disadvantages are that some researchers may take issue with applying interval-level statistical tests to attitudinal data, which is most often measured according to ordinal scales. These tests assume normality, but seldom in actual research practice is normality achieved. If researchers have access to *SPSS* software or some comparable data analysis package, they can test for kurtosis and skewness and determine whether normality exists for particular distributions of elements. Also, randomness is seldom achieved. If one or more assumptions underlying these tests are violated, then caution should be exercised when interpreting research findings. This is especially crucial if policy decision making is going to proceed on the basis of statistical test results.

Another weakness of these tests is that whenever deviant or outlier scores are present in a distribution, some distortion in statistical output will occur. Furthermore, whenever large samples of elements are studied, where N's > 500, standard error terms in statistical formulae are substantially reduced. Larger sample sizes usually mean much smaller standard error terms, which in turn inflate resulting observed statistical values. Therefore, while a statistically significant difference between a sample mean and hypothesized population mean may be disclosed, the substantive importance of this difference may be of little or no value. Good judgment is required to decide when to use statistical tests, whether assumptions are met, and how resulting findings ought to be interpreted. This is why many persons refer to statistical decision making as an "art."

TWO-SAMPLE TESTS: INDEPENDENT SAMPLES

Two-sample tests of significance are designed to determine whether two independent samples come from the same population relating to some measured characteristic. Are two sample means the same or different statistically? The two samples are either independent or related. Independent samples may be drawn at different times or created as subsamples from a single sample of elements. Related samples may involve persons in before-after experiments, matched pairs of elements, or two groups related through frequency distribution control matching. This section presents two tests: (1) the t test for determining the significance of difference between means; and (2) the Sandler A statistic, a two-related sample test.

The *t* Test for Differences Between Means

The **t test for differences between means** is a two-sample extension of the *t* test for a single sample described in the previous section. Therefore, almost all assumptions, advantages, and disadvantages underlying this procedure are the same as those that apply for single-sample situations. An example of the *t* test for differences between means is provided below.

James E. Lange, Mark B. Johnson, and Robert B. Voas (2005) conducted a study of racial profiling. Specifically, these investigators studied drivers on the New Jersey Turnpike. New Jersey State Troopers were known for stopping drivers who were speeding. Conversations with New Jersey State Troopers disclosed that troopers would tend to stop any speeder exceeding 15 miles per hour (mph) over the posted speed limit. Thus, if a driver were traveling at 80 mph in a 65 mph zone, he/she would be stopped and ticketed for speeding. Those exceeding the speed limit of 65 mph by 14 or fewer mph would not be stopped, according to state trooper authorities interviewed. Those traveling at speeds exceeding the posted speed limit of 65 mph but not equaling or exceeding 15 mph above this limit were designated as nonspeeders. Digital cameras posted strategically at different points along the New Jersey Turnpike would photograph both speeders and nonspeeders, so that they could be identified by police officers later. Interestingly, Lange, Johnson, and Voas found that troopers made frequent stops of nonspeeders as well as speeders. It is important to note that routinely, troopers would not stop nonspeeders as frequently as speeders, despite the fact that both types of drivers were exceeding the speed limit and any trooper stop of these vehicles would be justified.

Suppose that Lange, Johnson, and Voas wanted to know whether there were greater numbers of minority drivers among nonspeeders stopped by troopers and/or that minority drivers compared with whites were treated more harshly. If this outcome occurred, it might be evidence of possible racial profiling by the New Jersey State Troopers. Using some hypothetical information, suppose Lange, Johnson, and Voas obtained data from two samples of nonspeeders. Nonspeeder stops would be considered discretionary and more likely indicative of possible bias on the part of troopers concerning one's race or ethnicity. Suppose one sample of nonspeeders consisted of 55 whites, while the other sample of nonspeeders consisted of 45 minority motorists. Suppose Lange, Johnson, and Voas calculated the average speeds for both samples of drivers to determine if there were significant differences between them. It might be speculated that if such stops by New Jersey troopers of nonspeeders according to white/minority status showed significant differences in average speeds preceding such stops, an inference might be made whether racial profiling was occurring. Specifically, these researchers would suspect racial profiling was occurring if average speeds of minority nonspeeders were significantly less than average speeds of white nonspeeders. The following hypothesis set is used:

H_o: *White nonspeeders have the same or lower average speeds than minority nonspeeders.*

H_1: *White nonspeeders have higher average speeds than minority nonspeeders.*

$P \leq .01$ (one-tailed test)

The wording of these hypotheses is important. The null hypothesis must be worded in such a way that if it is rejected, a specific research hypothesis believed true by these researchers will be supported. The level of significance was set at .01. Average speeds were calculated for both white and minority nonspeeders, where $\overline{X}_1$ was the mean speed for the sample of white nonspeeders, and $\overline{X}_2$ was the mean speed for the sample of minority motorists. In symbolic terms, the hypotheses being tested were estimates of average population speeds among nonspeeders for both whites and minorities. The following hypothesis set illustrates the hypotheses tested:

$H_o: \mu_1 \leq \mu_2$ estimated by $\overline{X}_1 \leq \overline{X}_2$

$H_1: \mu_1 > \mu_2$ estimated by $\overline{X}_1 > \overline{X}_2$

$P \leq .01$ (one-tailed test)

The following hypothetical information is available from the collected data:

$\overline{X}_1 = 76.6$	$s_1 = 4.23$	$N_1 = 55$
$\overline{X}_2 = 69.4$	$s_2 = 3.71$	$N_2 = 45$

With this information, a t test for the significance of difference between means is applied by using the following formula:

$$t = \frac{\overline{X}_1 - \overline{X}_2}{s_{\overline{x}_1 - \overline{x}_2}}$$

or

$$t = \frac{\overline{X}_1 - \overline{X}_2}{\sqrt{\dfrac{s_1^2}{N_1} + \dfrac{s_2^2}{N_2}}}$$

where

N_1 and N_2 are the two sample sizes

$\overline{X}_1$ and $\overline{X}_2$ are the two sample means

$s_{\overline{x}_1} - s_{\overline{x}_2}$ are the standard error of the difference between two means.

s_1^2 and s_2^2 are the two sample variances

The **standard error of the difference between two means** functions in precisely the same way as does the standard error of the mean for a single sample. In this case, there are two samples being compared. Thus, there are two sources of sampling error. Sampling error comes from sample 1 and from sample 2 and is combined or "pooled" into the denominator term. Using the given values from the present problem, we can now solve for t:

$$t = \frac{76.6 - 69.4}{\sqrt{\dfrac{(4.23)^2}{55} + \dfrac{(3.71)^2}{45}}}$$

$$t_{obs} = \frac{7.2}{\sqrt{\dfrac{17.89}{55} + \dfrac{13.76}{45}}}$$

$$t_{obs} = t = \frac{7.2}{\sqrt{.6312}} = \frac{7.2}{.79}$$

$$t_{obs} = 9.114$$

The observed value of $t = 9.114$. Table A.3, Appendix A, p. 446–447 is entered to determine the significance of this t_{obs}. Since we are dealing with two samples instead of one, df are calculated differently. In this case, df are computed as follows:

$$df \text{ for two-sample case} = (N_1 - 1) + (N_2 - 1)$$

BOX 8.2
SPSS Alternative Application

The example above was based on hypothetical data, where means were artificially created to illustrate how the observed *t* was computed and the hypotheses were tested. In this example for *SPSS* users, suppose we have 16 female and 17 male prison inmates convicted of various offenses. Further suppose that we have ascribed a crime severity score to their respective conviction offenses. These scores associated with gender are shown below.

N	Gender	Crimesevertity	*N*	Gender	Crimesevertity
1	1.00	33.00	18	2.00	42.00
2	1.00	31.00	19	2.00	40.00
3	1.00	35.00	20	2.00	45.00
4	1.00	37.00	21	2.00	43.00
5	1.00	39.00	22	2.00	40.00
6	1.00	42.00	23	2.00	40.00
7	1.00	30.00	24	2.00	35.00
8	1.00	28.00	25	2.00	28.00
9	1.00	28.00	26	2.00	39.00
10	1.00	31.00	27	2.00	42.00
11	1.00	36.00	28	2.00	43.00
12	1.00	45.00	29	2.00	50.00
13	1.00	41.00	30	2.00	46.00
14	1.00	42.00	31	2.00	45.00
15	1.00	37.00	32	2.00	29.00
16	1.00	36.00	33	2.00	30.00
17	2.00	38.00			

Based on this information, we will illustrate how *SPSS* can analyze these data and yield a *t* value.

1. Activate your *SPSS* program and go to the Data Editor window. Using the "Variable View" at the bottom of the screen, label the first "var" column "Gender" and the second "var" column "Crimeseverity." Going back to the Data View, these newly named variables head the two columns as "Gender" and "Crimeseverity." Starting with the "Gender" column, type in 16 "1" values for female, and 17 "2" values for male. Next, go to the "Crimeseverity" column and type in the numbers as shown in the table, beginning with 33, 31, 35, and so on, ending with 30. You should now have 33 numbers entered.

2. Click on "Analyze," then "Compare Means," then "Independent-Samples *T* Test." This will bring up a screen with three windows. The left-hand window contains "Gender" and "Crimeseverity." Highlight "Gender" and use the arrow to move it to the "Grouping Variable." Highlight the Grouping Variable and this reveals a new screen with two empty windows: Group 1 and Group 2. Enter a "1" in the Group 1 window and a "2" in the Group 2 window. Click "Continue." This action will now show the original screen with the Grouping Variable indicated as Gender (1 2).

3. Highlight "Crimeseverity" and use the arrow to move it to the right-hand window "Test variable(s)." Click on "OK."

4. This action will yield several summary tables. The two most relevant tables for your use are the Group Statistics table and the Independent Samples Test table. The Group Statistics table shows Gender, *N*, means, standard deviations, and standard error terms. This table confirms that you

(continued)

(*continued*)

have 16 "1"s or females and 17 "2"s or males. The means are 35.6875 and 40.4706 respectively. The standard deviations and standard error terms are also displayed.

Group Statistics

	Gender	N	Mean	Std. Deviation	Std.Error Mean
VAR00001	1.00	16	35.6875	5.23729	1.30932
	2.00	17	40.4706	6.74646	1.63626

Independent Samples Test

		t-Test for equality of means			
		t	df	sig. (2-tailed)	Mean difference
VAR00001	Equal variances assumed	−2.265	31	.031	−4.78309
	Equal variances not assumed	−2.282	29.951	.030	−4.78309

5. Examine the Independent Samples Test table. Two *t* observed values are displayed: −2.265 and −2.282. These *t* values indicate that the two means differ and that the first mean is smaller than the second one. Had we predicted that female inmates would have lower crime severity scores, which is logical and consistent with the literature, we would know initially that at least the correct direction of mean difference had been predicted. Notice also in this table that the two observed *t* values are for situations where either equal variances are assumed or not assumed. Where equal variances are not assumed, slightly larger *t* values are yielded compared with *t* values yielded under the "equal variances" assumption. Let's proceed on the assumption that the variances for the two samples are not equal.

6. The table shows $df = 31$ as well as a two-tailed probability of .030 under the "unequal variances" assumption. This probability is for a two-tailed, nondirectional hypothesis test. Had we made a nondirectional test of the hypothesis at the .05 level that females and males differ in the crime severity of their conviction offenses, we would first locate the critical value of *t* for a two-tailed test from Table A.3 in Appendix A. Entering this table with 31 *df* would put us on the 30 *df* line. Where 30 *df* intersects with the two-tailed probability of .05 defines the critical value of *t*, which is ±2.042. With this information, we could reject the null hypothesis that the means are equal and conclude that they are unequal. The $t_{obs} = -2.282$ is equal to or larger than the two-tailed critical value of $t = \pm 2.042$ Had a directional prediction been made and we had forecast in our research hypothesis that female inmates would have lower crime severity scores associated with their conviction offenses, then we would have the probability shown in the above table, or .030/2 = .015. Since the correct directional prediction occurred concerning their respective means, the null hypothesis would have been rejected and H_1 would have been supported at $P \leq .05$.

In this instance, we have $(55 - 1) + (45 - 1) = 54 + 44 = 98$ *df*. With this *df*, we search the left-hand column seeking 98 *df*. There is no 98 *df*, although 98 *df* lies between 60 *df* and 120 *df*. Therefore, we select the smaller *df* or 60 *df* to find our critical value of *t*. We locate the level of significance, $P \leq .01$ (one-tailed test) across the top of the table, and where this probability intersects with $df = 60$ defines the critical value of t that must be equaled or exceeded by the observed t value. This critical t value (t_{cv}) = 2.390. Under our research hypothesis, H_1, it was predicted that $\overline{X}_1$ would be greater than $\overline{X}_2$. We observe that a correct directional prediction was made. Is the difference between means significant? Does the $t_{obs} = 9.114$ equal or exceed the critical t value of 2.390? Yes. Thus, H_o is rejected and H_1 is supported, tentatively concluding that minority nonspeeders are stopped and ticketed at speeds significantly lower than for white nonspeeders. This finding supports the idea that state troopers stop minority nonspeeders and ticket them at significantly lower speeds compared with white nonspeeders. This finding is significant at the .01 level of significance. There is 1 chance in a 100 that we could be wrong in making this conclusion and supporting H_1.

Had a two-tailed, nondirectional test been made of the same hypotheses, the nondirectional critical t value, from Table A.3, would be 2.660, slightly larger than the one-tailed t critical value of 2.390. Again, the null hypothesis would have been rejected because the magnitude of the observed $t = 9.114$ equaled or exceeded the critical value required.

ASSUMPTIONS, ADVANTAGES, AND DISADVANTAGES OF THE *t* TEST   The assumptions of the t test for differences between means are: (1) randomness; (2) the interval level of measurement; (3) independent samples; (4) normally distributed sets of scores for both groups; and (5) equal sample variances. The "equal sample variances" assumption is frequently relaxed in t test two-sample applications. A formula for pooled variances exists, although the results of this formula yield t values that are negligible and will not be illustrated here. In the *SPSS* example in Box 8.2, for instance, the two t values where equal variances were assumed and not assumed were -2.265 and -2.282 respectively.

The advantages of the t test are that (1) it is well known and widely applied; (2) it is quick and easy to interpret using tabled values; (3) it has no sample size restrictions; and (4) it is the most powerful test for differences between two independent samples. The t test for differences between means also functions as a standard against which several nonparametric tests of significance are compared.

Among the t test's disadvantages are the fact that the interval level of measurement is assumed. Because so much attitudinal information is analyzed according to ordinal scales, the t test is frequently applied despite this level-of-measurement assumption violation. In most social science research, the t application in these instances is conventional and accepted. However, test outcomes should be interpreted cautiously and conservatively. Despite one or more assumption violations, the t test has been demonstrably **robust**. **Robustness** is the ability of a test to yield decisions about hypotheses tested despite one or more assumption violations. Thus, the robustness argument is sometimes advanced to defend the use of tests such as the t test when some of its assumptions are violated by the data analyzed.

TWO WAYS OF DRAWING ERRONEOUS CONCLUSIONS ABOUT *t* TEST RESULTS   When observed t values are significant, this means that the two sample means are different. The inference is that the two population means, μ_1 and μ_2, are also different since the two sample means represent them. This may or may not be an accurate inference. Two possible erroneous conclusions about sample mean differences may be made. Suppose we had information relating to two population distributions with different μ's, as shown in Figure 8.1.

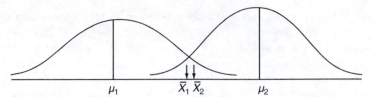

FIGURE 8.1 **Two Widely Different Population Distributions with Similar Sample Means**

Notice that two μ values have been indicated for the two population means. There is also some overlap of these two distributions. Two sample means have been identified and located adjacent to one another in both population distribution tails. For the population distribution with μ_1, the sample mean, $\overline{X}_1$, occurs in the far right tail of it. A second sample mean, $\overline{X}_2$, is located in the far left tail of its distribution with μ_2. These sample means are considered representative of their respective population means. But we can see in Figure 8.1 that the sample means are located far away from their respective μ values. If we were to apply the t test to these two sample means, we would likely fail to reject the null hypothesis that says the two population means are the same. This would be an erroneous conclusion because we can see that the two population means are very different. But since we don't know either population mean value, we rely on sample means to represent these values instead. A level of significance is always used in hypothesis tests, therefore. If we were to reject a null hypothesis that two populations are the same based on different sample means, there would always be a .05, .01, or .001 chance or probability that we might be wrong in making such a conclusion. This fact underscores the importance of using probabilities for all hypothesis tests. There is always the possibility that we could be wrong in deciding to reject null hypotheses when they are true and should not be rejected.

An alternative scenario we may face is shown in Figure 8.2. Figure 8.2 shows two population means that are almost the same. In this case, however, the two sample means that represent them are found in the far left and far right tails of these respective distributions. Both sample means are poor estimates of their respective population parameters. But we don't know this because we don't know each μ value. If we tested the significance of difference between the two sample means, our tentative conclusion would be that the population μ's are also different. The level of significance or probability at which the hypothesis is tested would

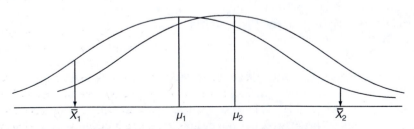

FIGURE 8.2 **Two Similar Population Distributions with Widely Different Sample Means**

protect us, however. There would always be some chance that we could be wrong in our conclusion about the mean differences. For instance, for the two sample means shown in Figure 8.2, we would probably reject H_o that the two population μ's are the same and conclude H_1 that the μ's are different, but there would be a 5 percent or 1 percent chance of being wrong in making this decision. This is why levels of significance always accompany hypothesis sets and statistical decision making. This is one reason why criminologists continue to re-examine the same types of problems over and over, seeking more consistent and complete information about the variables they study. Over time, some consistency emerges as our certainty about relations between variables increases.

When more than two samples are being compared, such as k-sample comparisons, our problems illustrated in Figure 8.1 and 8.2 are compounded. In a later section of this chapter, we will examine some k-sample tests of significance. Similar types of problems accompany these k-sample tests just like two-sample tests.

TWO-SAMPLE TESTS: RELATED SAMPLES

The Sandler *A* Test for Related Samples

A two-sample statistical test designed for related-sample applications is the **Sandler *A* test**. The Sandler *A* test is applied whenever researchers have related samples either through matched pairs of elements or when persons act as their own controls in before-after experiments. The *A* test is designed to determine significant differences between related sets of scores when those scores have been derived from an interval-level variable. A hypothetical example is provided below.

Sally Simpson, Leana Bouffard, Joel Garner, and Laura Hickman (2006) studied the influence of legal reform on domestic violence cases. These investigators gained access to Battered Spouse Reports from Maryland over a given time interval of 7 years. Simpson et al. found that various legislative changes expanded police powers in making arrests in domestic violence situations. Also, police department policy changes were significant in reducing the incidence of spousal assault incidents over time. These policy changes and legislative initiatives came at a time when mandatory arrest policies went into effect for many police departments. That is, whenever a domestic violence incident was reported to police and they responded to the incident, it was standard protocol for investigating officers to make a mandatory arrest of one spouse or the other. More often than not, the male in the family was arrested and charged with domestic violence or spousal assault. During the intervening period between arrest and trial, the arrested spouse would be exposed to various treatments, such as counseling and anger management. In many instances, such intervention techniques proved useful in reducing the incidence of domestic violence.

Suppose these investigators wanted to determine the impact of an anger-management technique on a group of spousal abusers, persons who were arrested for domestic violence. Suppose a sample of 20 spousal abusers was selected and subjected to an intervention designed to raise their level of awareness of their partner's feelings and needs. Simpson et al. might have designed a counseling and anger-management program which would subject these 20 spousal abusers to experiences calculated to increase their empathy with their abused spouses. Let's assume that between January 2007 and June 2008, 20 spousal abusers engaged in a program to heighten their level of awareness of others and their needs. These investigators had devised an interval-level scale to measure spousal abusers' amenability to change, so that they could settle their differences in nonviolent ways. Such a scale might be labeled the Compatibility Index (CI). By exposing these spousal abusers to an 18-month program and computing their CI scores both before and after the intervention program, we might have the following scores as shown in Table 8.2. The following hypothesis set might be tested by applying Sandler's A test:

H_o: There is no difference among 20 spousal abusers on their CI scores before and after exposure to a spousal abuse intervention program; if there is a difference, CI scores will be lower after the program.

H_1: CI scores for 20 spousal abusers will be higher following a spousal abuse intervention program.

$P \leq .01$ (one-tailed test)

A one-tailed or directional test at the .01 level of significance is being made here, since these researchers anticipate that the CI test scores for this sample will increase over time as the result of the spousal abuse intervention program. The larger the score on this CI, the more likely spousal abusers would be to resolve conflicts in nonviolent ways and avoid

TABLE 8.2 Compatibility Index Scores for 20 Spousal Abusers, 2007–2008, Before and After a Spousal Abuser Intervention Program

Spouse Arrestee	Year 2007	2008	Difference (D)	D^2
1	41	49	+8	64
2	22	26	+4	16
3	16	30	+14	196
4	40	37	−3	9
5	29	29	0	0
6	36	45	+9	81
7	24	29	+5	25
8	16	15	−1	1
9	22	32	+10	100
10	45	40	−5	25
11	32	35	+3	9
12	18	20	+2	4
13	21	33	+11	121
14	25	50	+25	625
15	25	30	+5	25
16	34	40	+6	36
17	18	30	+12	144
18	22	31	+9	81
19	48	40	−8	64
20	35	36	+1	1
Totals			$\Sigma D = 107$	$\Sigma D^2 = 1{,}627$

abusing their spouses. The before-after results for these 20 spousal abusers are shown in Table 8.2.

Table 8.2 is constructed as follows. Each spousal abuser's score for both time periods, 2007 and 2008, is placed in the two "Year" columns as shown. Each pair of scores is examined, and the difference between each pair is placed in the next column to the right, D. Each of these differences is squared and placed in the D^2 column. Both the D and D^2 columns are summed. The Sandler A test is applied by using the following formula:

$$A = \frac{\Sigma D^2}{(\Sigma D)^2}$$

Using the values from Table 8.2, we may calculate A_{obs} as follows:

$$A_{obs} = \frac{1,627}{(107)^2} = \frac{1,627}{11,449}$$

$$= .142$$

The $A_{obs} = .142$. In order to interpret the significance of A, we must turn to Table A.18 of Appendix A, p. 460, and determine the critical value of A. Table A.18 contains critical values of A for different significance levels and for one- and two-tailed tests. The left-hand column contains degrees of freedom (df), defined as $N - 1$, where $N =$ the total number of pairs of scores. Since the pairs of scores $= 20, 20 - 1 = 19\ df$. With 19 df down the left-hand side of the table, we move across the top of the table until we find the one-tailed level of significance associated with our hypothesis test, $P \le .01$. In this case, the critical value of A is .197. If our observed A (A_{obs}) is equal to or smaller than the one shown in the body of the table, we may reject the null hypothesis and support H_1. In this case, our $A_{obs} = .142$ which is equal to or smaller than the critical value of $A = .197$. We may reject H_o and conclude tentatively that at least for this sample of spousal abusers, their CI scores improved significantly between 2007 and 2008.

It is apparent from the score changes noted in column D in Table 8.2 that the scores between the years 2007 and 2008 are consistent with the direction predicted under our research hypothesis (H_1). Investigators making one-tailed hypothesis tests should always check first to see whether they have predicted score changes in the direction specified under the research hypothesis. The fact that most score changes were positive indicates that directionally, at least, the score differences were consistent with what was predicted under H_1. The Sandler A test answered the question about whether these score changes were significant statistically. In this case, they were significant.

ASSUMPTIONS, ADVANTAGES, AND DISADVANTAGES OF THE SANDLER A STATISTIC The assumptions underlying the application of the A test are: (1) randomness; (2) interval level of measurement underlying the scores analyzed; (3) related samples; (4) normality of distribution for both sets of scores.

The major advantages of Sandler's A statistic are that (1) it is quick and easy to apply; (2) a table exists for a rapid determination of its significance; (3) it applies to related samples where the scores are measured according to an interval scale; (4) there are no sample size restrictions; and (5) the A test exhibits test power equivalent with the t test. Since the t test assumes independent samples, the A test is an excellent alternative procedure for determining differences between two samples whenever the samples are related and not independent. The

BOX 8.3

SPSS Alternative Applications

While no Sandler A procedure exists for testing related-sample score differences at the interval level of measurement, there is a paired-sample t test described in *SPSS*. The procedural steps are outlined below.

1. Activate your *SPSS* software. Go to *SPSS* Data Editor and enter both columns of values from Table 8.2., beginning with the first "var" column. Enter all 20 values, beginning with 41, 22, 16, and so on, until 35 is reached. Repeat this process, but in the second "var" column. Enter 49, 26, 30, 37, and so on, until the last score of 36 is entered. You should now have two variables, VAR00001 and VAR00002 with 20 scores in each column.
2. Click on "Analyze," then "Compare Means," then "**Paired-Samples T Test**." This action brings up a screen with two windows. The left window contains VAR00001 and VAR00002. Highlight both of these variables and use the arrow to move both to the right-hand window, "Paired Variables." Click "OK."
3. This action generates several summary tables. The first summary table shows the means for VAR00001 (28.45) and VAR00002 (33.85). A second table, Paired Samples Correlation, may be ignored. A third table, "Paired Samples Test," contains a t value, -3.223. The fourth table contains a two-tailed significance level for t, which is .004. This significance value may be compared with the level of significance at which your hypothesis is being tested. The level of significance being used for the hypothesis set test in the above example was .01 for a one-tailed test. Since our two-tailed observed t value for the paired-samples t test was .004, doubling this probability $(.004)(2) = .008$, would yield the one-tailed probability. Again, consistent with the Sandler A statistic result, we would have rejected H_o at the .01 level of significance. The paired-samples t test is very similar to the Sandler A statistic, therefore, in that very similar findings are yielded by applying either test.

primary disadvantage of A test is the fact that it requires data measured according to an interval scale. Thus, the A statistic's use with attitudinal data might be limited. Since the t test is often applied conventionally to attitudinal data, however, this restriction is not especially strong. Any applications to data measured according to ordinal-level data should be interpreted with caution in any case.

k-SAMPLE TESTS OF SIGNIFICANCE

k-sample tests of significance technically apply to two or more samples of elements. In this text, however, k refers to three or more samples, since specific two-sample tests and several other tests have already been presented. It is possible to apply any k-sample test to a two-sample situation. However, k-sample procedures typically involve more complex computations compared with tests designed specifically for two samples.

In this section, two k-sample tests are illustrated. The first is the F test for analysis of variance, or simply the F test. This test determines whether k independent samples differ on some interval-level dependent variable. Thus, the F test would be suitable if we were examining average professionalism differences among several samples of police officers from different divisions; differences in the average use of force to control inmate behavior among correctional officer samples taken from federal, state, or county facilities; assessing average sentencing-disparity variations among different samples of judges whose courts have different sentencing schemes. There are many uses of the F test for analysis of variance.

A second procedure for k-sample situations is the two-way analysis of variance. This test is an extension of the F test, and it involves a third variable to be controlled. Besides answering questions about whether k groups differ on some dependent variable, it also answers whether the addition of a second independent variable has any impact upon a dependent variable, and whether the second independent variable interacts with the first independent variable to enhance its predictive power relative to the dependent variable. Thus, two-way analysis of variance enhances the explanatory power of two independent variables in relation to a dependent variable, as well as the interaction effects of the two independent variables operating together to influence a dependent variable.

Several stringent assumptions are associated with both the F test for analysis of variance and two-way analysis of variance. One of these assumptions is homogeneity of variance or equal variances. There are many tests to measure whether k-sample variances are equal. Two of these, the Hartley F_{max} test and the Cochran C test, will be described.

Finally, once an overall determination has been made that a significant difference exists somewhere between k sample means following an F-test application, it is necessary to probe for differences between all pairs of sample means to see which pairs differ significantly. The F test merely answers whether a difference between all means exists somewhere. It doesn't answer which mean differences are significant. The presumption is that if an overall F value is significant, then at least the largest and smallest sample means are different. But what about difference between the largest and next smallest sample mean? What about the difference between the smallest and second largest sample mean? Two postmortem tests used as probes are the Newman–Keuls procedure and the Scheffé procedure. These are alternative k-sample probes applied whenever a significant F value is observed. It answers the question of where the significant mean differences occur. Each of these procedures will be explained with accompanying illustrations.

The *F* Test for Analysis of Variance

The ***F* test for analysis of variance** is a procedure that examines k samples and determines whether a significant difference exists between them on some interval-level characteristic. Actually, the F test is an extension of the t test discussed earlier in this chapter. Therefore, when the researcher has more than two samples of elements and is examining differences among them on some interval-level characteristic, one possible option might be to examine differences between two groups at a time with the t test. But researchers would be faced with multiple applications of the t test in order to examine all of these differences between pairs of sample means. For example, if investigators were examining differences among eight groups, there would be the following number of separate two-sample t tests required:

$$\frac{k(k-1)}{2}$$

where $k =$ the number of sample means

Therefore, there would be $(8)(8-1)/2 = 56/2 = 28$ different t tests to be computed. The results of 28 separate t tests would tell researchers which groups differed from one another, but a great amount of time would be spent in tedious computational work. Fortunately, a procedure is available that examines all of these mean differences simultaneously. This procedure is the F test. The F test answers the following question: Does a significant difference exist anywhere among k samples on the variable measured? The answer to the question is either "Yes" or "No." The F test doesn't specify where differences between groups are found, just that there are differences or not among the groups. An example of the application of the F test is provided below.

Mark J. Strickland (2006) studied stress among correctional officers. He found that correctional officer stress arises for a variety of reasons. There are health risks. Corrections officers are exposed to deadly diseases on a daily basis, such as tuberculosis and AIDS. They may lack support from their supervisors or at least think that they lack such support. They work around dangerous offenders who have the capability of harming them in different ways. Many other sources of stress have been identified. Stress often leads to burnout, which may cause some correctional officers to have low morale or leave corrections for a different kind of work.

Suppose Strickland wanted to study how correctional officer stress might be affected by the dangerousness of the institution where different officers are employed. Suppose he identified four different types of institutions, arranged according to supermax, maximum security, medium security, and minimum security. Each of these designations suggests that offenders who pose varying degrees of dangerousness might be placed in one type of institution or another. For example, the most dangerous offenders are often placed in supermax facilities, which are sometimes referred to as admin max or maxi-maxi facilities. These inmates would pose the greatest risk to correctional officers who work around them. Next might be maximum-security facilities. These facilities also contain dangerous offenders, but they do not require the amount of control and supervision required of those offenders placed in supermax facilities. A third type of institution houses medium-security inmates. These may include dangerous offenders, but their behaviors are such that they only need moderate amounts of control. Finally, a fourth type of institution houses minimum-security inmates, who are considered the least dangerous. These types of institutions are gradated and shown below.

Least Dangerous			Most Dangerous
Minimum	Medium	Maximum	Supermax

Suppose Strickland were able to obtain samples of correctional officers from each of these four types of institutions. Further suppose that Strickland administered a Stress Index (SI) to correctional officers at all four facilities. The SI might result in a maximum of 30 points, indicative of high stress levels, while 0 points would be indicative of no stress or low stress levels. Based upon Strickland's theorizing about stress levels of correctional officers and the dangerousness of the institutions to which they are assigned, he might hypothesize the following:

H_0: *There is no difference in stress levels among four samples of correctional officers assigned to prisons that vary according to the dangerousness of inmates.*

H_1: *There is a difference in stress levels among four samples of correctional officers assigned to prisons that vary according to the dangerousness of inmates.*

$P \leq .01$ (two-tailed test)

Table 8.3 shows hypothetical distributions of correctional officers from each of four types of prisons, where $N_1 = 18, N_2 = 19, N_3 = 14,$ and $N_4 = 15$. Raw scores on the SI measure are designated for each of the samples, together with the computation of the four sample means as shown. Additional computational work in Table 8.3 includes determining the sums of

TABLE 8.3   Hypothetical Distribution of Correctional Officers from Four Different Correctional Institutions and Stress Index Scores

Institution							
Supermax ($N_1 = 18$)		Maximum ($N_2 = 19$)		Medium ($N_3 = 14$)		Minimum ($N_4 = 15$)	
X_1	X_1^2	X_2	X_2^2	X_3	X_3^2	X_4	X_4^2
22	484	19	361	19	361	3	9
19	361	14	196	18	81	9	81
14	196	13	169	12	144	12	144
24	576	22	484	12	144	9	81
21	441	28	784	14	196	7	49
20	400	17	289	12	144	18	324
24	576	14	196	10	100	7	49
23	529	15	225	7	49	9	81
17	289	12	144	9	81	14	196
16	256	9	81	11	121	10	100
29	841	19	361	12	144	9	81
15	225	22	484	21	441	8	64
26	676	20	400	11	121	8	64
23	529	19	361	13	169	10	100
23	529	17	289			11	121
28	784	11	121				
21	441	14	196				
25	625	17	289				
		17	289				

$\Sigma X_1 = 390$ $\Sigma X_1^2 = 8758$ $\Sigma X_2 = 319$ $\Sigma X_2^2 = 5719$ $\Sigma X_3 = 181$ $\Sigma X_3^2 = 2539$ $\Sigma X_4 = 144$ $\Sigma X_4^2 = 1544$

$\overline{X}_1 = 21.7$ $\overline{X}_2 = 16.8$ $\overline{X}_3 = 12.9$ $\overline{X}_4 = 9.6$

$\overline{X}_T = 15.7$

scores and sums of all squared scores for the four samples. Finally, a grand mean or mean of means has been calculated.

An inspection of the different sample means in Table 8.3 shows that stress scores vary from one type of prison to the next, moving from left to right, which is consistent with Strickland's predictions about stress and prison dangerousness. In fact, stress levels, as measured by the SI, appear to decline as the dangerousness of the prison declines as well. The main question to be answered by the F test is whether there is a statistically significant difference in SI scores among these four samples of correctional officers. The mean differences indicate differences between the officer groups. But are these differences significant statistically? In order to answer this question, we must construct an **analysis-of-variance summary table (ANOVA)** such as that shown in Table 8.4.

An examination of the ANOVA summary in Table 8.4 shows two sources of variation in the scores from Table 8.3. These two sources are **between-group variation** and **within-group**

TABLE 8.4 Analysis-of-Variance (ANOVA) Summary Table

Source of Variation	SS	df [a]	MS	F_{obs} [b]
Between Groups	1329.0	3	443.0	26.69
	(SS_{bet})	(df_{bet})	(MS_{bet})	
Within Groups	1031.7	62	16.6	
	(SS_{within})	(df_{within})	(MS_{within})	
Total	2360.7	65		
	(SS_{total})	(df_{total})		

[a] Between-groups $df = k - 1$ where $k =$ the number of groups; within-groups $df = \Sigma(N_k - 1)$, where $N_k =$ each sample size; and total $df = \Sigma N_k - 1$.

[b] $F_{obs} = MS_{bet}/MS_{within} = 443/16.6 = 26.69$.

variation. Between-group variation refers to differences in scores between k samples. The fact that there are average SI differences means that there is some between-group variation. If all of the four group means were identical, there would be no between-group variation. Whenever k groups are being compared, this scenario almost never occurs. There is always some between-group variation.

Within-group variation exists when scores within any given sample differ from one another. By inspecting the scores in Table 8.3, we can see that individual raw scores vary within each group. This means that there is some within-group variation. It is extremely unlikely that all persons in any given group would have the same score on any variable we might administer. Thus, for almost every application of the F test, there is always some between-group and within-group variation. Also, for both between- and within-group variation, there are **sums of squares** (SS), **degrees of freedom** (df), and **mean squares** (MS) to be computed. After computing these values, we determine an **F ratio**, which is found in the upper right-hand corner of the ANOVA summary in Table 8.4. This F ratio becomes our $F_{observed}$ for deciding whether there are significant differences among the four samples of officers according to their CI scores. But there is considerable work to do before reaching that point, however.

With the computations we have made and our knowledge of the four sample means, the grand mean, and individual sample sizes from Table 8.3, we may solve for the various values across the top of Table 8.4. We will solve for these values systematically, moving from left to right, across the top of the table. The first set of values we must determine is in a column, SS. SS refers to the sums of squares. We must calculate the sums of squares for both between and within groups. These are designated respectively as SS_{bet} and SS_{within}. Once we have calculated these values, their sum will become SS_{total}. Each of these values is calculated as shown below. Sums of squares for between groups is:

$$SS_{bet} = \Sigma N_k (\overline{X}_k - \overline{X}_T)^2$$

where

$N_k =$ sample size for the kth sample

$\overline{X}_k =$ mean for the kth sample

$\overline{X}_T =$ grand mean for all elements

Within-group variation is:

$$SS_{within} = \Sigma(X_{ik} - \overline{X}_k)^2$$

where

X_{ik} = each individual score across k samples (i.e., the ith score, kth sample), and

$\overline{X}_k$ = the kth sample mean.

Total variation, SS_{total}, is the sum of both SS_{bet} and SS_{within}. A formula for this value is:

$$SS_{total} = \Sigma(X_{ik} - \overline{X}_T)^2$$

where

X_{ik} = the ith score in the kth sample

$\overline{X}_T$ = the grand mean

The SS_{bet} and SS_{within} values are critical to our problem solution in that they help to determine our observed F value or F_{obs}. The SS_{total} is not an essential formula component, although it does enable us to check our computational accuracy through the so-called short method for determining each of the sums of squares. This short method is illustrated as follows. We must compute three numerical terms,

1. $\dfrac{(\Sigma X_T^2)}{\Sigma N_k}$

where

ΣX_T = the sum of all scores across all groups

ΣN_k = the sum of all sample sizes

2. $\Sigma X^2{}_k$ or the sums of all squared scores across all samples

3. $\Sigma\left(\dfrac{\Sigma X_k^2}{N_k}\right)$

where

ΣX_k = the sum of scores for each sample

N_k = the sample size for each sample.

Carrying out these computations for the three terms from the information computed in Table 8.3, we have:

1. $\dfrac{(390 + 319 + 181 + 144)^2}{18 + 19 + 14 + 15} = \dfrac{(1034)^2}{66}$

$$= \dfrac{1,069,156}{66}$$

$$= 16,199.3$$

2. $(8758 + 5719 + 2539 + 1544) = 18,560$

3. $\dfrac{(390)^2}{18} + \dfrac{(319)^2}{19} + \dfrac{(181)^2}{14} + \dfrac{(144)^2}{15}$

$$= \frac{152,100}{18} + \frac{101,761}{19} + \frac{32,761}{14} + \frac{20,736}{15}$$
$$= 8450 + 5355.8 + 2340.1 + 1282.4$$
$$= 17,528.3$$

With these terms calculated, we can now solve for SS_{bet}, SS_{within}, and SS_{total} as follows:

$$SS_{bet} = (3) - (1) = 17,528.3 - 16,199.3 = 1329.0$$
$$SS_{within} = (2) - (3) = 18,560 - 17,528.3 = 1031.7$$
$$SS_{total} = (2) - (1) = 18,560 - 16,199.3 = 2360.7.$$

Rounding error may result in slight differences in values when using the longer method compared with the "shorter" method. These are minor differences and do not affect our resulting F value significantly.

After determining the sums of squares, our next step is to determine degrees of freedom. Notice in the ANOVA summary, Table 8.4, that there are df for between-group variation (df_{bet}), df for within-group variation (df_{within}), and df for total variation (df_{total}). The df's for each of these sources of variation are computed as follows. df for between groups is simply $k - 1$, where k = the number of groups. Thus, with four groups, $4 - 1 = 3$ df. For within-group variation df, we must subtract "1" from each sample size and sum these results, or $(N_1 - 1) + (N_2 - 1) + (N_3 - 1) + (N_4 - 1)$. For the information in Table 8.3, we have $(18 - 1) + (19 - 1) + (14 - 1) + (15 - 1) = 17 + 18 + 13 + 14 = 62$ df. Thus, we have 62 df for within-group variation. We place these degrees of freedom in Table 8.4 as shown. Total df is calculated simply as a computational check on our accuracy. We may obtain this value in two ways. One is to sum the df for between- and within-group variation. Thus, $3 + 62 = 65$. The other way is to sum all sample sizes and subtract 1, or $18 + 19 + 14 + 15 = 66$, and $66 - 1 = 65$ for our total df.

The fourth column, MS, stands for mean square. Mean squares for between groups and within groups are determined by dividing their respective dfs into their sums of squares or SS's. These calculations are illustrated as follows:

$$MS_{bet} = \frac{SS_{bet}}{df_{bet}}$$
$$= \frac{1,329}{3}$$
$$= 443$$

$$MS_{within} = \frac{SS_{within}}{df_{within}}$$
$$= \frac{1031.7}{62}$$
$$= 16.6$$

MS_{total} is a meaningless value and therefore, there is no need to compute it. We are now ready to determine our observed value of F or F_{obs}. This is the ratio of our MS_{bet} to MS_{within}, or $443/16.6 = 26.69$ as shown in Table 8.4. We must now take our F_{obs} to the table of critical values of F in Appendix A, Table A.19, pp. 461–462. We must either equal or exceed the critical value of F, F_{cv}, shown in the body of Table A.19 with our F_{obs} value. Determining which critical value of F we must equal or exceed is done by determining where our between- and within-group degrees of freedom intersect in the body of the table. Entering Table A.19 with df's of 3 and 62 respectively (between- and within-group df), we first find our between group $df = 3$ across the top of the table. Down the left-hand side of the table are various values for within-group degrees of freedom.

Inspecting this table shows no $df = 62$. The closest df are for 60 df and 65 df respectively. Whenever we are between two df points in this table, we will always select the smaller df, since smaller df values yield slightly larger critical values of F_{cv} which we must equal or exceed with our F_{obs}. This is a conservative choice. Thus, where 3 df and 60 df intersect in the body of the table defines two critical values of F. Values shown in *boldface* are for the .01 level of significance, whereas the other values are for the .05 level of significance.

With 3 df and 60 df respectively at the .01 level of significance, the F_{cv} which we must equal or exceed with our $F_{obs} = 4.13$. If our F_{obs} equals or exceeds 4.13, then there is a significant difference in stress levels among these four samples of correctional officers. Our $F_{obs} = 26.69$ which is equal to or larger than 4.13. There is a difference in stress levels among these groups of correctional officers on the SI measure. Again, we could be wrong in rejecting H_0 and supporting H_1 about 1 percent of the time, given the level of significance at which our hypotheses were tested. For subsequent applications of the F test, Table A.19 contains a useful headnote that explains how degrees of freedom are calculated in determining critical values of F for various significance levels.

A two-tailed test of the hypotheses was made in the case of Strickland's research. In almost all situations involving the F test for differences between k samples of elements, researchers are interested in whether the k samples differ on the measured characteristic. If the direction of differences between groups is important, then directionality can be accomplished easily by inspecting the arrangement of means across the k samples. For example, moving from left to right in Table 8.3, each sample of correctional officers has a lower mean value on their SI scores. This means that directionally, at least, as we move from more dangerous facilities (supermax) to the least dangerous ones (minimum security), correctional officer stress decreases systematically as indicated by these SI score averages.

If we wanted to find out whether specific pairs of samples differed from one another, the F test would not answer this question. Essentially what we have determined by applying the F test to the data in Table 8.3 is that there is a difference in SI scores somewhere among these four samples of correctional officers. We don't know where all possible mean differences are located. What we do know, however, is that at least the largest and smallest means differ (21.7 and 9.6) as the only result of this F application. Thus, there is at least a significant difference between SI means for the supermax officer sample and the minimum-security officer sample. In order to find out whether other sample combinations differ (e.g., maximum security/medium security, supermax/minimum security), another type of test will have to be applied. Two tests are discussed later in this chapter. These include the Newman-Keuls procedure and Scheffé test. These tests will disclose where significant differences exist between different pairs of sample means for the data in Table 8.3.

ASSUMPTIONS FOR THE F TEST   The assumptions underlying the F test include: (1) randomness; (2) independent samples; (3) the interval level of measurement underlying the trait measured; (4) normal distribution for each distribution of scores analyzed; and (5) homogeneity of variances or equal variances. The homogeneity of variance assumption does not mean literally that all sample variances (squares of standard deviation values) must be precisely equal to one another. We might observe several sample variances of 25.3, 24.6, 23.9, 25.1, and 26.7. These variances are different, but they may not be different statistically. The homogeneity-of-variance

---

BOX 8.4

SPSS Alternative Applications

---

1. Activate your *SPSS* software and go to the *SPSS* Data Editor. You have four groups being compared. From Table 8.3, you observe that there are the following numbers of persons in each group: 18, 19, 14, and 15. You must begin in the first "var" column and type in 18 "1"s, then 19 "2"s, 14 "3"s, and then 15 "4"s. These numbers designate persons in each of the four groups. Next, go to the first set of raw scores for group 1 and begin typing these 18 scores into the second "var" column, beginning with 22, 19, 14, and so forth, until you finish the first set of scores with 25. Continue with the second set of scores, typing these next in the second column, following the last score of 25. Type in 19, 14, 13, 22, and so forth, until the final score, 17, is entered. Move to the third set of scores in Table 8.3 and continue entering values, beginning with 19, 18, 12, 12, and so forth until the last score of 13 is entered. Finally, move to the last column in Table 8.3 and continue entering values, beginning with 3, 9, 12, 9 and so forth, until the last value, 11, is entered. You should now have 66 entries. The first column, VAR00001, defines groups 1 through 4. The second column, VAR00002, defines the raw scores from each of the four groups. These scores should match up with the respective group numbers entered in VAR00001.

2. Click on "Analyze," then "Compare Means," then "One-Way ANOVA." This brings up two windows. The left window contains VAR00001 and VAR00002. Highlight VAR00001 and enter it in the "Factor" window. Highlight VAR00002 and enter it with the arrow in the "Dependent List." Click "OK."

3. This action generates a screen which is an ANOVA Summary Table. Notice that it is identical to the ANOVA Summary Table shown in Table 8.4, with minor rounding discrepancies. Overall, the significance is the same. There is a significant difference among these *k*-sample means and stress among correctional officers depending on the type of institution where they work. The significance of an $F_{obs} = 25.622$ is .000, which is well below what is required for these groups to significantly differ from one another.

---

assumption presumes that the variances are equal statistically. As we know, there is some latitude with respect to statistically significant differences between means, and this also applies to differences among several sample standard deviations. The Hartley F_{max} test and the Cochran C test exist as methods for determining whether homogeneity of variance exists for k samples. These tests are illustrated using some of the data from Table 8.3.

THE HARTLEY F_{max} TEST FOR HOMOGENEITY OF VARIANCE **Homogeneity of variance** is essentially equal variances. It is an assumption underlying the F test. Even though k variances may appear unequal, they may not differ significantly from one another. Several tests are available to determine whether homogeneity of variance or equal variances exists. One such test is the **Hartley F_{max} test** that determines whether there are significant differences among k-sample variances. Since we have four samples of correctional officers in the illustration in Table 8.3, we might think that a test would have to be made about all of these sample variances. This is not so. This test is very simple. We only need to test whether the largest sample variance is different statistically from the smallest sample variance. The computation of Hartley's F_{max} is:

$$F_{max} = \frac{s^2_{largest}}{s^2_{smallest}}$$

From Table 8.3, we have determined the four sample variances as follows: 17.1, 19.1, 14.2, and 10.8 (these computations were made following the standard deviation and variance formulae in Chapter 4). Using the largest and smallest sample variances, we may carry out our computation of F_{max}:

$$F_{max \ observed} = \frac{19.1}{10.8} = 1.77.$$

Our observed $F_{max} = 1.77$. To interpret our observed F_{max} value, we must turn to Table A.21 of Appendix A, p. 463–464. This table contains critical values of F_{max}, or $F_{max \ critical \ values}$. Across the top of Table A.21 are various values of k. These refer to the numbers of variances we are analyzing. Since there are four samples in the original analysis-of-variance problem when the F test was applied, $k = 4$.

Down the left-hand side of Table A.21 are degrees of freedom (df). These are calculated as $N - 1$, where $N =$ the largest sample size among all samples being compared. In this case, the largest sample size is 19. Therefore, $N - 1 = 19 - 1 = 18 \ df$. Notice that no precise df of 18 exists. Since 18 df is between 15 df and 20 df, we will use the 20 df point. Again, this is a conservative decision on our part, since slightly smaller critical values of F_{max} are yielded by selecting larger df sizes. Finding where $k = 4$ and $df = 20$ intersect in the body of the table defines the critical value of F_{max}. Note that there are pairs of values. The first values in these pairs is the F_{max} critical value for the .05 level of significance, while the lower or second value is the .01 critical value of F_{max}. Since we made our original F test at the .01 level of significance, we will continue to use this significance level for additional work relating to these four samples of correctional officers. Thus, with .01, we must observe a value of F_{max} that is equal to or smaller than the critical value, 4.3, shown in Table A.21. Since our observed F_{max} is only 1.77, this is equal to or less than 4.3. Our sample variances are equal statistically and homogeneity of variance is satisfied. Failing to achieve homogeneity of variance will not rule out the application of the F test, however. Even if we fail to have homogeneity of variance, it has been demonstrated repeatedly under different research conditions that nearly the same F results are obtained compared with F values yielded when this assumption is satisfied.

THE COCHRAN C TEST The **Cochran C test** is slightly more complex to apply than the Hartley F_{max} test. It is determined by the following formula:

$$C = \frac{s^2_{largest}}{s^2_k}$$

where

$s^2_{largest} =$ the largest sample variance

$s^2_k =$ the sum of all sample variances

Using the information we have about the sample variances by using the squared sample standard deviations in Table 8.3, we have

$$C = \frac{19.1}{17.1 + 19.1 + 14.2 + 10.8}$$
$$= \frac{19.1}{61.2}$$
$$= .31.$$

Next, we turn to Table A.22, p. 465, and select k across the top of the table, which is equal to the number of sample variances, $k = 4$. Next, we move down the left-hand column, df (degrees of freedom). In this case, df's are determined in the same way that we determined df's for the Hartley F_{max} test, or $df = N - 1$, where $N =$ any sample size if sample sizes are equal; or $N =$ the largest sample size if the sample sizes are unequal. In this case, the largest sample size is 19. Therefore, $df = 19 - 1 = 18\ df$. Since this df is between the 16 and 36 df shown, we will select the larger of the two df points as our reference.

Where $k = 4$ and 36 df intersect in the body of the table identifies critical values of C. There are pairs of C critical values presented in this table as well. The first of the two values of C is the critical value for the .05 level of significance. The second critical value of C is appropriate for the .01 level. The critical value of C we are seeking, therefore, is .4057 (.01 level of significance). If our observed C value is equal to or larger than .4057, then we do not have homogeneity of variance. In this case, our observed C or $C_{obs} = .31$, which is smaller than .4057, the C critical value. Therefore, we can assume that homogeneity of variance exists.

When both the Hartley F_{max} test and the Cochran C test were applied to the same data in Table 8.3, homogeneity of variance was achieved. The results of both of these tests are very similar. Thus, either test is acceptable to use when determining if homogeneity of variance exists when applying the F test. Neither the Hartley F_{max} test nor the Cochran C test is included in the *SPSS* software program. Other comparable tests for homogeneity of variance are treated, however.

ADVANTAGES AND DISADVANTAGES OF THE *F* TEST   When the stringent assumptions associated with the F test have been satisfied, this test is the most powerful measure of mean differences between k samples. It is easy to apply and is an integral part of many software programs, such as *SPSS*. However, because of its stringent assumptions, it is likely that more than one of these assumptions will be violated when applying this test. But the F test is popular and has widespread conventional usage in social research. There are no sample size restrictions associated with this test. Like the t test, the F test is robust with respect to certain assumption violations. For instance, if sample variances are unequal, the F test continues to disclose reliable information about the mean differences being assessed because of its robustness.

The main weakness of the F test is that it does not tell us where significant differences between groups exist. It merely says that a difference exists somewhere between the groups. While we can ordinarily assume that at least the largest and smallest sample means differ significantly from one another, it cannot be assumed that significant differences exist among other pairs of group means. One way of approaching this problem is to compare the samples of elements, taking two samples at a time, and computing t tests. This is time-consuming and unnecessary. For the four-sample case, this would involve $4(4 - 1)/2 = 12/2 = 6$ mean comparisons or six separate t tests. There is a better way of making this determination following the F test achieving statistical significance. Several postmortem tests have been created to assess where significant differences exist between means after an F test has shown significance. Two such tests will be described in the following section.

POSTMORTEM OR POST HOC TESTS

Postmortem tests or **post hoc tests** are designed to function as probes that work to find each pair of samples that is significantly different on the measured characteristic being studied. The F test for analysis of variance seeks to answer whether there is a difference somewhere among k samples. Once this question is answered, researchers only know that at least the largest and smallest sample means are significantly different from one another. But they do not know if all other mean comparisons are also significantly different. If four samples are being studied, the following six sample combinations are possible: 1–2, 1–3, 1–4, 2–3, 2–4, and 3–4. Suppose the largest mean is associated with the first sample, while the smallest mean is associated with the fourth sample. This means that if the F test is significant, then the l–4 mean comparison is significant. But what about mean combinations 1–2, 1–3, 2–3, 2–4, and 3–4? Are they significant too? The F test doesn't tell you. This is where postmortem tests are useful.

There are numerous postmortem procedures. These include such tests as the Box procedure, the Tukey A and Tukey B procedures, the Scheffé procedure, the h.s.d. (honest significant difference) procedure, and the l.s.d. (least significant difference) procedure. Presented here are two of the most simple (and conservative) postmortem tests, the Newman-Keuls procedure and the Scheffé procedure. These tests are one-time test applications for all mean differences being examined. Both of these tests show which sample means differ significantly from one another as well as which ones do not.

The Newman–Keuls Procedure

The Newman-Keuls procedure is a rapid test for determining the significance of difference between all sample means simultaneously. To illustrate the Newman-Keuls procedure, the data presented earlier in Table 8.3 will be used. In that example, a significant F value was obtained, meaning that there was a significant mean difference somewhere among the four sample means. These means reflected average SI (stress index) scores for four samples of correctional officers at prisons classified according to their dangerousness. To carry out this test, we must arrange our four sample means as shown in Table 8.5. This is known as a **table of ordered means.**

In Table 8.5, all sample means are arranged from lowest to highest across the top of the table and from lowest to highest down the left-hand side of the table as shown. Where each of these mean differences intersect, the mean differences are entered. The next step is to determine q values that will be entered in the next to the last column. These q values are obtained from Table A.20 in Appendix A, the Distribution of the Studentized Range Statistic, pp. 462–463.

Turning to Table A.20, the q values are determined as follows. Across the top of the table is r, the number of steps between ordered means. The r we will select is equal to the number of means we are comparing, in this case, $r = 4$. (If we were examining ten mean differences, $r = 10$; if we were examining eight mean differences, $r = 8$, and so on.) Down the left-hand side of Table A.20 are df. These are df for within-group variation taken directly from the ANOVA summary table, Table 8.4. This $df = 62$. Notice that in Table A.20, there are no exact degrees of freedom for 62.

TABLE 8.5 Table of Ordered Means for the Newman-Keuls procedure

	9.6	12.9	16.8	21.7	(q)	$(q)(s_{\bar{x}})$
9.6	—	3.3	7.2*	12.1*	4.60	5.01
12.9		—	3.9	8.8*	4.28	4.66
16.8			—	4.9*	3.76	4.10
21.7				—		

*Significant mean differences

However, we find two df points, 60 and 120, respectively. Therefore, we must choose one of them. We will select the smaller df in this case, since a larger value of q will be obtained. This choice will make it slightly more difficult to achieve significance between any given pair of mean differences. It is considered a conservative step in this process.

After selecting a $df = 60$, we determine where $r = 4$ and $df = 60$ intersect in the body of the table. Where these values intersect defines the first value of q we will use and place in the table of ordered means as shown. Again, we encounter a pair of q values at the intersecting point. The first or upper q value is for the .05 level of significance, while the second or lower q value is for the .01 level of significance. Since our original hypothesis test where the F test was used involved the .01 level of significance, we will use this same level of significance for the Newman-Keuls procedure.

It is important not to change significance levels when conducting a postmortem test of mean differences after the F test has been applied. The reason is simple. For instance, if we find an overall significant difference among k sample means at the .05 level, then that same level of significance must be used for any subsequent probes of mean differences. It would not make good sense, for instance, to conduct an F test at the .05 level of significance, find a significant F value, and then use the .01 significance level for determining other mean differences that may be significant with a postmortem test such as the Newman–Keuls procedure. In effect, whatever is significant at the .05 level of significance may not be significant at the .01 level of significance (a more stringent or rigorous significance level).

Using this guideline, our first value of q is 4.60 (.01 level), and we enter it in the q column of Table 8.5 as shown. The other q values for this column are found by moving exactly one space to the left of the $q = 4.60$ in Table A.20 (to the column where $r = 3$). Moving one space to the left will identify the next q value. The next $q = 4.28$. We place this value as shown in the q column in Table 8.5. The final q value is found by moving again to the left one column (where $r = 2$) and using the $q = 3.76$. We enter this value in Table 8.5 as shown. The final column in Table 8.5, $(q)(s_t)$, is the product of each q value and a value called the **standard error of the treatment means**, or s_t. The formula for s_t is

$$s_{\bar{t}} = \sqrt{\frac{MS_{within}}{N}}$$

where

  MS_{within} = the mean square within value taken from the ANOVA summary (in this case, Table 8.4)

  N = any sample size if the sample sizes are equal; if the sample sizes are unequal, then the smallest of the sample sizes

Since the smallest sample size is 14 and our MS_{within} from Table 8.4 is 16.6, we may solve for s as follows:

$$s_{\bar{t}} = \sqrt{\frac{16.6}{14}}$$
$$= \sqrt{1.186}$$
$$= 1.09$$

With an $s = 1.09$, we multiply all values of q in Table 8.5 by this value, or

  $(4.60)(1.09) = 5.01$
  $(4.28)(1.09) = 4.66$
  $(3.76)(1.09) = 3.76$

These products are placed in the last column in Table 8.5 as shown. These values are critical values that our mean differences in the body of the table must equal or exceed in order to be significantly different at the .01 level.

Lines are drawn in our table of ordered means (Table 8.5) as shown and are designated as sectors associated with each of the critical values. The first sector will contain only one mean difference, 12.1, the largest mean difference between the means of 9.6 and 21.7. The second sector will contain two mean differences (8.8 and 7.2), and the third sector will contain three mean differences (4.9, 3.9, and 3.3). (If there were a fourth and fifth sector, these sectors would contain four and five mean differences respectively; a sixth sector would contain six mean differences, and so on.).

The first critical value, 5.01, is compared with the only mean difference in its sector, 12.1. This is the largest mean difference. Since this mean difference equals or exceeds 5.01, it is significant at the .01 level. Therefore, we place an asterisk (*) beside it to indicate its significance. The next critical value is 4.66 and it is compared with all mean differences in its sector. Since the mean differences of 8.8 and 7.2 both equal or exceed 4.66, they are also significant at the .01 level and are asterisked as well. In the third sector, the critical value, 4.10 is compared with the three mean differences in that sector. Only one mean difference of 4.9 is significant at the .01 level, while the other mean differences are not significant (they do not equal or exceed the critical value of 4.10). After placing asterisks beside all significant mean differences, we may summarize our findings. The following mean differences are significant at the .01 level of significance, based upon our application of the postmortem Newman-Keuls procedure:

9.6 is significantly different from 21.7

9.6 is significantly different from 16.8

12.9 is significantly different from 21.7

16.8 is significantly different from 21.7

All other mean differences are not significant (i.e., 9.6 is not significantly different from 12.9, and 12.9 is not significantly different from 16.8). The Newman-Keuls procedure is completed. Had we applied t tests to all of these mean differences, the results would have shown at least the same mean differences as significant. But the t test is less conservative than the Newman–Keuls procedure and therefore, it is likely that more significant mean differences may have been found.

The Scheffé Procedure

The **Scheffé procedure** is an alternative to the Newman–Keuls procedure, and it accomplishes the same purpose but in a different way. The Scheffé procedure is even more conservative than the Newman–Keuls procedure, since fewer significant mean differences will be reported when using this test. Suppose we carry out the Scheffé procedure on the same data from Table 8.3. We will utilize some of the information from Table 8.4 as well (the ANOVA summary table).

When applying the Scheffé procedure, a critical F value is determined as follows:

$$F_{cv} = (k - 1)(F)$$

where

$k =$ the number of samples compared

$F =$ the original F_{cv} from the interpretive table, Table A.19, in Appendix A

Using information from the F test described earlier, we can solve for the F_{cv} as follows:

$$F_{cv} = (4 - 1)(4.13)$$
$$= (3)(4.13)$$
$$= 12.39.$$

All mean differences are evaluated by computing a special F_{obs} value for each pair of sample means by using the following formula:

Where

$$F_{obs} = \frac{(\overline{X}_1 - \overline{X}_2)^2}{\dfrac{MS_w(N_1 + N_2)}{(N_1)(N_2)}}$$

$\overline{X}_1$ and $\overline{X}_2$ = any pair of sample means to be compared

MS_w = mean-square within-group variation taken from the ANOVA summary table

N_1 and N_2 = the sample sizes for the two means being compared in the numerator term

For example, suppose we assess the difference between $\overline{X}$ and $\overline{X}_2$ from Table 8.3. We determine that the respective means are $\overline{X}_1 = 21.7$ ($N_1 = 18$) and $\overline{X}_2 = 16.8$ ($N_2 = 19$). With these data and with the MS_{within} value of 16.6 from Table 8.4, we can determine our first observed F value as follows:

$$F_{1obs} = \frac{(21.7 - 16.8)^2}{\dfrac{(16.6)(18 + 19)}{(18)(19)}}$$

$$= \frac{24.01}{\dfrac{615.68}{342}}$$

$$= \frac{24.01}{1.80}$$

$$= 13.34$$

A second computation will be helpful here. Suppose we examine another pair of means, such as $\overline{X}_1$ and $\overline{X}_3$:

$$F_{2obs} = \frac{(21.7 - 12.9)^2}{\dfrac{(16.6)(18 + 14)}{(18)(14)}}$$

$$= \frac{77.44}{\dfrac{532.48}{252}}$$

$$= \frac{77.44}{2.11}$$

$$= 36.70.$$

We continue using this formula until all of the different mean comparisons have been made. A table of ordered means similar to our Newman–Keuls table is constructed and is shown as

TABLE 8.6 Table of Ordered Means Showing Significant Mean Differences with the Scheffé Method

	9.6	12.9	16.8	21.7
9.6	—	$F_6 = 4.74$	$F_5 = 26.05^*$	$F_3 = 71.98^*$
12.9		—	$F_4 = 7.38$	$F_2 = 36.70^*$
16.8			—	$F_1 = 13.34^*$
21.7				—

*Significant mean differences at the .01 level of significance. The critical value of F for the Scheffé method = 12.39. Any observed F values in the body of the table which equal or exceed 12.39 are significant at the .01 level of significance, as designated by asterisks. These are F_{obs} values that equal or exceed 12.39.

Table 8.6. Table 8.6 has been arranged so as to display the sample means from lowest to highest across the top of the table and from lowest to highest down the left-hand side of the table. The body of the table shows various observed F values. We compare these F values, which are actually F_{obs} values, with the F_{cv} which we originally determined to be 12.39. Any F_{obs} value which equals or exceeds the F_{cv} of 12.39 will be significant at the .01 level of significance. We shall place an asterisk (*) beside each of the F_{obs} values shown in the body of the table. These asterisks will designate which of the mean differences are significant.

Our summary of significant mean differences is as follows:

9.6 is significantly different from 21.7

9.6 is significantly different from 16.8

BOX 8.5

SPSS Alternative Applications

1. All of the steps leading to completing the one-way ANOVA test eventually request options of the investigator. These options pertain to both homogeneity of variance tests and postmortem tests or post hoc tests as *SPSS* terms them. Several post hoc tests may be checked before actually carrying out the final tabular result of an ANOVA Summary. One of these post hoc tests is the Scheffé procedure illustrated earlier. In fact, the Scheffé procedure was conducted using the *SPSS* software program and results were identical to those manually computed. The Newman–Keuls procedure is not among the *SPSS* choices, although it is one of the most simple and conservative tests to apply to evaluate multiple mean differences. It involves minimal manual calculations. By the same token, the Hartley F_{max} procedure is not included nor is the Cochran C statistic. However, other optional tests may be performed to determine homogeneity of variance. These other tests can simply be clicked by the *SPSS* user and instant results can be obtained. It is likely that some of these tests will yield conflicting results, meaning that some tests will disclose that homogeneity of variance exists among groups, whereas other tests may show that it doesn't exist. This means that some tests are more or less conservative than others. The Hartley and Cochran procedures used in the present example were selected because they are located in the middle range of conservatism–liberalism regarding homogeneity of variance tests. Individual researchers may decide which tests are their favorite choices.

12.9 is significantly different from 21.7

16.8 is significantly different from 21.7

In this example, the Scheffé procedure yielded the same number of significant mean differences as did the Newman–Keuls procedure. Under certain circumstances, the Scheffé procedure may show fewer significant mean differences compared with the Newman–Keuls procedure. In a 20-mean comparison, for instance, the Newman–Keuls procedure might report 15 mean differences as significant, whereas the Scheffé procedure applied to the same data might show 13 or 14 significant mean differences. It is in this sense that the Scheffé procedure is slightly more conservative.

k-SAMPLE TESTS WITH ADDITIONAL VARIABLES

In the previous section, we examined four hypothetical samples of correctional officers at different prisons housing inmates of varying degrees of dangerousness and how these samples differed regarding their levels of stress. It was hypothesized that different levels of stress would be found, since the four correctional settings contained different types of prisoners of varying degrees of dangerousness. The *F* test was used to determine the significance of difference between these samples of officers on the stress variable.

Sometimes researchers may want to determine if other factors may be influential in affecting correctional officer stress scores. For instance, Strickland (2006) may have suspected that an officer's work experience might be a significant factor influencing stress levels. Strickland may have believed that more experienced officers with more years of service might have lower stress scores than newer officers with less work experience. It may have been predicted that those officers with longer years of service would tend to exhibit less stress compared with officers with fewer years of service. This would require using an additional variable in our analysis: length of service as correctional officers. We could solve this problem by using the two-way analysis-of-variance test, an extension of the *F* test.

Two-Way Analysis of Variance

The **two-way analysis-of-variance test** allows us to determine the influence of two independent variables acting upon a dependent variable, in this case, officer stress. Its results will show the influence of each of the independent variables as they each affect the dependent variable. The test also shows any **interaction effects** that occur between the two independent variables and whether our explanation for variation on the dependent variable is affected by these interaction effects. It is not expected that students will carry out two-way ANOVA tests in this or other chapters. But a short presentation of this test enables students to understand that different variables may be introduced to an original one-way ANOVA test if it is suspected that these other variables may have a significant impact on the group differences originally exhibited. You will not be required to actually perform a two-way ANOVA test. The purpose here is strictly to understand what this test does and why it is important. Suppose we were to recast the original data from Table 8.3 and arrange the raw scores for each of the four samples according to whether officers have 7 or more years of experience or 1 to 6 years of experience. This new arrangement is shown in Table 8.7.

Table 8.7 is a cross tabulation of years of service as a correctional officer (down the left-hand column) and correctional institution (across the top of the table). Years of service has been dichotomized according to 7 or more years and 1 to 6 years. Those correctional officers with 1 to

TABLE 8.7 Two-Way Analysis of Variance: Corrections Officers by Length of Service

Type of Institution

Length of Service	Supermax X_i	Supermax X_i^2	Maximum X_i	Maximum X_i^2	Medium X_i	Medium X_i^2	Minimum X_i	Minimum X_i^2
1 to 6 years	22	484	19	361	19	361	3	9
	14	196	13	169	12	144	7	49
	21	441	28	784	14	196	9	81
	24	576	14	196	10	100	9	81
	17	289	12	144	9	81	8	64
	29	841	19	361	12	144	8	64
	26	676	20	400	11	121	10	100
	23	529	17	289				
	21	441	14	196				
			17	289				
	$\Sigma X_i = 197$ $\Sigma X_i^2 = 4473$		$\Sigma X_i = 173$ $\Sigma X_i^2 = 3189$		$\Sigma X_i = 87$ $\Sigma X_i^2 = 1147$		$\Sigma X_i = 54$ $\Sigma X_i^2 = 448$	
	$N_1 = 9$ $\overline{X}_1 = 21.9$		$N_2 = 10$ $\overline{X}_2 = 17.3$		$N_3 = 7$ $\overline{X}_3 = 12.4$		$N_4 = 7$ $\overline{X}_4 = 7.7$	
							$\overline{X}_{1R} = 15.5$ $\Sigma X_i^2 = 9257$	
7 + years	19	361	14	196	18	324	9	81
	24	576	22	484	12	144	12	144
	20	400	17	289	12	144	9	81
	23	529	15	225	7	49	18	324
	16	256	9	81	11	121	7	49
	15	225	22	484	21	441	14	196
	23	529	19	361	13	169	10	100
	28	784	11	121			11	121
	25	625	17	289				
	$\Sigma X_i = 193$ $\Sigma X_i^2 = 4285$		$\Sigma X_i = 146$ $\Sigma X_i^2 = 2530$		$\Sigma X_i = 94$ $\Sigma X_i^2 = 1392$		$\Sigma X_i = 90$ $\Sigma X_i^2 = 1096$	
	$N_5 = 9$ $\overline{X}_5 = 21.4$ $\overline{X}_{1C} = 21.7$		$N_6 = 9$ $\overline{X}_6 = 16.2$ $\overline{X}_{2C} = 16.8$		$N_7 = 7$ $\overline{X}_7 = 13.4$ $\overline{X}_{3C} = 12.9$		$N_8 = 8$ $\overline{X}_8 = 11.2$ $\overline{X}_{4C} = 9.6$	
							$\overline{X}_{2R} = 15.8$ $\Sigma X_i^2 = 9393$	
							$\Sigma X_T = 523$	

6 years of service are placed in the first row in the upper half of Table 8.7, while those with 7 or more years of service are placed in he second row or lower half of the table. The raw scores shown are the SI (Stress Index) scores originally presented in Table 8.7. Separate means are computed for each of the table's eight subparts. For instance, the first subpart in the upper left-hand corner of Table 8.7 consists of correctional officers at a supermax prison with 1 to 6 years of service. The average SI score is computed as 21.9. In another part of the table, for example, those correctional officers at the medium-security prison with 7 + years of service have average SI scores of 13.4.

After all means have been computed for each of the Table 8.7's subparts, grand means are computed for the rows. [Grand means for the columns are the original sample means (e.g., 21.7, 16.8, 12.9, and 9.6) for the four groups of correctional officers taken directly from Table 8.3. Computing grand means for the two rows yields overall SI means of 15.5 and 15.8 for those officers with 1 to 6 and 7 + years of experience respectively. Note that although these average SI values are not very different, they are in the general direction we originally predicted in our theorizing about correctional officer work experience and stress.

We will label length of service as a correctional officer as factor 1. Factor 2 will be assigned to the different samples according to their work setting (i.e., supermax, maximum-security, medium-security, and minimum-security).

We are interested in answering three questions: (1) What is the main effect of factor 1 (length of service as a correctional officer) on stress? (2) What is the main effect of factor 2 (different correctional settings) on stress? and (3) What is the interaction effect of both factors on stress scores? Therefore, we need to understand two additional concepts. These are main effects and interaction effects. **Main effects** are effects on score values (dependent variables) which are likely attributable to one or more independent variables, such as length of service or type of correctional institution assigned as a work setting. Interaction effects are the indication of the significance of the interplay between different factors on SI scores.

The main effect of factor 1 (length of service as a correctional officer) is evaluated by determining whether there is a significant difference between row grand means. The main effect is assessed by determining whether differences exist between the column grand means. Interaction effects exist if substantial differences are found among SI means of groups in different work settings with different amounts of work experience. Differences between the following pairs of means in Table 8.7 do not appear to be substantial: means 1 and 5, means 2 and 6, and means 3 and 7. The difference between means 4 and 8 is the largest mean difference, but we do not know yet whether this particular mean difference is sufficiently large enough to produce a statistically significant interaction effect.

To evaluate the two main effects (factor 1 and factor 2) on SI scores and to learn of the significance of any interaction between length of service as a correctional officer and type of correctional setting assigned to work, we must construct a two-way analysis-of-variance summary table such as the one shown in Table 8.8. One of the exercises at the end of this chapter will provide some practice with a two-way ANOVA summary table.

Table 8.8 is computed as follows. We must first determine sums of squares (SS) for six different terms: (1) SS total (SS_{total}); (2) SS between groups (SS_{bet}); (3) SS within groups (SS_{within}); (4) SS for factor 1 (SS_{f1}) (length of service as a correctional officer); (5) SS for factor 2 (SS_{f2}) (type of correctional work setting assigned); and (6) SS for factor 1 and factor 2 interaction ($SS_{interaction}$). These terms are computed by using the following formulae:

$$SS_{total} = \Sigma X_T^2 - \frac{(\Sigma X_T)^2}{N_T}$$

TABLE 8.8 Two-Way ANOVA Summary Table

Source of Variation	SS	df	MS	F
Between				
Factor 1	2.3	1[a]	2.3	.137 n.s.
Factor 2	1329.0	3[b]	443.0	26.350*(P < .01)
Interaction				
Factor 1 × Factor 2	54.3	3[c]	18.1	1.077 n.s.
Within	975.1	58[d]	16.812	
Total	2360.7	65[e]		

[a] Factor 1 *df* = the number of row categories −1, or 2 − 1 = 1 *df*
[b] Factor 2 *df* = the number of column categories −1 or 4 − 1 = 3 *df*
[c] Interaction of Factor 1 and Factor 2 *df* = (Factor 1*df*)(Factor 2*df*) = (1)(3) = 3 *df*
[d] Within *df* = *N* − number of subcategories or *N* − 8 or 66 − 8 = 58 *df*
[e] Total *df* = total *N* − 1 or 66 − 1 = 65 *df*

where

$\Sigma X_T^2 = \Sigma X_i^2$, sum of the squared scores across all samples (eight subsamples in this case)

ΣX_T = sum of scores across all samples (eight subsamples in this case)

N_T = sum of sample sizes across all samples

$$SS_{total} = 18,560 - \frac{1,034}{N_T}$$

$$= 18,560 - 16,199.3$$

$$= 2,360.7$$

where

$$SS_{bet} = \Sigma\left[\frac{(\Sigma X_i)^2}{N_i}\right] - \frac{(\Sigma X_T)^2}{N_T}$$

ΣX_i = sum of scores for each sample or the *i*th sample

N_i = sample size for the *i*th sample

ΣX_T = sum of the scores across all samples

N_T = sum of sample sizes across all samples

Therefore,

$$SS_{bet} = \frac{(197)^2}{9} + \frac{(173)^2}{10} + \frac{(87)^2}{7} + \frac{(54)^2}{7} + \frac{(193)^2}{9} +$$

$$\frac{(146)^2}{9} + \frac{(94)^2}{7} + \frac{(90)^2}{8} - \frac{(1034)^2}{66}$$

$$= 4312.1 + 2992.9 + 1081.3 + 416.6 + 4138.8$$
$$+ 2368.4 + 1262.3 + 1012.5 - 16,199.3$$

$$= 17,584.9 - 16,199.3$$

$$= 1385.6$$

$$SS_{\text{within}} = SS_{\text{total}} - SS_{\text{within}}$$

$$= 2360.7 - 1385.6$$

$$= 975.1$$

$$SS_{f_1}(SS \text{ for factor } 1) = \Sigma\left[\frac{(\Sigma X_{TR})^2}{N_{iR}}\right] - \frac{(\Sigma X_T)^2}{N_T}$$

where

ΣX_{TR} = sum of scores for each row

ΣX_T = sum of scores across all samples

N_T = sum of all sample sizes across all samples

N_{iR} = sum of sample sizes for each row

Therefore,

$$SS_{f_1} = [(511)^2 + (523)^2] - \frac{(1034)^2}{66}$$

$$= 7912.8 + 8288.8 - 16,199.3$$

$$= 16,201.6 - 16,199.3$$

$$= 2.3.$$

$$SS_{f_2}(SS \text{ for factor } 1) = \Sigma\left[\frac{(\Sigma X_{TC})^2}{N_{iC}}\right] - \frac{(\Sigma X_T)^2}{N_T}$$

where

ΣX_{TC} = sum of scores for each column

N_{iC} = sum of sample sizes for each column

ΣX_T = sum of the scores across all samples

N_T = sum of all sample sizes across all samples

Therefore,

$$SS_{f_2} = \left[\frac{(390)^2}{18} + \frac{(319)^2}{19} + \frac{(181)^2}{14} + \frac{(144)^2}{15}\right] - \frac{(1,034)^2}{66}$$

$$= 8,450 + 5,355.8 + 2,340.1 + 1,382.4 - 16,199.3$$

$$= 17,528.3 - 16,199.3$$

$$= 1,329.$$

$$SS_{\text{interaction}} 1 \times 2 = SS \text{ for interaction between factor } 1 \text{ and factor } 2$$

$$= SS_{\text{between}} - SS_{f_1} - SS_{f_2}$$

$$= 1,385.6 - 2.3 - 1,329$$

$$= 54.3.$$

These values are now placed in the two-way ANOVA summary table, Table 8.8, as shown in the *SS* column. The degrees of freedom for each *SS* value are determined as follows. For factor 1 *df*, we determine the number of row categories and subtract 1, or $2 - 1 = 1$ *df*. For factor 2 *df*, we determine the number of column categories and subtract 1, or $4 - 1 = 3$ *df*. For interaction *df*, we multiply factor 1 *df* by factor 2 *df*, or $(1)(3) = 3$ *df*. For within *df*, we take the total *N* and subtract from this *N* the number of subcategories or rows × columns, or $N - (2)(4) = 66 - 8 = 58$ *df*. These *df* computations are also provided as footnotes in Table 8.8 for subsequent applications of two-way analysis of variance.

Once we have determined *df* for each *SS* value, we divide each *SS* value by its accompanying *df*. This result will yield the various mean square (*MS*) values shown in the fourth column. For instance, $2.3/1 = 2.3 = MS$ for factor 1. For factor 2, we have $1,329.0/3 = 443$, and so on. To maximize our computational accuracy, the various *SS* values in the second column should *sum* to SS_{total}, or 2360.7 as shown. The *df* for each *SS* should also *sum* to df_{total} or 65 *df*.

We are now ready to determine the significance of each of the main effects (factors 1 and 2) and the interaction effects (factor 1 *by* factor 2) on the dependent variable, stress or SI scores. The significance of these effects will be evaluated by the magnitude of various *F*-observed values computed from the *MS* terms. The F_{obs} value for factor 1 is determined by dividing the *MS* for factor 1 by MS_{within} or $2.3/16.812 = .137$. This F_{obs} is placed in Table 8.8 as shown.

The F_{obs} for factor 2 is determined by dividing the *MS* for factor 2 by MS_{within} or $443.0/16.812 = 26.350$. This second F_{obs} value is placed in the table as shown. Finally, the F_{obs} for interaction effects of factor 1 and factor 2 is determined by dividing the *MS* for interaction ($MS_{interaction}$) by the MS_{within} value, or $18.1/16.812 = 1.077$. This F_{obs} value is placed in the table as shown.

We now enter Table A.19 to determine the critical values of F (F_{cv}) that we must equal or exceed with our various F_{obs} values. This is the same table we used for our previous *F*-test application and interpretation. The critical value of *F* for the .01 level of significance (used here because of its use in the earlier *F* test) is the *boldface* value where 1 *df* and 58 *df* intersect in the body of the table. We find 1 *df* across the top of the table and 58 *df* down the left-hand side. Since there is no 58 *df*, we use the closest *df* which is smaller than 58 *df*. Where 1 *df* and 55 *df* intersect in the body of the table defines the critical value of $F = 7.12$. Our first F_{obs} value, .137, must equal or exceed 7.12 in order to be significant statistically at the .01 level. In this case, factor 1, or years of service as a correctional officer, is not significant statistically. We may place an n.s. (meaning *not significant*) beside the first F_{obs} value.

For factor 2, the critical value of *F* is determined where 3 *df* and 58 *df* intersect in the body of the table. We again turn to 55 *df* since there is no exact 58 *df*. The critical value of *F* in this instance is 4.16. If our observed *F* value of 26.350 equals or exceeds the critical value, 4.16, we may conclude that the correctional setting where these officers work acts upon their stress scores significantly as one of the main effects. It does appear to make a difference where correctional officers are located according to our findings.

Finally, to assess the significance of any interaction effects between factor 1 and factor 2 upon stress or SI scores, we determine the critical value of *F* where 3 *df* and 58 *df* intersect in the *F* table. Using 55 *df* again, the critical value of *F* is 4.16, and therefore, our observed $F = 1.077$ fails to equal or exceed this value and is not significant (n.s.). There is no significant interaction effect upon SI or stress scores. Thus, the fact that some officers have been on the job longer than others does not appear to influence their stress scores compared with the differences in the dangerousness of their respective correctional work settings. This completes the two-way ANOVA for these data.

BOX 8.6

SPSS **Alternative Applications**

It is beyond the scope of this book to provide an example of the detail required to perform two-way ANOVA for these data. A practice two-way ANOVA summary table will be presented as an exercise at the end of this chapter, however.

ASSUMPTIONS, ADVANTAGES, AND DISADVANTAGES The assumptions of the two-way ANOVA are: (1) randomness; (2) the interval level of measurement for the variable measured; (3) homogeneity of sample variances; (4) independent samples; (5) normality of distribution for each set of sample scores.

One of the primary advantages of the two-way ANOVA test is that it permits us to see the effects of different variables on whatever we have selected as the dependent variable. Also, it permits us to assess the significance of interaction between several independent variables as they jointly act upon the dependent variable.

A primary drawback of this procedure is the tediousness associated with the computational work. When one's sample size exceeds 100, two-way ANOVA becomes extremely cumbersome to apply. Fortunately, there are many types of software programs, such as *SPSS*, available to handle large quantities of data and make such ANOVA tests rapidly. Thus, it is primarily important to know how such ANOVA tests should be interpreted rather than the specifics of numerical calculations. The stringent assumptions underlying two-way ANOVA tend to restrict its application in much the same way as the *F* test is restricted. But conventional usage may override any concerns that arise because certain assumptions may be violated when applying this test. Tables exist containing critical values of *F* and assist researchers in decision-making situations regarding tests of their hypotheses.

Summary

This chapter has sought to describe a variety of parametric procedures that might be used to analyze collected data. All procedures presented in this chapter assume normality of the distribution and the interval level of measurement underlying the traits or characteristics measured. For single-sample situations, the *Z* and *t* tests may be applied. The *Z* test is identical in form to the *t* test, although two different distributions are used for interpreting these respective values. For applications of the *t* test, the distribution of *t* is used. This distribution becomes identical to the unit normal distribution as our sample sizes approach infinity. But the *t* table should be used for applications where sample sizes are less than 120. For sample sizes 120 or larger, either the unit normal distribution or the *t* distribution may be used for interpretive purposes.

Two-sample tests of significance include the *t* test for differences between means and Sandler's *A* statistic. The *t* test is applicable when researchers have two independent samples, while Sandler's *A* test is used when the two samples are related in some way, usually through matching or when persons are used as their own controls in before-after experiments. Both the *t* test and the *A* test are the most powerful parametric tests available for determining differences respectively between independent and related samples.

When researchers have more than two samples to analyze, they may use the F test for analysis of variance. This test is an extension of the t test and also exhibits high power relative to rejecting false null hypotheses. It determines whether k sample means differ, although it does not indicate specifically where these significant mean differences are located. Thus, a postmortem procedure, the Newman-Keuls procedure, may be used. Among the F test's several stringent assumptions is homogeneity of variances or equal variances. A test for homogeneity of variance, Hartley's F_{max} test, was illustrated. Finally, a two-way ANOVA test that allows researchers to assess the impact of a second independent variable in relation to a dependent variable was presented. The stringent assumptions associated with the F test also accompany applications of the two-way ANOVA procedure.

Key Terms

analysis-of-variance
   summary table 185
between-group
   variation 185
Cochran C test 191
degrees of freedom, df 169
F ratio 186
F test for analysis of
   variance 183
Hartley F_{max} test 190
homogeneity of variance 190
interaction effects 198
k-sample tests of
   significance 182

main effects 200
mean squares (MS) 186
Newman-Keuls
   procedure 193
paired-sample t test 182
point estimates 167
post hoc tests 192
postmortem tests 192
robust 177
robustness 177
Sandler A test 179
Scheffé procedure 195

standard error of the
   difference between two
   means 174
standard error of the
   treatment means 194
sums of squares (SS) 186
table of ordered means 193
t test 167
t test for differences between
   means 173
within-group variation 185
Z test 167

Questions for Review

1. What are some differences between the t test for a single sample and a Z test for a single sample? Discuss the nature of how such tests are applied.
2. What is a population estimate? How do single-sample tests of significance utilize such population estimates in their computation? Explain.
3. What is the most popular test for determining differences between two means? Why is it popular? What makes this test difficult to apply in criminology and criminal justice? Explain.
4. Whenever samples are related and the investigator has interval-level data, which test might be the best to apply to determine whether there are significant differences between two related samples? Discuss the test you have chosen.

5. What does the Newman-Keuls procedure do for you that the F test cannot do?
6. What additional features are there associated with the two-way analysis-of-variance test compared with the F test? Explain.
7. What assumptions make both the F test for analysis of variance and the two-way analysis of variance difficult to apply in criminology and the social sciences generally? Explain.
8. What are postmortem tests? Describe their functions and give two examples. How do such postmortem tests compare with conducting several t tests, taking two means at a time, and testing their differences statistically? Explain.

9. What is meant by homogeneity of variance? Why is it considered an important assumption underlying the proper application of the F test? Explain.

10. What are two procedures for determining homogeneity of variance? Describe each.

11. Under what conditions should you use the Sandler A statistic?

12. In what sense is the Newman-Keuls procedure more conservative than using multiple t tests to determine differences between 20 means?

13. If a significant difference is found among k sample means through the use of the F test, what does the F result mean? Does the F test disclose where significant mean differences are located? Why or why not? Discuss.

14. If the t test for differences between two means is applied and significance is found at the .01 level, what are two possible problems facing researchers when making assumptions about population mean differences that the sample means purportedly estimate? Explain these problems.

Exercises

All of the following exercises are designed to familiarize you with interpreting ANOVA summary tables, working with critical t and Z values and their interpretation, and understanding interval-level tests of significance and their application. Limited manual computations are required. SPSS software may be used alternatively for some of the numerical problems below.

8.1. Given the data below, determine whether the following two groups differ using the t test for significance of difference between means. Use the .05 level of significance (two-tailed test). Determine the requested values.

Group 1	Group 2
25	28
29	24
22	30
24	29
26	31
28	27
22	26
26	21
31	26
22	24

$H_0: \overline{X}_1 = \overline{X}_2$
$H_1: \overline{X}_1 \neq \overline{X}_2$
$P \leq .05$ (two-tailed test)
   a. t_{obs}
   b. t_{cv}
   c. df
   d. mean difference
   e. Decision about mean difference

8.2. Determine if a significant difference exists between the means below. Use the information provided.

SPSS Alternative Application: If you have access to *SPSS* software, you may use this method for determining the correct answer. Use Table A.3 of Appendix A to obtain your critical value of t. A step-by-step *SPSS* application for the t test was presented within the chapter. Use the same procedure in solving this problem.

Means = 114.7 and 119.3
Ns = 77 and 85
Standard deviations = 16.9 and 19.3
H_0: *The two means are the same.*
H_1: *The two means are different.*
$P \leq .01$ (two-tailed)
   a. $t_{obs} =$
   b. $t_{cv} =$
   c. df
   d. Decision about mean difference.

8.3. Carry out a simple one-way ANOVA F test for the following five samples at the .05 level of

Group 1	Group 2	Group 3	Group 4	Group 5
9	7	4	10	1
3	10	5	6	2
5	4	4	8	3
9	3	6	12	6
9	6	2	5	5

significance. Does a significant difference in samples exist? Determine the requested values.

a. df_{bet}
b. df_{within}
c. df_{total}
d. F_{obs}
e. F_{cv}
f. Decision about differences between sample means

> **SPSS Alternative Application:** If you have access to *SPSS* software, you may follow the directions given within the chapter for solving for *F*. Use Table A.19 for determining your critical value and in making your decision about the significance of *F*.

8.4. Below is an ANOVA summary table. Given the following values, including 7 Xs, 7 s^2 values, and 7 Ns, fill in the ANOVA summary table. (Hint: This is a fill-in-the-blanks type of question. Minimal manual computation is required. Several of these answers can be determined by inspection. Use the known information and work forwards or backwards to determine missing values requested. The MS_{within} and $SS_{between}$ values have already been supplied for the ANOVA summary table. The *key* to solving this and similar problems below is first determining the *df* for both between- and within-group variation. Once *df* have been computed, you can work forwards or backwards in the ANOVA summary table to determine the various values for MS_{bet} and SS_{within}. For instance, solving for missing values in this problem, simply multiply the MS_{bet} value by *df* for between-group variation to determine SS_{bet} and divide the SS_{within} value by the *df* for within-group variation to determine MS_{within}. The total SS is the simple sum of the SS_{bet} and SS_{within}. A knowledge of individual scores is unnecessary for these computations. The number of means and Ns can be counted for determining *df* values. Variances are also given so that the F_{max} test may be computed and a decision can be made about homogeneity of variance. An ANOVA summary table has been provided here as a guide, although you can simply sketch your own and fill in the known information to solve for the unknown information.

Means = 14, 12, 19, 21, 16, 17
Ns = 15, 10, 12, 13, 20, 29
Standard deviations = 3.1, 6.8, 1.9, 4.5, 4.1, 5.4
MS_{within} = 6.93

SS_{bet} = 156
$P \le .05$

a. SS_{within}
b. MS_{bet}
c. F_{obs}
d. F_{cv}
e. F_{max} observed
f. F_{max} critical value
g. df_{bet}
h. df_{within}
i. df_{total}
j. SS_{total}
k. Decision about *F* test
l. Decision about F_{max} test

ANOVA Summary Table

Source	SS	df	MS	F
Between				
Within				

8.5. For the six means in problem 8.4 above and using relevant information, carry out the Newman-Keuls procedure using the table of ordered means below. Fill in the table of ordered means, providing all values of *q* and the s_t. Asterisk (*) all significant mean differences. Determine the value of s_t.

$s_t = .83$
q values: 4.16, 3.98, 3.74, 3.40, 2.83
critical values = 3.45, 3.30, 3.10, 2.82, 2.34
Table of Ordered Means
$q (s_t)(q)$

a. s_t
b. *q* values
c. $(s_t)(q)$ values
d. Pairs of means that are significant

8.6. Given the following data, determine the values requested:

Means = 14.7, 15.8, 17.6, 19.9, 25.3
Standard deviations: 4.6, 5.3, 3.2, 7.5, 4.9
Ns: 22, 16, 28, 32, and 41
SS_{bet} = 2090.8 and MS_{within} = 79.8, $P \le .05$

ANOVA Summary Table

Source	SS	df	MS	F
Between				
Within				

a. SS_{within} =
b. MS_{bet} =
c. df_{bet} =

d. df_{within} =

e. df_{total} =

f. SS_{total} =

g. F_{obs} =

h. F_{cv} =

i. F_{max} observed =

j. F_{max} critical value =

k. Decision about mean differences

l. Decision about Hartley F_{max} test.

8.7. Given the following values, carry out a t test for significance of difference between means.

Means = 45.3 and 51.4

N's = 37 and 63; s's = 2.8, 2.4

$H_o: \mu_1 = \mu_2$

$H_1: \mu_1 \neq \mu_2$

$P \leq .01$ (two-tailed)

a. t_{obs}

b. t_{cv}

c. df

d. Decision about mean difference

e. Change the level of significance to .001. What is the new critical value of t?

f. Decision about mean difference with $P \leq .001$

8.8. You have the following sample variances as a part of applying a one-way ANOVA F test. You want to know whether homogeneity of variance exists at the .05 level of significance. Carry out the Cochran C test by applying the appropriate formula. Show your results in the answers below. Fill in all values requested.

N = 12, 14, 10, 17

s^2s = 29.5, 35.3, 40.1, 18.2

a. Sum of variances

b. Largest variance

c. C_{obs}

d. C_{cv}

e. k

f. df

g. Decision about homogeneity of variance

8.9. Given following information, test hypothesis set using t test:

$H_o: \mu_1 = \mu_2$

$H_1: \mu_1 \neq \mu_2; P \leq .10$ (two-tailed test)

Means: 92, 99

standard error of the difference between means = 3

Ns = 52 and 108

a. t_{cv}

b. t_{obs}

c. df

d. Decision about t test

8.10. You have six samples, with a total N = 94. These six samples consist of prisoners taken from six different prisons. The prisons range in type from minimum security to maximum security. You have divided these prisoners into two groups according to how long they have been confined, from 1 to 3 years, and 4 or more years. You measure their prison adjustment using a standard prison adjustment inventory. First, you want to learn whether the type of prison where these inmates are confined has an impact on their average scores on the prison adjustment inventory. Next, you want to determine if the length of time the inmates have been in prison has influenced their prison adjustment score. Also, you want to see if there are any interaction effects present between type of prison and length of confinement on these prison adjustment scores. You decide to carry out a two-way ANOVA test. Below is information useful in constructing a two-way ANOVA summary table. Construct your own two-way ANOVA summary table, fill in the known information, and determine the requested values. For solving requested values for this problem, a knowledge of raw scores, means, and grand means is not necessary. This problem is similar to filling in the blanks based on your knowledge of available information provided below. You performed similar tasks in one-way ANOVA problems earlier.

Main effect 1 (factor 1) = type of prison where inmates are confined

Main effect 2 (factor 2) = length of time confined

Interaction effect = type of prison where confined and length of time confined

Dependent variable = prison adjustment score

$P \leq .05$

Total N = 94

SS for factor 1 = 36.15

MS for factor 2 = 18.52

SS within groups = 625

a. df for main effect factor 1

b. df for main effect factor 2

c. df for interaction effects

d. df within groups

e. total df

f. MS for factor 1

g. SS for factor 2

h. MS for within groups

i. F_{obs} for main effect factor 1

j. F_{obs} for main effect factor 2

k. F_{obs} for interaction effects

l. F critical value for factor 1

m. F critical value for factor 2

n. F critical value for interaction effects

o. Decisions about main effects (factors 1 and 2) and interaction effects on prison adjustment scores

References

Lange, James E., Mark B. Johnson, and Robert B. Voas (2005). "Testing the Racial Profiling Hypothesis for Seemingly Disparate Traffic Stops on the New Jersey Turnpike." *Justice Quarterly* **22:**193–222.

Mallett, Christopher A. (2006). "Juvenile Court Probation Supervised Youths: At Risk in Cuyahoga County, Ohio." *Corrections Compendium* **31:**1–5, 27–33.

Simpson, Sally S., Leana Allen Bouffard, Joel Garner, and Laura Hickman (2006). "The Influence of Legal Reform on the Probability of Arrest in Domestic Violence Cases." *Justice Quarterly* **23:**297–316.

Strickland, Mark J. (2006). "Causations of Stress Among Correctional Officers." *American Jails* **20:**69–77.

CHAPTER 9

Nominal-Level Nonparametric Tests of Significance

Chapter Outline

Chapter Objectives

After reading this chapter, the following objectives will be realized:

1. understanding the concept of "goodness of fit" as it pertains to chi-square tests of significance;

2. describing elementary tabular construction and the application of statistical tests of significance;

3. differentiating between one-variable and two-variable tables for chi-square analyses;

4. understanding chi square–based statistical procedures and their significance;

5. understanding the meaning of degrees of freedom applied to chi square–based tests;

6. describing the chi-square test for single-sample, two-sample, and *k*-sample applications, proportions; and

7. describing related-sample tests such as the McNemar test for significance of change and Cochran's *Q* test.

INTRODUCTION

This chapter examines several popular nonparametric statistical tests that are of value to criminal justice professionals and criminologists. These tests are designed for data applications appropriate for the nominal level of measurement. Generally, these procedures are the least restrictive in their application.

This chapter is organized as follows. First, an explanation is provided of "goodness of fit" statistical tests. These are sometimes referred to as chi square–based tests. Chi-square tests are popular, and they are easy to apply, having few restrictive assumptions underlying their application for criminological data. A presentation illustrating tabular construction is provided. Chi-square tests are applicable for data arranged in cross-tabulations. One-variable, two-variable, and *k*-variable tables will be illustrated for chi-square use. Together with these illustrations, degrees of freedom (*df*) will be explained. Degrees of freedom are used to enter Table A.4 in Appendix A, the distribution of χ^2, and determining critical values of chi-square.

The chapter next presents the chi-square test for a single sample. A discussion of the chi-square test's assumptions, advantages and disadvantages, and suggested applications will be given. Useful examples from the criminological literature will be the bases for how this and other chi square–based tests can be applied in criminological research.

The following section describes a two-sample chi-square test for two independent samples. A synopsis of its assumptions, advantages and disadvantages, and potential research applications will be provided. Next is a discussion of a two-related-sample test known as the McNemar test for significance of change. The McNemar test will be illustrated with an example from the criminal justice literature. The McNemar test is also a chi square–based statistical procedure.

The last part of the chapter examines two *k*-sample tests of significance. The first test is an extension of the chi-square test for two independent samples for *k*-sample situations. The second test is the Cochran *Q* test for *k*-related samples, also chi-square based. In each case, the assumptions, advantages and disadvantages, and potential applications for criminal justice and criminology will be presented. *SPSS* illustrations will be provided for all tests presented. Several numerical problems are provided at the end of this chapter for student practice. These procedures lend themselves to *SPSS* alternative solutions as well, if students have access to such software.

GOODNESS OF FIT AND CHI SQUARE–BASED MEASURES

All statistical procedures presented in this chapter are **goodness-of-fit tests. Goodness of fit** refers to the fit or match between what is observed and what is expected according to chance. Another way of viewing goodness of fit is the fit between **observed frequencies** and **expected frequencies**. Observed frequencies are what investigators see whenever they collect and organize data. These are scores taken from questionnaires, raw data from interviews, and other quantified information. Expected frequencies are defined according to chance expectations, which are usually determined by the number of categories into which our data are divided.

An example might be a hypothetical sample of 100 convicted rapists in Minnesota for 2008. Suppose that we knew absolutely nothing about the characteristics of these rapists, including their gender. Expected frequencies are defined by the number of categories into which they are divided. For example, if we distributed 300 persons across three different categories, we would expect to find 100 persons in each of the three categories. Our expected frequencies would be defined as N/k, where N = the number of persons and k = the number of categories. In our hypothetical example, if N = 300 and k = 3, then 300/3 = 100 frequencies per category. Thus, we would expect 100 persons to be found in each of the three categories. Applying the N/k formula to our hypothetical sample of 100 Minnesota rapists, we would create two gender subclasses: male and female. Determining how many rapists of each gender would be expected according to chance, we would simply divide 100 by 2, or 100/2 = 50 to yield the following as shown in Table 9.1.

In this example, according to chance, the number of rapists in the two gender subclasses would be 50. In Table 9.1, we have placed our expected 50 male rapists into cell a and our expected 50 female rapists into cell b. What if we tabulate the actual numbers of 100 Minnesota rapists who are male and female? We might observe the following distribution in Table 9.2.

These frequencies are known as observed frequencies, since they are what we actually observe when we tabulate our collected information about the 100 Minnesota rapists. We have found that 90 rapists are male placed in cell a of Table 9.2. The remaining 10 rapists are female placed in cell b of Table 9.2. The goodness of fit is the discrepancy or difference between what is observed in Table 9.2 and what is expected according to chance in Table 9.1. A comparison is made of the expected 50–50 split and the observed 90–10 split to determine goodness of fit.

There is a poor fit between these observed and expected frequencies. The greater the discrepancy between what we expect and observe, the greater the significance of difference. If we were to apply a goodness-of-fit test to evaluate the significance of this difference, our test results would likely show statistical significance. Had our observed numbers of rapists been more evenly distributed, such as a 55–45 split, the goodness of fit is closer and the

TABLE 9.1 Expected Numbers of 100 Male and Female Minnesota Rapists

Expected Numbers of Male and Female Minnesota Rapists

Gender

Male	Female	
50a	50b	N = 100

TABLE 9.2 Observed Numbers of 100 Male and Female Minnesota Rapists

Observed Numbers of Male and Female Minnesota Rapists

Gender		
Male	**Female**	
90a	10b	$N = 100$

likelihood of significance of difference decreases. This is where the chi-square test can be useful in evaluating the significance of these divisions of frequencies on selected variables.

ELEMENTARY TABLE CONSTRUCTION

One-Variable Tables

Before proceeding with illustrations and applications of actual statistical tests, let's examine simple table construction. The absolute smallest tables we can generate for data analyses are illustrated in Tables 9.1 and 9.2. In the examples of different table sizes below, we will use letters to define **cells** in our tables. We have already seen two cells namely a and b in Tables 9.1 and 9.2. Any table we construct consists of one or more rows (r) or columns (c) and is expressed as $r \times c$. Therefore, we know the specific shape of any given table if we know the number of rows, r, and the number of columns, c. Tables of different $r \times c$ sizes are illustrated by the following examples. Tables 9.3 and 9.4 show 1×2 and 2×1 sizes respectively. Cells in each table have been labeled a and b.

Notice that in Table 9.3 there is one row, r_1 and two columns, c_1 and c_2. In Table 9.4, there is only one column, c_1 and two rows, r_1 and r_2. These two table sizes are the smallest table sizes that can exist for simple tabular data analysis.

TABLE 9.3 A 1 × 2 Table

	c_1	c_2
r_1	a	b

TABLE 9.4 A 2 × 1 Table

	c_1
r_1	a
r_2	b

TABLE 9.5 A 2 × 2 Table

	c_1	c_2
r_1	a	b
r_2	c	d

Two-Variable Tables: The $r \times c$ Case

Table 9.5 shows a **2 × 2 table**. This table has two rows and two columns and is the most common table observed in criminal justice and criminological literature.

In Table 9.5, there are four cells: *a*, *b*, *c*, and *d*. These cells represent a **cross tabulation** of two variables according to two subclasses each. The columns represent two subdivisions on the first variable, the independent variable, while the two rows represent subclasses on another variable, the dependent variable. Such 2 × 2 tables are often used to show whether any variation exists on the dependent variable subclasses that might be attributable to or caused by variation on the independent variable subclasses.

k-Variable Tables

If we add a third subclass to the independent variable, we can generate a 2 × 3 table as shown in Table 9.6. The columns in Table 9.6 might be three samples or *k* = 3. Or they can be viewed simply as three subdivisions on the independent variable.

In Table 9.6, the different cells have been labeled *a*, *b*, *c*, *d*, *e*, and *f*. This 2 × 3 table would be a *k*-sample table, since there are three subclasses on the independent variable. These subclasses could easily represent three different samples of persons, such as different types of inmates, different ethnicities or races, different religious faiths, different political affiliations, or different social backgrounds. Any 2 × 3 table or larger is considered a *k*-sample table for purposes of statistical analysis and chi-square applications.

Degrees of Freedom, *df*

Degrees of freedom, *df*, are defined as $(r-1)(c-1)$ for any **$r \times c$ table**. For the smallest table sizes where there is only one column or one row (e.g., 2×1, 1×2), $df = r - 1$ or $c - 1 = 2 - 1 = 1$ *df*, or $k - 1$ in the general case. *k* simply refers to the number of categories into which the data are divided. Thus, *k* can be either the number of rows or the number of columns.

If there are two rows and two columns, then $(r - 1)(c - 1) = (1)(1) = 1$ *df*. For larger tables, such as a 4 × 4 table, $df = (4 - 1)(4 - 1) = (3)(3) = 9$ *df*. For a 6 × 6 table, $df = (6 - 1)(6 - 1) = (5)(5) = 25$ *df*, and so on. These *df* are taken to Table A.4 of Appendix A, p. 448, where they are found down the left-hand side of the page. Probabilities at which hypotheses are being tested are found across the top of the table for both one- and two-tailed tests.

TABLE 9.6 A 2 × 3 Table

	c_1	c_2	c_3
r_1	a	b	c
r_2	d	e	f

Test Power and Its Meaning

One of the criteria for choosing one test of significance over others is the power of the test, or the ability of the test to reject null hypotheses whenever they are false and ought to be rejected. Chapters 9 and 10 contain a variety of nonparametric tests which have fewer restrictive assumptions associated with their application compared with the tests which were covered in Chapter 8. The tests in Chapter 8 were parametric tests, in that certain distributional assumptions were required, such as the normal distribution. No test in this chapter makes such an assumption. Another feature of parametric tests is that they usually require interval-level data. Nonparametric tests require only nominal- and ordinal-level data.

Chapter 7 examined various decision rules, including the level of significance, the sampling distribution of a statistic, and critical regions or regions of rejection. Type I and Type II errors were described and discussed. Power was determined to be $1 - \beta$, and it was found to be indirectly affected by one's sample size, the level of significance selected (Type I error or α error), and the sampling distribution of a statistic. Since the advantages and disadvantages of the tests in this chapter and those in Chapter 10 will include their comparative power relative to the most powerful tests presented in Chapter 8, a brief discussion of power and how it is determined is included here. The purpose of this discussion is to show what power is and how it is determined. Illustrations of the different factors that affect power are provided. Thus, subsequent comparisons of nonparametric tests and their power will be more meaningful.

The following examples are designed to assist in understanding the meaning of the power of a test and how it is affected by factors such as the level of significance, sample size, and the location of various observed sample means in relation to some hypothesized mean. Also, it makes a difference for test power whether the test is one-tailed (directional) or two-tailed (nondirectional). A simple single-sample Z test will be used. Suppose we were to test the following:

$H_o: \mu = 100$

$H_1: \mu \neq 100$

$P \leq .05$ (two-tailed test)

The following information is provided: $\overline{X}_{obs} = 110$, $s_{\overline{x}} = 5$.

To determine the power of this test, we begin by drawing a sampling distribution of the sample mean or a distribution shaped like the normal curve, designated a $\mu = 100$ at the center of the horizontal axis. Next, we would create and draw critical regions on this distribution, using the level of significance ($P > .05$, two-tailed) being used. We would divide the .05 level of significance into two equal parts. Each of these parts would be placed in the left and right tails of the curve we have just drawn. Thus, $.05/2 = .025$. We would place .025 in each of the curve tails to the left and right. This is illustrated in the first example, Example 1, shown in Figure 9.1.

Example 1. In this example, we would locate the proportion of curve area in Table A.2 of Appendix A that corresponds with and leaves .0250 of the curve area in each tail. This Z value is ± 1.96. Notice that ± 1.96 cuts off .4750 of curve area, leaving .0250 of it in each tail.

Next, identify a second normal curve, one having an observed $= 110$ as the mean of it. We are assuming that our distributions of scores are normal in order to use the sampling distribution of the means. The second curve we draw is positioned to the right of the first curve, since 110 is larger than or to the right of the hypothesized $\mu = 100$, as Example 1 illustrates. The small shaded portions of the first curve are the critical regions. Note also that a line has been extended upward at the point of the critical region of the first curve, where $+ 1.96$ is

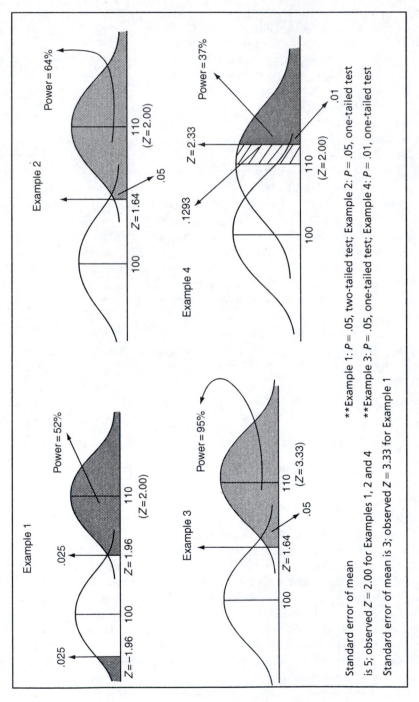

FIGURE 9.1 Four Examples of Determining Statistical Test Power.

found. There is a shaded portion of the second curve lying to the right of this line. All of this shaded portion of the second curve area is the power of the test or the probability of rejecting a null hypothesis when it is false and ought to be rejected.

For now, it is only important to know that the power of this particular test is all of the proportion of second curve area lying to the right of the critical region point of the first curve we have drawn. The vertical line drawn defining the right critical region area intersects the second curve area. Thus, all of the area of the second curve to the right of this vertical line is test power. Determining the amount of this second curve area lying to the right of the critical region of the first curve will require us to apply what was learned about the normal curve and its properties from Chapter 6.

For instance, we know that over half of the second curve area lies in the rejection region or critical region of the first curve. We can see this directly from the curves we have drawn. But for the present, we don't know how much more than 50 percent of the second curve lies to the right of the critical region of the first curve. We must therefore assign a Z value to our observed $\overline{X} = 110$. This can be done by dividing the difference between the observed and hypothesized means by the standard error of the mean, or $s_{\overline{x}} = 5$, or $(110 - 100)/5 = 10/5 = +2.00$. Notice the similarity between this procedure and the t test computed in Chapter 8. This Z value becomes our Z value for the observed $\overline{X} = 110$.

Next, we must determine the difference between the two Z values, the $+1.96$ which defines the critical region of the first curve and the $+2.00$ that is associated with the observed $\overline{X} = 110$. The absolute Z value difference is $|2.00 - 1.96| = .04$. This value is also a Z value. We can look up this Z value in Table A.2 and determine that it cuts off .0160 of curve area. Let's round this proportion, .0160, to .02. Now we know how much of the second curve area actually lies between the critical region of the first curve, defined by the $+1.96$, and the mean of the second curve, or 110. We simply add this .02 to the known 50 percent of the second curve area lying to the right of the mean of 110, or $.5000 + .0200$ (or .02), and this yields our power of .52. Thus, $1 - \beta = .52$ as Example 1 illustrates. We have now actually computed the power of this particular test and it is known.

What if we were to keep all of the facts the same from Example 1, except this time we will change the hypothesis set from a two-tailed example to a one-tailed, directional example. This is illustrated as Example 2.

$H_o: \mu \leq 100$

$H_1: \mu > 100$

$P \leq .05$ (one-tailed test)

Assume an $\overline{X}_{obs} = 110, s_{\overline{x}} = 5$.

Example 2 is the new hypothesis set, and we have made a directional, one-tailed prediction that μ will be greater than 100. By inspection, we can see that our observed $\overline{X}$ is greater than 100. Therefore, at least we have made a correct directional prediction. We will now repeat what was done in the two-tailed test presented in Example 1. We will draw the first curve, a sampling distribution of the mean, with a $\mu = 100$ placed at the center of the horizontal axis. However, this time we will not halve the significance level of .05. Rather, we will place all of this .05 in the right tail of this curve. We know the curve tail where this probability should be located, since we know the prediction made under H_1 which states that $\mu > 100$. We will repeat the steps followed in Example 1 and now we have a new first curve/second curve scenario as shown in Figure 9.1, Example 2.

Example 2 shows that more than 50 percent of the second curve area lies to the right of the critical region of the first curve. A new Z value $= +1.64$ has been determined by consulting

Table A.2 of Appendix A. We selected + 1.64 since this Z value cuts off .4500 of curve area, leaving .0500 or 5 percent of it in the right tail of our first curve. Again, we must determine how much more than 50 percent of the second curve area is actually included between the Z value of + 1.64 and our $\overline{X}_{obs} = 110$. This means that we must again convert our observed mean of 110 into a Z value. This Z value would be determined by taking the difference between the hypothesized μ and our observed $\overline{X}$ and dividing this difference by $s_{\overline{x}} = 5$, or $(110 - 100)/5 = 10/5 = 2.00$. The Z value associated with our observed $\overline{X}$ of $110 = 2.00$, as shown in Example 2 in Figure 9.1. The absolute difference between these two Z values, or $|1.64 - 2.00| = .36$. This value is also a Z value and we determine that a $Z = .36$ cuts off .1406 of curve area. This amount of curve area is now added to the 50 percent of the second curve area lying to the right of the mean of 110. Therefore, we have $.5000 + .1406 = .6406$, or rounded to .64. Power for Example 2 is .64. This new power computation is based on a one-tailed hypothesis test using the .05 level of significance. The only difference between Example 1 and Example 2 is the fact that we changed the second test from a two-tailed, nondirectional test to a one-tailed directional test. The purpose of these first two examples is to illustrate that under the same level-of-significance conditions, with all other factors being equal, one-tailed tests where correct directional predictions are made are *more powerful* than two-tailed tests where no directional prediction is made.

Another example will be provided, this time showing what happens if we change the sample size being studied. It is known that test power can usually be increased if our sample size increases. If we were to double our sample size, for instance, this larger sample size would influence the denominator term in our computation of the standard error of the mean formula. One direct result of increasing the sample size would be to reduce the magnitude of the standard error of the mean, $s_{\overline{x}}$. Suppose we increased our sample size so that the new standard error term, $s_{\overline{x}} = 3$ instead of 5. Using our one-tailed hypothesis set example, Example 2, and keeping all other facts in the example the same, including significance level, direction of our hypothesis test prediction, and the same observed and hypothesized means, we would do exactly what was done earlier to create the graphic scenario in Example 2. Except we now have a different amount of second curve area lying in the critical region of the first curve. This fact is illustrated in Example 3 in Figure 9.1.

Notice that although 110 and 100 do not change in relation to one another, the distance between them, as measured by $s_{\overline{x}}$ units, changes. Using the new $s_{\overline{x}} = 3$, a new Z value must be determined. This new calculation is $(110 - 100)/3 = 10/3 = 3.33$. Thus, the new Z value for the observed $\overline{X} = 3.33$. Again, we calculate the absolute difference between these two Z values, that is, the one defining our critical region on the first curve, or + 1.64, and the new Z of 3.33 associated with the sample mean of 110, the mean of the second curve, or $|1.64 - 3.33| = 1.69$. This 1.69 is also a Z value, and we determine from Table A.2 that it cuts off .4545 of curve area. This is the shaded portion of second curve area between the mean of 110 and the Z of 1.64 defining the critical region of the first curve. We must add this amount of curve area to that lying to the right of 110, or $.5000 + .4545 = .9545$, which we will round to .95. Thus, our new test power = 95 percent. Increasing our sample size substantially greatly increased the test power under those changed conditions. Sample size does indeed influence test power.

One additional example is provided. This time we will illustrate what happens if the level of significance is changed when we make a hypothesis test. Let's retain all of our factual information used in Example 2, using the same hypothesis set, and where $s_{\overline{x}} = 5$, the observed $\overline{X} = 110$, and $\mu = 100$, and a one-tailed hypothesis test is made, predicting under H_1 that $\mu > 100$.

This time the level of significance will be changed from .05 to .01. We can examine in Example 4, Figure 9.1, the effect of this change in the level of significance on test power. Notice that the Z value changes from 1.64 to 2.33. This is because the right area of the first curve will contain .01 instead of .05. The Z value cutting off .4900 of curve area is 2.33. Now the mean of the second curve, 110, lies to the left of the critical region rather than to the right of it. This means that less than half of the second curve area lies in or to the right of the critical region of the first curve. On the basis of this Z comparison, we would fail to reject H_0 because our observed Z value = 2.00 does not equal or exceed the critical value of Z = 2.33. Anytime we fail to reject an H_0, test power will always be less than 50 percent. Notice in Example 4 that in order to determine test power under these new conditions, we again determine a Z value for our known mean of 110, which is 2.00 from our previous computation, and then we determine the absolute difference between these two Z values, or $|2.00 - 2.33| = .33$. This is also a Z value. Looking up this value in Table A.2, we determine that .1293 of curve area is included as shown in Example 4. But now, instead of adding this amount of .5000 of the second curve area, we must subtract it from .5000. Doing this, $.5000 - .1293 = .3707$ rounded to .37. This means that only 37 percent of the second curve area lies in the critical region of the first curve. This time, power is only 37 percent. Briefly summarizing, we can conclude about power that:

1. Nondirectional tests are generally less powerful than directional tests, provided that we make correct directional predictions under our H_{1s}.
2. Changing the level of significance from .05 to .01 reduces our Type I or α error, but it also increases our Type II or β error. In turn, this reduces our test power, or $1 - \beta$. This is not a direct, one-to-one change, however, as has been illustrated by these examples.
3. Increasing sample size will generally cause increases in test power, since the magnitude of the standard error of the mean is reduced. This makes it possible for observed means to have larger Z values, and thus the distance between observed and hypothesized means is made more statistically significant, simply by increasing the size of one's sample.

Why is test power important to know? Test power is one of several important test selection criteria in this chapter and Chapter 10 where tests of significance for different levels of measurement are discussed. More powerful tests of hypotheses are generally more desirable compared with less powerful tests, but we must not overlook the fact that many less powerful statistical tests are not that much less powerful compared with other more powerful tests. Some nonparametric tests have power equal to 95 percent or more compared with their parametric equivalent tests designed to make similar decisions about samples studied. Thus, while parametric statistical procedures are generally more powerful than nonparametric statistical procedures, many of these nonparametric tests are more realistic to apply in the social sciences. Much of the data examined by researchers are measured according to nominal and ordinal scales, and the most powerful parametric tests almost always assume the data are measured according to interval scales. Furthermore, it is difficult to meet the normality assumption in any test application, parametric or nonparametric.

What can be said about the power we have computed for the four examples illustrated in Figure 9.1? Below is a brief interpretation of the power we have determined for each of these examples.

Example 1: With a power = 52 percent, there is a 52 percent chance of rejecting H_0 when it is false and ought to be rejected. This was a two-tailed test at the .05 level of significance.

Example 2: With a power = 64 percent, there is a 64 percent chance of rejecting H_0 when it is false and ought to be rejected. This is a one-tailed test of the same hypothesis set from Example 1, where a correct directional prediction is made.

Example 3: With a power = .95, there is a 95 percent chance that H_0 is false and ought to be rejected. In this case, our observed mean occurred far away from the hypothesized μ.

But remember that we decreased the size of the standard error of the mean term by increasing sample size. Thus, this illustrates how power may be maximized by simple sample size increases. If you want more powerful statistical tests, add more people to your sample.

Example 4: Whenever we change the level of significance or α from .05 to .01, this makes it more difficult for us to reject our null hypotheses. The level of significance, α, is the probability that we are wrong if H_o is rejected. No one likes to be wrong and so more than a few researchers set very high standards for themselves, using significance levels such as .01 or .001. These levels permit only 1 time in 100 times or 1 time in a 1,000 times of being wrong if H_o is rejected. But there is a penalty incurred if our α error is decreased substantially. That error makes it very difficult to reject H_os, even when they're false and ought to be rejected.

Examine what happened in Example 4. The significance level was changed to .01. This yielded a new critical value of $Z = 2.33$. The lesser standard of $Z = 1.64$ from Example 1 was eliminated as a result. Now we discovered that our observed $\overline{X} = 110$ isn't far enough away from the hypothesized μ to be considered significantly different from it. In this case power or $1 - \beta = .37$, and thus, there is only a 37 percent chance of rejecting H_o when it is false and ought to be rejected. This is one reason why significance levels such as .05 are considered reasonable. Power is one of several important evaluative criteria for determining which statistical tests to apply under certain circumstances.

In this and subsequent chapters examining tests of significance of difference, the power of statistical tests will be reviewed. The traditional standards against which power of statistical tests are compared are the *t* test and *F* test, which we have already examined in Chapter 8. These are the most powerful tests available for determining the significance of difference between two or more samples on some interval-level characteristic we study. Thus, all of the tests in this chapter and Chapter 10 are less powerful compared with *t* or *F* test. But the power differential isn't always great. In some tests to follow, particularly some of those discussed in Chapter 10, we will find that the power associated with them is nearly the same as these parametric equivalents. One test, the Mann-Whitney *U* test, for instance, has about 95 percent power compared with the *t* test for determining the significance of difference between two groups. Other tests have fairly high power as well. Thus, just because a test is nonparametric and by definition less powerful than its parametric counterpart, it doesn't mean we should discount the test or avoid it in research. There are a number of advantages associated with using nonparametric tests as we will discover. The standards for applying such tests are not as stringent as parametric test standards. This is one distinct advantage of nonparametric tests over parametric ones.

SINGLE-SAMPLE TESTS OF SIGNIFICANCE

The Chi-Square Test, χ^2

The **chi-square test**, χ^2, is the most popular goodness-of-fit procedure used in social science literature today. An example of the use of chi-square is a study by Mark Renzema and E. Mayo-Wilson (2005), who were interested in the impact of using electronic monitoring (EM) on moderate to high-risk offenders and their subsequent recidivism. EM has been touted as a powerful supervisory technique for reducing recidivism among probationers. EM devices are electronic wristlets and anklets that emit signals that can be intercepted by monitoring probation agencies. Theoretically, those probationer/clients fixed with

EM devices are more inclined to be law-abiding and adhere to the requirements of their probation programs, because they know that they are being monitored. It may be, however, that probationer/clients considered low risk, compared with those considered moderate or high risk might exhibit differences in recidivism even when monitored by EM. Suppose Renzema and Mayo-Wilson wanted to study a single sample of EM probationer/clients who were also recidivists and who were classified into low, moderate, and high risk. Renzema and Mayo-Wilson may not know how these groupings of probationer/client recidivists will differ, but they expect them to differ on amount of recidivism anyway. Table 9.7 shows a hypothetical distribution of 150 recidivist-probationers on EM divided according to low, moderate, and high risk.

Suppose Renzema and Mayo-Wilson had hypothesized the following:

H_o: *There is no difference among EM low, moderate, and high-risk probationer/clients according to their recidivism.*

H_1: *There is a difference among EM low, moderate, and high-risk probationer/clients according to their recidivism.*

$P \leq .02$ (two-tailed test)

The hypothesis set being tested here is that Renzema and Mayo-Wilson expect that EM low, moderate, and high-risk probationers will differ according to their recidivism. The .02 level of significance is used for a two-tailed, nondirectional test. These researchers would apply the following formula if using the chi-square test for a single sample:

$$\chi^2 = \Sigma \left[\frac{(O_k - E_k)^2}{E_k} \right]$$

where

O_k = the observed frequencies in the kth cell

E_k = the expected frequencies in the kth cell

Where the sample size is 150 and the elements have been divided into three categories, the expected cell frequencies would be defined as N/k. This would yield $150/3 = 50$ probationer/clients per cell. As can be seen from Table 9.7, this equal distribution of frequencies does not exist. To what extent do the observations in Table 9.7 differ from what would be

TABLE 9.7 Hypothetical Sample of Recidivist Probationer/Clients on Electronic Monitoring Divided According to Low, Moderate, and High Risk

	Low Risk	Moderate Risk	High Risk	Total
EM Recidivist Probationers	36	49	65	$N = 150$
%	24%	33%	43%	100%

expected according to chance (e.g., the 50, 50, 50 division expected)? For the data in Table 9.7, we may use the χ^2 formula and carry out our computations as follows:

$$\chi^2_{obs} = \frac{(36-50)^2}{50} + \frac{(49-50)^2}{50} + \frac{(65-50)^2}{50}$$

$$= \frac{(-14)^2}{50} + \frac{(-1)^2}{50} + \frac{(15)^2}{50}$$

$$= \frac{196}{50} + \frac{1}{50} + \frac{225}{50}$$

$$= 3.92 + 0.02 + 4.5$$

$$\chi^2_{obs} = 8.44$$

The observed chi-square (χ^2) value = 8.44.

To determine the significance of this observed χ^2, we turn to Table A.4, Appendix A, p. 448. Across the top of the table are both one-and two-tailed probabilities. Down the left-hand side of the table are degrees of freedom, df. For the single-sample application of χ^2, $df = k-1$, where k = the number of categories into which the sample has been divided. In this case, $k = 3$, and so $df = k-1$ or $3-1$ or $df = 2$. Entering Table A.4 with 2 df at the .02 level of significance with a two-tailed test, we determine where these values intersect in the body of the table. This defines the critical value of χ^2, or 7.824. If our observed χ^2 value equals or exceeds 7.824, then we can reject H_o and support H_1. Since our observed χ^2 value of 8.44 equals or exceeds the critical value in Table A.4, we support H_1 that there is a difference among EM low, moderate, and high-risk probationers according to their recidivism.

Headnotes or helpful instructions in Table A.4 are useful for applying the table for one-tailed hypothesis tests as well as two-tailed tests. Whenever one-tailed χ^2 applications are desired for single-sample tests, we must inspect our observed frequencies to see whether the distribution is in the direction we might expect for H_1. Had we predicted that high-risk probationers would tend to have higher recidivism compared with low-risk or moderate-risk probationer clients, for instance, then our hypothesis set would have been as follows:

H_o: *There is no difference between EM probationer/clients according to their recidivism; if there is a difference, low- and moderate-risk EM probationer/clients will have higher recidivism compared with high-risk probationer/clients.*

H_1: *High-risk probationer/clients will have higher recidivism compared with low-risk and moderate-risk probationer/clients.*

$P \leq .025$ (one-tailed test)

Since our first hypothesis set had a probability of .02 (two-tailed, nondirectional), our second hypothesis test is one-tailed. There is no exact .02 level of significance for a one-tailed probability in Table A.4, but the .025 level of significance comes close to it. If we were to use the .025 level of significance and make a one-tailed test of this hypothesis, the critical value of chi-square, $\chi^2_{cv} = 4.991$. Does our observed χ^2 equal or exceed 4.991? Yes, the $\chi^2_{obs} = 8.44$ equals or exceeds the critical value. Notice that for similar significance levels, the critical values of statistics for one-tailed directional tests tend to be smaller than for two-tailed tests. This is because we can take advantage of the knowledge of what is expected and make a directional prediction. Provided we can make an accurate directional prediction, it is usually easier to reject H_os when they are false and ought to be rejected. One-tailed tests, therefore, are more powerful than two-tailed tests,

BOX 9.1

SPSS Alternative Applications

1. Activate your *SPSS* software program and go to the Data Editor screen. Click on the "Variable View" at the bottom of the screen. Go to the top of the first column and type in "Recidivism" in the blank space. Next, click "Data View." You will see "Recidivism" at the top of the column.

2. Type in 36 as a "1" value, 49 as a "2" value, and 65 as a "3" value for a total of 150 values in the Recidivism column. These match up with and stand for "low," "moderate," and "high risk." This is a tedious process. In actual practice, researchers will have already entered their data, including recidivism scores.

3. Click on "Analyze," then "Nonparametric," and then "Chi Square." This action opens a screen with "Recidivism" in the left-hand window. Highlight "Recidivism" and using the arrow, move it to the "Test Variable List" window. Underneath these windows under "Expected Range," click "Get from data" and "All Categories Equal." Next, click "OK."

4. This action produces two summary tables. These are shown below in this box. The first is "Recidivism" which shows 1, 2, and 3 down the left-hand side and the observed and expected *N*s. Double check to see that there are 36 "1"s, 49 "2"s, and 65 "3"s. The total should be 150.

Chi-Square Test

Frequencies

recidivism

	Observed N	Expected N	Residual
1.00	36	50.0	−14.0
2.00	49	50.0	−1.0
3.00	65	50.0	15.0
Total	150		

Test Statistics

	recidivism
Chi-Square[a]	8.440
df	2
Asymp. sig.	.015

5. The second table is called "Test Statistics." It shows the observed chi-square value = 8.440, 2 *df*, and a two-tailed probability of .015. This is the "Asymp. Sig" or significance level. In the manual computation of chi-square, the observed $\chi^2 = 8.44$, which is the same as what was obtained through the *SPSS* program. If any minor discrepancies occur between manual computations and *SPSS*-generated values, these are most often attributed to rounding error and considered unimportant. The final result is unaffected.

6. Compare the probability, .015, with the probability at which the hypothesis was tested, or .02 (two-tailed). Since .015 is equal to or smaller than .02, H_o can be rejected and H_1 is supported.

7. Had a one-tailed, directional test of this hypothesis been made, the probability .015 would be halved, or .015/2 = .0075. Thus, we have changed the two-tailed probability into a one-tailed probability. This one-tailed probability is equal to or smaller than .025 and therefore the null hypothesis can be rejected and the research hypothesis supported. There is a .025 chance of being wrong in making this decision.

especially where information exists that enables researchers to make one-tailed predictions of outcomes such as in this scenario we have presented. Also, one-tailed tests always require careful inspection of the distribution of observed cell frequencies to make sure they are in the predicted direction as specified in our H_1s.

ASSUMPTIONS, ADVANTAGES, AND DISADVANTAGES OF CHI-SQUARE.   Three assumptions of the chi-square test are: (1) randomness; (2) the nominal level of measurement; and (3) a sample size equal to 25 or larger. The chi-square test is easy to apply and interpret. It has both one-and two-tailed applications and may be applied to any data in categorical form. An interpretive table (Table A.4 in Appendix A) exists for a rapid determination of critical values of this statistic. A major weakness of the chi-square test is the sensitivity of the test to very small or very large samples. The reasonable operating range for the chi-square test is a sample size variation from 25 to 250. This doesn't mean that chi-square cannot be applied to smaller or larger samples. But greater distortions in the magnitude of the resulting chi-square value occur when one's collected data is outside of this range. The greater the departure from this range of Ns, the greater the distortion. In turn, probabilities are affected and our interpretations of test results are likewise affected.

This sensitivity of chi-square to sample size can be illustrated by using the data from Table 9.7. For example, the distribution of frequencies throughout the three cells in the table was 36, 49, and 65. What if we were to double these in the three cells? We would have $(2)(36) = 72$, $(2)(49) = 98$, and $(2)(65) = 130$, or a total $N = 300$. Our original chi-square observed was 8.44 based on the distribution of the original frequencies. If we double these frequencies exactly as they occur in these cells, we have twice as many frequencies. But what is the impact on our application of the chi-square test to the doubled frequencies in a new table, with 72, 98, and 130 frequencies in the three cells? The effect is an exact doubling of the chi-square value, or $(2)(\chi^2) = (2)(8.44) =$ 16.88. (This new value of chi-square, 16.88, is left as an exercise.) The point is that nothing has been done to change the proportionate distribution of these frequencies. But the statistical significance of what we have observed has increased immensely. This example illustrates the sensitivity of chi-square to larger samples. The statistical significance of whatever is observed is enhanced, but it means nothing. The original proportionate distribution of frequencies is the same.

Another problem is that the frequencies are converted to percentages, some researchers will use the percentages as the bases for their chi-square computations. Chi-square should never be applied to percentages. Every time our frequencies are converted to percentages, this is the equivalent of treating our sample size as 100 rather than 150 or some other actual total number of frequencies.

A TWO-SAMPLE TEST

In this section, a two independent-sample test is presented. This is the chi-square test for two independent samples.

The Chi-Square Test for Two Independent Samples

The **chi-square test for two independent samples** is an extension of the single-sample chi-square test. The two-sample chi-square test is applied to data that are cross tabulated, usually into 2×2 tables. An application of the chi-square test for two independent samples is a study conducted by Min Xie et al. (2006), who studied victim reporting of crimes to police and previous police response to past victimizations. Xie et al. learned that whatever victims report to police is influenced greatly by how police officers have handled previous victimizations that have been reported. Perhaps some crime victims have reported prior crimes to police officers and no perpetrators were ever caught. If property was stolen, it was never recovered. Yet other victims may have had positive experiences with police responses to their own victimizations. Xie et al. argued that the probability that victims would report crimes to the police relates positively to whether arrests are made and the level of investigatory effort by police following previous victimizations. Essentially, Xie et al. hypothesized that crime victims would more likely report crimes to the police if they or other household members had positive experiences as the result of their crime reporting. Suppose that Xie et al. wanted to study repeat victimizations. They might obtain a sample of 228 crime victims and divide them according to whether police had been called when other household members had been victimized previously at least once. They could cross tabulate this information with whether police were called when they were victims themselves and had been victimized once before. Such information might be shown in Table 9.8. They might hypothesize the following:

> H_o: *Crime victims who have had other household members who reported prior victimizations to the police will not differ in reporting their own victimizations compared with crime victims who have not had other household members report prior victimizations to the police.*

> H_1: *Crime victims who have had other household members who reported prior victimizations to the police will differ in reporting their own victimizations compared with crime victims who have not had other household members report prior victimizations to the police.*

> $P \le .01$ (two-tailed test)

The frequencies shown in Table 9.8 are called the observed cell frequencies. In order to calculate the chi-square observed (χ^2_{obs})for the data in Table 9.8, we must calculate the expected cell frequencies. This will enable us to apply the formula we used earlier in this chapter for the single-sample application of the chi-square test, or

$$\chi^2 = \Sigma \left[\frac{(O_k - E_k)^2}{E_k} \right]$$

where

O_k = the observed frequency for any given cell

E_k = the expected frequency for any given cell

TABLE 9.8 Hypothetical Distribution of Crime Victims Who Have and Have Not Had Other Household Members Report Prior Crime Victimizations to the Police and Whether They Report Their Own Victimizations

		Police Called When Other Household Members Were Victimized Once or More		
		Yes	No	Totals
Police Called When Respondent Victimized At Least Once	Yes	68a	35b	103(a + b)
	No	29c	96d	125(c + d)
	Totals	97 (a + c)	131 (b + d)	228 = N

Expected cell frequencies are determined for each cell by multiplying the row total in which any given cell is found by the column total in which that cell is found and then dividing the product by the total number of frequencies for the table. Row and column totals are called the **marginal totals**. Essentially, **expected cell frequencies** are determined from the marginal totals. Symbolically expressed, each expected frequency for cells a, b, c, and d would be calculated as follows:
Cell

$$a = (a + b)(a + c)/N$$
$$b = (a + b)(b + d)/N$$
$$c = (c + d)(a + c)/N$$
$$d = (c + d)(b + d)/N$$

Using the actual marginal totals, we would calculate expected cell frequencies as follows:
Cell

$$a = (103)(97)/228 = 43.8$$
$$b = (103)(131)/228 = 59.2$$
$$c = (125)(97)/228 = 53.2$$
$$d = (125)(131)/228 = 71.8$$

With these expected cell frequencies determined, we may compute the observed χ^2 value:

$$\chi^2 = \frac{(68 - 43.8)^2}{43.8} + \frac{(35 - 59.2)^2}{59.2} + \frac{(29 - 53.2)^2}{53.2} + \frac{(96 - 71.8)^2}{71.8}$$
$$= 13.4 + 9.9 + 11.0 + 8.2$$
$$= 42.5$$

The resulting chi-square is 42.5. This is observed chi-square, or $\chi^2_{obs} = 42.5$. Using Table A.4 of Appendix A, p. 448, with $(2 - 1)(2 - 1)$ degrees of freedom $(r - 1)(c - 1) = 1$ df, where the .01 level of significance for a two-tailed test intersects with 1 df defines the critical value of chi-square, χ^2_{cv}. We must equal or exceed this critical value with our observed χ^2 in order to reject H_o. The critical value of chi-square $= 6.635$. In this case, our observed $\chi^2 = 42.5$ easily equals or exceeds this value and we can reject H_o and support H_1 at the .01 level of significance (two-tailed test). The two groups differ significantly. Crime victims who have had other members of their household victimized at least once previously differ from those who have not had other household members victimized according to whether they will report their own victimizations to the police.

There is no reason to treat the large value of the observed $\chi^2 = 42.5$ with greater significance than a smaller observed value of it. The simple decision made is whether the critical value of χ^2 is equaled or exceeded in Table A.4. Larger observed chi-square values are primarily a function of larger sample sizes, such as an $N = 228$. Notice that the .001 critical value of chi-square was also exceeded. Sometimes researchers will express their findings as follows: $\chi^2_{obs} = 42.5$, $P < .01 < .001$ (two-tailed test). This expression says that the statistical finding was not only significant at .01, but it was also significant at the .001 level. Sometimes this information is added to make a stronger impression on those seeking more rigor in hypothesis testing.

BOX 9.2

SPSS Alternative Application

1. Activate your *SPSS* software program and open the Data Editor window. From the data provided in Table 9.8, the independent variable is "Police Called When Other Household Members Were Victimized Once or More." "Yes" and "No" are the two subdivisions on this variable. There were 97 "Yes" responses and 131 "No" responses. These will be designated numerically as "1" for "Yes" and "2" for "No." Using the Variable View at the bottom of the Data Editor screen, type in "twoormore." In the second column, type in "once." Switch back to the Data View and begin typing in 97 as a "1" value in the "twoormore" column, and then continue typing in 131 as a "2" value for a total of 228 values.

2. Go to the second column, "once," which is the dependent variable. It is also divided into "Yes" and "No" categories. We will label "Yes" responses with a "1," while "No" responses will be labeled with a "2." Using cell *a* first, type in 68 as a "1" value in the "once" column. Continue typing 29 as a "2" value in the same column from cell *c*. Move next to cell *b* and type in 35 as a "1" value, and finally, type in 96 as a "2" value. Column 2, "once," should now have 228 values in it.

3. Next, click on "Analyze," then "Descriptives," then "Crosstabs." This brings up a screen with several windows. You can see in the left-hand window "once" and "twoormore." Highlight "once" and move it with the arrow to the "Row(s)" window. Highlight "twoormore" and use the arrow to move this variable to the "Column(s)" window.

4. Next, click "Statistics" at the bottom of the screen and this brings up numerous correlation coefficients. Notice in the upper left-hand corner of the options is "Chi Square." Click the space beside this option. Next, click "Continue." This brings you back to the previous screen. Now click "OK."

5. Three tables are generated and are shown below. The first table, "Case Processing Summary," shows that indeed, you have an $N = 228$. The second table should look exactly like the distribution of frequencies originally found in Table 9.8. This table is called "once*twoormore

Case Processing Summary

	Cases					
	Valid		Missing		Total	
	N	**Percent**	**N**	**Percent**	**N**	**Percent**
once*two or more	228	100.0%	0	.0%	228	100.0%

once*twoormore Crosstabulation
Count

		two or more		
		1.00	2.00	Total
once	1.00	68	35	103
	2.00	29	96	125
Total		97	131	228

(continued)

(continued)

Chi-Square Tests

	Value	df	Asymp. Sig. (2-sided)	Exact Sig. (2-sided)	Exact Sig. (1-sided)
Pearson Chi-Square	42.357[b]	1	.000		
Continuity Correction[a]	40.623	1	.000		
Likelihood Ratio	43.539	1	.000		
Fishwe's Exact Test				.000	.000
Linear-by-Linear Association	42.171	1	.000		
N of Valid Cases	228				

[a]Computer only for a 2 × 2 table
[b]0 cells (.0%) have expected count less than 5. The minimum expected count is 43.82

Crosstabulation." If there are discrepancies, you made a mistake during data entry and should recheck your work. If everything matches, proceed.

6. The third table, "Chi-Square Tests," contains the most important interpretive information. Your primary objective was to determine the observed χ^2 value. Although there are several different values shown in this table, the most important one is "Pearson Chi-Square." Notice that it is 42.357, with 1 *df*, and an Asym. Sig. = .000. This means that the chi-square observed was significant at least at the level of significance used in the original problem, $P \leq .01$. Again, the Asym. Sig. designation is the probability level at which the observed chi-square of 42.357 is significant. Notice that the two chi-square observed values, the one computed manually, 42.5, and the *SPSS*-generated value, 42.357, are not exact but close. Again, rounding error is responsible for this minor difference and the difference can be ignored.

ASSUMPTIONS, ADVANTAGES, AND DISADVANTAGES OF THE CHI-SQUARE TEST. The assumptions of the chi-square test for two samples are: (1) randomness, (2) two independent samples, and (3) nominal-level data. The chi-square test for two independent samples is comparable to the single-sample application of it, with the exception of how *df* are computed. The test is easy to apply and interpret. There are few restrictive assumptions governing its application.

YATES' CORRECTION FOR CONTINUITY. Whenever sample sizes in a 2 × 2 table range from 25 to 75, a correction factor has been used that reduces the size of the resulting observed chi-square value. This correction factor is called **Yates' correction for continuity**. Essentially, it consists of reducing the difference between observed cell frequencies and expected cell frequencies by .5 for each of the four cells. Thus, if there were a difference between an observed cell frequency and expected cell frequency for cell *a* of 3.5, this difference would be adjusted to 3, a reduction of .5 points. For each of the four table cells, this .5 correction would reduce slightly the resulting chi-square value. This is a conservative procedure that reduces the likelihood of yielding significant chi-square values. It is included here for two reasons. First, it is sometimes used in the social science literature whenever chi-square tests are used. Second, it is often displayed in software programs where data are expressed in 2×2 tabular form. For larger sample sizes, such as $N > 75$, Yates' correction is negligible to the final chi-square result.

TWO-SAMPLE TESTS: RELATED SAMPLES

The McNemar Test for Significance of Change, χ^2_m

The **McNemar test for significance of change** is one of the only tests of its kind for use with related samples of elements. In this case, it works best whenever persons are used as their own controls in before-after experiments. The McNemar test is a chi square–based statistic designed to measure whether persons change their behaviors between two time periods, usually as the result of an intervening or experimental variable. An application of the McNemar test is illustrated with some research conducted by Seave (2006), who studied the incidence of spousal abuse in selected California jurisdictions, particularly physical violence among spouses and the battering phenomenon. One solution to the problem of battering investigated by Seave was the issuance of restraining orders or protective orders to bar batterers from coming near or harming their spouses. Suppose Seave wished to investigate the problem of battering through the use of an intervention involving anger management. If batterers were required to participate in anger-management counseling, would this have any deterrent value on their propensity to commit spousal assault and be considered batterers? Suppose Seave investigated the impact of an anger-control intervention, where a sample of wife batterers participated in a 10-week program designed to curb their propensity for physical violence toward their spouses. Assume that Seave obtained a sample of 186 batterers who had measurably different anger levels according to a well-known anger scale. Perhaps Seave believed that batterers' exposure to the 10-week course in anger control would tend to reduce their anger levels and, accordingly, their propensity to commit physical violence against their spouses. According to these 186 batterers' scores on the anger scale, Seave might divide the sample of batterers into two groups: those with high anger levels and those with low anger levels. After the 10-week course, Seave might measure the anger levels of these persons again to determine whether the course had any impact on changing their anger levels from one time period (before the course) to the next (after the course). Seave might create a table such as that shown in Table 9.9.

TABLE 9.9 Anger Levels of 186 Batterers Before and After a 10-Week Intervention on Anger Management

		Anger Level After 10-Week Course		
		High	Low	Total
Anger Level Before 10-Week Course	High	30a	72b	102
	Low	45c	39d	84
	Total	117	69	$N = 186$

Table 9.9 shows four cells labeled *a*, *b*, *c*, and *d*. Cell *a* contains batterers who had high anger levels both before and after the 10-week course. Cell *b* contains batterers who changed from high anger levels to low anger levels following the course. Cell *c* contains batterers who changed from low to high anger levels after completing the course, while cell *d* shows those persons with low anger levels both before and after the course.

One major question Seave might seek to answer by using the McNemar test is whether significant changes occurred among batterers before and after the 10-week anger-management course. The following hypothesis set could be tested:

H_o: *There will be no change in anger levels among batterers participating in a 10-week anger-management program; if there is a change, batterers with low anger levels will change to higher anger levels.*

H_1: *Batterers with high anger levels will exhibit lower anger levels following participation in a 10-week anger-management program.*

$P < .01$ (one-tailed test)

The hypothesis set says that Seave expects that the anger-management program will change batterers' behavior, presumably toward lower anger levels. Thus, a one-tailed or directional prediction is made. A preliminary inspection of the table frequencies shows that 72 batterers changed their anger levels from high to low from before to after the anger-management program. Interestingly, 45 batterers changed from low to high anger levels during the program as well. A total of $30 + 39 = 69$ batterers did not change as a result of the program. The question Seave must answer is whether there is a significant difference in the changes that were observed between the two time periods. The significance of this change can be assessed with the McNemar test and is applied as follows:

$$\chi_m^2 = \frac{(c_1 - c_2 - 1)^2}{c_1 + c_2}$$

where

c_1 and $c_2 =$ the cells containing persons who changed from either high to low or low to high.

Examining the data in Table 9.9, c_1 and c_2 are cells *b* and *c* respectively. These cells contain frequencies of 72 and 45 as shown. The frequencies in the other cells, 30 and 39, are ignored for purposes of this test application. Using these values in the formula, we have

$$\chi_m^2 = \frac{(72 - 45 - 1)^2}{72 + 45} = \frac{(27 - 1)^2}{117} = \frac{676}{117} = 5.778$$

We may now interpret our observed χ_m^2 value of 5.778 by using Table A.4 in Appendix A, p. 448, with 1 *df*. *Df*'s for all McNemar tests are $(r-1)(c-1) = (2-1)(2-1) = 1$ *df*. Because the hypothesis set is being tested at the .01 level and a one-tailed, directional test is being made, we determine where these values, .01 (one-tailed) and $df = 1$, intersect in the body of the table. This point defines our critical value which is a $\chi^2 = 5.412$. If our observed χ_m^2 equals or exceeds 5.412, then we can reject the null hypothesis. Our observed $\chi_m^2 = 5.778$ and equals or exceeds 5.412. A significant change in anger levels among the batterers participating in the anger-management program occurred.

BOX 9.3

SPSS Alternative Application

1. Activate the *SPSS* program and go to the Data Editor window. Using the Variable View, identify the first column as "After" and the second column as "Before." In the "After" columns, notice that there are "High" and "Low" designations which we will label as "1" and "2" respectively. Also, in the row designation, "Before," there are also "High" and "Low" categories which we will label as "1" and "2" respectively. Go to the first column, "After," and type in 117 "1" values. Continue typing in 69 "2" values.

2. Next, go to column 2, or "Before," and type in 30 "1" values from cell *a*. From cell *c*, type in 45 "2" values. Go to cell *b* and type in 72 "1" values, and then type in 39 "2" values from cell *d*. You should now have 186 values for both columns.

3. Click "Analyze," then "Nonparametric Tests," then "Two-Related Samples." This brings up a screen with several windows. In the left-hand window are "Before" and "After." Click on "After" first and then click "Before." Notice that this action moves these to Variable 1 and Variable 2 below the window. Once both time periods have been placed in these variable designations, use the arrow to move them to the right window.

4. Under "Test Type" at the bottom of the same screen, click on "McNemar." Make sure the other tests, such as Wilcoxon and Sign, are not checked. Then click "OK."

5. This action produces two summary tables shown below. These summary tables show the data from Table 9.9. These are the "Before & After" and "Test Statistics" tables. The Before & After table should resemble the data in Table 9.9. Sometimes the *SPSS* program may distribute these data different from how they are shown in Table 9.9. But a close inspection shows that there are 30 persons who have "high" anger levels before and "high" anger levels after the course, 72 persons who have "high" anger levels before and "low" anger levels after the course, 45 persons who have "low" anger levels before and "high" anger levels after the course, and 39 persons who have "low" anger levels before and "low" anger levels after the course.

McNemar Test

Crosstabs

Before & After

Before	After	
	1	2
1	30	72
2	45	39

Test Statistics[b]

	Before & After
N	186
Chi-Square[a]	5.778
Asymp. Sig.	.016

[a]Countinuity Corrected
[b]McNemar Test

(continued)

(*continued*)

6. The "Test Statistics" table shows $N = 186$, a Chi-Square = 5.778, matching precisely the manual calculation, and the probability (Asymp. Sig.) = .016. This is a two-tailed probability which must be halved for a one-tailed interpretation. Accordingly, $.016/2 = .008$. This probability is equal to or smaller than .01, the level of significance at which the hypothesis set was originally tested. The null hypothesis can be rejected and the research hypothesis is supported. The anger-management course appeared to change the anger levels of the participants significantly and in the predicted direction.

ASSUMPTIONS, ADVANTAGES, AND DISADVANTAGES OF THE MCNEMAR TEST FOR SIGNIFICANCE OF CHANGE. The assumptions underlying the McNemar test include (1) randomness; (2) two related samples; and (3) the nominal level of measurement. Because the McNemar test is a chi square–based test, this procedure should be restricted to Ns ranging from 25 to 250 without causing distortion in any observed chi-square value. For purposes of applying the McNemar test, N is defined as the sum of those persons who change between two time periods, or $72 + 45 = 117$ from the data in Table 9.9.

The McNemar test is easy to use and is easily interpreted. One limitation is that the McNemar test cannot be applied to matched samples. Also, data must be arranged in a before-after format in a 2×2 table. If investigators wanted to determine the significance of difference between matched sets of individuals on some nominal variable, a two-sample variation of a k-related sample test, such as the Cochran Q test presented later in this chapter, would have to be used. Although the Cochran Q test is a k-related sample test, it may be applied to any two-sample case as can all other k-sample tests.

K-SAMPLE TESTS

k-sample tests are designed to determine the significance of difference between three or more samples. Any k-sample test can be applied to two-sample situations as well. In this section, two k-sample tests are presented. These include (1) the chi-square test for k independent samples and (2) Cochran's Q test for k-related samples.

The Chi-Square Test for *k* Independent Samples

The third and final version of the chi-square test in this chapter is the **chi-square test for *k* independent samples**. Essentially, it is a simple extension of the two-sample chi-square test illustrated earlier. An illustration of the application of this test is provided with research conducted by Pauline K. Brennan (2006), who investigated sentencing of female misdemeanants in New York City's criminal court. Brennan was interested in learning more about the influence of race and ethnicity on sentencing disparities, particularly among female offenders. An investigation of the criminological literature on the relation between race/ethnicity and sentencing suggested to Brennan that the findings were mixed, although greater numbers of minority defendants convicted of misdemeanors were more likely to serve jail time compared with their counterpart white defendants. Factors disclosed by Brennan in her research and that influenced these sentencing disparities in different ways included socioeconomic status, community ties, prior record, prior pending cases, and charge severity.

Suppose that Brennan investigated 173 female misdemeanants convicted of similar offenses in New York City's criminal court during a three-month period in 2006. Using

TABLE 9.10 Hypothetical Samples of White, Hispanic, and Black Female Misdemeanants and Jail Sentences in New York City Criminal Courts, October–December 2006

		Race/Ethnicity			
		White	Hispanic	Black	Totals
Jail Sentence	Yes	24a	31b	46c	101
	No	36d	21e	15f	72
Totals		60	52	61	N = 173

race/ethnicity as the independent variable and jail/no jail as the dependent variable, suppose she were to generate a table such as that shown in Table 9.10.

Table 9.10 is constructed as follows. Samples of white, Hispanic, and black female defendants convicted of misdemeanor offenses during October–December 2006 are distributed across three categories on the independent variable. These women are cross-tabulated with whether they are sentenced to jail or no jail, shown down the left-hand side of the table. The table frequencies are shown in cells a, b, c, d, e, and f. Row and column totals have been calculated. In this particular instance, there are 60 white female convicts, 52 Hispanic female convicts, and 61 black female convicts. These make up the three rows, each row indicating an independent sample of female offenders. Down the left-hand side of the table, two rows have been created. The first row shows women who have been sentenced to jail, while the second row shows women not sentenced to jail.

A preliminary inspection of table frequencies shows a pattern of jail incarceration consistent with what Brennan has previously observed in the research literature. A majority of white female offenders have been sentenced to no jail time, while a majority of Hispanic and black female offenders have been given jail time. The question Brennan seeks to answer, therefore, is whether these patterns are significant statistically. Does the race/ethnicity of convicted female offenders significantly influence whether they are jailed for their crimes?

The chi-square test for k independent samples can be used as follows based on the data in Table 9.10:

$$\chi^2 = \Sigma \left[\frac{(O_k - E_k)^2}{E_k} \right]$$

where

O_k = the observed frequencies for the kth cell

E_k = the expected frequencies for the kth cell

Brennan might hypothesize the following:

H_o: *There is no difference between women of different races/ethnicities and whether they are jailed or not jailed for misdemeanor convictions.*

H_1: *There is a difference between women of different races/ethnicities and whether they are jailed or not jailed for misdemeanor convictions.*

$P \leq .001$ (two-tailed test)

This hypothesis set says that according to H_1, Brennan expects that there will be differences among women of different races/ethnicities and whether they will be jailed. The null hypothesis, H_o, states there will be no differences among these women and whether they are jailed.

Expected cell frequencies must be computed. Each expected cell frequency is determined by multiplying the row total in which any given cell is found by the column total in which that cell is found and dividing this product by the total N in the table, in this case 173. Since there are six cells in this table, a through f, we must make six separate calculations. Once these six calculations are made, we can apply the chi-square test and determine our observed chi-square value, χ^2_{obs}. The calculations for the six expected cell frequencies are determined as follows:

$$a = \frac{(101)(60)}{173}, b = \frac{(101)(52)}{173}, c = \frac{(101)(61)}{173},$$

$$d = \frac{(72)(60)}{173}, e = \frac{(72)(5)}{173}, f = \frac{(72)(61)}{173}$$

The following are the expected cell frequencies:

$a = 35.1$

$b = 30.4$

$c = 35.6$

$d = 25.0$

$e = 21.6$

$f = 25.4$

With a knowledge of these expected cell frequencies, we may now apply the chi-square formula:

$$\chi^2 = \frac{(24 - 35.1)^2}{35.1} + \frac{(31 - 30.4)^2}{30.4} + \frac{(46 - 35.6)^2}{35.6} + \frac{(36 - 25.0)^2}{25.0}$$

$$+ \frac{(21 - 21.6)^2}{21.6} + \frac{(15 - 25.4)^2}{25.4}$$

$$= \frac{(-11.1)^2}{35.1} + \frac{(0.6)^2}{30.4} + \frac{(10.4)^2}{30.4} + \frac{(11)^2}{35.6} + \frac{(0.6)^2}{25.0} + \frac{(10.4)^2}{21.6}$$

$$= 3.510 + 0.012 + 3.038 + 4.840 + 0.017 + 4.258$$

$$\chi^2 = 15.675.$$

Our observed chi-square value, χ^2_{obs}, is 15.675. A critical value must be selected from Table A.4. Degrees of freedom, df, are $(r - 1)(c - 1) = (2 - 1)(3 - 1) = (1)(2) = 2 \, df$. Taking our 2 df to Table A.4 of Appendix A, p. 448, we locate the intersection point for the .001 two-tailed value and 2 df. This is the critical value of chi-square, χ^2_{cv}, or 13.815. Does our observed $\chi^2 = 15.675$ equal or exceed the critical value of 13.815? Yes. Therefore, H_o is rejected and H_1 is supported. The researcher may conclude that race/ethnicity influences whether women are jailed, at least in New York City criminal courts.

ASSUMPTIONS, ADVANTAGES, AND DISADVANTAGES OF THE CHI-SQUARE TEST FOR K INDEPENDENT SAMPLES. The assumptions underlying the chi-square test are (1) randomness; (2) k independent samples; (3) nominal-level data; and (4) a recommended

BOX 9.4

SPSS Alternative Application

1. Activate your *SPSS* software program and go to the Data Editor window. Inspecting the data shown in Table 9.10, go to Variable View in the Data Editor window and type in "Raceethnicity" in the first column. Go to the second column and type in "Jailtime." Go to Data View. This action will show column labels for "raceethnicity" and "jailtime" respectively.

2. We will code "White," "Hispanic," and "Black" as "1," "2," and "3" respectively. Type in 60 as a "1" value; continue typing in 52 as a "2" value; and finally continue typing in 61 as a "3" value.

3. Go to the second column. Using the same data in Table 9.10, we will code "Yes" on "Jailtime" as "1" and "No" as "2." Begin typing 24 as a "1" value, then 36 as a "2" value. Continue typing 31 as a "1" value, then 21 as a "2" value. Continue with 46 as a "1" value and then 15 as a "2" value. This should sum to 173 values for both columns as are shown in Table 9.10. Any errors at this point should be corrected.

4. Click on "Analyze," then "Descriptive Statistics," then "Crosstabs." This will bring up a screen with several windows. Highlight "raceethnicity" in the left-hand window and use the arrow to move it to the "Column(s)" window. Highlight "jailtime" and use the arrow to move it to the "Row(s)" window.

5. Click on "Statistics" at the bottom of the window. This brings up a display of various tests you can run. You want to check "Chi Square" in the upper left-hand corner. Then click "Continue." This action returns you to the variables windows. Click "OK."

6. Three tables are displayed and are shown below in this box. The first table is "Case Processing Summary" and basically shows that you are examining 173 cases. This is a check on your work. The second table is "Jailtime/Raceethnicity Crosstabulation." It should resemble precisely the display of cell frequencies shown in Table 9.10. If it doesn't show this table precisely, you have entered data incorrectly and must go back and check your work. If everything matches, then proceed with further examination of the next table.

Case Processing Summary

	Cases					
	Valid		Missing		Total	
	N	Percent	N	Percent	N	Percent
jailtime*raceethnicity	173	100.0%	0	.0%	173	100.0%

jailtime*raceethnicity Crosstabulation

Count

		raceethnicity			Total
		1.00	2.00	3.00	
jailtime	1.00	24	31	46	101
	2.00	36	21	15	72
Total		60	52	61	173

(continued)

(*continued*)

Chi-Square Tests

	Value	df	Asymp. Sig. (2-sided)
Pearson Chi-Square	15.656[a]	2	.000
Likelihood Ratio	15.981	2	.000
Linear-by-Linear Association	15.511	1	.000
N of Valid Cases	173		

[a]0 cells (.0%) have expected count less than 5. The minimum expected count is 21.64

7. The third table, "Chi-Square Tests," shows the Pearson Chi-Square = 15.656 with 2 *df* and a two-tailed probability (Asymp.Sig. 2-sided) = .000. Inspect the probability at which the hypothesis set is being tested, .001 (two-tailed test) in this case. Since the probability, .000, is equal to or smaller than .001, you may reject H_o and support H_1. It does appear in this instance that jail sentences of female misdemeanants are affected by their race/ethnicity. Notice that the chi-square generated by the *SPSS* program, 15.656, is not precisely equal to the one computed manually, or 15.675. This difference is due to rounding error in the manual calculation and can be ignored.

sample size range from 25 to 250. The principal advantages of the chi-square test are that it does not assume a normal distribution. It is well known and easy to apply. Almost every software program, including *SPSS*, includes chi-square as a nonparametric test of significance. The chi-square test has approximately 80–85 percent power compared with the parametric *F* test for rejecting false null hypotheses. The primary disadvantage of chi-square is that is not useful for related samples. However, a *k*-related sample test exists. It is the Cochran *Q* test and is presented in the next section.

The Cochran Q Test

It is not unusual for criminologists to track persons over time to determine whether they change their behavior as the result of an experimental stimulus, behavioral intervention, or some other factor designed to produce change. Attitudinal change can be tracked over time as the result of participating in counseling sessions, courses, and other instructional/educational settings/experiences. These changes in attitudes are reflected by ordinal score changes over time, often in before-after experiments, where the experimental time dimensions are represented as time 1 (t_1) and time 2 (t_2). Some experiments involve multiple time periods, perhaps as many as six or seven, over which ones' scores are tracked. The time intervals between interventions may be a week, two weeks, a month, two months, or longer.

In most cases where persons are tracked over time, they are used as their own controls. This means that researchers can assume that any changes detected in measured attitudes are more likely attributable to interventions rather than personality or individual differences among persons who are being tested.

Where investigators have simple indicators of change rather than raw score changes on attitudinal indices, such as a positive or negative reactions to interventions at different intervention periods, such changes can be tracked as well. The Cochran Q test is a chi square–based test designed to determine significant differences among persons used as their own controls over k time periods or between matched sets of N persons, where the dependent variable is a simple dichotomy, such as "yes" or "no" or "agree" or "disagree." An illustration of the application of the **Cochran Q test** is provided by Lorenn Walker, Ted Sakai, and Kat Brady (2006) who investigated the impact of restorative justice circles on the reentry process for samples of Hawaiian prison inmates. Restorative justice circles consist of three-hour group planning sessions for individual inmates, their families, and prison staff. Often, victims of these offenders are invited to participate in the intervention process. The result of restorative justice circles as an intervention experience is a written transition plan for inmate planning to leave prison. These plans include the need for reconciliation with loved ones, victims, and whatever the group considers important to repair the harm done by the inmate. Reconciliation may be as simple as "staying clean and sober" or "forgiving myself" or "apologizing to victims."

Suppose Walker, Sakai, and Brady wanted to track the impact of restorative justice circles on a sample of 29 prerelease inmates facing subsequent reentry. They might experiment with a new variation of restorative justice circles and track inmate response to these experiences over four time periods. They might expect that as the result of the restorative justice circle intervention, participating inmates would acquire more positive views of themselves and their future circumstances as they confront the reentry process. They might hypothesize the following:

> H_0: *There is no change among inmates in their positive views toward reentry as the result of participation in restorative justice circles; if there is a difference, inmates will have negative views toward reentry.*
>
> H_1: *Inmates will have positive views toward reentry as the result of participating in restorative justice circles.*
>
> $P \le .0005$ (one-tailed test)

This hypothesis set says that these researchers believe, under H_1, that the result of participating in restorative justice circles among Hawaiian inmates will generate positive views among them toward reentry into their communities. The null hypothesis, H_0, says that either there is no change in these inmates' views toward reentry as the result of participating in restorative justice circles, or their experiences will lead to negative views toward reentry. Walker, Sakai, and Brady could test this hypothesis set using the .0005 level of significance for a one-tailed test, since the direction of change is being predicted. Table 9.11 is generated based on some hypothetical results.

Table 9.11 is constructed as follows. All 29 inmates are listed down the far left-hand side of the table. Four time periods are identified across the top of the table as shown. In each of these time periods, positive or negative scores are recorded, depending on individual inmates' reactions to restorative justice circle experiences. Positive experiences for inmates are recorded as a "1," while negative experiences are recorded as a "0." The positive experiences for inmates in each of the four time periods are summed and placed as S_1, S_2, S_3, and S_4 as shown. The positive experiences or "1"s are recorded across the table for each inmate and placed in a column, F, as shown. Each of these F sums is squared, and each inmate has an F^2 value recorded. Both sums, the F values and the F^2 values, are summed and listed as ΣF and ΣF^2 as are shown.

TABLE 9.11 Positive and Negative Views of 29 Hawaiian Inmates Facing Reentry and Participation in Restorative Justice Circles Over Four Time Periods

Inmate	Time 1	Time 2	Time 3	Time 4	F	F^2
1	0	0	1	1	2	4
2	0	1	1	1	3	9
3	0	0	1	1	2	4
4	1	1	1	1	4	16
5	0	1	0	1	2	4
6	1	1	1	1	4	16
7	1	1	0	1	3	9
8	0	0	1	1	2	4
9	0	1	1	1	3	9
10	0	1	1	1	3	9
11	0	1	0	1	2	4
12	0	0	1	1	2	4
13	0	0	1	1	2	4
14	0	1	1	1	3	9
15	1	1	1	1	4	16
16	0	1	1	1	3	9
17	0	1	1	0	2	4
18	1	1	1	1	4	16
19	0	1	1	1	3	9
20	0	0	1	1	2	4
21	0	0	1	1	2	4
22	0	0	1	1	2	4
23	0	1	1	1	3	9
24	0	0	0	1	1	1
25	0	0	1	1	2	4
26	0	0	0	1	1	1
27	0	1	0	1	2	4
28	0	0	0	1	1	1
29	0	1	0	1	2	4
	$S_1 = 5$	$S_2 = 17$	$S_3 = 28$	$S_4 = 28$	$\Sigma F = 71$	$\Sigma F^2 = 195$

Based on these sums, the Cochran Q formula is applied:

$$Q = \frac{(k - 1)[k\Sigma S_i^2 - (\Sigma F)^2]}{k(\Sigma F) - \Sigma F^2}$$

where

k = number of samples or time periods

S_i = number of favorable responses for each sample in each time period

F = total number of favorable responses per person across time periods

F^2 = sum of squared total of favorable responses for each individual across the k time periods

Substituting the symbols in the formula for the values from Table 9.11, we can carry out our Cochran Q computations as follows:

$$Q = \frac{(3)(1,549) - 5,041}{89} = \frac{(3)(1,115)}{89} = \frac{3,345}{89} = 37.58.$$

The resulting $Q_{obs} = 37.58$. This Q value is interpreted as a chi-square value. Table A.4 of Appendix A, p. 448, contains critical values of Q, which is a chi-square value. We find the level of significance across the top of the table, .0005 for a one-tailed test, and df down the left-hand side of the table. For the data in Table 9.11, $df = k - 1$, where k = the number of time periods. These df are calculated as $4 - 1 = 3$ df. Where 3 df intersects with the .0005 level of significance for a one-tailed test defines the critical value of $\chi^2 = 16.268$. Does our observed χ^2 equal or exceed the critical value? Yes, 37.58 equals or exceeds 16.268. Therefore, Walker, Sakai, and Brady can reject H_o and support H_1 and conclude that the restorative justice circles promote positive views toward reentry among the 29 inmates studied.

BOX 9.5

SPSS Alternative Application

1. Open your *SPSS* software program and go to the Data Editor window. Create four columns. Each of these columns will represent a time period. Starting with the first "var" column, type in the first set of Time 1 scores from Table 9.11, until you enter all 29 scores. Next, go to the second "var" column and type in Time 2 scores of "1" or "0" for the 29 inmates. Repeat this process for the third and fourth columns. You now have 29 scores each of "1" or "0" values in four columns, VAR00001, VAR00002, VAR00003, and VAR00004. If you want to label each of these columns as Time1, Time2, Time3, and Time4, you may do so through the Variable View function at the bottom of the screen. This has been done for purposes of this *SPSS* application.
2. Click on "Analyze," then "Nonparametric Tests," then "*k*-Related Samples." This brings up a screen with two windows. The left-hand window shows time1, time2, time3, and time4. Highlight each, one at a time, and use the arrow to move the variable to the right window, "Test Variables." You should now have time1, time2, time3, and time4 in the right window.
3. Check the Cochran Q test below the window and then click "OK."
4. This action brings up two summary tables, one being "Frequencies" and the other "Test Statistics." These are shown below in this box.

Cochran Test

Frequencies

	Value	
	0	1
time1	24	5
time2	12	17
time3	8	21
time4	1	28

(continued)

(continued)

Test Statistics

N	29
Cochran's Q	37.584
df	3
Asymp. Sig.	.000

5. The first table, "Frequencies," shows the number of "1" and "0" values for each of the four time periods. Notice that the "0" values decline from time1 to time 4. Also, the number of "1" values increase from time1 to time4. These changes in frequencies indicate changes in positive views about restorative justice. Are these changes significant?

6. An examination of the "Test Statistics" table shows $N = 29$, Cochran's $Q = 37.584$, $df = 3$, and a two-tailed probability = .000 (Asymp. Sig.). This probability is compared with the same critical value of chi-square reported in the discussion above, $\chi^2 = 16.268$ (.0005, one-tailed test). The observed probability is equal to or smaller than .0005 and therefore the null hypothesis can be rejected. There is a difference among the time periods concerning positive inmate attitudinal change, probably as the result of restorative justice circle participation. In this instance, the manually computed chi-square equaled precisely that generated by the Cochran Q test, or 37.58 (rounded).

ASSUMPTIONS, ADVANTAGES, AND DISADVANTAGES OF THE COCHRAN Q TEST. The assumptions of the Cochran Q test include (1) randomness; (2) nominal-level data; and (3) k-related samples, where each person acts as his/her own control over k-time periods, or k-matched samples under k-treatment conditions. The advantages of Cochran's Q test are that it is easy to apply for nominal data. This test works fine whenever persons act as their own controls over k-time periods or for matched sets of persons compared according to k treatments.

The Cochran Q test is the only test of its kind to assess nominal-level variables for k-related samples. Another advantage is that the Cochran Q test is that it is a chi square–based test. Therefore, Q values are easily interpreted. The Cochran Q test seemingly is an extension of the McNemar test for significance of change, but this is misleading. The two tests are unrelated. The McNemar test is also restricted to situations where persons act as their own controls in before-after experiments. It cannot be applied to matched sets of persons. The Cochran Q test can function as its own probe if researchers want to investigate two samples at a time. For those with access to an *SPSS* program, two-sample comparisons are quite easy. Any two time periods are designed for comparison and the Q test is calculated. The Cochran Q test is 80–85 percent powerful compared with parametric k-related sample tests.

Summary

Several important goodness-of-fit tests for the nominal level of measurement were examined. Goodness-of-fit tests evaluate differences between one's observations and what might be expected according to chance. All tests discussed here are chi-square based. They do not have numerous restrictive assumptions and are easy to apply. Software programs such as the *SPSS* have these and other tests available for use.

The chi-square test is applied to one-sample, two-independent sample, and *k*-independent sample situations. All chi square–based tests have recommended sample ranges for optimum application, where *N*s vary between 25 and 250. For two related samples, the McNemar test for significance of change was presented and illustrated. The McNemar test is also a chi square–based procedure and assumes nominal-level data. It is also easy to apply and interpret.

For *k*-sample situations, a *k*-sample extension of chi-square was illustrated and discussed. This test is merely an extension of the two-sample case, and all of the assumptions, advantages, and disadvantages of two-sample applications also apply to the *k*-sample case. For *k*-related samples, the Cochran *Q* test was presented. It, too, is a chi square–based test.

Key Terms

cells *213*
chi-square test, χ^2 *220*
chi-square test, two
    samples *224*
chi-square test, *k*
    samples *232*
Cochran *Q* test *237*

cross tabulation *214*
expected cell frequencies *226*
goodness of fit *212*
goodness-of-fit tests *212*
marginal totals *226*
McNemar test for significance
    of change *229*

observed frequencies *212*
$r \times c$ table *214*
2×2 table *214*
yates' correction for
    continuity *228*

Questions for Review

1. What is the chi-square test? What is meant by the fact that tests are chi-square based?

2. Relate assumptions made for the chi-square test for a single sample to assumptions associated with two-sample and *k*-sample versions of the chi-square procedure.

3. What is the smallest single-variable table? Give two examples of how such a table might be constructed.

4. Compare and contrast the weaknesses and strengths of the two-sample chi-square test, and the *Z* test for differences between proportions.

5. In what way is the *Z* test for differences between proportions similar to the parametric *Z* test? Explain.

6. What are the primary assumptions, advantages, and disadvantages of the McNemar test for significance of change?

7. Compare and contrast the Cochran *Q* test with the chi-square test for *k*-independent samples.

8. What are the primary features of the chi-square test that make it a desirable test for those testing hypotheses involving two independent samples?

9. Under what circumstances would the chi-square test be applicable for sample sizes larger than 25? Explain.

10. What is the most popular table size in criminological research? Why do you think this is the case? Explain.

Exercises

9.1. Forty-seven correctional officers have participated in a program to improve their discretionary ability in prison inmate–officer confrontations. Carry out the McNemar test for significance of change for the data below to determine whether an improvement in their discretionary ability

		After Program		Totals
		High Ability	Low Ability	
Before	High Ability	12	6	18
	Low Ability	26	3	29
Program				
Totals		38	9	47

actually occurred. Assume a nondirectional, two-tailed hypothesis test made at the .0l level of significance.

  a. What is the observed chi-square value?
  b. What is the critical value of chi-square?
  c. How many degrees of freedom are associated with the above table?
  d. What is your decision about the correctional officers' change of attitude, if any? Describe your findings in a short paragraph.

9.2. You have two groups of parolees under close and general supervision by their parole officers. These parolees have been cross tabulated with their recidivism, and this variable has been dichotomized into high and low. Test the following hypothesis set using the chi-square test.

H_o: There is no difference in type of parolee supervision and recidivism.

H_1: There is a difference between parolee supervision and recidivism.

$P < .05$ (two-tailed test)

		Nature of Offender Supervision		
		Close	General	Totals
Recidivism Rate	High	25	17	42
	Low	12	43	55

  a. What is the observed chi-square value for this table?
  b. How many degrees of freedom are there in this table?
  c. What is the critical value of chi-square?
  d. What is your decision regarding H_o? Write a short paragraph describing what you found.

9.3. You have three matched sets of 15 drug offenders. Each has been exposed to a three-month treatment program, Treatment A, Treatment B, and Treatment C. Using the Cochran Q test,

determine whether there is a significant difference between these drug offenders in their response to treatments using the .05 level of significance (two-tailed test). A "1" indicates no favorable reaction to treatment, while a "2" indicates favorable reaction to treatment. Answer the questions below.

Drug Offender	Treatment A	Treatment B	Treatment C
1	1	2	2
2	1	2	2
3	2	2	2
4	1	1	1
5	1	2	1
6	2	2	2
7	2	1	2
8	1	1	2
9	1	1	1
10	1	2	2
11	1	2	2
12	2	2	2
13	1	1	2
14	1	1	2
15	1	1	2

  a. What is the observed Q for these data?
  b. What are the df?
  c. What is the critical value of Q?
  d. What is your decision regarding the differences between treatment programs, using the level of significance stated above?

9.4. A distribution of a sample of juvenile probation officers has been divided into four categories of effectiveness, ranging from low to high. These are shown below. Is there a significant difference between what is observed and what is expected according to chance, using a chi-square test for a single sample? Use the .05 level of significance (two-tailed test).

Juvenile Probation Officers				
Low	Moderately Low	Moderately High	High	
15	25	40	20	$N = 100$

a. What is the chi-square observed?
b. What is the critical value of chi-square?
c. What is your decision about whether significance exists?

9.5. A sample of 140 police officers is obtained. These are divided according to a measure of their professionalism. Their personal records are examined and they are classified into two categories on the basis of citizen complaints filed against them. An absence of complaints is given a "Satisfactory" designation, while "Unsatisfactory" is given to officers with one or more citizen complaints. Is there any significance associated with the distribution of officers below, using the chi-square test for k independent samples, assuming a $P \leq .01$ (two-tailed test)?

Professionalism of Officers

	High	Medium	Low	Totals
Satisfactory	42	18	10	70
Unsatisfactory	21	14	35	70
Totals	63	32	45	$N = 140$

a. What is the chi-square observed?
b. What is the critical value of chi-square?
c. What are the df?
d. What is your conclusion about these officers and their professionalism and their satisfactory/unsatisfactory classification? Write a short answer for this question.

9.6. Provide df for the following table sizes:
a. 2×5
b. 4×7
c. 1×8
d. 5×5
e. 5×1

9.7. What are critical values of chi-square for the following degrees of freedom (df) and levels of significance?
a. $df = 5, P \leq .001$ (two-tailed test)
b. $df = 9, P \leq .01$ (one-tailed test)
c. $df = 15, P \leq .10$ (two-tailed test)
d. $df = 11, P \leq .025$ (one-tailed test)

References

Brennan, Pauline K. (2006). "Sentencing Female Misdemeanants: An Examination of the Direct and Indirect Effects of Race/Ethnicity." *Justice Quarterly* **23**:60–95.

Renzema, M. and E. Mayo-Wilson (2005). "Can Electronic Monitoring Reduce Crime for Moderate to High-Risk Offenders." *Journal of Experimental Criminology* **1**:215–237.

Seave, P.L. (2006). "Disarming Batterers Through Restraining Orders: The Promise and the Reality in California." *Evaluation Review* **30**:245–265.

Walker, Lorenn, Ted Sakai, and Kat Brady (2006). "Restorative Circles: A Reentry Planning Process for Hawaii Inmates." *Federal Probation* **70**:33–37.

Xie, Min et al. (2006). "Prior Police Contact and Subsequent Victim Reporting: Results from the NCVS." *Justice Quarterly* **23**:481–500.

CHAPTER 10

Ordinal- and Interval-Level Nonparametric Tests of Significance

Chapter Outline

Chapter Objectives

After reading this chapter, the following objectives will be realized:

1. understanding the nature of ordinal-level tests of significance and their potential for use in criminological research;

2. learning about single-sample applications of ordinal-level tests, including the Kolmogorov–Smirnov one-sample test;

3. comparing two-independent sample tests and determining their respective applications and power;

4. learning about the median test as a related-sample test and how it can be applied;

5. understanding the Kruskal-Wallis *H* test and its use in criminal justice and criminological research;

6. learning about the Friedmann two-way analysis of variance test as an ordinal-level test of the significance of difference between *k*-related samples;

7. understanding differences between two two-sample interval-level nonparametric tests for small-sample applications;

8. learning about the Wilcoxon matched-pairs signed-ranks test and how it can be applied for interval-level data where two samples are related; and

9. determining the relative effectiveness of different tests and their power relative to the *t* test for differences between sample means.

INTRODUCTION

This chapter is probably one of the most important of the entire book. Let's face it. We're studying attitudes and personal characteristics of people all the time in criminology and criminal justice. We focus on their gender, socioeconomic status, race, political affiliation, their type of crime, whether a felony or misdemeanor, their prior records, ethnicity, jail/prison inmate status, and so forth. Most of the scaling procedures we use to measure any attitudinal variables yield ordinal-level data at best. This chapter presents a wide array of tests of significance of difference for these types of data. If you're studying attitudes and testing hypotheses about them, chances are you're using a Likert scale to measure those attitudes. Don't worry. You're in good company. Likert scaling procedures are used by over 90 percent of all criminologists. Read any article from criminal justice or criminological literature, older or more current, and the chances are 9 out of 10 that if attitudes are being investigated, the author is probably using a Likert-type scaling procedure. This chapter relates directly to tests of significance applied to data measured according to ordinal scales.

Besides this very utilitarian feature, there are several very useful nonparametric tests presented here whenever the interval level of measurement is attained. Studying age or income? You're in the interval-level realm. Studying years in prison or on the job as a probation or parole officer? Again, you're studying interval-level data.

Compared with all of the tests of significance discussed in Chapter 8, which are useful for analyses of data measured according to a nominal scale, these procedures utilize ordinal-level properties of variables and are most appropriate for analyses of attitudinal data. Investigators usually achieve the ordinal level of measurement whenever Likert, Thurstone, or Guttman scaling procedures are applied to derive attitudinal scores. Any good research methods text will cover such scaling procedures. Ever see "Strongly Agree," "Strongly Disagree," "Very Favorable," "Very Unfavorable," and "Undecided, But Probably Agree" on questionnaires? These are usually indicative of Likert-based scales.

This chapter is organized as follows. A single-sample test, the Kolmogorov–Smirnov test, will be presented and discussed. Two two-independent-sample tests will follow: (1) the Wald-Wolfowitz runs test and (2) the Mann-Whitney U test. When the investigator has two related samples, the sign test may be used. A second test, the Wilcoxon matched pairs-signed ranks test, may also be employed for a similar purpose. Technically the Wilcoxon test requires interval-level data for its appropriate application. However, most researchers use it for ordinal-level data analyses for two related samples.

Whenever k-independent samples are being analyzed, one test is presented. This is the Kruskal-Wallis H test. For k-related samples, the Friedman two-way analysis of variance test may be applied. For all tests presented, the assumptions, advantages, and disadvantages of these procedures will be discussed.

ONE-SAMPLE TEST: THE ORDINAL LEVEL OF MEASUREMENT

The Kolmogorov–Smirnov Single-Sample Test

When researchers have data measured according to an ordinal scale, then they can establish graduated categories and compute the **Kolmogorov–Smirnov single-sample test** (**K-S test**). The K-S test is a goodness-of-fit procedure similar to the chi-square test. A distribution of frequencies is arranged throughout k-ranked or graduated categories. This observed distribution of frequencies is compared with a hypothetical distribution based on an equal distribution of frequencies throughout the k categories. The actual comparison is made between cumulative frequencies from one category to the next. If there is a substantial variation between the two cumulative frequency distributions (e.g., between what is observed and what is expected if the data were equally divided across the k categories), the observed frequency distribution would be considered significantly different from what would be expected according to chance. An example of a K-S test application is provided below.

Jail suicides have been an increasingly popular topic in the correctional literature. Much of this interest has been fueled by growing jail incarceration rates throughout the nation. Jail suicides are increasingly frequent in those settings that are more densely populated and depending on the average incarcerative period of inmates (Farber, 2007). Bernard J. Farber has argued, for instance, that inmates subjected to greater overcrowding conditions might be more likely to commit suicide than those inmates where overcrowding is less intense. The thinking seems to be that the closeness of inmate proximity triggers suicidal thoughts and subsequent reactions among some inmates who feel too cramped and cloistered, especially where such population density is intense and lengthy.

Suppose Farber wished to test whether jail overcrowding actually had an impact on jail inmate suicides for a given year. Suppose he gathered information for 312 jail suicides for the year 2007 from reported jail information in a selected jurisdiction. It might be possible to devise graduated categories of jail overcrowding, based upon jail square footage, rated jail capacity, and the actual average daily jail inmate population. Hypothetically, let's assume that Farber devised such jail overcrowding measure and that the measure gave the actual ratio of the average daily jail inmate population to the rated jail capacity. If the average daily jail inmate population were 120 for a given jail, for example, and the rated jail capacity were 100 for that same jail, then the ratio would be 120/100 = 1.2. This would yield a ratio of 1.2:1. The jail inmate population would exceed its rated capacity by 20 percent. Using these ratios, Farber could then classify all inmate suicides into several discrete categories. In the present example, let's assume that Farber established three categories of jail overcrowding density: low, moderate, and high. After examining the records of the 312 jail inmate suicide victims for 2007, Farber could classify them according to the overcrowding density categories he created. A hypothetical distribution of jail inmate suicides for 2007 for the jails studied is shown in Table 10.1. Let's assume that Farber wishes to use the K-S test to see if the jail suicide victims vary according to jail population density.

The K-S test is applied as follows. Table 10.1 consists of five rows. The first row (R_1) is the observed distribution of jail inmate suicide victims according to the overcrowding density levels associated with jails in which they were confined. Row 2 (R_2) is the expected distribution for these same inmates. Expected frequencies are determined in the same way these expected values were calculated for the chi-square test, or N/k, where N = the number of jail inmate suicide victims and k = the number of overcrowding density categories. In this case, N/k = 312/3 = 104. Therefore, 104 inmates would theoretically fall into each of these three categories, according to chance.

The third row (R_3) is the cumulative observed frequency distribution for Row 1. The first cell contains 18 frequencies out of 312, or 18/312. These are added to the frequencies in the next cell, 120, to yield 18 + 120/312 or 138/312. The third cell contains the frequencies of all previous cells added to those in the third cell, or 138 + 174/312 or 312/312. Row 4 (R_4) consists of the expected cumulative frequency distribution for Row 2 (R_2), where the expected cell frequencies of each cell are added to the frequencies in successive cells. Thus, the first cell has 104 frequencies out of 312, and these would yield 104/312. The next cell would contain all previous cell frequencies added to the present cell total, or 104 + 104/312 or 208/312. The third cell consists of all previous frequencies added to the previous cell total, or 208 + 104/312 or 312/312. The fifth row, R_5, consists of the absolute difference between the observed and expected cumulative frequency distributions Farber has determined. Thus, Farber would have (18/312) − (104/312) = 86/312,

TABLE 10.1 Hypothetical Distribution of Jail Inmate Suicide Victims for 2007 according to Three Levels of Jail Overcrowding Density

	JAIL OVERCROWDING DENSITY			
	Low	**Moderate**	**High**	**Total**
(R_1) Observed number of jail inmate suicide victims	18	120	174	312
(R_2) Expected number of jail inmate suicide victims	104	104	104	312
(R_3) Cumulative observed frequencies	$\dfrac{18}{312}$	$\dfrac{138}{312}$	$\dfrac{312}{312}$	100%
(R_4) Cumulative expected frequencies	$\dfrac{104}{312}$	$\dfrac{208}{312}$	$\dfrac{312}{312}$	100%
(R_5) Absolute difference between cumulative observed and cumulative expected frequencies	$\dfrac{86}{312}$	$\dfrac{70}{312}$	—	
Observed proportionate differences (D)	.280	.220	—	

$(138/312) - (208/312) = 70/312$, and $(312/312) - (312/312) = 0$. Finally, these absolute proportionate differences are converted to proportions, where $86/312 = .280$, and $70/312 = .220$. These values are the observed proportionate differences, or D as shown.

The following hypothesis set is tested:

H_0: *There is no difference among jail inmate suicide victims and jail overcrowding density.*

H_1: *There is a difference among jail inmate suicide victims and jail overcrowding density.*

$P \le .01$ (two-tailed test)

In order to test this hypothesis set, Farber would identify the largest D value shown in Table 10.1. In this case, the largest $D = .280$. This D becomes Farber's observed D value. Farber would next turn to Table A.5 in Appendix A, p. 449, "Critical Values of D in the Kolmogorov–Smirnov One-Sample Test," to determine the critical proportionate difference of D which must be equaled or exceeded by the observed proportionate difference. Table A.5 contains critical proportionate differences, or Ds, for different levels of significance, for different sample sizes, and for one-and two-tailed hypothesis tests. Smaller sample size values of D are tabled up to an $N = 35$. Since our observed $N = 312$, we must use the "Over 35" line to determine the critical D value.

Our hypothesis test is being made at the .01 level of significance (two-tailed test), and therefore, we use the formula, $1.63/\sqrt{N}$ to determine the critical D value. This becomes $1.63/\sqrt{312} = 1.63/17.66 = .090$. The critical D value $= .090$. We must equal or exceed .090 with our observed D value. Since our observed $D = .280$, this D equals or exceeds .090 and therefore, H_0 is rejected and H_1 is supported, meaning that there is a difference among jail inmate suicide victims according to jail overcrowding density.

Had a one-tailed, directional test of the hypothesis been desired, we might have predicted under H_1 that greater numbers of jail inmate suicides would be found in those jails with higher overcrowding densities. Our null hypothesis would have been that either there is no difference among jail inmate suicide victims according to jail overcrowding density or if there is a difference, then more inmate suicides would be found in those jails with lower over-crowding density levels. The probabilities in Table A.5 would be halved (e.g., $.10/2 = .05$) in order to determine one-tailed, directional values of D. An explanatory headnote in Table A.5 describes this process in detail.

In one-tailed K-S tests, we must inspect the distributional arrangement of our observed inmate suicides to make sure that they are consistent with the direction predicted under our H_1. Had large numbers of jail suicides been found to occur in the low overcrowding density category and small numbers of jail suicides found in the high overcrowding density category, this finding would nullify our one-tailed test. In short, we would have made a directional prediction, but the prediction would have been made in the wrong direction. Thus, this demonstrates the risk of making one-tailed hypothesis tests. Unless we are reasonably certain of a difference in a particular direction, it is far more conservative to make two-tailed hypothesis tests rather than one-tailed ones. Two-tailed hypothesis tests require only that the difference between observed and expected cumulative frequency distributions be sufficiently large, in either direction, to equal or exceed the tabled two-tailed critical D values shown for different significant levels.

ASSUMPTIONS, ADVANTAGES, AND DISADVANTAGES OF THE K-S TEST The K-S test has three assumptions: (1) randomness; (2) the ordinal level of measurement; and (3) continuous data. The continuous data assumption is often symbolic, since we almost always collapse our continuous data into k discrete categories. This does not discourage our application of the

BOX 10.1

SPSS **Alternative Application**

The application of *SPSS* for the numbers of categories and sample size involved here is more complicated than the manual calculation. Therefore, it will not be presented.

K-S test, however. Such collapsing is common whenever attitudinal data are being examined. In this instance, it is apparent that we have taken advantage of the ordinality of the measured variable, jail overcrowding density, and that the K-S test is relatively easy to apply and interpret. The interpretive Table A.5 in Appendix A is also an advantage. No complex calculations are required, and the significance of our observed D values can be simply and directly determined. Relative to parametric tests that are designed for similar single-sample applications, such as the t test, the K-S test has power of approximately 80 to 90 percent for rejecting false null hypotheses. Finally, the K-S test is superior to the chi-square test for a single sample because it exploits the ordinality inherent in the graduated categories we have created.

TWO-INDEPENDENT SAMPLE TESTS: THE ORDINAL LEVEL OF MEASUREMENT

In this section, we examine three useful procedures for evaluating differences between two independent samples according to some ordinal-level characteristic. Each of these tests answers the question of whether the two distributions of scores are the same or different. In this respect, they may be compared with the t test for differences between means. It will be illustrated that each of these tests answers this question of whether significant group differences exist by approaching this problem in unique ways. These tests also vary in their power relative to t-test applications. They are presented in order, from the least powerful alternative to the t test to the most powerful alternative to the t test. These tests are (1) the Wald-Wolfowitz runs test, (2) the Kolmogorov–Smirnov two-sample test, and (3) the Mann-Whitney U test.

The Wald-Wolfowitz Runs Test

The **Wald-Wolfowitz runs test** is the most conservative procedure for determining whether two groups differ on some ordinal characteristic. It is also the most direct method for determining the significance of difference between two independent samples. The test is relatively easy to apply, since it involves a simple rank ordering of raw scores from either high to low or low to high. Scores from the same group that are immediately adjacent to one another are grouped and labeled as runs, hence the name, the **runs test**. The greater the number of runs between the two sets of ranked scores, the greater the homogeneity between groups. The fewer the number of runs, the less the homogeneity between the two groups. The following example illustrates this procedure.

Ann Adalist-Estin and Jim Mustin (2003) were interested in studying female inmates who were also mothers. One program they investigated was involved with connecting older children with inmate mothers. The goal of the program they studied was to provide opportunities for mothers to spend quality time with their children and deepen the relationship between mothers and their children during the years when the child is most impressionable. The program provided parenting classes and parent/child workshops for female inmates who were also parents. It was believed that participation in the program would reduce recidivism and break the cycle of child abuse and neglect. Participants learned about effective parenting skills in classes that focused on the basic issues of self-esteem, communication, effective discipline, and emotional and social development. The program lasted for eight weeks, with each week devoted to a 90-minute unit of formal curriculum.

Suppose that Adalist-Estin and Mustin created a scale that measures parenting sensitivity and maturational achievement among inmate mothers. Further suppose that this scale was been administered to 20 inmate mothers, 10 of whom participated in a Program for Caring Parents initiative and 10 inmate mothers who did not participate in the program. Table 10.2 shows hypothetical sensitivity and maturational achievement scores for 20 inmate mothers divided according to whether they participated or did not participate in this program.

Although hypothetical, the raw scores shown in Table 10.2 are based on a minimum–maximum score range from 180 to 330. Thus, it was possible for inmate mothers to obtain a low score of 180 and a high score of 330, although no inmate mother achieved such a score in the hypothetical distribution shown in Table 10.2. In this illustration, the lowest score achieved by any female inmate was 199, while the highest score was 322. It is assumed that the higher the score, the greater the sensitivity and maturational development of the inmate mother. The following hypothesis set was tested:

H_o: *There is no difference between inmate mothers on sensitivity and maturational development and whether they participated in the Program for Caring Parents.*

H_1: *There is a difference between inmate mothers on sensitivity and maturational development and whether they participated in the Program for Caring Parents.*

$P \leq .05$ (two-tailed test)

TABLE 10.2 Hypothetical Sensitivity and Maturational Development Scores for 20 Inmate Mothers Involved and Not Involved in the Program for Caring Parents

Program for Caring Parents	
Female Inmate Participants $(N_1 = 10)$	**Female Inmate Nonparticipants** $(N_2 = 10)$
(Scores on Sensitivity and Maturational Development)	
253	308
221	237
229	245
257	249
259	202
296	203
285	310
288	215
275	322
304	199

Do the two samples of inmate mothers come from the same population in terms of their sensitivity and maturational development scores? This is a commonly asked question and one that we have seen before. Essentially it means whether the two groups are the same (come from the same population) or different (don't come from the same population) according to the scores they received. Is there a significant difference between the two samples of inmate mothers according to the sensitivity and maturational development scale? The Wald-Wolfowitz runs test can answer these questions.

First, the data in Table 10.2 are rearranged from low to high (based on score magnitude), regardless of the group possessing particular scores. That is, the scores are rank-ordered regardless of one's group affiliation. The following distribution of scores is observed:

1	3	5
199 202 203 215 221 229 237 245 249	253 257 259 275 285 288 296 304	308 310 322
2	4	

Next, a line is drawn over each of the scores from the sample of inmate mothers who did not participate in the Program for Parents, while a line is drawn under the scores of inmate mothers who participated in the program as shown. It is apparent that several of the scores from female inmates in the same groups are immediately adjacent to one another. These consecutive scores from the same sample make up one **run**. One of more scores from each group that run together make up a run. As can be seen from the number of runs (e.g., the scores from the same sample that run together), there are five runs of scores between the two inmate mother samples. The total observed number of runs is equal to R. Therefore, $R = 5$. The fewer the number of runs or R, the greater the difference between the two groups of inmate mothers on their sensitivity and maturational development scores.

We must turn to Table A.6, p. 450, which contains various critical values of R. This will aid us in assessing the significance of the $R = 5$ that we have observed. Table A.6 is designed for smaller samples of elements, where N_1 and N_2 are both no larger than 20. Where our $N_1 = 10$ and $N_2 = 10$ intersect in the body of the table identifies the critical number of runs. Our observed number of runs, $R = 5$, must be equal to or less than the critical R shown in the body of the table in order to reject H_o and support H_1 at the .05 level of significance. The critical $R = 6$, and since our observed $R = 5$, we may reject H_o and support H_1 at the .05 level of significance. There is a significant difference between participants and nonparticipants in the Program for Caring Parents concerning their sensitivity and maturational development. This significance is for the .05 level for a two-tailed, nondirectional test.

Whenever either N_1 or N_2 exceed 20, Table A.6 cannot be used. In that event, an approximation of a Z value may be calculated by using the following formula:

$$Z = \frac{\left| R\left(\frac{2N_1N_2}{N_1 + N_2} + 1\right)\right| - .5}{\sqrt{\frac{2N_1N_2(2N_1N_2 - N_1 - N_2)}{(N_1 + N_2)^2(N_1 + N_2 - 1)}}}$$

where

R = the observed number of runs

N_1 and N_2 = the number of elements in each sample

The resulting Z value can be interpreted like any other Z value. Table A.2 would be used to determine the critical value of Z for various significance levels. The larger the Z value, the greater the significance of difference between two distributions of scores. (If you have access to *SPSS*, then you can enter data for larger sample sizes even when either N exceeds 20.) Remember that Z formula approximations used for nonparametric tests such as the runs test do not assume normality or any other distributional assumptions previously discussed with the parametric Z test application for single-sample or two-sample hypothesis tests.

ASSUMPTIONS OF THE WALD-WOLFOWITZ RUNS TEST   The assumptions of the runs test include (1) randomness, (2) independent samples; and (3) the ordinal level of measurement.

ADVANTAGES AND DISADVANTAGES OF THE RUNS TEST   The primary advantage of the runs test compared with the other tests discussed in this section is that the raw scores may be rearranged directly rather than transformed into ranks or categories. For smaller groups of

---

BOX 10.2

SPSS Alternative Application

1. Activate your *SPSS* program. Go to the *SPSS* Data Editor window and click "Enter Data."
2. Using the information from Table 10.2, type in 10 "1" values in the first "var" column. Continue entering 10 additional values in the same column, this time "2" values. You should now have a VAR00001 column consisting of 10 "1"s and 10 "2"s.
3. Go to the second "var" column and type in the first list of 10 scores, beginning with 253, 221, 229, and so on. When you finish these 10 scores, continue entering the next 10 scores from the second list of values in Table 10.2, beginning with 308, 237, 245, and so on. You will now have two lists of variables: VAR00001, consisting of 10 "1" values and 10 "2" values, and your second variable, VAR00002, which will begin with 253 and end with 199.
   There will be 20 scores in the VAR00002 column.
4. Click on "Analyze," then "Nonparametric Statistics," then "2 Independent Samples."
5. The "2 Independent Samples" option shows VAR00001 and VAR00002. VAR00001 is the "Grouping Variable" and it must be highlighted and moved with the arrow to the "Grouping Variable" side on the right. The second variable, VAR00002, should be highlighted and moved to the right in the "Test Variable List."
6. Next, click "Define Groups" under the "Grouping Variable." This will show two boxes, Group 1 and Group 2. Type in "1" and "2" in boxes Group 1 and Group 2 respectively.
7. Next, click the Wald-Wolfowitz runs test box and then click OK.
8. A Wald-Wolfowitz test pair of summary tables will appear showing the two groups on VAR00001 (1.00, 2.00). You will also see a "Test Statistics" table, showing the exact number of runs, which is 5 in this case. A Z value, -2.527, will be displayed, together with an exact probability of .004.
9. Compare this probability of .004 to the .05 (two-tailed) probability at which the hypothesis set was tested. Your conclusion will be to reject H_o and support H_1 that the two groups differ at the .05 level of significance.[**]

[**]This same procedure may be followed to define two groups where sample sizes are in excess of 20, and thus the lengthy Z formula may be avoided for above samples > 20 if you wish to use the *SPSS* Data Entry feature and if it is available to you. The same instructions may be followed, except with larger sample sizes for your next application.

numbers, this feature is a distinct advantage that other comparable tests do not have. The runs test is quick and easy to apply and there are no sample-size restrictions. It provides the researcher with the most conservative evaluation of differences between two sets of scores.

Compared with the parametric *t* test, the runs test is approximately 75 to 80 percent as powerful for rejecting false null hypotheses.

The major disadvantage of the runs test is the possible presence of a large number of tied scores. These tied scores may interfere with the effectiveness of the runs test results. Tied scores present the researcher with a special problem. Suppose that two groups of 10 persons each have the following scores, arranged from low to high:

```
       A              A                      A
_____    _____    _____
1 2 3 4 5 6 7 8 8 8 8 9 10 11 12 13 14 15 16 17
        ‾                ‾
        B                B
```

If we designate scores belonging to one group as *A* scores and to the other group as *B* scores as has been done above, we can determine the number of runs readily. There are 5 runs shown. But there are four tied scores of 8. However, if all of these tied scores of "8" belong to persons in group *A*, the arrangement above is appropriate. Or, if all of the scores of "8" belong to members of group B, then we might see the following with a similar result.

```
            B                     B
    _____    _____
1 2 3 4 5 6 7 8 8 8 8 9 10 11 12 13 14 15 16 17
‾                      ‾                      ‾
A                      A                      A
```

Again there are 5 runs. These two situations are not problematic for investigators, because the scores of "8" can be blended in with other scores belonging to the same group. But what if the tied scores are distributed equally between the two groups. Suppose that each group has two scores of "8." Any number of runs arrangements could be determined. The number of runs could be minimized as was done with the previous two examples. Or the numbers of runs could be maximized as shown below.

```
          B       B   B           B
    _____    ___ ___    _____
1 2 3 4 5 6 7 8 8 8 8 9 10 11 12 13 14 15 16 17
‾                 ‾ ‾ ‾                      ‾
A                 A A A                      A
```

In this new arrangement of the four "8" values, 9 runs have been created. The impression is that the two groups are sufficiently similar as to come from the same population. Thus, it would be possible to rearrange these "8" values so that some variation in the number of runs between 5 and 9 could be obtained. This situation is a good example of how easily numbers can be manipulated so as to fit investigator objectives and indulge their biases, if they are inclined to do so. Whenever researchers encounter such a situation, the recommendation is to maximize the number of runs. This is a conservative option that greatly lessens the likelihood of rejecting H_o. If the investigator were to minimize the number of runs and increase the likelihood of rejecting H_o, investigator bias may be alleged. Thus, where tied scores belong to both groups being compared, the safest alternative would be to select another test to see whether the two groups differ on the measured variable. The Mann-Whitney *U* test, presented later in this section, would be the superior alternative, although the Mann-Whitney *U* test is slightly more complicated to implement.

The Kolmogorov–Smirnov Two-Sample Test

The **Kolmogorov–Smirnov two-sample test** is an extension of the K-S test for a single sample. In the single-sample case, the K-S test evaluated the significance of difference between an observed and an expected cumulative frequency distribution. The present version of the K-S test evaluates the significance of difference between two independent samples, where the samples have been arranged into a cumulative frequency distribution throughout k categories. The greatest proportionate difference between the two samples in any given category is used for hypothesis testing purposes. Consider the following example.

Angus Reed (2001) reported the use of a new jail inspection program at the Fulton County Jail in Atlanta, Georgia. The new jail inspection program was designed to provide jail administrators with both a quantitative and qualitative measure of the sanitary conditions of the housing units and the support areas. Various points were given as ratings for the quality of different jail amenities, characteristics, and services, including showers, walls, windows, doors, fixtures, floors, trash, and clutter. As a result of using the new jail inspection program, jail administrators were able to determine the overall quality of the jail being inspected, and to anticipate which areas of concern should be addressed throughout future corrective action.

Suppose that Reed wanted to determine whether the new jail inspection program could work in other large jail jurisdictions. One way of determining whether the new jail inspection program worked would be to implement new jail inspections in other jails as a regular part of jail quality assessment. Over time, jails using the new jail inspection method would be compared with jails using traditional jail inspection methods, and overall jail quality could be assessed. As a result, if the new jail inspection program enabled those jails using it to improve the quality of their characteristics and services, the program might be adopted on a larger scale by other comparable jails. Let's assume that Reed obtained two samples of jails. In the first sample, $N_1 = 188$, Reed might have examined jails that used traditional inspection methods. In the second sample, $N_2 = 226$, Reed might have examined jails using the new jail inspection method. Further, he might have devised four categories to reflect general jail quality, ranging from high, moderately high, moderately low, and low. The following hypothesis set could be tested:

H_o: *There is no difference in jail quality between those jails using traditional jail inspection methods compared with new jail inspection methods.*

H_1: *There is a difference in jail quality between those jails using traditional jail inspection methods compared with new jail inspection methods.*

$P \leq .001$ (two-tailed test)

Suppose Table 10.3 were created. Table 10.3 is constructed as follows. Based on an assessment of overall jail quality, four categories of graduated responses are created from high to low, as shown across the top of the table. The two samples of jails are distributed across the four jail quality categories, according to the scores the jails received from their assessments. Rows 1 and 2 (R_1 and R_2) contain the two distributions of frequencies throughout the four categories created.

Row 3 (R_3) is a cumulative frequency distribution of the frequencies in row 1. The frequencies from the first cell in row 3 are added to those of the second cell, and so on. These have also been transformed into cumulative proportions. For instance, 42/188, or 42 jails out of 188, becomes .223; and $119/188 = .633$. Row 4 (R_4) consists of a cumulative frequency distribution of the data in row 2. This row has been determined in the same manner from the data in row 3.

TABLE 10.3 A Comparison of Jails Using the New Jail Inspection Method and Traditional Inspections According to Jail Quality

	Jail Quality				
	High	Moderately High	Moderately Low	Low	Totals
Traditional Jail Inspection (R_1)	42	77	50	19	$N_1 = 188$
New Jail Inspection (R_2)	47	90	53	36	$N_2 = 226$
Cumulative Traditional (R_3)	$\dfrac{42}{188}$	$\dfrac{119}{188}$	$\dfrac{169}{188}$	$\dfrac{188}{188}$	
Cumulative Proportion	(.223)	(.633)	(.899)	(1.000)	
Cumulative New Inspection (R_4)	$\dfrac{47}{226}$	$\dfrac{137}{226}$	$\dfrac{190}{226}$	$\dfrac{226}{226}$	
Cumulative Proportion	(.208)	(.606)	(.841)	(1.000)	
Absolute Difference (R_5) Between R_3 and R_4	.015	.027	.058	—	

Finally, row 5 (R_5) consists of the absolute proportionate difference between each pair of cells in rows 3 and 4. For instance, the absolute difference between the pair of cells in rows 3 and 4 for jail quality scores would be .223 − .208 = .015. The absolute difference for the second pair of cells would be .633 − .606 = .027. The absolute differences in the two cumulative frequency distributions (expressed in proportion terms) have been entered in row 5. Focusing on the largest absolute proportionate difference, which is .058, we are now ready to evaluate the statistical significance of this proportion. This is the largest proportionate difference and becomes our observed D value.

We now turn to Table A.7 of Appendix A, p. 451, "Critical Values in the Kolmogorov–Smirnov Two-Sample Test." In the left-hand column are one-and two-tailed probabilities. The body of the table to the right of these probabilities contains formulas that will yield critical values of D. Since our hypothesis test is being made at the .001 level of significance, we use the formula,

$$1.95\sqrt{\frac{N_1 + N_2}{N_1 N_2}}$$

to obtain the critical D value. The critical D values that are obtained by using the formulas in Table A.7 are actually critical proportions that our largest observed proportionate difference must equal or exceed in order to be significant statistically. We will refer to the largest difference between the two cumulative proportion differences in Table 10.3 as our observed D value. The critical value of D that we must equal or exceed is determined as follows:

$$\text{Critical value of } D = 1.95\sqrt{\frac{188 + 226}{(188)(226)}} = 1.95\frac{\sqrt{414}}{42,488}$$

$$= 1.95\sqrt{.0097} = (1.95)(.098) = .191.$$

The resulting critical D value = .191. We must obtain an observed D equal to or larger than .191 with our observed D in order to reject the null hypothesis. With an observed D = .058, we fail to reject H_0. Therefore, we may conclude that there is no significant difference between the traditional and new jail inspection methods according to jail quality assessments, at least in this particular study. This decision is made at the .001 level of significance with a two-tailed, nondirectional test. More study is needed.

Had a one-tailed test of the hypothesis been made, the researcher would have used the one-tailed probability column shown in Table A.7 to obtain the critical value of D. In the one-tailed hypothesis test situation, however, the researcher would be obligated to examine the two distributions of frequencies in order to determine if the direction predicted under H_1 was consistent with the two frequency distributions. If Reed had predicted that the new jail inspection method would more likely result in higher jail quality assessments, then a majority of jails subjected to the new jail inspection method would have been found in the high or moderately high jail quality categories, while a majority of jails subject to traditional inspection methods would have been found in the low to moderately low jail quality categories.

BOX 10.3

SPSS Alternative Application

1. Activate your *SPSS* software program. Go to the *SPSS* Data Editor. Examine the data shown in Table 10.3. Your task is to enter the data from this table. Notice that there are 188 traditional jail inspections and 226 new jail inspections. Across the top of the table are four categories of jail quality ranging from high to low. In order enter data in the *SPSS* Data Editor, go to the first "var" column and type in 188 "1" values to stand for traditional jail inspections. Continue typing in 226 "2" values which stand for new jail inspections. As a result, you will have a VAR00001 column with 414 cases, 188 "1"s and 226 "2"s.

2. Go to the second "var" column. Inspect Table 10.3 and note that there are four categories of jail quality, ranging from high to low. These can be assigned 4, 3, 2, and 1 respectively. Begin data entry in the second "var" column by typing in 42 "4" values, 77 "3" values, 50 "2" values, and 19 "1" values. You should have 188 entries thus far. This matches the number of traditional jail inspections from column 1 (as a check on the accuracy of your work). Continue entering jail quality values for the new jail inspection (value "2" in the VAR00001 column), beginning by entering 47 "4" values, 90 "3" values, 53 "2" values, and 36 "1" values. When finished, you will have 226 additional values beyond the original 188 you typed in. These will sum to 414 (again as a check on your work).

3. You are now ready with this data to perform the Kolmogorov–Smirnov two-sample test. Click on "Analyze," then "Nonparametric Tests," then "2 Independent Samples." This will bring up a screen with several windows. In the left-hand window will be VAR00001 and VAR00002. Highlight VAR00001 and use the arrow to move it to the "Grouping Variable" window. Underneath this window is "Define Groups." Click on "Define Groups" and this will yield Group 1 and Group 2 with blank windows. Type a "1" in the Group 1 window and a "2" in the Group 2 window. Then click "Continue."

4. Next, highlight VAR00002 and use the arrow to move it to the right screen under "Test Variable List." Underneath these windows are several test options. Click "Kolmogorov–Smirnov Z." Next, press "OK."

5. This action will yield two summary tables. The first shows "Frequencies" where the number of "1" and "2" values entered will equal 188 and 226 respectively. These sum to 414. Again, this is primarily used as a check on your work.

6. The second table shows the most extreme differences between proportions from Table 10.3. As we saw in the original manually computed problem, the largest absolute difference shown

(continued)

(continued)

in the "Test Statistics" table is .058, the same as was found in the original problem above. A Kolmogorov–Smirnov Z value is shown of .590. The significance level, under "Asymp. Sig." (2-tailed) is .877. This is not impressive at all. Recall that a two-tailed test was being conducted regarding differences between jail quality and types of jail inspections. The actual probability of the significance of difference between proportions is .877, far away from .001. We learned from Table A.7 in the Appendix that a critical proportion of .191 or larger was required in order to reject H_o at the .001 level for a two-tailed test. The .058 observed as the largest proportionate difference between these two groups failed to equal or exceed this critical proportion. The actual probability level yielded was .877. Therefore, our null hypothesis could not be rejected and the research hypothesis could not be supported.

7. It should be noted that for extremely large samples of 188 and 226 respectively, a lot of work is needed to enter data into the *SPSS* Data Editor for using *SPSS* software. Sometimes it is simply easier to make these calculations by hand using a hand calculator. The proportions in Table 10.3 are easily calculated, and proportionate differences can be determined in a matter of a few minutes. The critical value also required a minimum of work, given the values from Table 10.3. Therefore, an *SPSS* application, though rapid once data have been entered into the Data Editor, is not the most rapid way of yielding proportionate differences in a test such as the Kolmorogov–Smirnov two-sample test. By the time a researcher had entered numbers into the two columns, VAR00001 and VAR00002, another researcher working with these same data with a hand calculator could have completed five or six of these types of problems. Therefore, *SPSS* is not always better.

ASSUMPTIONS OF THE K-S TWO-SAMPLE TEST   The assumptions of the K-S two-sample test are (1) randomness; (2) two independent samples; and (3) the ordinal level of measurement.

ADVANTAGES AND DISADVANTAGES OF THE K-S TEST   Compared with the Wald-Wolfowitz runs test, the K-S test is approximately 85 to 90 percent as powerful compared with its parametric t test counterpart for rejecting false null hypotheses. The greater power differential of the K-S test makes it a more desirable alternative compared with the runs test.

The K-S test also deals with tied scores effectively. Any cell containing more than one frequency is a tied-score situation. In Table 10.3, for instance, there are 42 tied scores in the first cell in row 1, 77 tied scores in the second cell in row 1, 90 tied scores in the second cell in row 2, and so on. The researcher must create k categories into which the data for the two samples can be distributed. The raw scores cannot be dealt with directly as was the case with the runs test.

The K-S test is particularly useful for comparing two distributions of elements on some ordinal characteristic. The researcher simply identifies an attitudinal or behavioral variable, divides the variable logically into k-graduated subclasses or categories, and compares the resulting cumulative frequency distributions according to the proportionate differences between them. An interpretive table is available for determining critical D values for hypothesis-testing purposes. The K-S test is easy to compute and is not subject to any sample-size restrictions. It has no restrictive distributional assumptions such as normality, and it is properly regarded as one of the better nonparametric two-sample tests at the ordinal level of measurement. There are no serious disadvantages associated with the K-S test. Furthermore, an *SPSS* formula exists to solve these problems, although entering data for larger sample sizes is sometimes quite tedious.

The Mann-Whitney *U* Test

The **Mann-Whitney *U* test**, or simply the *U* test, is the most powerful nonparametric equivalent to the parametric *t* test. It is used for determining whether a difference exists between two independent samples on some ordinal-level or characteristic such as an attitude or other rankable variable. An example from the criminal justice literature is provided.

M. Nellis (2006) investigated the use of electronic monitoring in a selected jurisdiction as a part of a juvenile electronic monitoring project. Electronic monitoring is increasingly used as a means of verifying the whereabouts of certain low-risk offenders. Some offenders are permitted to go about their daily activities and perform their jobs outside of prisons or jails, provided that they wear electronic wristlets or anklets which emit signals that may be received at some other location. Probation officers may conduct "drive bys," where they drive by the residences of offenders and verify their presence with electronic receivers that are equipped to receive the signals emitted by the wristlets and anklets worn by probationers or parolees. Some forms of electronic monitoring involve special telephonic equipment, where probationers are called at random times by a computer. The probationers insert their wristlets into special equipment and their particular signal and/or vocal transmission is "verified" by computer analyses. Thus, those involved in electronic monitoring programs are more intensively supervised, at least electronically, than those on standard probation programs.

Nellis' research focused, in part, upon the effectiveness of electronic monitoring used by different segments of the probation population, particularly those persons, both adult and juvenile, who participated in a community-based corrections program. Suppose that the program had included provisions for educating and preparing youths to take the G.E.D., signifying their completion of high school requirements. Let's further suppose that we have devised a measure of mathematical and verbal aptitude, a G.E.D. skills test, for all juvenile delinquents in our jurisdiction. Because of the greater supervisory potential of electronic monitoring over standard probation, would youths subject to electronic monitoring tend to do better on our measure of mathematical and verbal aptitude compared with standard juvenile probationers? The *U* test can help us answer this question.

To demonstrate the application of the *U* test, assume that Nellis has obtained two samples of delinquents. One sample consists of 14 youths who wear electronic wristlets and participate in the electronic monitoring program. The other sample consists of 12 youths from the same juvenile court jurisdiction, but who only receive standard probation (i.e., weekly face-to-face visits from their probation officers and/or periodic telephone calls). Additionally, suppose these 26 youths have participated in a six-week educational training course designed to improve their mathematical and verbal skills. The program includes independent study and homework. At the end of the six-week period, we administer the G.E.D. skills test and attempt to determine whether electronically monitored youths performed at a higher level compared with those youths on standard probation. In this case, the larger the scores on our G.E.D. skills test, the better the performance. Table 10.4 shows hypothetical G.E.D. skills test scores for two independent samples of delinquent youths. Nellis might hypothesize the following:

H_0: *Electronically monitored juveniles will do no better on a G.E.D. skills test than youths on standard probation; if there is a difference, youths on standard probation will have higher scores.*

H_1: *Electronically monitored juveniles will do better on a G.E.D. skills test compared with youths on standard probation.*

$P \leq .05$ (one-tailed test)

TABLE 10.4 Hypothetical G.E.D. Skills Test Scores for Electronically Monitored and Standard Probation Juvenile Offenders

Raw Scores, G.E.D. Skills			
Electronically Monitored Juveniles		Standard Probation Juveniles	
N_1 = 14	R_1	N_2 = 12	R_2
51	1	41	10
47	4	44	6
43	7	32	17.5
29	20.5	37	15
40	12	30	19
28	22.5	22	26
46	5	25	25
41	10	28	22.5
33	16	26	24
32	17.5	48	3
29	20.5	42	8
39	13	41	10
49	2		
38	14		
	ΣR_1 = 165		ΣR_2 = 186

Table 10.4 contains raw scores for both groups of youths, those participating in an electronic monitoring program and those on standard probation. Further, the scores across groups have been rank-ordered from high to low, where the highest score of 51 receives a rank of "1," 49 receives a rank of "2," 48 receives the rank of "3," and so on. Whenever tied scores are encountered, these tied scores are counted and given the average of the ranks they would otherwise occupy. Thus, there are two raw scores of 32. The ranks these scores would otherwise receive if slightly different would be 17 and 18. Therefore, the scores are given the average of these ranks or 17 + 18/2 = 35/2 = 17.5. The two scores of 29 have been given ranks of 20.5 each, because they would otherwise occupy ranks 20 and 21 (20 + 21/2 = 41/2 = 20.5). It makes no difference which group has specific scores. All rank-ordering is done across both groups, disregarding the groups where the scores actually occur. Once this rank-ordering has been completed, the ranks for both groups are summed as shown. These are designated respectively R_1 and R_2. The formula for the U test is:

$$U = N_1N_2 + \frac{(N_1)(N_1 + 1)}{2} - \Sigma R_1$$

where

N_1 and N_2 = the two sample sizes

and R_1 = the smaller of the two sums of ranks

Using the values from Table 10.4, we may compute our observed U value as follows:

$$U = (14)(12) + \frac{(14)(14 + 1)}{2} - 165$$

$$= 168 + \frac{210}{2} - 165$$

$$= 168 + 105 - 165$$

$$= 273 - 165$$

$$= 108.$$

Once we have determined this U value, we must determine a U' value, actually a second U value, as follows:

$$U' = N_1 N_2 - U$$

$$= (14)(12) - 108$$

$$= 168 - 108$$

$$= 60.$$

We now have two U values, 108 and 60. The reason for computing two U values is that we need the smaller of the two U values as our critical value of U. We are interested only in the *smaller* of the two U values, or 60. This becomes our observed U. Tables A.8–A.17, Appendix A, pp. 441–459, contain critical values of U for different sample sizes and different levels of significance. These tables are designed for smaller sample sizes, where the larger of the two Ns ranges from 3 to 20. Tables A.8–A.13 are for situations where the larger of the two Ns is 8 or smaller. Tables A.14–A.17 are for situations where the larger of the two sample sizes ranges from 9 to 20. Since the level of significance is .05 and a one-tailed test is being made, we will use Table A.15, p. 457. In this case, we locate the larger of the two Ns, 14, across the top of the table, and the smaller N, 12, down the left-hand side. Where these values intersect in the body of the table, the critical value, $U = 51$, is found. If we observe a U equal to or smaller than the critical value of U shown in the body of the table, then we may reject the null hypothesis and support our research hypothesis.

Explanatory headnotes in all Mann-Whitney interpretive tables describe how to interpret all observed U values. Since our observed $U = 60$, this value is not equal to or smaller than the critical U value of 51. Therefore, we fail to reject H_o and tentatively conclude that there is no significant difference in G.E.D. skills scores between the two groups at the .05 level (one-tailed test). However, an inspection of the two sums of ranks as well as the raw scores of both groups discloses that directionally at least, the electronically monitored youths appeared to have slightly higher scores on the G.E.D. skills test compared with those youths on standard probation. While this difference was not significant statistically when the U test was applied, at least a correct directional prediction was made under H_1, and this fact should be reported for reader interest.

For applications of the U test where either sample size exceeds 20 and Tables A.14–A.17 cannot be applied, a Z test approximation has been devised as follows:

$$Z = \frac{U - \left(\dfrac{N_1 N_2}{2}\right)}{\sqrt{\dfrac{(N_1 N_2)(N_1 + N_2 + 1)}{12}}}$$

where

N_1 and N_2 = the sample sizes

U = the smaller of the two U values

The resulting Z value is interpreted like any other Z value through the use of Table A.2. This does not mean that the normal distribution assumption is required for U-test applications. Rather,

---

BOX 10.4

SPSS Alternative Application

1. Activate your *SPSS* software. Go to the *SPSS* Data Editor screen and enter the two sets of scores from the data in Table 10.4. The first column, "var," will contain 14 "1" values and 12 "2" values. These represent the two groups of boys, 14 and 12 respectively. The second "var" column will be the ranks of the scores for the electronically monitored juveniles in the R_1 column from Table 10.4. These will begin with the ranks of 1, 4, 7, and so on, until the last rank of 14 is entered. We will continue entering ranks for the second group, R_2, beginning with 10, 6, 17.5, 15, and so on, until the last rank of 10 is entered. When finished, we will have two columns, VAR00001 which will consist of 14 "1" values and 12 "2" values, and a second column, VAR00002, which will contain a continuous listing of ranks for the two sets of youths. The first rank in the column will be "1," while the last rank will be "10." There will be a total of 26 entries in both columns. Double-check your entries to ensure that they are accurate.

2. Next, click on "Analyze," then "Nonparametric Tests," then "2 Independent Samples." This will display a screen with several windows. The left window will contain VAR00001 and VAR00002. On the right are two windows, "Test Variable List" and "Grouping Variable."

3. Highlight VAR00001 and using the arrow, move it to the "Grouping Variable" window. Click "Define Groups" and this will bring up "Group 1" and "Group 2" screens. Type "1" in Group 1 and "2" in Group 2. Click "Continue." Highlight VAR00002 and using the arrow, transfer it to the "Test Variable List." At the bottom of the screen, you are given several test options. Click the Mann-Whitney *U* option, then "OK."

4. This should yield two summary tables for the Mann-Whitney *U* Test. The first table verifies that 14 and 12 persons (a total of 26 persons) were analyzed. These are defined by subclasses of "1" and "2" under VAR00001. The second table is the more important one. This table contains the following information. First, it shows the smaller of the two *U* values yielded by the manual procedure used in the above example, 60. It also provides a Wilcoxon *W* which we can ignore. It produces a Z value of -1.236 and a one-tailed significance level of .231.

5. We now compare this significance level, .231, with the level of significance at which our hypothesis set was tested. This probability was .05 (one-tailed). Since our observed probability of .231 fails to equal or fall below our significance level of .05, we fail to reject H_o that the two groups are the same on the characteristic measured. This finding is consistent with the interpretation made using the test manually.

6. It is important to note that if an *SPSS* program can be accessed, then ranks can be entered for any number of persons across two groups, especially in excess of 20. This means that there is no use for the Appendix Tables A.8 through A.17. These tables may be conveniently bypassed. Again, this is a positive feature of having access to an *SPSS* software program. While all *SPSS* programs have restrictions, most researchers never approach these restrictions with the numbers of persons they study. Different sample sizes of 50 or 100 can be studied easily with some easy data entry programming, and usually, both one- and two-tailed probabilities can be obtained quickly for most statistical test applications.

the Z value here is only an approximation that permits us to evaluate the significance of observed U values for larger Ns whenever they are encountered. As our observed U values become smaller, the larger the Z value becomes, and the more significant the difference between the two samples on the ranked sets of scores.

ASSUMPTIONS, ADVANTAGES, AND DISADVANTAGES OF THE *U* TEST   The assumptions underlying the application of U test are: (1) randomness; (2) two independent samples; and (3) the ordinal level of measurement. Favorably, the U test is easy to apply and has either convenient interpretive tables or a large N formula to determine the significance of difference between two groups on a ranked variable. Furthermore, the U test is the most powerful nonparametric equivalent compared with the parametric t test for differences between means, with a power level of 95 percent. Thus, even if researchers have achieved the interval level of measurement with some of the data they have collected, certain assumption violations may exclude the t test from being applied. Although treating raw scores as ranked data, the Mann-Whitney U test offers a convenient substitute for the t test without a significant power loss relative to rejecting false H_os. An *SPSS* program for entering data and analyzing it for differences between two independent samples exists and is a useful alternative as well.

A COMPARISON OF TWO INDEPENDENT SAMPLE NONPARAMETRIC TESTS WITH THE PARAMETRIC *t* TEST

The hypothesis test power reported for the Wald-Wolfowitz runs test, the Kolmogorov–Smirnov test, and the Mann-Whitney U test relates to how each of these procedures compares with the t test for differences between means. The least powerful test compared with the t test is the runs test, while the most powerful test is the Mann-Whitney U test. This section illustrates how each of these tests compares with the t test applied to the same data. In each of these three test applications, the same question is being asked. Do two groups differ on some measured characteristic? The calculations for all tests have been performed in advance, with critical and observed values of the different test outcomes supplied. Students may wish to carry out their own calculations to verify the accuracy of these results. Also, each of the tests has been arranged from the most powerful to least powerful for rejecting false H_os.

Suppose we are testing the following hypothesis set at the .05 level of significance with a one-tailed test for two samples of 13 persons each:

H_o: *There is no difference between two samples on characteristic X; if there is a difference, group 2 will have lower scores on characteristic X than group 1.*

H_1: *Group 2 will have higher scores than group 1 on characteristic X.*

$P \leq .05$ (one-tailed test)

Group 1	Group 2	Group 1	Group 2
14	19	12	33
13	22	11	21
21	16	10	14
28	32	24	17
22	19	13	35
17	25	30	16
13	29	$\bar{X}_1 = 17.5$	$\bar{X}_2 = 22.9$

1. *t* Test Application

$t_{obs} = -2.061$; critical value of $t = 1.711$ (.05 level of significance, one-tailed test, 24 *df*)

Conclusion: Reject null hypothesis, support research hypothesis at .05 level of significance, one-tailed test, 24 *df*, where $(N_1-1) + (N_2-1) = (13-1) + (13-1) = 12 + 12 = 24$ *df*.

The remaining three tests are nonparametric and thus have fewer restrictive assumptions compared with *t* test applications to interval-level data. In fact, these are ordinal-level tests of significance. Generally, these are less powerful tests, but this statement is somewhat deceptive. The Mann-Whitney *U* test is less powerful than the *t* test, but the power differential is about 95 percent. In other words, the Mann-Whitney *U* test is about 95 percent as powerful as the *t* test applied to the same data. This power differential is almost inconsequential. Other tests compared with the *t* test in this section are somewhat less powerful. The power differentials in these other tests are in the 75–85 percent power range, a substantial reduction in test power compared with the *t* test. The purpose of this section is to illustrate how different tests applied to same set of information can yield different conclusions and decisions about hypothesis tests involving identical data. Power varies among these tests and is one important consideration researchers take into account when selecting statistical tests for data analyses. These ranks are based on the same scores used for the *t* test comparison above.

2. Mann-Whitney *U* Test Application
(ranked scores across groups)

Group 1	Group 2
19.5	13.5
22	9.5
11.5	17.5
6	3
9.5	13.5
15.5	7
22	5
24	2
25	11.5
26	19.5
8	15.5
22	1
4	17.5
$R_1 = 215$	$R_2 = 136$

Observed $U = (13)(13) + (13)(13 + 1)/2 - 136$,
Second observed $U = 169 + 91 - 215 = 45$;
$45 = $ smaller observed U
Critical value of $U = 51$; we must observe a U equal to or smaller than 51 in order to reject the null hypothesis at the .05 level, one-tailed test.

Conclusion: Reject null hypothesis, support research hypothesis (.05 level of significance, one-tailed test).

3. Kolmogorov–Smirnov Two-Sample Test Application

	10–16	17–23	24–29	30–35	10–16
Group I	7	3	2	I	$N_1 = 13$
Group 2	3	5	2	3	$N_2 = 13$
Critical proportion = .478					

Largest observed difference between cumulative proportions = .309; in order to reject null hypothesis, largest proportionate difference must equal or exceed critical proportion. These scores are also based on the original scores used for the t test in the first example above.

Conclusion: We fail to reject the null hypothesis at .05 level, since .309 fails to equal or exceed .478.

4. Wald-Wolfowitz Runs Test Application
Wald-Wolfowitz Runs Test:

10 11 12 13 13 13 14 14 16 16 17 17 17 19 19 21 21 22 22 24 25
28 29 30 32 33 35

Observed $r = 16$
Critical number of runs (r_{cv}) = 8; if observed number of runs is equal to or smaller than critical number of runs, we can reject null hypothesis. Calculating the number of runs in left as an exercise.

Conclusion: We fail to reject null hypothesis (.05 level of significance, one-tailed test).

What does this comparison reveal? First, the relative efficiency of these three tests at rejecting the same null hypothesis varies. Notice that the application of the most powerful nonparametric equivalent of the t test, the Mann-Whitney U test, resulted in rejecting the null hypothesis. However, the least powerful Wald-Wolfowitz runs test failed to reject the null hypothesis.

Second, this comparison shows how each test treats the same data in different ways to arrive at the decision whether to reject or fail to reject the null hypothesis. In the case of the t test, we averaged the scores and conducted a t test for significance of difference between the two sample means. In the Mann-Whitney U test, the two sets of scores were rank-ordered across the two groups. Then the rank sums were compared to yield the final result, which was the same result yielded by the t test. This is logical, because the U test is about 95 percent as powerful as the t test for differentiating between two samples. In other words, the two procedures are almost equivalent in their power.

The Kolmogorov–Smirnov two-sample test dealt with these data in a cross tabulation. The two groups compared were grouped according to shared scores across four categories. Cumulative proportions of scores were calculated and these cumulative proportions were compared. The largest cumulative proportionate difference was used as the basis for this test result. In this case, the largest cumulative proportionate difference was .309, which was not equal to or larger than the critical proportion of .478. Thus the null hypothesis could not be rejected at the .05 level of significance.

For the Wald-Wolfowitz runs test, the null hypothesis could not be rejected either. In the runs test application, all 26 scores were ordered from low to high, and the contiguous numbers of scores for the two groups, resulting in a certain number of runs, were counted. The maximum number of observed runs was compared with the critical number of runs as shown in Appendix Table A.6. For these sample sizes and level of significance, the critical number of runs was 8, while the observed number of runs was 16. We would have had to observe 8 or fewer runs between the two samples in order to conclude that the samples were different at the .05 level of significance. There were simply too many runs, which meant that there was too much similarity between the two groups for them to be considered different.

The conclusion reached, therefore, is that the most powerful test for rejecting null hypotheses is the *t* test. The least powerful test is the Wald-Wolfowitz runs test. The most conservative test is the runs test; the least conservative test is the *t* test. When making test selections from those presented here, therefore, if the stringent assumptions of the *t* test cannot be met, then the investigator should choose the next most powerful test. In this case, the Mann-Whitney *U* test would be next best test of choice. Almost always, if a more conservative nonparametric test is applied to data and the null hypothesis is rejected, more powerful nonparametric tests would yield similar results. Different criteria must be considered when making test selections for different types of data analysis.

A TWO RELATED-SAMPLE TEST: THE ORDINAL LEVEL OF MEASUREMENT

Whenever investigators have two samples that are matched in some way, either through individual matching or where persons are used as their own controls in before-after experiments, several procedures are available to assess the significance of difference between these two samples. One statistical procedure is presented here. This is the sign test.

The Sign Test

When investigators have two matched sets of subjects or whenever persons are used as their own controls in before-after experiments, and where an ordinal-level variable has been used, the sign test may be applied to determine the significance of difference between the two groups according to score differences or changes. The **sign test** is a straightforward technique that examines the directionality associated with score differences. It performs a function similar to the Wilcoxon matched pairs-signed ranks test, although the sign test does not examine the *magnitude* of score changes or score differences. The application of the sign test can be illustrated with an example from the criminological literature.

Tomislav V. Kovandzic (2001) was interested in learning about the impact of Florida's habitual offender law (HOL) on crime prevention. He examined various initiatives in different states, such as California's "three-strikes-and-you're-out" laws and other get-tough measures to make punishments more stringent for persistent felony offenders. Kovandzic indicated that by 1995, 24 states had passed "three strikes" laws designed to deter offenders. The primary aim of these laws was to lengthen prison sentences for the most criminally active offenders, insuring the decline of current crime levels, because these offenders would be unable to commit more crimes while incarcerated (2001:179). Kovandzic disclosed that Florida implemented a HOL in 1988.

Suppose Kovandzic was interested in whether the law had any appreciable effect on repeat offenders, persistent offenders, or hardcore recidivists, and whether these persons might be inclined to refrain from further criminal activity if they became aware of the harsher punishments associated with the Florida habitual offender statute. Further suppose that Kovandzic obtained two samples of Florida recidivists matched according to a number of salient characteristics. These two samples of 18 recidivists each were obtained at different times. The first sample of recidivists, N_1, was obtained in 1986, prior to 1988 before the HOL was enacted. The second sample, N_2, was obtained in 1991, three years after passage of the HOL. Next, suppose that Kovandzic administered a Pro-Social Attitudinal Scale (PSAS) to all of these offenders. The PSAS purportedly measures the degree to which offenders believe that they should be law-abiding and refrain from further offending. The larger the score on the PSAS, the more pro-social the attitude of the offender. Based on the rationale underlying the passage of the HOL, the following hypothesis set might be generated:

H_0: *There is no difference on PSAS scores for two groups of recidivists prior to and after passage of the HOL; if there is a difference, scores on the PSAS will be greater for recidivists prior to the passage of the HOL than for recidivists after the passage of the HOL.*

H_1: *Recidivists after the passage of the HOL will have greater PSAS scores than recidivists prior to the passage of the HOL.*

$P \leq .05$ (one-tailed test)

Suppose Kovandzic found the following information for his matched set of recidivists as shown in Table 10.5.

TABLE 10.5 Recidivists Prior to and After Passage of the Florida Habitual Offender Law (HOL) Measured According to Pro-Social Attitudinal Scores (PSAS)

PSAS Scores		
Recidivists Prior to HOL	Recidivists After HOL	Sign Associated with Change in Score
25	29	+
27	28	+
16	21	+
29	28	−
19	29	+
15	25	+
19	20	+
28	26	−
32	33	+
32	31	−
29	26	−
30	33	+
23	26	+
29	31	+
19	17	−
20	30	+
19	21	+
23	26	+
$N = 18$	Sum of fewer signs = $m = 5$	

Table 10.5 is easily constructed. The first two columns consist of raw PSAS scores for the two matched samples of recidivists. The third column contains the signs (either + or −) associated with the difference between each pair of scores. The less frequently occurring signs are summed and designated as m.

From the data in Table 10.5, we see that 13 of the score differences were positive, and 5 score differences were negative. Therefore, $m = 5$. We are now ready to evaluate the significance of our observed $m = 5$ by turning to Table A.23, Appendix A, p. 466. Table A.23 contains one-tailed exact probabilities for various numbers of ± score changes. We find the sample size (numbers of pairs of scores), $N = 18$, down the left-hand column. Across the top of the table, we locate the m value. Where $N = 18$ intersects with $m = 5$ defines the probability associated with our particular distribution of signs. This probability is .048. Since this probability is equal to or less than the .05 level of significance at which our hypothesis is tested, we can reject H_o and support H_1 that PSAS scores are higher for the recidivists after the HOL was enacted compared with the sample of recidivists before the HOL was enacted. This means that at least for these samples of recidivists, the passage of the HOL seemed to influence higher pro-social scores among recidivists.

For two-tailed applications where $N > 25$, the probabilities in Table A.23 must be doubled. Had we made the hypothesis test at the .05 level of significance for a two-tailed nondirectional test instead of the one-tailed test, the probability associated with a 13–5 split for our 18 pairs of recidivists would have been $(.048)(2) = .096$. With a probability this large, we would not have been able to reject H_o at the .05 level.

Whenever we exceed 25 pairs of scores, Table A.23 cannot be used. In such cases, an approximation of a Z value may be determined by using the following formula:

$$Z = \frac{2m - N}{\sqrt{N,}}$$

where

$m =$ the sum of the less frequently occurring signs

$N =$ the number of pairs of untied scores

Had we examined a sample of 35 persons and observed a 27–8 split in the positive (+) and negative (−) signs, our observed $m = 8$. The observed Z value would be computed as follows:

$$Z = \frac{(2)(8) - 35}{\sqrt{35}} = \frac{-19}{5.9} = -3.22.$$

The resulting Z value is −3.22 and would be interpreted as any other Z value by using Table A.2. Again, despite the fact that a Z approximation is rendered for use with the sign test here, there is no normal distribution assumption accompanying this application. Rather, this Z value is merely an approximation. For example, the critical value of Z for the .05 level of significance for a two-tailed test would be ±1.96. Thus, any H_o we would have tested would be rejected at the .05 level with an observed Z value as large as −3.22. This Z value would have permitted a rejection of H_o at the .001 level as well. Sometimes, investigators wish to indicate this potential result and express it as follows: $Z = -3.22, P < .05 < .001$ (two-tailed test). This notation underscores the significance achieved with the matched pairs of scores and the differences in scores observed.

BOX 10.6

SPSS **Alternative Application**

1. Activate your *SPSS* software program. Go to the *SPSS* Data Editor. Using the data from Table 10.5, enter the raw scores from column 1, "Recidivists Prior to HOL" into the first "var" column, beginning with 25, 27, 16, and so on, until the last score of 23 is entered. Move to the second "var" column and enter the second set of scores beginning with 29, 28, 21, and so forth, until the last score of 26 is entered. You should now have two variable columns, VAR00001 and VAR00002.

2. Click on "Analyze," then "Nonparametric Tests," then "2 Related Sample Tests." This will reveal two windows, one containing VAR00001 and VAR00002. The second window will be "Test Pair(s) List." Highlight VAR00001 and VAR00002 and use the arrow to move them to the "Test Pair(s) List." Click "OK."

3. This action will generate two Sign Test summary tables. The first table will contain the 5–13 breakdown, showing 5 negative differences and 13 positive differences. The second table shows the two-tailed probability at which these changes in sign are significant. This probability is .096. Since a one-tailed probability is being made of this hypothesis set, this two-tailed probability must be halved, or .096/2 = .048. Notice that .048 matches up perfectly with what was obtained manually for the above problem. Again, we can reject the null hypothesis that there was no significant change from one time period to another among the 18 recidivists. .048 is equal to or less than .05, the significance level used in our hypothesis test.

4. It is significant to note that if one has access to *SPSS* software, more than 25 pairs of scores may be compared without having to resort to the manual *Z* test procedure. Exact probabilities for both one- and two-tailed tests can be conducted quickly and easily through data entry and subsequent analysis as described above.

ASSUMPTIONS OF THE SIGN TEST   The assumptions of the sign test are (1) randomness; (2) the ordinal level of measurement; and (3) two related samples.

ADVANTAGES AND DISADVANTAGES OF THE SIGN TEST   Besides being a rapid method of determining the significance of difference between two related samples, the sign test gives us a conservative appraisal of differences between two groups on some ordinal-level characteristic. The sign test has power relative to the *t* test equivalent to 75 percent for rejecting false H_os.

One drawback of the sign test is that all pair of elements are eliminated from where no differences in scores exist from one time period to the next or where there are tied scores between matched sets of persons. For instance, if we observed 50 pairs of scores and 10 pairs of scores were the same or tied across two time periods, these 10 pairs of scores would be dropped, leaving us with an $N = 40$. There were no tied scores in Table 10.5 for the 18 pairs of recidivists. Had there been several pairs of scores that had been tied, these score pairs would have been eliminated, and our resulting N would be less than 18.

If a substantial number of score pairs are tied, this condition could seriously impair our use of the sign test for assessing score pair differences. Sometimes, observing no change in score pairs is as important as observing score changes. In any case, the researcher should acknowledge the number of tied score pairs when reporting research results. This is valuable information for the readership.

Another advantage is that a table of probabilities exists for samples up to 25, and an approximation of *Z* can be calculated for assessing the significance of *m*, the sum of the less frequently occurring sign. It is also an advantage that the column containing the signs can be scanned easily to determine the overall impact of differences or changes between groups. This advantage is especially useful when one-tailed directional tests of hypotheses are being made. Investigators can give the column of signs a quick glance and determine instantly whether the correct directional prediction has been made. The question then becomes whether the numbers of score changes are significantly different. As we have seen, the sign test answers this question fairly quickly. Finally, an *SPSS* program exists for determining test results once data have been entered through the Data Editor. There are no sample size restrictions when the *SPSS* program is used, if available.

k INDEPENDENT SAMPLE TESTS: THE ORDINAL LEVEL OF MEASUREMENT

The Kruskal-Wallis *H* Test

Considered by many researchers as a *k*-independent sample extension of the Mann-Whitney *U* test, the **Kruskal-Wallis *H* test (*H* test)** is applicable to three or more samples where the data have been measured according to an ordinal scale. As is the case with all other *k*-sample procedures, the test may be applied to the two-sample case, but its application would be cumbersome. In the two-sample case, the Mann-Whitney *U* test would be preferred because it would be more rapid and far easier to apply where two independent samples are encountered. When three or more samples exist, however, the *H* test becomes the test of choice. An example of the *H* test from the criminological literature is presented as follows.

Joyce Fogg, Charles J. Kehoe, and Timothy O. Kestner (2007) examined the work performance among several samples of older corrections officers. These investigators assessed their work performance according to several criteria, including years of formal education, on-the-job experience, and other forms of training. They found that oldest correctional officers had formal educational levels well beyond the minimum educational levels required to perform their present tasks. Suppose these researchers had devised a professionalism scale and wished to learn whether there are differences in professionalism among corrections officers compared with probation and parole officers from different jurisdictions. The *H* test would be useful in helping them to determine whether these three types of corrections personnel differ according to their degree of professionalism.

Let's assume that Fogg, Kehoe, and Kestner obtained three random samples of correctional personnel from a given jurisdiction, consisting of 10 parole officers, 12 probation officers, and 15 corrections officers. Further assume that they have made assessments of these persons according to the scores received on a professionalism scale. Assuming that the larger or higher the score, the greater the professionalism, some hypothetical data about these samples and their amounts of professionalism have been placed in Table 10.6.

The following hypothesis set could be tested:

H_0: *There is no difference in professionalism among samples of parole, probation, and corrections officers.*

H_1: *There is a difference in professionalism among sample of parole, probation, and corrections officers.*

$P \leq .01$ (two-tailed test)

TABLE 10.6 Professionalism Scores of Alaskan Parole, Probation, and Corrections Officers

Parole Officers		Probation Officers		Corrections Officers	
$N_1 = 10$	R_1	$N_2 = 12$	R_2	$N_3 = 15$	R_3
32	37	48	15	64	1
50	14	46	17.5	56	8.5
38	32.5	59	5	45	19
41	25	42	22	62	3
43	20	41	25	59	5
38	32.5	40	28.5	47	16
35	36	55	10	41	25
36	35	46	17.5	63	2
38	32.5	42	22	42	22
40	28.5	38	32.5	58	7
		40	28.5	56	8.5
		40	28.5	51	13
				54	11.5
				54	11.5
				59	5
$\Sigma R_1 = 293$		$\Sigma R_2 = 252$		$\Sigma R_3 = 158$	

In order to perform the H test, all scores across the three groups must be ranked from high to low. The rank of "1" will be assigned to the high score of 64 occurring in the corrections officer sample; the rank of "2" will be assigned to the score of 63 in the same sample; the rank of "3" will be assigned to the score of 62 in the same sample, the rank of "4" (the average of the next three ranks) will be assigned to the tied scores of 59 occurring in the probation officer and corrections officer groups, and so on, until all scores have been rank-ordered. Notice that whenever tied scores are encountered, the different ranks these scores would otherwise occupy are averaged and assigned, depending on the group where they occur. Next, the ranks for the three groups are summed. Once these rank sums have been calculated as shown in Table 10.6, the H formula is applied:

$$H = \frac{12}{N(N + 1)} \Sigma \left(\frac{\Sigma R^2}{N_i} \right) - [k(N + 1)]$$

where

N = the total number of people in the k samples

N_i = the number of people in the ith sample

R_i = sum of ranks for the ith sample

k = number of samples

Using the information from Table 10.6, we carry out our H computation as follows:

$$H = \frac{12}{(37)(37 + 1)}\left[\frac{(293)^2}{10} + \frac{(252)^2}{12} + \frac{(158)^2}{15}\right] - [(3)(37 + 1)]$$

$$= \frac{12}{1406}\left[\frac{85,849}{10} + \frac{63,504}{12} + \frac{24,964}{15}\right] - 114$$

$$= (.00853)(8,584.9 + 5,292 + 1,664.27) - 114$$

$$= (.00853)(15,541.17) - 114 = 132.6 - 114 = 18.566.$$

Our observed H value is 18.566. Since H is an approximation of a chi-square value with $k - 1$ degrees of freedom, where $k =$ the number of samples, $df = 3 - 1 = 2$ df. Since our hypothesis test is being made at the .01 level of significance (two-tailed test), we enter Table A.4 of Appendix A, p. 448, and where .01 intersects with 2 df defines the critical value of H which we must equal or exceed with our observed H value. Our critical value of $H = 9.210$. Since our observed value of $H = 18.566$, this value equals or exceeds our critical value. Therefore, Fogg, Kehoe, and Kestner could reject H_o and conclude tentatively that there is a difference among these officers according to their professionalism.

Had these investigators wanted to make a one-tailed test, they could have indicated which groups might be expected to have greater degrees of professionalism, inspected Table 10.6 initially to see whether the professionalism scores were in the direction predicted under their one-tailed H_1, and then carried out the test. Then they would have interpreted the H value using the one-tailed probability shown in Table A.4. When applying the H test to k samples, directionality can be determined by inspecting the rank sums. The lowest rank sums indicate which group contains the highest scores on the ranked variable. Had these investigators predicted that corrections officers would have higher professionalism scores, an inspection of Table 10.6 would show that, indeed, this sample had the lowest rank sum (R_3). These researchers could have rejected their directional H_o and tentatively concluded this observation.

ASSUMPTIONS, ADVANTAGES, AND DISADVANTAGES OF THE H TEST   The assumptions underlying the H test include (1) randomness; (2) ordinal-level measurement, and (3) k independent samples.

The primary advantages of the H test include the fact that it is the most powerful nonparametric equivalent to the F test for analysis of variance, with power approximating 95 percent. In this respect, the H test compares with the F test in the same way the Mann-Whitney U test compares with the parametric t test. Also, just like the F test, the H test merely answers the question: Does a difference exist somewhere between k samples on some ordered characteristic? Yes or no? If yes, then the H test does not disclose which samples differ from one another, only that there is a difference somewhere. Unfortunately, the H test has no postmortem tests that are similar to the Newman–Keuls or Scheffé procedures used following a significant F value. There are some limited choices, however, if investigators wish to know which samples actually differ significantly. The two-sample Mann-Whitney U test can be used as a probe in this instance. This would mean that investigators would have to take two samples at a time and use the U test for each pair compared. This method of comparing groups seems cumbersome, and it is. But it is the only way we can be sure of which differences between specific sample pairs are significant statistically.

A strong advantage of the H test is that it is a goodness-of-fit procedure, where the H value is an approximation of a chi-square value with $k - 1$ degrees of freedom. Unfavorably, however, because the H statistic is also chi square-based, applications of H to samples where

BOX 10.7

SPSS Alternative Application

1. Activate your *SPSS* software and go to the *SPSS* Data Editor window. Go to the first "var" column and type in 10 "1" values, 12 "2" values, and 15 "3" values. These values stand for the 10 persons in group 1 (parole officers), group 2 (probation officers), and group 3 (corrections officers) respectively. This will yield a VAR00001 column containing 37 values, 10 "1"s, 12 "2"s, and 15 "3"s.

2. Next, go to the second "var" column and begin typing in the ranks from column 1 in Table 10.6, beginning with 37, 14, 32.5, and so on, until the last rank of 28.5 is entered. Move to the second column in Table 10.6 and continue typing in the second set of ranks, beginning with 15, 17.5, 5, 22, and so forth, until the last rank of 28.5 is entered. Move to the third column in Table 10.6 and continue entering ranks, beginning with 1, 8.5, 19, 3, 5, and so forth, until the last rank of 5 is entered. You will now have a second column labeled VAR00002, and this column will contain 37 ranks from the 3 groups. The ranks for the first group (the "1" values in the VAR00001 column should match up with the "1"s, the ranks for the second group (the "2" values) will match up with the "2"s, and the 15 ranks for the third group (the "3" values) will match up with the 15 ranks entered from Table 10.6. Double-check your work to make sure that all ranks match the groups where they were found from Table 10.6.

3. Now click "Analyze" at the top of the *SPSS* Data Editor screen, then "Nonparametric Statistics," then "*K* Independent Samples." This will yield a screen with several windows. The far left window will contain VAR00001 and VAR00002. Highlight VAR00001 and use the arrow to move it to the "Grouping Variable" window. Click on "Define Range" and you will see "Minimum" and "Maximum" windows. Type a "1" in Minimum and a "3" in Maximum. Click "Continue."

4. Next, highlight VAR00002 and use the arrow to move it to the "Test Variable List" window. Click "OK."

5. Two summary tables will appear next, showing Kruskal-Wallis Test results. The first table, "Ranks," merely functions as a check on your work. It shows that you started with three groups, with 10, 12, and 15 persons in the three groups, totaling 37 persons. This figure should tally with the number of entries you made in the *SPSS* Data Editor window for VAR00001.

6. The second table, Test Statistics, shows the observed chi-square, df, and the probability at which the chi-square is significant. In this case, the observed chi-square = 18.719, df = 2, and the probability level is .000. Notice that the manually computed H value (a chi-square value) is 18.566, slightly different from the one produced with the *SPSS* program. This is due to rounding error between the two formulae and is unimportant.

7. Next, compare the observed chi-square = 18.719 with the critical value of H, which is 9.210 from the problem described above. Since the observed chi-square of 18.719 equals or exceeds the critical chi-square value, 9.210, there is a significant difference between the three groups of officers at the .001 level, the level of significance at which the hypothesis set was originally tested. Therefore, H_o can be rejected and H_1 supported, meaning that there is a significant difference in professionalism among the three groups of officers.

sample sizes fall below 25 or exceed 250 should be cautiously interpreted. Positively, H is easy to apply, is unaffected by tied scores across groups, and requires no correction factor when excessive numbers of ties are observed. It is a popular k-sample test of significance for data measured according to an ordinal scale, and it is an excellent alternative to the parametric F test when the stringent assumptions of the F test cannot be met by one's data. An *SPSS* program for H exists. It requires data to be entered through a Data Editor, but once such data are entered, it is easily computed. This is an advantage for those with access to *SPSS* software.

k-SAMPLE TESTS: RELATED SAMPLES

The Friedman Two-Way Analysis of Variance Test

A useful k-related sample test for data measured according to an ordinal scale is the **Friedman two-way analysis of variance test**, or simply, the Friedman test. The Friedman test determines whether a sample differs on some ordered characteristic over k time periods. It also assesses whether k samples of matched individuals differ. An example from the probation literature illustrates an application of the Friedman test.

M. Chan et al. (2005) examined case management services and intensive supervision programs (ISP) for female probationers who were formerly drug involved. It is widely known that many former drug-dependent offenders, both male and female, face numerous obstacles when released back into their communities following criminal convictions. It is difficult to adjust to normal community living, and there is great temptation to return to drug use through simple associations with active drug users. One method of regulating the behaviors of female probationers might be to supervise them more intensively, requiring more frequent face-to-face visits, random drug testing, impositions of curfews, and other restrictive measures. Suppose that Chan et al. had a random sample of 10 probationers assigned to an Arizona intensive supervision program (ISP), and that they wanted to observe the progress of these probationers over five different time periods at four-week intervals. Further suppose that they kept track of the number of program infractions (e.g., violation of curfew, consumption of alcohol, positive drug testing, and failure to attend counseling session) committed by each probationer in each of these time periods. These investigators might arrange this information as is shown in Table 10.7.

In Table 10.7, the numbers of infractions for each of the ten probationers enrolled in the Arizona ISP have been identified over five different time periods at four-week intervals. Next, the scores for each probationer are ranked across the five time periods. Thus, if probationer 1 had an infraction pattern of 5, 4, 3, 2, and 1 for each of the five time periods, Chan et al. would

TABLE 10.7 A Hypothetical Sample of ten Arizona Female Probationers Participating in an ISP over Five Time Periods According to Number of Program Infractions

Client	T_1	R_1	T_2	R_2	T_3	R_3	T_4	R_4	T_5	R_5
1	5	1.5	4	3	3	4.5	5	1.5	3	4.5
2	4	1.5	4	1.5	3	3	2	4.5	2	4.5
3	6	3	7	1.5	7	1.5	5	4.5	5	4.5
4	4	1	3	2	2	3.5	2	3.5	1	5
5	3	1.5	3	1.5	2	4	2	4	2	4
6	4	2.5	5	1	4	2.5	3	4.5	3	4.5
7	6	1	5	2.5	5	2.5	4	4	3	5
8	3	2.5	3	2.5	4	1	2	4.5	2	4.5
9	7	1	5	2	4	3	3	4.5	3	4.5
10	4	1	3	3	3	3	2	5	3	3
$\Sigma N = 10$		$\Sigma R_1 = 16.5$		$\Sigma R_2 = 20.5$		$\Sigma R_3 = 28.5$		$\Sigma R_4 = 40.5$		$\Sigma R_5 = 44$

Time Period, Raw Scores, Ranked Scores[*]

[*]T_k = each time period

rank these scores 1, 2, 3, 4, and 5 respectively, assigning a "1" to the most infractions and a "5" to the least infractions. Where the number of infractions within two or more time periods is the same, the average of the ranks otherwise occupied by these infraction numbers would be assigned as shown. Therefore, in Table 10.7, each clients' infraction numbers have been ranked across the five time periods. Next, the ranks of all 10 clients for each of the time periods are summed and shown as rank sums of R_k.

Chan et al. would want to know whether the ISP made a difference in changing the number of infractions among these female probationers over five different time periods. He and his associates might test the following hypothesis set:

H_0: *There is no difference between a sample of ten probationers across five time periods and the number of their program infractions.*

H_1: *There is a difference between a sample of ten probationers across five time periods and the number of their program infractions.*

$P \leq .001$ (two-tailed test)

The formula for applying the Friedman test is shown below:

$$\chi_r^2 = \left[\frac{12}{Nk(k+1)} \Sigma(\Sigma R_i)^2 \right] - [3N(k+1)]$$

where

k = the number of groups or time periods

$(\Sigma R_i)^2$ = square of the sum of the ranks under each of the experimental conditions or time periods

N = the number of individuals under each of the different time periods

Using the information in this formula supplied from Table 10.7, we have the following:

$$\chi_r^2 = \frac{12}{10(5)(5+1)[(16.5)^2 + (20.5)^2 + (28.5)^2 + (40.5)^2 + (44)^2]} - [(3)(10)(5+1)]$$

$$= \frac{12}{300(5081)} - 180$$

$$= (.040)(5081) - 180$$

$$= 203.24 - 180$$

$$\chi_r^2 = 23.24$$

This chi-square value may be taken to Table A.4 in Appendix A, p. 448, with $k - 1$ degrees of freedom, where k is defined as the number of time periods. In this case, there are five different time periods, and therefore, $k = 5$. Thus, $df = k - 1$ or $5 - 1 = 4\ df$. Where 4 df intersects with the .001 level of significance (two-tailed test) across the top of the table defines the critical value of χ_r^2 that we must equal or exceed with our observed chi-square value in order to reject H_0. A headnote provides helpful information about entering the table and determining critical values for both one- and two-tailed test applications. The critical value of $\chi_r^2 = 18.465$. Therefore, with an observed $\chi_r^2 = 23.24$, we can reject H_0 and support H_1 that there is a difference among female probationers across the five different time periods and the numbers of their infractions. The ISP program seemed to make a difference in reducing the numbers of program infractions across the five time periods.

Had Chan et al. wanted to make a one-tailed or directional test of the hypothesis, they could have done so easily. In this case, they would have inspected Table 10.7 to determine first that the numbers of program infractions among the 10 probationers tended to decrease across the five time periods. If they believed that the ISP program would decrease the number of female probationer program infractions over time, this outcome would be predicted under a directional H_1. An inspection of the rank sums (R_is) would disclose that the smaller the rank sums, the more infractions would be committed by these probationers. The larger the rank sums, the fewer the program infractions. Directionally, it would appear that the number of infractions among the 10 female probationers decreased over the five time periods. This trend of the rank sums was 16.5, 20.5, 28.5, 40.5, and 44 as shown in Table 10.7. The Friedman test would simply confirm whether these rank sum differences across the five time periods were significant statistically.

It should be noted that the sample of probationers could also be compared across two time periods only. Since the two samples would be related, we could use the Friedman test as its own two-sample probe in this case. We might also use the sign test as an alternative.

BOX 10.8

SPSS Alternative Application

1. Activate your *SPSS* software program and go to the *SPSS* Data Editor
2. In the first five "var" columns, enter the 10 ranks from each column, R_k. Place all ranks from the first column (summing to 16.5) in the first "var" column, the second set of ranks (summing to 20.5) in the second "var" column, and so forth, until all ranks have been entered in five "var" columns. You will now have VAR00001, VAR00002, VAR00003, VAR00004, and VAR00005, indicating ranks for five different time periods.
3. Next, click on "Analyze" at the top of the *SPSS* Data Editor, then "Nonparametric Tests," then "K Related Samples."
4. Clicking on the "K Related Samples" option will pull up a screen with two windows. The first window to the far left will have a list of variables from VAR00001 through VAR00005. Highlight each variable and use the arrow to move it to the right window, "Test Variables." This involves highlighting each VAR individually. These variables cannot be grouped and transferred.
5. Once these variables have been transferred to the Test Variables window, check "Friedman" at the bottom of the screen in the appropriate box and then click "OK."
6. Two summary tables will appear with your Friedman test results. The "Ranks" table can be ignored. The second table, however, contains N, the chi-square value observed, df, and the significance level achieved. In this case, $N = 10$, chi-square $= 26.112$, $df = 4$, and the probability $= .000$. This means that significance has been achieved equal to or less than .001, the level of significance used in the original hypothesis test.
7. Note that the two chi-square values, the one yielded manually and the one yielded through the *SPSS* program, do not match up perfectly although they are close (23.24 versus 26.112). Minor differences in calculation functions between the manual formula and the *SPSS* program account for such discrepancies, although most of the time, the two figures will be identical or nearly identical. Often these discrepancies are due to rounding error, which can occur. These small differences are inconsequential, however, since the critical chi-square value was 18.465 and both observed chi-square values, manually derived or *SPSS* derived, greatly exceed this value. In both cases, the results are the same. H_0 is rejected at the .001 level. There is a significant difference across the five time periods among the 10-female Arizona probationers and the numbers of their program infractions as the possible result of their participation in an ISP program.

ASSUMPTIONS OF THE FRIEDMAN TEST   The assumptions of the Friedman test are (1) randomness; (2) the ordinal level of measurement; and (3) k related samples through individual matching or using persons as their own controls over k time periods.

ADVANTAGES AND DISADVANTAGES OF THE FRIEDMAN TEST   The Friedman test is a chi square–based statistical procedure with $k - 1$ degrees of freedom. Whenever sample sizes are quite large, the procedure becomes cumbersome. However, most software programs include the Friedman test as a standard feature, and thus computations are simplified. The results of the Friedman test are easily interpreted for both one- and two-tailed hypothesis tests.

The Friedman test is one of the very few procedures that can be applied to ordinal-level data for k-related samples. This is one of its key advantages. Furthermore, it has a power equivalent to 85–90 percent for rejecting false H_0s compared with the F test for analysis of variance. Since the Friedman test uses the chi-square distribution for its interpretation, investigators should be aware that this test is sensitive when applied to extremely small or extremely large sample sizes (e.g., less than 25 or greater than 250).

Like the Kruskal-Wallis H test, the Friedman test answers the question, Does a significant difference exist somewhere between k related samples? Yes or no. If yes, and if investigators wish to determine which time periods differ significantly from one another, a two-sample probe is necessary. The sign test is one appropriate alternative, although it should be recalled that one weakness of the sign test is a loss of data if there are numerous tied scores which are dropped from the overall sample N.

One additional option is to use the Friedman test itself as its own two-sample probe. Any k-sample test can function as its own probe in any two-sample situation. Thus, the Friedman test could be applied to each pair of time periods. For the probationers in Table 10.7, for example, with five different time periods, there would be $k(k - 1)/2$ or $5(5 - 1)/2 = 20/2 = 10$ different Friedman tests which would need to be performed to determine which time periods differed significantly from one another. Unfortunately, there are no equivalent Newman–Keuls or Scheffé postmortem procedures that can be applied to k-related samples at the ordinal level of measurement. On the positive side, an *SPSS* program exists for computing the Friedman test. It requires data entry through the Data Editor function of this software, however. But once data have been entered, the data are analyzed easily and exact probabilities are yielded for hypothesis test purposes. This is a definite advantage for those with access to *SPSS* programming.

INTERVAL-LEVEL NONPARAMETRIC TESTS OF SIGNIFICANCE

There are more than a few occasions when researchers have interval-level data at their disposal, but they do not meet certain rigorous assumptions underlying various popular parametric tests, such as the t test for differences between means. For instance, the distribution of scores under investigation may be nonnormal or badly skewed to the left or right. Kurtosis may be present. For various reasons, normality cannot be assumed. Under such conditions, therefore, it might be unwise to apply the t test, although there have been abundant applications of it when some or all of its assumptions have been violated. For investigators who wish to adopt a more conservative approach to the data they analyze, there are several nonparametric options. These options enable them to make decisions about differences between two independent samples of elements where no normality assumption exists.

In this section, we will examine one-test of significance of difference that does not assume a normal distribution. Furthermore, this test maximizes the usefulness of the interval-level properties of scales used by investigators without reducing the information to the ordinal level. This test is the Wilcoxon matched pairs-signed ranks test.

The Wilcoxon Matched Pairs-Signed Ranks Test

The **Wilcoxon matched pairs-signed ranks test** is a nonparametric test that determines whether two related samples differ according to some interval-level variable. The Wilcoxon test may be used whenever researchers have related samples, either through individual matching or where persons act as their own controls in before-after experiments. The following example is provided from the criminal justice literature.

Harry E. Allen and Julie C. Abril (1997) investigated the reintroduction of chain gangs in the United States in selected jurisdictions as punishments for various types of offenders. Chain gangs are not new. They were used in the eighteenth century in the North and in New England. Chain gangs involved linking prison or jail inmates together in work groups with chains. Thus, inmate groups would be chained together and sent to particular locations to perform manual labor, such as clearing fields or roads of brush and debris. In the mid-1900s, chain gangs were abandoned in virtually every jurisdiction, because it was believed that such chain gangs violated one's right against cruel and unusual punishment. In a recent turn of events, chain gangs in Alabama, Arizona, and several other states have been reintroduced. However, the conditions under which modern chain gangs operate are considerably different from chain gang operations of the 1940s. One Arizona county sheriff, for instance, has used chain gangs in the Phoenix area as a punishment for various types of offenders. He dresses inmates in striped uniforms and places them in conspicuous public areas where they work at various public projects in plain view of passersby. He believes that the chain gang experience itself is humiliating and functions as a deterrent to others who might contemplate violating the law.

Suppose Allen and Abril wanted to know whether chain gang usage in the United States as it is presently being used has any significant deterrent effect and will decrease recidivism among those assigned to chain gangs. Further suppose that these investigators have created a scale to measure the deterrent effect of chain gangs. Questions asked of a sample of chain gang members might pertain to whether they consider the chain gang experience to be an effective crime deterrent. Suppose Allen and Abril devised a scale that yielded scores reflecting the amount of deterrence fostered by the chain gang experience. Such a scale might be comprised of a 10 items, where the scores range from a low of 10 to a high of 60. Suppose that a score of 10 is "low deterrence," while a score of 60 is "high deterrence." Maybe Allen and Abril might obtain a sample of offenders who are about to be assigned to a chain gang. Prior to their exposure to the chain gang experience, time 1, these offenders might be given the deterrence scale. Then, after being placed on a chain gang for 90 days, these offenders would be given the deterrence scale again in time 2. Their scores for the two time periods would be compared. It might be anticipated that the chain gang experience would result in deterrence score changes. Allen and Abril might test the following hypothesis set:

H_0: A chain gang experience will have no effect on deterrence scores for chain gang members.

H_1: A chain gang experience will change deterrence scores for chain gang members.

$P \leq .05$ (two-tailed test)

Table 10.8 shows deterrence scores for 21 chain gang offenders both before and after exposure to a chain gang experience of 90 days. Table 10.8 shows raw deterrence scores, where it is assumed that the larger the score, the greater the deterrence.

TABLE 10.8 Hypothetical Deterrence Scores for 21 Chain Gang Members

| Chain Gang Member | Deterrence Scores | | Difference D | Rank D | Rank with Less Frequent Sign, (T) |
	Before Chain Gang Experience	After Chain Gang Experience			
1	21	31	10	18	
2	28	29	1	2.5	
3	26	25	−1	−2.5	2.5
4	23	25	2	5.5	
5	25	28	3	7.5	
6	25	33	8	15.5	
7	22	20	−2	−5.5	5.5
8	19	23	4	10	
9	28	33	5	12.5	
10	31	30	−1	−2.5	2.5
11	32	31	−1	−2.5	2.5
12	20	31	11	19	
13	24	33	9	17	
14	27	35	8	15.5	
15	24	28	4	10	
16	23	29	6	14	
17	20	25	5	12.5	
18	24	28	4	10	
19	22	34	12	20	
20	28	42	14	21	
21	33	36	3	7.5	
					$\Sigma T = 13.0$

Table 10.8 is constructed as follows. First, deterrence scores are recorded for 21 chain gang members both prior to and after their assignment to the chain gang experience. The difference in scores for each offender for the two time periods is recorded in a column, D, as shown. The signs (either + or −) are recorded in the D column, depending upon whether there was a positive change in score or a negative change in score. Next, disregarding the direction of the score changes, all score changes are rank-ordered from the smallest score difference to the largest score difference for all 21 offenders. These ranks are placed in a column, D, which means the absolute rank associated with score changes, disregarding the sign associated with the score changes. For instance, in the D column, there are four score changes of 1, which is the smallest score change. These four score changes of 1 are assigned the average of the ranks they would otherwise occupy if different from one another, or ranks 1, 2, 3, and 4. Averaging the first four ranks would yield 2.5. Thus, each of these score differences of 1 receives a rank of 2.5. The next smallest score change is 2. Since there are two score changes of 2, we will assign these score differences the average of the next two ranks we would assign, or ranks 5 and 6. The average of ranks 5 and 6 would be 5.5. Thus, 5.5 is assigned to each of the score changes of 2. We proceed with our ranking of score differences until all 21 offenders have had their score differences ranked.

Next, we enter all ranks associated with the less frequently occurring sign (+ or −). An inspection of Table 10.8 shows that the less frequently occurring sign is negative, and therefore, we place all ranks with negative signs in this final column. These ranks with the less frequent sign are summed, for a $T = 13.0$.

We are now ready to assess the significance of difference between these two sets of scores. We turn to Table A.24 of Appendix A, pps. 467–468, which contains critical values of T for both one- and two-tailed tests and for an N ranging from 6 to 50. In this table, N refers to the number of matched or paired scores. For our sample, $N = 21$. Where $N = 21$ intersects with the .05 level of significance for a two-tailed test identifies the critical value of T. We must observe a T equal to or smaller than the T critical value shown in the table. The critical value of $T = 59$. Our observed $T = 13.0$, which is equal to or less than 59. Therefore, we can reject the null hypothesis and conclude that at least in this instance, the chain gang experience changes deterrence scores of participating inmates.

When larger samples are encountered (i.e., whenever $N > 50$), Table A.24 cannot be used. Instead, there is an approximation of a Z value which can be determined with the following formula:

$$Z = \Sigma T - \frac{\dfrac{N(N + 1)}{4}}{\sqrt{\dfrac{N(N + 1)(2N + 1)}{24}}}$$

where

$\Sigma T = $ the sum of the ranks with the less frequent sign

$N = $ the number of pairs of scores

$$Z = \frac{13 - \dfrac{(21)(21 + 1)}{4}}{\sqrt{\dfrac{(21)(21 + 1)(42 + 1)}{24}}} = \frac{-102.5}{\sqrt{\dfrac{19,866}{24}}} = \frac{-102.5}{\sqrt{827.75}} = \frac{-102.5}{28.8} = -3.56.$$

The values of 4 and 24 are constants and are used regardless of the value of N or T. The resulting Z value is interpreted as we would interpret any Z value for the Z test of significance for either one- or two-tailed applications. For instance, had we used the observed $T = 13$ in this formula, we would have an observed Z value of −3.56 (the direction of the Z value is irrelevant for a two-tailed test) would be significant at $P \leq .01$, where a critical value of ± 2.58 would be equaled or exceeded.

ASSUMPTIONS OF THE WILCOXON MATCHED PAIRS-SIGNED RANKS TEST The assumptions of the Wilcoxon matched pairs-signed ranks test are (1) randomness; (2) the interval level of measurement; and (3) related samples. Since the magnitudes of score differences are rank-ordered, some investigators have utilized the Wilcoxon test for data measured according to an ordinal scale. Conventionally, the Wilcoxon test, therefore, is applied to ordinal data, although a strict application of the level of measurement rule would restrict its use to the interval level only. This is because the *magnitude* of score differences is assessed prior to rank-ordering scores.

ADVANTAGES AND DISADVANTAGES OF THE WILCOXON MATCHED PAIRS-SIGNED RANKS TEST One advantage of the Wilcoxon test is that it may be applied to larger numbers of paired scores compared with the more restricted randomization test for matched pairs. In a

BOX 10.9

SPSS Alternative Application

1. Activate your *SPSS* program. Go to the *SPSS* Data Editor screen and enter two columns of values, using the first and second "var" columns. In the first "var" column, begin typing 21, 28, 26, and so forth, until 33 is entered from the first column of scores in Table 10.8. This will become VAR00001 and contain 21 scores. Repeat this process, entering all scores in the second "var" column in the second column of Table 10.8. This second "var" will become VAR00002.
2. Once these values have been entered, click "Analyze," then "Nonparametric Tests," then "2 Related Samples." This screen will give you several options. Click "Wilcoxon test."
3. Two screens are visible. The one on the left contains two variables, VAR00001 and VAR00002. Highlight both variables and use the arrow to move them both to the "Test Pair(s) List," the window to the right. Click "OK."
4. This action will yield a Wilcoxon Signed Ranks Test pair of tables. The first table, "Ranks," displays the number of negative and positive ranks, 4 and 17 respectively. There are no tied ranks. This table is significant if the investigator wishes to predict the direction of difference between the two columns of paired scores. For instance, 17 changes were observed to occur in a positive direction. That is, 17 scores in the second column were larger than scores in the first column. Only 4 scores exhibited negative differences where the second-column scores were smaller than the first-column scores. Since the test being made in the actual example was a two-tailed one, direction of difference in scores was irrelevant. But had a one-tailed test been made, this useful table could have indicated directionality very clearly.
5. The second table, "Test Statistics," shows the Z observed, which is -3.568 (again, direction of Z is irrelevant since a two-tailed, nondirectional test is being made). The significance of this Z value is .000, meaning that it is well below the required significance level of .05 for a two-tailed test. There is a significant difference between the two pairs of scores.
6. An additional dimension and advantage of this test in its *SPSS* format is that if the N limit of 50 associated with Table A.24 in the Appendix is exceeded, more pairs of scores in excess of 50 could be entered through the Data Editor, and this *SPSS* computational process could be repeated, thus bypassing the need to perform a Z test manually when Table A.24 is inapplicable. This is one especially advantageous feature of using the *SPSS* program.

sense, therefore, the Wilcoxon test in application begins where the randomization test ends. It is amenable to both one- and two-tailed test interpretations, and the researcher can readily determine the directionality associated with score changes if these changes had been predicted. In Table 10.8, for example, it is clear that the predominant direction of change was positive, indicating that most scores changed toward greater deterrence. Had a one-tailed prediction been made, an inspection of the table would have confirmed their prediction under H_1.

Another advantage is that the Wilcoxon test is easy to compute. A table for quick interpretation of T values for Ns ranging from 6 to 50 exists and is conveniently referenced. For larger sample sizes where N exceeds 50, an approximation of the Z test can be used through an alternative Z formula. The Wilcoxon test is probably the best nonparametric procedure equivalent to the t test for differences between means when related samples are found. It is approximately 95 percent as powerful as t. This test has no normality assumption, and therefore would be superior to the Sandler A statistic, its direct parametric equivalent, if normality for a distribution of scores did not exist. For those with access to *SPSS* programming, once data have been entered through the Data Editor of the *SPSS* program, the Wilcoxon test is easily calculated and exact probabilities may be determined.

Summary

Several useful nonparametric tests of significance have been devised whenever investigators have data measured according to ordinal or interval scales. No test has a normality assumption. Compared with their parametric counterparts, these procedures are relatively powerful for rejecting false H_os.

For single-sample applications, the Kolmogorov–Smirnov single-sample test is available. The K-S test uses cumulative frequencies in k categories and compares proportionate distributions to determine whether an observed distribution differs significantly from an expected one. For two-sample comparisons, three tests included the Wald-Wolfowitz runs test and the Mann-Whitney U test. These are arranged from the most conservative and least powerful to the least conservative and most powerful. A comparative example was provided, showing three tests and their results when applied to a common set of scores from two independent samples. The U test is probably the most powerful nonparametric equivalent to the t test for assessing differences between two independent samples on some ordinal variable. When two related samples are studied, the sign test may be applied. Persons are either individually matched or used as their own controls in before-after experiments.

Where k independent samples exist, the Kruskal-Wallis H test is applicable. This test is chi-square based and has limitations similar to those with conventional applications of chi-square for nominal-level data. The H test is an extension of the U test. In this respect, it has comparable power. For analyses of ordinal-level data where k samples are related, the Friedman two-way analysis of variance test can be used. It is also a chi square–based test.

Whenever investigators have interval-level data but fail to meet the more stringent assumptions associated with popular parametric tests such as t and F, several nonparametric options are available. Of several alternative tests that could be discussed here, the most flexible test was presented. This test was the Wilcoxon matched pairs-signed ranks test, which is applicable whenever interval-level data are encountered. All of procedures presented in this chapter have large-sample Z approximations when such samples are studied. Examples of the use of *SPSS* software were provided with most tests of significance presented.

Key Terms

Friedman two-way analysis of variance test *273*

Kolmogorov–Smirnov single-sample test *246*

Kolmogorov–Smirnov two-sample test *254*

Kruskal-Wallis H test (H test) *269*

Mann-Whitney U test *258*

run *251*

runs test *249*

sign test *265*

Wald-Wolfowitz runs test *249*

Wilcoxon matched pairs-signed ranks test *277*

Questions for Review

1. What are several advantages of tests of significance for the ordinal level of measurement?
2. How does the Mann-Whitney U test treat two samples differently compared with the Kolmogorov–Smirnov two-sample test? Explain.
3. What are some major advantages of the Mann-Whitney U test over the runs test and the Kolmorogov–Smirnov two-sample test?
4. In what respects are ordinal-level tests of significance generally less powerful compared with interval-level tests of significance?

5. How does the power associated with ordinal-level tests of significance differ compared with the power associated with nominal-level tests of significance? Explain.

6. What is the most powerful nonparametric equivalent to the *t* test for differences between means? Which is the least powerful nonparametric test for the same purpose and discussed in this chapter?

7. If the level of significance for a hypothesis test is changed from .10 to .01, what is the effect of this change on the power of a test in a general sense? Explain.

8. Can *k* sample tests of significance of difference function as their own probe to determine significant differences between two groups of scores at a time, if there is an overall showing of significance for all groups on some measured characteristic? Why or why not? Explain.

9. If a significant difference between groups is disclosed by the Kruskal-Wallis *H* test, how can we learn which groups are significantly different from each other? Explain.

10. What is the primary usefulness of the Wilcoxon matched pairs-signed ranks test? What are its primary advantages? Can the Mann-Whitney *U* test be applied to the same data as the Wilcoxon test? Why or why not? Explain.

Exercises

10.1. For the data below, carry out the Kolmogorov-Smirnov one-sample test, using the .05 level of significance (two-tailed). Is this distribution different from what would be expected according to chance?

		Categories		
Very Unfavorable	Favorable	Very Unfavorable	Unfavorable	Totals
29	16	43	71	$N = 159$

a. What is your decision? Do these data differ from what would be expected according to chance? Why or why not?
b. Could the chi-square test be applied to these same data? Why or why not?

***SPSS* Alternative Application:** If you have *SPSS* software, determine these answers with the method illustrated in the chapter.

10.2. Carry out the Mann-Whitney *U* test for the following data. Assume an hypothesis test at the .05 level of significance (two-tailed). The null hypothesis would be that there is no difference between the two groups on the attitude scores.

Attitude Scores	
Group 1	Group 2
$N_1 = 11$	$N_2 = 13$
45	53
47	59
52	40
44	41
43	51
51	55
43	57
33	62
45	50
51	58
56	63
	47
	56

a. What is your decision about rejecting (or failing to reject) the null hypothesis between the two groups of scores above? Explain briefly.
b. Could the *t* test be applied to these same data? Why or why not?

***SPSS* Alternative Application:** If you have *SPSS* software available, carry out the procedures requested, given the scores above. Discuss your results.

10.3. Four groups of probation office employees are shown below. These employees, paraprofessionals, have been matched with one another according to several salient characteristics. They have been subjected to four different supervisory methods. Does a significant difference exist among these four groups on a measure of job satisfaction (the raw scores shown are job satisfaction scores, with the larger scores indicative of high satisfaction and the smaller scores indicative of low satisfaction)? Apply the Friedman test to these data. Assume the .05 level of significance and a two-tailed, nondirectional test.

Job Satisfaction Scores			
Group 1	Group 2	Group 3	Group 4
18	21	23	29
15	14	17	19
10	18	14	21
11	10	15	22
16	21	20	23
19	18	19	25
20	19	20	21
22	22	23	25
16	14	19	28

a. Define k and N. How many degrees of freedom are associated with these data? What distribution is approximated by the Friedman test results?

b. What is your decision about the differences between the matched pairs on the job satisfaction variable?

c. What two-sample probe could be used to determine the significance of difference between each pair of groups above? Explain your rationale for this choice.

10.4. Three samples of police officers have been selected and measures have been obtained on some attitudinal characteristic. Raw scores for the three samples are shown below. Carry out the Kruskal-Wallis H test, using the .01 level of significance and a two-tailed, nondirectional test, and determine whether a difference exists somewhere among them.

Attitudinal Scores		
Group 1	Group 2	Group 3
35	42	41
28	43	37
27	55	49
19	57	43
29	41	46
31	63	44
32	56	47
29	49	43
22	51	46
19	39	33
20	57	42
17	58	
16		
$N_1 = 13$	$N_2 = 12$	$N_3 = 11$

a. What conclusion do you reach about differences among the three groups? Support your conclusions by providing the critical H value and the observed H value.

b. Could the Friedman test be applied to these same data? Why or why not? Explain.

c. How many degrees of freedom are associated with the data above?

d. What distribution is approximated by the H value?

e. What two-sample test would be preferred as a probe for differences between each pair of groups? Explain your choice.

10.5. Given the following information, carry out the Wilcoxon matched pairs/signed ranks test assuming the .05 level of significance for a one-tailed test.

Scores for Matched Groups	
Group 1 Scores	Group 2 Scores
15	25
18	16
23	29
15	17
18	21

a. Based on your test results, is there a significant difference between the two sets of scores for the two time periods?

BOX 10.10

SPSS Alternative Application

1. Activate your *SPSS* program. Go to the Data Editor screen. Notice for the three sets of scores above, there are 13 scores in group 1, 12 scores in group 2, and 11 scores in group 3. In the first "var" column, therefore, type in 13 "1" values, 12 "2" values, and 11 "3" values. These will represent your three groups to be compared. Once you finish this task, the column will be labeled VAR00001.

2. In the second "var" column, begin typing in the scores from the first group, with 35, 28, 27, and so on, until all of these scores have been entered. Continue entering scores from group 2 in the same column (beginning with 42, 43, 55, 57, and so on) until all 12 of these scores have been entered. And finally, continue entering scores for the remaining 11 persons (beginning with 41, 37, 49, 43, and so on) in group 3. You should have a total of 13 + 12 + 11 = 36 scores. This second column will now appear as VAR00002.

3. Click on "Analyze" then "Nonparametric Statistics," then "*K* Independent Samples."

4. A window will be displayed with VAR00001 and VAR00002 displayed. Highlight VAR00001 and move it by clicking on the arrow to the "Grouping Variable." At this point, you will be asked to "Define Range." Click on "Define Range," and two windows will appear: "Minimum" and "Maximum." Type a "1" in the "Minimum" window and a "3" in the "Maximum" window. You are analyzing differences between 3 groups. Therefore, the minimum number of groups is 1 and the maximum number is 3. You should see something like this: VAR00001 (1 3), which now appears in the "Grouping Variable" window. Click "Continue."

5. Now, highlight VAR00002 and using the arrow, move this variable to the "Test Variable List." You have a choice of two tests or both. You can choose the Kruskal-Wallis *H* test or the Median test. Check the Kruskal-Wallis test. Then press "OK."

6. Two summary tables appear, one showing the three groups of 13, 12, and 11 persons and their "Mean Rank." This is satisfying and shows that you entered all 36 persons correctly in the VAR00001 column. The second table has Test Statistics and shows significance = .000. This means that the differences between the three groups on the measured variable are significant at .000, clearly equal to or less than .01 (two-tailed test). The chi-square observed is 25.882, which is the basis for this probability, and 2 *df* is consistent with $k - 1$ or $3 - 1$, where 3 groups are being compared. The hypothesis that the three groups are the same can be rejected at the .01 level at least. Even if a more rigorous standard of .001 had been used, the null hypothesis would still be rejected. Clearly there is a significant difference among the 3 groups on the measured variable.

10.6. A probation department recently received a directive to improve probation office effectiveness. The probation office supervisor interpreted this directive to mean that more probationer/clients should be assigned to the probation officers. Therefore, new procedures were implemented. A follow-up study was conducted of the number of clients supervised by a sample of 22 probation officers across two time periods, time 1 before the change in number of probationers supervised, and time 2 after the change in numbers of probationers supervised. Carry out the sign test to determine if there was a significant change in probation officer caseload from time 1 to time 2 using the $P \leq .10$ level of significance (two-tailed test):

a. What is your decision regarding the application of the sign test? Is there a significant difference between the two time periods at

BOX 10.11

SPSS Alternative Application

1. Activate your *SPSS* program. Go to the Data Editor screen and enter the scores for the two matched pairs of scores in the first two "var" columns. This will create VAR00001 and VAR00002. VAR00001 will contain scores 15, 18, 23, 15, and 18, while VAR00002 will contain 25, 16, 29, 17, and 21.
2. Click on "Analyze," then "Nonparametric Tests," then "2 Related Samples."
3. Two variables will appear in a screen: VAR00001 and VAR00002. Highlight both variables by clicking on each, and then use the arrow to move these to the "Test Pairs List" window.
4. You have several test choices. You may use the Wilcoxon test, the sign test, or the McNemar test. Click on the Wilcoxon test. Then click "OK."
5. This next screen displays the results of the Wilcoxon signed ranks test. The two-tailed probability displayed is .104. To obtain the one-tailed probability, this probability must be halved, or $.104/2 = .052$. You are using the .05 level of significance for a one-tailed test. Unfortunately, you do not achieve .05 or less with your probability associated with this test. You are close with .052 but you cannot reject the null hypothesis that the scores are different between the matched pairs of subjects. Perhaps had you been less rigorous in your choice of significance levels and used the .10 level of significance instead of .05, then you could have concluded that the two sets of scores were different statistically. Some researchers may indicate their close proximity to .05 with the .052 observed probability anyway, just to illustrate that the difference between the two sets of scores is almost significant at the probability level used. Thus, readers can make up their own minds to conclude whether the two groups differ significantly. This was a close call, but this is why standards such as levels of significance are used. They remove arbitrary interpretations from the decision-making process. The cold fact is that the matched groups did not differ in their scores, regardless of how close we came to concluding they differed.

Caseloads			Caseloads		
Probation Officers	Time 1	Time 2	Probation Officers	Time 1	Time 2
1	225	229	12	230	220
2	215	214	13	215	219
3	235	250	14	244	240
4	210	211	15	223	226
5	216	213	16	220	223
6	200	210	17	231	233
7	245	245	18	216	218
8	247	250	19	214	213
9	221	220	20	218	215
10	214	219	21	210	220
11	221	225	22	229	230

the .05 level of significance with a two-tailed test? What is your proof for the conclusion you have reached?

b. Could the Mann-Whitney *U* test be applied to these data? Why or why not? Explain briefly.

10.7. For the following data, determine if any significant difference exists using the Mann-Whitney *U* test.

a. What is the significance of difference between the two groups of scores, using the .05 level of significance for a one-tailed test?

BOX 10.12

SPSS Alternative Application

1. Open your *SPSS* program and go to the Data Editor.
2. Click on the first "var" and type in the scores for time 1. This is a part of the data entry process. "VAR00001" will appear with the first list of scores.
3. Click on the second "var" and type in the scores for time 2. This is the second part of the data entry process. "VAR00002" will appear with the second list of scores.
4. Go to "Analyze" and click on "Nonparametric Tests."
5. Click on "2 Related Samples."
6. Two variables, VAR00001 and VAR00002, will appear in a box. Highlight both of these by clicking on each. Then use the arrow to move them to a box labeled "Test Pairs List."
7. You have a choice of tests: the Wilcoxon, Sign, or McNemar tests. Click on the "Sign" and then click "OK." (Actually, you can click on all three tests if you want, and the program will calculate and show all three sets of test results.)
8. A tabular summary will appear of the sign test results. The display will show an exact two-tailed probability of .189 for these data. Another part of the summary will show negative differences = 7, positive differences = 14, and ties = 1. These are the score differences for the two columns of variables you created through Data Entry.
9. Since you made a simple nondirectional prediction about score changes between time 1 and time 2 at the .10 level, the scores for the pairs of 22 persons did not change significantly. You would need to observe a probability equal to or smaller than .10 (two-tailed) in order to conclude there was a significant score change. The two-tailed probability was .189. Therefore the null hypothesis could not be rejected that the groups are the same in both time periods. However, if you had made a directional prediction, namely that the scores of officers would increase from time 1 to time 2, then you would simply halve the .189, or .189/2 = .095. This would be the one-tailed, directional probability of the significance of change you observed. In this event, .095 is equal to or smaller than the one-tailed probability of .10, and therefore the groups differ in the direction you predicted. Specifically 14 out of 22 pairs of scores changed positively between time 1 and time 2.

Scores	
Group 1	Group 2
23	29
28	28
18	32
17	15
19	21
25	27
13	22
30	35
12	41
	43
	39
$N_1 = 9$	$N_2 = 11$

b. Can the runs test be applied to these same data? Why or why not? Explain. In what respects would the Mann-Whitney U test be superior to the runs test, if at all? Explain.

This problem also asked about the Wald-Wolfowitz runs test. Notice that this test was one of four options you were given initially. If you were to go back, repeat everything you did to compute the Mann-Whitney U test, and then click "Wald-Wolfowitz runs test," the test results would also appear, together with the Mann-Whitney U test results. In this case, however, the results of the runs test are not impressive. A table is displayed showing a total of 10 runs. This is far too many runs to be statistically significant. The actual one-tailed probability is only .43. This is far greater than the .05 or smaller one-tailed probability required to reject the null

BOX 10.13

SPSS Alternative Application

1. Activate your *SPSS* program. Go to the Data Editor window. Indicate that you want to enter data.
2. You will be using two "var" columns for this test. The first "var" column will stand for the two groups you are comparing. There are 9 persons in group 1 and 11 persons in group 2. In the first "var" column, put "1"s in the first nine spaces. Then follow with 11 "2"s. You should have 9 "1" values in the first "var" column as well as 11 "2"s. The column label will now read "VAR00001."
3. In the second "var" column, type in the scores from the first group, beginning with 23, 28, 18, 17, and so forth, until all 9 values are entered. This will create a VAR00002 column label. Continue entering values in the VAR00002 column from the second group, beginning with 29, 28, 32, 15, and so on. When you finish, you will have two VAR columns, VAR00001 and VAR00002. The first column will represent persons from two groups, 1 and 2. The second column, labeled "VAR00002," will contain the scores for the 9 persons in the first 9 slots in VAR00001, and the next 11 scores will be associated with the next 11 persons in the VAR00001 column. These scores in the VAR00002 column are the scores to be compared.
4. Click on "Analyze." Next, click on "Nonparametric tests." Select "2 Independent Samples" and click on that option.
5. A window is displayed showing VAR00001 and VAR00002. Highlight VAR00001 and using the arrow for "Grouping Variable," click it. This moves VAR00001 to the "Grouping Variable" window.
6. Under the grouping variable is "Define Groups." Click on this box and Group 1 and Group 2 are displayed, with open windows. Type "1" in the Group 1 window and "2" in Group 2 window. Click "Continue" when finished.
7. Next, highlight VAR00002 and using the arrow, move this variable to the "Test Variable List."
8. A window is now displayed giving you four test options: the Mann-Whitney *U* test, the Moses Extreme Reactions test, the Kolmogorov–Smirnov test, and the Wald-Wolfowitz runs test. You may click on one, two, three or all four of these tests. For the purpose of the present problem, click on the "Mann-Whitney *U* test." Next, press "OK."
9. A screen will appear with summary statistics for the Mann-Whitney *U* test. One table will display the 9 and 11 persons in the two groups (VAR00001) and the Sum of Ranks. This table verifies that you began with the right number of persons in each group. A second table is displayed containing the significance of difference between the two groups. The exact probability for a one-tailed test using the Mann-Whitney test is .020. This means that the two samples differ at .02, which is equal to or smaller than the .05 one-tailed probability you were using when you tested the hypothesis that the two groups were different. This result means that you can reject the null hypothesis that the two groups are the same and conclude that they are different at the .05 level of significance (one-tailed test).

hypothesis that the two groups are the same. Therefore, you cannot reject the null hypothesis.

The two statistical applications, the Mann-Whitney *U* test and the Wald-Wolfowitz runs test, show vastly different outcomes. The Mann-Whitney *U* test is the most powerful nonparametric equivalent to the *t* test. It resulted in showing a statistically significant difference between the two groups. The Wald-Wolfowitz runs test did not disclose a significant difference between the two groups. One reason is that this test is far less powerful than the Mann-Whitney test. Even if the Kolmogorov–Smirnov two-sample test had been computed, it would have disclosed a two-tailed probability of .16 and a one-tailed probability of .08 (.16/2 = .08). Again, this result would not be significant statistically. You may compute the Kolmogorov–Smirnov two-sample test if you wish, since it is one of four options you were given when you started this procedure.

References

Adalist-Estin, Ann and Jim Mustin (2003). *Women in Prison Project.* Palmyra, VA: Children of Prisoners Library.

Allen, Harry E. and Julie C. Abril (1997). "The New Chain Gang: Corrections in the Next Century." *American Journal of Criminal Justice* **22:**1–13.

Chan, M. et al. (2005). "Evaluation of Probation Case Management (PCM) for Drug-Involved Women Offenders." *Crime and Delinquency* **5:**447–469.

Farber, Bernard J. (2007). "Civil Liability for Prisoner Suicide." *AELE Monthly Law Journal* **2:**301–310 (February).

Fogg, Joyce, Charles J. Kehoe, and Timothy O. Kestner (2007). "The Long Gray Line: Older Workers and the Correctional Work Force." *Corrections Today* **69:**26–29.

Kovandzic, Tomislav V. (2001). "The Impact of Florida's Habitual Offender Law on Crime." *Criminology* **39:**179–204.

Nellis, M. (2006). "Surveillance, Rehabilitation, and Electronic Monitoring: Getting the Issues Clear." *Criminology and Public Policy* **5:**103–108.

Reed, Angus S. (2001). "The Utilization of a Statistically Based Jail Inspection Program at the Fulton County Jail." *American Jails* **15:**19–21.

CHAPTER 11

Measures of Association I: Nominal and Ordinal Levels of Measurement

Chapter Outline

Chapter Objectives

After reading this chapter, the following objectives will be realized:

1. understanding the meaning of association and relationships between variables;

2. understanding proportional reduction in error (PRE);

3. understanding the strength and significance of measures of association;

4. learning about two-variable measures of association for nominal- and ordinal-levels of measurement.

INTRODUCTION

This chapter examines measures of association between two variables, where the variables are measured according to the nominal- or ordinal-levels of measurement. Criminal justice professionals and criminologists are always attempting to illustrate relationships between variables by using measures of association. This comprehensive chapter examines an array of some of the most frequently used measures of association for two-variable relationships. These measures depict the degree of agreement or association between two variables under various circumstances.

This chapter is organized as follows. First, we will examine several different meanings of association in our research work. The words "association" and "relationship" are sometimes misleading. We may believe, for instance, that if two variables appear to be correlated, then they must be causally related in some way. That is, one variable is causing the other variable to change in value or influences it in some way. It is easy to understand why some investigators believe this. All causal relations between variables must first be preceded by some type of demonstrable relationship or correlation. But more than a few researchers see a simple observed association between variables conclude prematurely that a causal relation exists between them. As will be demonstrated, this is not always the case. Thus, several cautions will be discussed about the generalizations we can make about observed associations between variables. Other ways of interpreting our coefficients of association will be examined.

Not everyone interprets measures of association the same way. Some investigators attach great meaning to the statistical significance of an association. Others are persuaded that a causal relation exists according to the degree of association they observe. Yet others turn to the strength of the association as indicated by the magnitude of the numerical result. Other interpretations of association include the explanatory value one variable contributes to another. Therefore, some investigators look at error or variation in one variable and the amount of error or variation that can be reduced by using another variable as a predictor of it. This reasoning employs a proportional-reduction-in-error calculation, which assesses the amount of variation (or error) explained in one variable by using another as a predictor of it. Sometimes variable relationships are interpreted according to their mutual predictability. A more descriptive approach is to examine the nature of an association between variables. Each of these ways of assessing association or relationships between variables will be examined and explained. The relative merits of these different kinds of interpretation will be presented.

Several popular measures of association for two variables will be examined. These measures have been divided according to the level of measurement associated with their application. The first two measures of association discussed include those where two variables are measured according to the nominal level of measurement. These measures are followed by two measures appropriate for when investigators are examining two ordinal-level variables. Not all measures of association under each grouping are equivalent with one another in the practical application to criminological problems. Some measures of association are better than others. Most measures of association can yield coefficients ranging from ± 1.00, although some measures cannot achieve perfect association without a correction factor being applied. In other instances, different table sizes or uneven distributions of frequencies in various $r \times c$ tables make achieving ± 1.00 impossible. These situations will be discussed. Also, each measure of association presented has weaknesses and strengths that make them compare favorably or unfavorably with other measures of association. Certain measures of association presented here are clearly favored by investigators. The reasons for these preferences will be explained and illustrated.

All of these measures also have tests of significance that may be applied to resulting correlation coefficients. Therefore, we can always determine the statistical significance of any coefficient of association. But sometimes, statistical significance is different from substantive significance, or the practical meaning of the coefficient we have calculated. As we have seen for different tests of significance of difference, numerical values are quite sensitive to variations in sample sizes. Larger sample sizes often yield statistical significance, despite the fact that little or no substantive significance exists. The same is true of measures of association. Coefficients of association are influenced greatly by fluctuations in sample sizes, from one study to the next. Also, if we were to apply several measures of association to the same sets of scores, the different correlation coefficients yielded would be different depending upon the measures used. Attention will be focused on the meaning of each correlation coefficient yielded from each measure of association, therefore. Explanations for why these different measures yield varying numerical results will be given and discussed.

THE MEANING OF MEASURES OF ASSOCIATION

Numerical expressions of the degree to which two variables are associated or correlated are called **coefficients of association**. The measures that yield these coefficients are called **measures of association**. Tests of theory or theoretical schemes often rely upon measures of association for support. To what extent are two variables correlated? To what extent does a relationship exist between two variables? For instance, we might believe that an association exists between poverty and crime. From subsequent data we collect, it may appear that persons in lower socioeconomic statuses have higher arrest rates compared with those in higher socioeconomic statuses. This association would support our belief about the relation between poverty and crime.

In another scenario, we may believe that young boys whose mothers work have a greater likelihood of becoming delinquent compared with boys whose mothers do not work. Examining a sample of boys whose mothers either work or do not work and finding that a relationship exists supporting our belief that working and nonworking mothers tend to have delinquent or nondelinquent boys respectively might lead us to conclude that a causal relation exists between these variables, delinquency of boys, and working/nonworking status of mothers. High correlations between these two variables would be numerical proof of our beliefs. We would interpret such findings as support for our theory about delinquency and working mothers.

These scenarios are only two of an infinite number of scenarios that could be advanced about different variable relationships. Regardless of the variables we are examining and correlating, any observed correlation between them might be sufficient numerical evidence to support our beliefs about their causal association.

Essentially, measures of association function as platforms for making causal assertions about variables. We use terms such as **relationship**, **correlation**, and **association** when describing two variables and how they covary. Some investigators see little or no difference in these terms and use them interchangeably. But there are subtle differences in meaning among them. Association seems to be the most conservative term, because it merely describes covariation between two variables. Other words such as relationship and correlation seem stronger and loaded. For some investigators, at least, they imply causality between variables. To say that a relationship exists between variables or that two variables are correlated seems to suggest that a causal relation exists between them and that one variable is influencing the other to change in value. Because cause–effect relations between variables are quite difficult to establish empirically, the simple appearance of an association between variables may be misleading. Simple associations between variables are insufficient to assume that a causal relation exists between them. Ultimately, we are certainly interested in establishing causal relations between variables. This is what our research work seeks to accomplish. But our knowledge of which factors influence others in predictable ways is incomplete. Therefore, we approach the task of observing associations between variables with some amount of caution and conservatism. This is the context within which this chapter is couched.

Four primary ways of assessing association coefficients are: (1) the strength of an association; (2) the statistical significance of an association; (3) the direction of an association; and (4) the proportional reduction in error (PRE).

The Strength of an Association

The **strength of an association** is based on an artificially contrived set of coefficients, ranging from 0.00 or no association to ±1.00 (perfect positive or perfect negative association). Using this method, a strong association between variables is determined according to how closely +1.00 (a perfect positive association) or −1.00 (a perfect negative association) is approached with our observed coefficient. No association is indicated by zero or "0." Association coefficients are either positive or negative and are typically expressed to the nearest hundredth (e.g., .02, .35, .42, .88, and so forth). A conventional interpretation of coefficients of association of ±.30 or larger are considered strong in the criminological literature. The following arbitrary guide may be used to assess the general strength of association coefficients:

±.00 to .25 = no association or low association (weak association)

±.26 to .50 = moderately low association (moderately weak association)

±.51 to .75 = moderately high association (moderately strong association)

±.76 to 1.00 = high association (strong association) up to perfect positive or negative association.

While these coefficients and their interpretation are strictly arbitrary and subjective, they give investigators preliminary and general indications about how strongly two variables may be associated. All of the measures of association presented in this chapter may be interpreted using these general guidelines when discussing one's findings. However, if investigators wanted a more definitive interpretation of any coefficient they calculate, other more objective methods are available.

Figures 11.1 and 11.2 illustrate (1) a perfect positive association between variables X and Y, and (2) a perfect negative (inverse) association between variables X and Y. In Figure 11.1, a unit increase on variable X is followed by a unit increase on variable Y. The vertical and horizontal lines are called **axes**. One **axis**, the horizontal axis, is X, while the vertical axis is Y. These represent graduated score values for two variables. Two sets of scores for a sample of elements are paired and plotted. The resulting plot of intersecting score points is called a **scatter plot**. These points where the scores intersect on hypothetical variables X and Y are marked, and a line is drawn through them as shown in Figure 11.1. Since this line is straight, it is also **linear**. This type of association is considered positive, since every unit increase on variable X is accompanied by a unit increase on variable Y. The straight line drawn illustrates **linearity**, and this feature will have relevance for several measures of association discussed later in this chapter.

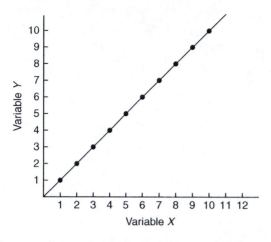

FIGURE 11.1   Perfect Positive Association Between Variables X and Y

In contrast, Figure 11.2 shows another pairing of scores with intersecting points for a sample of elements, where each unit increase on variable X is accompanied by a unit decrease on variable Y. When the intersectional points are plotted in Figure 11.2, another straight line is illustrated, but this time, the line is in the opposite direction of the line shown in Figure 11.1. This is also a linear (straight line) association, but in this case, the line portrays a perfect negative or inverse association between variables X and Y. Positive associations between variables are represented with coefficients ranging from +.01 to +1.00 (perfect positive association), while negative associations between variables are represented with coefficients ranging from −.01 to −1.00 (perfect negative association).

Nonlinear associations between variables occur whenever straight lines do not exist between intersectional points of scores on variables X and Y. Sometimes associations between variables are curved. These are called **curvilinear** since the scatter plot of intersecting points is curved.

Figure 11.3 is a scatter plot showing a curvilinear association between variables X (*VAR00001*) and Y (*VAR00002*), which has been generated by an *SPSS* software program. A line has been drawn through the intersecting points of scores, which are the dots in the scatter plot. It is a curved line rather than a straight one. **Curvilinearity** exists when variable increases (or decreases) with another variable to a certain point then decreases (or increases).

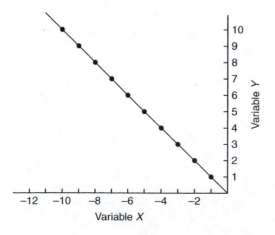

FIGURE 11.2   Perfect Negative (Inverse) Association Between Variables X and Y

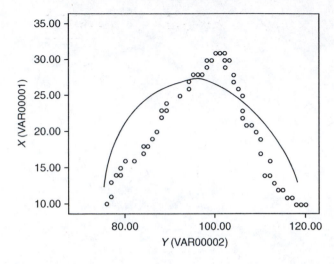

FIGURE 11.3 **Curvilinear Association Between Variables**

For example, adding more management levels in a police department may generate greater police officer effectiveness, but if more management levels continue to be added, police officer effectiveness may begin to decline. Another example might be that adding conditions to probation plans for offender/clients may reduce their recidivism, but if more conditions are added to these probation plans, offender/client recidivism may begin to increase. Greater recidivism arises, perhaps, from greater offender/client resentment over added and more onerous probation plans. The following scores for two hypothetical variables, VAR00001 and VAR00002, are those upon which the curvilinear scatter plot is based.

Notice that the scores in VAR00001, the first variable, start out at 10 and gradually increase up to 31, and then they decrease to 10. The scores in the second column, VAR00002,

VAR00001	VAR00002	VAR00001	VAR00002
10	76	23	88
11	77	24	89
13	77	25	92
14	78	26	94
14	79	27	94
15	79	28	95
16	80	28	96
16	82	28	96
17	84	28	97
18	84	29	98
18	85	30	98
19	86	30	99
19	86	30	99
20	87	31	100
22	88	31	101
23	89	31	102

VAR00001	VAR00002	VAR00001	VAR00002
31	102	19	110
30	102	17	110
30	103	14	111
29	102	16	112
28	104	14	113
27	104	13	114
26	105	12	115
26	105	12	116
25	106	11	117
23	106	11	118
22	106	10	119
21	107	10	119
21	108	10	120
20	109		

begin with a low score of 76 and continuously increase to a high score of 120. Thus, one variable increases for a time then decreases, while the other continuously increases. There is correlation between these variables, but it is a curvilinear one.

Associations between variables are either linear or nonlinear. Some measures of association require that linearity must exist between variables, while other measures of association do not have this requirement. If linearity is an assumption underlying the application of a particular measure of association discussed, it will be noted. For instance, the Pearson r is discussed later in Chapter 12. It is a measure of association that requires linearity. If it were applied to these scores, which are related in a curvilinear way, the numerical result would be a correlation near zero or no association. But it is apparent from Figure 11.3 that a curvilinear association exists. Special measures of association have been devised to measure association between variables when curvilinearity exists. One such measure is eta, the correlation ratio, and it will be discussed at length in Chapter 12. Applied to these same data, for instance, eta will yield a very strong **degree of association** between the two variables, whatever they may be. The degree of association refers to the amount of departure a coefficient is from 0 or no association. Most measures of association presented here do not require linearity, however. Linearity can be measured, although a discussion of linearity measurement is beyond the scope of this book.

The **slope** of the lines shown in Figures 11.1 and 11.2 is also indicative of the strength of the association between variables. Figures 11.1 and 11.2 show +1.00 and −1.00 coefficients, which are perfect positive and perfect negative association respectively. Seldom do two variables correlate with one another perfectly in criminological research, however. When associations between variables are not perfect, the slope of the line drawn through the intersectional points of scores on the two variables lies closer to one line of scores or the other, as is shown in Figures 11.4 and 11.5. Depending on the particular scatter plot of intersecting points we observe between two variables, we can refer to this distribution of intersecting points as the **nature of association** as well.

Figure 11.4 shows a flatter line reflecting a low but positive degree of association between variables. A low negative degree of association is shown by the line drawn between

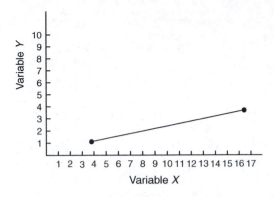

FIGURE 11.4   **A Low Positive Association Between Two Variables**

intersectional points in Figure 11.5. In these instances, the scatter plots of intersecting points between pairs of scores on variables *X* and *Y* are distributed in a way that yields such low-lying lines. Therefore, we can see a low degree of association by observing simple scatter plots of intersecting points if we choose to draw such graphs. Coefficients of association may also be computed to determine the strength of the association between the two variables.

The Statistical Significance of an Association

Another way of assessing association is according to the **statistical significance of an association**. Each measure of association can be assessed according to the difference between the observed coefficient and zero, 0, or no association. All measures of association have statistical tests of significance. If investigators observe a correlation coefficient of .64, for example, they might interpret this coefficient as significant at the .05 level of significance, whenever they apply the accompanying statistical test. But tests of significance applied to coefficients of association may be misleading and inappropriate. A correlation coefficient's statistical significance is influenced greatly by sample size. Larger sample sizes yield greater statistical significance than smaller sample sizes. This is because the greater the sample size, the smaller the standard error term. All tests of significance for observed coefficients of association have standard error terms. These are always denominator values which are divided into numerator

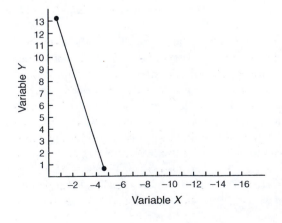

FIGURE 11.5   **A Low Negative Association Between Two Variables**

values. Numerator values involving coefficients of association almost always are the differences observed between the actual coefficient of association calculated and zero (0) or no association. Is the difference between no association and the observed coefficient of association large enough to be significantly different at some probability level, such as .05 or .01? The numerical result is an observed statistical value that is compared with a critical statistical value for a particular sample size. One's sample size is crucial here. If extremely large sample sizes are used in one's computations, the correlation coefficients generated may be significant statistically but they may not mean much.

For instance, suppose researchers are examining job satisfaction and job effectiveness of a sample of 2,000 probation officers from six states. If a particular measure of association is applied, where job satisfaction scores of these 2,000 officers are correlated with job effectiveness, the resulting coefficient may be .13. Using the arbitrary method described earlier for assessing the magnitude of this coefficient, we might say that there is either no association or a low degree of association between the two variables. However, if we apply a statistical test of significance to the difference of our observed coefficient, .13, from 0.00 (no association), the standard error term we calculate based on the sample of 2,000 may be so small that when it is divided into .13 (i.e., the difference between no association, 0, and .13), this .13 difference may be significant at the .001 level. Thus, although .13 would be statistically significant, how meaningful would it be? This scenario might lead us to say that yes, our coefficient is significant statistically but it doesn't mean anything. Or it has little value for explaining the relation between job satisfaction and job effectiveness.

Despite the flaws of applying statistical tests of significance to measures of association, these significance tests will be presented anyway. Therefore, if statistical significance is desired, it may be computed easily. *SPSS* programs almost always calculate the statistical significance of coefficients of association routinely. Investigators may choose to use these test results or not use them when discussing the significance of whatever they have found. However, a far superior way of discussing any measure of association is according to its **predictive utility**. How well does a given measure of association help us to predict relationships between variables?

The Direction of An Association

The **direction of an association** refers to whether the association between variables is positive or negative. A **positive association** exists whenever one variable, variable *X*, increases, while the other variable, variable *Y*, also increases. Also, if one variable decreases while the other variable decreases, this too is a positive association. However, if one variable increases while the other decreases, or if one variable decreases while the other variable increases, then the association between these variables would be negative. Sometimes we might refer to positive associations between variables as direct, while negative associations are inverse.

An example of a **direct association** or positive association between variables may be the relation between job satisfaction in a probation agency and the amount of participation in decision making allowed for probation officers. The more probation officers participate in decision making (a variable *X* increase), the more satisfied they may be with their jobs (a variable *Y* increase). We might use pay and job satisfaction to illustrate a direct or positive association in a different way. Suppose pay reductions were to occur in a probation agency undergoing financial cutbacks. With decreased pay (variable *X*), we might expect to find decreased satisfaction with work (variable *Y*) among probation officers. Thus, in the first instance above, two variables, X and Y, increase together, while in the second instance, two variables, X and Y, decrease together. These changes of two variables in the same direction, either upward or downward, are considered direct or positive.

A **negative association** or **inverse association** between variables might be illustrated with the example of increasing the number of police officers on city streets during evening hours and changes in crime rates in those areas. It might be assumed that those areas with increased police presence (variable X), there may occur a decrease in crime rates (variable Y). Alternatively, decreased police presence (variable X) may be accompanied by increased crime rates (variable Y).

Positive or direct associations between variables are symbolically expressed with either a plus sign, +, or no sign, and negative or inverse associations are indicated by a minus sign (−). The symbol, r, is often used as an association measure. If $r = +.33$, or simply .33, this is considered a positive or direct association between variables X and Y. If $r = -.33$, then the association between variables X and Y is considered negative or inverse. The direction of association is important in cases involving one-tailed or directional tests of hypotheses, where direction of association may be predicted. If one variable is expected to increase (or decrease) as the result of an increase (or decrease) in the other variable, the r observed should be positive. If the prediction is that as one variable increases (or decreases), the other variable decreases (or increases), then the resulting r will be negative or inverse. If researchers are simply interested in knowing whether an association exists between two variables, then they rely on the strength or statistical significance of an association rather than the direction of it.

Proportional Reduction in Error (PRE) Interpretations

We are seriously interested in a variable's ability to explain variation or fluctuation in other variables. How well does knowing the socioeconomic or minority status of a sample of youths enable us to predict whether these youths will or will not be delinquent? How much does it help to know one's political affiliation in order to predict accurately their attitude toward the death penalty? There is an infinite list of associations between different variables that can be cited.

Let's use "attitude toward the death penalty" as an example of a variable we wish to predict. Let's also assume that we believe that one's support for the death penalty varies according to his/her political affiliation, such as Democrat or Republican. In other words, we believe that by knowing one's political affiliation, we can predict one's response on the "attitude toward the death penalty" variable. Another way of looking at this is saying that we can explain the variation in attitude toward the death penalty by using political affiliation as a predictor of it. In fact, there is considerable research in criminology suggesting that Republicans express greater support for the death penalty than Democrats (Cochran, Boots, and Chamlin, 2006). Whether this is a true assumption or holds true for most Republicans and Democrats is irrelevant. Let's assume that we believe it is true. Hypothetically, if we drew a random sample of 150 Democrats and Republicans from a given population and asked them their opinions about the death penalty, then we would expect a majority of Republicans to be for the death penalty while a majority of Democrats would be against it. If our sample consisted of 75 Democrats and 75 Republicans, and if all Democrats in our sample said they were against the death penalty and all Republicans said they were in favor of the death penalty, we might observe a table as shown in Table 11.1.

Table 11.1 is an **error-free association** between political affiliation and attitude toward the death penalty. What is an error-free association between variables? An error-free association exists whenever two variables correlate with one another perfectly and all persons

TABLE 11.1 Error-free Association Between Political Affiliation and Attitude Toward the Death Penalty

		Political Affiliation		
		Democrat	Republican	Total
Death Penalty Attitude	Pro	0 *a*	75 *b*	75
	Con	75 *c*	0 *d*	75
Total		75	75	N = 150

expected to give particular responses given those responses. In Table 11.1, no Democrats said they were for the death penalty, and no Republicans said they were against the death penalty. Had 30 Democrats said they were for the death penalty, these sample elements would be considered 30 errors. And if 25 Republicans had said they were against the death penalty, then there would have been 25 errors. The total errors would be $30 + 25 = 55$ errors. Errors, therefore, consist of elements expressing opinions they are not expected to express. They do or say things we do not expect them to do or say. In this sense, then, errors do not refer to mistakes on examinations or quizzes. They are strictly inconsistent outcomes between what we expect (or predict) and what we observe.

In Table 11.2, the table cells *a* and *d* contain errors, or responses that go against what we expect. In almost every study where samples of persons are investigated, these kinds of errors will occur. Consider the hypothetical redistribution of responses of our Democrats and Republicans in Table 11.2. Table 11.2 discloses an imperfect relation between political affiliation and one's attitude toward the death penalty.

Table 11.2 contains 30 errors. There are 20 Democrats who favor the death penalty and 10 Republicans who oppose it. $20 + 10 = 30$ errors. Again, these persons are counted as errors because they express an opinion different from our perfect forecast of what we think they believe as shown in Table 11.1. How much variation in attitude toward the death penalty did we explain or account for by using one's political affiliation as a predictor of this attitude?

TABLE 11.2 Imperfect Relation Between Political Affiliation and Attitude Toward the Death Penalty

		Political Affiliation		
		Democrat	Republican	Total
Death Penalty Attitude Nondelinquent	Pro	20 *a*	65 *b*	75
	Con	55 *c*	10 *d*	75
Total		75	75	N = 150

We were able to explain variation in attitude toward the death penalty, either pro or con, by using one's political affiliation as a predictor of it in $55 + 65 = 120$ cases. But we also failed to account for the remaining 30 cases. Thus, our prediction was wrong 30 times for 150 elements in our sample. We can look at how much variation in attitude toward the death penalty was not explained by political affiliation as a predictor of it in an alternative way. We can approach this question by asking how much error in explaining attitude toward the death penalty was reduced by using political affiliation as a predictor of it. Therefore, two kinds of variation are being discussed here. **Explained variation** is the amount of variation we account for in one variable by using another variable as a predictor of it. **Unexplained variation** is how much variation we fail to explain by using another variable as a predictor of it.

Explained variation can be reduced to a numerical expression and gives us a concrete measure of the predictive utility of one variable as an explanation for another variable. Table 11.1 contained no errors and there was 100 percent explained variation and 0 percent unexplained variation in attitude toward the death penalty when we used one's political affiliation as a predictor. If we began our study with 100 percent error or no knowledge of what might explain variation on the attitude toward the death penalty variable, we reduced that error by 100 percent with the distribution of elements in Table 11.1. However, in Table 11.2, we didn't explain all of the error in predicting attitude toward the death penalty. Table 11.2 contained 30 errors. But we predicted 120 elements' attitudes toward the death penalty correctly. Therefore, with a knowledge of one's political affiliation in Table 11.2, for example, we have reduced our prediction error in attitude toward the death penalty as follows:

$$\frac{\text{original total error} - \text{error using political affiliation variable as predictor}}{\text{original error}} \times 100$$

$$= \frac{150 - 30}{150} \times 100$$

$$= \frac{120}{150} \times 100$$

$$= .80 \times 100$$

$$= 80 \text{ percent.}$$

This means that we have explained 80 percent of the variation in attitude toward the death penalty by using one's political affiliation as a predictor of it. Political affiliation as a predictor of one's attitude toward the death penalty accounted for 80 percent of the variation. We reduced the total number of errors, 150 to 30, an 80 percent error reduction. This **proportional reduction in error** is labeled **PRE**. The remaining percentage is unexplained variation. It can be calculated as

$$1 - \text{explained variation, or } 1 - .80 = .20 \text{ or } 20 \text{ percent.}$$
Unexplained variation was 20 percent therefore.

As an alternative way of assessing the coefficients yielded by different measures of association, we can use the strength of an association, the statistical significance of the coefficient, and also the amount of variation in a variable that we can explain by using another variable as a predictor of it, or PRE.

PRE AND COEFFICIENTS OF ASSOCIATION   Measures of association may be evaluated according to the PRE yielded by their coefficients. However, some measures of association have PRE interpretations while other measures of association do not. Generally, measures of association having PRE interpretations are preferred over those not having such interpretations. This is because PRE is an assessment of how well certain variables predict variation in other variables. Thus, whether measures have PRE interpretations or do not have them becomes a very important criterion used to select which measure of association should be used in our data analyses. In fact, PRE is perhaps the most important criterion used for selecting coefficients of association.

Using coefficients of association with a PRE interpretation, we can compare several different variables to see which ones are better predictors of variables we wish to explain. In most cases where measures of association have a PRE interpretation, they have a **symmetric PRE interpretation**. This means both variables predict each other equally. Hypothetically, if we use X as a predictor of Y, we might observe a coefficient of .50. And then if we use variable Y as a predictor of X, we will observe the same coefficient of .60. However, some measures of association have an **asymmetric PRE interpretation**. An asymmetric interpretation means that we can determine which variable is the better predictor of the other. For instance, if we use X to predict Y, we may observe a coefficient = .60. But if we use Y to predict X, we may observe a coefficient = .40. This asymmetric outcome enables us to say that X is a better predictor of Y than Y is of X. When we test our theories using a measure of association with an asymmetric PRE interpretation, we may gain a greater understanding of how specific variables are associated with one another therefore.

Measures of Association for Two Nominal-Level Variables

THE NOMINAL LEVEL OF MEASUREMENT   The largest category of measures of association has been designed for two-variable associations where each variable is measured according to a nominal scale. Common categorizations might be delinquent/nondelinquent, property/violent offender, civil/criminal judge, prosecutor/defense counsel, jail/correctional officer, misdemeanor/felony, conviction/acquittal, or male/female inmate. Actually, any data measured according to higher levels of measurement may be reduced to the nominal level for the purpose of applying one or more of these measures. For instance, "age," an interval-level variable, may be dichotomized into "old inmate"/"young inmate" or "old judge"/"young judge." Years of educational attainment may also be reduced: more educated/less educated, college/noncollege graduate, and so on. An unlimited number of attitudinal variables, normally measured according to ordinal-level Likert or Thurstone scales, may also be reduced to nominal categories: high stress/low stress, high job satisfaction/low job satisfaction, high or strong professionalism/weak or low professionalism, high commitment/low commitment, or high cynicism/low cynicism. While specific measures of association exist for variables at higher measurement levels, sometimes researchers want a preliminary and rapid indicator of association between the variables they are studying.

There are many measures of association for two nominal-level variables. Four of the most popular measures will be presented here. These include (1) Pearson's C, the coefficient of contingency; and (2) Cramer's V; (3) the phi coefficient, φ; and (4) lambda, λ, Guttman's coefficient of predictability. Each of these measures has certain advantages and disadvantages compared with one another, and they may be calculated by using *SPSS*.

PEARSON'S COEFFICIENT OF CONTINGENCY, C   This is a nonparametric index of association between two variables cross-tabulated into any $r \times c$ table. This is a chi square (χ^2)–based coefficient, since a chi-square value derived from a chi-square test earlier applied to the table is used in the calculation of C. Following the application of the chi-square test, Pearson's C can be calculated to determine how strongly the variables are associated. Pearson's C is derived by the following formula:

$$C = \sqrt{\frac{\chi^2}{N + \chi^2}}$$

where

χ^2 = the observed chi-square value from the $r \times c$ table

N = the sample size

For example, W.L. Hicks (2006) studied police pursuit policies, written or unwritten, and whether police officers tended to engage in high, and potentially deadly, pursuits of fleeing suspects. Some of these high-speed pursuits have involved chasing drivers for traffic violations and who attempt to elude police and have occurred in congested traffic areas with serious consequences, where bodily injury or death have occurred. Many police departments have written policies for when their officers should engage in high-speed pursuits of motorists. It might be expected that those departments with written policies about such pursuits would have fewer of them, while those departments without such policies would have more of them. Hypothetically, suppose Hicks studied a sample of 90 police departments, 50 of which had high-speed pursuit policies and 40 not having them. Suppose further that Hicks cross-tabulated this information with high and low numbers of high-speed pursuits, where high = 5 or more high-speed pursuits per month and low = fewer than 5 high-speed pursuits per month. Hicks might generate a table such as that shown in Table 11.3. The hypothesis tested might be:

H_o: $C = 0$

H_1: $C \neq 0$

$P \leq .05$ (two-tailed test)

TABLE 11.3   Police Departments With and Without High-Speed Pursuit Policies and Numbers of High-Speed Pursuits

		High-Speed Pursuit Policy Yes	High-Speed Pursuit Policy No	Total
Numbers of High-Speed Pursuits	High	12	25	37
	Low	38	15	53
	Total	50	40	$N = 90$

An observed chi-square, $\chi^2 = 12.8$ was determined to be significant at the .001 level (two-tailed test, 1 df). With this observed chi-square value and the sample size, 90, from Table 11.3, the following Pearson's C was computed:

$$C = \sqrt{\frac{12.8}{90 + 12.8}}$$
$$= \sqrt{.1245}$$
$$= .35$$

The resulting C observed $= .35$. This observed $C = .35$ is a moderately low association between police department written or unwritten high-speed pursuit policies and numbers of high-speed pursuits. H_o would be rejected in any event, since the chi-square value of 12.8 was determined to be significant at the .001 level (two-tailed test).

ASSUMPTIONS, ADVANTAGES, AND DISADVANTAGES OF PEARSON'S C   The assumptions associated with C are: (1) the data must be arranged into a $r \times c$ table; (2) randomness; (3) sample size >25 and <250; and (4) the nominal level of measurement. The sample size limitation stems from the fact that C is based upon the observed chi-square value, and the chi-square test has the same sample size restriction. Applications of C to smaller or larger Ns would distort resulting C values.

The advantages of C are that (1) it can be computed for tables of any $r \times c$ size; (2) it can be computed directly from N and the observed χ^2 value; and (3) it is easy to compute. The disadvantages are that (1) C is a simple index number; (2) it has no PRE interpretation; (3) all C values are positive, despite existing negative or inverse associations; and (4) C never reaches +1.00 or perfect association. In order to artificially create a C value comparable with +1.00, a correction factor must be divided into the observed C. This correction factor, based on the table's $r \times c$ size, inflates an observed C value to a corrected C or (read: C bar). Correction factors for Pearson's C are found in Table A.29 of Appendix A, p. 475. Observed Cs are divided by the appropriate correction factor matching the table's $r \times c$ size and the result makes the resulting comparable with 1.00. Table A.29 of Appendix A presents artificial correction factors for table sizes ranging from 2×2 to 10×10. In the present example, we might take our observed $C = .25$ and correct it as follows: $.35/.707 = .49$. The .707 correction factor was taken from Table A.29, Appendix A and should be used with 2×2 tables.

The purpose of correcting observed C values is to compare them with other C values, even though table sizes may vary. Uncorrected C values cannot be compared directly with one another, unless (1) they have been computed for tables of the same size and (2) the tables have identical marginal totals. Given the corrected C value $= .49$, this greatly raises it from the original .35 observed. Again, it reflects a moderately low degree of association between the two variables examined. And it is statistically significant. We know this because the chi-square value that was originally calculated was significant at the .001 level. The significant chi-square value makes this C value significant also. Because C values are always positive, the direction of the association must be deduced by inspecting the table of frequencies directly. The *SPSS* program which can be used to solve for C does not provide correction factors as are shown in Table A.29. This correction must be done manually, although it is simple to perform.

BOX 11.1

SPSS Alternative Application

1. Open your *SPSS* program and go to the *SPSS* Data Editor. In the first column "var," type in 50 "1"s and 40 "2"s. This action will convert the first "var" column to VAR00001. Next, go to the second "var" column, and begin typing in the following: 12 "1" values; 38 "2" values; 25 "1" values; and 15 "2" values. You should now have two columns, titled VAR00001 and VAR00002, with a total of 90 values entered for both columns.
2. Click on "Analyze," then "Descriptive Statistics," then "Crosstabs." This will pull up a screen with several windows. In the left-hand window are VAR00001 and VAR00002.
3. Highlight VAR00001 and use the arrow to move this variable to the "Column(s)" window. Highlight VAR00002 and use the arrow to move this variable to the "Row(s)" window.
4. Click on "Statistics" at the bottom of the screen, and this will bring up a large variety of measures of association, together with chi-square, with boxes to check. Check the "Chi square" box and the "Contingency Coefficient" box. Then click "Continue."
5. This action will return you to the screen with the rows and columns. Click "OK" and several summary tables will be generated.
6. The "Case Processing Summary" simply shows all 90 cases were entered. The "VAR00002-VAR00001 Crosstabulation" shows information identical to what is found in Table 11.3. This functions as a check on your work. The cell frequencies should match.
7. The "Chi-Square Tests" table shows a variety of measures, including "Pearson Chi-Square," which shows 13.606. Notice that chi-square value is slightly different from the chi-square value in our manual problem above, which is 12.8. This slight difference is due to rounding error from the manual problem. Ignore the rounding error. Also ignore the next table, "Directional Measures."
8. Look at the last table, "Symmetric Measures," which contains Phi, Cramer's *V*, and the Contingency Coefficient, the last value is the Pearson's *C* we are seeking. It is .362. In our original problem, our observed *C* = .35. This minor discrepancy is again attributable to rounding error when chi-square was manually computed. It will not affect our interpretation of this value and the final results reported in the original manually performed problem. A *C* = .36 (rounded) is a moderately low degree of association between the two variables, high-speed-pursuit policy and numbers of high-speed pursuits. The significance of the *C* value is shown in the far right column. The probability of .000 means that we are able to reject H_o at the .001 level (two-tailed test) and conclude that there is a significant correlation between these two variables. $C \neq 0.00$. It should be noted that the test of significance of any *C* value is the chi-square itself. Any time the chi-square value is significant, any correlation based on chi-square is also statistically significant. But we must also describe how correlated these two variables are. This *C* value was a moderately low degree of association, not especially high. Thus, this example is good at illustrating the difference between statistical significance and substantive significance. The *C* value is statistically significant but it is not especially strong.

CRAMER'S V An improvement over Pearson's *C* is **Cramer's V**. This measure of association is also nonparametric and based upon a preliminary χ^2 test applied to a $r \times c$ table. The primary improvements are that (1) *V* values can achieve +1.00; (2) no correction factor needs to be made to inflate *V* values; and (3) *V* has no sample size restrictions, despite the fact that it's value is based on the observed χ^2 value. Cramer's *V* is derived from the following formula:

$$V = \sqrt{\frac{\chi^2}{(N)(a-1)}}$$

where

> N = the sample size
>
> χ^2 = the observed chi-square
>
> a = the smaller of the rows and columns in the $r \times c$ table

If we were to apply Cramer's V to the same information hypothetically derived from Hicks' (1960) study of police departments with or without written high-speed pursuit policies and higher or lower numbers of high-speed pursuits, we would enter the following information in our V formula to yield

$$V = \sqrt{\frac{12.8}{(90)(2 - 1)}}$$
$$= \sqrt{.1422}$$
$$= .38$$

Cramer's V for the same data shown in Table 11.3 is .38. Again, this is a moderately low degree of association between the two variables. If we were to compare this value with our uncorrected Pearson's C value = .35, it would be almost the same. Despite this small difference, it still possesses the same statistical significance as Pearson's C since it is based on the chi-square test which is a test of the significance of it. The hypothesis set would have been:

> H_o: $V = 0$
>
> H_1: $V \neq 0$
>
> $P \leq .05$ (two-tailed test)

Under these circumstances, H_o would have been rejected at the .05 level as was done when C was applied earlier.

ASSUMPTIONS, ADVANTAGES, AND DISADVANTAGES OF CRAMER'S V The assumptions of Cramer's V are (1) nominal level of measurement; (2) randomness. Advantages of Cramer's V include the fact that there are no sample size restrictions. It can be applied to tables of any $r \times c$ size, although as the table size increases, the general effect on V is to decrease it in relation to comparable measures, such as Pearson's C. Compared with C, it generates a more reliable measure of association between two nominal variables. It is quite easy to compute and interpret. Its value

BOX 11.2

SPSS Alternative Application

1. Follow all steps as outlined above for Pearson's C, the coefficient of contingency. A set of tables will be yielded, including Cramer's V. From our table generated from the computation of C from the earlier example, Cramer's V was .389. The manually computed Cramer's V was .38. Again, this slight discrepancy is attributable to rounding error in the manual calculation of chi-square. The same conclusion is reached about Cramer's V as was reached about C. The null hypothesis is rejected, this time at the .05 level of significance (two-tailed test), and it may be concluded that there is a significant relation between the two variables studied.

can range from 0.00 (no association) to +1.00, or perfect association. The significance of Cramer's V is known in advance, since it is test of significance of the chi-square test. Thus, if we know in advance that a chi-square test result is significant for a particular $r \times c$ table, then the Cramer's V computed for that table is also statistically significant.

Disadvantages include that Cramer's V has no PRE interpretation. It is always positive, despite the fact that a negative association may exist between variables. Thus, the table frequencies must always be inspected to determine the direction of association rather than to rely on the actual coefficient produced.

THE PHI COEFFICIENT, φ This is a nonparametric nominal-level measure of association for data arranged into a 2×2 table. Let's examine an application of it to some hypothetical data based on criminological research. T. Zink et al. (2006) studied lifetime intimate partner violence among older women. They acknowledged that little is known about how older women cope in long-term abusive intimate relationships. Therefore, these researchers wanted to learn more about how older women over 55 years of age coped with and remained in long-term abusive relationships. Their research led to interviews with a sample of 38 women over 55 who admitted to being in long-term abusive relationships with intimate partners. Some women said that they coped by finding meaning in a situation (the abusive relationship) that was virtually unchangeable. For instance, they coped by refocusing their energies into certain roles, setting limits with their abusers, and reached out to others, including friends (emotion-focused strategies). Other women simply survived, maintaining the external appearance to others of conjugal unity (i.e., passivity). Suppose Zink et al. wanted to know whether the amount of time these older women spent in abusive relationships with intimate partners was associated with their coping strategies (i.e., using emotion-focused strategies or simply staying in the relationship and doing nothing, or passivity)? Using a hypothetical distribution for these 38 women, suppose Zink et al. found the following distribution as shown in Table 11.4. The following hypothesis set was tested:

H_o: $\varphi = 0$
H_1: $\varphi \neq 0$
$P \leq .05$ (two-tailed test)

TABLE 11.4 Association Between Length of Time Spent in Abusive Intimate Partner Relationship and Type of Coping Among 38 Women

		Length of Time in Abusive Relation with Intimate Partner		
		10 or fewer years	More than 10 years	
Method of Coping	**Emotion-focused**	7 a	12 b	19($a + b$)
	Passivity	14 c	5 d	19($c + d$)
	Total	21($a + c$)	17($b + d$)	$N = 38$

Table 11.4 shows 38 older women (over age 55) who have been in long-term abusive relationships according to 10 or fewer years or more than 10 years. The following formula for the phi coefficient may be applied:

$$\phi = \frac{ad - bc}{\sqrt{(a + b)(c + d)(a + c)(b + d)}}$$

where a, b, c, and d = cells in the 2×2 table, and $(a + b)$, $(c + d)$, $(a + c)$, $(b + d)$ = marginal totals in 2×2 table.

Inserting the cell and marginal total values into the phi formula, we have

$$\phi = \frac{(7)(5) - (12)(14)}{\sqrt{(7 + 12)(14 + 5)(7 + 14)(12 + 5)}}$$

$$= \frac{35 - 168}{\sqrt{(19)(19)(21)(17)}}$$

$$= \frac{-133}{\sqrt{128,877}}$$

$$= \frac{-133}{358.99}$$

$$= -.37.$$

The resulting phi coefficient, φ is equal to $-.37$, a moderately low degree of association between length of long-term intimate partner abuse and method of coping (i.e., emotion-focused or passivity). The direction of phi is indicated as $-.37$, but the direction of phi is irrelevant since a two-tailed, nondirectional test of the hypothesis was being made. This amount of association, $-.37$, would disclose that a moderately low degree of association occurred between these two variables. No interpretive tables exist to determine the significance of phi magnitude. If a one-tailed directional interpretation were desired, an inspection of the frequencies in Table 11.4 would be in order. Such an inspection of Table 11.4 discloses that older women in abusive relationships with intimate partners for more than 10 years tend to use emotion-focused coping strategies, while women in these relationships for less than 10 years or less show passivity or acceptance. One tentative interpretation is that the longer older women are in abusive relationships, the more likely they are to use emotion-focused coping strategies. Women in these relationships for shorter periods seem willing to be passive and accepting of these abusive conditions. The sample is small, however, and more research would be needed to justify these tentative interpretations.

ASSUMPTIONS, ADVANTAGES, AND DISADVANTAGES OF THE PHI COEFFICIENT, φ The assumptions of the phi coefficient are (1) nominal-level data or data capable of being dichotomized into a 2×2 table; (2) randomness. Advantages of the phi coefficient are (1) coefficients of ± 1.00 can be achieved; (2) the direction of phi is indicated because phi yields both positive $(+)$ and negative $(-)$ values; and (3) the phi coefficient has a PRE interpretation. Disadvantages of phi include (1) phi can only be applied to 2×2 tables; (2) independent and dependent variable subclasses must be equal in order for phi to achieve ± 1.00; otherwise, unequal numbers of elements in subclasses will yield phi coefficients smaller than ± 1.00; and (3) data are confined to 2×2 tables only.

The PRE interpretation of the phi coefficient is especially important. Phi is one of only a few nominal-level measures of association to have one. The PRE interpretation of the phi coefficient is symmetric, and it is measured by φ^2 or $(-.37)^2 = .14$. This PRE of .14 means

BOX 11.3

***SPSS* Alternative Application**

1. Activate your *SPSS* software program and go to the *SPSS* Data Editor. Go to the first column, "var," and from Table 11.4 type in 21 "1" values. Next, type in 17 "2" values. You will now have 38 values in the first column, now designated as VAR00001. Next, go to the second "var" column, type in 19 "1" values and 19 "2" values.
2. Go to the second column, "var," and type in 7 "1" values, 14 "2" values, 12 "1" values, and 5 "2" values. This will yield VAR00002. You should now have two columns, VAR00001 and VAR00002, with a total of 38 pairs of "1" and "2" values.
3. Click on "Analyze," then "Descriptive Statistics," then "Crosstabs." This action will produce a screen with several windows. In the far left window will be VAR00001 and VAR00002. Highlight VAR00001 and use the arrow to move it to the right screen designated as "Column(s)." Highlight VAR00002 and use the arrow to move it to the "Row(s)" screen.
4. At the bottom of the screen is "Statistics." Click on this function and it will pull up a variety of measures from which to select. Click the box for "Phi and Cramer's *V*." Click "Continue."
5. Next, click "OK." This action produces several summary tables similar to those produced when the Pearson *C* and Cramer's *V* actions were performed. The phi coefficient shown in the last table, "Symmetric Measures," is −.37. This is the precise measure of φ yielded manually in the original problem above.
6. The *SPSS* program produces an exact probability for the observed φ value. The significance of the φ value is .02. This exact probability is equal to or less than .05, the level of significance at which the above hypothesis set was tested. A manual test of the significance of φ is shown in subsequent discussion in this section. The null hypothesis can be rejected, therefore, and the research hypothesis can be supported. There is a relation between women's methods of coping and the amount of time spent in an abusive spousal relationship.

that 14 percent of the variation in coping with intimate partner abuse has been explained by using length of time in the abusive relationship. Unexplained variation is measured by $1 - \varphi^2$ or $1 - .14 = .86$. Thus, 86 percent of the variation in coping with abusive intimate partner abuse has not been explained by the "length of time in the relationship" variable.

Should we be content with an explanation, length of time in an abusive relation with intimate partners, that only explains 14 percent of how women cope with this abusive relationship? This is a subjective question. Each investigator has his/her own standards about how much predictive utility or explanatory power is acceptable or good. Clearly some of this variation in coping has been explained by the time factor, or length of time in the abusive relation. But other variables may have greater predictive power. Also, as we will see in later chapters, using more than a single variable or multiple variables to predict how women cope with abuse is possible and definitely more productive than using single-variable predictors.

THE STATISTICAL SIGNIFICANCE OF THE PHI COEFFICIENT, φ   The statistical significance of the phi coefficient is determined by a chi-square test:

$$\chi^2 = N\varphi^2 \ (1 \ df)$$

Therefore, the significance of phi would be $\chi^2 = (38)(.14) = 5.32$. Using Table A.4 in Appendix A with 1 *df*, the critical value of chi-square (1 *df*) for the .05 level of significance for a two-tailed test = 3.841. Our observed chi-square of 5.32 equals or exceeds 3.841, and therefore our phi coefficient $= -.37$ is significant at the .05 level (two-tailed test). Had we predicted that women who stay longer in abusive intimate partnerships use emotion-focused coping strategies compared with women in such relationships for shorter time intervals, this would have been a directional or one-tailed test, and our chi-square observed would have been significant at .025. H_o would have been rejected under these circumstances. Interestingly the exact probability of φ produced by the *SPSS* program was .022, very close to .025.

LAMBDA, λ, GUTTMAN'S COEFFICIENT OF PREDICTABILITY   The best nonparametric measure of association between two nominal-level variables is lambda, λ, **Guttman's coefficient of predictability**. Lambda is calculated as follows:

$$\lambda = \frac{\sum f_r + \sum f_c - (F_r + F_c)}{2N - (F_r - F_c)}$$

where

f_r = largest frequency occurring in a row

f_c = largest frequency occurring in a column

F_r = largest marginal frequency occurring among the rows

F_c = largest marginal frequency occurring among the columns

N = number of observations for the table

An application of λ is based on information from a study conducted by Anthony W. Flores et al. (2005). These investigators were interested in studying agency awareness of measuring risk/need factors and effective treatment strategies for juvenile delinquents. Flores and his associates investigated three types of agencies in a Midwestern state: the state department of youth services; a county juvenile probation department; and a county juvenile rehabilitation center. According to Flores et al., these three types of agencies represent a continuum of correctional treatment for delinquent youths ranging from traditional probation supervision to secure, long-term, institutional placement. Through surveys, Flores et al. asked staff from each agency or institution to provide information about their current treatment programs. Some questions pertained to agency or institutional awareness of juveniles' criminogenic needs and treatment strategies. Risk factors assessed included antisocial attitudes of juvenile clients, associates, personality, and criminal history. The investigators wanted to know if there was an association between identifying criminogenic needs of juvenile offenders and the type of agency surveyed.

Suppose Flores et al. believed that more practitioner-oriented agencies/institutions, such as secure institutions, would be more likely to be aware of and identify the criminogenic needs of youthful inmates compared with larger agencies, such as the state department of youth services or the county-level probation department? If Flores et al. had drawn samples of administrators and employees from each of these agencies and asked them to indicate whether they identified a youth's criminogenic needs, they may have generated some hypothetical information such as that presented in Table 11.5.

Table 11.5 shows a cross tabulation of different agencies (secure institution, county probation department, and state youth agency) with awareness/unawareness of the criminogenic needs of juveniles. Thus, a total of 140 persons are represented here: 42 persons from a juvenile correctional institution, 40 persons from a juvenile probation department, and 58 persons from a state youth agency were surveyed. The type of agency/institution is shown across the top of the table. Down the left-hand side are "aware/measured" and "unaware/unmeasured," meaning that persons either indicated an awareness of these criminogenic needs and measured them or

TABLE 11.5 Three Youth Agencies/Institutions and Awareness of Criminogenic Needs of Youthful Offenders

Awareness of Criminogenic Needs of Youths	Agencies/Institutions			
	Secure Institution	County Probation	State Youth Agency	Total
Aware/Measured	32 _a_	26 _b_	11 _c_	69
Unaware/Unmeasured	10 _d_	14 _e_	47 _f_	71
Total	42	40	58	N = 140

were not aware of these needs and did not measure them. What degree of association exists between these variables? Suppose we were to test the following hypothesis set:

$H_o: \lambda = 0$

$H_1: \lambda \neq 0$

$P \leq .05$ (two-tailed test)

The lambda formula is:

$$\lambda = \frac{\Sigma f_r + \Sigma f_c - (F_r + F_c)}{2N - (F_r - F_c)}$$

where

f_r = largest frequency occurring in a row

f_c = largest frequency occurring in a column

F_r = largest marginal frequency occurring among the rows

F_c = largest marginal frequency occurring among the columns

N = number of observations in the table.

Applying these values from Table 11.5, we have

$$\lambda = \frac{(32 + 47) + (32 + 26 + 47) - (71 + 58)}{(2)(140) - (71 + 58)}$$

$$= \frac{(79 + 105) - 129}{280 - 129}$$

$$= \frac{55}{151}$$

$$= .36.$$

The observed $\lambda = .36$. There are no direct interpretive tables for evaluating the significance of λ. We must rely, therefore, on the strength of lambda exhibited by the coefficient.

In terms of the strength of this lambda coefficient, we would say that there is a moderately low degree of association between type of agency/institution and awareness/unawareness of a youth's criminogenic needs. However, lambda is also interpretable as a PRE measure. In this instance, the absolute value of lambda, .36 as indicated here, is directly interpretable as a PRE measure. Therefore, 36 percent of the variation between the two variables has been explained. Unexplained variation is $1 - \lambda$, or $1 - .36 = .64$. Thus, 64 percent of the variation in the two variables is unexplained by their association.

This particular lambda formula yields a symmetric PRE interpretation, meaning that regardless of which variable is used as the independent variable, both would predict the variation in the other 36 percent of the time. But lambda has a feature that most other measures of association do not have. It has an asymmetrical PRE interpretation as well. This means that we can determine which variable is the better predictor of the other. In the case of the data in Table 11.5, for example, is the type of agency/institution a better predictor of awareness/unawareness of a youth's criminogenic needs, or is awareness/unawareness of one's criminogenic needs a better predictor of the type of agency/institution? In order to make these asymmetric PRE interpretations, we need to use an alternative lambda formula. The asymmetric lambda formula, yielding a lambda a coefficient, λ_a, is

$$\lambda_a = \frac{\Sigma f_i - F_d}{N - F_d}$$

where

$f_i =$ largest frequency occurring within each subclass of the independent variable

$F_d =$ largest frequency found within the dependent variable subtotals

$N =$ total number of observations for the table

Applying this formula to the information shown in Table 11.5, we would be identifying type of agency/institution as the independent variable and awareness/unawareness of a youth's criminogenic needs as the dependent variable. This is probably how Flores et al. (2005) envisioned this association. The computational work to yield lambda a, or λ_a, is shown as follows:

$$\lambda_a = \frac{(32 + 26 + 47) - 71}{140 - 71}$$

$$= \frac{105 - 71}{71}$$

$$= \frac{34}{71}$$

$$= .49.$$

In this instance, our lambda a value, $\lambda_a = .49$. Thus, when we use type of agency/institution to predict awareness/unawareness of youth criminogenic needs, we now account for 49 percent of the variation in awareness/unawareness by using type of agency/institution as a predictor of it. And we fail to explain 51 percent of the variation as well.

Now, let's rearrange the data in Table 11.5 so that we switch the independent (predictor) variable with the dependent one. In this case, we will now recast these data and use awareness/unawareness of a youth's criminogenic needs as the predictor or independent variable and type of agency/institution as the dependent variable as shown in Table 11.6.

TABLE 11.6 Awareness/Unawareness of Youth Criminogenic Needs as a Predictor of Type of Agency/Institution

		Awareness of Criminogenic Needs of Youths		
		Aware/Measured	Unaware/Unmeasured	Total
	Secure Institution	32	10	42
Type of Agency/ Institution	County Probation	26	14	40
	State Youth Agency	11	47	58
	Total	69	71	$N = 140$

A new λ_a may be computed, based upon this new tabular arrangement, as follows:

$$\lambda_a = \frac{(32 + 47) - 58}{140 - 82}$$
$$= \frac{79 - 58}{82}$$
$$= \frac{21}{82}$$
$$= .26.$$

The second λ_a is now .26. We only account for 26 percent of the variation in type of agency/institution when we use awareness/unawareness of a youth's criminogenic needs as a predictor. Comparing the two λ_as, type of agency/institution is a better predictor of awareness/unawareness of a youth's criminogenic needs, with 49 percent of the variation explained compared with only 26 percent of the variation explained by using awareness/unawareness of a youth's criminogenic needs as a predictor of type of agency/institution.

This example illustrates the importance of λ as an asymmetric PRE measure. It should be noted that averaging the two λ_a values will yield approximately the same symmetric λ originally derived. This is demonstrated as follows: $(.26 + .49)/2 = .37$, very close to the earlier symmetric lambda value of .36.

ASSUMPTIONS, ADVANTAGES, AND DISADVANTAGES OF LAMBDA The assumptions for λ are: (1) randomness; (2) the nominal level of measurement; and (3) data in a form that can be cross-tabulated into some $r \times c$ form.

The major advantage of λ over other nominal-level measures of association is its ability to yield both symmetric and asymmetrical λ values that have a PRE interpretation. Lambda requires no correction factor and may be directly interpreted as a PRE measure. It is unrestricted regarding table size and may achieve +1.00. The only disadvantage of lambda is that occasionally, because of certain distributions of table frequencies, λ values may be 0.00 even though an association actually exists between the variables. An *SPSS* software program also exists, where available, to yield these same values through use of the *SPSS* Data Editor and running appropriate analyses and cross tabulations.

BOX 11.4

SPSS Alternative Application

1. Activate your *SPSS* software program and go to the *SPSS* Data Editor. Go to the first "var" column and type in 42 "1" values; 40 "2" values; and 58 "3" values. This produces 140 1s, 2s, and 3s in the first column, now labeled VAR00001.
2. Next, go to the second "var" column, and type in 32 "1" values; 10 "2" values; 26 "1" values; 14 "2" values; 11 "1" values; and 47 "2" values. These should total 140 values of 1s and 2s matched with the values of 1, 2, and 3 in column VAR00001. All of these values have been taken from Table 11.5.
3. Next, click on "Analyze," then "Descriptive Statistics," then "Crosstabs." This action will yield a screen with several windows. VAR00001 and VAR00002 are in the far left-hand window. To the right are two windows labeled "Row(s)" and "Column(s)." Highlight VAR00001 and use the arrow to move it to the "Column(s)" window. Highlight VAR00002 and move it with the arrow to the "Row(s)" window.
4. At the bottom of the screen is "Statistics." Click on this feature and this brings up a screen with several alternative procedures. Click the "Lambda" box, then click "Continue."
5. This action will return you to the original screen, showing the variables, VAR00001 and VAR00002 in the column and row windows. Click "OK." Several summary tables are generated. The first "Case Processing Summary" shows $N = 140$, and it functions as a check on your work. The second table, "VAR00002-VAR00001 Crosstabulation," shows the distribution of frequencies essentially viewed in Table 11.5. If these frequencies do not match those in Table 11.5, one or more errors have been made in the *SPSS* Data Editor when entering data and you must first correct them. However, if the table is consistent with Table 11.5, this functions as an additional check on your work.
6. The last table is very important here. It shows λ from three different perspectives: (1) as a symmetric measure; (2) as an asymmetric measure where VAR00002 is dependent, and (3) as an asymmetric measure where VAR00001 is dependent. Note that these different values of λ are .36, .49, and .25 respectively. They match up perfectly with the manual calculations described in an earlier section.
7. An additional feature of this table is that the statistical significance of each of these lambda values is displayed in a column to the far right. All are significant at .001 or less. Thus, the null hypothesis being tested in the hypothesis set in the above discussion can be rejected at the .05 level of significance (two-tailed test). If directional tests of hypotheses were being conducted using each variable as a predictor of the other, these null hypotheses would be rejected as well.
8. It is significant to note that this last summary table shows that VAR00001, the type of agency/institution, is a better predictor of awareness of the criminogenic needs of juvenile offenders (.49) than criminogenic needs of youths is as a predictor of the type of agency/institution (.25). The mutual predictability of the two variables is .36, which means that 36 percent of the variation between the two variables is explained by their mutual predictability.

Measures of Association for Two Ordinal-Level Variables

THE ORDINAL LEVEL OF MEASUREMENT The measures presented in this section are useful whenever attitudinal data have been measured according to conventional procedures, such as Likert or Thurstone scaling techniques (Champion, 2006). Three measures are presented here. These include (1) Kendall's tau, τ; (2) Somers' d_{yx}; and (3) Goodman's and Kruskal's gamma, γ.

KENDALL'S TAU, τ This is a useful nonparametric measure of association for two sets of scores which have been measured according to an ordinal scale. This procedure is appropriate for data arranged into ranks and not in cross-tabulated form such as an $r \times c$ table. The following example from the criminal justice literature is provided.

William L. White et al. (2005) were interested in studying a sample of Illinois probation officers and examining the impact of various stressors in their lives that might affect their work performance and effectiveness. Stressors can erode professional performance and personal health, and they can include role ambiguity, role conflict, safety concerns, low pay and promotional opportunities, excessive paperwork, and a lack of administrative support. In White et al.'s study, 15 county probation departments in Illinois were targeted for investigation, and a sample of probation officers was surveyed by completing questionnaires about different aspects of their jobs.

One frequently studied variable is participation in decision making. Suppose White et al. wanted to know whether greater participation in decision making among a sample of probation officers would be associated with greater work effectiveness. White et al. would need to measure the degree of one's participation in decision making as well as develop some indicator of officer effectiveness. Suppose such measures had been devised and 25 probation officers were studied to determine the amount of association between these two ordinal-level variables. In Table 11.7, two sets of scores are shown. Scores on a "participation in decision making" variable are indicated in one column and range from 135 (high) to 90 (low), while "officer effectiveness" according to hypothetical administrator ratings of one's actual work effectiveness are shown in a second column, ranging from 74 (high) to 39 (low). The following hypothesis set might be tested:

H_o: $\tau = 0$

H_1: $\tau \neq 0$

$P \leq .05$ (two-tailed test)

Table 11.7 is constructed as follows. The raw "participation in decision making" scores for the 25 probation officers are arranged from high to low (135 to 90). Then, their corresponding officer effectiveness scores are placed beside the participation scores in a second column. These scores are left unranked. It is seldom the case in research that one array of scores is identical in distribution from high to low compared with another array of scores, unless perfect association between the two variables exists. Next, in a column, R_1, the "participation in decision making" scores are ranked from 1 to 25 as shown. Column R_2 consists of the respective ranks assigned to the raw officer effectiveness scores from 1 to 25 also, based on the magnitude of individual raw scores presented. Column R_2 becomes the focus of our attention for determining the values for the final two columns.

In the column, "number of higher ranks," we focus upon the first rank of the first probation officer, which is 2. We count the number of ranks below 2 that are higher than 2. In this instance, 23 ranks are higher, and we place this value adjacent to the rank of 2 as shown. The next rank of 1 also has 23 ranks below it which are higher. We continue down this column until we have entered all values as shown in the "number of higher ranks" column.

The final column, "number of lower ranks," represents the number of ranks below each rank in column R_2 which are lower than that rank. For instance, the first rank of 2 has only one rank below it (i.e., 1) that is lower than 2. The rank of 16 farther down the column has 7 ranks

TABLE 11.7 Hypothetical Officer Effectiveness and Participation in Decision-Making Scores Among 25 Probation Officers

Probation Officer	Participation in Decision Making	Officer Effectivenes	R_1	R_2	Number of Higher Ranks	Number of Lower Ranks
1	135	72	1	2	23	1
2	134	74	2	1	23	0
3	133	69	3	4	21	1
4	132	71	4	3	21	0
5	128	65	5	7	18	2
6	127	64	6	8	17	2
7	126	63	7	9	16	2
8	125	62	8	10	15	2
9	124	49	9	16	9	7
10	123	68	10	5	15	0
11	122	66	11	6	14	0
12	121	55	12	11	13	0
13	120	51	13	14	10	2
14	119	54	14	12	11	0
15	116	50	15	15	9	1
16	114	42	16	23	2	7
17	113	47	17	18	6	2
18	110	48	18	17	6	1
19	108	46	19	19	5	1
20	106	45	20	20	4	1
21	100	53	21	13	4	0
22	99	39	22	25	0	3
23	96	43	23	22	1	1
24	92	44	24	21	1	0
25	90	41	25	24	0	0
					$\Sigma H = 264$	$\Sigma L = 36$

below it that are lower than 16 (i.e., 5, 6, 11, 14, 12, 15, and 13). We carry out this procedure until all values have been determined for the final column. We sum these values. With these two columns of sums, we may carry out the formula for Kendall's tau, which is

$$\tau = \frac{\Sigma H - \Sigma L}{\dfrac{N(N-1)}{2}}$$

where

H and L = sums of the number of higher and lower ranks respectively

N = number of probation officers in our sample

With the data from Table 11.7, we may compute as follows:

$$\tau = \frac{264 - 36}{\dfrac{(25)(25 - 1)}{2}}$$

$$\tau = \frac{228}{30}$$

$$= .76$$

The observed $\tau = .76$. This coefficient can be interpreted as a strong (or high) association between participation in decision making and probation officer job effectiveness. Kendall's tau also has a PRE interpretation. Making a PRE interpretation of our observed τ value, it appears that 76 percent of the variation in officer job effectiveness and participation in decision making has been accounted for or explained by the mutual predictability of these variables. Only 24 percent of this variation $(1 - \tau)$ remains unexplained. This is a symmetrical PRE interpretation. Kendall's tau has no asymmetrical PRE interpretative capability similar to the lambda coefficient discussed earlier in this chapter.

ASSUMPTIONS OF KENDALL'S TAU   The assumptions of Kendall's tau are (1) randomness and (2) two variables measured according to an ordinal scale. There are no distributional

---

BOX 11.5

SPSS Alternative Application

1. Open your *SPSS* program and go to the *SPSS* Data Editor. Enter two columns of values from Table 11.7. These are the ranks in columns labeled R_1 and R_2. The first "var" column, which will eventually become VAR00001, begins with 1, 2, 3, 4, 5, and so forth, until rank 25 is entered. Essentially, this is a simple ranking of values from 1 through 25. The second column "var" (which will become VAR00002) contains the ranks from the second R column in Table 11.7, beginning with 2, 1, 4, 3, and so on, until the rank of 24 is entered. Note that Kendall's tau cannot be calculated from the raw scores in the first two columns of Table 11.7. You must rank these variables first. Tau is computed based on the ranks associated with the raw scores rather than the raw scores themselves.
2. Once the data have been entered, click on "Analyze," then "Correlate," then "Bivariate."
3. You will see a screen with two windows. The left window contains VAR00001 and VAR00002. Highlight each variable and move it to the "Variables" window. Both VAR00001 and VAR00002 should now be in the "Variables" window.
4. You will be given a choice of several correlation coefficients to compute, including Kendall's tau. Click the box indicating "Kendall's tau-*b*." Now press "OK."
5. A summary table is generated called "Correlations." This table shows the actual value calculated for Kendall's tau *b*, one version of Kendall's tau, and the one being used for the problem described above. It also provides the sample size, 25. The τ value $= .76$, which is equal to the τ manually calculated from the information provided in Table 11.7. The significance level is also included, which is .000. This probability means that we can reject the null hypothesis that $\tau = 0$ and support the research hypothesis at the .05 level of significance (two-tailed test). Most hypotheses of association are two-tailed anyway.

assumptions, such as normality or linearity. Applications of Kendall's tau, however, can be improved whenever used with Ns larger than 10.

ADVANTAGES AND DISADVANTAGES OF KENDALL'S TAU   Kendall's tau is specifically designed for scores in a format similar to that shown in Table 11.7. It also has a symmetrical PRE interpretation. Values of the tau coefficient can equal ±1.00. When data are cross tabulated, Kendall's tau would not be appropriate, however. This is because tau is not suitable for use where excessive numbers of tied scores and ranks are present. Tied scores exist in each cell of an $r \times c$ table. Even when data are presented in a format similar to Table 11.7, the value of Kendall's tau may be impaired because of tied scores, which may exist. This situation may cause resulting tau values not to equal ±1.00. Thus, where tied scores exist, some caution should be used when interpreting tau values.

THE SIGNIFICANCE OF KENDALL'S TAU   Kendall's tau may be assessed in terms of its statistical significance. Tau's statistical significance may be determined by using the following formula, which results in an approximation of a Z value:

$$Z = \frac{\tau}{\sigma_r}$$

where

τ = the observed Kendall's tau value

σ_r = the standard error of tau, defined as

$$\sigma_r = \sqrt{\frac{2(2N + 5)}{9N(N - 1)}}$$

With our observed tau = .76, the test of significance becomes

$$Z = \frac{.76}{\sqrt{\dfrac{2(2N + 5)}{9N(N - 1)}}}$$

$$= \frac{.76}{\sqrt{\dfrac{(2)(50 + 5)}{9(25)(25 - 1)}}}$$

$$= \frac{.76}{\sqrt{\dfrac{110}{5400}}}$$

$$= \frac{.76}{\sqrt{.0204}}$$

$$= \frac{.76}{.143}$$

$$= 5.31.$$

The observed $Z = 5.31$. Using Table A.2 from Appendix A, we can determine the significance associated with this value. For instance, we would need to equal or exceed a $Z = \pm 2.58$ in order for the observed tau value to be significant statistically at the .01 level (two-tailed). Since our observed $Z = 5.31$ equals or exceeds this critical Z value, tau coefficient is significant at the

.01 level (two-tailed). H_o can be rejected at the .05 level of significance. This finding is consistent with what the *SPSS* program generated and the probability level achieved. However, the *SPSS* program did not print out a *Z* value, only a probability level.

IMPROVEMENTS ON KENDALL'S TAU Subsequent to Kendall's development of tau, other versions of tau were devised which improved on the original tau coefficient. Thus, the Kendall's tau presented here, the first one developed for two ordinal-level variables, became known as tau *a*. Two other versions of tau were created: tau *b* and tau *c*. These statistical procedures are discussed elsewhere (Walker, 1999:170–177). Kendall's tau *b* and tau *c* are considered improvements over tau *a*, since they can be calculated for various $r \times c$ tables. Both have symmetric PRE interpretations and raise the predictive value of their respective τ values by yielding larger observed tau coefficients compared with tau *a*. The primary difference between the two tau values is that tau *b* is designed for square $r \times c$ tables where $r = c$, whereas tau *c* is designed for rectangular $r \times c$ tables where $r \neq c$. Examples of these ls of the tau coefficient will not be presented here, since other superior measures are discussed, including Somers' *d* and Goodman's and Kruskal's gamma, γ.

Somers' d_{yx}

A nonparametric measure of association designed for cross-tabulated data measured according to an ordinal scale, **Somers' d_{yx}** provides investigators with a relatively simple method for determining which variable is a better predictor of the other. Therefore, it is strictly an asymmetric PRE measure. Because of this fact, it is necessary to use switch each of these variables and use each as independent in order to evaluate which one is the better predictor. The following example is provided.

Bruce G. Taylor, Robert C. Davis, and Christopher D. Maxwell (2001) investigated a treatment program for batterers, or those who physically abuse their spouses. Among other aspects of their investigation, these researchers sought to characterize batterers by describing their social circumstances and other factors. Frequently, those convicted of spousal assaults have prior histories of being physically abused as children by their own parents. Furthermore, many batterers report that their own parents battered each other fairly frequently. Thus, much of their battering behavior seemed to be learned as they grew up in violent familial circumstances. Suppose that Taylor, Davis, and Maxwell wanted to know whether there was any correlation between the level of home early childhood violence, as disclosed by a sample of convicted batterers, and the receptivity of these batterers to a treatment program designed to assist batterers in understanding and possibly changing their battering behaviors and propensities. Perhaps these researchers might obtain a sample of 150 convicted batterers and obtain impressions from them concerning the level of violence in their own homes as children. Next, these researchers might want to measure their level of receptivity to a batterer treatment program offered by a community corrections agency. Receptivity to a batterer treatment program might indicate how much these batterers wanted to become involved in the program and how willing they might be to understand and change their prior battering behaviors. A table such as that shown in Table 11.8 might be constructed. The following hypothesis set might be tested:

H_o: $d_{yx} = 0$

H_1: $d_{yx} \neq 0$

$P \leq .001$ (two-tailed test)

Each cell in Table 11.8 is lettered to follow the computational work. Since Somers' d_{yx} is asymmetric, two *d* values must be computed. One value, d_{yx}, will yield a coefficient that indicates

TABLE 11.8 Hypothetical Scores for 150 Convicted Batterers According to the Level of Home Childhood Violence and Receptivity to a Batterer Treatment Program

Receptivity to Treatment Program (Variable Y)	Level of Home Childhood Violence (Variable X)			Total
	Low	Medium	High	
Low	25 a	18 b	10 c	53
Medium	12 d	13 e	15 f	40
High	8 g	17 h	32 i	57
Total	45	48	57	N = 150

how much variation in variable Y will occur as a function of variable X as a predictor of it. The other coefficient, d_{xy}, will indicate the variation in predicting variable X by using variable Y as a predictor of it. These respective formulae are as follows. Where X is the predictor of Y,

$$d_{yx} = \frac{\Sigma f_a - \Sigma f_i}{\Sigma f_a + \Sigma f_i + T_y}$$

Where Y is the predictor of X,

$$d_{xy} = \frac{\Sigma f_a - \Sigma f_i}{\Sigma f_a + \Sigma f_i + T_x}$$

where

    f_a = the frequency of agreements

    f_i = the frequency of inversions

    T_y and T_x = the pairs of scores tied on Y and on X

These values are determined as follows from the cell frequencies in Table 11.8:

    $\Sigma f_a = (a)(e+f+h+i) + (b)(f+i) + (d)(h+i) + (e)(i).$

    $\Sigma f_i = (c)(d+e+g+h) + (b)(d+g) + (f)(g+h) + (e)(g).$

    $T_x = (a)(d+g)(g) + (b)(e+h) + (e)(h) + (c)(f+i) + (f)(i).$

    $T_y = (a)(b+c) + (b)(c) + (d)(e+f) + (e)(f) + (g)(h+i) + (h)(i).$

Using the frequencies from Table 11.8, each of these terms is computed as follows:

    $\Sigma f_a = (25)(13 + 15 + 17 + 32) + (18)(15 + 32) + (12)(17 + 32) + (13)(32)$

        $= 1{,}925 + 846 + 588 + 416$

        $= 3{,}775.$

    $\Sigma f_i = (10)(12 + 13 + 8 + 17) + (18)(12 + 8) + (15)(8 + 17) + (13)(8)$

        $= 500 + 360 + 375 + 104$

        $= 1{,}339.$

$$\Sigma T_x = (25)(12 + 8) + (12)(8) + (18)(13 + 17) + (13)(17) +$$
$$(10)(15 + 32) + (15)(32)$$
$$= 500 + 96 + 540 + 221 + 470 + 480$$
$$= 2{,}307.$$

$$\Sigma T_y = (25)(18 + 10) + (18)(10) + (12)(13 + 15) + (13)(15) +$$
$$(8)(17 + 32) + (17)(32)$$
$$= 700 + 180 + 336 + 195 + 392 + 544$$
$$= 2{,}347.$$

Summarizing these values, we have

$$\Sigma f_a = 3{,}775$$
$$\Sigma f_i = 1{,}339$$
$$T_y = 2{,}347$$
$$T_x = 2{,}307.$$

We may now determine our d values:

$$d_{yx} = \frac{(3{,}775 - 1{,}339)}{(3{,}775 + 1{,}339 + 2{,}347)}$$
$$= \frac{2{,}436}{7{,}461}$$
$$= .326.$$

$$d_{xy} = \frac{(3{,}775 - 1{,}339)}{(3{,}775 + 1{,}339 + 2{,}307)}$$
$$= \frac{2{,}436}{7{,}421}$$
$$= .328.$$

Based on these two d values, it seems that neither variable is the better predictor. This is probably attributable to the distribution of frequencies in Table 11.8. Usually, Somers' d yields different values whenever the independent variable is switched to be the dependent variable. These values have been carried out to three places where $d_{yx} = .326$ and $d_{xy} = .328$. Variable Y had an almost imperceptible edge in predictive utility over variable X. Receptivity to the treatment program influenced one's childhood perception of family violence slightly more, therefore, than one's childhood perception of family violence influenced one's receptivity to the treatment program. Logically, this doesn't make a whole lot of sense. However, these differences in the two d values are essentially negligible. This is why it is important for researchers to examine carefully the theoretical foundations of their research and not rely totally on association coefficients in order to make meaningful interpretations of whatever they have found. This finding also shows that successful predictions are not always made, and important findings are not always disclosed.

Both asymmetric coefficients of .33 (rounded) suggest that approximately 33 percent of the variation in the two variables has been explained by their mutual predictability. This results from averaging the two d values to yield a symmetric PRE interpretation. However, 67 percent

BOX 11.6

SPSS Alternative Application

1. Open up your *SPSS* program and go to the *SPSS* Data Editor screen. From Table 11.8, in the first "var" column, type in 45 "1" values; 48 "2" values; and 57 "3" values. Next, go to the second "var" column and type in the following: 25 "1"s; 12 "2"s; 8 "3"s; 18 "1"s; 13 "2"s; 17 "3"s; 10 "1"s; 15 "2"s; and 32 "3"s. You will have created two columns, VAR00001 (level of home childhood violence) and VAR00002 (receptivity to treatment program). The column totals will be 150 as a check on your work.

2. Next, click on "Analyze," then "Descriptive Statistics," then "Crosstabs." Several windows will be displayed. The far left window contains VAR00001 and VAR00002. You want to highlight VAR00001, the independent variable, and use the arrow to place it in the "Column(s)" window. Next, highlight VAR00002, the dependent variable, and use the arrow to place it in the "Row(s)" window.

3. Next, click on "Statistics" at the bottom of the screen, and several correlational options will appear. Click the Somers' *d* box, then "Continue." Next, click "OK."

4. A list of summary tables appears, including a "Case Processing Summary," a "VAR00001-VAR00002 Crosstabulation," and a "Directional Measures" table. The first table shows how many persons were sampled, or 150. The second table shows how the data were displayed in Table 11.8. If there are any discrepancies, then you must return to the *SPSS* Data Editor and verify that you typed in the values correctly for both columns. However, if the table matches 11.8, then this is an additional check on your work accuracy.

5. The last table shows different values of Somers' *d*. The symmetric Somers' *d* is shown as .327. This is consistent with what the manual computation yielded. This table also discloses which variable is the better predictor of the other. When VAR00001 is the independent variable, it explains .326 of the variation in VAR00002. When VAR00002 is the independent variable, it explains .328 of the variation in VAR00001. Thus, VAR00002 is a slightly better predictor than VAR00001. But these differences are negligible. One additional disclosure in this table is the probability at which these Somers' *d*s are significant. These probabilities are .000, meaning that our original null hypothesis could have been rejected at the .001 level.

of the variation in the two variables remains unexplained. Thus, the two variables are not especially good predictors of each other's variation. Furthermore, it would appear that a moderately low correlation exists between receptivity to treatment and the level of childhood home violence. Notice also that the statistical significance of a Somers' *d* value is not available through conventional means. In order to yield probabilities, we must have a software program such as *SPSS*.

ASSUMPTIONS, ADVANTAGES, AND DISADVANTAGES OF SOMERS' d_{yx} The assumptions for Somers' d_{yx} are (1) randomness and (2) two variables measured according to an ordinal scale. Favorably, Somers' d_{yx} can achieve perfect negative or perfect positive association, ± 1.00, depending upon the distribution of table frequencies. The asymmetric PRE interpretation of Somers' *d* also makes it attractive for use in criminological research. The strength of the association can also be assessed by examining the absolute value of the *d*.

Adversely, compared with other measures of association we have examined thus far, Somers' *d* is somewhat more complicated to compute. However, the *SPSS* is available to yield asymmetric values of d for both variables examined, and the asymmetric property of d gives it a strength that other measures in this section do not possess. An additional advantage of d is that it can be computed for any $r \times c$ table, regardless of whether $r = c$ or $r \neq c$. In this respect, at least, Somers' d is superior to both Kendall's tau b and tau c.

GOODMAN'S AND KRUSKAL'S GAMMA, γ The best nonparametric measure of association for two variables measured according to an ordinal scale is **Goodman's and Kruskal's gamma, γ.** Gamma is strictly a symmetric PRE measure, however, regardless of which variable is designated in cross tabulations as either independent or dependent.

An application of γ from the criminological literature is presented. Michael Reisig, Kristy Holtfreter, and Merry Morash (2006) studied a sample of female parolees and the predictive utility of the Level of Supervision Inventory-Revised (LSI-R) in forecasts of recidivism. The LSI-R is an actuarial tool used to classify offenders into "high," "medium," or "low" recidivism risks. It is frequently used to assess the effectiveness of community programs involving offenders who are placed on probation or parole. Two research sites were used in the actual study. One was the Minneapolis-St. Paul area of Minnesota, and the other was two counties in Oregon. Do LSI-R scores assigned to female offenders in these jurisdictions enable supervising parole agencies to predict their likelihood of reoffending? Reisig, Holtfreter, and Morash defined recidivism as either a violation of supervision conditions, a rearrest, or a reconviction. Suppose these investigators obtained a sample of 150 female parolees who had recently been released from prison. Further suppose that these female parolees were studied over a 36-month period and their recidivism was tracked by these investigators.

Table 11.9 shows a hypothetical distribution of these female parolees distributed according to their LSI-R scores divided into high, medium, and low categories, and their actual recidivism, also divided into high, medium, and low classifications. Each cell in Table 11.9 has been lettered, from a to i, in order to simplify the computational work for calculating γ. Suppose the following hypothesis test were made:

$H_o: \gamma = 0$

$H_1: \gamma \neq 0$

$P \leq .05$ (two-tailed test)

TABLE 11.9 Attitudes of Hypothetical Sample of 150 Community Residents Toward Capital Punishment and the Brutalization Hypothesis

		LSI-R Scores Indicating Potential for Recidivism			
		High	Medium	Low	Total
	High	25 _a_	18 _b_	10 _c_	53
(Y) Degree of Recidivism	Medium	12 _d_	13 _e_	15 _f_	40
	Low	8 _g_	17 _h_	32 _i_	57
	Total	45	48	57	$N = 150$

The formula for gamma is

$$\gamma = \frac{\Sigma f_a - \Sigma f_i}{\Sigma f_a + \Sigma f_i}$$

where

Σf_a = the frequency of agreements

Σf_i = the frequency of inversions

The computational procedures for determining the frequency of agreements, Σf_a, and the frequency of inversions, Σf_i, are the same as were used for Somers' d_{yx} described in the previous discussion. It will also be noted that for purposes of comparison, the identical tabular frequencies have been used in Table 11.9 as were used in Table 11.8. In this instance, however, the row and column labels have been changed to match the research problem raised by Reisig, Holtfreter, and Morash. Based upon the tabular information, it is determined that Σf_a = 3,775 and Σf_i = 1,339. With these values, we may easily compute gamma as follows:

$$\gamma = \frac{3,775 - 1,339}{3,775 + 1,339}$$

$$= \frac{2,436}{5,114}$$

$$= .48.$$

We would interpret the absolute value of $\gamma = .48$ as a moderately strong association between the two variables, LSI-R scores and recidivism. A PRE interpretation would be that 48 percent of the variation in the two variables has been accounted for by their mutual predictability. If we had reconstructed this table such that LSI-R scores were the dependent variable and

BOX 11.7

SPSS Alternative Application

1. Open your *SPSS* software program and go to the *SPSS* Data Editor. Do precisely all of the steps you performed when computing Somers' *d*.
2. The result will yield three summary tables as before, a "Case Processing Summary," a "VAR00001-VAR00002 Crosstabulation," and "Symmetric Measures" table. The first table verifies your work in that 150 persons were examined. The second table duplicates the data in Table 11.8. If there are discrepancies, these must be corrected in your *SPSS* Data Editor before proceeding further. If these frequencies match those in Table 11.8, then continue.
3. The data in the third table disclose the γ value of .48 (rounded). This is consistent with the manual application of gamma described in the above discussion. Since gamma is a symmetric PRE measure, this .48 means that 48 percent of the variation in the two variables has been accounted for by their mutual predictability. But $1 - .48 = .52$ or 52 percent of the variation remains unexplained. See the discussion below for a manual calculation of a *Z* value for determining the significance of a γ value. For the present, however, the probability associated with a gamma this large is .000, and the null hypothesis can be rejected. There is a significant difference between 0 and the observed gamma = .48. By inference, we assume there is a significant association between the two variables.

recidivism were the independent one, the same γ coefficient of .48 would have resulted. Unexplained variation would be $1 - \gamma$ or $1 - .48 = .52$. In other words, 52 percent of the variation between LSI-R scores and recidivism is unexplained under these particular circumstances. It is interesting to note that Somers' d_{yx} applied to the same tabular data yielded a coefficient of .33. Thus, the gamma coefficient tends to yield stronger coefficients where all other circumstances are equal in any $r \times c$ table.

ASSUMPTIONS, ADVANTAGES, AND DISADVANTAGES OF γ The assumptions of γ include: (1) randomness and (2) two variables measured according to an ordinal scale. The favorable features of γ include that its absolute value is interpreted as a symmetric PRE measure. The range of γ values extends from ± 1.00, without the necessity of correction factors. Gamma has no specific limitations relating to either sample size or table size. In fact, of all the existing measures of association currently available for two ordinal-level variable situations, γ is most frequently recommended as the measure of association of choice. An *SPSS* program exists where data can be entered from any $r \times c$ table and gammas can easily be calculated, with probabilities disclosed.

One weakness of γ is that under certain conditions, perfect associations between variables of ± 1.00 will result when, in fact, perfect association doesn't exist. These situations occur whenever there are no frequencies in certain cells in an $r \times c$ table. These are extreme situations, however. Almost never will investigators have tabular arrangements featuring cells with no frequencies in them.

THE SIGNIFICANCE OF GAMMA, γ If a significance test of γ is desired, a Z approximation is available through the formula:

$$Z = (\gamma)\sqrt{\frac{\Sigma f_a - \Sigma f_i}{N(1 - \gamma^2)}}$$

Using our observed $\gamma = .48$ as well as other information from our example above, we can solve for Z as follows:

$$Z = (.48)\sqrt{\frac{3775 - 1339}{(150)(1 - .48^2)}}$$

$$= (.48)(4.592)$$

$$= 2.20.$$

Our resulting $Z = 2.20$. With a Z this large, we may conclude that our observed Z is significant at the .05 level of significance (± 1.96 are the critical Z values for the .05 level, two-tailed test) and H_o would have been rejected.

Finally, when γ is applied to 2×2 tables, it is identical to another measure of association known as Yule's Q. Yule's Q is a measure of association applied to 2×2 tables. Yule's Q is a measure of association for two nominal-level variables. Although gamma is designed for use with two ordinal-level variables, whenever variables at higher measurement levels are dichotomized, their ordinality is virtually eliminated and two nominal categories result. This fact means that collapsing ordinal-level larger tables into dichotomous 2×2 tables involves a loss of data. The data loss results from originally having ordinal-level data at one's disposal and eventually treating that same data in a dichotomous fashion (e.g., agree–disagree, weak–strong, high–low) which essentially reduces it to the nominal level of measurement.

Summary

Measures of association have been designed for different variable combinations under different conditions. Terms such as relationship and correlation seem more loaded than association, since causality between variables is mildly implied. Association may be viewed in terms of its strength, direction, nature, and significance. The strength of an association refers to how much the coefficient observed departs from "0" or no association. Subjective interpretive tables suggest that .00–.25 refer to low or no association; .26–.50 to moderately low association; .51–.75 to moderately high association; and .76–1.00 to high or strong association. The strength of an association is merely impressionistic, however. Better interpretations of coefficients are available.

We can also determine the direction of an association, whether it is positive or negative. Positive or direct associations between variables are reflected by positive coefficients of association, while negative or inverse associations between variables are indicated by negative signs. Sometimes, we must inspect our data to determine whether association coefficients seemingly positive are in fact negative, or whether a negative coefficient is positive. All of this depends on the formula used to generate the coefficient desired. Simply looking at one's data can often disclose the direction of the association in any event.

Association can also be assessed in terms of its statistical significance. However, there are limitations to making significance interpretations of coefficients. One of these limitations is that sometimes, large sample sizes used in research investigations are too large, and the sampling error is reduced to such a degree that just about any coefficient we observe might be statistically significant. Thus, an observed coefficient of .02 might be statistically significant at the .01 level of significance, but in reality, it means nothing. Thus, there is a difference between statistical and substantive significance. This is why we should exercise caution whenever applying tests of significance to measures of association.

The most productive way of looking at association coefficients is through proportional reduction in error or PRE. PRE is a measure of the amount of variation accounted for by the different variables being associated. This is frequently far more meaningful than the statistical significance or strength of an association. For instance, we may find statistical significance with a coefficient of .36, but such a coefficient may only explain 36 percent of the variation among variables. Viewed in those terms, $1 - .36 = .64$ means that 64 percent of the variation among the variables remains unexplained. Coin flips are better at predicting variation under such circumstances than actual associations between the variables themselves. Some coefficients must be squared in order to yield PRE interpretations. This sometimes makes the situation worse. In the case of a .36 coefficient, if we square it to get a PRE interpretation, this means that $(.36)^2 = .16$. In turn, this means that only 16 percent of the variation among variables is accounted for, while 84 percent of the variation is unexplained variation. For use in hypothesis testing as well as tests of theories, however, PRE interpretations seem to be most sound compared with other forms of coefficient interpretations.

This chapter has focused upon two-variable measures of association for nominal- and ordinal-level data. Such data are quite commonly encountered in the social sciences, including criminology and criminal justice. Attitudinal scores are most often measured according to ordinal-level scales, and numerous variables are dichotomous (e.g., felony/misdemeanor, first offense/prior record, male/female, and so forth). Other higher-level measures of association are discussed in Chapter 12.

For the first scenario of dealing with two variables measured according to the nominal level of measurement, seven measures of association were presented. Each of these measures is usually displayed in computer printouts from software programs such as *SPSS*. It is important for us to know the weaknesses, strengths, and assumptions underlying these different measures in order to know when to correctly apply them and how they should be interpreted.

Most of these nominal-nominal variables are chi-square based, meaning that they can be computed following the application of the chi-square test, and where a chi-square value is an integral part of their formula. As is known from prior discussion in previous chapters, the chi-square test is a test of significance of difference. Thus, if we know that a particular chi-square value is significant at some probability level, this means that resulting coefficients of association applied to the same data will be significant at those probability levels also, regardless of their magnitude. This is because tests of significance for chi square–based measures of association are chi-square tests themselves.

A chi square–based measure of association includes Pearson's C, the coefficient of contingency. This yields an index number which must be corrected in order to reach +1.00. The most desirable feature of C is that it is calculated directly from a chi-square value and is easily interpreted. Unfortunately, C has no PRE interpretation. In contrast, lambda is vastly superior to C. It has both a symmetric and an asymmetric PRE interpretation. Thus, we can not only account for the mutual predictability among variables, but we can also determine which variable is the better predictor of the other.

Ordinal-ordinal level variable measures of association include Somers' d_{yx} and Goodman's and Kruskal's γ. Each of these measures has a PRE interpretation. More flexibility is found in applications of gamma, however, and thus it is considered superior to Somers' d_{yx}. If we are able to achieve higher measurement levels with our data, then more sophisticated and informative measures of association may be applied. Some of these are presented in Chapter 12.

Key Terms

association *291*
asymmetric PRE
    interpretation *301*
axes *292*
axis *292*
coefficients of association *291*
correlation *291*
Cramer's V *304*
curvilinear *293*
curvilinearity *293*
degree of association *295*
direct association *297*
direction of an association *297*

error-free association *298*
explained variation *300*
Goodman's and Kruskal's
    gamma, γ *322*
Kendall's tau, τ *314*
Guttman's coefficient of
    predictability, λ *309*
inverse association *298*
linear *292*
linearity *292*
measures of association *291*
nature of association *295*
negative association *298*

Pearson's C, the coefficient of
    contingency *302*
Phi coefficient, φ *306*
positive association *297*
PRE *300*
relationship *291*
slope *295*
Somers' d_{yx} *318*
statistical significance of an
    association *296*
strength of an association *292*
symmetric PRE
    interpretation *301*

Questions for Review

1. What is meant by association, correlation, and relationship? How does each differ? Explain.
2. What is meant by the strength of an association? How is such strength determined? What is the meaningfulness of interpreting coefficients of association in terms of their strength? Explain.
3. What is the significance of an association? What are some of the problems encountered whenever tests of significance are applied to coefficients of association? Give some examples.
4. What is meant by PRE? How is PRE used as a way of selecting measures of association for use in data analyses? Explain.

5. What is meant by unexplained variation?
6. What is the best nominal-nominal variable measure of association and why? Explain.
7. What are chi square–based measures of association? How do chi-square values influence coefficients of association in chi square–based measures?
8. Differentiate between symmetric and asymmetric PRE measures.
9. What are some advantages of gamma over Kendall's tau and Somers' d_{xy}? Explain.
10. Differentiate between linearity and curvilinearity. Why is linearity important for some measures of association?
11. Do any of the measures discussed in this chapter require linearity? Why or why not? Explain.

Exercises

11.1. For the data in the table below, determine the requested values:

	Male	Female
Felon	55	32
Misdemeanant	36	98

a. Compute Pearson's C.
b. What can be said in terms of PRE about C? Explain.
c. What is the level of significance achieved by the chi-square observed?
d. What are the phi coefficient and Cramer's V for these data?
e. What is the chi-square observed for these data?

SPSS Alternative Application: If you have access to an *SPSS* program, you can follow the steps for computing this value from the chapter explanation.

11.2. For the following data, determine the requested values:

	Probation Officer Caseload			
	Low	Moderately Low	Moderately High	High
Job Satisfaction High	44	36	27	22
Medium	25	27	21	29
Low	18	19	26	44

a. Compute gamma and Kendall's tau. What PRE interpretation does each measure provide here? What interpretation can you make?
b. What is the statistical significance of gamma? Explain.

SPSS Alternative Application: If you have access to *SPSS*, you may compute gamma, Kendall's tau, and gamma. Theta, however, is not included among correlation coefficients computed by an *SPSS* program. Follow the steps outlined in each of the discussions in the chapter for *SPSS* Alternative Applications in order to determine these coefficients.

11.3. For the following table, determine the requested values:

		Type of Supervision	
		Close	General
Offender Recidivism	High	46	21
	Low	15	38

a. Determine Pearson's C for these data. What is the corrected C value? How should it be interpreted?
b. What is the chi-square observed for this table?
c. What are the phi coefficient and Cramer's V respectively?

SPSS Alternative Application: If *SPSS* software is available, follow the steps outlined in the chapter and compute the required values.

11.4. Determine the requested values for the data below:

		Type of Inmate Security			
		Minimum	Medium	Maximum	Admin. Max
Security Classification	High	14	18	24	28
	Medium	12	14	18	12
	Low	22	18	16	3

a. Determine lambda. Which variable is the better predictor of the other?
b. What is a symmetric PRE interpretation that can be made of these data using lambda?
c. What is this table size?

> **SPSS Alternative Application:** If *SPSS* software is available, you can compute these values by following the steps as outlined in the chapter discussion of lambda.

11.5. Determine the requested values for the information below:

		Victimized By Criminals	
		Yes	No
Fear of Crime	High	48	22
	Low	27	39

a. What is the coefficient of contingency, *C*, for these data? What is the corrected *C*, for these data? What is the PRE interpretation, if any? Explain.
b. What are the phi coefficient and Cramer's *V* respectively? Are either of these measures interpretable as a PRE measure?
c. What is the chi-square value for this table?

> **SPSS Alternative Application:** If *SPSS* software is available, enter the data from this table and make the necessary computations.

References

Champion, Dean John (2006). *Research Methods for Criminal Justice and Criminology*, 3/e. Upper Saddle River, NJ: Pearson/Prentice Hall.

Cochran, John K., Denise Paquette Boots, and Mitchell B. Chamlin (2006). "Political Identity and Support for Capital Punishment: A Test of Attribution Theory." *Journal of Crime and Justice* 29:45–80.

Flores, Anthony W. et al. (2005). "Evidence of Professionalism or Quackery: Measuring Practitoner Awareness of Risk/Need Factors and Effective Treatment Strategies." *Federal Probation* 69:9–14.

Hicks, W.L. (2006). "Police Vehicular Pursuits: A Descriptive Analysis of State Agencies' Written Policy." *Policing: An International Journal of Police Strategies and Management* 29:106–124.

Reisig, Michael D., Kristy Holtfreter, and Merry Morash (2006). "Assessing Recidivism Risk Across Female Pathways to Crime." *Justice Quarterly* 23:384–405.

Taylor, Bruce G., Robert C. Davis, and Christopher D. Maxwell (2001). "The Effects of a Group Batterer Treatment Program: A Randomized Experiment in Brooklyn." *Justice Quarterly* 18:171–201.

Walker, Jeffrey T. (1999). *Statistics in Criminal Justice: Analysis and Interpretation*. Gaithersburg, MD: Aspen Publishers, Inc.

White, William L. et al. (2005). "The Other Side of Burnout." *APPA Perspectives* 29:26–31.

Zink, T. et al. (2006). "Accuracy of Five Domestic Screening Questions with Non-Graphic Language." *Clinical Pediatrics* 46:127–134.

Measures of Association II: Interval Level and Alternative Level of Measurement Procedures

Chapter Outline

Chapter Objectives

After reading this chapter, the following objectives will be realized:

1. understanding measures of association for use when the interval level of measurement has been achieved;

2. describing several measures of association when two variables are measured according to two different level-of-measurement combinations; and

3. understanding the process of making proper measure-of-association choices.

INTRODUCTION

This chapter examines measures of association where the interval level of measurement has been achieved for both variables. In all cases, assumptions underlying the application of these measures, as well as their weaknesses and strengths, will be presented. All of these measures of association yield coefficients of association, or numerical expressions ranging from −1.00 (perfect negative association) to +1.00 (perfect positive association). These numerical expressions cannot always be compared directly with one another, and they have different meanings according to the measures used to derive them. These coefficients will be described and discussed. Some of these coefficients of association are parametric, while others are nonparametric. These will be indicated.

In criminological research, it is often the case that two variables to be correlated are measured according to different levels of measurement. For instance, one variable may be measured according to the nominal level of measurement, such as type of crime, while another may be measured according to an interval scale, such as the number of years of a prison sentence. Attitudinal variables are almost always measured according to the ordinal level of measurement. Therefore, specific measures of association are presented that exploit fully these different level-of-measurement variable combinations. Specific nominal–ordinal, nominal–interval, and ordinal–interval measures of association will be presented and discussed. Their assumptions will be presented and described. Again, each measure has a test of significance that may be applied. Also, the weaknesses and strengths of each of these measures will be examined.

The chapter concludes with a description of the criteria used in choosing the best measure of association for one's data analysis, where measures of association for two variables will be applied. Standard *SPSS* programs compute and display most of these measures for collected data or data sets. Thus, we are often faced with a variety of choices in deciding which measures of association are most suitable for our variables studied. A decision tree of sorts will be presented that will assist us in making the best choices among these various measures of association.

INTERVAL-LEVEL MEASURES OF ASSOCIATION FOR TWO VARIABLES

Whenever researchers obtain information measured according to interval scales, they may wish to apply measures of association that exploit these measurement levels achieved. Certainly variables such as income, years of education, sentencing terms, or magnitude of fines assessed would be examples of factors measurable according to an interval scale. At least two measures of association may be applied. These include (1) Spearman's rho, ρ and (2) Pearson's r or the product-moment correlation coefficient.

Spearman's Rho, ρ

A nonparametric measure of association for two interval-level variables that is extremely limited in its application is **Spearman's rho**, ρ. This procedure has conventionally been applied to data measured according to ordinal scales, although its arithmetic operations technically require that the data be measured according to an interval scale. Also, Spearman's ρ has a sensitivity to tied scores, similar to Kendall's tau, τ, and this sensitivity tends to undermine its effectiveness when considerable numbers of tied scores exist. An example of Spearman's ρ applied to criminology is provided.

James L. Johnson (2006) was interested in studying sex offenders and identifying those factors most likely to result in their probation revocation. Johnson investigated factors such as offender demographics (e.g., age, race, religious beliefs, socioeconomic status), criminal history or prior offending, time spent on probation prior to being revoked for a program violation, employment, and education. While there are numerous factors that might explain one's probation program revocation, suppose Johnson focused upon the employment records of sex offenders placed in probation programs. For sex offenders, is there an association between the amount of time these offenders spend on probation and employment stability? It might be argued, for instance, that those offenders who have stronger employment records also remain violation-free for longer periods compared with those offenders who have weak employment records or are underemployed or unemployed. Two scores must be calculated. First, a calculation needs to be made of the number of months a probationer is in a probation program before that program is revoked for one or more program violations. Second, a measure of the amount of time offenders are employed during their probation programs needs to be devised.

Suppose that Johnson focused upon a random sample of 20 sex offender/probationers for his research. In this instance, Johnson's focus would be upon those sex offenders whose programs had been revoked for one or more reasons. Johnson could easily determine when each of these offenders had been placed on probation, and thus he could calculate the number of months these sex offenders remained violation-free before having their programs revoked. He could also determine through monthly reports required of these probationers the percentage of time each was employed at different jobs. Thus, some sex offenders might be employed 100 percent of the time, some 80 percent of the time, some 10 percent of the time, and so forth. Both of these variables, time on probation prior to revocation and percentage of time employed while on probation, may be determined easily and ranked. Such rankings might be displayed in Table 12.1 for a random sample of 20 sex offenders whose probation programs were revoked.

Table 12.1 is constructed as follows. The numbers of months sex offenders have been on probation prior to the revocation of their programs is rank-ordered from most (1) to least (20). These ranks are placed in the first column as shown, ranging from 1 to 20. Suppose in this case the most number of months a sex offender was on probation was 32, while the least number of months was 6. The second column consists of the ranks assigned to each of the sex offenders according to the percentage of time they were employed while on probation. Suppose in this case the percentage of time employed ranged from 90 percent to 5 percent. These percentages have simply been converted to ranks. Column D represents the absolute differences between the two sets of ranks for both variables. Thus, sex offender 1 was on probation the longest, and he received the rank of "1." But the same sex offender 1 had the rank of "3" indicating he had the third highest amount of employment during his probation period. Sex offender 14 ranked 14

TABLE 12.1 Twenty Sex Offenders Whose Probation Programs Have Been Revoked According to Length of Time on Probation and Percentage of Time Employed

Revoked Probationer	Time on Probation Prior to Revocation Rank[a]	Percentage of Time Employed Rank[b]	D	D²
1	1	3	2	4
2	2	4	2	4
3	3	1	2	4
4	4	5	1	1
5	5	2	3	9
6	6	7	1	1
7	7	9	2	4
8	8	10	2	4
9	9	8	1	1
10	10	6	4	16
11	11	11	0	0
12	12	15	3	9
13	13	14	1	1
14	14	12	2	4
15	15	13	2	4
16	16	20	4	16
17	17	18	1	1
18	18	17	1	1
19	19	16	3	9
20	20	19	1	1
			ΣD^2 =	94

a = ranking of time on probation, most to least number of months
b = ranking of percentage of time employed while on probation, most to least amount
   of time

and 12 on length of time on probation and percentage of time employed, and so forth. These ranks of percentage of time employed while on probation are placed along side the ranks assigned the numbers of months on probation before revocation occurred. These D values are squared and placed in the final column, D^2. These D^2 are summed to determine the ΣD^2. The formula for Spearman's ρ may now be applied and is shown below:

$$\rho = 1 - \left[\frac{6\Sigma D^2}{N(N^2 - 1)} \right]$$

where

D^2 = squared differences between the two sets of ranks

N = sample size

6 = a constant value

Entering the values from Table 12.1, we determine rho as follows:

$$\rho = 1 - \left[\frac{(6)(94)}{(20)(400 - 1)} \right]$$

$$= 1 - \frac{564}{7{,}980}$$

$$= 1 - .07$$

$$= .93.$$

Our observed $\rho = .93$. A ρ this large is interpreted as a strong or high, positive association between the two columns of ranks. Rho has a symmetric PRE interpretation. In order to obtain a PRE interpretation for ρ, we must square the ρ value, or $(.93)^2 = .86$. Thus, 86 percent of the variation in the two variables is explained by their mutual predictability. Only $1 - .86 = .14$ or 14 percent of the variation in the two variables remains unexplained. There does appear to be a strong association between the length of time these sex offenders are on their probation programs and the percentage of time they are employed during that same period.

ASSUMPTIONS, ADVANTAGES, AND DISADVANTAGES OF RHO, ρ   The assumptions underlying ρ are: (1) randomness; (2) two variables measured according to interval scales; and (3) fewer than 25 percent tied ranks. Whenever 25 percent or more of the ranks on the two variables are tied, the meaningfulness of ρ diminishes. An elaborate correction procedure is described in Siegel (1956) and is beyond the scope of this book. It is highly unlikely that such large numbers of tied scores would ever exist under most research conditions, however. Furthermore, the result of correcting for tied ranks is negligible, even where large numbers of tied ranks exist. In short, even in the case of large numbers of tied ranks between variables, ρ would remain largely unchanged.

Spearman's ρ is easy to use, straightforward, and included in *SPSS* as well as other software programs used for data analyses. It has a symmetric PRE interpretation which is desirable.

BOX 12.1

SPSS Alternative Application

1. Activate your *SPSS* program and go to the *SPSS* Data Editor. Enter the two sets of values in the first two "var" columns. The first column will be ranks from 1 to 20. The second column will be unordered ranks. Once completed, you will have two columns, VAR00001 and VAR00002.
2. Click on "Analyze," then "Correlate," then "Bivariate."
3. This action will open a screen with two windows. Highlight VAR00001 and VAR00002 in the left-hand window and using the arrow, move these variables to the "Variables" right-hand window.
4. Click "Spearman," then "Two-Tailed," then "OK."
5. This action will display a summary table showing Spearman's rho, which is .929 or .93 rounded. This is the same result obtained from our manual calculations. The significance of this degree of association is displayed as .000, which means ρ is highly significant. The $N = 20$ is a check on your work to ensure that the proper number of persons whose ranked scores were correlated was entered.

Also, ρ has no distributional assumption, such as normality. Thus, whenever researchers have sets of ranked data with few ties, Spearman's ρ would be applicable without being required to meet stringent assumptions.

A TEST OF SIGNIFICANCE FOR RHO, ρ   Suppose we wished to test the significance of rho. We might hypothesize the following:

$H_o : \rho = 0$

$H_1 : \rho \neq 0$

$P \leq .01$ (two-tailed test)

If a significance test of ρ is desired, a Z approximation is available. This approximation is:

$$Z = \frac{\rho}{\rho_s}$$

where ρ_s = the standard error of ρ or

$$\rho = \frac{1}{\sqrt{N - 1}}$$

For the present problem, this Z would be calculated as follows:

$$Z = \frac{.93}{\dfrac{1}{\sqrt{20 - 1}}}$$

$$= \frac{.93}{\dfrac{1}{\sqrt{19}}}$$

$$= \frac{.93}{\dfrac{1}{4.359}}$$

$$= \frac{.93}{.23}$$

$$= 4.04.$$

A $Z = 4.04$ would be significant at the .001 level of significance (two-tailed test), since 4.04 equals or exceeds ± 2.58, the .01 critical Z value. While this Z approximation works best whenever our sample sizes exceed 30, it has been applied here to illustrate the application of Z. Whenever $N < 30$, a convenient interpretative table has been provided for evaluating the significance of ρ values. Table A.31 of Appendix A, p. 477, shows various critical values of ρ for the .05 and .01 levels of significance for one-tailed or directional tests and .10 and .02 significance levels for two-tailed or nondirectional tests. In Table A.31, our observed $\rho = .93$ clearly equals or exceeds the .01 critical ρ value for $N = 20$ (one-tailed test), which is .53. Therefore, using this table, we would say that our ρ value was significant at $P < .01$ (one-tailed test). While a directional test could have been made here since it was predicted that numbers of months on probation by sex offenders would be positively associated with the percentage of time employed while on probation, a simple nondirectional test was performed.

The Pearson r

The best-known parametric measure of association is the **Pearson product-moment correlation coefficient, r,** or simply the **Pearson r.** Until the mid-1950s, the Pearson r was the most favored measure of association used for correlating two interval-level variables. This was because the Pearson r was one of the only correlation options available to social scientists and others at the time. Only since the mid-1950s have we seen a proliferation of measures of association for different levels of measurement (e.g., nominal, ordinal) that are more appropriate for most variables studied in criminal justice and criminology. However, when all assumptions of the Pearson r are satisfied, the Pearson r is the most superior measure of association to apply. Unfortunately, the popularity of r and its stringent assumptions have led to numerous misapplications of it in the research literature. We will examine these limitations and restrictions of r in this section. The Pearson r is illustrated by the following example.

Daniel Nagin, Alex Piquero, Elizabeth Scott, and Laurence Steinberg (2006) investigated public preferences for rehabilitation versus incarcerating juvenile offenders. Their focus was partially upon punitive get-tough policies developed by politicians to combat rising juvenile violence. Get-tough policies often favor incarcerating juvenile offenders, and for longer periods in secure facilities, particularly if their offenses are especially violent. While Nagin et al.'s study focused upon a resident survey of whether juveniles should be incarcerated or rehabilitated for specific acts of violence, suppose they had wanted to know whether any relation existed between numbers of months incarcerated and severity of violent juvenile offenders. Suppose Nagin et al. studied a random sample of violent juvenile offenders who had been incarcerated for various periods in state juvenile facilities and had recently been released. Further suppose that Nagin et al. had obtained violence scores for each of these juveniles according to their adjudication offenses. Quantifying numbers of months incarcerated would be easy. As another step, Nagin et al. would have to assign "level of violence" scores to the adjudication offenses of offenders who had done institutional time. Suppose all violent juvenile offenses had been listed and "level of violence" numbers had been assigned to each of these crimes. To carry out this particular part of their study, Nagin et al. would simply have to correlate the two arrays of numbers, "number of months incarcerated" and "level of violence" scores. Table 12.2 shows a hypothetical distribution of such scores for 18 youths Nagin et al. may have studied.

If these researchers wanted to test a hypothesis about the association between the number of months incarcerated and the level of violence scores for the 18 youths studied, they would have developed a hypothesis set as follows:

H_o: $r_{xy} \leq 0$

H_1: $r_{xy} > 0$

$P \leq .05$ (one-tailed test)

The null hypothesis says that the association between variables X and Y (number of months incarcerated and level of violence scores) is "0" or no association or less than "0," meaning a negative or inverse association. The research hypothesis, H_1, says that there is a positive association between the two variables. In this case, the .05 level of significance is used for this hypothesis test. A test of significance for the Pearson r is available and is in the form of a Z approximation. It will be used to evaluate the observed r_{xy} later in this discussion.

Table 12.2 is constructed as follows. Two columns, X and Y have been created to show the number of months incarcerated (X) and the level of violence (Y) associated with their adjudication offense (1 = most violent, 20 = least violent). Three additional columns have

**TABLE 12.2 Numbers of Months Incarcerated in a Juvenile Facility and Level of Violence
Scores for 18 Violent Juveniles**

Juvenile	Numbers of Months Incarcerated (*Variable X*)	Level of Violence (*Variable Y*)	X^2	Y^2	XY
1	18	4	324	16	72
2	16	2	256	4	32
3	13	6	169	36	78
4	24	1	576	1	24
5	21	3	441	9	63
6	14	16	196	256	224
7	13	10	169	100	130
8	22	8	484	64	176
9	29	1	841	1	29
10	33	2	1089	4	66
11	21	4	441	16	84
12	10	7	100	49	70
13	7	9	49	81	63
14	19	12	361	144	228
15	15	8	225	64	120
16	19	7	361	49	133
17	14	9	196	81	126
18	13	2	169	4	26
	$\Sigma X = 321$	$\Sigma Y = 111$	$\Sigma X^2 = 6447$	$\Sigma Y^2 = 979$	$\Sigma XY = 1744$

been calculated. The third column is the squares of the "number of months" scores, X^2, $Y^2 =$ the squared level of violence scores, and XY is the product of the "months incarcerated" and "level of violence" scores respectively. With a knowledge of this information, we may compute the Pearson r for these data by applying the following formula:

$$r = \frac{N\Sigma XY - (\Sigma X)(\Sigma Y)}{\sqrt{[N\Sigma X^2 - (\Sigma X)^2][N\Sigma Y^2 - (\Sigma Y)^2]}}$$

where

$N =$ sample size

X and $Y =$ values on variables X and Y

X^2 and $Y^2 =$ squared values on variables X and Y

$XY =$ products of scores on variables X and Y

Substituting the values from the Table 12.2, we have.

$$r = \frac{(18)(1,744) - (321)(111)}{\sqrt{[(18)(6,447) - (321)^2][(18)(979) - (111)^2]}}$$

$$= \frac{31,392-35,631}{\sqrt{(13,005)(5,301)}}$$

$$r = -4,239/8,303$$

$$r = -.51$$

The resulting $r = -.51$. This negative r value is not in the direction originally predicted between months served in a juvenile institution and level of violence scores. This $r = -.51$ is a moderately high negative association between the two variables. Directionally, the association suggests that level of violence is inversely associated with longer time served. An explanation for this finding is beyond the scope of this text.

The absolute value of a Pearson r has a symmetric *PRE* interpretation. However, we must square this r value, where $r^2 = $ PRE. In this case, $r^2 = (-.51)^2 = .26$. Thus, 26 percent of the variation in the two variables has been accounted for by their mutual predictability. However, $1 - r^2$ is the amount of unexplained variation. With $1 - .26 = .74$, 74 percent of the variation in the two variables remains unexplained by their mutual predictability. This finding is not impressive. The directional association is inconsistent with what was expected as well. If these researchers, Nagin et al., had made such a finding, they would have to look elsewhere for explanations of variation in these variables.

THE STATISTICAL SIGNIFICANCE OF A PEARSON r.   The statistical significance of an r is easily determined by using a Z approximation, which is

$$Z = \frac{r}{s_r}$$

where

$r = $ observed r value

$s_r = $ the standard error of r, or

BOX 12.2

SPSS Alternative Application

1. Activate your *SPSS* software and go to the *SPSS* Data Editor. Create two columns, VAR00001 and VAR00002, for the first two "var" columns.
2. Enter the scores for number of months incarcerated from Table 12.2 in column 1, VAR00001. Enter the scores for level of violence in VAR00002, the second column.
3. Click "Analyze," then click "Correlate," then "Bivariate."
4. Two variables will appear in the left box, VAR00001 and VAR00002. Both variables should be highlighted and moved with the arrow to the right box, the "Variables" window.
5. Check the "Pearson r" box and "One-Tailed," since a one-tailed correlation is being made. Click "OK."
6. An output box will appear, showing the r value $-.51$ and the one-tailed significance of this value, which is .015. The N is also shown as a check on your work to make sure that you entered the proper number of persons with scores to be correlated.
7. A comparison of the significance level indicated, .015, is compared with the significance level at which the hypothesis was tested, .05 (one-tailed). Since .015 is equal to or smaller than .05, then H_o is rejected and H_1 is supported. Given the correlation's directionality, an appropriate interpretation is made of these results. As noted in the general discussion of findings, the result was in the opposite direction of that predicted. This was not the finding expected by these researchers.

$$\frac{1}{\sqrt{N-1}}$$

or

$$\frac{r_s}{\dfrac{1}{\sqrt{N-1}}}$$

For our observed $r = -.39$, we derive Z as follows:

$$Z = \frac{-.51}{\dfrac{1}{\sqrt{18-1}}}$$

$$= \frac{-.51}{.24}$$

$$= -2.13.$$

A $Z = -2.13$ is significant at the .05 level of significance, since critical values of Z of ±1.64 or higher are required for this level, making a one-tailed test. Two-tailed Z values for .05 are ±1.96. Had this level of significance been used, the observed Z would be significant. Since a directional prediction was made, that number of months incarcerated in a juvenile institution would be associated with the level of violence associated with these juveniles' level of violence, the resulting $Z = -2.13$ is significant statistically. However, Nagin et al. would have been disappointed in these results for two reasons: the direction of the association between variables was the opposite of that predicted under H_1. Not only was the association in the opposite direction predicted, but it was significantly in the opposite direction. A second disappointment would be that only 26 percent of the variation between the two variables was accounted for by their mutual predictability, while 74 percent of this variation was unaccounted for using a PRE interpretation.

ASSUMPTIONS, ADVANTAGES, AND DISADVANTAGES OF PEARSON r. There are five assumptions underlying the appropriate application of the Pearson r. These include: (1) randomness; (2) two interval-level variables; (3) linearity; (4) bivariate normal distribution; and (5) homoscedasticity. We are familiar with the first three assumptions. Linearity is manifested by the straight-line relationships between two variables illustrated in Chapter 11. Figure 11.3 illustrated curvilinearity. If the Pearson r had been applied to these data, the result would have been a Pearson $r = -.04$. This is essentially no association between the two variables. However, as was seen in Figure 11.3, a true curvilinear association between the two hypothetical variables existed. Had eta been applied, the result would have been an eta value $= .52$. This would be a moderately high degree of association between the two variables.

If the relation between the two variables in our present example, level of violence and number of months confined, had been nonlinear, then there is a good chance that a "canceling out" effect occurred, where increasing and decreasing values for one variable offset one another when correlated with the other variable. Failing to achieve linearity, therefore, may lead to small values of r, when in fact there may actually be a larger degree of association between the variables being correlated. The Pearson r is always unreliable under conditions of nonlinearity. When nonlinearity occurs, researchers might wish to use an alternative procedure, eta, the correlation ratio, η, discussed in the following section. Eta overcomes this distributional limitation and takes into account curvilinearity to show more accurate coefficients.

The **bivariate normal distribution** assumption is that both variables, X and Y, are normally distributed. It is very difficult for investigators to meet this assumption, since many distributions of scores encountered in criminological research of any kind are nonnormal. The assumption of homoscedasticity refers to how intersecting points of scores on variables X and Y are distributed around the line drawn through them. This line drawn through the intersecting points is referred to as the **regression line** or **best-fitting line**, where the distances between intersecting points of scores from the line are minimized. These lines are similar to those illustrating linearity in Figures 11.1 and 11.2 in Chapter 11. When investigators examine their data to determine if linearity exists, the intersecting points around the line drawn form an ellipse, shaped very much like a football. Figure 12.1 illustrates **homoscedasticity**. Any shape or pattern of intersecting points other than the one similar to that shown in Figure 12.1 fails to meet the assumption of homoscedasticity. Figures 12.2 and 12.3 show examples of scatter plots around regression lines that also do not exhibit homoscedasticity.

In order for r to be applied properly, all of these assumptions should be satisfied. Whenever one or more of these assumptions are not met, particularly the distributional assumptions of

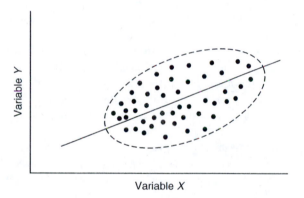

FIGURE 12.1   Homoscedasticity Between Two Variables

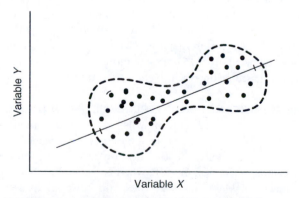

FIGURE 12.2   Scatterplot with no Homoscedasticity

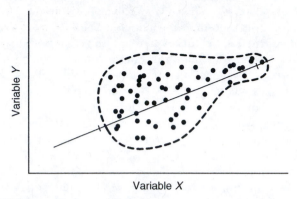

FIGURE 12.3   Scatterplot with no Homoscedasticity

linearity, a bivariate normal distribution, and homoscedasticity, there is a great likelihood that resulting r values will have little or no meaning. Thus, interpretations and discussions of subsequent meaningless r values are equally meaningless. Interestingly, much of the research literature where r is used does not indicate whether these distributional assumptions have been met. Thus, reported r values and discussions about them should be viewed with caution.

Favorably, the Pearson r is the best-known measure of association for data measured at the interval level of measurement. However, this popularity is both a blessing and a curse. It is a familiar measure, to be sure. It is reported in *SPSS* and all other software programs involving data analyses. We understand it and how it should be interpreted. But the sheer popularity of r doesn't necessarily mean that it is the most suitable measure for all criminological or criminal justice applications, however. Other alternative measures exist that can determine the degree of association between variables and do not have these restrictive assumptions.

The absolute value of r^2 is interpreted as a symmetric PRE measure. This is a positive feature of r. Further, it is unnecessary to rank scores in order to compute r values. Although the example used here involved a small sample size, r has no sample-size restrictions. Many students are overwhelmed by the complexity of the r formula. Luckily, virtually every computer program automatically computes r for any entered sets of scores. Thus, researchers can simply enter data into their computer programs and these complex mathematical operations are completed in seconds.

Disadvantages of r include the fact that several restrictive assumptions exist that severely limit the application of r in social research. But in actual practice, some or all of these assumptions are often ignored and Pearson r's are computed and interpreted anyway. This is where convention dominates in the professional literature. Another factor is that more complex prediction models frequently use r values. Thus, in order to use these more advanced techniques for elaborate data analyses, researchers must assume that their r values are sound and meaningful.

DETERMINING THE SIGNIFICANCE OF DIFFERENCE BETWEEN TWO PEARSON *r*s.   Before leaving the discussion of r, one final operation will be illustrated. Sometimes investigators seek to correlate several variables, two at a time. They may discover coefficients for multiple variables of .38, .42, .55, .62, .68, and so forth. These different coefficients mean that each variable has different explanatory power, or PRE, when correlated with some common variable. For example, if we have variable X and wish to explain it, we might use variables A, B, C, D, and E as predictors. Our separate two-variable coefficients, therefore, would reflect different degrees of association for *XA*, *XB*, *XC*, *XD*, and *XE*. It might be helpful for us to know whether two correlation coefficients differ from one another significantly. A test of significance of difference between two *r* values has been devised. This is the **Fisher Z approximation** or **Fisher Z transformation** and its formula is:

$$Z = \frac{Z_{F_1} - Z_{F_2}}{s_{Dz}}$$

where

Z_{F_1} and Z_{F_2} = Fisher Z values

s_{D_z} = the standard error of the difference between two Z_F values.

The s_{D_z} formula is determined by the following formula:

$$s_{D_z} = \sqrt{\frac{1}{(N_1 - 1)} + \frac{1}{(N_2 - 1)}}$$

where N_1 and N_2 are the two sample sizes for the *r* coefficients being compared. The hypothesis set we might use would be illustrated as follows:

$H_o: r_{xa} = r_{xb}$

$H_1: r_{xa} \neq r_{xb}$

$P \leq .05$ (two-tailed test)

Suppose Nagin et al. (2006) had correlated the number of months in a juvenile secure facility with prior record, r_{xa}, and also with offender needs, r_{xb}, where variables *A* and *B* were prior record and offender needs respectively. Prior record would include prior felonies, misdemeanors, and other offenses charged against incarcerated juveniles, while offender needs might refer to their level of need for counseling, drug addiction or dependency, and other services. Suppose Nagin et al. had obtained the following coefficients for the two variable combinations:

$r_{xa} = .66, N_1 = 60$

$r_{xb} = .79, N_2 = 60$

In this instance, both sample sizes are the same because Nagin et al. would have studied the same group of institutionalized youths. Had Nagin et al. studied two different samples of institutionalized delinquents, it is possible these sample sizes would be different. This situation might have occurred if Nagin et al. had studied youths from two different institutions who had completed their incarceration. For purposes of demonstrating the Fisher Z approximation, let us assume that both N values are 60. With a knowledge of the two Ns, we may calculate s_{Dz}. This value is calculated as follows:

$$s_{D_z} = \sqrt{\frac{1}{(60 - 1)} + \frac{1}{(60 - 1)}}$$
$$= \sqrt{.0170 + .0170}$$
$$= .1843.$$

The next step in determining the significance of difference between these two observed *r* values, .66 and .79, involves converting these coefficients to **Fisher Z values**. In order to do this, we must take these coefficients and compare them with coefficients found in Table A.26 of

Appendix A, p. 470. In Table A.26, various values of r are presented. Associated with each r value is a Fisher Z value, Z_F. The following Fisher Z values have been drawn from Table A.26:

$$r_{xa} = .66 = \text{Fisher } Z, Z_{F_1} = .7928$$
$$r_{xb} = .79 = \text{Fisher } Z, Z_{F_2} = 1.0714$$

With this information, we may now calculate our Z approximation:

$$Z = \frac{.7928 - 1.0714}{.1843}$$

$$= -\frac{.2786}{.1843}$$

$$= -1.51.$$

This Z value is interpreted as any other Z value using Table A.2 of Appendix A. The one- and two-tailed critical values of Z for the .05 level of significance are ±1.64 and ±1.96 respectively. In this instance, with a $Z_{obs} = -1.51$, these two r values do not differ from one another significantly even though r_{xb} is larger, .79, than r_{xa}, or .66. We would be unable to reject H_o under these circumstances. The only thing we can say about the two variables is that prior record correlates more strongly with length of time served compared with the level of offender needs for the juveniles studied.

OTHER MEASURES OF ASSOCIATION FOR DIFFERENT VARIABLE COMBINATIONS

This last section examines several useful measures of association that take advantage of different variable combinations, such as nominal/ordinal, nominal/interval, and ordinal/interval. Before investigators became aware of these specific measures of association, they typically reduced the higher-level-of-measurement variable to fit the lower-level-of-measurement variable, much like reaching the least common denominator. For instance, if investigators had information relating to type of crime and sentencing severity, "type of crime" might be measured according to a nominal scale, with categorical distinctions such as misdemeanor/felony or property/violent. Sentencing severity could be measured in years imposed as one's sentence. "Years" would be an interval-level variable. If investigators wanted to correlate type of crime with years sentenced, this would be a nominal/interval variable relation, since one nominal-level measure and one interval-level measure were being correlated.

Standard operating procedure for researchers would be to reduce the variables to the lowest level of measurement both would have in common. Since the properties of nominal scales are an integral part of interval scales, the interval-level variable would be reduced to the nominal level of measurement. Thus, we would take actual "years" of sentences and change them into "severe" and "not severe" or "harsher" or "less harsh." This categorical treatment of years of sentence would destroy the interval-level properties of the scale, since two discrete categories would be created that would be nominal at best. This would be "throwing away" the interval properties of the "years of sentence" variable and treating it as though it were a nominal scale. But such action would have to be taken, since mixed-variable measures of association were unfamiliar to most social scientists.

During the 1950s, Sidney Siegel (1956) broke new ground and provided a readable and comprehensive textbook about nonparametric statistics for the behavioral sciences.

This book also included an extensive discussion of previously lesser-known or unknown measures of association that would preserve the levels of measurement achieved by each variable's scaling procedure.

This section describes three measures of association that exploit fully the levels of measurement we have achieved in our research work. There is no longer any need to seek the lowest common denominator as researchers once did. The interval- and ordinal-level properties of different variables can now be preserved, and coefficients may be computed without throwing away valuable data properties. Also, these measures of association have become an integral part of software programs for data analyses, such as *SPSS*. Their application to criminological problems and determining associations between different variables will be illustrated here.

Three measures of association described here include (1) Wilcoxon's theta, the coefficient of differentiation, θ (designed for nominal/ordinal variable combinations); (2) eta, the correlation ratio, η (designed for nominal/interval variable combinations) and (3) Jaspen's *M* (designed for ordinal/interval variable combinations).

Wilcoxon's Theta, the Coefficient of Differentiation, θ

Theta, the coefficient of differentiation, θ, is a useful nonparametric measure of association between two variables when one variable is measured according to a nominal scale and the other variable is measured according to an ordinal scale. An example of the application of θ is provided as follows.

Carroll Seron, Joseph Pereira, and Jean Kovath (2006) conducted a study of citizen attitudes toward police officers and the actions taken by these officers in a series of hypothetical vignettes involving minority citizens. The vignettes presented various situations which involved different types of police misconduct in police–citizen encounters. A sample of persons was asked to indicate their thoughts about the severity of punishment that should be applied whenever officers engage in misconduct described in these vignettes. This study is one of many investigating police actions relative to minority citizens and how officers treat these citizens.

Suppose Seron, Pereira, and Kovath wished to learn if there was any relation between a citizen's race and police use of force when making citizen arrests. Suppose these investigators had collected data from a sample of arrested citizens and interviewed them concerning how much force was used by police when these citizens were arrested. These researchers may have selected a random sample of 131 black arrestees and 111 white arrestees. Then they could have cross tabulated these citizens according to their race and the amount of force officers used when arresting them, as shown in Table 12.3.

TABLE 12.3 Hypothetical Distribution of 242 Citizens According to Race of Citizen and the Use of Force by Police When Making Arrests

| | Police Use of Force in Making Arrests | | | | | | |
| | Low | | | | | High | |
Citizen Race	1	2	3	4	5	6	Total
Blacks	12	16	18	22	28	35	131
Whites	29	22	24	15	12	9	111
Total	41	38	42	37	40	44	$N = 242$

Table 12.3 shows some hypothetical information that indicates the amount of force used by police officers when arresting black and white citizens. A low amount of force or no force is represented with a "1," while the greatest amount of force is represented with a "6" in the table. Table 12.3 represents a situation we might likely encounter where one variable is measured according to a nominal scale (race) and the other according to an ordinal scale (police use of force).

A preliminary inspection of Table 12.3 suggests that the arrested black citizens sampled were subjected to greater force compared with the sample of arrested white citizens. Theta can be applied here to determine the degree of association between these two variables. The formula for theta is:

$$\theta = \frac{\Sigma D_i}{T_2}$$

where

D_i = absolute difference between the total frequencies above each rank and below each rank for pairs of nominal subclass variables, or; $|f_a - f_b|$

T_2 = each total frequency on the nominal subclasses multiplied by every other total frequency; these products are summed to give T_2

The procedure for determining theta is as follows. We begin with the first category (1), for low use of force, and multiply the cell frequency, 12, on the black subclass by the sum of all cell frequencies below and to the left of it on the white subclass. Since there are no frequencies below and to the left of 12, we move to the next cell to the right (2), and multiply the frequencies on the black subclass, 16, by the sum of all frequencies below and to the left of it on the white subclass. This is (16)(29). We proceed successively to the right until we have done this for all categories [the last category is (35)(29 + 22 + 24 + 15 + 12)]. The sum of these products yields our first value in the formula for D_i. The value we obtain is the f_a value.

Next, we move back to the first cell on the use-of-force variable, (1), and multiply the first frequency on the black subclass by the sum of all frequencies below and to the right of it on the white subclass. This becomes (12) (22 + 24 + 15 + 12 + 9). We continue moving to the right, one cell at a time, carrying out this procedure until we have determined all products. The sum of these products will yield our f_b value. The computation of f_b is left as an exercise:

$$f_a = (12)(0) + (16)(29) + (18)(29 + 22) + (22)(29 + 22 + 24)$$

$$+ (28)(29 + 22 + 24 + 15) + (35)(29 + 22 + 24 + 15 + 12)$$

$$= 464 + 918 + 1,650 + 2,520 + 3,570$$

$$= 9,122.$$

Once we have determined these values, we must determine the absolute difference between them, ΣD_i, or $9,122 - 3,306 = 5,816$. With a difference of 5,816 as shown, we divide this numerator term by T_2. This term is the product of all different category sums on the race variable or nominal variable. Since there are only two nominal variable subclass sums, 131 and 111, $T_2 = (131)(111) = 14,541$. With these values we may carry out theta, or $\theta = 5,816/14,541 = .40$.

Our observed θ is .40. This observed θ would be interpreted as a moderately low degree of association between the two variables. Since θ values are always positive (because of how the numerator term is determined), we must inspect the table to determine the direction of this coefficient. In this case, the association is inverse or negative. Thus, this theta coefficient would best be portrayed as $-.40$. Black citizens experience greater use of force by police, while whites experience less force, at least based on this hypothetical distribution of 242 frequencies.

BOX 12.3

SPSS **Alternative Application**

There is no *SPSS* application for Theta.

The absolute value of theta is directly interpreted as a symmetric PRE measure. In this case, 40 percent of the variation in the two variables, race and use of force by police, has been explained by their mutual predictability. Logically, race would be designated as "independent" in this instance, and "use of force by police" would be labeled as "dependent." Since theta is a symmetric PRE measure, rearranging the variables will not change its value.

TEST OF SIGNIFICANCE FOR THETA.   The computational procedure for determining the statistical significance of theta values is beyond the scope of this text and will not be discussed here. It is sufficient to use its PRE interpretation as the best way of understanding the association between variables in any event.

ASSUMPTIONS, ADVANTAGES, AND DISADVANTAGES OF θ.   The assumptions underlying the application of θ are: (1) randomness; and (2) one variable measured according to a nominal scale and the other measured according to an ordinal scale. There are no tabular or sample-size restrictions relating to theta's application. Theta computations become increasingly tedious for larger table sizes, although theta coefficients can be yielded rapidly through *SPSS* and other data analysis software programs. That theta has a symmetric PRE interpretation is a favorable feature of this coefficient. We do not need to square it or correct it to yield such an interpretation. Also, different theta values may be compared directly with one another, regardless of the differences in table sizes where theta values have been computed.

Eta, η, the Correlation Ratio

In an earlier discussion of the stringent assumptions associated with the application of the Pearson r, two distributional drawbacks of this measure were the requirement of linearity and a bivariate normal distribution. Eta, η, the correlation ratio, avoids these restrictive assumptions. Eta, η, a nonparametric measure of association, may be computed for two variables under one of two circumstances. The first circumstance is that both variables are measured according to an interval scale and one is treated as though it were measured according to the nominal level of measurement as a dichotomy. The second circumstance is that one variable is measured according to an interval scale, while the other is actually a nominal-level dichotomous variable. An example of the application of η is illustrated as follows.

Connie Stivers Ireland and JoAnn Prause (2005) studied samples of parolees who had been released under different paroling methods: mandatory or discretionary parole release. Under mandatory release, prison inmates are automatically discharged from prison after having served a specified prison term. Discretionary release is the practice of parole board review and determining prison release for inmates sentenced under indeterminate sentencing. Discretionary releases are subject to questioning by parole board members, and their parole chances are affected by several factors, including subjective opinions of parole board members about each inmate's potential to integrate into their communities successfully after being released. Mandatory releases are not subject to such subjective early-release decision making.

Subsequent comparisons of mandatory and discretionary parolees have disclosed contradictory information about their recidivism.

Suppose that Ireland and Prause wanted to study samples of recidivists from a jurisdiction with both mandatory and discretionary release policies. This scenario is possible because a state legislature can change the method of parole release for newly sentenced prisoners rather quickly. Thus, a prison inmate population may contain both those eligible for mandatory release as well as discretionary release. If Ireland and Prause were to examine a hypothetical random sample of recidivists, 13 inmates who had been released from prison under mandatory release and 14 inmates who had been released under discretionary release, they could count the number of months between release and a conviction for a new offense. Thus, mandatory release/discretionary release would be the dichotomous nominal-level variable, while number of months to reconviction for a new offense would be the interval-level variable. Such information might be presented in Table 12.4. Ireland and Prause might wish to know whether there is any association between the method of release from prison and recidivism, as measured by the number of months before a reconviction for a new offense. Thus, they might hypothesis the following:

$$H_o : \eta = 0$$
$$H_1 : \eta \neq 0$$
$$P \leq .01 \text{ (two-tailed test)}$$

TABLE 12.4 Method of Release from Prison (Variable X) and Recidivism

Mandatory ($N_1 = 13$)		Discretionary ($N_2 = 14$)	
Months to Reconviction for New Offense (Variable Y)			
Y_1	$Y_1{}^1$	Y_2	$Y_2{}^2$
27	729	28	784
40	1600	35	1225
19	361	42	1764
35	1225	39	1621
37	1369	41	1681
41	1681	47	2209
33	1089	62	3844
28	784	58	3364
26	676	41	1681
22	484	33	1089
27	729	29	841
26	676	47	2209
42	1764	49	2401
		42	1764

$\Sigma Y_1 = 403$ $\Sigma Y_1{}^2 = 13{,}167$ $\Sigma Y_2 = 593$ $\Sigma Y_2{}^2 = 26{,}377$

$\overline{Y}_1 = 31.0$ $\overline{Y}_T = 36.9$ $\overline{Y}_2 = 42.4$

(group 1 mean)   (grand mean)   (group 2 mean)

$\Sigma Y_1{}^2 + \Sigma Y_2{}^2 = \Sigma Y_T{}^2 = 13{,}167 + 26{,}377 = 39{,}544$

H_o says that there is no association between the two variables, whereas H_1 says that there is an association between the two variables. The level of significance is .01 (two-tailed test). The direction of association is not predicted in this instance since these researchers simply want to know if an association exists.

Table 12.4 has been constructed as follows. Variable X is the method of release from prison and is dichotomized into "mandatory release" and "discretionary release" and is the nominal-level variable. Variable Y would be designated as the interval-level variable, the number of months from release from prison to reconviction for a new offense. In Table 12.4, the Y variable values (numbers of months) are indicated for both mandatory and discretionary releases, Y_1 and Y_2 respectively. These values are summed and squared to yield ΣY_1^2 and ΣY_2^2. All columns are summed. Sample means are computed for the months figures for both groups as well. A grand mean is also computed. Finally, both columns of the sums of the squared scores are combined to yield ΣY_T^2. With these values, we may compute η, the correlation ratio, using the following formula:

$$\eta = \sqrt{1 - \frac{\Sigma Y_T^2 - (N_1)(\overline{Y}_2)^2 - (N_2)(\overline{Y}_2)^2 - (N_3)(\overline{Y}_3)^2 - (N_4)(\overline{Y}_4)^2}{\Sigma Y_T^2 - (N_1 + N_2 + N_3 + N_4)(\overline{Y}_T)^2}}$$

where

N_1 and N_2 = two sample sizes
Y_T = grand mean for groups 1 and 2 combined
$\overline{Y}_1$ and $\overline{Y}_2$ = mean scores for groups 1 and 2
ΣY_T^2 = sum of squared scores across both samples

Using the information from Table 12.4, we have:

$$\eta = \sqrt{\frac{1 - 39{,}544 - (13)(31)^2 - (13)(31)^2 - (14)(42.4)^2}{39{,}544 - (13 + 14)(36.9)^2}}$$

$$= \sqrt{\frac{1 - 39{,}544 - 12{,}493 - 25{,}168.64}{39{,}544 - 36{,}763.47}}$$

$$= \sqrt{\frac{1 - 1{,}882.36}{2{,}780.53}}$$

$$= \sqrt{1 - .68}$$

$$= \sqrt{.32}$$

$$= .56.$$

The resulting η value = .56. This would indicate a moderately high or strong association between income level and type of attorney.

THE STATISTICAL SIGNIFICANCE OF η. A statistical test of the significance of η values is obtained by a formula which approximates F values:

$$F = \frac{\eta^2 (N - k)}{(1 - \eta^2)(k - 1)}$$

BOX 12.4

***SPSS* Alternative Application**

═══

1. Activate your *SPSS* program and go to the *SPSS* Data Editor window. In the first "var" column, enter 13 "1"s and 14 "2"s, which will stand for "Mandatory" and "Discretionary" methods of release from prison. You will have 27 entries when finished.
2. In the second "var" column, begin typing in the months to reconviction, beginning with the first "Mandatory" group, or 27, 40, 19, 35, and so on. Continue entering these values until the last value of 42 is entered. Continue entering months in this same column (which is now VAR00002), continuing with 28, 35, 42, and so on, until the last value of 42 is entered. You will now have 27 entries in both columns VAR00001 and VAR00002.
3. Click on "Analyze" at top of screen, then "Descriptive Statistics," then "Crosstabs."
4. A window will open, showing VAR00001 and VAR00002 on the left-hand side, and "Row" and "Column" on the right-hand side. Highlight VAR00001 and move it with the arrow to "Row." Highlight VAR00002 and move it with the arrow to "Column."
5. Click the "Statistics" button at the bottom of the screen. This will bring up many correlation options. Among these is "Eta" for Nominal-Ordinal use. Check the Eta box, then click "Continue."
6. This action will return you to the screen with Rows and Columns marked with VAR00001 and VAR00002. Click "OK," and several tables will now be generated as a "Case Processing Summary." The last table shows "Directional Measures," Nominal by Interval, with VAR00001 Dependent and VAR00002 Dependent. Two values are shown, .761 and .557. Round the smaller value, .557 to .56. This is eta, the correlation ratio and is consistent with the .56 derived from the original formula presented in the general discussion of eta's computation.

═══

Using our observed $\eta = .56$, we can test its statistical significance as follows:

$$F = \frac{(.31)(27 - 2)}{(1 - .31)(2 - 1)}$$

$$= \frac{7.75}{.69}$$

$$= 11.23.$$

This observed F value of 11.23 may be interpreted by using the F table, Table A.19 in Appendix A, pps. 461–462. We enter this table with $k - 1$ degrees of freedom (across the top of the table), and $N - k$ degrees of freedom down the left-hand side. Where these values intersect in the body of the table define .05 (lightface type) and .01 (boldface type) critical values of F which must be equaled or exceeded by our observed F value. These degrees of freedom are $2 - 1 = 1$ df and $27 - 2 = 25$ df respectively. The critical value of F for the .01 level of significance is 7.77 in this case. In this instance, we may say that our observed η value is statistically significant at the .01 level. There is a statistically significant association between the method of release from prison and the number of months to first reconviction for a new offense among recidivists. Ireland and Prause can reject H_o and support H_1 in this instance.

ASSUMPTIONS, ADVANTAGES, AND DISADVANTAGES OF η. The underlying assumptions of η are: (1) randomness; (2) one variable measured according to an interval scale and one measured according to a nominal scale; (3) a continuous distribution for the interval-level variable; and (4) curvilinearity. While sample size recommendations pertaining to η have been for

Ns larger than 30, η is also appropriate for sample sizes <30 without significant distortion in the resulting coefficient.

The primary advantage of η is that it may be used as an alternative to the Pearson r whenever linearity cannot be assumed. There are no sample-size restrictions. η is easy to apply and interpret, and it has a symmetrical PRE interpretation. In order to make a symmetric PRE interpretation of η, we must square this value, or η^2 or $(.56)^2 = .31$. Thus, 31 percent of the variation in the two variables has been accounted for by their mutual predictability. Having a PRE interpretation is a distinct advantage of η. Alternatively, $1 - \eta^2 =$ unexplained variation. In this case, $1 - .31 = .69$, meaning that 69 percent of the variation in the two variables cannot be accounted for by their mutual predictability. Depending upon the investigator's standards, this amount of unexplained variation may be important.

Another positive feature of η is that its values may achieve 1.00 and can be compared with one another directly. Most computer software programs, such as *SPSS*, include η. There are no disadvantages of η for this specialized application, where one variable is measured according to a nominal scale and the other according to an interval scale.

Jaspen's *M*, the Coefficient of Multiserial Correlation

Jaspen's *M* is a nonparametric measure of association, is fairly unique and useful, since it is designed to determine the amount of association between variables where one is measured according to an ordinal scale and the other is measured according to an interval scale. Thus, attitude/income relationships and socioeconomic status/years of sentence are only a few of its many applications. An example from the professional literature illustrates the application of Jaspen's *M*.

Rick Ruddell and Robert Main (2006) were interested in jail officer training delivery programming. They noted that particularly for jail officers working in smaller jails, much of their work experience is hands-on, on-the-job experience, and that because of long distances from schools, it is simply impractical for many of them to travel to training centers or educational facilities to get more formalized training or accreditation as jail officers. Increasingly states mandate that all jail officers (and correctional officers in state prisons) must receive some type of refresher training as a part of labor agreements. Changes in the laws affecting inmate rights, new U.S. Supreme Court and state supreme court rules, and other factors are often not made available to all officers in an up-to-date fashion. The fact that there are numerous challenges that thwart conventional classroom training and other types of training delivery services has led to the creation of various E-learning or online methods for delivering needed remedial or refresher work. While not everyone in the correctional community is familiar with or accepting of E-learning methods, the fact is that such training does offer those officers in remote locations the opportunity to acquire accreditation and greater knowledge about their jobs through nontraditional means over the Internet.

The cost-effectiveness of E-learning is undisputed. It is cheaper to educate jail staff and others through the Internet as opposed to sending them great distances to attend seminars and special training sessions. This cost savings appeals to many community leaders and those in charge of funding jails. Suppose that Ruddell and Main wanted to know whether one's years on the job as jail officers/administrators were associated with their amount of knowledge acquired through an E-learning delivery system. Suppose these investigators were able to quantify the amount of information learned through particular E-learning courses. They might divide a larger sample of 47 jail officers into five subclasses on a "level of E-learning" variable, measured according to an ordinal scale. Furthermore, suppose they identified the years of service as jail officers/administrators accumulated by persons in the different subclasses. In order to determine

TABLE 12.5 Five Samples of Jail Officers According to Their Level of E-Learning and Years of Correctional Service

E-Learning Achievement Scores (Variable X)				
(High)				(Low)
5	4	3	2	1
Years of Correctional Service (Variable Y)				
15	16	5	10	2
17	12	10	12	5
19	8	12	10	11
23	3	4	8	4
14	20	10	2	6
28	14	9	7	4
22	13	8	5	7
12	12		5	9
9	10		5	6
15	10			
22				
21				
$\Sigma Y_1 = 217$	$\Sigma Y_2 = 118$	$\Sigma Y_3 = 58$	$\Sigma Y_4 = 64$	$\Sigma Y_5 = 54$
$\overline{Y}_1 = 18.1$	$\overline{Y}_2 = 11.8$	$\overline{Y}_3 = 8.3$	$\overline{Y}_4 = 7.1$	$\overline{Y}_5 = 6.0$
$N_1 = 12$	$N_2 = 10$	$N_3 = 7$	$N_4 = 9$	$N_5 = 9$

$$\Sigma Y = 511 \qquad \Sigma Y^2 = 7275 \qquad s_y = 6.05$$
$$N_T = 47 \text{ (i.e., } N_1 + N_2 + N_3 + N_4 + N_5)$$

whether the amount of E-learning was associated with years of service as jail officers/administrators, they might generate a table such as that shown in Table 12.5.

Table 12.5 is constructed as follows. Measuring one's level of E-learning according to an ordinal scale, they might divide the overall sample of 47 correctional officers into five groups, ranging from high E-learning achievement scores (5) to low E-learning achievement scores (1). After arranging these officers accordingly, they could enter the numbers of years each person has been as a jail officer/administrator. These years of service are shown for each sample according to their level of E-learning achievement. Subsequently means for each sample are determined, reflecting the average number of years each sample of jail officers has been affiliated with their jail. Additional computations include summing all years across groups, ΣY. Also, all individual scores are squared and summed, yielding a ΣY^2. All sample sizes are indicated. Finally, a s_y value is computed, which is the standard error of Y. This is computed by using the following formula,

$$s_y = \sqrt{\frac{\Sigma Y^2 - \frac{(\Sigma Y)^2}{N_T}}{N_T}}$$

using the values from Table 12.5.

With these values from Table 12.5, we may determine s_y as follows:

$$s_y = \sqrt{\frac{1719.234}{47}}$$

$$= \sqrt{36.579}$$

$$= 6.05.$$

The observed $s_y = 6.05$. We must now create an additional table. Table 12.6 shows the ranks of professional commitment, arranged from high to low, in the far left column. The next column contains the means for each sample. The third column, p, contains the proportion of each sample to the total number of officers, or 47 officers. The fourth column, C_p, is a cumulative proportion based upon the proportion values in the p column immediately to the left. The next column, o_b, contains ordinates for each of the cumulative proportion values in the column immediately to the left of it. These values may be found by turning to Table A.28, Appendix A, pps. 472–474. This table is arranged so that the various proportions may be found in either the far left column or far right column. Although these values are reported only to three places under "B, the larger area," we need to find the proportions that match each cumulative proportion in the C_p column. The first proportion, for instance, .26, has an ordinate value of .3244 associated with it. This ordinate column is the center column in each page of Table A.28. We proceed in this fashion until we have determined all ordinates and placed them as shown in Table 12.6.

Moving to the next column, o_a, these are ordinates that are above any ordinate shown in column o_b. Since there are no ordinates above .26 (from column C_p), we enter a "0." Moving down the o_a column, the first ordinate above .47 (from column C_p) is .3244 (from column o_b). We enter this value in column o_a as shown. Notice that column o_a is a repeat of column o_b down to and including the last ordinate of .2714.

The next column, $o_b - o_a$, is the difference between ordinates placed in columns o_b and o_a. These values are then squared and placed in the next column $(o_b - o_a)^2$. The values in this column are then divided by the corresponding proportion from column p. In other words, $.1052/.26 = .4046; .0054/.21 = .0257$, and so on.

The final column is the product of each sample mean with the value adjacent to it in the $(o_b - o_a)$ column. For example, the first product would be $(18.1)(.3244) = 5.8716$. Our primary

TABLE 12.6 Summary Table for the Jaspen's *M* Computation

Ranks	$\overline{Y}_i$	p	C_p	o_b	o_a	$o_b - o_a$	$(o_b - o_a)^2$	$\dfrac{(o_b - o_a)^2}{p}$	$(\overline{Y}_i)(o_b - o_a)^2$
5	18.1	.26	.26	.3244	0	.3244	.1052	.4046	5.8716
4	11.8	.21	.47	.3978	.3244	.0734	.0054	.0257	.8661
3	8.3	.15	.62	.3808	.3978	−.0003	.0003	.0020	−.1411
2	7.1	.19	.81	.2714	.3808	−.1094	.0120	.0632	−.7767
1	6.0	.19	1.00	0	.2714	−.2714	.0737	.3879	−1.6284
						0		.8834	4.1915

$$\Sigma \left[\frac{(o_b - o_a)^2}{p} \right] = .8834 \qquad \Sigma(\overline{Y}_i)(o_b - o_a) = 4.1915$$

interest is in these last two columns of values. The sums of these columns are shown in Table 12.6. With this information and the information from Table 12.6, we may compute M as follows:

$$M = \frac{\sum (\bar{Y}_i)(o_b - o_a)}{(s_y) \sum \left[\frac{(o_b - o_a)^2}{p} \right]}$$

Using the information from Tables 12.5 and 12.6 in the formula for M, we have

$$M = \frac{4.1915}{(6.05)(.8834)}$$

$$= \frac{4.1915}{5.344}$$

$$= .78.$$

Our observed $M = .78$. This would be interpreted as a strong or high association between one's professional commitment to corrections work and years of affiliation with the ACA. A symmetrical PRE interpretation is available by squaring this M value. Thus $(.78)^2 = .61$. We can conclude that 61 percent of the variation in the two variables has been accounted for by their mutual predictability. Sixty-one percent of the variation on the length of service as jail officers and E-learning achievement variables has been accounted for by their mutual predictability.

THE STATISTICAL SIGNIFICANCE OF A JASPEN'S *M*.   If a test of significance is desired for Jaspen's M, we might test the following hypothesis:

$H_o : M = 0$

$H_1 : M \neq 0$

$P \leq .01$ (two-tailed test)

In order to determine the statistical significance of Jaspen's M in this instance, we must convert our M value to an equivalent Pearson r value by using the following formula:

$$r = (M) \sqrt{\sum \left[\frac{(o_b - o_a)^2}{p} \right]}$$

Using the information we have determined from Table 12.6, we compute the desired r value as follows:

$$r = (.78) \sqrt{.8834}$$

$$= (.78)(.9399)$$

$$= .73.$$

BOX 12.5

SPSS Alternative Application

There is no *SPSS* formula for Jaspen's M.

Our observed r value is .73. We must now turn to Table A.30 in Appendix A, pps. 475–476 with N_T degrees of freedom. This table contains critical values of r for various levels of significance. For our example, with a $df = 47 - 2 = 45$, we would need to observe an $r > .372$ to achieve statistical significance at the .01 level. Our observed $r = .73$ is clearly statistically significant at .01 (two-tailed test). In turn, this means that we can reject H_o and support H_1, and conclude that our observed M is significant at the .01 level.

ASSUMPTIONS, ADVANTAGES, AND DISADVANTAGES OF JASPEN'S M.   The assumptions associated with Jaspen's M include: (1) randomness; (2) one variable measured according to an ordinal scale, and one variable measured according to an interval scale; and (3) the ordinal-level variable must be capable of being standardized or normalized. This is accomplished through the convenient procedure for determining ordinates.

A primary advantage of M is that it is suitable for two-variable associations where one ordinal-level variable and one interval-level variable are being associated. M has a symmetrical PRE interpretation which is also a desirable feature. M is included in many social science computer programs and is easily interpreted. On the negative side, it is obvious, even with applications for smaller sample sizes, that M is extremely tedious to apply manually. Existing software programs easily overcome these manual operations, however.

SUMMARY OF TWO-VARIABLE MEASURES OF ASSOCIATION

Table 12.7 is a convenient summarization of all two-variable measures presented in Chapters 11 and 12. The table is a cross tabulation of these measures according to different levels of measurement. The boxes contain appropriate alternative measures that may be applied whenever researchers have data where certain measurement levels have been achieved.

TABLE 12.7 Two-Variable Summary for Different Level-of-Measurement Combinations

	Nominal	Ordinal	Interval
Nominal	Pearson's C Cramer's V Phi, ψ Lambda, λ	Theta, θ	Eta, η
Ordinal		Gamma, γ Kendall's tau, τ Somers' d_{yx}	Jaspen's M
Interval			Spearman's rho, ρ Pearson's r

K-VARIABLE MEASURE OF ASSOCIATION

Kendall's Coefficient of Concordance, *W*

Kendall's **coefficient of concordance,** *W*, is a nonparametric measure of association for determining the degree of agreement between *k* variables where each has been measured according to an ordinal scale. For instance, perhaps we have data concerning the ratings of six state prison systems according to three different federal prison inspectors. These inspectors have examined each of six state prison systems and rank-ordered them from high to low according to the degree to which they are in compliance with certain federal standards of health and safety. Table 12.8 shows a hypothetical ranking of six different state prison systems by three different federal inspectors.

Table 12.8 is constructed as follows. Rankings from the three prison inspectors are assigned to each of the six state prison systems from 1 to 6 (high to low). In the case of a tie between ranks, the average of the ranks otherwise assigned would be given to both state prison systems. In the case of federal prison inspector 2, for instance, California and North Carolina were both ranked highest. Therefore, they are given the average of ranks 1 and 2, or 1.5 each as is shown. Next, the ranks assigned to each state prison system by each of the three federal prison inspectors are summed across each state prison system. For California, the sum of ranks would be $1 + 1.5 + 1 = 3.5$. This is done for each of the six state prison systems. Once these sums have been determined, these sums are summed as well. We will label this value as the sum of the rank sums, ΣRS.

The next step is to determine a distribution of rank sums based on the idea that all state prison systems receive equal rankings. This distribution is the equivalent to an expected set of cell frequencies that we might determine if we were to compute the chi-square test. In this case, we must take the *RS* and divide it by *N*, the number of state prison systems ranked. The sum of the rank sums, $RS = 63$, is divided by 6, or $63/6 = 10.5$. If there were perfect disagreement and all categories were ranked so that each rank sum was identical, 10.5 would be the expected rank sum for each of the state prison systems. We would expect rank sums for each prison system as shown in Table 12.9.

TABLE 12.8 Rankings of Six Prison Systems by Three Federal Prison Inspectors

Prison System	Prison Inspector			Rank Sum
	1	2	3	
California	1	1.5	1	3.5
Georgia	2	5	3	10
North Carolina	3	1.5	2	6.5
Florida	4	3	5	12
West Virginia	5	6	6	17
Louisiana	6	4	4	14
			$\Sigma RS = 63$	

TABLE 12.9 Expected Rank Sums for the Data in Table 12.8

State Prison System	Rank Sums
California	10.5
Georgia	10.5
North Carolina	10.5
Florida	10.5
West Virginia	10.5
Louisiana	10.5
	$RS = 63.0$

Next, we determine an S value, which is the sum of all squared differences between the expected and observed rank sums. This value, S, is defined as follows:

$$S = (10.5 - 3.5)^2 + (10.5 - 10)^2 + (10.5 - 6.5)^2$$
$$+ (10.5 - 12)^2 + (10.5 - 17)^2 + (10.5 - 14)^2$$

$$= 49 + .25 + 16 + 2.25 + 42.25 + 12.25$$

$$= 122.$$

The resulting $S = 122$. Once we have completed these operations, we may apply the following formula for W, the coefficient of concordance:

$$W = \frac{S}{(\frac{1}{12})k^2 (N^3 - N)}$$

where

$S =$ the sum of the squares of the observed deviations from the expected sum of ranks

$k =$ the number of persons doing the ranking

$N =$ the number of prison systems being ranked

Using the information from Tables 12.8 and 12.9, and with an $S = 122$, we determine W as follows:

$$W = \frac{122}{(.083)(3)^2 (6^3 - 6)} = \frac{122}{(.075)(216 - 6)} = \frac{122}{157.5} = .77.$$

With a resulting $W = .77$, we would interpret this W to indicate a strong or high degree of association that exists between the ratings of the three federal prison inspectors who examined six different state prison systems.

Another example might provide additional application potential of W. Suppose that we observed eight individuals in an organization, such as a probation department. These persons

TABLE 12.10 Rankings of Eight Probation Department Employees for Satisfaction with Pay, Working Hours, Work Associates, and Supervisors

| | | Satisfaction with: | | | Rank Sums | |
| | | Working | Work | | | |
Individual	Pay	Hours	Associates	Supervision	Observed	Expected
1	2	1	1	3	7	18
2	1	3	3	2	9	18
3	3	2	2	1	8	18
4	5	4	6	4	19	18
5	4	8	5	5	22	18
6	8	7	4	6	25	18
7	7	6	8	8	29	18
8	6	5	7	7	25	18
					$\Sigma RS = 144$	$\Sigma RS = 144$

completed questionnaires which measured the following variables: satisfaction with one's pay, working hours, work associates, and supervision. Assuming that if we ranked all raw scores for these variables for the eight persons examined, we might observe some hypothetical data, such as those shown in Table 12.10.

In Table 12.10, each person has been ranked according to the intensity of his or her score on each of the four variables. Each person's ranks are summed, and the resulting sum of rank sums, $\Sigma RS = 144$ as shown. Next, we determine the expected rank sum for each individual if all individuals were distributed equally for each of the four variables. This would be $\Sigma RS/N = 144/8 = 18$. If there were equal rank sums for all eight individuals, these rank sums would be 18. Note that these values have been placed conveniently in an expected column of rank sums.

The next step is to determine the value of S. Again, this is the sum of the squared differences between each expected rank sum and the adjacent observed rank sum, or

$$S = (18 - 7)^2 + (18 - 9)^2 + (18 - 8)^2 + (18 - 19)^2$$
$$+ (18 - 22)^2 + (18 - 25)^2 + (18 - 29)^2 + (18 - 25)^2$$

$$= 121 + 81 + 100 + 1 + 16 + 49 + 121 + 49$$

$$= 538.$$

The resulting $S = 538$. With this information and with the information in Table 12.10, we may compute W as follows:

$$W = \frac{538}{(.083)(4)^2(8^3 - 8)} = \frac{538}{(1.328)(512 - 8)} = \frac{538}{669.3} = .84.$$

An observed $W = .84$ is again a strong degree of association among the four variables: satisfaction with pay, working hours, work associates, and supervision. It would appear that persons who are highly satisfied with pay are also highly satisfied with the other work

> **SPSS Alternative Application:** There is no application for Kendall's *W* in *SPSS* software programs.

specifications indicated. Also, those persons who are less satisfied with one variable are also less satisfied with the others.

ASSUMPTIONS OF *W*.   Kendall's coefficient of concordance, *W*, assumes ordinal-level or rankable data for each and every variable correlated. Random sampling is also assumed.

ADVANTAGES AND DISADVANTAGES OF *W*.   When researchers are interested in determining the degree of agreement between *k* variables measured according to an ordinal scale, *W* is one of the only procedures that can be used to provide a fairly easy solution. There is no limit to the number of variables that can be correlated. There are no sample-size restrictions or distributional requirements underlying the proper application of *W*. The coefficient is interpreted in much the same way as any other measure of association for a two-variable situation. It does not have a *PRE* interpretation, however. Criminologists should find the *W* useful for *k*-ordinal variable associations. A chi-square test of significance may be applied to determine the statistical significance of a *W* value. This test is discussed elsewhere (Champion, 1981). This is an integral part of any *SPSS* program.

Summary

For two interval-level variables, two measures of association were presented. Spearman's rho and the Pearson *r* were described. Spearman's rho squared is a PRE measure, just as is the Pearson *r*. However, more complex measures of association presented in later chapters rely heavily on Pearson *r* values in their formulae to make the Pearson *r* the preferred coefficient.

This chapter has also described three very useful measures designed to take advantage of different levels of measurement associated with variables to be correlated. Their uniqueness enables special applications for different variable combinations without throwing out valuable data. Data are lost, for instance, where two variables are reduced to their lowest common level of measurement. If one variable is measured according to an interval scale and the other according to a nominal scale, in the past it was common practice to treat both variables as nominal ones and carry out a two nominal-variable measure of association such

as *C*, phi, or Cramer's *V*. With these special measures of association, however, we no longer have to disregard the higher measurement level properties of variables. Now we can treat each variable as it is measured. The three special measures included theta, eta, and Jaspen's *M*.

Theta, the coefficient of differentiation, is perhaps the most frequently applied measure of association, given the fact that it correlates one nominal-level variable with one ordinal-level variable. These types of two-variable associations are the most frequently occurring in criminological research. For two-variable associations where one nominal- and one interval-level variable are examined, eta, the correlation ratio, is applicable. This particular measure of association overcomes the distributional limitations associated with the Pearson *r*. Linearity and homoscedasticity do not have to exist. These less restrictive assumptions enable investigators to determine more reliable coefficients of association between variables, even if they are forced to dichotomize one interval-level variable and treat it as though it were nominal. This trade-off of giving up the intervalness of one variable in exchange for more reliable coefficients of association between variables make eta a definite contender whenever measures of association are sought for variables measured according to the interval measurement level. The last measure treated, Jaspen's M, is the most complex of all measures of association. It determines the degree of agreement or association between one ordinal and one interval-level variable. It's uniqueness in this respect renders it a very valuable measure of association indeed. A convenient summary table of all two-variable measures of association is presented in Chapters 11 and 12.

The chapter concluded with a description of a simple k-variable measure of association. This was Kendall's coefficient of concordance, W. This measure required no special knowledge other than the raw scores of k samples of subjects. Thus, a preliminary view of k-variable association measures was provided to show how k variables can easily be correlated.

Key Terms

best-fitting line *249*
bivariate normal
    distribution *249*
eta, η, the correlation
    ratio *345*
Fisher Z approximation *251*
Fisher Z transformation *251*
Fisher Z values *251*

homoscedasticity *249*
Jaspen's M *349*
Kendall's coefficient of
    concordance, W *263*
Pearson product-
    moment correlation
    coefficient, r *245*
regression line *249*

Spearman's rho, ρ *241*
Wilcoxon's theta, the
    coefficient of
    differentiation, θ *343*

Questions for Review

1. What are five assumptions associated with the Pearson r?
2. Does the Pearson r have a PRE interpretation? How is it interpreted?
3. Can we determine the significance of difference between two Pearson r values? What would be some advantages for being able to do so? Explain.
4. What is Jaspen's M? What are some limitations of it? Discuss.
5. What is eta, the correlation ratio? Under what circumstances should it be used? What other measure of association does eta replace as a desirable measure of association of certain distributional assumptions are violated? Explain.
6. What is theta, the coefficient of differentiation? What are its advantages and disadvantages?

Why is this measure especially popular among criminologists?
7. Compare and contrast the assumptions and applications of Spearman's rho with the Pearson r. Which is the better of the two measures and why? Explain.
8. What is meant by homoscedasticity? Why is it important? What measure of association assumes homoscedasticity?
9. What are the governing criteria for choosing a particular measure of association for determining the amount of association between variables? Explain each.
10. What is the value of knowing both the strength and significance of an association coefficient? Explain.

Exercises

12.1. For the following scores, determine Spearman's rho and the Pearson r.

Attitude Toward Job	Income (thousands)
18	56
15	44
19	74
22	68
13	41
15	45
18	52
26	55
25	57
21	40
31	52
24	36
29	59

a. What is the Pearson r for these data?
b. What is the statistical significance of it?
c. What is the PRE associated with the r observed?
d. What is Spearman's rho?
e. What is the PRE associated with rho?

> **SPSS Alternative Application**: If you have access to *SPSS* software, enter these values through the Data Editor and carry out the necessary computations.

12.2. For the following scores, determine Spearman's rho.

Variable X	Variable Y
21	58
32	45
26	51
29	55
19	44
15	43
12	40
20	50
33	65
31	28
35	45
34	68
14	36

a. Calculate the Spearman's rho for the above data.
b. What is the Pearson r for the same data?

> **SPSS Alternative Application**: If you have *SPSS* software, enter these data through the Data Editor and carry out the necessary computations as explained earlier in this chapter.

12.3. Observe the following data:

Years on Job	Correctional Officer Moderately		Job Satisfaction Moderately	
	Low	High	High	High
10+ years	15	22	28	35
5–9 years	21	26	22	28
1–5 years	52	38	17	10

a. Using theta, the coefficient of differentiation, determine the amount of association between the two variables.
b. How much variation in the two variables is explained by their mutual predictability?
c. How strong is the association between the two variables?

d. How would you interpret the results of the association between years on the job and correctional officer job satisfaction?

> **SPSS Alternative Application**: There is no application in the *SPSS* software for the theta coefficient.

12.4. Given the following scores for variables X and Y, determine the Pearson r.

Variable X	Variable Y
115	29
122	35
139	41
120	30
117	31
114	35
122	24
119	28
122	31
125	33
131	32
148	26
159	21
142	19
146	29
141	27
138	26
128	28
129	22
150	21
129	19
120	22
116	29
147	28
151	25
148	15
139	30
136	29
135	33
122	35
120	37
123	39
125	42
145	36
157	29
162	30

a. Calculate the Pearson r for the above data.
b. What is the statistical significance of the Pearson r you computed?
c. What is the PRE for the observed r? What interpretation can be made of this PRE?
d. What is Spearman's rho for the same data?
e. What are the major assumptions associated with applying the Pearson r?

SPSS Alternative Application: Use your *SPSS* software program, if available, and perform the steps necessary to carry out the Pearson *r* and Spearman's rho computations.

12.5. Below are various values for months to recidivism and parolee gender. Determine eta, the correlation ratio, for these data.

Months to Recidivism	Parolee Gender
22	Male
32	Female
21	Female
16	Male
24	Female
19	Male
30	Male
24	Male
18	Female
19	Female
12	Male
14	Male
18	Male
22	Male
31	Female
28	Male
27	Female
21	Female
17	Male
19	Male
10	Male
12	Female
15	Female
18	Female
21	Male
15	Male
18	Female
16	Female
19	Male

a. What is the observed eta value for these data?
b. Does eta have a PRE interpretation? Discuss.
c. What is the strength of association between these two variables? Provide a brief statement.

SPSS Alternative Application: Utilize your *SPSS* software, if available, and make your computation for eta.

12.6. For the following scores, determine Spearman's rho.

Individual	Variable X	Variable Y
1	9	7
2	17	10
3	16	5
4	10	6
5	8	9
6	14	11
7	18	15
8	7	4
9	15	8
10	6	3

a. What is the observed rho value?
b. Does rho have a PRE interpretation? If so, what is it?
c. Determine a Pearson's r for these same data.

> **SPSS Alternative Application**: If you have *SPSS* software, make the necessary computations by entering data through the Data Editor, and then carry out your analysis.

References

Champion, Dean J. (1981). *Basic Statistics for Social Research, 2/e.* New York: Macmillan.

Ireland, Connie Stivers and JoAnn Prause (2005). "Discretionary Parole Release: Length of Imprisonment, Percent of Sentence Served, and Recidivism." *Journal of Crime and Justice* **28**:27–49.

Johnson, James L. (2006). "Sex Offenders on Federal Community Supervision: Factors that Influence Revocation." *Federal Probation* **70**:18–32.

Nagin, Daniel S., Alex R. Piquero, Elizabeth S. Scott, and Laurence Steinberg (2006). "Public Preferences for Rehabilitation versus Incarceration of Juvenile Offenders: Evidence from a Contingent Validation Survey." *Criminology and Public Policy* **5**:627–652.

Ruddell, Rick and Robert Main (2006). "Evaluating E-Learning for Staff Training." *American Jails* **20**:39–43.

Seron, Carroll, Joseph Pereira, and Jean Kovath (2006). "How Citizens Assess Just Punishment for Police Misconduct." *Criminology* **44**:925–960.

Siegel, Sidney (1956). *Nonparametric Statistics for the Behavioral Sciences.* New York: McGraw-Hill.

CHAPTER 13

An Introduction to Multivariate Statistics

Chapter Outline

Chapter Objectives

After reading this chapter, the following objectives will be realized:

1. understanding the foundation of multivariate statistics and multiple regression;
2. understanding the concept of interaction;
3. examining the idea of linearity;
4. knowing what causation is and the steps important to causality;
5. understanding part and partial correlation and their difference;
6. understanding the meaning of robustness; and
7. understanding the interpretation of parsimony.

INTRODUCTION

It has been said that you can make the world spin with only two variables, orbit and axis. But do these two variables fully explain how the world revolves, and are there other factors that may also be part of the equation? The previous chapters have discussed assessment of relationships among variables. Most of the tests of these associations covered thus far have only dealt with two variables. Rarely, however, do social scientists and criminologists only consider two variables in attempts to explain the nature of our reality, or in our efforts to further understand phenomenon. In Chapter 12, several techniques were presented that allow us to examine how two variables are associated or related with one another, such as a bivariate correlation, or Pearson's *r*. However, these techniques do not allow us to assess the effect of a third variable in a relationship, or a fourth, fifth, or even sixth variable. If you were asked to name a variable that relates to criminal activity, such as robbery, most of you would name different variables. One cause for robbery might be prior record of the offender. Another might be poor socioeconomic circumstances or indigence. You might believe income or unemployment is also related to robbery. Family values and attitudes toward society may also influence the incidence of robbery. Age, gender, and education may also be listed as possible factors that relate in some way to robbery. The fact is that whenever explaining something as complex as crime, it is seldom the case that only one variable is causally related. The reality is that many variables influence robbery and its occurrence.

Similarly, when attempting to predict human behavior, many associations between numerous factors might be found. Often, some of the factors that predict phenomena such as crime are also related with each other. **Multivariate statistical analyses** allow us to account for several causally related factors. Multivariate statistics, such as those discussed here, as well as the multivariate techniques presented in Chapters 14 and 15, permit social scientists and others to explain sociological and criminological phenomenon such as crime as a dependent variable using modeling that accounts for all of the factors or independent variables that we believe may be related with variable we are interested in predicting. This chapter discusses the foundations of multivariate statistics as well as their theoretical and methodological limitations. This discussion will become especially important for understanding the various multivariate techniques discussed in Chapters 14 and 15 as well as their use and interpretation.

MULTIVARIATE REGRESSION ANALYSIS

Regression is an extension of Pearson's product-moment correlation, or the Pearson *r*. The goal of regression is to find the best-fitting line in a scatter plot of data points. In Chapter 12, it was learned that the Pearson's *r* examined relationships between two interval-level variables. An extension of the Pearson *r* is regression analysis, which assesses relationships among two or more variables. Relationships between a dependent variable and multiple independent variables are examined in such a way so as to provide the best corresponding value of *Y* for any value of *X*. If a straight line can be drawn through a scatter plot of points representing two variables, it is said that they are linearly related. **Linearity** is a primary assumption underlying multiple regression. Assuming linearity among variables allows us to be able to predict scores on a dependent variable, given a knowledge of scores on other independent variables.

This predictive ability can be illustrated with simple algebra. If variables are linearly related, we can represent the straight line between them with a mathematical equation. A linear equation is simply an equation that establishes that the points produced by the equation will yield a straight line as opposed to some other relation. Exact linearity means that for each data point on X, there is only one point on Y (Lewis-Beck, 1980). For each value on the independent variable, there is only one value on the dependent variable. For research in the social sciences in general and criminal justice specifically, few relationships between variables are exact, and therefore some error exists in all predictions or forecasts. An equation for a linear regression will be given in the following chapter, and this equation has an error term. **Linear regression** is a technique that can calculate the straight line in a scatter plot of data points, and the ordinary least squares regression method is the technique permitting us to find the best-fitting line.

If we have two independent variables believed to be factors in predicting some dependent variable, these two variables are said to have an additive effect. **Additivity** is the result of multiple variables each influencing the variance of a dependent variable. Each variable contributes in some way and to some degree to the explanation of the dependent variable. Therefore, with multiple independent variables we can gauge the independent effects each has on the dependent variable and then sum the total amount of variance these variables jointly explain in the dependent variable. This type of interaction between variables can be assessed through the Pearson r discussed in Chapter 12.

As with the Pearson r, regression examines the relationships between variables. However, this type of prediction becomes more difficult as more variables are added to our explanatory scheme. As the example above illustrates in accounting for various causes of crime such as robbery, we know that there are multiple factors that predict crime. One problem is isolating the relationships between each independent variable with the dependent variable, because often, the independent variables are also related with one another in some manner. For example, suppose it is believed that income is a factor that leads someone to commit robbery. We would likely use a measure of income as one independent variable in our prediction of robbery. Suppose we also believe that educational level influences robbery and its occurrence. Again we would devise and use a measure of educational level as an independent variable in our prediction of robbery. We want to know how much influence a person's income and educational level have on predicting likelihood of robbery. But then we recognize that one's income often depends on the educational level one has, and thus both income and education are related in some way to jointly influence robbery. Is education directly related to robbery, or does education only have indirect effects because it is also related to income? In this example we might say that education and income are interacting with one another jointly to produce an overall effect on the incidence of robbery.

In statistics, **interaction** refers to a change in one variable that is caused, or is associated with a change in another variable. In the robbery example, interaction would be the influence of two or more independent variables (education, income, prior record) on the dependent variable (robbery). Indeed, regression is a technique that can assess the combined effects or correlation of all independent variables on a dependent variable. But regression also gives us the separate effects of each independent variable on the dependent variable. Similar to a Pearson r analysis, regression asks what is the correlation between each of the independent variables and the dependent variable? In essence, **multiple regression** assesses the effects of multiple independent variables in predicting a single dependent variable. It conducts numerous Pearson r's simultaneously.

Figure 13.1 illustrates the problem with assessing effect on one dependent variable with two or more independent variables using the robbery example we have already used. In Figure 13.1, the dependent variable, robbery, and two independent variables, income and education, are depicted. These two variables have an effect on robbery, as illustrated by the circles for income and education overlapping the circle for robbery. However, the circles for

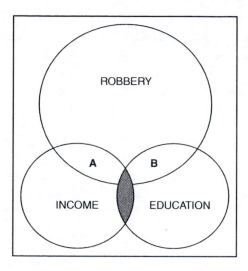

FIGURE 13.1 **Effects of Two Independent Variables, Income and Education, on a Single Dependent Variable, Robbery**

income and education overlap each other as well. This means that they are also correlated with one another, and that there is also a segment where overlapping areas of income and education are found within the circle of robbery. This means that these variables are interacting with one another to have an effect on robbery as well. Income and education have individual, separate effects on robbery, but they also interact to have a combined effect on robbery. One of the most important tasks of regression is to try to isolate the effects of independent variables used in our prediction scheme. If these variables overlap in their influence, our task of isolating their respective effects on robbery becomes more difficult. Since income and education are correlated or overlapped, our difficulty becomes isolating the independent effects of income and education on robbery, as shown in Figure 13.1 by the letters A and B. A and B in the illustration represent the independent or separate effects of income and education on robbery. The area shaded in Figure 13.1 indicates the area the two independent variables share with one another. This is the correlation between income and education, and also the area of the dependent variable, which is difficult to explain. If this shaded area is large, it is difficult to isolate the independent effects of each independent variable on the dependent variable.

As we will discuss in Chapter 14, one of the assumptions of regression is that there is little correlation or overlap between the independent variables. In statistical terms, this phenomenon is referred to as collinearity. If a great deal of collinearity exists between two variables, our regression analysis will be difficult to conduct. The primary reason the regression will not be difficult to conduct is that it is too problematic to calculate a coefficient that indicates the relationship between each of the independent variables' influence on the dependent variable because of their excessive overlap with one another. However, assessing the independent effects and the amount of overlap among variables can be done with formulae that have been created expressly for this purpose. This means that multiple Pearson r's need to be computed in order to assess the relationship between variables. This can be done through a **bivariate correlation matrix** or a **matrix of intercorrelations**. This can be computed in an *SPSS* program, which gives a table that represents every variable correlated with every other variable. Table 13.1 is a bivariate correlation table computed for sentencing data on offenders. From this table, we can judge the relationships between any and all variables. The equations for determining these relationships follow as do the brief description of the part and partial correlation.

TABLE 13.1 Bivariate Correlation Table.[a]

	X_1	X_2	X_3	X_4	X_5	X_6	X_7	X_8	X_9	X_{10}
X_1	1	.340	.150	−.150	−.095	.030	.012	−.082	−.026	−.042
X_2		1	−.450	.029	.111	−.049	−.058	.201	−.085	−.001
X_3			1	.020	.011	−.009	.007	.032	.137	−.004
X_4				1	.055	−.038	−.003	.037	.032	.006
X_5					1	.047	−.009	.683	.050	.015
X_6						1	.016	.037	.015	.022
X_7							1	−.016	−.025	.030
X_8								1	.025	.004
X_9									1	.013
X_{10}										1

[a] X_1 = conviction; X_2 = offender's age; X_3 = number of codefendants; X_4 = type of attorney; X_5 = offender's race; X_6 = offender's gender; X_7 = pretrial status; X_8 = offender's ethnicity; X_9 = number of charges; X_{10} = disposition type.

To illustrate the partial correlation between variables, we focus on three variables from Table 13.1: (1) conviction, (2) offender's age, and (3) the number of codefendants. The smaller bivariate correlation matrix of these three variables is reproduced below.

	X_1	X_2	X_3
X_1	1.00	.34	.15
X_2		1.00	−.45
X_3			1.00

Using these values, we can apply the following formula for the partial correlation. Using this formula, we can assess the strength of the relationship between the independent variable and a dependent variable, holding the effect of a third variable constant. In this case, we want to examine the relationship between offender's age and conviction while holding the number of codefendants constant. We also want to gauge the relationship between the number of codefendants and conviction while holding age constant. Therefore, the partial correlation is indicated by $r_{12.3}$, with the number to the right of the decimal indicating the controlled variable. The partial correlation between X_1 and X_3 would be $r_{13.2}$. Because these calculations may become complex as we add more variables as controls, researchers often use computer programs such as *SPSS* that can calculate these correlations rapidly. Indeed, multiple regression calculates the independent effects of a particular variable on a dependent variable, while holding all other variables constant. However, using only three variables, the partial correlation may be calculated manually. The calculations for the above variables would appear as follows:

$$r_{12.3} = \frac{r_{12} - r_{13}\,r_{23}}{(\sqrt{1 - r^2_{13}})(\sqrt{1 - r^2_{23}})}$$

$$= \frac{.34 - (.15)(-.45)}{(\sqrt{1 - .15^2})(\sqrt{1 - .45^2})}$$

$$= \frac{.34 - (-.067)}{(\sqrt{1 - .0225})(\sqrt{1 - .203})}$$

$$= \frac{.34 - (-.067)}{(\sqrt{.978})(\sqrt{.797})}$$

$$= \frac{.407}{(.99)(.893)}$$

$$= \frac{.407}{.884}$$

$$= .46$$

$R_{12.3} = .46$. This value may be interpreted as a moderate degree of association between an offender's age and conviction, where the number of codefendants is held constant. Next, we must calculate the relationship between the number of codefendants and conviction while holding age constant. This computation becomes:

$$r_{13.2} = \frac{r_{13} - r_{12} r_{23}}{(\sqrt{1 - r^2_{12}})(\sqrt{1 - r^2_{23}})}$$

$$= \frac{.15 - (.34)(-.45)}{(\sqrt{1 - .34^2})(\sqrt{1 - .45^2})}$$

$$= \frac{.15 - (-.153)}{(\sqrt{1 - .116})(\sqrt{1 - .203})}$$

$$= \frac{.303}{(\sqrt{.884})(\sqrt{.797})}$$

$$= \frac{.303}{(.94)(.893)}$$

$$= \frac{.303}{.839}$$

$$= .36$$

Again, although smaller than the first partial correlation, this coefficient is interpreted as a moderately low degree of association between the number of codefendants and conviction, holding the offender's age constant. The partial correlation between offender's age and conviction is .46, while controlling for number of codefendants. The partial correlation between number of codefendants and conviction is .36, while controlling for offender's age. Since the partial correlation for an offender's age (.46) is greater than the partial correlation for number of codefendants (.36), offender's age has a stronger impact on conviction. Therefore, we can compare the explanatory power among these and other variables. The variable with the largest partial correlation coefficient also has the strongest relationship with the dependent variable.

All of the assumptions that apply to the Pearson r for two interval-level variables also apply to multiple association measures that are comprised of multiple r values. Linearity, homoscedasticity, randomness, a bivariate normal distribution, and the interval level of measurement are the other assumptions underlying the proper application of the Pearson r. As we increase the number of variables to be correlated, however, we also increase the number of

BOX 13.1

SPSS Alternative Application

To obtain partial correlation coefficients for a number of independent variables, use the following steps:

1. To get partial correlation coefficients in *SPSS*, open the *SPSS* program and a data set of interest.
2. Next click on the tab at the top that says "Analyze", then click on "Correlate", then on "Partial". This will bring up a new window. It is in this window that you will have options to enter the dependent and independent variables from a list.
3. The next step would involve highlighting the variables of interest from the left hand window and moving it over to the appropriate box in the right hand window. In this instance we would want to use a number of variables. Find the variables you are interested in then highlight them and move them into the box labeled variables.
4. Next, highlight any variables you want to control for, and move them to the box on the right labeled "Controlling for".
5. Click on the tab "OK" and *SPSS* will calculate the partial correlations. A new window will pop up giving us our output for these calculations.

relationships between variables that may not be linear. We increase the likelihood of errors in interpretation of combined effects on the dependent variable as we increase the number of variables to be correlated. A common source of error in interpretation stems from the fact that a matrix of intercorrelations may combine variables that are not theoretically connected. For instance, the matrix of intercorrelations may correlate variables such as one's political affiliation, religion, and prior record. It is silly to believe that a true association exists between these variables. But when all variables imported from a survey or questionnaire are entered into a computer program, the program does not recognize the variables themselves but rather, the numbers only. All numbers are correlated, regardless of what these numbers represent. This is where meaningless correlations are obtained. Also, the variables correlated may be measured at different levels of measurement besides the interval level. Pearson r values should not be correlated unless both variables are measured according to an interval scale. Although many researchers use Pearson r computations for ordinal-level variables, including most attitudinal scales, it is simply wrong to use Pearson r computations for nominal-level variables such as gender, race/ethnicity, political affiliation, or religion.

For instance, suppose that a researcher were to gather data from a survey. A questionnaire containing 40 or 50 different variables could be administered. Sex, years of education, political affiliation, religious preference, age, socioeconomic status, fear of crime, any victimizations, race, ethnicity, satisfaction with the police, and many other variables could be included on the questionnaire. A bivariate correlation matrix will correlate all of these variables with one another. Pearson r's will be computed for the association between race and fear of crime, religious preference and political affiliation, years of education and satisfaction with the police, and any other nonsensical associations. Multiple correlations indiscriminately computed for these variables will be meaningless. Therefore, it is necessary that the researcher develops a consistent theoretical scheme that sets forth certain logical variable associations to be examined in detail. Multiple correlations are meaningfully interpreted only when they are generated from a coherent theoretical scheme. All too often, students accept as valid all information derived from or produced by computer printouts. Computers are not programmed to discern one variable or measurement level from another. Researchers must exercise discretion when interpreting computer printout information. The foundations behind the partial correlation are described in more detail below. The part correlation is also discussed, as it is sometimes important to see the unique variance between a particular independent variable and the dependent variable, or the contribution of an independent variable on the dependent variable that is not shared with any other variable.

Part and Partial Correlations

Partial correlation refers to the relationship between two variables, less the correlation or overlap from each of them. Thus, it is the effect of an independent variable on the dependent variable, less the overlap only between the independent variables, and not the overlap of the dependent variable. Therefore, it is the effect of an independent variable on a dependent variable, including the effect that another variable may interactively exert. The partial correlation between income and robbery in Figure 13.1 would therefore be section A including the shaded area of A, or the effect only, and excluding the shaded area between income and education. The partial correlation between income and robbery may actually overestimate the effect of income on robbery because it is including the effect of income on robbery that can also be attributed to education. The part correlation, therefore, will always be less than the partial correlation because the part correlation excludes the effect of variables such as income on robbery that can also be explained by education. The part correlation is a more conservative estimate of the effect of a particular independent variable on the dependent variable.

 Part correlation, sometimes called **semi-partial correlation**, is the foundation for multiple regression. The part correlation is the separate effect of an independent variable on the dependent variable, controlling for the other independent variables. Controlling variables means to hold other independent variables constant in order to assess the independent or unique effect of a particular independent variable on a dependent one. When the part correlation is squared, a **unique variance** is obtained. The unique variance is the amount of variance, or amount of the dependent variable explained, by an independent variable after the overlap with other variables has been eliminated. In Figure 13.1, this is the amount of robbery explained by income after eliminating the overlap with education. The unique variance for income on robbery would be section A less the shaded area, including the part of section A that is shaded. An easier way of understanding the difference between the partial and part correlation is illustrated by Figures 13.2 and 13.3.

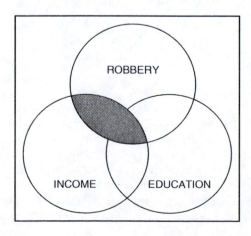

FIGURE 13.2   Partial Correlation Between Income and Robbery

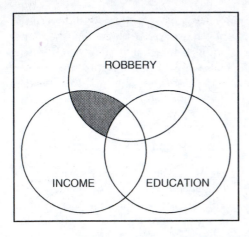

FIGURE 13.3 Part Correlation Between Income and Robbery

The partial correlation between income and robbery is shown in Figure 13.2. The part correlation between income and robbery is shown in Figure 13.3.

The formula for the part correlation is:

$$r_{1(2.3)} = r_{1.23} - r_{1.3}$$

The part correlation can be calculated easily from a knowledge of the partial correlation. We can use this formula and our results from the partial correlation to calculate the part correlation for the same variables. First, let's calculate the part correlation for offender's age with conviction. Remember that this will be the correlation between conviction and only that portion of an offender's age which cannot be due to number of codefendants.

$$r_{1(2.3)} = .46 - .15$$
$$= .31$$

The coefficient, .31, is the part correlation between offender's age and conviction, excluding the shared influence of offender's age upon the number of codefendants. If we square this value, $(.31)^2$, we can obtain the unique variance, or the proportion of explained variance in conviction that can be uniquely attributed to the age of the offender. Thus, $(.31)^2 = .096$. The offender's age is explaining nearly 10 percent of the variance in conviction. Let's calculate the part correlation for the number of codefendants with conviction, excluding the influence from the offender's age. This calculation becomes:

$$r_{1(3.2)} = r_{1.32} - r_{1.2}$$
$$= .36 - .34$$
$$= .02$$

Based on our calculations, the influence of number of codefendants on conviction is not as large as is the offender's age. If we square this value, we obtain .0004. This value represents the unique variance that the number of codefendants has with conviction. The number of codefendants explains less than 1 percent of the variance in conviction. This variable is not very influential. The part correlations are also usually less than the partial correlations we might obtain from the same information. Most of the partial correlation obtained for the number of codefendants was attributable to the overlap with offender's age. Again the two variables together may have a synergistic influence on the dependent variable, and this may add up to greater influence than the unique influence of each variable acting independently. An easier way of distinguishing the difference between the partial and part correlation, using the figures above, is that the partial correlation between two variables resembles a football, whereas the part correlation between two variables resembles a Pontiff's hat. Figures 13.2 and 13.3 illustrate these forms.

Both the part and partial correlations can be calculated fairly easily. For instance, we may have only two independent variables in our model. Again, this is unrealistic for criminal justice and the social sciences, because most models would use many independent variables, and a multiple regression technique is more useful for devising a satisfactory explanatory scheme.

In Chapter 14, it will be seen that in multiple regression, the combined effect of all of the independent variables together on the dependent variable can be considered and determined. This additivity of effects is represented by an R^2, or the **coefficient of determination**, sometimes called the **coefficient of multiple determination**. This coefficient discloses the amount of variance explained in the dependent variable where all of the independent variables have been combined. We cannot simply sum the unique variance of each independent variable to derive the variance explained by them simultaneously. This is because some of the independent variables are also correlated with one another. R^2, therefore, indicates the unique variance that each independent variable explains in the dependent variable, as well as variance explained by the correlation between all independent variables. The combined effects of variables would more satisfactorily explain a greater amount of variation in the dependent variable compared with the sum of the separate effects of individual independent variables. Again, part correlation coefficients are always smaller than the partial correlation coefficients.

BOX 13.2

SPSS Alternative Application

To obtain the part and partial correlation coefficients for the independent variables, the following steps may be used:

1. Open the *SPSS* program and a data set of interest.
2. Next click on the tab at the top that says "Analyze", then click on "Regression", then on "Linear". This will bring up a new window for the regression analysis. It is in this window that you will have options to enter the dependent and independent variables from a list.
3. The next step would involve highlighting the variables of interest from the left-hand window and moving it over to the appropriate box in the right-hand window. In this instance we would want to use a number of variables. Find the dependent variable and highlight it, then move it to the box for Dependent.
4. Next, the independent variables that you are interested in need to be highlighted on the left and moved to the box on the right entitled covariates.
5. Before you click "OK," click on the tab labeled "Statistics". This will open up a new window where you will have various options. Place a check mark in the boxes for part and partial correlation. Click "Continue" You will now be back to the window where you entered your variables of interest.
6. Click on the tab "OK" and *SPSS* will run the regression. A new window will pop up giving us our output for the logistic regression analysis, including the part and partial correlation coefficients.

For example, we know that being detained versus being released prior to trial has a positive effect on whether someone will receive a lengthy prison sentence. Those who are detained receive longer prison sentences than those who are released. We also know that going to trial and being convicted as opposed to pleading guilty through plea bargaining will most likely result in a longer prison sentence. If these factors are examined together, they may be explain more of the variation in prison sentence length than the amount each of them would explain if considered separately. Being detained and being found guilty through a trial may be very influential in explaining prison sentence length. These are some of the types of questions multivariate regression answers. In multivariate statistics, it is essential to know about the different interaction effects that are occurring between variables. If we have three independent variables, A, B, and C, and we believe that each influences a particular dependent variable, X, then there are three Pearson r's that must be calculated: A with the dependent variable, X; B with the dependent variable, X; and C with the dependent variable, X. There are also three interactions among the independent variables: A interacting with B; B interacting with C; and A interacting with C. Also, there may be further interaction between all three of these variables jointly on the dependent variable: A, B, and C with the dependent variable, X. These four interactions, therefore, are important in explaining the effects of our independent variables on the dependent variable.

The interaction between variables can be assessed through **path analysis**. Path analysis is an extension of regression analysis, and it assesses the effects of connections between variables in a causal model (Wright, 1921, 1934). It can be used to determine which of our hypothesized causal paths is best supported by our data. Path analysis uses a goodness-of-fit function and has assumptions similar to regression. Especially important are those assumptions that state that no relevant independent variables have been excluded from the model and no irrelevant variables have been included because these would clearly have an effect on the paths and coefficients that are produced by the model.

Path analysis estimates the significance and magnitude of our hypothesized relationships. It also gives us a more complete picture of a theoretical model and how the results of our analysis might appear. Essentially, a path diagram illustrates relationships between variables by illustrating connecting arrows between the related variables under investigation. The arrows are labeled with the coefficients of metric effects that describe each relationship between the connecting variables. These coefficients show the direction, significance, and strength of each relationship.

Brennan (2006) used a path diagram to illustrate the relationships between the likelihood of a jail sentence and various defendant characteristics for a sample of female misdemeanants. Some of these characteristics included age, prior convictions, educational level, employment status, pretrial release, and whether the females were married. Brennan was particularly interested in whether race and ethnicity directly influenced the likelihood of a jail sentence. Suppose Brennan was interested in diagrammatically illustrating relationships between several variables, but she wanted to show the relationship between certain variables and the likelihood of conviction. She could use the data from Table 13.1. Suppose she wanted to show what the relationship between offender's age (X_2) and the number of codefendants (X_3) would be on the likelihood of conviction and how such a relationship would appear in a causal diagram. Most likely it would look like the diagram in Figure 13.4.

Figure 13.4 shows the numbers used as labels for the arrows and they represent the partial regression coefficients for the relationships between variables. Both offender's age and number of codefendants are positively associated with conviction. However, offender's age has a stronger effect on conviction than the other variables. Offender's age is negatively

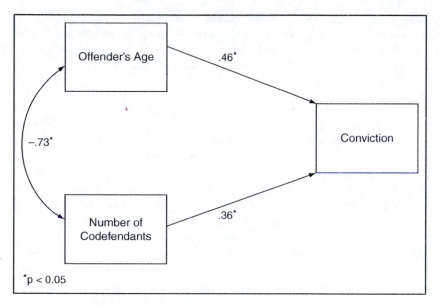

FIGURE 13.4 **Path Diagram of the Influence of Offender's Age and the Number of Codefendants on Conviction**

associated with the number of codefendants. Learned from this path diagram is the fact that both of our variables have a significant influence on the dependent variable, and also that they are somehow related with one another. We can better understand the relationships between variables in a path diagram, even if we do not have a full understanding of the statistical analyses underlying its application.

Path diagrams are important for a more advanced technique called **structural equation modeling** (SEM). SEM is also a technique for testing causal models of the relationships between variables. SEM is suitable for theoretical tests because it begins with hypotheses, then measures the variables of interest and tests the theoretical model. SEM is superior for calculating the relationships between multiple independent, dependent, and even latent variables (Kline, 1998). **Latent variables** are variables not directly measured, but rather, they can be estimated in the model from those variables that do have direct effects. Both path analysis and SEM are regularly used in criminology and criminal justice research. A comprehensive explanation of SEM is beyond the scope of this book, however.

SOLVING THE CAUSALITY PROBLEM

Examining the relationships and interactions among variables is also important for another dimension of our research. When assessing relationships between variables, we attempt to show **causality**. For instance, the bivariate correlation techniques discussed in Chapter 12 included some cautionary advice. That advice was that we should be careful when inferring causality between two variables because we have not controlled for other potentially important variables that may or may not be influential in our theoretical scheme. These precautions are especially important when doing research in the social sciences. Even in multiple regression, where we believe we have included and controlled for all important independent variables, we still exercise caution when making causal inferences between variables. Solving the causality problem involves three key steps: (1) establishing that a relationship or association exists among variables; (2) determining the time order or establishing that the cause comes before the effect; and (3) proving nonspuriousness, or eliminating rival causal factors.

Association

Establishing a relationship among variables is the first step in any research investigation. Although often in the social sciences this is not difficult because every variable seems to be slightly related to every other variable, if there is not at least some relationship between the variables studied, then further research is fruitless. Determining that an association exists is important because if the variables are not related in any way, then there can be no causal relation. Again, techniques discussed in previous chapters, especially those that examined bivariate relationships, are an integral part of this process. If association between variables is present, we are generally interested in two things about the association: (1) the strength of the relationship, and (2) the consistency to which it exists. The strength of the relationship, such as was illustrated by the Pearson r, is important because a strong association will be better in establishing causality than a weak association. However, consistency is concerned with how constant the relationship is over time and under various circumstances. For instance if males are always more likely than females to participate in criminal activity, no matter what the crime is, gender seems to have a consistent relationship with crime. If the bivariate correlations show strong relationships, or differences between males and females and crime as well, we can be fairly certain that indeed, a causal relationship exists between gender and crime. However, association by itself cannot infer cause–effect relations between variables. Indeed, since crime has been recorded, males have been more likely the perpetrators of it, however, true causality is difficult to infer and involves several important steps.

Time Order

The second step in establishing a causal relationship is to determine a **time order** between variables. In research, we usually examine variables at different times and assess any changes that may have occurred. This is important because in order to infer cause, the independent variable must be shown to either precede the dependent variable in time, or it must be shown that a change in the independent variable occurs before the dependent variable changes. We are primarily interested in changes in Y that seem to follow changes in X. If a change in the independent variable does not occur first, or if there is no change in the independent variable but a change occurs in the dependent variable, then it is difficult to establish a cause–effect relation. However, if there is an association between two variables, and if there is a change in the independent variable followed by a change in the dependent variable, then it is likely that there is some degree of causation which warrants further examination.

NonSpuriousness

The final step in resolving the causality problem is ensuring that no other variable is responsible for the original two-variable relationship. **Nonspuriousness** involves eliminating **rival causal factors**. Rival causal factors are any factors, other than the independent variable under investigation, that may be responsible for the change in the dependent variable. These variables are sometimes called **confounding variables**. In social sciences, there may be numerous confounding variables that might limit the researcher's ability to infer cause. If there are confounding variables unknown to the researcher, then the analysis and explanation of a causal relationship between variables is precarious. For both applied and theoretical types of research, if we have not included all possible influential variables, we cannot accurately infer cause–effect relations. This problem can be solved either through the analysis itself or by reference to theoretical principles. Using a criminological example, it is frequently believed that strong family ties are vital to whether someone will engage in criminal activity. On its face, this hypothesis is too one-dimensional. Obviously, this is not the case for everyone who commits a criminal act, as there are many persons engaging in illegal behavior who have strong bonds with their families. As well, there are many individuals who do not have close ties with their families, but nonetheless, they do not engage in law-breaking behavior. To test the theory that family ties are related to criminal activity, a more comprehensive model must be constructed which includes measures of family ties, bonds, and relationships. Unless other factors are included in the model because they are relevant variables, or factors are excluded from the model based on theoretical considerations, we will not have an accurately specified model. Sometimes it is difficult to determine which variables should be included and which ones should be excluded. Determining nonspuriousness through eliminating rival causal factors is a tedious process. We cannot always conduct experiments in the controlled environment of a laboratory setting. For instance, crime does not occur in a laboratory, and thus controlling for every confounding variable related to crime is seldom if ever achievable as is explaining every possible influential variable. In the study of human behavior, rival causal factors are numerous, and it is highly unlikely that criminologists and criminal justice researchers will be able to account for every possible factor related to a particular phenomenon.

However, researchers can use path analysis or SEM, which use both confirmatory factor analysis and path analysis to examine various relationships among variables. Nonetheless, solving the causality problem is a vital process in attempts to explain causal relationship among variables. Even if these three steps are followed, causality may still remain elusive. But satisfying each of these steps at least demonstrates a reasonable probability that relationships exist and some evidence is provided for an argument supporting a cause–effect relation.

OTHER KEY CONCEPTS FOR MULTIVARIATE ANALYSIS

A brief discussion of some additional concepts that are important in multivariate analysis is in order. Considering the idea that not every known variable can be incorporated into any analytical model, the following concepts become important when conducting explanatory statistical tests. These concepts are also addressed at length in Chapters 14 and 15. These include (1) error; (2) parsimony; and (3) robustness.

Error

Error is ever present in research. Researchers are aware of this error and attempt to control for it. Error exists in many forms, including random error, systematic error, observational error, and measurement error. When researchers control for error, an error term is always used in their statistical models. The regression formula, $Y = a + bX + e$, contains an error term. The "e" in the formula is the symbol for random error in this model. The "e" is also accounting for what is unknown. It has been said that truth is our knowledge plus our ignorance. The same seems true in research; we rarely know the exact truth, but we can better understand it if we admit there is some ignorance and include error in our statistical models. For instance, if we were testing the theory of differential association, stating that behavior is learned and delinquency is one learned experience, we would want to account for all types of relationships other variables may have with delinquency. We might want to look at relationships with peers, co-workers, and even family members. In a very practical sense, however, we cannot account for all possible variables that may measure these different relationships. If we can only adequately measure two of the types of relationships of importance for the theory, then we must include error in the model to account for the missing information we could not collect or have overlooked. Error must always be accounted for in multivariate statistical techniques. This is why a great deal of thought must be given to the theoretical and methodological planning of any multivariate analysis. Error is a fundamental part of any statistical model and must be given consideration in any research project. Several important assumptions regarding regression analyses deal directly with the error terms in our statistical models.

Parsimony

Parsimony means explaining the most with the least. A parsimonious model is one where no irrelevant variables remain in the model. If a variable contributes nothing to the overall explanation of a dependent variable, it is omitted from the analysis. We rarely have a complete picture of any phenomenon and why it occurs, and even when we do have a complete picture, we are often not in a position to include every concept in a form that accurately measures the true nature of the concept. Sometimes researchers attempt to capture all concepts or seek comprehensive tests of some phenomenon, including every imaginable variable. Although the resulting model may result in a slight increase in the amount of explained variation in the dependent variable, the model becomes far more complex than it needs to be. Probably most of the additional variables will not add much to the overall variation in the dependent variable.

Often used is an adjusted R^2 to gauge the variance explained, as this measure adjusts for the number of independent variables in the model. If there are variables in the model that explain only minimal variation, the total variance explained may be reduced. In short, the best model is the one that explains the most with the least. Attempting to achieve this type of model by adhering to the assumptions of including only relevant independent variables and excluding irrelevant ones is the nature of parsimony.

When studying phenomena such as crime, for instance, there are numerous factors that probably have a small influence on crime, but these can be measured and included in an accurate way so as to add to the models' explanatory power. **Occam's razor** is a principle that was developed by William of Ockham, which states that the simplest model is the best one. The minimum number of variables needed to explain the most variance is the best of several competing models. Basically, if one of our variables can be removed from the model without severely affecting the outcome, it should be removed from the model. However, if a variable has been proved in the past to be influential, or the theory states that the variable is an important indicator of a given phenomenon, perhaps the variable(s) should remain in the model. Ultimately, this decision is up to individual investigators, although if two models have fairly equal explanatory power, the simpler model should be chosen.

Robustness

There are numerous assumptions that must be met in order to be able to conduct multivariate regression analyses. Some of these are rather rigorous, especially for social science applications.

Robustness is the condition that under certain conditions, some of the assumptions of statistical analyses may be violated without serious repercussions or consequences for the subsequent numerical results. For example, in some instances, ordinal-level data may be used in analyses requiring the interval level of measurement if our N is large enough. However, this assumption may be relaxed or violated where other more important assumptions are met. For instance, the data must be normally distributed in order to conduct data analyses. There is some subjectivity about how robust techniques should be under certain assumption violations. Some researchers conduct analyses of data despite assumption violations, whereas others have serious reservations about their numerical results where one or more assumptions are violated. Robustness and robust statistics allow us to determine how much departure from the traditional assumptions is tolerable for the model before it becomes unreliable.

Mathematicians have continually researched how much deviation can be accepted before unreliability occurs. In 1953, Box used the term "robust" in statistics, and it has since been used to refer to procedures that will endure despite violations of one or more critical assumptions underlying various tests of significance. Some techniques provide accurate results even though interval-level measurement is not achieved, or if the data is slightly skewed or has kurtosis. Some procedures, such as the F test, have been determined to be robust despite various assumption violations, such as homogeneity of variance. As was seen in Chapter 4, the median as a measure of central tendency compared with the mean is a robust statistic when dealing with outlier scores. Robustness is important for those who conduct multivariate analyses because depending on the nature of the data being studied, the analytic technique chosen may depend on the robustness of it. In Chapter 14, ordinary least squares (OLS) regression will be discussed. This type of regression relies on the variance and the mean to calculate coefficients, and as such, it is not considered to be a robust technique. The choice to use OLS regression, therefore, depends upon the belief that all the assumptions have been clearly met.

Summary

This chapter has introduced multivariate statistics, or statistics for use with two or more variables. Some of the concepts and concerns important to multivariate techniques were introduced. Chapters 14 and 15 will provide a more comprehensive discussion of various types of multivariate regression techniques that are widely used in the social sciences and criminal justice. The discussion presented in this chapter, however, is intended to provide an introduction to and an initial understanding of the fundamentals underlying the use of multiple variables in research. These underlying foundations will be very important for implementing new research. Multivariate techniques are expansions of the bivariate techniques presented earlier in Chapter 12. In social science attempts are made to predict human behavior. In criminology, attempts are made to explain crime and delinquency and the factors contributing to these phenomena. These phenomena are associated with many factors that may be influential in explaining them. Also, we can almost always find associations between various factors and the phenomena we attempt to predict. Multivariate statistical analyses allow us to account for many of the variables that we believe are causally related. Indeed, causality is at the crux of all of our research activity. In order to solve the causality problem or attain greater certainty about causal relationships between variables, we must pay attention to three factors. First, does an association or relationship exist between key variables studied. Second, a time order between variables must be established. We must demonstrate that the cause preceded the effect, or that at least a change in the independent variable occurred before the dependent variable changed in value. Finally, rival casual factors must be eliminated. Controlling for or ruling out any other variables that could have produced the change in the dependent variable is important for establishing causality. If there is a variable that was not considered but could account for the outcome of the dependent variable, then assuming causality resulting from the chosen independent variables is very tenuous.

Linearity and additivity are also important to multivariate regression. Variables must be linearly related in order for regression to be successfully applied. The assumption of linearity among variables aides in prediction, as we are able to assess the scores on the dependent variable, given a knowledge of scores on independent variables. Additivity is that multiple variables should each contribute to the variance of the dependent variable. Basically, the influence of the independent variables is cumulative, as each variable adds something to explaining the dependent variable. Because of this assumption, we can also gauge the independent or separate effects that each independent variable has on the dependent variable. Assessing the separate effects as well as the interactive effects two or more independent variables may contribute to the dependent variable can be done with part and partial correlational procedures. Part correlation is the foundation for multiple regression, and it is the separate effect of an independent variable on

the dependent variable, controlling for the other independent variables. When the part correlation is squared, the result is the unique variance. The unique variance is the amount of the dependent variable that can be explained or accounted for by an independent variable after we have eliminated any interactions it may have with other variables. In contrast, the partial correlation is the relationship existing between two variables less the correlation between them that is influential. It gives us the effect of an independent variable on a dependent variable including the effect that the correlation may have with another variable.

Finally, the concepts of error, parsimony, and robustness are also important to discussions of multivariate techniques. There are numerous instances in multivariate regression analyses where these concepts are extremely important. Some of the most widely used statistical techniques for assessing the influence of multiple independent variables on a single dependent variable will be discussed in Chapters 14 and 15. These include OLS regression, logistic regression, ordinal regression, multinomial regression, and Poisson and negative binomial regression. Other techniques have been developed for assessing the relationships between multiple independent variables and a dependent variable, and the techniques that appear here are those most often used by criminologists and criminal justice researchers. In Chapters 14 and 15, interpretations of the effects each independent variable has on the dependent variable will be examined, as well as how to interpret the overall combined effect that the independent variables jointly exert on the dependent variable.

Key Terms

additivity *274*
association *284*
bivariate correlation
    matrix *275*
causality *283*

coefficient of
    determination *281*
confounding
    variables *284*
error *285*

interaction *274*
latent variables *283*
linearity *273*
linear regression *274*
multiple regression *274*

Questions for Review

1. Describe linearity and additivity as they relate to linear regression analysis.
2. What do we mean when we say that two variables interact?
3. What is a bivariate correlation matrix? What does it allow us to do?
4. What is the difference between the part and partial correlation? What is the unique variance and how can it be calculated?
5. What is the coefficient of multiple determination? What can it tell us?

6. What is the purpose of a path diagram?
7. What are the important steps in solving the causality problem? Explain each.
8. What do we mean when we say that we must have parsimony in our models? Why is parsimony important?
9. What does it mean to say that a particular technique is statistically robust? What does robustness allow us to do?

Exercises

13.1. From the bivariate correlation matrix in the chapter, calculate the partial correlations between the variables type of attorney and offender's race and conviction. The Pearson r's are provided in the table below.

	X_1	X_4	X_5
X_1	1.00	−.15	−.095
X_4		1.00	.055
X_5			1.00

SPSS Alternative Application: If you have access to *SPSS* software, open a data set of your choice and run the partial correlations as explained earlier in the chapter.

13.2. Calculate the part correlation for the above variables of type of attorney and offender's race.
    a. Figure out the unique variance for these variables.
    b. How much of the variation in conviction are we explaining with each of these variables?

    c. How do the partial correlations compare to the part correlations for these variables?
    d. Which of the variables has the stronger relationships with conviction?

13.3. Calculate the partial correlation for variables X_6 (offender's gender) and X_7 (pretrial status) with conviction from Table 13.1. Which of these partial correlations shows the strongest effect on conviction?
    a. Calculate the part correlation for these two variables.
    b. From the part correlation calculate the unique variance for these two variables.
    c. Which of the four variables (X_4, X_5, X_6, X_7) shows the strongest relationship with conviction?
    d. Which of the four variables (X_4, X_5, X_6, X_7) explains the most variation in the dependent variable conviction?

13.4. Draw a path diagram for the above four variables using arrows to show the relationships between variables. Link the four independent variables with each other.

References

Brennan, Pauline, K. (2006). "Sentencing Female Misdemeanants: An Examination of the Direct and Indirect Effects of Race/Ethnicity." *Justice Quarterly* **23**:60–95.

Kline, Rex B. (1998). *Principles and Practice of Structural Equation Modeling.* New York, NY: The Guilford Press.

Lewis-Beck, M. S. (1980). *Applied Regression: An Introduction.* Newbury Park: Sage Publications.

Wright, S. (1921). "Correlation and Causation." *Journal of Agricultural Research* **20**:557–585.

Wright, S. (1934). "The Method of Path Coefficients." *Annals of Mathematic Statistics* **5**:161–215.

CHAPTER 14

Multivariate Statistics: Multiple Regression

Chapter Outline

Chapter Objectives

After reading this chapter, the following objectives will be realized:

1. understanding the assumptions of ordinary least squares regression;

2. examining the limitations of multiple regression;

3. understanding multicollinearity and how to assess its presence;

4. knowing what remedies are available for correcting collinearity;

5. understanding the concept of dummy variables;

6. examining interaction effects using dummy variables; and

7. understanding the interpretation of a multiple regression output.

INTRODUCTION

Many researchers conduct studies using univariate and bivariate techniques. Few dependent variables, however, can be explained with a single independent variable. Often researchers use multivariate techniques. For those engaging in more in-depth research, multivariate analysis is warranted. Multivariate statistics, as well as some of the fundamental mathematics important to this analysis, were discussed in Chapter 13. This chapter will extend these ideas as well as explore multiple regression strategies more intensively. There are numerous types of multiple regression techniques available for researchers but probably the most widely used, at least in criminology and criminal justice, is OLS or ordinary least squares regression. Suppose investigators wanted to find out what influences a judge's decision about sentence lengths they will impose on convicted offenders? Do judges only consider legal factors? Or do they also consider extralegal factors, including defendant age, gender, or race/ethnicity when imposing sentences? These are just some of the many questions that can be answered using multiple regression techniques. Suppose researchers wanted to learn about the influence of all of these factors together as they might impact sentence lengths? But what if they also wanted to determine the independent effects of gender or race and their specific influence of how one's sentence might be affected? **OLS regression** is an appropriate technique for this kind of question because it can determine the combined effect of all relevant independent variables on the dependent variable, as well as determine the independent effects of each variable separately on the dependent variable. With OLS regression, a researcher can determine how much variance in sentence length is explained with all the independent variables together as well as the separate effects each independent variable, such as gender or race/ethnicity, have on the sentence lengths of different types of offenders.

ORDINARY LEAST SQUARES REGRESSION

Ordinary least squares (OLS) regression is a widely used technique in criminology and criminal justice research, and it is usually the first technique covered about multiple regression in a statistics class. This does not mean that it is the easiest statistical technique, but rather, when researchers refer to regression, they are referring to OLS regression. Other regression techniques, such as regression with limited dependent variables and for variables at the ordinal level of measurement, will be discussed in Chapter 15. OLS regression is used for dependent variables that are measured at the interval level. It is an extension of Pearson's product-moment correlation coefficient (r). The goal of regression is to determine the best-fitting line in data values with two or more variables in such a way so as to provide the best corresponding value of y for any value of x. Regression uses least squares analysis, which selects the straight line that minimizes the **sum of the squares** of the errors. This technique minimizes the distances between X and Y values. It is an estimation method that calculates coefficients by minimizing the sum of the squared **residuals**, which are the differences between the actual Ys and the predicted Ys from the regression analysis. OLS regression therefore minimizes the sum of the difference between the actual and predicted Y. Multiple regression allows us to assess the linear effects of an independent variable on the dependent variable while controlling for all the other independent variables. We can also gauge the influence of all the independent variables together on the dependent variable.

ASSUMPTIONS

OLS regression analysis is not a difficult technique to undertake because of various statistical software programs that are available today. But in order to utilize OLS regression, there are several assumptions that must be met. Frequently, meeting these assumptions is one of the most difficult parts of regression analysis. The following is a list of the assumptions of OLS regression and the consequences of violating one or more of them. See Studenmund (1997), Lewis-Beck (1980), and Berry (1993) for a more extended discussion of these assumptions and the consequences for violating them.

Assumptions Regarding the Variables

The assumptions underlying OLS regression are: (1) the variables for study are measured at the interval level; (2) the relation between the variables X and Y is linear; (3) no relevant independent variables have been excluded from the model; (4) no irrelevant independent variables have been included in the model; (5) the independent variable is quantitative and dichotomous; and (6) the dependent variable is quantitative and continuous.

Regression analysis uses the **variance** and the mean as its roots, and if data are not amenable to using the variance or mean, then they are not suitable for regression analysis. Regression analysis also assumes that the independent variables are quantitative or **dichotomous** and that the dependent variable is quantitative, continuous (meaning it can take on any value), and unbounded. Because we assume scores on the dependent variable are a result of scores on each of the independent variables, the dependent variable must be able to assume any value. If this is not the case and the dependent variable is not quantitative (interval level), continuous, and unbounded, the scores predicted for the dependent variable might occur outside of the possible range of the dependent variable.

Specification Error

The next set of assumptions has to do with **specification error**. Are we using the proper equation that accounts for changes in the dependent variable? Under this set of assumptions, the relationship between X and Y must be linear in the coefficients and error terms. If the relationship is nonlinear, OLS regression is not appropriate even if the variables are strongly associated with each other. The easiest way to determine whether linearity exists is to examine bivariate scatter plots. When looking at a scatter plot of the residuals plotted against the predicted values, no visible pattern should be present. If nonlinearity exists, there are transformations that can be made. However, a discussion of such transformations is beyond the scope of this chapter. Not all variables are amenable to linear transformations. Whenever a transformation is conducted, it should be supported in both practical and theoretical ways.

Two other critical assumptions regarding specification error are that no relevant independent variables have been excluded from the model, and no irrelevant independent variables have been included in the model. We do not want to omit any important causes of our dependent variable, and we do not want to include any irrelevant variables that will undermine the influence of the other more meaningful independent variables. We also do not want to include variables that should be in the model but are not measured correctly. Incorrect measurements would violate the assumption of linearity. We also do not want to include in the model two variables that are highly correlated with one another. If two variables which are highly correlated are incorporated into the model, the regression will not be able to distinguish between the independent effects of each of these variables. Detecting these specification errors requires that researchers reexamine the theoretical foundations of their studies or methodologies involved rather than anything that can be statistically identified. If there are variables in the model that should not be there, they can simply be removed from the analysis. After these variables are removed, if there is little change in the R^2, the variable can safely be eliminated from the analysis. If a variable needs to be integrated into the model because of its theoretical relevance, then some amount of specification error can be tolerated. Regression analyses should always be driven by theory. Therefore, if an independent variable isn't significantly influencing the dependent variable, but if it is important theoretically, it can always be included in the model. Deciding whether all the important variables are included in the model is a misspecification problem that is more difficult to resolve. Again, we should revisit our theory to determine which variables are relevant predictors. If an R^2 is low, this could indicate that important variables are missing from the equation. Whatever those variables happen to be, however, can only be known from one's theoretical or methodological frameworks. Lastly, we can determine whether two variables are highly correlated by examining the bivariate correlation of all of the independent variables. If two independent variables are highly correlated, their standard errors on the regression output may be quite large.

Assumptions About the Error Terms

The remaining assumptions about regression involve the **error term**. As with any other statistical technique, a degree of error is involved in regression analysis. Our intent is to try to minimize the amount of error that occurs in the analysis. If we have a great deal of error present in our regression model, the results may be unstable or unpredictable and produce an inflated impression of the variance explained. The first assumption regarding the error term is that the residuals have a mean of zero. In other words, the deviation of the mean of residuals must sum to zero. The points on the regression line have to be averages so that our residuals will have a mean of zero. If we do not meet this assumption, our coefficients will not be biased, however, the intercept, or starting point of the regression line will be incorrect.

The second assumption is that our errors are homoscedastic. This simply means that our errors about the regression line are constant and form an ellipses. Homoscedasticity was discussed in Chapter 12 in relation with Pearson's r. The average variance of the errors about the regression line must remain constant along the entire regression line. If this is not the case, then we have **heteroscedasticity** which means that the variance of the error terms depends on which case we are examining. Heteroscedasticity may occur when we have a data set where the difference between the smallest and largest observed values is large. If we have homoscedastic error terms, we can assume that all of the observations of the error term come from the same distribution.

Another assumption is that we also have no autocorrelation among errors. **Autocorrelation** means that errors for cases in close proximity with each other are correlated. We do not want to have autocorrelation. If this occurs, our coefficients may be biased and the standard errors associated with our b-coefficients will be underestimated. The next assumption is that the independent variables in the model must not be correlated with the error term. If they are correlated, some of the influence of an independent variable will inflate the error term and reduce that independent variable's actual influence, thereby making the *b*-coefficient for that independent variable biased.

Another assumption dealing with the error term is that the errors are normally distributed about the regression line. In other words, there are more errors close to the line than far away from it. This is the normality assumption not with the variables themselves, but rather their errors. Normality must also hold across the entire regression line. If these error terms are not normally distributed, our significance tests will be invalid.

The last assumption dealing with the error term is that we can have no perfect **multicollinearity**. This means that we can have no independent variable or group of independent variables that is perfectly correlated with another independent variable or group of independent variables. In a regression analysis, we want our independent variables to be correlated with our dependent variable but not with the other independent variables. **Collinearity** is when two variables are correlated with one another, whereas multicollinearity is when this condition occurs among more than two variables (Studenmund, 1997). In social science research, criminal justice, and criminology, there will always be some degree of collinearity between the variables that we study. In dealing with social science phenomena and behavioral variables, almost every variable is related to some degree. For example, in studying the causes of crime, we may believe that income, education and age are influential in determining whether someone will engage in criminal activity. However, income is sometimes dependent on education and education is often correlated with age. Regression analysis is robust enough to be utilized with some collinearity among the different variables used. Diagnosing the situation and making regression work appropriately with some degree of collinearity will be examined later in this chapter.

When these above assumptions of regression are fully met, we can be certain that our regression coefficients will be unbiased. The **Gauss-Markov theorem** states that if the above assumptions are met, the OLS regression is the best linear unbiased estimator (Studenmund, 1997). Our coefficients will be designated as minimum variance, meaning that the sampling distribution of coefficients will be centered and tightly clustered about the mean of *b*. OLS regression gives us the smallest standard error of any regression technique. The standard deviation of the distribution of *b*-coefficients is called the standard error of *b*. Whenever we have a tightly clustered distribution like the one OLS gives us, the smaller the standard error will become. Lastly, the distribution of coefficients will be normally distributed when we meet the assumptions, and this will allow us to carry out tests of significance. If any of these assumptions are violated, the *b*-coefficients for our regression will be biased estimates of the effect of our independent variables on the dependent variable. Therefore, it is important that the assumptions of OLS regression are met in order to be able to run the regression model. We will also be more certain of the accuracy of our interpretation of the output from this analysis.

THE REGRESSION EQUATION

Multivariate analysis formulae can be very complex and difficult to understand. Because of this complexity, the formula for OLS regression will be given, although it will only be briefly discussed. Indeed, several mathematical calculations are involved but are very tedious when calculated by hand. Multiple regression is a statistical technique that allows us to explain changes in one variable (the dependent variable) based on changes in other variables (independent variables) with a single equation. The reason we can interpret the *b*-coefficient as the change in *Y* for a unit change in *X* from an ordinary regression is because the *b*-coefficient is the **first order partial derivative** of a linear additive model. The first derivative (dy/dx or $\Delta y/\Delta x$) of the equation for a dependent variable is the rate of change in Y for a change in X. The simple regression formula is given with the following equation:

$$Y = a + bX + e$$

In this equation Y is the predicted value of an independent variable, a is the intercept, b is the slope of the regression line, X is the value for the independent variable, and e is the error associated with the model. This formula is probably recognizable as the same one that is associated with Pearson's r. In algebra, this is also the equation for the slope/intercept of a straight line. In a multiple regression equation, this simple formula is expanded to include the number of independent variables that will be in the regression model. Thus, a multiple regression equation would be displayed as follows:

$$Y = a + b_1 X_1 + b_2 X_2 + \cdots b_k X_k + e$$

In this equation, each of the bs represents a coefficient that is associated with an independent variable and the Xs represent the value of an independent variable in the multiple regression model. In this equation, the predicted value of Y depends on a number of independent variables, including error.

In order to assess the goodness of fit of a multiple regression equation we utilize the R^2, or the coefficient of multiple determination. The R^2 of a regression equation will give us the proportion of variation in our dependent variable (Y) that is explained by all the independent variables. This formula and its statistic, which comes out as part of the regression output can be easily obtained through statistical software programs, is as follows:

$$R^2 = \frac{\Sigma(\hat{Y} - Y)^2}{\Sigma(\hat{Y} - Y)^2}$$

In a regression output, it is desirable to have a high R^2 because it means that you have a more absolute explanation of the phenomenon you are studying. A large R^2 means that more of the variation in the dependent variable is being explained with the independent variables in the model. Multiple regression, therefore, can be used for both prediction and explanation.

OLS REGRESSION ANALYSIS AND INTERPRETATION

Although regression analysis is one of the simplest regression procedures, there are many other complex procedures that could be used when conducting an OLS regression analysis. A very concise description of the procedure will be examined here. The OLS regression procedure can be easily undertaken with an *SPSS* program. Using OLS regression analysis, for example, Paula Kautt and Cassia Spohn (2002) studied federal narcotics offenders. They were interested in determining whether the race of the defendant, the type of drug in the case, or the sentencing statute used against the defendant influence the length of the sentence that a defendant receives. Kautt and Spohn found that there are different factors that influenced sentence lengths for white and black defendants. For instance, if black defendants receive a substantial assistance departure, the magnitude of their sentence discount is greater than that for whites. However, criminal history, number of conviction counts, the final offense level, and going to trial, all result in longer sentences for blacks than for whites. They also found that the drug type has little effect on sentences, but that the type of sentencing statute the defendant is sentenced under will affect the factors that influence sentence lengths net of other effects.

Suppose Kautt and Spohn wanted to judge the effects of ethnicity, in addition to race, on defendant sentence lengths and further wanted to examine whether one's citizenship status influences the length of sentence given. Moreover, suppose that they hypothesized that Hispanic defendants and those who were not U.S. citizens would receive the largest sentences. Let's say that these researchers obtained a sample of defendants sentenced for narcotics violations in four southwestern districts in the United States. Let's also suppose that they decided to examine whether sentence lengths vary by district for defendants in the sample. The dependent variable in this instance would be the number of months in prison that a convicted defendant receives. A number of independent variables would be chosen because of their relevance, according to the U.S. Sentencing Commission, on the length of sentence. With this analysis and using regression, Kautt and Spohn would attempt to explain the factors that influence judicial sentencing decisions for narcotics offenders in the southwestern districts. In this case, the data would probably be acquired from the U.S. Sentencing Commission. When collected, the data must be cleaned to ensure that no random or systematic error in coding variables exists. It must be determined whether the variables in this data set, and the way in which they are measured, are appropriate for regression analysis. As discussed previously the data should be measured at the interval level and the dependent variable must be continuous and unbounded. If some of the variables fail to meet this assumption they will be dropped from the analysis or will need to be transformed.

After the variables are selected for study, univariate statistical analysis must be conducted. The goal is to examine the data to determine whether the variables are measured at the appropriate level as well as to determine if the data are appropriate for regression analysis by ensuring that none of the assumptions have been violated. The variables must be examined by looking at means, standard deviations and skewness and kurtosis. Looking at univariate statistics can assist investigators in being certain that the variables are normally distributed. As is the case is presented here, if the data were collected by a government agency, researchers must rely on the agency's data collection methods. Sometimes not all of the variables researchers want to utilize are collected. Sometimes the variables are not coded in ways that are useful for the researchers' purposes. If these situations occur, the data will need to be "cleaned up"; some cases may need to be omitted and some variables will need to be recoded and/or recomputed. Therefore, it is very important that researchers examine the data in this way to ensure that everything is in order to properly run a regression analysis.

After unvaried analyses are run, a bivariate analysis of variables for study should be conducted. This involves running a correlation analysis of the variables. A correlational procedure looks at relationships between variables and it is a good test for determining whether we will have problems with multicollinearity among our variables. Conducting a correlation analysis between independent and dependent variables can also give us a preliminary idea of what we can expect from the regression analysis. When all of these initial steps have been taken to ensure that the data are ready and if none of the assumptions have been violated, the actual regression analysis is ready to be conducted. Running the actual regression can be a simple procedure when using statistical software programs. However, we must not be misled to believe that regression is a simple procedure. There are many steps that need to be carefully considered during the procedure. Most researchers believe that the variables to be included in the regression model need to be entered within the context of one's theoretical framework. For instance, in the proposed study above the variables would be entered according to the current research and literature on sentencing. In this way, the investigators will be testing theory and presenting the results accordingly no matter the outcome. Some researchers believe that a regression model should be manipulated sufficiently so that much of the variance in the dependent variable is explained. In other words, these researchers should run the analysis, scan the results and then rerun the analysis omitting all insignificant variables and keeping only the most significant variables relevant for the model. This is called model building rather than theory testing and it is generally regarded as a poor strategy. It is probably best to allow theory and literature guide which variables will be included in the regression analysis and place all of them into a regression model simultaneously. This is referred to as the "Enter" method of regression.

Below is an example of a regression output similar to one that might be observed if the *SPSS* Alternative Application in Box 14.1 is followed. The dependent variable in this case was the total number of months of imprisonment. The independent variables placed in the regression model include: (1) the offender's age; (2) the offender's gender; (3) the offender's citizenship; (4) the presumptive sentence; (5) if the offender was Hispanic; (6) if the offender was black; (7) if the offender was detained; (8) if the offender received a downward departure; (9) if the offender received a departure for substantial assistance; (10) whether the offender graduated from high school; (11) whether the offender had some college education; and the last three variables are dummy variables for the different districts. These are all variables that have been shown to be theoretically linked to judicial decisions related to the length of imprisonment. The demographic variables above would be included as controls. **Control variables** are those that hold the characteristics of defendants constant. Including these variables in the regression will allow us to determine whether judges consider extralegal factors in their decision making the about sentence lengths that they give to defendants.

The output for our regression analysis will appear very quantitative and this statistical barrage may be initially intimidating. This is partially because of the mathematical calculations (iterations) involved in regression analysis and partially because of the number of variables

---

BOX 14.1

SPSS Alternative Application

1. In order to conduct an OLS regression analysis in the *SPSS* statistical software, open *SPSS* and activate a data set of choice. Next click on the tab at the top that says "Analyze", then click on "Regression", then on "Linear". It is in this new window that you will have options to enter the dependent and independent variables from a list. Linear regression in *SPSS* is the procedure for OLS regression.

2. The next step would involve highlighting the variables of interest from the left-hand window and moving it over to the appropriate box in the right-hand window. In this instance, we would want to use a number of variables. Highlight your dependent variable from the left hand-window and move it to the box for Dependent.

3. Next, the independent variables that you are interested in need to be highlighted on the left and moved to the box on the right labeled independents.

4. Next, click on the "Statistics" tab, this will allow you to place a check mark for various statistics you want *SPSS* to give you in the output. You may want to place a check mark in the box for part and partial correlations, this would give you the coefficients like the ones we calculated in Chapter 13. This however, is not a necessity for OLS regression as you will see the *b*-coefficients give us similar statistics. Click Continue.

5. Click on the tab "OK" and *SPSS* will run the regression. A new window will pop up giving us our output for the logistic regression analysis.

included as a part of attempting to explain judicial sentencing practices. An example of the *SPSS* output for the OLS regression is presented in Table 14.1a–c.

The first two boxes in the regression output in Table 14.1a and b refer to our overall regression model and give us information about whether our regression model was significant as well as how much of the variance we explained in the dependent variable with the independent variables we entered. The last box, Table 14.1c lists the regression statistics and coefficients

TABLE 14.1 a. *SPSS* Output for OLS Regression; b. ANOVA; c. Regression Coefficients

(a)

Model	R	R^2	Adjusted R^2	Std. Error of the Estimate
1	.491[a]	.241	.239	39.705

[a]Predictors: (Constant), California, OFFENDER'S GENDER, presump, black, DEFENDANT'S AGE AT TIME OF OFFENSE, Somecollege, pretrialdet, NewMexico, Subasst, HSgrad, departdown, DEFENDANT'S CITIZENSHIP, Arizona, Hispanic

(b)

Model		Sum of Squares	df	Mean Square	F	Sig.
1	Regression	2380618	14	170044.155	107.865	.000[a]
	Residual	7503926	4760	1576.455		
	Total	9884544	4774			

ANOVA[b]

[a]Predictors: (Constant), California, OFFENDER'S GENDER, presump, black, DEFENDANT'S AGE AT TIME OF OFFENSE, Somecollege, pretrialdet, NewMexico, Subasst, HSgrad, departdown, DEFENDANT'S CITIZENSHIP, Arizona, Hispanic
[b]Dependent Variable: TOTAL number of MONTHS IMPRISONMENT ORDERED

(c)

Coefficients[a]

Model		Unstandardized Coefficients		Standardized Coefficients		
		b	Std. Error	β	t	Sig.
1	(Constant)	44.478	2.688		16.545	.000
	DEFENDANT'S AGE AT TIME OF OFFENSE	.452	.057	.102	7.973	.000
	OFFENDER'S GENDER	−12.593	1.780	−.091	−7.075	.000
	DEFENDANT'S CITIZENSHIP	−12.455	1.408	−.137	−8.845	.000
	PRESUMPTIVE	.042	.002	.235	18.332	.000
	HISPANIC	1.301	1.728	.012	.753	.451
	BLACK	31.698	2.964	.151	10.693	.000
	PRETRIALLY DETAINED	−21.334	1.633	−.178	−13.060	.000

(continued)

TABLE 14.1 *Continued*

Model		b	Std. Error	β	t	Sig.
	DOWNWARD DEPARTURE	−8.116	1.426	−.080	−5.690	.000
	SUBSTANTIAL ASSISTANCE	−4.335	1.821	−.032	−2.381	.017
	HS GRAD	4.191	1.501	.038	2.792	.005
	SOME COLLEGE	3.334	1.816	.025	1.835	.067
	NEW MEXICO	−11.251	1.870	−.084	−6.017	.000
	ARIZONA	−22.696	1.516	−.227	−14.974	.000
	CALIFORNIA	−23.195	1.716	−.210	−13.513	.000

[a]Dependent Variable: TOTAL number of MONTHS IMPRISONMENT ORDERED

for the effects of each of the independent variables. Again, these statistics may look intimidating but are actually fairly easy to interpret. For most research articles you will be reading about OLS regression, the results from the three boxes in *SPSS* will be presented in one table to make reporting of the results more straightforward and simplified. Table 14.2 is an example of how the information from the three boxes in Table 14.1 would be formatted into a single tabular format for publication purposes.

The information in Table 14.2 makes it much easier to examine the results of the regression analysis. Both of these tables are presented to outline the differences between output received from a statistical software program and the type of information that would be published in a research article. The information about the R^2 is placed at the bottom of Table 14.2, and the column for whether the variable is significant is eliminated from Table 14.1 and an asterisk is simply placed by the *b*-coefficient in Table 14.2 to denote that the variable was significant.

Before we actually interpret the information given in Tables 14.1 and 14.2, we must learn the important steps involved in evaluating an OLS regression. After we learn these important steps, we will then use them to evaluate the information from our tables. There are generally five important steps in evaluating any multiple regression output (Roncek, 1993). The first step is determining whether the regression model is significant. The significance of the model can be determined by looking at the significance associated with the *F* test. In most statistical software programs, a probability associated with *F* is given as part of the output. We can simply look at this significance associated with *F* and if it is less than .05, we judge our regression model to be significant. If this significance was not readily available from our output, then we would simply look at the **F statistic** and go to a table of critical *F* values (Table A.19 of Appendix A, p. 461), with our degrees of freedom and appropriate probability level. If the number we received from the output is equal to or greater than the number in the table, we judge our regression model to be significant. If the significance associated with *F* is not less than .05, we need to stop our work here. A nonsignificant model means that we must go back to the drawing board and determine whether we have the appropriate variables or if any of the assumptions have been violated.

The second step in interpreting a regression output is an examination of the power of our model. How much of the variance in the dependent variable have we explained with our independent variables? The answer can readily be determined by looking at the multiple coefficient of determination symbolized by R^2. The R^2 that is generated by most statistical software programs,

TABLE 14.2 The Sentence Length Decision: OLS Regression of Narcotics Offenders in Southwestern Districts

Variable	b	SE	β	Rank
Presumptive Sentence	.042*	.002	.235	1
Downward Departure	−8.116*	1.426	−.080	10
Substantial Assistance Departure	−4.335*	1.821	−.032	12
Offender is Black	31.7*	2.964	.151	5
Offender is Hispanic	1.3	1.728	.012	8
Offender is Female	−12.6*	1.78	−.091	7
Offender's Age	.452*	.057	.102	
Offender Education				
No High School Degree (reference)				
High School Degree	4.191*	1.501	.038	11
Some College	3.334	1.816	.025	
Offender not Detained	−21.3*	1.633	−.178	4
Offender is a Noncitizen	−12.45*	1.408	−.137	6
District				
Texas South (Reference)				
New Mexico	−11.25*	1.87	−.084	9
Arizona	−22.7*	1.516	−.227	2
California South	−23.19*	1.716	−.210	3
Constant	44.47	2.688		
Adjusted R^2	.239			
N = 4,774				

*$P = <.05$

multiplied by 100, yields the percentage of what our model actually explained when predicting the dependent variable. This R^2 is equal to the Pearson's r in a bivariate regression. Like the Pearson's r, the R^2 for a multiple regression is the correlation between the dependent variable and all of the independent variables and is an indicator of how well our model fits the data. Values of R^2 range from 0 percent, which would indicate that we haven't explained anything, to a maximum of 100 percent, which means that we have explained all of the variance in the dependent variable with the independent variables we have chosen. If the R^2 is .50, for example, we have only explained half of the variation in the dependent variable with the variation in our independent variables. In this case, the other half of the variation in the dependent variable, $1 - R^2$, is due to other factors that we have not included in our model. The larger the R^2, the better our model fits the data. It is rare in the prediction of social science phenomena that all variance in the dependent variable is ever explained. Obviously, the larger the R^2 the better, but in the social sciences an R^2 of .60 or .70 is generally considered good. Sometimes, the adjusted R^2 is favored over the R^2, because the adjusted R^2 accounts for the number of cases in the sample. The formula for the **adjusted R^2** is as follows:

$$R^2 \text{ adjusted} = \frac{R^2 - k(1 - R^2)}{N - k - 1}$$

where k = the number of independent variables.

In order to be **parsimonious** we will use the adjusted R^2 because the regular R^2 will not decrease if a variable is added that does not predict the dependent variable. The adjusted R^2 therefore controls for the number of variables in the equation. With the adjusted R^2 only the correct explanatory variables are counted.

The third step in interpreting an OLS regression output is to determine which of our independent variables in the model are significant predictors of our dependent variable. If our overall model is significant and we have examined how much of the dependent variable we have predicted, we can next examine each independent variable to assess its contribution to the dependent variable. What we want to know about our independent variables is whether they have a significant effect on the dependent variable. This is accomplished by examining the significance associated with the t statistic in the *SPSS* output. Similar to the F statistic, if the significance associated with t is less than .05, the independent variable is significant. In Table 14.2, we have indicated whether the variable is significant with an asterisk. We do not interpret those variables which are not significant. Again, as is consistent with our model's overall significance, if the statistical software did not yield a significance associated with t, then we would have to resort to looking at a table of critical t values and determine whether the number associated with t in our model was larger than the number in the Table of critical t values (Table A.3 of Appendix A, p. 447)

The fourth step is to interpret the independent variables that indicate significant contributions to the dependent variable. In other words, what are the effects of our independent variables on our dependent variable? These effects are usually represented in our output by a "b". The numbers in this "b" column are referred to as **b-coefficients** and represent the **unstandardized effect** of our independent variables. The column next to the b is usually the standard error associated with that b-coefficient. These statistics are important and are shown in both Tables 14.1c and 14.2. We label this the unstandardized effect because it relies on how the independent variable has been measured. The unstandardized coefficient has many qualities. First, it minimizes the sum of squared errors. Second, it adjusts the scale of the independent variable to the scale of the dependent variable. Third, it converts the units of the independent variable into the units of the dependent variable. Fourth, it tells us how the value of the dependent variable will change with an increase or decrease in the independent variable. The unstandardized coefficient can be interpreted in the following way: We can expect an (increase/decrease) of (value of b-coefficient) in the (dependent variable) for a one unit change in the (independent variable). The values and characteristics that we enter into the parentheses will change according to the data and variables we are using. In the first parenthesis, it will be an increase or a decrease depending on the sign associated with the b-coefficient. A negative sign is associated with a decrease; a positive sign is associated with an increase. This will become easier to understand as we move through these steps for the sample outputs that are provided in Tables 14.1c and 14.2. The b-coefficients are important in explaining our results for practical purposes. The only limitation of the b-coefficient is that we cannot judge its relative importance to the other independent variables because it has been computed based upon how the individual independent variables were measured. In order to examine which of the independent variables are most important, we must examine the standardized effects.

The fifth step in interpreting an OLS regression analysis is examining the relative importance of each of the independent variables. The **standardized effects** are usually denoted by the Greek symbol for Beta (β). The Beta or **Beta weight** is the standardized correlation coefficient. This allows a comparison of the magnitude of effects of the independent variables because it is not calculated according to how the independent variables have been measured. These standardized values are computed by converting the raw data to Z scores. Standardizing puts the mean at 0 and the standard deviation at 1. In this way, the Beta weights can be compared to each other. We will be able to rank order our independent variables in importance of influence on the dependent variable. The Beta weight is equal to the effect on the standard deviation of the dependent variable for a change of 1 standard deviation in an independent variable. The rule of thumb is that the larger the Beta weight in absolute sense, the greater the importance it has for the model. Basically, the independent variable that has the largest Beta weight is the most important variable. The second largest Beta weight associated with an independent variable makes this variable the next most important variable and so on. This standardized coefficient compared to the unstandardized b-coefficient is important for testing theory.

Table 14.3 provides a convenient summary of the five steps in interpreting an OLS regression output and the statistics associated with determining each of the steps. Let's use Table 14.3 as a guide to interpret the results of the OLS regression in Tables 14.1 and 14.2.

1. Is our overall regression model statistically significant? What is the probability the results could have occurred by chance?

In our regression output from *SPSS* (Table 14.1b) our F statistic is 107.865 and the significance associated with it is .000. This is shown in the significance column to the right of the F statistic. Since this significance is less than .05, we can be assured that our model is significant at this probability level. This means that the results that we have in our output are not due to chance and therefore we may proceed to step 2.

2. How good is our model? What percentage of the variance in the dependent variable has been explained with our independent variables?

This step is answered by looking at the R^2 (Table 14.1a) In this model the R^2 is .241. When we multiply this by 100 we get 24.1, which means we have explained 24 percent of the variation in sentence length for narcotics offenders with our independent variables. Our variables are only explaining about 24 percent of what influences decision making about the length of sentence a defendant will receive. Approximately 76 percent of this variation is unexplained. Again, in the social sciences, getting a large R^2 is very rare. Remember also that the adjusted R^2 corrects for the number of independent variables. In this case the adjusted R^2 is .239, which is not much different from the R^2.

3. Which independent variables are statistically significant?

We can determine the significance of the independent variables by looking at the significance associated with the t statistic in Table 14.1c or the asterisked variables in Table 14.2.

TABLE 14.3 Five Steps for Interpreting an OLS Regression

Step	Questions to Ask	Statistic
1	Is our overall regression model statistically significant? What is the probability the results could have occurred by chance?	F test—$P < 0.05$
2	How good is our model? What percentage of the variance in the dependent variable has been explained with our independent variables?	R^2
3	Which independent variables are statistically significant?	T test—$P < 0.05$
4	What is the interpretation of the unstandardized effect of the independent variables that are statistically significant?	b
5	What is the relative importance of the magnitude of our independent variables?	β

In this case, all of the variables are significant except the variable for Hispanic defendants and the variable measuring college education. This means most of the variables we have chosen for study do have a statistically significant relationship with the dependent variable (the sentence length imposed on defendants). With this information, we can now move to step 4 and interpret those variables that are statistically significant.

4. What is the interpretation of the unstandardized effect of the independent variables that are statistically significant?

Again, we will use Tables 14.1c and 14.2 and the scores under the "*b*" columns. Interpreting the **unstandardized effects** of the independent variables means that we need to examine whether they are continuous or dichotomous in nature. For the continuous variables, we will interpret the *b*-coefficients as a change in the dependent variable for a 1-unit change in the independent variable. The variable for presumptive sentence measures all the legally relevant factors and shows that we can expect an increase of 0.42 months in sentence length for each unit of change in presumptive sentence. This is a fairly negligible effect. Age is also a continuous variable. From our *b*-coefficient, we can expect an increase of .452 months in sentence length for an increase of one year in age. On the average in this case, as age increases the sentence length will also increase about half a month per year.

The dichotomous variables are more straightforward to interpret. For these, the independent variable can assume only one of two values. In these cases, however, we must remember how the variables are coded. For instance, the variable for downward departure was coded as a 1 for receiving a downward departure and a 0 for not receiving a downward departure. If we look at our output, we can see that the sentence length decreases 8.116 months for those who get a downward departure. In other words, moving from a 0 (not receiving a departure) to a 1 (receiving a departure) on the independent variable, results in an average decrease in sentence length of 8 months. Similarly by receiving a substantial assistance departure, defendants on the average, will receive 4 months less in sentence lengths. The variable for females is significant and reveals that on the average, females receive prison sentences that are 12 months less than males. Likewise, those defendants who are not U.S. citizens receive on average of one year less in prison compared with citizens. Finally, those who are not detained receive sentences that are 21 months less, on the average, compared with those who are detained.

The remaining variables are referred to as dummy variables. Dummy variables will be discussed later in this chapter but can be interpreted similarly as dichotomous independent variables. For instance, the variable for "black" reveals that those defendants who are African American compared with white (Caucasian) defendants receive on average sentences that are 31.7 months longer. The effect of this variable shows the difference in sentence length attributable to being black or white. It may be recalled that the variable for "Hispanic" was not significant and so we do not interpret its *b*-coefficient. The dummy variables for education reveal that those defendants who have a high school degree receive on average 4.191 more months in prison than those who do not have a high school diploma. Finally, if we examine the dummy variables for the districts, we will see that defendants in New Mexico, Arizona, and the Southern District of California receive sentences that are on the average 11, 22, and 23 months less than defendants from the Southern District of Texas.

5. What is the relative importance of the magnitude of our independent variables?

To answer this question, we must examine the Beta weights. This is represented by the column labeled "Beta" for both Tables 14.1c and 14.2. Remember, the larger the Beta weight, the better. If we were to rank order the significant variables according to Beta weights, we would determine that the variable for presumptive sentence is the most important variable in the model that influences our dependent variable. This is because it has the largest Beta weight at .235. This finding shows that judges rely heavily on the legal variables that are measured in the presumptive sentence variable when deciding on sentence lengths for defendants. Table 14.2 actually includes a column labeled "rank" that shows the rank ordering of variables as determined from the Beta weights. The second and third most important variables are the dummy variables for the districts Arizona and California South. The least important variable in the model is the variable for substantial assistance departure. It must be remembered that the sign of the Beta weight does not matter. What does matter is the size of the Beta weight.

OLS Regression Limitations

Although a very popular and widely used statistical technique, OLS regression does have several limitations. Regression is not considered by statisticians to be a very robust technique. This is largely because large sample sizes have a great impact on the regression results. For very large samples, regression will often indicate significance where the association between variables is extremely weak and would not be significant using other techniques. Also because regression depends greatly on the **sums of squares**, serious problems may arise if relationships between variables are not linear, the interval level of measurement is not achieved and/or if normality does not exist. There are also sometimes limited uses of OLS regression for dependent variables that researchers in criminal justice usually study. Dependent variables that are continuous and unbounded are rarely found. For these nonnormal, or limited, dependant variables, we must turn to other regression techniques that are more complex. Some of these techniques will be discussed in Chapter 15.

DUMMY VARIABLES AND INTERACTION EFFECTS

Some of the variables that are available in our data sets may not be measured at the interval level or may be incapable of being quantified. For example, race and gender variables are variables conceptualized at and limited to the nominal level of measurement. Being Asian does not mean that you have more or less race than being Native American. Likewise being female does not mean you have more or less gender than a male. These variable subclasses are simply categories to distinguish between persons according to nominal attributes that are different but unrankable. However, investigators have determined ways of quantifying these nominal-level variables by dichotomizing them or making them binary. **Dummy variables** are dichotomized, or made binary by forcing them to assume either a 0 or 1 value. In the case of the gender variable, we recode the variable and make all males in the data = 0 and all females = 1. By doing this, we can now assess the influence on the dependent variable for a change in our independent variable. In this case what is the effect on our dependent variable for changing from a 0 (male) to a 1 (female)? In essence, we are deceiving our regression analysis into believing that defendants can change from being male to female, and our regression analysis will tell us the effects of that change on some dependent variable. Obviously, this change cannot occur in real life (other than through sex reassignment surgery, which is rare), but in creating a dummy variable for gender we can now assess the change in the dependent variable for a male/female distinction.

In the race example, we would use the same technique, only we would have more variables. Measuring race, we would generate five categories. We would essentially create five dummy variables by recoding the original nominal variable for race. For instance, we would create a new variable for Native American and assign all Native Americans = 1 and all other races = 0. We now have a dummy variable for Native American. We would create variables in this fashion for each nominal category of race of interest to us and then we would place each of these variables in the regression equation except one. This variable, the omitted variable, would be called the reference category. The **reference category** becomes the basis upon which we may compare all of the other dummy variables. We can then gauge that (if we leave the variable for white as the reference category) for instance, what is the change in the dependent variable for the difference between whites and all the other categories of race. Forcing nominal-level variables into the interval level of measurement is also referred to as scaling. In **scaling** variables, researchers are able to meet various stringent assumptions of statistical tests and utilize important variables that would otherwise violate (according to the level-of-measurement) assumptions accompanying the proper application of these tests.

Another instance where dummy variables become useful is when we believe that two or more of our variables may interact so as to produce more pronounced and/or differing effects on the dependent variable. In our sentencing example, for instance, we found through our regression results that ethnicity had no effect on sentence outcomes. Let's argue, however, that we believe that ethnicity would only have an impact on male defendants. In other words, we believe that gender and ethnicity will interact together to produce the harshest sentences for those defendants who are both male and Hispanic. If this is one of our hypotheses, we are essentially saying that ethnicity (being Hispanic) by itself will not directly affect a defendant's sentence; however, the interaction of ethnicity and gender will cause ethnicity to become a predictor of sentence outcomes. In order to test this hypothesis we would again have to create dummy variables that would enable us to gauge the **interaction effects** of these two variables.

Similar to the example we have been using, we would have to create new variables that would represent four categories of ethnicity/gender: non-Hispanic male, non-Hispanic female, Hispanic male, Hispanic female. If we put these new variables into our regression equation, less the non-Hispanic male variable as the reference category, we will be able to judge the effects on sentence length of a defendant who is a non-Hispanic female, a defendant who is an Hispanic male, and a defendant who is an Hispanic female compared with defendants who are non-Hispanic males. Let's suppose that our regression results with these newly created variables indicate that there is no significant difference between average sentence lengths of non-Hispanic males and Hispanic females, but that non-Hispanic females receive significantly shorter sentences than non-Hispanic males and Hispanic males receive significantly longer sentences than non-Hispanic males. With these results, we can now see the interactive effects of gender and ethnicity. In this case, gender only matters for non-Hispanics; Hispanic females didn't have sentence lengths significantly different from non-Hispanic males; likewise, ethnicity matters, but only for males, where Hispanic males received significantly longer sentences than non-Hispanic males. By testing these interaction effects, researchers can disclose effects that otherwise would be masked in models not testing for such interactions.

For instance, in our original regression model we found that gender matters and that females receive significantly shorter sentences, but the ethnicity variable was not significant. This means that the ethnicity of a defendant does not matter relating to sentence lengths. In testing for interaction effects of gender and ethnicity, however, we may reveal that the gender effect on sentence lengths was only relevant for non-Hispanics, and that ethnicity actually does have significant effects on sentence lengths but only for males. Testing for these interaction effects has revealed some significant results that were masked, or that were not significant in the original regression.

COLLINEARITY AND MULTICOLLINEARITY

The above discussion thus far has involved meeting the assumptions of regression, running an OLS regression analysis and interpreting OLS regression output. These are all important components of conducting multiple regression analysis. However, there are additional components of regression that must be considered. After we have completed the five easy steps discussed earlier, we will also have to ensure that there is no collinearity between variables in the model. As stated earlier, when studying social science phenomenon, often our independent variables are interconnected. If some of our variables are too correlated with each other, then we have multicollinearity in our model. It has been noted that one of the assumptions of OLS regression is an absence of multicollinearity. While correlation among independent variables occurs with most criminal justice and social science data, too much correlation, or a perfect relationship, between variables is very problematic for OLS regression. If two or more independent variables are highly correlated, they can bias both the unstandardized and standardized coefficients as well as the tests of significance.

"Collinearity" is the term used whenever we have two variables that are highly correlated. "Multicollinearity" is when more than two of the variables examined are highly correlated with each other (Studenmund, 1997). Researchers usually use these two terms interchangeably, however, and the presence of multicollinearity can seriously distort the interpretation of an OLS regression model. The next section will explore the methods involved in assessing collinearity as well as several methods for remedying collinearity. Assessing multicollinearity is a very important task of regression, especially in the social sciences, where variables are usually interrelated. As such researchers consider it to be a fundamental prerequisite for conducting any multivariate regression techniques. It will also be an important step in Chapter 15, which deals with regression for limited dependent variables.

Collinearity Diagnostics

The easiest and probably most frequently utilized method for assessing collinearity is simply to scan the zero-order correlations among the independent variables. This is usually done before we conduct our regression by computing a Pearson's r. This will reveal relationships between the independent variables we are going to use in our regression model. If the Pearson's r between two variables is .70 or higher, there may be problems with collinearity in our model. The reason we use .70 as a rule is because the Pearson's r is a **PRE measure**, which is a proportional-reduction-in-error measure. This means that if we square the Pearson's r of .70 we get .49, meaning that these two variables share about half of the variance with each other. If this is the case, it will be difficult for regression to differentiate the independent effects of each of these two variables. Pearson's r, however, is insufficient for concluding that we have a multicollinearity problem because it only assesses relationships between two variables. In conducting multiple regression, we are examining several independent variables simultaneously, which means that even if two variables were not highly correlated in a Pearson's r test, they may become highly correlated in multiple regression because of interactions that may occur as in our discussion about dummy variables. Therefore, utilizing Pearson's r or zero-order correlation is necessary, although we must use other diagnostic procedures to ensure the non-existence of multicollinearity.

In statistical software packages like *SPSS*, there are many options available to assess the presence of multicollinearity. The two most widely used options are the **Tolerance**, and the **Variance Inflation Factor Scores (VIF)**. These statistics are easily added to a regression output in *SPSS*. Table 14.4 shows how the output of these two statistics appears in a regression output.

In Table 14.4 under the collinearity statistics heading, we can see both the Tolerance and the VIF scores. The Tolerance statistic tells us how much of the variance of an independent variable is not dependent on other independent variables. This value ranges from 0 to 1, and the closer the value is to 1, the more independence the variable has. A value close to 0 indicates the presence of multicollinearity. The general rule of thumb regarding the Tolerance statistic is that if we have any values below .40, then we may have a multicollinearity problem. In Table 14.4 none of our variables are below .40, and most are close to 1, indicating that these variables are highly independent. Therefore, no possibility of collinearity exists among them.

The next statistic in the regression output is the VIF scores. These are probably the most frequently used statistics to assess whether multicollinearity exists. This statistical procedure is popular because it not only tells us if we have a problem with collinear variables, but it also indicates which of the independent variables are collinear. This statistic can also assess the severity of the collinearity problem as well as how much greater our standard error is. Calculating the square root of the VIF score tells us how much greater our standard error is compared with what it would be if our variable were not correlated with any of the other independent variables in the

TABLE 14.4 OLS Regression Output with Collinearity Diagnostics

Model		Unstandardized Coefficients		Standardized Coefficients				Collinearity Statistics	
		b	Std. Error	β	t	Sig.		Tolerance	VIF
1	(Constant)	44.478	2.688		16.545	.000			
	DEFENDANT'S AGE	.452	.057	.102	7.973	.000		.976	1.024
	GENDER	−12.593	1.780	−.091	−7.075	.000		.969	1.032
	NONCITIZEN	−12.455	1.408	−.137	−8.845	.000		.668	1.497
	PRESUMPTIVE	.042	.002	.235	18.332	.000		.971	1.029
	HISPANIC	1.301	1.728	.012	.753	.451		.631	1.585
	BLACK	31.698	2.964	.151	10.693	.000		.800	1.251
	PRETRIALLY DETAINED	−21.334	1.633	−.178	−13.060	.000		.861	1.162
	DOWNWARD DEPARTURE	−8.116	1.426	−.080	−5.690	.000		.812	1.231
	SUBSTANTIAL ASSISTANCE	−4.335	1.821	−.032	−2.381	.017		.880	1.136
	HS GRAD	4.191	1.501	.038	2.792	.005		.849	1.177
	SOME COLLEGE	3.334	1.816	.025	1.835	.067		.889	1.124
	NEW MEXICO	−11.251	1.870	−.084	−6.017	.000		.827	1.210
	ARIZONA	−22.696	1.516	−.227	−14.974	.000		.694	1.441
	CALIFORNIA SOUTH	−23.195	1.716	−.210	−13.513	.000		.658	1.520

BOX 14.2

SPSS **Alternative Application**

1. Follow the steps above in the *SPSS* Alternative Application to running an OLS Regression.
2. This time, however, after adding the dependent and independent variables, click on the "Statistics" tab. This will open a new window in which you have many options. Place a check mark in the box for collinearity diagnostics.
3. Click Continue.
4. Now when you click "OK" to tell *SPSS* to run the regression, these statistics will automatically become a part of the regression output.

---

model. VIF scores range from 1 to infinity. The larger the score, the more severe the problem. The general rule of thumb for this statistic is that if all the VIF scores are below 4, there are no problems with collinearity among variables. Looking at Table 14.4, all of the VIFs are below 4, indicating that there is no multicollinearity in the model. If there were collinearity between two variables, the VIFs associated with those variables would be above 4. In this way, we can easily determine which variables are the problematic ones.

There are other diagnostic tests that can be used to assess multicollinearity in a regression model. For instance, if in using the five easy steps for interpreting an OLS regression, the overall model is significant, although none, or few, of the independent variables are significant, then multicollinearity is probably present. This is because the regression is significant, but the model cannot separate the independent effects of each variable, thereby rendering them nonsignificant. Finally, if our Beta weights have an absolute value greater than 1, we may have multicollinearity issues. Beta weights can only take on values from −1 to +1. If any of the scores are outside of this range, then it may be indicative of a multicollinearity problem.

Remedies for Collinearity

If we detect the presence of multicollinearity with any of the diagnostic procedures mentioned above in our model, there are several options for attempting to correct this problem. The first remedy is to do nothing. If the multicollinearity is not severe, then attempting to make corrections may not change any of the significance levels associated with our independent variables. Or the *b*-coefficients may not change in any meaningful way from the model that shows a degree of collinearity.

The second method of correcting for collinearity would be to drop one of the collinear variables from the model and rerun the analysis. This correction is probably the easiest way to deal with collinearity. However, dropping a variable that is important to our model can cause other problems that are more severe than collinearity. These problems include making specification error, because of the assumption violation that no important variables are left out of the equation, and/or producing *b*-coefficients that are biased. If we are using theory to guide our model, then excluding variables that are important theoretically may be more injurious than keeping them in the model with some degree of multicollinearity present.

Another method is to use more data, or attempt to increase the size of the sample studied. If sample size is increased, the effects of collinearity on the standard errors in the model will be diminished. The standard errors in our model are based on our sample size and the correlation between our independent variables. Sometimes, however, increasing our sample size proves to be a difficult task, either because we have enumerated the entire population of offenses for study, or additional data collection cannot be done quickly, or without incurring significant additional expense. Most people do not use this method of correcting for multicollinearity.

A better method would be to combine the collinear variables, especially if they are measured similarly, or transform them so as to reduce the problem. This involves recoding the problematic variables into a new variable. For example, similar to the discussion of interaction effects earlier in the chapter, suppose we have a collinearity problem between the variables for detention status and citizenship status. The problem with collinearity in this case could arise because logically we would suppose that those who are noncitizens are more likely detained, whereas citizens are more likely to have an option to bond out. In short, a majority of defendants detained were noncitizens. Therefore, regression is having difficulty separating the independent effect of being detained and being a noncitizen on the length of sentence. To correct for this problem, we may want to combine the variables for detention status and citizenship status. This would involve dummy coding. Since each variable has only two possible values, we would need to create four new dummy variables (detained citizens, detained noncitizens, released citizens, and released noncitizens). Now, if we use these four new variables in our regression model with the one omitted as the reference category, regression will calculate the independent effects for each of the four categories. But in doing this, we must be careful to insure that there are sufficient cases in each category for comparison. For example, if most of the noncitizens were detained, there is the possibility that in our newly coded dummy variables, there are very few cases where a defendant was a noncitizen but not detained. If there are not at least 30 cases in each of these new categories, we will not have sufficient numbers for comparative purposes. With the creation of these four new variables, we have removed the collinearity between being detained and being a noncitizen. For a more in-depth discussion of multicollinearity, its causes, cures and which remedies are the best choices for any given situation, see Lewis-Beck (1980) and Studenmund (1997).

Summary

This chapter has provided a basic introduction to multiple regression analysis, its interpretation and limitations. Multiple regression is useful to researchers because it allows us to see the combined effects of multiple independent variables on a dependent variable, and it also gives us the separate or independent effects each of our independent variables have on the dependent variable. The inner workings and steps involved in multiple regression analysis are indeed more difficult than what was discussed here, and may take many years and a great deal of practice to master. This chapter has provided the basic information needed for students to get started with running multiple regression techniques as well as better understand and interpret the results of research articles they may be required to read involving such methods.

The assumptions of a multiple regression technique like OLS are very important to its fundamental application. These assumptions have to do with ensuring that the variables for study are appropriate, specifying the correct model, and the properties associated with the error terms. If these assumptions are met, the Gauss-Markov theorem states that OLS will be the best (minimum variance) linear unbiased estimator. If one or more of these assumptions are violated, the consequences could include that the b-coefficients from our regression will be biased. They may not be accurate estimates of the effect of our independent variables on the dependent variable.

Finally, there are other statistics that must be considered when running a regression analysis. Mostly these have to do with whether collinearity is present in our model. *SPSS* and other statistical packages are able to include statistics like tolerance and VIF scores with regression output, thus making it easier to determine whether this problem is present. However, in social science, most variables are more or less related, and some amount of multicollinearity is therefore acceptable for most regression techniques. If collinearity is too severe, however, several remedies may be applied to fix the problem. These include dropping a variable from the equation, increasing sample size if possible, and conducting some type of transformation of the collinear variables. Often researchers decide that the best option is to do nothing, depending on how severe the collinearity is. Regression is robust with some collinearity present. Doing nothing may

be the best strategy especially if the theoretical foundations specify that the problem variables are important to the model. Learning and using a statistical software program that can easily help with running a regression is a very helpful tool today in being able to understand academic research, test theories about social science phenomena and perform real-world research. Once the fundamentals of OLS regression are understood and *SPSS* protocol is mastered, understanding other forms of multiple regression will be considerably easier. These other regression techniques will be discussed in Chapter 15.

Key Terms

adjusted R^2 *391*
autocorrelation *384*
b-coefficients *392*
beta weight *392*
collinearity *385*
control variables *388*
dummy variables *395*
error term *384*
first order partial
    derivative *385*
F statistic *390*

Gauss-Markov
    Theorem *385*
heteroscedasticity *384*
interaction effects *396*
multicollinearity *385*
multivariate analysis *385*
OLS regression *382*
parsimonious *392*
PRE measure *397*
R^2 *391*
reference category *396*

residuals *382*
scaling *396*
specification error *383*
standardized effects *392*
sum of squares *382*
tolerance *398*
unstandardized effects *394*
variance *383*
variance inflation factor
    scores *398*

Questions for Review

1. What are the primary aims of OLS regression technique?

2. What are six assumptions associated with OLS regression?

3. What statistic does OLS regression use to determine significance? What type of statistic is used to determine which of our independent variables in the model are statistically significant?

4. What is collinearity? What is multicollinearity? How can we diagnose whether it is present in our model? What are the remedies if it does exist?

5. What is the R^2? Why is it important for regression? How is R^2 interpreted? Explain.

6. What are control variables? Why do we include them in the regression model?

7. What are the five steps to interpreting an OLS regression output?

8. What are some of the limitations of the OLS regression procedure?

9. What are dummy variables? What are interaction effects? How can dummy variables be used to test for interaction effects?

10. Select two journal articles that use OLS regression analysis as the main statistical

technique. For each article: (a) look at the variables being used in the study, do they meet the assumptions for conducting an OLS regression analysis? (b) review the tables the authors use to display their results, attempt to analyze this output using the five easy steps for interpreting a regression analysis. Do you get the same findings as the authors? (c) discuss the limitations present in the studies. How are they different or similar to the ones discussed in this chapter?

Exercises

14.1. A researcher has run a regression analysis attempting to predict whether various extra-legal factors play a role in determining the length of sentence a narcotic's defendant receives in Texas. The researcher obtains the following output from *SPSS*. Examine these results and explain the statistics that are important to an OLS regression.

a. Is the overall regression model significant?
b. Which of the variables are significant in the model?
c. Look at the adjusted R^2, how much of the variance is explained in the dependent variable with these independent variables?

d. Rank-order the significant variables in the order of importance. Which is the most important predictor?

Model Summary

Model	R	R^2	Adjusted R^2	Std. Error of the Estimate
1	.126[a]	.016	.012	715.221

[a]Predictors: (Constant), Somecollege, OFFENDER'S GENDER, black, DEFENDANT'S AGE AT TIME OF OFFENSE, DEFENDANT'S CITIZENSHIP, HSgrad, hispanic

ANOVA[b]

Model		Sum of Squares	df	Mean Square	F	Sig.
1	Regression	141.4	7	20.2	3.951	.000[a]
	Residual	3489.949	1711	511.54		
	Total	3722.297	1718			

[a]Predictors: (Constant), Somecollege, OFFENDER'S GENDER, black, DEFENDANT'S AGE AT TIME OF OFFENSE, DEFENDANT'S CITIZENSHIP, HSgrad hispanic
[b]Dependent Variable: TOTAL number of MONTHS IMPRISONMENT ORDERED

Coefficients[a]

Model		Unstandardized Coefficients		Standardized Coefficients		
		b	Std. Error	*β*	*t*	Sig.
1	(Constant)	−89.382	80.252		−1.114	.266
	DEFENDANT'S AGE	5.042	1.774	.069	2.841	.005
	DEFENDANT'S GENDER	−77.086	53.154	−.035	−1.450	.147
	NON-CITIZEN	26.102	38.666	.018	.675	.500
	HISPANIC	−6.533	56.258	−.004	−.116	.908
	BLACK	24.28	18.2	.087	2.960	.003
	HS GRADUATE	5.6006	14.1	.034	1.359	.174
	SOME COLLEGE	5.8273	15.5	.026	1.048	.295

[a]Dependent Variable: TOTAL number of MONTHS IMPRISONMENT ORDERED

14.2. The researcher in the above question also obtains the following collinearity diagnostics output from *SPSS*. Examine these tests and determine whether the researcher has a problem with collinearity among variables. Also explain how you came to your conclusion.

Coefficients[a]

Model		Collinearity Statistics	
		Tolerance	VIF
1	DEFENDANT'S AGE AT TIME OF OFFENSE	.979	1.021
	OFFENDER'S GENDER	.986	1.041
	DEFENDANT'S CITIZENSHIP	.846	1.181
	hispanic	.609	1.642
	black	.670	1.493
	HSgrad	.901	1.110
	Somecollege	.923	1.083

[a]Dependent Variable: TOTAL # Months IMPRISONMENT ORDERED

References

Berry, W.D. (1993). *Understanding Regression Assumptions.* Newbury Park, CA: Sage Publications.

Kautt, P.M. and C. Spohn. (2002). "Cracking Down on Black Drug Offenders? Testing for Interactions Between Offender Race, Drug Type, and Sentencing Strategy in Federal Drug Sentences." Justice Quarterly 19:1–36.

Lewis-Beck, M.S. (1980). *Applied Regression: An Introduction.* Newbury Park, CA: Sage Publications.

Roncek, D. (1993). "When Will They Ever Learn that First Derivatives Identify the Effects of Continuous Independent Variables or 'Officer, You Can't Give Me a Ticket, I Wasn't Speeding for an Entire Hour.'" *Social Forces* 71:1067–1078.

Studenmund, A.H. (1997). *Using Econometrics: A Practical Guide.* Reading, MA: Addison-Wesley.

CHAPTER 15

Multivariate Statistics: Multiple Regression with Limited Dependent Variables

Chapter Outline

Introduction

Limited Dependent Variables
  Assumption Violations

Logistic Regression

Analysis and Interpretation
  Limitations of Logistic Regression
  Interaction Effects With Logistic Regression

Other Logistic Regression Techniques
  Ordered Logistic Regression
  Multinomial Logistic Regression
  Interpreting Effects in Multinomial Logit
  Poisson and Negative Binomial Regression
  Poisson and Negative Binomial Interpretation
  Limitations of Poisson and Negative Binomial Regression
  Multicollinearity for Logistic Regression Techniques

Summary

Key Terms

Questions for Review

Exercises

References

Chapter Objectives

After reading this chapter, the following objectives will be realized:

1. understanding the assumptions that are violated with limited dependent variables;
2. understanding logistic regression;
3. examining the limitations of logistic regression;
4. understanding how to interpret a logistic regression output;
5. understanding Poisson and negative binomial regression;
6. understanding the concept of overdispersion;
7. understanding ordinal regression; and
8. understanding multinomial regression.

INTRODUCTION

Chapter 14 examined multiple regression for dependent variables that were continuous and measured at the interval level. However, dependent variables frequently violate one or more of the assumptions associated with OLS regression. From our previous discussion of OLS regression we know that there are several important assumptions that must be met in order to use the statistical technique properly. Quantitative methods have had a long history of use in the social science literature. The statistical techniques employed in social science research have become both increasingly advanced and complex. We have progressed well-beyond putting straight lines through a scatter plot points. As increasingly complex issues in criminology and criminal justice are further explored and our data have become more intricate and detailed, the notion of a straight-line relationship between independent and dependent variables has been challenged. Often investigated dependent variables have only two possible outcomes. They are either dichotomous in nature, such as prison or probation, or they may consist of ordered categories (e.g., strongly agree, agree, disagree, and strongly disagree). Some of these dependent variables are censored or truncated (i.e., values on the dependent variable are clustered around a given point), or only nominal-level data are involved (religious affiliation, race/ethnicity, or gender). This chapter examines various alternative regression techniques for use with limited dependent variables, or those that do not adhere to the traditional requirements of continuous data and the interval level of measurement assumption.

Although there have been attempts made to linearize variables that are skewed, semi-logged in x or semi-logged in y (Menard, 2002; Studenmund, 1997; Roncek, 1993), increasingly criminal justice and other social scientific data do not fit the idea of a straight line through a scatter plot and they cannot be forced into linear transformations (Aldrich and Nelson, 1984). Examples of such data sets are sentencing information which often involves binomial outcomes (e.g., in/out decisions or receipt or nonreceipt of a departure). Although logged transformations (i.e., where each point of data is multiplied by the value of its natural logarithm) did much toward linearizing data, gradually additional data collected about crime and justice was not amenable to being forced into linearity. As advances in data collection and data gathering techniques occurred, and as researchers developed increased interest in examining the true nature of outcomes regarding these types of phenomena, statistical techniques to accommodate these advances were also developed. Many of these advances in developing statistical techniques using criminal justice data have been made for limited dependent variable applications.

LIMITED DEPENDENT VARIABLES

When we have a dependent variable that is binary, or dichotomous, in nature, it means that there are only two possible outcomes on the dependent variable. For example, in sentencing data, the outcome for whether or not someone is sentenced to prison has only two possibilities: (1) being sent to prison, or (2) not being sent to prison. Any dependent variable with only two possibilities is typically coded "0" and "1." The variable would be coded as a "1" if the defendant was sentenced to prison and a "0" if the defendant was not sentenced to prison. These dichotomous dependent variables are not amenable to OLS regression because several important assumptions underlying them are violated.

Assumption Violations

A binary or dichotomous dependent variable obviously violates two important traditional OLS regression assumptions. The first assumption is that the dependent variable should be continuous and unbounded (Menard, 2002; Studenmund, 1997; Liao, 1994; Aldrich and Nelson, 1984). The second assumption is that the independent and dependent variables have a linear relationship. The assumption of continuity in logistic regression is dealt with by treating the dependent variable as the probability of taking on the value of "1." When attempting to explain the effect of an independent variable on a dependent variable, and when the dependent variable has only two outcomes, the primary problem is that the only possible change on a dichotomous dependent variable is a change from "0" to "1" or vice versa. Therefore, **logistic regression** functions instead, not by gauging whether the outcome is a "0" or a "1," but rather what the probability is that the outcome is a "1" on the dependent variable. But by doing this, the assumption of unboundedness is also violated. By its very definition, treating the dependent variable as a probability bounds it between "0" and "1." Logistic regression deals with these assumption violations in several ways. First, it uses odds because they are continuous and unbounded at the high end (Studenmund, 1997). Second, it uses the log of the odds because it unbounds the lower end (Studenmund, 1997).

A second problem with a dichotomous dependent variable is that the linearity assumption becomes unreasonable (Liao, 1994). If the values of the dependent variable are limited to only two possibilities, and if linearity is assumed, then no data would be needed. Using a straight line as the relationship between x and y would yield nothing in the middle of the scatter plot. This problem is resolved in logistic regression by using the natural log. Although the relationship between x and y is not linear, x is said to have a linear relationship with the logit (log of the odds) of P (probability of being "1"). Other important assumptions are violated when using dichotomous dependent variables and either continuous or dichotomous independent variables. These assumption violations involve the error terms.

There are three basic assumptions underlying the error term (as indicated earlier about OLS regression) that are violated in dealing with a dichotomous dependent variable (Aldrich and Nelson, 1984). First, the errors are normally distributed across the entire regression line or the mean of errors is equal to zero. Second, the error terms are homoscedastic, meaning that the errors around the regression line are constant for all values of x. Finally, there is no autocorrelation among the error terms. The error terms are not correlated with each other across the cases. As seen earlier in our discussion of OLS regression, other assumptions exist regarding the error terms, although these three errors are especially problematic in the case of dichotomous dependent variables.

The first assumption about error terms, that these errors have a mean of 0, is violated with dichotomous dependent variables because determinations of error terms depend on the probability of being "0" or "1." The error terms are related to the probability of the dependent variable being either "0" or "1," and therefore these terms cannot be assumed to have a mean $= 0$. The values of error terms depend upon whether the dependent variable can be dichotomized into a "0" or a "1." We could take the variance, the expected value of the square of the error term, and say that it is equal to PR (where P is the probability of $x = 1$ and R is the probability of $x = 0$, or $1 - P$). Therefore, as P increases, R decreases and vice versa. But by inserting different numbers for P and R into the variance equation, we will fail to have a constant error term.

The second assumption pertains to homoscedasticity and is also violated with dichotomous dependent variables. Because the value of the error terms change with the values of the independent variables, and with the probability of the dependent variable being either "1" or "0," the error term heavily depends on the value of the dependent variable whenever it is dichotomous. Our error term fluctuates based on values of the independent and dependent variables, therefore. If the variance of the error term is not constant (indicated by the first assumption violation), the errors are not homoscedastic but rather heteroscedastic. In Chapter 14, it was shown that heteroscedastic errors yield biased coefficients, leading to inaccurate conclusions about relationships between variables in our data. In this case, logistic regression provides a better model specification, and therefore it ameliorates some of these problems.

The third assumption violation concerning autocorrelation among the error terms relates again to the nature of a dichotomous dependent variable. Logistic regression deals with the probability of taking one of the binary values on the dependent variable, a "0" or a "1." When the probability of a dependent variable taking on one of the values is exactly 1 minus the probability of the dependent variable taking the other value, these probabilities (and their error terms) are absolutely correlated with each other. This perfect autocorrelation may bias our coefficients. Logistic regression takes a clear-cut approach in resolving this problem. If we know the probability that our dependent variable will have one value is 1 minus the probability that it will have the other value, we can easily interpret the probability of having either value. Thus, by knowing the chance of taking on one value, we automatically know the chance of taking on the other value. So, saying there is a 60 percent chance of going to prison also lets us know that there is a 40 percent chance of not going to prison.

Therefore, because of the nature of dichotomous dependent variables, as well as the subsequent problems regarding the error terms that accompany them, the relationship between independent variables and dichotomous dependent variables is not linear. With a dichotomous dependent variable, because the effect of x on y changes with values of x, OLS regression cannot calculate a straight line fitting the data. This violates the regression assumption of linearity and OLS is therefore inappropriate as an analytic technique with these data. According to Studenmund (1997), other problems with a dichotomous dependent variable are that the predicted values would be unlikely to be in the 0, 1 range. Furthermore, the R-squared and adjusted R-squared would be rendered meaningless and they would no longer be good measures of fit. Where data have dichotomous dependent variables, logistic regression is more appropriate because of several relaxed assumptions with its application.

LOGISTIC REGRESSION

Logistic regression (sometimes called **binary logistic regression, dichotomous regression,** or **logit**) is an analytical technique that can be employed where the dependent variable is dichotomous because it has assumptions that are less rigorous than the assumptions of OLS regression. Logistic regression refers to a technique that can be used where the researcher has both continuous and dichotomous independent variables and a dichotomous dependent variable. Logit finds the best-fitting equation, as does OLS, but alternative methods are used to accomplish this task (Liao, 1994). That is, instead of using least squares deviation criterion to find the best fit, logit uses a maximum likelihood technique called **maximum likelihood estimation**. Maximum likelihood estimation is a technique where the program estimates the coefficients, gauges how close its estimated model comes to reality, and then recalculates the model until the likelihood of getting a group of coefficients with the same proportion of "0"s and "1"s that are in the data is maximized (Roncek, 1993). Thus, logit resolves the problem of unboundedness by using the log of the odds that a score on the dependent variable will be 1. The logit equation is therefore

$$\ln\left(\frac{P}{1-P}\right) = a + b_1 x_1 + b_2 x_2 + \ldots$$

where

$\ln$ = the natural log

P = the probability of an event occurring (being a "1" on the dependent variable).

The formula to the right of the equal sign is the same as that for a regression line. In the logit formula, both the independent and dependent variables become unbounded, with a range of infinity (when $P = 1$) to negative infinity (when $P = 0$).

Dichotomous dependent variables violate several of the assumptions underlying OLS regression; however, there are some assumptions that are the same as those for OLS regression. Box 15.1 lists some of the important assumptions for logistic regression. Notice that in Box 15.1

BOX 15.1

Logistic Regression Assumptions

Assumptions that differ from OLS Regression:

Logistic regression does not assume that a linear relationship exists between the dependent variable and the independent variables.

In Logistic regression, the dependent variable does not need to follow the normal distribution.

Logistic regression does not assume that the error terms are normally distributed.

Logistic regression does not require that the dependent variable is homoscedastic at each level of the independent variables.

Logistic regression does not require that the independent variables be measures at the interval level.

Logistic regression does not require that the independent variables be unbounded.

Assumptions that are the same as OLS Regression:

All relevant variables must be included in the model.

No irrelevant variables have been included in the model.

Logistic regression does not assume linearity but assumes that there is a linear relationship between the independent variable and the logit (log of the odds) of P (probability of being 1).

In logistic regression, the error terms are assumed to be independent.

In logistic regression, additivity in the model is assumed.

In logistic regression, we can have no perfect multicollinearity. In other words, no independent variable or group of independent variables can be perfectly correlated with another independent variable or group of independent variables.

the assumptions are the same as those for OLS regression as well as those that are different from OLS regression.

Although OLS regression may produce somewhat acceptable results for dichotomous dependent variables for moderate, or centered, values of X, for extreme values on the independent variable, OLS regression will yield regression coefficients that are biased or inaccurate, usually underestimates of the effects of the independent variables. Since OLS regression analysis is inappropriate for dichotomous dependent variables, binary logistic regression, which has relaxed assumptions that can more easily be met with these type of variables, may be used.

ANALYSIS AND INTERPRETATION

The logistic regression technique can be used through the application of the latest version of *SPSS* software. Using binary logistic regression for example, Hartley, Maddan, and Spohn (2007) studied federal crack and powder cocaine offenders to determine what factors were influential in predicting which types of defendants were likely to receive a substantial assistance departure. Using both legal and extralegal factors as well as differentiating the type of drug and the sentencing statute used against defendants, the authors found that different factors influence the receipt of a departure for substantial assistance based upon the type of drug and the type of case. Specifically, prosecutors were less likely to file substantial assistance departure motions for offenders charged with offenses involving crack cocaine (rather than powder cocaine), but they were more likely to file motions for those offenders facing mandatory minimum sentences. Offenders charged with more serious crimes and with more substantial criminal histories (in some instances) had a greater likelihood of receiving departures, as did female offenders, white offenders, and more educated offenders.

In this instance, the dependent variable was the receipt of a substantial assistance departure. At the federal level, prosecutors may file motions so that defendants who provide substantial assistance may get departures from what their punishments normally would be. For example, if defendants give information about other offenders or assist the prosecutor in other cases, their punishments may be reduced through a departure. Considering that punishments are fairly severe in the federal system for those convicted of narcotics offenses, a departure for substantial assistance becomes an important mechanism to mitigate the punishment of defendants who cooperate with prosecutors. In determining who gets these type of departures, it is important to identify which factors are most influential in a prediction of when prosecutors seek this type of departure. If extralegal factors are playing an important role, then these types of departures may be a source of disparity in sentencing these and other offenders.

Suppose we wanted to conduct a study similar to Hartley et al. (2007), but we also wanted to see whether how the case is disposed influences the receipt of a substantial assistance departure. Suppose that we also want to know whether if a defendant pleads guilty versus pleading not guilty and going to trial matters in a decision about whether they will receive a departure for substantial assistance. For this type of study, several independent variables would be chosen because of their relevance to receipt of a substantial assistance departure. With this type of analysis and by using logistic regression, we would be able to examine the factors that are influential in prosecutorial decisions about which types of defendants receive these departures. For this analysis, data would probably be acquired from the U.S. Sentencing Commission. As in OLS regression, the data must be examined carefully to ensure that no random or systematic errors in coding variables exist. Also, it must be determined whether the variables in the data set and the ways in which they are measured are appropriate for logistic regression analysis. Are all of the assumptions of regression satisfied to the extent that we can utilize the logistic regression technique with these data? These and other questions can be resolved by conducting univariate and bivariate statistical analyses discussed in Chapter 14.

Running the actual logistic regression can be a simple procedure when using statistical software programs such as *SPSS*. But we must not be misled to believe that logistic regression is a simple procedure. Again, variables chosen and the method for which they are included in the analyses should be conducted according to one's theoretical framework for study. For instance, in this example, the variables would be entered according to the current research and literature on sentencing.

The dependent variable for this study is also a dichotomous one, substantial assistance departure or no substantial assistance departure. The dependent variable would be coded as a "1" for receiving a substantial assistance departure and a "0" would be assigned for not receiving a substantial assistance departure. The independent variables would be selected because of their relevance to sentencing as well as to examine the effects of demographic characteristics of defendants on this decision. Using logit, we could gauge what the effects of the seriousness of the crime would be for receiving this type of departure. We would also be able to predict whether pleading guilty versus pleading not guilty and going to trial affects this decision. We could further examine what the effect of being female or being a non-citizen would exert on sentencing decisions. Finally, we could also examine the influence of race/ethnicity and one's pretrial detention status and whether defendants will receive departures for substantial assistance. The results of the logistic regression analysis for a study such as this would be very similar to the output shown in Tables 15.1a and Tables 15.1b.

The first two boxes in the regression output in Table 15.1a refer to the overall regression model and give us information about whether our regression model was significant as well as how much of the variance we explained in the dependent variable with the independent variables we entered. Table 15.1b lists the regression statistics and coefficients for the effects of each of the independent variables we used in the analysis. Again, these statistics may look intimidating and can sometimes be complex to interpret. As such, it is critical to follow the five important steps in logistic regression interpretation listed below. For most

TABLE 15.1 a. SPSS Output for Logistic Regression;
b. SPSS Regression Coefficients

a. Omnibus Tests of Model Coefficients

		x_2	df	Sig.
Step 1	Step	1230.886	12	.000
	Block	1230.886	12	.000
	Model	1230.886	12	.000

Model Summary

Step	−2 Log Likelihood	Cox and Snell R^2	Nagelkerke R^2
1	10291.003[a]	.126	.176

[a]Estimation terminated at iteration number 7 because parameter estimates changed by less than .001.

b. SPSS Regression Coefficients

		b	SE	Wald	df	Sig.	Exp(B)
Step 1[a]	Criminal History	.083	.015	29.036	1	.000	1.087
	Offense Level	.069	.005	223.377	1	.000	1.071
	Number of Counts	−.038	.024	2.523	1	.112	.963
	Disposition = Trial	−3.727	.266	197.013	1	.000	.024
	Offense = Trafficking	.429	.109	15.498	1	.000	1.536
	Offender was Detained	−.517	.057	81.780	1	.000	.596
	Offender is Female	.280	.075	13.884	1	.000	1.323
	Drug Type = Crack	−.159	.059	7.165	1	.007	.853
	Offender is Noncitizen	−.381	.075	25.718	1	.000	.683
	Sentenced under Mandatory Minimum	.462	.073	39.774	1	.000	1.588
	Offender is Black	−.532	.077	47.700	1	.000	.587
	Offender is Hispanic	−.679	.086	61.758	1	.000	.507
	Constant	−2.874	.242	140.810	1	.000	.056

[a]Variable(s) entered on step 1: xchissr, xfolsor, nocounts, disposit, monofftp, present, monsex, drugtyp1, icitizen, statute, black, hispanic.

BOX 15.2

SPSS Alternative Application

To conduct an analysis similar to the study above, a data set including variables containing information on federal narcotics offenders would be needed. A data set that includes a variable containing information on whether or not a defendant received a departure for substantial assistance.

1. To conduct a logistic regression analysis using *SPSS* software, open the *SPSS* program and a data set of interest.
2. Next click on the tab at the top that says "Analyze," then click on "Regression," then on "Binary logistic." This will bring up a new window for the logistic regression analysis. It is in this window that you will have options to enter the dependent and independent variables from a list. Binary logistic regression in *SPSS* is the procedure for logistic regression.
3. The next step would involve highlighting the variables of interest from the left-hand window and moving it over to the appropriate box in the right-hand window. In this instance, we would want to use a number of variables. The dependent variable is whether or not the defendant received a substantial assistance departure. Find the variable measuring this and highlight it, then move it to the box for Dependent.
4. Next, the independent variables that you are interested in need to be highlighted on the left and moved to the box on the right entitled covariates. Variables entered as covariates or our independent variables may include: the offense seriousness score, criminal history category, number of conviction counts, sex, race, disposition, citizenship status, type of drug, and type of case, offense type and pre-trial detention status. These are some of the variables that have been shown to be theoretically linked to decisions regarding departures. The demographic variables above would be included as controls.
5. Click on the tab "OK" and *SPSS* will run the regression. A new window will pop up giving us our output for the logistic regression analysis.
  The output that comes out for a logistic regression analysis in *SPSS* will look similar to the OLS regression output in Chapter 14, very quantitative and somewhat confusing. The *SPSS* output for the logistic regression example is presented in Table 15.1a and 15.1b.

TABLE 15.2 Decision on Receipt of a Substantial Assistance Departure: Logistic Regression of Federal Crack and Cocaine Offenders

Variable	b	SE	Exp(B)	B_R	Rank
Criminal History	.083*	.015	1.087	.0012	10
Offense Level	.069*	.005	1.071	.0004	11
Number of Counts	−.038	.024	.963	.0009	
Disposition = Trial	−3.72*	.266	.024	.9895	1
Offense = Trafficking	.429*	.109	1.536	.0467	3
Offender was Detained	−.517*	.057	.596	.0295	6
Offender is Female	.280*	.075	1.323	.0210	8
Drug Type = Crack	−.159*	.059	.853	.0093	9
Offender is Noncitizen	−.381*	.075	.683	.0285	7
Sentenced under Mandatory Minimum	.462*	.073	1.588	.0337	5
Offender is Black	−.532*	.077	.587	.0409	4
Offender is Hispanic	−.679*	.086	.507	.0583	2
Constant	−2.874	.242			
Nagelkerke R^2	.176				
N = 9,127					
P = < .05					

research articles using logistic regression, the results from Table 15.1a and b will be presented in a single table in order to simplify reporting one's results. Table 15.2 is an example of how the information from Table 15.1a and b might be formatted into a single tabular format for article purposes.

Interpretation of the output in logistic regression is done in a manner similar to that of OLS regression but with some important modifications. As in Chapter 14, the five important steps for interpreting regression output will be provided. These are summarized in Table 15.3. The first interpretive step in logit regression is a determination of the overall significance of the model. In logistic regression this can be done by inspecting the likelihood ratio statistic. Logistic regression uses a **chi-square test** variation with the **−2 log likelihood**. This test compares the −2 log likelihood of the intercept and covariate (with all of the independent variables) model with the "intercept only" model. Again we verify whether the significance associated with this statistic is less than .05. This significance level is shown in the Omnibus Tests of Model Coefficients section. As shown by this example, the overall model is significant (looking at the stepwise block under the Sig. column) because it is 0.000. In the second part of Table 15.1a, the −2 log Likelihood for the model is given. If *SPSS* did not yield the significance associated with this number, then this −2 log likelihood number could also be compared with critical chi-square values obtained from Table A.4, Appendix A, using the appropriate degrees of freedom (*df*). If the calculated number of the −2 log likelihood exceeds the critical value of chi-square shown in Table A.4, then we can consider our overall model significant statistically at the probability level we have chosen.

The second step is to look at how much of the variance in the dependent variable our model explained. In logistic regression, there is no mathematical counterpart to the R^2, and so a pseudo R^2 is utilized. *SPSS* provides both the **Cox and Snell R^2** and the **Nagelkerke R^2**. Both

TABLE 15.3 Five Steps for Interpreting a Logistic Regression

Step	Questions to Ask	Statistic
1	Is our overall regression model statistically significant? What is the probability the results could have occurred by chance?	−2 Log Likelihood Chi-Square −$P < 0.05$
2	How good is our model? What percentage of the variance in the dependent variable has been explained with our independent variables?	Cox and Snell R^2, or Nagelkerke R^2
3	Which independent variables are statistically significant?	Wald test −$P < 0.05$
4	What is the interpretation of the unstandardized effect of the independent variables that are significant?	Sign of the b, Odds Ratio Exp(B), or better yet, Predicted Probabilities $(P = e^{a+bx} / 1 + e^{a+bx})$
5	What is the relative importance of the magnitude of our independent variables?	β_R (b*SE)

can be considered a PRE statistic, and they are analogs to the R^2 given in an OLS regression output. This is shown in Table 15.1a adjacent to the −2 log Likelihood. Notice the note at the bottom of the model in Table 15.1a. This note tells us how many iterations the logit model went through to obtain the greatest likelihood of our patterns of "0"s and "1"s that best represent the true number in our data.

The third step involves a determination of which of the independent variables were statistically significant. To make this determination in logit, a chi-square test is used. The **Wald statistic** divides the b-coefficients by their standard errors and squares them. Again, these can be compared with critical values of chi-square in Table A.4 in Appendix A, using the appropriate *df*. Again, if the observed chi-square value exceeds the critical value shown in Table A.4, then that variable is considered to be statistically significant. A much easier way is to simply look at the probability associated with the variables. If the probability is below .05, then the particular independent variable is statistically significant. In logistic regression it is a good idea to check for multicollinearity as was done and illustrated in OLS regression. If multicollinearity is present, our resulting b-coefficients could be biased. This can be done easily by placing the dependent and independent variables used into an OLS regression analysis in *SPSS* and click the tab for collinearity diagnostics. Again if the Variance Inflation Factor scores are below four, we have no collinearity problems.

The fourth step is an interpretation of the unstandardized effects of the independent variables that were found to be statistically significant. In Table 15.1b, *SPSS* yields a b-coefficient similar to that produced in OLS regression. This is known as the **logit coefficient**. However, this coefficient is not a measure of the change in the dependent variable (y) for a unit change in an independent variable (x) because we are using a dichotomous dependent variable. Actually it is the **log of the odds** of a change in y for a change in x. Because our independent variables can assume only two possible values on our dependent variable, we must explain the results in terms of the change in the log of the odds for a given coefficient. We can also look at the **odds ratio** denoted by **Exp(B)**, which is also shown in Table 15.1b, to determine how many times more likely it is that the value on the dependent variable will be "1" given the value of the independent variable. Therefore, we should look at the b-coefficient for the sign ($\pm$) and the Odds ratio Exp(B) for the metric effects.

It should also be noted that because the odds ratio refers to the odds that the value of the dependent variable will be 1, the closer that the Exp(B) is to 1, the more the likelihood is that the values of the independent variable are not influential in predicting the dependent variable. For instance, if the b-coefficient and the Exp(B) for the independent variable for citizenship status were -23 and 1.23 respectively, and the citizenship variable was coded "0" for citizens and "1" for noncitizens, we would conclude that noncitizens are less likely to receive a departure. However, since the Exp(B) is close to 1, it means that the odds of receiving a departure are not that much different for citizens and noncitizens although noncitizens have a slightly lesser chance due to the negative sign of the b-coefficient. However, if the b-coefficient and the Exp(B) for the citizenship variable were .23 and 4.1 respectively, we would conclude that noncitizens are more likely than citizens to receive a departure. We would also conclude that noncitizens have more than 4 times greater likelihood of receiving this departure than do citizens.

Although this may seem like a direct interpretation, the log of the odds is not an especially convenient way to interpret the effects of x on y; logit results are usually calculated into probabilities (Roncek, 1991, 1993). In fact, interpreting effects in logit is probably one of the most difficult and misunderstood steps in using this statistical technique (Roncek, 1991). In the long run, it is better to transform the logit coefficients into probabilities. In the original logit formula $\ln (P/1 - P) = a + bx$, if we exponentiate the right side of the equation and carry out the simple algebra, we will see that the probability is $P = e^{a + bx}/1 + e^{a + bx}$. This will then yield the effect on the dependent variable of a particular value on the independent variable. This should be done for meaningful values of x. This is far more practical and more easily understood as the effect of x on y.

Effects can be interpreted for both continuous and dichotomous independent variables (Roncek, 1991, 1993). For continuous variables, Stolzenberg's (1979) principles are used. Assume the first derivative and find a convenient interpretation. In logistic regression, the first-order partial derivative is an equation that must be solved for by using various values of x: $\partial P/\partial X_i = b_i^* \, e^{a + bx}/(1 + e^{a + bx})^2$. This leaves b_1 as the proportional effect on y for a unit change in x, multiplying b_1 by 100 will give the percent change in y for a unit change in x. Maximum and minimal effects should be calculated to obtain a range. Roncek (1991) says that this should be done at $0.25b_1$ for maximum effects and $0.09b_1$ for minimal effects. With independent variables that are dichotomous, this process is somewhat easier. There are only two values assumed by the independent variable (e.g., citizen/noncitizen). Therefore, the effects of having one value on a particular independent variable will also result in the effects of having the other value. Select values of variables that represent important cases. Then calculate the probabilities associated with these and subtract them to get the effects for the other value.

The fifth step is an assessment of the standardized effects. This allows for the rank-ordering of the independent variables according to their importance. Since a logit regression does not have a standard y, the standard deviation is not 1 as in other normal distributions. Rather, the standard deviation is $\pi/\sqrt{3}$ (Roncek, 1991). We can standardize these coefficients by dividing them by the standard deviation of the logit distribution. However, an easier alternative has been developed by Roncek (1997). **Roncek's semi-standardized coefficient (B_R)** can be calculated by multiplying the b-coefficient by its standard deviation, which will yield the proportional effect on y for a standard deviation change in x. The bigger the standardized coefficient (in absolute value) the more important it is. Note this semi-standardized coefficient is not available in *SPSS* output and must be calculated by other means.

Table 15.3 can be used as a guide to interpret the results of the OLS regression presented in Tables 15.1a and b.

Step 1: ***Is our overall regression model statistically significant?*** In our regression output from *SPSS* (Table 15.1a), the significance associated with the *chi-square* statistic for the −2 log likelihood is .000. This is shown in the significance column to the right of the chi-square statistic under the Omnibus Tests of Model Coefficients heading. Since this significance is less than .05, we can be assured that our model is significant at this probability level. This means that the results that we have in our output are not due to chance, and therefore we may proceed to step 2.

Step 2: ***How good is our model? What percentage of the variance in the dependent variable has been explained with our independent variables?*** This step is accomplished by examining either the Cox and Snell R^2 or the Nagelkerke R^2 (Table 15.1a). In this model, the Cox and Snell R^2 is .126, and the Nagelkerke R^2 is .176. Let's use the latter figure since it explains more. When we multiply this by 100 we get 17.6 which means we have explained almost 18 percent of the variation in who gets a substantial assistance departure with our independent variables. Therefore, our variables are explaining only about 18 percent of what influences decision making about the receipt of a substantial assistance departure. Again, in the social sciences, getting a large R^2 is very rare.

Step 3: ***Which independent variables are statistically significant?*** We can determine the significance of the independent variables by looking at the significance associated with the Wald statistic in Tables 15.1b or the asterisked variables in Table 15.2. Again if the significance associated with the Wald statistic is less than .05, we can say that the variable is significant. In this case, all of the variables are significant except the variable for number of counts of conviction. This means almost all of the variables we have chosen for study are significantly associated with the receipt of a substantial assistance departure. With this information we can now move to step 4 and determine which variables are statistically significant.

Step 4: ***What is the interpretation of the unstandardized effect of the independent variables that are statistically significant?*** Again, we will use Tables 15.1b and 15.2 and the coefficients in answering this question. Interpreting the unstandardized effects of the independent variables in a logistic regression can be very confusing. Although the log of the odds, or the odds ratios, have issues regarding their interpretation, most scholarly journals publish these. The odds ratio is interpreted as the likelihood of being a "1" on the dependent variable, in this case the likelihood of receiving a substantial assistance departure. We will use this complex but conventional method for interpreting the effects here. We need to interpret the effects in terms of whether the independent variables are continuous or dichotomous in nature. For the continuous variables we will interpret the b-coefficients as a likelihood change in the dependent variable for a 1-unit change in the independent variable. Continuous variables include the criminal history, the offense level, and the number of counts. The variable for criminal history and offense level are both positive and the Exp(B)s are approximately 1. This means that an increase in offense level and criminal history category does not result in large differences in the receipt of a departure. These effects are seemingly negligible. However, each increase in criminal history or offense level results in an increased chance of receiving this type of departure. And so, if we were to gauge the probability of a departure for someone who has committed a crime at the lowest offense level compared with someone whose offense level is at the highest, there may be larger differences in the likelihood of receiving a departure. The variable for number of counts was not significant, and therefore we do not need to interpret its effects.

Dichotomous variables are more straightforward to interpret. For these, the independent variable can assume only one of two values. However, in these cases we must remember how the variables are coded. For instance, the disposition variable was coded as "0" for someone who plead guilty and "1" for someone who plead not guilty and went to trial. Since the coefficient is negative, we may say that those who plead not guilty and go to trial are less likely to get a substantial assistance departure than those who plead guilty. The odds ratios under the Exp(B) column are negligible, meaning that those who go to trial indeed have a decreased chance, but the odds of this decreased chance are not large. The next variable is offense type, which was coded as "0" for simple possession and "1" for trafficking offenses. We can see that those who are convicted of trafficking offenses have a greater chance of receiving a departure than those convicted of simple possession offenses. The odds are one-and-a-half times greater.

The next variable is pretrial detention. Those detained were coded as "1." Examining the coefficient and odds, we can determine that those detained are less likely to receive a departure and the odds are about 0.6 times as likely. The variable for gender was coded as males = 0 and females = 1. The b-coefficient for this variable is positive, and therefore, we can say that females (because they are coded a "1") have a 1.3 times greater likelihood to receive a substantial assistance departure than males. The variable for type of drug was coded as "0" for cocaine and "1" for crack. The b-coefficient is negative, and therefore those convicted of a crack offense have a decreased likelihood to receive this type of departure, although the odds are minimal at .853. The variable for citizen was coded as "0" for a U.S. citizen and "1" for noncitizen. The coefficient is negative, meaning that noncitizens have decreased odds of receiving a departure. Again, looking at the Exp(B) we see that effects are minimal. The variable for type of case was coded as "0" for guidelines cases and "1" for mandatory minimum cases. We see that those sentenced under mandatory minimum cases have a 1.5 times greater likelihood of receiving a departure. Finally, the variables for being black and Hispanic show that blacks are less likely than whites, and Hispanics are less likely than non-Hispanics, to receive a departure. However, the odds ratios are negligible.

Step 5: *What is the relative importance of the magnitude of our independent variables?* In order to answer this question, we must examine the standardized effects. It will be recalled in logistic regression that we do not obtain a standardized effect through the *SPSS* output. Therefore, we must calculate the standardized effects manually. We can calculate Roncek's semi-standardized coefficient easily by multiplying the b-coefficient by its standard error. These two statistics are provided in *SPSS* output under the columns B and S.E. It is generally the case that the greater the standardized effect, the better, in absolute value. Most researchers will include a standardized effect in their research reports. In Table 15.2, it is seen that there is a column where Roncek's semi-standardized coefficient is reported under the column B_R, together with another column showing the rank order of the variables. If we examine this column, we observe that the most important variable in the model of whether someone will receive a substantial assistance departure is the variable for the disposition of the case. In step four it was shown that those who go to trial are less likely to receive a departure. The variable we are interested in studying appears to be the most important predictor in the model of whether someone will receive a departure. Why would this be the most important variable in the model? One guess is that prosecutors are more likely to negotiate with defendants who are willing to plead guilty. People who plead guilty are more likely to receive concessions from the prosecutor, which may include departures from the presumptive sentence. The second most important variable is whether the offender was a Hispanic. The third most important variable is whether the offense was for trafficking or simple possession. The least important variables are the variables for offense level and criminal history. This means that a defendant's offense seriousness and criminal history are not especially important for influencing a prosecutor's decision about who will receive departure for substantial assistance.

Limitations of Logistic Regression

One of the most frequently cited criticisms of logistic regression is that the effects on the dependent variable rely on the values of the independent variables (Liao, 1994). While this is not problematic for situations where large samples are used, it can become problematic when smaller data sets are analyzed. One rule of thumb used to gauge whether there are sufficient numbers of cases for a study is that the number of cases for the lower of the two dichotomous outcomes (for instance, if more persons were sent to prison than not in your data, the rule applies to the number of cases that did not go to prison) should be at least 10 times the number of independent variables you are using in the analysis. If you have 10 independent variables, you should have at least 100 cases where the defendant did not go to prison. Other problems involve multicollinearity, which can make it difficult for regression to isolate and separate out the independent effects. Another problem in logistic regression may be **influence**. Influential cases are outliers, or those cases outside the distribution of the rest of the cases. These can alter the results of logit regression output. Data can be scanned for problematic or influential cases, and if necessary, these cases can be deleted. Finally, because logit is a maximum likelihood estimation technique, validity becomes a problem where sample sizes are small. If this is the case, there are more advanced techniques that have been developed. For instance, Metah and Patel (1995) have generated an exact logit technique for use with small samples.

Interaction Effects With Logistic Regression

Interaction terms and dummy variables can also be used in logit and are constructed similarly as they are for OLS regression analysis. They are also entered into the equation in a similar manner. Interaction terms can be added to a model by taking the product of the value of each variable. The section in Chapter 14 referring to constructing and imputing dummy variables for interaction terms in an OLS regression should be revisited. Follow the same steps for their use with logistic regression.

The next regression techniques discussed in this chapter violate similar assumptions associated with the logit technique previously described. Similarly, they can easily be conducted in the *SPSS* software program and interpreted using the five important steps with minor modifications. Therefore, the discussion of them will be less in-depth compared with our examination of logistic regression.

OTHER LOGISTIC REGRESSION TECHNIQUES

Ordered Logistic Regression

Many investigators in the social sciences administer surveys to subjects where their survey data almost always includes variables measured according to nominal and ordinal scales rather than interval scales (e.g., strongly agree, agree, disagree, and strongly disagree). In Chapter 14, it was determined that OLS regression assumes the interval level of measurement. Thus, ordinal-level data are not easily amenable as a dependent variable for regression analysis. However some advances have been made, as discussed earlier in the logistic regression section. One advance is the invention of a technique called **ordered logit regression**, sometimes referred to as ordinal logit regression. This technique is similar to binary logistic regression except that it is designed for use with dependent variables that have more than one outcome and are measurable according to an ordinal scale. And so rather than having a dependent variable with only two outcomes, as is the case with ordered logit, the dependent variable can have more than two outcomes, although it continues to be a limited dependent variable because it is measured at the ordinal level. The analysis and interpretation for ordered logit is similar to that for binary logit, with minor exceptions. Refer to the steps in Table 15.3 for interpreting logit results and applying them to ordered logit results.

In ordered logit, one additional step is needed to determine whether our data are amenable to its use. This additional step uses the **proportional odds assumption test**. This step is needed in situations where there are different categories on the dependent variable. The different categories will share a unique intercept, but the slopes related to each category must be similar. If this is the case, then ordered logit may be utilized. The proportional odds assumption test is a test that determines whether the slopes of the various categories are equal. In essence, it makes a determination of whether the proportional odds are different. We must be sure that the proportional odds are not proportionately different to permit the use of ordered logit. The proportional odds assumption procedure tests the null hypothesis that there is no difference in the proportions of the odds or the slopes. Therefore, unlike other significance tests, we must fail to reject the null hypothesis in order to validate the use of ordered logit. It will be recalled from a previous chapter that the *F* test for analysis of variance required homogeneity of variance or equal variances in order to be applied properly. Tests were presented to examine whether *k*-sample variances were equal. That situation was similar in that as investigators, we did not want to reject the null hypothesis that the sample variances were the same. We wanted the variances to be equal. Thus, our proportional odds assumption procedure is viewed similarly in that we want the different proportions of the odds of slopes to be the same.

James Unnever, Francis Cullen, and Bonnie Fischer (2007) used an ordinal logistic regression to determine what factors shape conservative political beliefs. They looked at several dependent variables that were measured on an ordinal level. They wanted to see what predicts opposition to guns laws, opposition to abortion, opposition to civil rights for

BOX 15.3

SPSS Alternative Application

Ordered logit is most often used with survey data. The dependent variable in survey research is often measured by Likert scales or some other similar scaling procedures. This type of dependent variable is ordinal rather than interval. This technique can be easily conducted with *SPSS* software.

1. To conduct an ordered logistic regression analysis in the *SPSS* software, open the *SPSS* program and a data set of interest.
2. Next click on the tab, "Analyze," then click "Regression," then "Ordinal." This will bring up a new window for the ordered logistic regression analysis. In this window, you will have options for entering the dependent and independent variables from a list. Ordinal logistic regression in *SPSS* is the procedure for ordered logit.
3. The next step involves highlighting the variables of interest from the left-hand window and moving it over to the appropriate box in the right-hand window. In this instance we would want to use a number of variables. The dependent variable would be one that has more than one outcome and is measured at an ordinal level. Find the variable of interest and highlight it, then move it to the box for "Dependent."
4. Next, the independent variables that you are interested in need to be highlighted on the left and moved to the box on the right entitled factors. Variables entered as factors will act as the independent variables.
5. Click on "OK" and *SPSS* will run the ordinal regression. A new window will be displayed with the output for the ordinal logistic regression analysis.

homosexuals, and other conservative political beliefs. They were most interested in whether being victimized or fear of crime was influential on these conservative beliefs. Suppose we wanted to conduct a similar analysis on fear of crime. In other words, we wanted to see what factors affect someone's fear of crime measured on a scale from 1 to 4, 1 being not fearful, 2 being not very fearful, 3 being somewhat fearful, and 4 being very fearful. These are attitudes measure on an ordinal level scale. In order to see what characteristics of persons causes them to be fearful of crime or not, we would have to conduct an ordinal logistic regression. Let's say we administered a survey to students in a criminal justice program and asked them to rate their fear of crime on a scale of 1 to 4. This is a very simple example for our purposes. In a full-scale survey, many questions would be asked about crime. Suppose we also asked them to record various demographic information as well. Information such as age, gender, year in school, whether they live with parents, whether they have ever been victimized, and whether they knew someone who has been victimized would be obtained. Next, we would dummy code these answers. Gender would be a "0" for males and a "1" for females; for year in school, we would create four separate variables for freshman, sophomore, junior, and senior and then leave freshman out as the reference category; we would code students living on their own a "0" and students living at home a "1"; students who had never been victimized would be coded a "0" and student who had been victimized would be coded "1"; similarly if students did not know someone who had been victimized, they would be coded a "0", if they knew someone who was victimized, they would be coded a "1." This information would be entered into *SPSS*, and the application for running an ordinal logistic regression would be followed. Next, we would want to enter the output into a table such as Table 15.4.

TABLE 15.4 Ordinal Logistic Regression on Fear of Crime for Criminal Justice Students

Variable	b	SE	Sig.
Age	−.05*	.015	.032
Female	.23*	.005	.021
Sophomore	.13*	.024	.014
Junior	−.72*	.066	.024
Senior	−.429*	.109	.003
Lives at Home	−.517*	.057	.007
Victimized	.25*	.075	.032
Know Someone Victimized	.159	.059	.853
Nagelkerke R^2	.247		
$N = 295$			
*$P < 0.05$			

Interpretation of an ordinal logistic regression is similar to the logistic regression with dichotomous dependent variables. Again use the five steps for interpretation:

Step 1: *Is the model as a whole statistically significant?* This can be determined by looking at the Likelihood ratio test, and the significance associated with the −2 Log Likelihood Statistic for dichotomous logit. It should be noted that there will also be more than one intercept presented in the output, there will be one less than the number of categories of the dependent variable, in our case there would be three intercepts because our dependent variables has four categories. Usually, the first intercept is for the category with the largest number.

Step 2: *How much does the model as a whole explain?* Again, we will use a pseudo R^2, in Table 15.4, the Nagelkerke R^2 is reported. Here it is .247, meaning that we have explained 25 percent of the variance in fear of crime with our independent variables.

Step 3: *Which independent variables are statistically significant?* Again, in Table 15.4, this can be judged by looking at the significance column, or by looking at the variables coefficients that are denoted by an asterisk. All of our variables except the one for whether the respondent knows someone who has been victimized are significant.

Step 4: *How much did each variable explain?* Similar to logistic regression, in interpreting the b-coefficient, we look at it as a proportional change in the odds for a change in x or by gauging minimum and maximum effects. There is no odds ratio given in an *SPSS* output, but if you multiply the b-coefficient by 100, you will get the percentage change in odds for a change in x. With a quick glance, however, we can see that by looking at the signs of the b-coefficients, the older students are, the less fearful of crime they are. Female students are more likely to be fearful of crime. Sophomores are more likely to be fearful of crime than freshman, however, both junior and seniors are less likely to be as fearful of crime as freshman. Those students who still live at home are less fearful. Being victimized does make students more fearful but simply knowing someone who has been victimized does not affect the level of fear of crime as this variable was not significant.

Step 5:   ***What is the relative importance of the magnitude of our independent variables?*** Again, calculate Roncek's semi-standardized coefficient and then rank order the significant variables in importance.

Multinomial Logistic Regression

Multinomial logistic regression, also referred to as **Multinomial logit** is for use with nominal-level dependent variables. For example, multinomial logit could be used for analyzing dependent variables such as political affiliation (Democrat, Republican, Independent, and Green Party). These variables violate the traditional regression assumptions that the dependent variable is continuous and unbounded. But as in logistic regression, these assumptions are overcome with the use of odds and the log of the odds. The multinomial logistic regression technique overcomes some of the assumption violations by testing the various categories of the dependent variable against one reference category. In this sense it is like a series of binary logits. For example, $\ln (P1/P4)$, $\ln (P2/P4)$, $\ln (P3/P4)$, $P4$ being the reference category. So, for the present example, the multinomial analysis would compare Democrats versus the Green Party, then Republicans versus the Green Party, and then Independents versus the Green Party. In this way, a number of logistic regressions are created, and the number of logit equations are equal to the number of categories minus one. Multinomial logit, however, requires an additional assumption because it is a series of dichotomous logits. This assumption is independence of irrelevant alternatives, in that the categories of the dependent variable must be real alternatives of each other (Roncek, 1991). None of these can be subcategories of another category. Also, the reference category should not be smaller than the other categories. For instance, we may want to use Democrats or Republicans as the reference category rather than the Green Party, since the former parties probably have more members than the latter party. If these additional assumptions have been met, the five important steps for interpretation can be utilized. However, step 4 is not completed in a multinomial logit because unstandardized effects cannot be calculated for this particular procedure.

King and Weiner (2007) used a multinomial logit in a study of, among other things, anti-Semitism. One of the dependent variables they used came from a question asked to respondents about their attitudes toward marrying a Jewish person. The three possible responses were: disapprove, indifferent, and approve. This type of variable is measured at the nominal level and consists of three categories, therefore, the appropriate technique is a multinomial logistic regression. These authors were interested to see what characteristics were influential in choosing any one of those three responses. Suppose that we were interested in examining the factors that influence a person's political affiliation. Much in the same way as King and Weiner, we could obtain a sample of persons, for instance, a random sample of persons who participated in the last census, and run a multinomial logistic regression on which characteristics are influential in a determination of whether persons classify themselves as Green Party, Democrat, or Republican. Some of the characteristics we would want information on to serve as independent variables might include age, race, ethnicity, education, gender, employment status, and marital status. If we were to follow the

---

BOX 15.4

SPSS **Alternative Application**

Multinomial logit is most often used where dependent variables are measured at the nominal level. For instance, we are often interested in how persons vary in their religious affiliations. We might be interested in the characteristics of persons who are members of different religious faiths which can be categorized. These categories of religious faiths are measured at the nominal level (e.g., Catholic, Presbyterian, Baptist, and Jewish). The multinomial logit technique can be easily conducted in *SPSS*.

1. To conduct a multinomial logistic regression analysis in the *SPSS* statistical software, open the *SPSS* program and a data set of interest.
2. Next click "Analyze," then "Regression," then "Multinomial Logistic." This will disclose a new window for the multinomial logistic regression analysis. It is in this window that you will have options to enter the dependent and independent variables from a list.
3. The next step involves highlighting the variables of interest from the left-hand window and moving it over to the appropriate box in the right-hand window. In this instance we would want to use a number of variables. The dependent variable would be the variable of interest that is measured at the nominal level. Find the variable of interest and highlight it, then move it to the box for Dependent.
4. An additional step is required here. Under the box for Dependent, there is a tab that is labeled "Reference Category". This tab must be clicked in order for you to tell *SPSS* which of the categories of the dependent variable you want to be the reference category or the category you want *SPSS* to compare with all other categories. You will have the option to choose the first or the last category as the reference. This is an important thing to remember when looking at the univariate statistics for your data set. Remember the rules of thumb regarding the selection of the reference category. We want the reference category to be the category that takes on the most values or has the largest number of cases. The variable may need to be recoded in order that either the first or last category is the one with the largest number of cases so that the multinomial logit regression technique will properly run.
5. Next, the independent variables that you are interested in need to be highlighted on the left and moved to the box on the right entitled factors. Variables entered as factors will act as the independent variables.
6. Click on the tab "OK" and *SPSS* will run the ordinal regression. A new window will pop up giving the output for the ordinal logistic regression analysis.

SPSS Alternative Application in Box 15.4, we would get *SPSS* output and report the information in a table such as Table 15.5.

Interpreting Effects in Multinomial Logit

The purpose of multinomial logit is to test the odds of being in a particular category of the dependent variable relative to the odds of being in the reference category. In this sense, the number of coefficients and equations will depend on the number of categories on the dependent variable. Therefore, the number of equations in a multinomial logit will be equal to the number of categories less 1. Interpretation for multinomial logit is similar to OLS and regular logistic regression. However, one difference is that more than one equation will be produced, and therefore more than one coefficient for each independent variable will be yielded. Another difference is that

TABLE 15.5 Multinomial Logistic Regression of Political Affiliation

Variable	EXP(B)	SE
Green Party versus Republican		
Age	.95*	.015
Female	1.03*	.005
Caucasian	−1.53*	.024
High School Graduate	−1.72*	.066
College Graduate	.429	.109
Unemployed	−.517*	.057
Married	−2.2*	.075
Hispanic	.159	.059
Democrat versus Republican		
Age	−1.2*	.054
Female	−.95*	.043
Caucasian	−1.6*	.034
High School Graduate	−.75	.042
College Graduate	1.24*	.061
Unemployed	−.89*	.067
Married	.75	.089
Hispanic	1.2*	.035
Nagelkerke R^2	.398	
$N = 1,245$		
*$P < 0.05$		

for multinomial logit, the best measure of the strength of the model or the amount of variance explained is again with a pseudo R^2. *SPSS* gives three options for the R^2, again, probably the Nagelkerke R^2 is the best of the three. Despite having a number of different categories and equations, there will only be one R^2. When interpreting the independent variables, interpret only those that are significant. Note, we do not get b-coefficients in a multinomial logistic regression, and so usually researchers will report odds ratios. Again, the same principles used in logistic regression apply here as well. For standardized effects and in order to rank variables in importance, we will use Roncek's (1997) semi-standardized coefficient.

In Table 15.5, the odds ratios are reported, denoted by Exp(B), this gives us the likelihood of being in the category of interest versus the reference category. Again, the same steps are used in interpreting a multinomial logit as for a regular binary logistic regression.

Step 1: *Is the model as a whole statistically significant?* This can be determined by looking at the Likelihood ratio test and the significance associated with the −2 Log Likelihood Statistic. If the significance is less than .05, our overall model is significant.

Step 2: *How much does the model as a whole explain?* Again, we will use a pseudo R^2, in Table 15.5, the Nagelkerke R^2 is reported. Here it is .398, meaning that we have explained almost 40 percent of the variance in political affiliation with our independent variables.

Step 3: ***Which independent variables are statistically significant?*** Again, in Table 15.5, this can be judged by looking at the variables that are denoted by asterisks. All of our variables except the ones for college graduate and Hispanic are significant for the Green Party versus Republican model, and all except high school graduate and being married are significant for the Democrat versus Republican model.

Step 4: ***How much did each variable explain?*** Remember that in multinomial logistic regression, there are no unstandardized effects that are produced, therefore researchers usually report odds ratios. In Table 15.5, for the Green Party versus Republican model, we can observe that age and gender are both positive but have negligible effects. In other words, older persons and females are more likely to be affiliate with the green party, but the odds are not that much greater. Regarding the other variables, being Caucasian and a high school graduate are negatively related with being affiliated with the Green party. In other words, being Caucasian and a high school graduate, the odds are over 1.5 times more likely that you will be Republican. Being unemployed also makes it less likely that you are affiliated with the Green Party but odds are negligible, and finally, those who are married are 2.2 times less likely to be a Green Party member versus Republican party member. For the model testing Democrat versus Republican, we can observe that older persons, females, and those not employed are less likely to be Democrats but the odds are small. Caucasians are 1.5 times less likely to be democrats. Finally, those who are college graduates and those who are Hispanic are 1.2 times more likely to be affiliated with the Democratic party.

Step 5: ***What is the relative importance of the magnitude of our independent variables?*** Again, calculate Roncek's semi-standardized coefficient and then rank-order the significant variables in importance.

Poisson and Negative Binomial Regression

In logistic, ordinal and multinomial regression, our dependent variables are categorical. However, **Poisson regression** is a technique useful for count data. Count data are data which are bounded. For example, suppose you were interested in the number of burglaries occurring in various neighborhoods in your city. Although the number of burglaries could be considered as a continuous variable, the variable does have a lower boundary, "0." There will be no neighborhoods with less than zero burglaries. Although OLS regression can be utilized with this type of dependent variable, Poisson regression is probably a better method for investigation of variables that are counts of events such as crimes. Most data in the social sciences are count data or counts of incidents. Like many of the dependent variables in the ordinal and multinomial logit, count variables violate the traditional regression assumptions of continuity and unboundedness. It is also likely that the errors are heteroscedastic and not normally distributed. In count data involving crime, the relationship between the independent variable and dependent variable is not linear. Rather, it takes the form of an L-shaped curve because of the high number of zero values. Therefore, Poisson regression relaxes the assumption required in OLS regression that the independent and dependent variable coefficients must be linear. Instead, Poisson regression assumes that there is a linear relationship between the log of lambda and sum of the independent variables. The equation therefore is:

$$\ln(\lambda) = \Sigma bx.$$

$\ln(\lambda)$ = the log of lambda

Σbx = the linear sum of the independent variables

For this equation, the log of lambda is a linear function of the independent variables. In using the log of λ in Poisson regression, the independent variables can assume any value, but Σbx will never be less than zero.

Poisson regression also has the assumption that the variance of the dependent variable equals its mean. In social science we rarely achieve this result, since our variances usually exceed our means. We have what is referred to in statistical terms as **overdispersion**. Generally, there are two ways of testing for overdispersion. One way involves a **test of the significance of the dispersion parameter (alpha)**. The second way is the **Cameron and Trivedi test**. Either of these tests will reveal if the data are overdispersed. Depending on the outcome of these two tests, we would use either Poisson regression (if the data are not overdispersed) or **negative binomial regression** (if the data are overdispersed). If the data are overdispersed, then we must use a technique called negative binomial regression. Negative binomial regression overcomes the problem of overdispersion by using the gamma distribution. Using the **gamma distribution** introduces another error term into the equation: $(\ln (\lambda) = a + \Sigma bx + \varepsilon)$. As a result, we have two error terms, the standard one, or the difference between the actual and predicted y, and a random one, Epsilon, which allows the errors to float by the gamma distribution. Negative binomial regression cannot be done using the *SPSS* program. Therefore, no alternative *SPSS* application will be provided here. Other software programs such as Statistical Analysis System (SAS) can readily perform analyses using Poisson or negative binomial regression.

Let's suppose that we were interested in investigating what factors about neighborhoods determine the number of residential burglaries that occur in those neighborhoods. The number of residential burglaries by neighborhood are counts of this type of crime. Therefore, we would have to use the technique that is appropriate for data that are counts of incidents. Here we would employ the use of Poisson regression. However, often data on crime are overdispersed, meaning that the variance is not equal to the mean. For instance, the number of burglaries in different neighborhoods varies considerably. In fact, the variance in burglaries by neighborhood is probably larger that the mean or average number of burglaries. We know that some neighborhoods will have zero burglaries, most will have a few, and still there will be others that have numerous burglaries. In this case the average number of burglaries may be small say 10 or 12, but the variance will be larger than that because we have many neighborhoods with no burglaries and some with possibly hundreds of burglaries. If this is the case, we say our data is overdispersed; if our data are overdispersed, we resort to employing a technique called negative binomial regression. Let's say we utilize the negative binomial regression technique as our dependent variable and we have various neighborhood characteristics for our independent variables. Characteristics such as: neighborhood population, percentage of dwellings that are rented, number of dwellings that are vacant, median housing value, median family income, and percentage young males. The output from a Negative Binomial Regression reported in tabular format would look similar to Table 15.6.

Poisson and Negative Binomial Interpretation

Again interpretation using this technique can be done by using the five important steps utilized in previous regression analyses:

Step 1: ***Is the model as a whole statistically significant?*** Assess overall significance by using the likelihood ratio statistic associated with the -2 log likelihood. Again, if the probability is less than .05, the overall model is significant.

Step 2: ***How much does the model as a whole explain?*** Assess the strength of the model. For Poisson and Negative Binomial Regression an Adjusted R^2 is calculated. For the

TABLE 15.6 Negative Binomial Regression on Neighborhood Characteristics on Burglaries

Variable	b	SE	Sig. [t]	B_R
Population	.052*	.015	.032	.79
Percent Rented	.093*	.005	.021	.34
Number of Vacant Houses	.031*	.024	.003	.24
Median Housing Value (thousands of $)	−.072*	.036	.024	−.11
Median Income (thousands of $)	−.042*	.009	.001	−.32
Percent Young Male	.517	.038	.596	.54
Adjusted R^2	.512			
N = 65				

results in Table 15.6, the Adjusted R^2 is .512, this means we have explained just over 50 percent of the variation in burglaries with our neighborhood variables.

Step 3: ***Which independent variables are statistically significant?*** Determine which of the independent variables are statistically significant. In most Poisson and negative binomial outputs (*SAS* for instance), both the coefficients and the probability associated with the *t* statistics are provided. Simply make a determination of the significant variables by examining which ones have probabilities associated with the *t* statistics that are less than .05. In tabular format, again, these are the variables denoted with asterisks. In Table 15.6, we can see that all of the variables are significant except the variable for the percentage of young males in the neighborhood.

Step 4: ***How much did each variable explain?*** Interpret unstandardized effects of the significant independent variables. To do this, follow the steps for interpreting unstandardized effects for logistic regression analysis. In this case we would multiply the *b*-coefficients by 100 and interpret as a percentage change in *Y* for a unit change in *X*. For instance, above for the variable population multiplied by 100, we would interpret this as an increase of 5 burglaries for a 1 percent increase in population. For percent-rented dwellings, we can expect an increase of 9.3 burglaries for a 1 percent increase in percentage of dwellings rented. We can also expect an increase of 3 burglaries for each additional house in the neighborhood that is vacant. Finally, we can expect a decrease of seven burglaries for each thousand dollar increase in median housing value, and a decrease of 4 burglaries for each 1000 dollar increase in median family income.

Step 5: ***What is the relative importance of the magnitude of our independent variables?*** Standardized effects can be determined using Roncek's semi-standardized coefficient for continuous independent variables or simply by multiplying the unstandardized effect by the standard deviation of *x*.

Limitations of Poisson and Negative Binomial Regression

Poisson and negative binomial analysis have several criticisms. One of these criticisms is that these techniques have assumptions that are especially harsh. For instance, Poisson requires that the variance equal the mean. The data must not be overdispersed. For social science data, and especially for crime data, this assumption will rarely be met, since the means of criminal events rarely are equal to their variances. For instance, we may have an average number of burglaries in a city per neighborhood of 10, but we know that some neighborhoods may have only 1 or 2 burglaries. A select few may have 60 or 70 burglaries, maybe even hundreds of them. Poisson regression also assumes that our counts of events are positive integers. This is not a problem for criminal events, since we cannot have negative burglaries in any neighborhood. However, Poisson regression assumes that these events occur independently. For criminal events, this assumption becomes problematic because it mandates that each event on the dependent variable occurs separately. We can't always say, for instance, that the burglaries in one neighborhood occurred independently of those in other neighborhoods, especially if the neighborhoods are in close proximity. This is a very stringent assumption to meet for criminologists and criminal justice practitioners. Therefore, these two techniques have limited application. Regardless, these techniques may be useful for criminal justice research. The techniques are designed for use with data that are of counts, they are easy to conduct, and they have interpretations similar to other logit regression techniques. They are also useful tools where their assumptions are met by the data being analyzed.

The previous procedures regarding regression with limited dependent variables are the most popular and widely used techniques. The techniques described thus far, however, are not the only ones available for use with dependent variables that are limited in nature. There are several other procedures that may be more appropriate for use with limited dependent variables and social science and criminal justice data. However, a comprehensive discussion of these various techniques is beyond the scope of this chapter. Nevertheless, several other techniques have been advanced for use with dependent variables that are limited and will be discussed briefly in the following section. These analytical procedures have played important roles in researching crime and social science phenomena.

Multicollinearity for Logistic Regression Techniques

Multicollinearity was mentioned briefly in the discussion of logit regression for dichotomous dependent variables. As we saw in Chapter 14, multicollinearity can have serious implications for OLS Regression. When using any of the regression techniques for limited dependent variables discussed in this chapter, multicollinearity is a pervasive problem and must be dealt with in ways similar to OLS. The primary problem is that when using the procedures described thus far, there are no handy tools available to examine the extent to which collinearity may exist among two or more variables. Multicollinearity exists only when two or more of our independent variables are highly correlated with one another, thus making it very difficult for regression to isolate and separate the independent effects that each of our independent variables exert on our dependent variable. A simple way of checking whether any collinearity exists in our models is to place the independent and dependent variables for whichever of the limited dependent variable techniques being used into an OLS regression procedure. Running an OLS regression analysis and using the collinearity diagnostics with the variables you are using for an ordered, multinomial, or Poisson or negative binomial procedure can assess whether multicollinearity may be a problem for your analysis. In this instance, you would only be interested in the collinearity diagnostics given on the output and not the actual regression results themselves. The regression output here is meaningless and inaccurate. This is because when using a limited dependent variable in an OLS regression, you have violated the primary assumptions of continuity, linearity, and unboundedness.

Looking at the collinearity diagnostics such as the variance inflation factor scores, the tolerance, or the condition numbers index test, you can determine if any multicollinearity exists. If, after using these diagnostics results, no collinearity seems to be present, then you can run the desired logit regression technique for your data. If multicollinearity is present, then you must use the remedies discussed in Chapter 14. It may seem unconventional to run an OLS with a limited dependent variable, but the key here is that you are only interested in the statistical tests that examine relationships among the independent variables, and not those that examine the nature of the relationship between the dependent variable and the independent variables. Tests for multicollinearity do not depend on the regression technique you are interested in using. Multicollinearity is assessed in the same way for all regression techniques.

Summary

Although limited dependent variables can be problematic to study because they violate some of the traditional assumptions of OLS regression, many advances in statistical techniques have allowed us to deal more effectively with the problems inherent in these variables, thus making it relatively easy to include these types of variables in our research. The techniques described here are by no means exhaustive. There are other techniques available for use with dependent variables that are of a limited nature. However, each of the techniques discussed in this chapter are the most conventional and widely used techniques. All of them were developed with limited dependent variables in mind. Statistics has continued to develop techniques to use with the ever-increasing amount and type of data that continues to be collected about criminal justice phenomena. The assumptions of all of the regression techniques discussed here are very important to their fundamental application and subsequent analysis and interpretation of social data. These assumptions pertain to ensuring that the appropriate technique is being used for the variables and data of interest.

Utilizing the proper technique will enable investigators to be confident about the accuracy and parsimony of their results and analysis models. If one or more assumptions associated with various tests are violated, or if an inappropriate technique is used, the consequences could be that the statistical results obtained from the output will be biased at best and meaningless at worst. Further, forcing data to run in analytic models for which it is unsuited will greatly affect our ability to make any statement regarding the true nature of the relationships between variables of study. All assumptions of any technique used should be inspected to insure that the regression procedures you have chosen are the best and most appropriate ones for your data analysis purposes.

This chapter has involved an overview of some of the techniques that can be used for limited dependent variables, as well as the assumptions, interpretations, and limitations involved in each of these procedures. These regression techniques have become very useful to researchers because they have allowed us to study phenomena that in the past have not been amenable to analytic statistical investigation. It must be remembered that regression in general allows us to examine the combined effects of multiple independent variables on a dependent variable as well as the separate or independent effects that each of our independent variables have on the dependent variable. The techniques presented here require increased attention to assumptions and other characteristics of the data that may not have been necessary for ordinary least squares regression. Those with a strong interest in learning more about some of these limited dependent variable techniques should pursue advanced reading and give further attention to data measurement as well as increased time and practical application in order to become more adept at mastering these procedures.

This chapter has provided the basic information needed to use some of the limited dependent variable regression techniques. It has equipped the reader with the skills to understand and interpret data analyses and research articles where such techniques are applied. Learning and using a statistical software program is a good way of running these regression models, testing theories about social science and criminal justice phenomena, and performing real-world applications of statistical theory. Once the fundamentals of each of these regression techniques is understood, and the application of *SPSS* is mastered, comprehending more advanced statistical techniques will become much easier.

Key Terms

−2 log likelihood *322*

test of the significance of the dispersion parameter (alpha) *335*

Cameron and Trivedi test *335*

chi-square test *322*

Cox and Snell R^2 *322*

gamma distribution *335*

influence *327*

logistic regression *316*

log of the odds *323*

maximum likelihood estimation *318*

multinomial logistic regression *331*

Nagelkerke R^2 *322*

negative binomial regression *335*

odds ratio *324*

ordered logit regression *328*

overdispersion *335*

Poisson regression *334*

proportional odds assumption test *328*

Roncek's semi-standardized coefficient (B_R) *324*

Wald statistic *323*

Questions for Review

1. What is the binary or dichotomous logistic regression used for?

2. What are the two traditional OLS regression assumptions that having a dichotomous dependent variable violates?

3. Name at least three other regression techniques that are based upon Logistic regression. For what kinds of dependent variables are these used?

4. How can we diagnose collinearity for logistic regression techniques?

5. For each of the techniques described in this chapter, give the type of R^2 given in the results. Why are these important?

6. What do we mean when we say we have a limited dependent variable? What is maximum likelihood estimation?

7. Can we still use the five steps for interpreting logistic regression output? What about the other logistic techniques?

8. What are some of the limitations of each of the procedures discussed in this chapter?

9. What is the proportional odds assumption test? When would we use it? What does it test? Do we want to accept or reject the null hypothesis in this case?

10. What is count data? What does it mean when we say data are overdispersed? Which technique do we have to resort to using if our data are overdispersed?

11. Select two journal articles that use any of the logistic regression analysis discussed in this chapter. For each article: (a) examine the variables being used in the study. Do they meet the assumptions for conducting a logistic regression analysis? (b) examine the tables the authors use to display their results. Attempt to analyze this output using the five easy steps for interpreting a regression analysis. Do you get the same findings as the authors? (c) discuss the limitations present in the studies. How are they different or similar to the ones discussed in this chapter?

Exercises

15.1. A researcher has run a regression analysis attempting to predict whether various extra-legal factors play a role in determining whether narcotics offenders in California will be sent to prison or not. The researcher obtains the following output from *SPSS*. Examine these results and explain the statistics that are important to a binary logistic regression.

a. Is the overall logistic regression model significant?

b. Which of the variables are significant in the model?

c. Look at the Nagelkerke R^2, how much of the variance is explained in the dependent variable with these independent variables?

d. Which variable increases the odds of going to prison the most? Which the least?

Omnibus Tests of Model Coefficients

		X	df	Sig.
Step 1	Step	39.172	6	.000
	Block	39.172	6	.000
	Model	39.172	6	.000

Step	−2 Log likelihood	Cox and Snell R^2	Nagelkerke R^2
1	3350.527[a]	.310	.340

[a]Estimation terminated at iteration number 4 because parameter estimates changed by less than .001.

		b	S.E.	Wald	Sig.	Exp(B)
Step 1[a]	Prior Convictions	−.044	.036	1.506	.040	.957
	Offenders age	−.001	.004	.095	.758	.999
	Private Attorney	−.131	.093	1.981	.159	.877
	Male	.363	.138	6.903	.009	1.438
	Not Detained	−.379	.084	20.573	.000	.685
	Trial	.899	.414	4.709	.030	2.457
	Constant	−.151	.465	.105	.746	.860

[a]Variable(s) entered on step 1: pfelc, oage, attny, ogen, prestat, disp.

15.2. The following table represents results of an ordinal logistic regression measuring citizen attitudes about satisfaction with the police using three responses, not satisfied, somewhat satisfied, and completely satisfied. The independent variables include the age, employment status, and gender of the respondent, whether the respondent has ever had to call the police, and whether the respondent has ever been the victim of a crime. Given the tabular results below, answer the following questions.

a. How much variance in satisfaction with the police is being explained here?

b. Which variables have a positive relationship with increased satisfaction? Which have negative effects?

c. Interpret the significant variables from this table. How did you know which variables had a significant effect?

Variable	b	Sig.	Sig.
Sig. Age	.05*	.015	.012
Female	3.23*	.005	.041
Ever Called Police	−1.13*	.024	.024
Ever Been Victimized	−2.2*	.075	.033
Employed	.159	.059	.853
Nagelkerke R^2	.365		
N = 495			

15.3. The following table represents the results of a multinomial regression asking citizens their attitudes toward the banning of assault weapons. Responses included approve, indifferent, and disapprove. The independent variables used in the model include the respondents' age and gender, as well as their educational, employment, and marital status. Answer the following questions based on the results below.

a. How much variance in the attitudes toward banning assault weapons is being explained here?

b. Which variables have a positive relationship with disapproving of assault weapons bans? Which have negative effects? Which are more likely to be indifferent rather than approve?

c. Interpret the significant variables from this table. How did you know which variables had a significant effect?

d. Which variables have the highest odds ratios for disapproval? Which the lowest?

Variable	Exp(B)	SE
Disapprove versus Approve		
Age	.95*	.054
Female	2.43*	.043
High School Graduate	−0.72*	.042
College Graduate	.622	.061
Unemployed	−.517*	.067
Married	−2.9*	.089
Indifferent versus Approve		
Age	−2.3*	.012
Female	−.95	.034
High School Graduate	−1.75	.078
College Graduate	−.94*	.032
Unemployed	−.89*	.046
Married	.75	.011
Nagelkerke R^2	.356	
$N = 842$		

References

Aldrich, J.H. and F.D. Nelson (1984). *Linear probability, Logit and Probit Models.* Beverly Hills, CA: Sage Publications.

Hartley, R.D., S. Maddan, and C. Spohn (2007). "Prosecutorial Discretion: An Examination of Substantial Assistance Departures in Federal Crack-Cocaine and Powder Cocaine Cases." *Justice Quarterly* **24:**382–407.

King, Ryan D. and M.F. Weiner (2007). "Group Position, Collective Threat and American Anti-Semitism." *Social Problems* **54:**47–77.

Liao, T.F. (1994). *Interpreting probability models: Logit, Probit, and other generalized linear models.* Thousand Oaks, CA: Sage Publications.

Menard, S. (2002). *Applied Logistic Regression Analysis.*Thousand Oaks, CA: Sage.

Metah, C.R. and M.R. Patel (1995). "Exact Logistic Regression: Theory and Examples."*Statistics in Medicine* **14:**2143–2160.

Roncek, D. (1991). "Using Logit Coefficients to Obtain the Effects of Independent Variables on Changes in Probabilities."*Social Forces* **70:** 509–518.

Roncek, D. (1993). "When Will They Ever Learn that First Derivatives Identify the Effects of Continuous Independent Variables or 'Officer, You Can't Give Me a Ticket, I Wasn't Speeding for an Entire Hour.' "*Social Forces* **71:**1067–1078.

Roncek, D. (1997). "Interpreting the Relative Importance of Negative Binomial and Poisson Regression Coefficients." Paper Presented to the 1997 annual meetings of The American Society of Criminology, San Diego, CA.

Stolzenberg, R. (1979). The Measurement and Decomposition of Causal Effects in Nonlinear and Nonadditive Models, 459–488, in Karl F Schuessler (ed.), Sociological methodology, Jossey-Bass.

Studenmund, A.H. (1997). *Using Econometrics: A Practical Guide.* Reading, MA: Addison-Wesley.

Unnever, J.D., Francis T. Cullen, and Bonnie S. Fischer (2007). " 'A Liberal Is Someone Who Has Not Been Mugged': Criminal Victimization and Political Beliefs." *Justice Quarterly* **24:**309–334.

APPENDIX A
Interpretive Tables

TABLE A.1 Table of Squares and Square Roots, 1–1000

n	n^2	$\sqrt{n}$	n	n^2	$\sqrt{n}$
1	1	1.0000	44	1936	6.6332
2	4	1.4142	45	2025	6.7082
3	9	1.7321	46	2116	6.7823
4	16	2.0000	47	2209	6.8557
5	25	2.2361	48	2304	6.9282
6	36	2.4495	49	2401	7.0000
7	49	2.6458	50	2500	7.0711
8	64	2.8284	51	2601	7.1414
9	81	3.0000	52	2704	7.2111
10	100	3.1623	53	2809	7.2801
11	121	3.3166	54	2916	7.3485
12	144	3.4641	55	3025	7.4162
13	169	3.6056	56	3136	7.4833
14	196	3.7417	57	3249	7.5498
15	225	3.8730	58	3364	7.6158
16	256	4.0000	59	3481	7.6811
17	289	4.1231	60	3600	7.7460
18	324	4.2426	61	3721	7.8102
19	361	4.3589	62	3844	7.8740
20	400	4.4721	63	3969	7.9373
21	441	4.5826	64	4096	8.0000
22	484	4.6904	65	4225	8.0623
23	529	4.7958	66	4356	8.1240
24	576	4.8990	67	4489	8.1854
25	625	5.0000	68	4624	8.2462
26	676	5.0990	69	4761	8.3066
27	729	5.1962	70	4900	8.3666
28	784	5.2915	71	5041	8.4261
29	841	5.3852	72	5184	8.4853
30	900	5.4772	73	5329	8.5440
31	961	5.5678	74	5476	8.6023
32	1024	5.6569	75	5625	8.6603
33	1089	5.7446	76	5776	8.7178
34	1156	5.8310	77	5929	8.7750
35	1225	5.9161	78	6084	8.8318
36	1296	6.0000	79	6241	8.8882
37	1369	6.0828	80	6400	8.9443
38	1444	6.1644	81	6561	9.0000
39	1521	6.2450	82	6724	9.0554
40	1600	6.3246	83	6889	9.1104
41	1681	6.4031	84	7056	9.1652
42	1764	6.4807	85	7225	9.2195
43	1849	6.5574	86	7396	9.2736

(continued)

TABLE A.1 (*Continued*)

n	n^2	$\sqrt{n}$	n	n^2	$\sqrt{n}$
87	7569	9.3274	129	16641	11.3578
88	7744	9.3808	130	16900	11.4018
89	7921	9.4340	131	17161	11.4455
90	8100	9.4868	132	17424	11.4891
91	8281	9.5394	133	17689	11.5326
92	8464	9.5917	134	17956	11.5758
93	8649	9.6437	135	18225	11.6190
94	8836	9.6954	136	18496	11.6619
95	9025	9.7468	137	18769	11.7047
96	9216	9.7980	138	19044	11.7473
97	9409	9.8489	139	19321	11.7898
98	9604	9.8995	140	19600	11.8322
99	9801	9.9499	141	19881	11.8743
100	10000	10.0000	142	20164	11.9164
101	10201	10.0499	143	20449	11.9583
102	10404	10.0995	144	20736	12.0000
103	10609	10.1489	145	21025	12.0416
104	10816	10.1980	146	21316	12.0830
105	11025	10.2470	147	21609	12.1244
106	11236	10.2956	148	21904	12.1655
107	11449	10.3441	149	22201	12.2066
108	11664	10.3928	150	22500	12.2474
109	11881	10.4403	151	22801	12.2882
110	12100	10.4881	152	23104	12.3288
111	12321	10.5357	153	23409	12.3693
112	12544	10.5830	154	23716	12.4097
113	12769	10.6301	155	24025	12.4499
114	12996	10.6771	156	24336	12.4900
115	13225	10.7238	157	24649	12.5300
116	13456	10.7703	158	24964	12.5698
117	13689	10.8167	159	25281	12.6095
118	13924	10.8628	160	25600	12.6491
119	14161	10.9087	161	25921	12.6886
120	14400	10.9545	162	26244	12.7279
121	14641	11.0000	163	26569	12.7671
122	14884	11.0454	164	26896	12.8062
123	15129	11.0905	165	27225	12.8452
124	15376	11.1355	166	27556	12.8841
125	15625	11.1803	167	27889	12.9228
126	15876	11.2250	168	28224	12.9615
127	16129	11.2694	169	28561	13.0000
128	16384	11.3137	170	28900	13.0384

(*continued*)

TABLE A.1 (*Continued*)

n	n²	√n	n	n²	√n
171	29241	13.0767	213	45369	14.5946
172	29584	13.1149	214	45796	14.6287
173	29929	13.1529	215	46225	14.6629
174	30276	13.1909	216	46656	14.6969
175	30625	13.2288	217	47089	14.7309
176	30976	13.2665	218	47524	14.7648
177	31329	13.3041	219	47961	14.7986
178	31684	13.3417	220	48400	14.8324
179	32041	13.3791	221	48841	14.8661
180	32400	13.4164	222	49284	14.8997
181	32761	13.4536	223	49729	14.9332
182	33124	13.4907	224	50176	14.9666
183	33489	13.5277	225	50625	15.0000
184	33856	13.5647	226	51076	15.0333
185	34225	13.6015	227	51529	15.0665
186	34596	13.6382	228	51984	15.0997
187	34969	13.6748	229	52441	15.1327
188	35344	13.7113	230	52900	15.1658
189	35721	13.7477	231	53361	15.1987
190	36100	13.7840	232	53824	15.2315
191	36481	13.8203	233	54289	15.2643
192	36864	13.8564	234	54756	15.2971
193	37249	13.8924	235	55225	15.3297
194	37636	13.9284	236	55696	15.3623
195	38025	13.9642	237	56169	15.3948
196	38416	14.0000	238	56644	15.4272
197	38809	14.0357	239	57121	15.4596
198	39204	14.0712	240	57600	15.4919
199	39601	14.1067	241	58081	15.5242
200	40000	14.1421	242	58564	15.5563
201	40401	14.1774	243	49049	15.5885
202	40804	14.2127	244	59536	15.6205
203	41209	14.2478	245	60025	15.6525
204	41616	14.2829	246	60516	15.6844
205	42025	14.3178	247	61009	15.7162
206	42436	14.3527	248	61504	15.7480
207	42849	14.3875	249	62001	15.7797
208	43264	14.4222	250	62500	15.8114
209	43681	14.4568	251	63001	15.8430
210	44100	14.4914	252	63504	15.8745
211	44521	14.5258	253	64009	15.9060
212	44944	14.5602	254	64516	15.9374

(*continued*)

TABLE A.1 (*Continued*)

n	n²	√n	n	n²	√n
255	65025	15.9687	297	88209	17.2337
256	65536	16.0000	298	88804	17.2627
257	66049	16.0312	299	89401	17.2916
258	66564	16.0624	300	90000	17.3205
259	67081	16.0935	301	90601	17.3494
260	67600	16.1245	302	91204	17.3781
261	68121	16.1555	303	91809	17.4069
262	68644	16.1864	304	92416	17.4356
263	69169	16.2173	305	93025	17.4642
264	69696	16.2481	306	93636	17.4929
265	70225	16.2788	307	94249	17.5214
266	70756	16.3095	308	94864	17.5499
267	71289	16.3401	309	95841	17.5784
268	71824	16.3707	310	96100	17.6068
269	72361	16.4012	311	96721	17.6352
270	72900	16.4317	312	97344	17.6635
271	73441	16.4621	313	97969	17.6918
272	73984	16.4924	314	98596	17.7200
273	74529	16.5227	315	99225	17.7482
274	75076	16.5529	316	99856	17.7764
275	75625	16.5831	317	100489	17.8045
276	76176	16.6132	318	101124	17.8326
277	76729	16.6433	319	101761	17.8606
278	77284	16.6733	320	102400	17.8885
279	77841	16.7033	321	103041	17.9165
280	78400	16.7332	322	103684	17.9444
281	78961	16.7631	323	104329	17.9722
282	79524	16.7929	324	104976	18.0000
283	80089	16.8226	325	105625	18.0278
284	80656	16.8523	326	106276	18.0555
285	81225	16.8819	327	106929	18.0831
286	81796	16.9115	328	107584	18.1108
287	82369	16.9411	329	108241	18.1384
288	82944	16.9706	330	108900	18.1659
289	83521	17.0000	331	109561	18.1934
290	84100	17.0294	332	110224	18.2209
291	84681	17.0587	333	110889	18.2483
292	85264	17.0880	334	111556	18.2757
293	85849	17.1172	335	112225	18.3030
294	86436	17.1464	336	112896	18.3303
295	87025	17.1756	337	113569	18.3576
296	87616	17.2047	338	114244	18.3848

(*continued*)

TABLE A.1 (*Continued*)

n	n²	√n	n	n²	√n
339	114921	18.4120	381	145161	19.5192
340	115600	18.4391	382	145924	19.5448
341	116281	18.4662	383	146689	19.5704
342	116964	18.4932	384	147456	19.5959
343	117649	18.5203	385	148225	19.6214
344	118336	18.5472	386	148996	19.6469
345	119025	18.5742	387	149769	19.6723
346	119716	18.6011	388	150544	19.6977
347	120409	18.6279	389	151321	19.7231
348	121104	18.6548	390	152100	19.7484
349	121801	18.6815	391	152881	19.7737
350	122500	18.7083	392	153664	19.7990
351	123201	18.7350	393	154449	19.8242
352	123904	18.7617	394	155236	19.8494
353	124609	18.7883	395	156025	19.8746
354	125316	18.8149	396	156816	19.8997
355	126025	18.8414	397	157609	19.9249
356	126736	18.8680	398	158404	19.9499
357	127449	18.8944	399	159210	19.9750
358	128164	18.9209	400	160000	20.0000
359	128881	18.9473	401	160801	20.0250
360	129600	18.9737	402	161604	20.0499
361	130321	19.0000	403	162409	20.0749
362	131044	19.0263	404	163216	20.0998
363	131769	19.0526	405	164025	20.1246
364	132496	19.0788	406	164836	20.1494
365	133225	19.1050	407	165649	20.1742
366	133956	19.1311	408	166464	20.1990
367	134689	19.1572	409	167281	20.2237
368	135424	19.1833	410	168100	20.2485
369	136161	19.2094	411	168921	20.2731
370	136900	19.2354	412	169744	20.2978
371	137641	19.2614	413	170569	20.3224
372	138384	19.2873	414	171396	20.3470
373	139129	19.3132	415	172225	20.3715
374	139876	19.3391	416	173056	20.3961
375	140625	19.3649	417	173889	20.4206
376	141376	19.3907	418	174724	20.4450
377	142129	19.4165	419	175561	20.4695
378	142884	19.4422	420	176400	20.4939
379	143641	19.4679	421	177241	20.5183
380	144400	19.4936	422	178084	20.5426

(*continued*)

TABLE A.1 (*Continued*)

n	n²	√n	n	n²	√n
423	178929	20.5670	465	216225	21.5639
424	179776	20.5913	466	217156	21.5870
425	180625	20.6155	467	218089	21.6102
426	181476	20.6398	468	219024	21.6333
427	182329	20.6640	469	219961	21.6564
428	183184	20.6882	470	220900	21.6795
429	184041	20.7123	471	221841	21.7025
430	184900	20.7364	472	222784	21.7256
431	185761	20.7605	473	223729	21.7486
432	186624	20.7846	474	224676	21.7715
433	187489	20.8087	475	225625	21.7945
434	188356	20.8327	476	226576	21.8174
435	189225	20.8567	477	227529	21.8403
436	190096	20.8806	478	228484	21.8632
437	190969	20.9045	479	229441	21.8861
438	191844	20.9284	480	230400	21.9089
439	192721	20.9523	481	231361	21.9317
440	193600	20.9762	482	232324	21.9545
441	194481	21.0000	483	233289	21.9773
442	195364	21.0238	484	234256	22.0000
443	196249	21.0476	485	235225	22.0227
444	197136	21.0713	486	236196	22.0454
445	198025	21.0950	487	237169	22.0681
446	198916	21.1187	488	238144	22.0907
447	199809	21.1424	489	239121	22.1133
448	200704	21.1660	490	240100	22.1359
449	201601	21.1896	491	241081	22.1585
450	202500	21.2132	492	242064	22.1811
451	203401	21.2368	493	243049	22.2036
452	204304	21.2603	494	244036	22.2261
453	205209	21.2838	495	245025	22.2486
454	206116	21.3073	496	246016	22.2711
455	207025	21.3397	497	247009	22.2935
456	207936	21.3542	498	248004	22.3159
457	208849	21.3776	499	249001	22.3383
458	209764	21.4009	500	250000	22.3607
459	210681	21.4243	501	251001	22.3830
460	211600	21.4476	502	252004	22.4045
461	212521	21.4709	503	253009	22.4277
462	213444	21.4942	504	254016	22.4499
463	214369	21.5174	505	255025	22.4792
464	215296	21.5407	506	256036	22.4944

(continued)

TABLE A.1 (*Continued*)

n	n²	√n	n	n²	√n
507	257049	22.5167	549	301401	21.1896
508	258064	22.5389	550	302500	21.2132
509	259081	22.5610	551	303601	23.4734
510	260100	22.5832	552	304704	23.4947
511	261121	22.6053	553	305809	23.5160
512	262144	22.6274	554	306916	23.5372
513	263169	22.6495	555	308025	23.5584
514	264196	22.6716	556	309136	23.5797
515	265225	22.6936	557	310249	23.6008
516	266256	22.7156	558	311364	23.6220
517	267289	22.7376	559	312481	23.6432
518	268324	22.7596	560	313600	23.6643
519	269361	22.7816	561	314721	23.6854
520	270400	22.8035	562	315844	23.7065
521	271441	22.8254	563	316969	23.7276
522	272484	22.8473	564	318096	23.7487
523	273529	22.8692	565	319225	23.7697
524	274576	22.8910	566	320356	23.7908
525	275625	22.9129	567	321489	23.8118
526	276676	22.9347	568	322624	23.8328
527	277729	22.9565	569	323761	23.8537
528	278784	22.9783	570	324900	23.8747
529	279841	23.0000	571	326041	23.8956
530	280900	23.0217	572	327184	23.9165
531	281961	23.0434	573	328329	23.9374
532	283024	23.0651	574	329476	23.9583
533	284089	23.0868	575	330625	23.9792
534	285156	23.1084	576	331776	24.0000
535	286225	23.1301	577	332929	24.0208
536	287296	23.1517	578	334084	24.0416
537	288369	23.1733	579	335241	24.0624
538	289444	23.1948	580	336400	24.0832
539	290521	23.2164	581	337561	24.1039
540	291600	23.2379	582	338724	24.1247
541	292681	21.0000	583	339889	24.1454
542	293764	21.0238	584	341056	24.1661
543	294849	21.0476	585	342225	24.1868
544	295936	21.0713	586	343396	24.2074
545	297025	21.0950	587	344569	24.2281
546	298116	21.1187	588	345744	24.2487
547	299209	21.1424	589	346921	24.2693
548	300304	21.1660	590	348100	24.2899

(*continued*)

TABLE A.1 (Continued)

n	n^2	$\sqrt{n}$	n	n^2	$\sqrt{n}$
591	349281	24.3105	633	400689	25.1595
592	350464	24.3311	634	401956	25.1794
593	351649	24.3516	635	403225	25.1992
594	352836	24.3721	636	404496	25.2190
595	354025	24.3926	637	405769	25.2389
596	355216	24.4131	638	407044	25.2587
597	356409	24.4336	639	408321	25.2784
598	357604	24.4540	640	409600	25.2982
599	358801	24.4745	641	410881	25.3180
600	360000	24.4949	642	412164	25.3377
601	361201	24.5153	643	413449	25.3574
602	362404	24.5357	644	414736	25.3772
603	363609	24.5561	645	416025	25.3969
604	364816	24.5764	646	417316	25.4165
605	366025	24.5967	647	418609	25.4362
606	367236	24.6171	648	419004	25.4558
607	368449	24.6374	649	421201	25.4755
608	369664	24.6577	650	422500	25.4951
609	370881	24.6779	651	423801	25.5147
610	372100	24.6982	652	425104	25.5343
611	373321	24.7184	653	426409	25.5539
612	374544	24.7386	654	427716	25.5734
613	375769	24.7588	655	429025	25.5930
614	376996	24.7790	656	430336	25.6125
615	378225	24.7992	657	431649	25.6320
616	379456	24.8193	658	432964	25.6515
617	380689	24.8395	659	434281	25.6710
618	381924	24.8596	660	435600	25.6905
619	383161	24.8797	661	436921	25.7099
620	384400	24.8998	662	438244	25.7294
621	385641	24.9199	663	439569	25.7488
622	386884	24.9399	664	440896	25.7682
623	388129	24.9600	665	442225	25.7876
624	389376	24.9800	666	443556	25.8070
625	390625	25.0000	667	444889	25.8263
626	391876	25.0200	668	446224	25.8457
627	393129	25.0400	669	447561	25.8650
628	394384	25.0599	670	448900	25.8844
629	395641	25.0799	671	450241	25.9037
630	396900	25.0998	672	451584	25.9230
631	398161	25.1197	673	452929	25.9422
632	399424	25.1396	674	454276	25.9615

(continued)

TABLE A.1 (*Continued*)

n	n^2	$\sqrt{n}$	n	n^2	$\sqrt{n}$
675	455625	25.9808	717	514089	26.7769
676	456976	26.0000	718	515524	26.7955
677	458329	26.0192	719	516961	26.8142
678	459684	26.0384	720	518400	26.8328
679	461041	26.0576	721	519841	26.8514
680	462400	26.0768	722	521284	26.8701
681	463761	26.0960	723	522729	26.8887
682	465124	26.1151	724	524176	26.9072
683	466489	26.1343	725	525625	26.9258
684	467856	26.1534	726	527076	26.9444
685	469225	26.1725	727	528529	26.9629
686	470596	26.1916	728	529984	26.9815
687	471969	26.2107	729	531441	27.0000
688	473344	26.2298	730	532900	27.0185
689	474721	26.2488	731	534361	27.0370
690	476100	26.2679	732	535824	27.0555
691	477481	26.2869	733	537289	27.0740
692	478864	26.3059	734	538756	27.0924
693	480249	26.3249	735	540225	27.1109
694	481636	26.3439	736	541696	27.1293
695	483025	26.3629	737	543169	27.1477
696	484416	26.3818	738	544644	27.1662
697	485809	26.4008	739	546121	27.1846
698	487204	26.4197	740	547600	27.2029
699	488601	26.4386	741	549081	27.2213
700	490000	26.4575	742	550564	27.2397
701	491401	26.4764	743	552049	27.2580
702	492804	26.4953	744	553536	27.2764
703	494209	26.5141	745	555025	27.2947
704	495616	26.5330	746	556516	27.3130
705	497025	26.5518	747	558009	27.3313
706	498436	26.5707	748	559504	27.3496
707	499849	26.5895	749	561001	27.3679
708	501264	26.6083	750	562500	27.3861
709	502681	26.6271	751	564001	27.4044
710	504100	26.6458	752	565504	27.4226
711	505521	26.6646	753	567009	27.4408
712	506944	26.6833	754	568516	27.4591
713	508369	26.7021	755	570025	27.4773
714	509796	26.7208	756	571536	27.4955
715	511225	26.7395	757	573049	27.5136
716	512656	26.7582	758	574564	27.5318

(*continued*)

TABLE A.1 (*Continued*)

n	n²	√n	n	n²	√n
759	576081	27.5500	801	641601	28.3019
760	577600	27.5681	802	643204	28.3196
761	579121	27.5862	803	644809	28.3373
762	580644	27.6043	804	646416	28.3549
763	582169	27.6225	805	648025	28.3725
764	583696	27.6405	806	649636	28.3901
765	585225	27.6586	807	651249	28.4077
766	586756	27.6767	808	652864	28.4253
767	588289	27.6948	809	654481	28.4429
768	589824	27.7128	810	656100	28.4605
769	591361	27.7308	811	657721	28.4781
770	592900	27.7489	812	659344	28.4956
771	594441	27.7669	813	660969	28.5132
772	595984	27.7849	814	662596	28.5307
773	597529	27.8029	815	664225	28.5482
774	599076	27.8209	816	665856	28.5657
775	600625	27.8388	817	667489	28.5832
776	602176	27.8568	818	669124	28.6007
777	603729	27.8747	819	670761	28.6182
778	605284	27.8927	820	672400	28.6356
779	606841	27.9106	821	674041	28.6531
780	608400	27.9285	822	675684	28.6705
781	609961	27.9464	823	677329	28.6880
782	611524	27.9643	824	678976	28.7054
783	613089	27.9821	825	680625	28.7228
784	614656	28.0000	826	682276	28.7402
785	616225	28.0179	827	683929	28.7576
786	617796	28.0357	828	685584	28.7750
787	619369	28.0535	829	687241	28.7924
788	620944	28.0713	830	688900	28.8097
789	622521	28.0891	831	690561	28.8271
790	624100	28.1069	832	692224	28.8444
791	625681	28.1247	833	693889	28.8617
792	627264	28.1425	834	695556	28.8791
793	628849	28.1603	835	697225	28.8964
794	630436	28.1780	836	698896	28.9137
795	632025	28.1957	837	700569	28.9310
796	633616	28.2135	838	702244	28.9482
797	635209	28.2312	839	703921	28.9655
798	636804	28.2489	840	705600	28.9829
799	638401	28.2666	841	707281	29.0000
800	640000	28.2843	842	708964	29.0172

(*continued*)

TABLE A.1 (*Continued*)

n	n²	√n	n	n²	√n
843	710649	29.0345	885	783225	29.7489
844	712336	29.0517	886	784996	29.7658
845	714025	29.0689	887	786769	29.7825
846	715716	29.0861	888	788544	29.7993
847	717409	29.1033	889	790321	29.8161
848	719104	29.1204	890	792100	29.8329
849	720801	29.1376	891	793881	29.8496
850	722500	29.1548	892	795664	29.8664
851	724201	29.1719	893	797449	29.8831
852	725904	29.1890	894	799236	29.8998
853	727609	29.2062	895	801025	29.9166
854	729316	29.2233	896	802816	29.9333
855	731025	29.2404	897	804609	29.9500
856	732736	29.2575	898	806404	29.9666
857	734449	29.2746	899	808201	29.9833
858	736164	29.2916	900	810000	30.0000
859	737881	29.3087	901	811801	30.0167
860	739600	29.3258	902	813604	30.0333
861	741321	29.3428	903	815409	30.0500
862	743044	29.3598	904	817216	30.0666
863	744769	29.3769	905	819025	30.0832
864	746496	29.3939	906	820836	30.0998
865	748225	29.4109	907	822649	30.1164
866	749956	29.4279	908	824464	30.1330
867	751689	29.4449	909	826281	30.1496
868	753424	29.4618	910	828100	30.1662
869	755161	29.4788	911	829921	30.1828
870	756900	29.4958	912	831744	30.1993
871	758641	29.5127	913	833569	30.2159
872	760384	29.5296	914	835396	30.2324
873	762129	29.5466	915	837225	30.2490
874	763876	29.5635	916	839056	30.2655
875	765625	29.5804	917	840889	30.2820
876	767376	29.5973	918	842724	30.2985
877	769129	29.6142	919	844561	30.3150
878	770884	29.6311	920	846400	30.3315
879	772641	29.6479	921	848241	30.3480
880	774400	29.6648	922	850084	30.3645
881	776161	29.6816	923	851929	30.3809
882	777924	29.6985	924	853776	30.3974
883	779689	29.7153	925	855625	30.4138
884	781456	29.7321	926	857476	30.4302

(*continued*)

TABLE A.1 (*Continued*)

n	n^2	$\sqrt{n}$	n	n^2	$\sqrt{n}$
927	859329	30.4467	964	929296	31.0483
928	861184	30.4631	965	931225	31.0644
929	863041	30.4795	966	933156	31.0805
930	864900	30.4959	967	935089	31.0966
931	866761	30.5123	968	937369	31.1127
932	868624	30.5287	969	938961	31.1288
933	870489	30.5450	970	940900	31.1448
934	872356	30.5614	971	942841	31.1609
935	874225	30.5778	972	944784	31.1769
936	876096	30.5941	973	946729	31.1929
937	877969	30.6105	974	948676	31.2090
938	879844	30.6268	975	950625	31.2250
939	881721	30.6431	976	952576	31.2410
940	883600	30.6594	977	954529	31.2570
941	885481	30.6757	978	956484	31.2730
942	887364	30.6920	979	958441	31.2890
943	889249	30.7083	980	960400	31.3050
944	891136	30.7246	981	962361	31.3209
945	893025	30.7409	982	964324	31.3369
946	894916	30.7571	983	966289	31.3528
947	896809	30.7734	984	968256	31.3688
948	898704	30.7896	985	970225	31.3847
949	900601	30.8058	986	972196	31.4006
950	902500	30.8221	987	974169	31.4166
951	904401	30.8383	988	976144	31.4325
952	906304	30.8545	989	978121	31.4484
953	908209	30.8707	990	980100	31.4643
954	910116	30.8869	991	982081	31.4802
955	912025	30.9031	992	984064	31.4860
956	913936	30.9192	993	986049	31.5119
957	915849	30.9354	994	988036	31.5278
958	917764	30.9516	995	990025	31.5436
959	919681	30.9677	996	992016	31.5595
960	921600	30.9839	997	994009	31.5753
961	923521	31.0000	998	996004	31.5911
962	925444	31.0161	999	998001	31.6070
963	927369	31.0322	1000	1000000	31.6228

Source: Compiled by author.

TABLE A.2 Areas Under the Normal Curve

This table contains Z scores and proportions of curve area included between 0 and a particular Z value. The values down the left-hand side of the table represent the first two digits of a Z score, while the values across the top of the table depict the third digit. If the proportion of curve area included by a $Z = 1.83$ is to be found, find 1.8 down the left-hand side and .03 across the top of the table. Where these values intersect defines the proportion of curve area included between 0 and a $Z = 1.83$. This proportion is .4664. Since the normal curve is perfectly symmetrical, these proportions are the same for negative Z values, such as $Z = -1.83$. The proportion of curve area between 0 and a $Z = -1.83$ is also .4664, the same as for $Z = +1.83$.

Z Scores	.00	.01	.02	.03	.04	.05	.06	.07	.08	.09
0.00	.0000	.0040	.0080	.0120	.0160	.0199	.0239	.0279	.0319	.0359
0.1	.0398	.0438	.0478	.0517	.0557	.0596	.0636	.0675	.0714	.0753
0.2	.0793	.0832	.0871	.0910	.0948	.0987	.1026	.1064	.1103	.1141
0.3	.1179	.1217	.1255	.1293	.1331	.1368	.1406	.1443	.1480	.1517
0.4	.1554	.1591	.1628	.1664	.1700	.1736	.1772	.1808	.1844	.1879
0.5	.1915	.1950	.1985	.2019	.2054	.2088	.2123	.2157	.2190	.2224
0.6	.2257	.2291	.2324	.2357	.2389	.2422	.2454	.2486	.2517	.2549
0.7	.2580	.2611	.2642	.2673	.2704	.2734	.2764	.2794	.2823	.2852
0.8	.2881	.2910	.2939	.2967	.2995	.3023	.3051	.3078	.3106	.3133
0.9	.3159	.3186	.3212	.3238	.3264	.3289	.3315	.3340	.3365	.3389
1.0	.3413	.3438	.3461	.3485	.3508	.3531	.3554	.3577	.3599	.3621
1.1	.3643	.3665	.3686	.3708	.3729	.3749	.3770	.3790	.3810	.3830
1.2	.3849	.3869	.3888	.3907	.3925	.3944	.3962	.3980	.3997	.4015
1.3	.4032	.4049	.4066	.4082	.4099	.4115	.4131	.4147	.4162	.4177
1.4	.4192	.4207	.4222	.4236	.4251	.4265	.4279	.4292	.4306	.4319
1.5	.4332	.4345	.4357	.4370	.4382	.4394	.4406	.4418	.4429	.4441
1.6	.4452	.4463	.4474	.4484	.4495	.4505	.4515	.4525	.4535	.4545
1.7	.4554	.4564	.4573	.4582	.4591	.4599	.4608	.4616	.4625	.4633
1.8	.4641	.4649	.4656	.4664	.4671	.4678	.4686	.4693	.4699	.4706
1.9	.4713	.4719	.4726	.4732	.4738	.4744	.4750	.4756	.4761	.4767
2.0	.4772	.4778	.4783	.4788	.4793	.4798	.4803	.4808	.4812	.4817
2.1	.4821	.4826	.4830	.4834	.4838	.4842	.4846	.4850	.4854	.4857
2.2	.4861	.4864	.4868	.4871	.4875	.4878	.4881	.4884	.4887	.4890
2.3	.4893	.4896	.4898	.4901	.4904	.4906	.4909	.4911	.4913	.4916
2.4	.4918	.4920	.4922	.4925	.4927	.4929	.4931	.4932	.4934	.4936
2.5	.4938	.4940	.4941	.4943	.4945	.4946	.4948	.4949	.4951	.4952
2.6	.4953	.4955	.4956	.4957	.4959	.4960	.4961	.4962	.4963	.4964
2.7	.4965	.4966	.4967	.4968	.4969	.4970	.4971	.4972	.4973	.4974
2.8	.4974	.4975	.4976	.4977	.4977	.4978	.4979	.4979	.4980	.4981
2.9	.4981	.4982	.4982	.4983	.4984	.4984	.4985	.4985	.4986	.4986
3.0	.4987	.4987	.4987	.4988	.4988	.4989	.4989	.4989	.4990	.4990
3.1	.4990	.4991	.4991	.4991	.4992	.4992	.4992	.4992	.4993	.4993

(continued)

TABLE A.2 (Continued)

Z Scores	.00	.01	.02	.03	.04	.05	.06	.07	.08	.09
3.2	.4993	.4993	.4994	.4994	.4994	.4994	.4994	.4995	.4995	.4995
3.3	.4995	.4995	.4995	.4996	.4996	.4996	.4996	.4996	.4996	.4997
3.4	.4997	.4997	.4997	.4997	.4997	.4997	.4997	.4997	.4997	.4998
3.5	.4998	.4998	.4999	.4999	.4999	.4999	.4999	.4999	.4999	.4999
Beyond 3.59	.49999									

Source: Compiled by authors.

TABLE A.3 Distribution of t

Degrees of freedom (df) are calculated as $N-1$ for single samples, and $(N_1-1) + (N_2-1)$ for two-sample applications and where the Ns are the two sample sizes. If the exact df cannot be found down the left-hand side of the table, always use the *smaller* of the two df values when your df is between two values (e.g., if you have 39 df in your actual sample, use $df = 30$, not 40, for your selection of the appropriate critical value of t. Across the top of the table are both one- and two-tailed levels of significance. The body of the table contains critical values of t which must be *equaled or exceeded* by the observed t value you are evaluating. For instance, if you have an observed t value = 2.845 with 20 df and are conducting a two-tailed test for the .01 level of significance, the critical value of t is 2.845 as shown. Since your observed t value equals the critical t value of 2.845, it is considered significant statistically at the .01 level of significance. Any larger t value would also be significant statistically at that level. Since the t distribution is perfectly symmetrical, both positive and negative observed t values may be assessed with the same critical t values shown in the table. Thus, the critical t values in the body of the table are technically ±t critical values. The direction (− or +) of t is only relevant in one-tailed directional hypothesis tests.

df	One-tailed level of significance	.10	.05	.025	.01	.005	.0005
	Two-tailed level of significance	.20	.10	.05	.02	.01	.001
1		3.078	6.314	12.706	31.821	63.657	636.619
2		1.886	2.920	4.303	6.965	9.925	31.598
3		1.638	2.353	3.182	4.541	5.841	12.941
4		1.533	2.132	2.776	3.747	4.604	8.610
5		1.476	2.015	2.571	3.365	4.032	6.859
6		1.440	1.943	2.447	3.143	3.707	5.959
7		1.415	1.895	2.365	2.998	3.499	5.405
8		1.397	1.860	2.306	2.896	3.355	5.041
9		1.383	1.833	2.262	2.821	3.250	4.781
10		1.372	1.812	2.228	2.274	3.169	4.587
11		1.363	1.796	2.201	2.718	3.106	4.437
12		1.356	1.782	2.179	2.681	3.055	4.318

(continued)

TABLE A.3 (*Continued*)

df	One-tailed level of significance Two-tailed level of significance	.10 .20	.05 .10	.025 .05	.01 .02	.005 .01	.0005 .001
13		1.350	1.771	2.160	2.650	3.012	4.221
14		1.345	1.761	2.145	2.624	2.977	4.140
15		1.341	1.753	2.131	2.602	2.947	4.073
16		1.337	1.746	2.120	2.583	2.921	4.015
17		1.333	1.740	2.110	2.567	2.898	3.965
18		1.330	1.734	2.101	2.552	2.878	3.922
19		1.328	1.729	2.093	2.539	2.861	3.883
20		1.325	1.725	2.086	2.528	2.845	3.850
21		1.323	1.721	2.080	2.518	2.831	3.819
22		1.321	1.717	2.074	2.508	2.819	3.792
23		1.319	1.714	2.069	2.500	2.807	3.767
24		1.318	1.711	2.064	2.492	2.797	3.745
25		1.316	1.708	2.060	2.485	2.787	3.725
26		1.315	1.706	2.056	2.479	2.779	3.707
27		1.314	1.703	2.052	2.473	2.771	3.690
28		1.313	1.701	2.048	2.467	2.763	3.674
29		1.311	1.699	2.045	2.462	2.756	3.659
30		1.310	1.697	2.042	2.457	2.750	3.646
40		1.303	1.684	2.021	2.423	2.704	3.551
60		1.296	1.671	2.000	2.390	2.660	2.460
120		1.289	1.658	1.980	2.358	2.617	3.373
∞		1.282	1.645	1.960	2.326	2.576	3.291

Source: Compiled by authors.

It is significant to note that for *df* of 120 through infinity (∞), the critical values of *t* are the equivalent of *Z* values from the Table of Areas of the Normal Curve for different significance levels. Critical values of *Z* for one- and two-tailed applications at the .05 and .01 levels of significance are 1.64, 1.96, 2.33, and 2.58 respectively. Compare these values with the critical values of *t* for the same levels of significance for one- and two-tailed tests on the infinity line: 1.645, 1.960, 2.326, and 2.576. Rounded, these *t* values become 1.64, 1.96, 2.33, and 2.58 respectively. Thus the *t* distribution approximates the normal distribution as *df* exceed 120 appreciably.

TABLE A.4 Distribution of χ^2

Degrees of freedom, *df*, are shown in the left-hand column. Both one- and two-tailed levels of significance, expressed as probabilities ranging from .50 to .001, are shown across the top of the table. Degrees of freedom are determined by *k*−1 for single samples, and (rows−1)(columns−1) or (*r*−1)(*c*−1) for 2 × 2 tables or larger. *df* range from 1 to 30. It is highly unlikely that *df* 30 or greater will ever be encountered in actual research situations. Critical values of χ^2 are shown in the body of the table. If one's observed χ^2 equals or exceeds the critical value of χ^2 shown for the given probability level, then the distribution of frequencies is significant at the level of significance shown. For instance, in a two-tailed test at the .05 level of significance and 5 *df*, the critical value of $\chi^2 = 11.070$. If the observed $\chi^2 = 11.222$, then it equals or exceeds 11.070 and is significant statistically. Even if the observed χ^2 value is 11.070, since it equals the critical value shown, it is considered statistically significant.

				Probabilities				
One-tailed	**.25**	**.15**	**.10**	**.05**	**.025**	**.01**	**.005**	**.0005**
df **Two-tailed**	**.50**	**.30**	**.20**	**.10**	**.05**	**.02**	**.01**	**.001**
1	.455	1.074	1.642	2.706	3.841	5.412	6.635	10.827
2	1.386	2.408	3.219	4.605	4.991	7.824	9.210	13.815
3	2.366	3.665	4.642	6.251	7.815	9.837	11.345	16.268
4	3.357	4.878	5.989	7.779	9.488	11.668	13.277	18.465
5	4.351	6.064	7.289	9.236	11.070	13.388	15.086	20.517
6	5.348	7.231	8.558	10.645	12.592	15.033	16.812	22.457
7	6.346	8.383	9.803	12.017	14.067	16.622	18.475	24.322
8	7.344	9.524	11.030	13.362	15.507	18.168	20.090	26.125
9	8.343	10.656	12.242	14.684	16.919	19.679	21.666	27.877
10	9.342	11.781	13.442	15.987	18.307	21.026	23.209	29.588
11	10.341	12.899	14.631	17.275	19.675	22.618	24.725	31.264
12	11.340	14.011	15.812	18.549	21.026	24.054	26.217	32.909
13	12.340	15.119	16.985	19.812	22.362	25.472	27.688	34.528
14	13.339	16.222	18.151	21.064	23.685	26.873	29.141	36.123
15	14.339	17.322	19.311	22.307	24.996	28.259	30.578	37.697
16	15.338	18.418	20.465	23.542	26.296	29.633	32.000	39.252
17	16.338	19.511	21.615	24.769	27.587	30.995	33.409	40.790
18	17.338	20.601	22.760	25.989	28.869	32.346	34.805	42.312
19	18.338	21.689	23.900	27.204	30.144	33.687	36.191	43.820
20	19.337	22.775	25.038	28.412	31.410	35.020	37.566	45.315
21	20.337	23.858	26.171	29.615	32.671	36.343	38.932	46.797
22	21.337	24.939	27.301	30.813	33.924	37.659	40.289	48.268
23	22.337	26.018	28.429	32.007	35.172	38.968	41.638	49.728
24	23.337	27.096	29.553	33.196	36.415	40.270	42.980	51.179
25	24.337	28.172	30.675	34.382	37.652	41.566	46.314	52.620
26	25.336	29.246	31.795	35.563	38.885	42.856	45.642	54.052
27	26.336	30.319	32.912	36.741	40.113	44.140	46.963	55.476
28	27.336	31.391	34.027	37.916	41.337	45.419	48.278	56.893
29	28.336	32.461	35.139	39.087	42.557	46.693	49.588	58.302
30	29.336	33.530	36.250	40.256	43.773	47.962	50.892	59.703

Source: Compiled by authors.

TABLE A.5 Critical Values of *D* in the Kolmogorov–Smirnov One-Sample Test

Critical proportions are found in the body of the table associated with different sample sizes shown down the left-hand side of the table. One- and two-tailed probabilities are shown across the top of the table. If a sample size that is encountered lies between two sample sizes, such as 25 and 30, use the smaller sample size of 25 to determine the critical proportion associated with the level of significance used. For samples over 35, we must use a formula to calculate critical proportions for different levels of significance. These formulas are shown in the table. Use the largest observed proportionate difference from your data to compare with the critical proportion fitting the sample size and level of significance you have chosen. Any observed proportion that is *equal to or larger than* the critical proportion shown in the body of the table means a statistically significant difference at the level of significance indicated.

Sample level of significance (one-tailed)	.10	.075	.05	.025	.005
Size level of significance (two-tailed)	.20	.15	.10	.05	.01
1	.900	.925	.950	.975	.995
2	.684	.726	.776	.842	.929
3	.565	.597	.642	.708	.733
4	.494	.525	.564	.624	.733
5	.446	.474	.510	.565	.669
6	.410	.436	.470	.521	.618
7	.381	.405	.438	.486	.577
8	.358	.381	.411	.457	.543
9	.322	.380	.388	.432	.514
10	.322	.342	.368	.410	.490
11	.307	.326	.352	.391	.468
12	.295	.313	.338	.375	.450
13	.284	.302	.325	.361	.433
14	.274	.292	.314	.349	.418
15	.266	.283	.304	.338	.404
16	.258	.274	.295	.328	.392
17	.250	.266	.286	.318	.381
18	.244	.259	.278	.309	.371
19	.237	.252	.272	.301	.363
20	.231	.246	.264	.294	.356
25	.210	.220	.240	.270	.320
30	.190	.200	.220	.240	.290
35	.180	.190	.210	.230	.270
Over 35	$1.07/\sqrt{N}$	$1.14/\sqrt{N}$	$1.22/\sqrt{N}$	$1.35/\sqrt{N}$	$1.63/\sqrt{N}$

Source: Compiled by authors.

TABLE A.6 Critical Values of R for the Runs Test for .05 Level of Significance

N_1 values are located down the left-hand side of the table, while N_2 values are located across the top of the table with Ns ranging from 2 to 20. In the body of the table are various critical values of R for various N sizes within the 2–20 range. Find your two N values and where these values intersect in the body of the table defines the critical number of runs (R). If your observed R is *equal to or smaller than* the R shown for your particular combination of Ns, then the difference between the two groups of scores is significant at the .05 level. However, if the observed number of runs is greater than the R shown, there is no difference between your two samples of scores. If either sample size exceeds 20, the Z formula at the bottom of this table can be used.

N_1	N_2 2	3	4	5	6	7	8	9	10	11	12	13	14	15	16	17	18	19	20
2											2	2	2	2	2	2	2	2	2
3			2	2	2	2	2	2	2	2	2	2	2	3	3	3	3	3	3
4				2	2	2	3	3	3	3	3	3	3	3	4	4	4	4	4
5			2	2	3	3	3	3	3	3	4	4	4	4	4	4	5	5	5
6		2	2	3	3	3	3	4	4	4	4	4	5	5	5	5	5	6	6
7		2	2	3	3	3	4	4	5	5	5	5	5	6	6	6	6	6	6
8		2	3	3	3	4	4	5	5	5	6	6	6	6	6	7	7	7	7
9		2	3	3	4	4	5	5	5	6	6	6	7	7	7	7	8	8	8
10		2	3	3	4	5	5	5	6	6	7	7	7	7	8	8	8	8	9
11		2	3	4	4	5	5	6	6	7	7	7	8	8	8	9	9	9	9
12	2	2	3	4	4	5	6	6	7	7	7	8	8	9	9	9	9	10	10
13	2	2	3	4	5	5	6	6	7	7	8	8	9	9	9	10	10	10	10
14	2	2	3	4	5	5	6	7	7	8	8	9	9	9	10	10	10	11	11
15	2	3	3	4	5	6	6	7	7	8	8	9	9	10	10	11	11	11	12
16	2	3	4	4	5	6	6	7	8	8	9	9	10	10	11	11	11	12	12
17	2	3	4	4	5	6	7	7	8	9	9	10	10	11	11	11	12	12	13
18	2	3	4	5	5	6	7	8	8	9	9	10	10	11	11	12	12	13	13
19	2	3	4	5	6	6	7	8	8	9	10	10	11	11	12	12	13	13	13
20	2	3	4	5	6	6	7	8	9	9	10	11	12	12	12	13	13	13	14

Source: Compiled by authors.

When either $N > 20$, the following formula can be used, where R = the observed number of runs and N_1 and N_2 are the two sample sizes, whichever N is larger than 20. The resulting Z value can be interpreted as either a one- or two-tailed test at the .05 or .01 levels, using 1.64 and 1.96 as one-tailed critical values, or 2.33 and 2.58 as two-tailed critical values.

$$Z = \frac{\left| R\left(\dfrac{2N_1N_2}{N_1 + N_2} + 1\right) \right| - .5}{\sqrt{\dfrac{2N_1N_2(2N_1N_2 - N_1 - N_2)}{(N_1 + N_2)^2(N_1 + N_2 - 1)}}}$$

TABLE A.7 Critical Values in the Kolmogorov–Smirnov Two-Sample Test

The left-hand column contains one- and two-tailed levels of significance for different values of D. The critical values of D are determined by formulae to the right of the significance levels. N_1 and N_2 are the respective sample sizes. The critical values of D based on the sample sizes must be *equaled or exceeded* by the observed D value in order to be significant statistically at the level of significance indicated.

Level of Significance		Observed values of D must equal or exceed the critical values shown below in order to reject H_o at a given level
One-tailed	Two-tailed	
.05	.10	$1.22\sqrt{\dfrac{n_1 + n_2}{n_1 n_2}}$
.025	.05	$1.36\sqrt{\dfrac{n_1 + n_2}{n_1 n_2}}$
.0125	.025	$1.48\sqrt{\dfrac{n_1 + n_2}{n_1 n_2}}$
.005	.01	$1.63\sqrt{\dfrac{n_1 + n_2}{n_1 n_2}}$
.0025	.005	$1.73\sqrt{\dfrac{n_1 + n_2}{n_1 n_2}}$
.005	.001	$1.95\sqrt{\dfrac{n_1 + n_2}{n_1 n_2}}$

Source: Compiled by authors.

TABLE A.8 Mann-Whitney U Test Exact Probabilities for Small Samples, $N \leq 3$

This table contains exact probabilities for various values of U based on samples of size 3 or smaller. The larger N is 3, while the second N, N_2, equal to or smaller than 3, is found across the top of the table. Various U values are found down the left-hand side of the table. Where the U value intersects with N_2 in the body of the table defines the exact probability at which the U value is significant statistically. The exact probabilities found in the body of the table may be compared directly with the level of significance at which the hypothesis is being tested. All probabilities are two-tailed.

U	N_2	$N_1 = 3$		
		1	2	3
0		.250	.100	.050
1		.500	.200	.100
2		.750	.400	.200
3			.600	.250
4				.500
5				.650

Source: Compiled by authors.

TABLE A.9 Mann-Whitney *U* Test Exact Probabilities for Small Samples, *N* ≤ 4

This table contains exact probabilities for various values of *U* based on samples of size 4 or smaller. The larger *N* is 4, while the second *N*, N_2, equal to or smaller than 4, is found across the top of the table. Various *U* values are found down the left-hand side of the table. Where the *U* value intersects with N_2 in the body of the table defines the exact probability at which the *U* value is significant statistically. The exact probabilities found in the body of the table may be compared directly with the level of significance at which the hypothesis is being tested. All probabilities are two-tailed.

		$N_1 = 4$			
U	N_2	1	2	3	4
0		.200	.067	.028	.014
1		.400	.133	.057	.029
2		.600	.267	.114	.057
3			.400	.200	.100
4			.600	.314	.171
5				.429	.343
6				.571	.343
7					.557
8					

Source: Compiled by authors.

TABLE A.10 Mann-Whitney *U* Test Exact Probabilities for Small Samples, *N* ≤ 5

This table contains exact probabilities for various values of *U* based on samples of size 5 or smaller. The larger *N* is 5, while the smaller *N*, N_2, equal to or smaller than 5, is found across the top of the table. Various *U* values are found down the left-hand side of the table. Where the *U* value intersects with N_2 in the body of the table defines the exact probability at which the *U* value is significant statistically. The exact probabilities found in the body of the table may be compared directly with the level of significance at which the hypothesis is being tested. All probabilities are two-tailed.

		$N_1 = 5$				
U	N_2	1	2	3	4	5
0		.167	.047	.018	.008	.004
1		.333	.095	.036	.016	.008
2		.500	.190	.071	.032	.016
3		.667	.286	.125	.056	.028
4			.429	.196	.095	.048
5			.571	.286	.143	.155
6				.393	.206	.111
7				.500	.278	.155
8				.607	.365	.210
9					.452	.274
10					.548	.345
11						.421
12						.500
13						.579

Source: Compiled by authors.

TABLE A.11 Mann-Whitney U Test Exact Probabilities for Small Samples, $N \le 6$

This table contains exact probabilities for various values of U based on samples of size 6 or smaller. The larger N is 6, while the smaller N, N_2, equal to or smaller than 6, is found across the top of the table. Various U values are found down the left-hand side of the table. Where the U value intersects with N_2 in the body of the table is an exact probability which may be compared directly with the level of significance at which the hypothesis is being tested. All probabilities are two-tailed.

		$N_1 = 6$					
U	N_2	1	2	3	4	5	6
0		.143	.036	.012	.005	.002	.001
1		.286	.071	.024	.010	.004	.002
2		.428	.143	.048	.019	.009	.004
3		.571	.214	.083	.033	.015	.008
4			.321	.131	.057	.026	.013
5			.429	.190	.086	.041	.021
6			.571	.274	.129	.063	.032
7				.357	.176	.089	.047
8				.452	.238	.123	.066
9				.548	.305	.165	.090
10					.381	.214	.120
11					.457	.268	.155
12					.545	.331	.197
13						.396	.242
14						.465	.294
15						.535	.350
16							.490
17							.469
18							.531

Source: Compiled by authors.

TABLE A.12 Mann-Whitney U Test Exact Probabilities for Small Samples, $N \le 7$

This table contains exact probabilities for various values of U based on samples of size 7 or smaller. The larger N is 7, while the smaller N, N_2, equal to or smaller than 7, is found across the top of the table. Various U values are found down the left-hand side of the table. Where the U value intersects with N_2 in the body of the table is an exact probability which may be compared directly with the level of significance at which the hypothesis is being tested. All probabilities are two-tailed.

		$N_1 = 7$						
U	N_2	1	2	3	4	5	6	7
0		.125	.028	.008	.003	.001	.001	.000
1		.250	.056	.017	.006	.003	.001	.001
2		.375	.111	.033	.012	.005	.002	.001
3		.500	.167	.058	.021	.009	.004	.002
4		.625	.250	.092	.036	.015	.007	.003

(continued)

TABLE A.12 (Continued)

					$N_1 = 7$			
U	N_2	1	2	3	4	5	6	7
5			.333	.133	.055	.024	.011	.006
6			.444	.192	.082	.037	.017	.009
7			.556	.258	.115	.053	.026	.013
8				.333	.158	.074	.037	.019
9				.417	.206	.101	.051	.027
10				.500	.264	.134	.069	.036
11				.583	.324	.172	.090	.049
12					.394	.216	.117	.064
13					.464	.265	.147	.082
14					.538	.319	.183	104
15						.378	.223	.130
16						.438	.267	.159
17						.500	.314	.191
18						.562	.365	.228
19							.418	.267
20							.473	.310
21							.527	.355
22								.402
23								.451
24								.500
25								.549

Source: Compiled by authors.

TABLE A.13 Mann-Whitney U Test Exact Probabilities for Small Samples, N ≤ 8

This table contains exact probabilities for various values of U based on samples of size 8 or smaller. The larger N is 8, while the smaller N, N_2, equal to or smaller than 8, is found across the top of the table. Various U values are found down the left-hand side of the table. Where the U value intersects with N_2 in the body of the table is an exact probability which may be compared directly with the level of significance at which the hypothesis is being tested. All probabilities are two-tailed.

					$N_1 = 8$				
U	N_2	1	2	3	4	5	6	7	8
0		.111	.022	.006	.002	.001	.000	.000	.000
1		.222	.044	.012	.004	.002	.001	.000	.000
2		.333	.089	.024	.008	.003	.001	.001	.000
3		.444	.133	.042	.014	.005	.002	.001	.001
4		.556	.200	.067	.024	.009	.004	.002	.001
5			.267	.097	.036	.015	.006	.003	.001

(continued)

TABLE A.13 (*Continued*)

U	N_2	1	2	3	4	5	6	7	8
					$N_1 = 8$				
6			.356	.139	.055	.023	.010	.005	.002
7			.444	.188	.077	.033	.015	.007	.003
8			.556	.248	.107	.047	.021	.010	.005
9				.315	.141	.064	.030	.014	.007
10				.387	.184	.085	.041	.020	.010
11				.461	.230	.111	.054	.027	.014
12				.539	.285	.142	.071	.036	.019
13					.341	.177	.091	.047	.025
14					.404	.217	.114	.060	.032
15					.467	.262	.141	.076	.041
16					.533	.311	.172	.095	.052
17						.362	.207	.116	.065
18						.416	.245	.140	.080
19						.472	.286	.168	.097
20						.528	.331	.198	.117
21							.377	.232	.139
22							.426	.268	.164
23							.475	.306	.191
24							.525	.347	.221
25								.389	.253
26								.433	.287
27								.478	.323
28								.522	.360
29									.399
30									.439
31									.480
32									.520

Source: Compiled by authors.

TABLE A.14 Mann-Whitney U Test Critical Values for .025 One-Tailed and .05 Two-Tailed Test for Ns Ranging from 9 to 20

This table is for a two-sample application where the larger sample ranges from 9 to 20 and where the level of significance is .025 (one-tailed) and .05 (two-tailed). The larger of the two Ns, N_1, is located across the top of the table, while the smaller of the two Ns, N_2, is found down the left-hand side. The body of the table where these respective Ns intersect defines critical values of U. If the observed value of U is *equal to or smaller than* the U shown in the body of the table, then the observed U is significant at either the .025 (one-tailed) or .05 (two-tailed) level of significance.

N_2	N_1	9	10	11	12	13	14	15	16	17	18	19	20
2		0	0	0	1	1	1	1	1	2	2	2	2
3		2	3	3	4	4	5	5	6	6	7	7	8
4		4	5	6	7	8	9	10	11	11	12	13	13
5		7	8	9	11	12	13	14	15	17	18	19	20
6		10	11	13	14	16	17	19	21	22	24	25	7
7		12	14	16	18	20	22	24	26	28	30	32	4
8		15	17	19	22	24	26	29	31	34	36	38	1
9		17	20	23	26	28	31	34	37	39	42	45	48
10		20	23	26	29	33	36	39	42	45	48	52	55
11		23	26	30	33	37	40	44	47	51	55	58	62
12		26	29	33	37	41	45	49	53	57	61	65	69
13		28	33	37	41	45	50	54	59	63	67	72	6
14		31	36	40	45	50	55	59	64	67	74	78	83
15		34	39	44	49	54	59	64	70	80	80	85	0
16		37	42	47	53	59	64	70	75	81	86	92	8
17		39	45	51	57	63	67	75	81	87	93	99	105
18		42	48	55	61	67	74	80	86	93	99	106	112
19		45	52	58	65	72	78	85	92	99	106	113	119
20		48	55	62	69	76	83	90	98	105	112	119	27

Source: Compiled by authors.

**TABLE A.15 Mann-Whitney *U* Test Critical Values for .05 One-Tailed and .10 Two-Tailed
Test for *N*s Ranging from 9 to 20**

This table is for a two-sample application where the larger sample ranges from 9 to 20, and where
the level of significance is .05 (one-tailed) and .10 (two-tailed). The larger of the two *N*s, N_1, is found
across the top of the table, while the smaller of the two *N*s, N_2, is found down the left-hand side. The
body of the table where these respective *N*s intersect defines critical values of *U*. If the observed value
of *U* is *equal to or smaller than* the *U* shown in the body of the table, then the observed *U* is
significant at either the .05 (one-tailed) or .10 (two-tailed) level of significance.

N_2N_1	9	10	11	12	13	14	15	16	17	18	19	20
1												
2	0	0	0	1	1	1	1	1	2	2	2	2
3	3	4	5	5	6	7	7	8	9	9	10	11
4	6	7	8	9	10	11	12	14	15	16	17	18
5	9	11	12	13	15	16	18	19	20	22	23	25
6	12	14	16	17	19	21	23	25	26	28	30	32
7	15	17	19	21	24	26	28	30	33	35	37	39
8	18	20	23	26	28	31	33	36	39	41	44	47
9	21	24	27	30	33	36	39	42	45	48	51	54
10	24	27	31	34	37	41	44	48	51	55	58	62
11	27	31	34	38	42	46	50	54	57	61	65	69
12	30	34	38	42	47	51	55	60	64	68	72	77
13	33	37	42	47	51	56	61	65	70	75	80	84
14	36	41	46	51	56	61	66	71	77	82	87	92
15	39	44	50	55	61	66	72	77	83	88	94	100
16	42	48	54	60	65	71	77	83	89	95	101	107
17	45	51	57	64	70	77	83	89	96	102	109	115
18	48	55	61	68	75	82	88	95	102	109	116	123
19	51	58	65	72	80	87	94	101	109	116	123	130
20	54	62	69	77	84	92	100	107	115	123	130	138

Source: Compiled by authors.

If either *N* > 20, use *Z* formula:

$$Z = \frac{U - \left(\dfrac{N_1N_2}{2}\right)}{\sqrt{\dfrac{(N_1N_2)(N_1 + N_2 + 1)}{12}}}$$

Where
N_1 and N_2 = respective sample sizes
U = smaller of the two observed *U* values
2 and 12 are constants in formula.

TABLE A.16 Mann-Whitney *U* Test Critical Values for .001 One-Tailed and .002 Two-Tailed Test for *N*s Ranging from 9 to 20

This table is for a two-sample application where the larger sample ranges from 9 to 20, and where the level of significance is .001 (one-tailed) and .002 (two-tailed). The larger of the two *N*s, N_1, is across the top of the table, while the smaller of the two *N*s, N_2, is found down the left-hand side. The body of the table where these respective *N*s intersect defines critical values of *U*. If the observed value of *U* is *equal to or smaller than* the *U* shown in the body of the table, then the observed *U* is significant at either the .001 (one-tailed) or .002 (two-tailed) level of significance.

$N_2 N_1$	9	10	11	12	13	14	15	16	17	18	19	20
1												
2												
3									0	0	0	0
4		0	0	0	1	1	1	2	2	2	3	3
5	1	1	2	2	3	3	4	5	5	6	7	7
6	2	3	4	4	5	6	7	8	9	10	11	12
7	3	5	6	7	8	9	10	11	13	14	15	16
8	5	6	8	9	11	12	14	15	17	18	20	21
9	7	8	10	12	14	15	17	19	21	23	25	26
10	8	10	12	14	17	19	21	23	25	27	29	32
11	10	12	15	17	20	22	24	27	29	32	34	37
12	12	14	17	20	23	25	28	31	34	37	40	42
13	14	17	20	23	26	29	32	35	38	42	45	48
14	15	19	22	25	29	32	36	39	43	46	50	54
15	17	21	24	28	32	36	40	43	47	51	55	59
16	19	23	27	31	35	39	43	48	52	55	60	65
17	21	25	29	34	38	43	47	52	57	61	66	70
18	23	27	32	37	42	46	51	56	61	66	71	76
19	25	29	34	40	45	50	55	60	66	71	77	82
20	26	32	37	42	48	54	59	65	70	76	82	88

Source: Compiled by authors.

TABLE A.17 Mann-Whitney U Test Critical Values for .01 One-Tailed and .02 Two-Tailed Test for Ns Ranging from 9 to 20

This table is for a two-sample application where the larger sample ranges from 9 to 20, and where the level of significance is .01 (one-tailed) and .02 (two-tailed). The larger of the two Ns, N_1, is across the top of the table, while the smaller of the two Ns, N_2, is found down the left-hand side. The body of the table where these respective Ns intersect defines critical values of U. If the observed U value is *equal to or smaller than* the U shown in the body of the table, then the observed U is significant at either the .01 (one-tailed) or .02 (two-tailed) level of significance.

N_2N_1	9	10	11	12	13	14	15	16	17	18	19	20
2					0	0	0	0	0	0	1	1
3	1	1	1	2	2	2	3	3	4	4	4	5
4	3	3	4	5	5	6	7	7	8	9	9	10
5	5	6	7	8	9	10	11	12	13	14	15	16
6	7	8	9	11	12	13	15	16	18	19	20	22
7	9	11	12	14	16	17	19	21	23	24	26	8
8	11	13	15	17	20	22	24	26	28	30	32	4
9	14	16	18	21	23	26	28	31	32	36	37	0
10	16	19	22	24	27	30	33	36	38	41	44	7
11	18	22	25	28	31	34	37	41	44	47	50	2
12	21	24	28	31	35	38	42	46	49	53	56	0
13	23	27	31	35	39	43	47	51	55	59	63	7
14	26	30	34	38	43	47	51	56	60	65	69	3
15	28	33	37	42	47	51	56	61	66	70	75	0
16	28	33	37	42	47	51	56	61	66	70	69	3
17	33	38	44	49	55	60	66	71	77	82	88	3
18	36	41	47	53	59	65	70	76	82	88	94	00
19	38	44	50	56	63	69	75	82	88	94	101	07
20	40	47	53	60	67	73	80	87	93	100	107	14

Source: Compiled by authors.

If either $N > 20$, use Z formula:

$$Z = \frac{U - \left(\dfrac{N_1N_2}{2}\right)}{\sqrt{\dfrac{(N_1N_2)(N_1 + N_2 + 1)}{12}}}$$

Where
N_1 and $N_2 =$ respective sample sizes
$U =$ smaller of the two observed U values
2 and 12 are constants in formula.

TABLE A.18 Table of Critical Values for the Sandler A Statistic* ‡

	Levels of Significance for One-Tailed Test				
	.05	.025	.01	.005	.0005
	Levels of Significance for Two-Tailed Test				
df	Critical Values of the Sandler A Statistic				
1	.512	.503	.500	.500	.500
2	.412	.369	.347	.340	.334
3	.385	.324	.286	.272	.254
4	.376	.304	.257	.238	.211
5	.372	.293	.240	.218	.184
6	.370	.286	.230	.205	.167
7	.369	.281	.222	.196	.155
8	.368	.278	.217	.190	.146
9	.368	.276	.213	.185	.139
10	.368	.274	.210	.181	.134
11	.368	.273	.207	.178	.130
12	.368	.271	.205	.176	.126
13	.368	.270	.204	.174	.124
14	.368	.270	.202	.172	.121
15	.368	.269	.201	.170	.119
16	.368	.268	.200	.169	.117
17	.368	.268	.199	.168	.116
18	.368	.267	.198	.167	.114
19	.368	.267	.197	.166	.113
20	.368	.266	.197	.165	.112
21	.368	.266	.196	.165	.111
22	.368	.266	.196	.164	.110
23	.368	.266	.195	.163	.109
24	.368	.265	.195	.163	.108
25	.368	.265	.194	.162	.108
26	.368	.265	.194	.162	.107
27	.368	.265	.193	.161	.107
28	.368	.265	.193	.161	.106
29	.368	.264	.193	.161	.106
30	.368	.264	.193	.160	.105
40	.368	.263	.191	.158	.102
60	.369	.262	.189	.155	.099
120	.369	.261	.187	.153	.095
∞	.370	.260	.185	.151	.092

*Between two df, use the *smaller df* for interpretation.

‡If A_{obs} is equal to or larger than the A critical value, then A_{obs} is significant at the level of significance shown.

Source: Compiled by authors.

TABLE A.19 Critical Values of F for the F Distribution, .05 and .01 Levels of Significance

Critical values of F are shown in the body of the table for various between- and within-group degrees of freedom (df). Across the top of the table are between-group degrees of freedom, while down the left-hand side of the table are within-group degrees of freedom. Between-group df are determined by $k-1$, where k = the number of groups being compared. Within-group degrees of freedom are determined by summing the numbers of persons in each group and subtracting from this total the number of groups. As an example, if there are 5 groups and a total of 75 persons across the 5 groups, then $75-5 = 70$ df. Therefore, one would look for the intersection of 4 (between-group degrees of freedom, $k-1$ or $5-1 = 4$) and 75–5 or 70 df for within-group degrees of freedom. Where these values intersect in the body of the table identify two critical values of F. One is light-faced type, and the other is bold-faced type. Light-faced type is the critical value of F for the .05 level of significance, while the boldfaced type is the critical value of F for the .01 level of significance. If the investigator has an observed F value equal to or larger than the value shown where the between-group and within-group df values intersect, then the groups are considered significantly different from one another on the characteristic being measured. Dfs of 4 and 70 intersect where 2.50 and 3.60 are found. 2.50 is the .05 level of significance for observed F values, while 3.60 is the .01 critical value. If the observed F value = 3.54, then the groups are considered different statistically at the .05 significance level but not at the .01 significance level. Our F observed value equals or exceeds 2.50 but fails to equal or exceed 3.60. Critical values of F are provided for up to 10 groups, while within-group df range from 25 to 1000. If the exact number of df for within-groups down the left-hand side cannot be found, then use the smaller df closest to the observed df. For instance, if there are 988 df, use 400 df instead of using 1,000 df.

Within-Group df	Between-Group df									
	1	2	3	4	5	6	7	8	9	10
25	4.24	3.38	2.99	2.76	2.60	2.49	2.41	2.34	2.28	2.24
	7.77	**5.57**	**4.68**	**4.18**	**3.86**	**3.63**	**3.46**	**3.33**	**3.21**	**3.13**
30	4.17	3.32	2.92	2.69	2.53	2.42	2.34	2.27	2.21	2.16
	7.56	**5.39**	**4.51**	**4.02**	**3.07**	**3.47**	**3.30**	**3.17**	**3.06**	**2.98**
40	4.08	3.23	2.84	2.61	2.45	2.34	2.25	2.18	2.12	2.07
	7.31	**5.18**	**4.31**	**3.83**	**3.51**	**3.29**	**3.12**	**2.99**	**2.88**	**2.80**
50	4.03	3.18	2.79	2.56	2.40	2.29	2.20	2.13	2.07	2.02
	7.17	**5.06**	**4.20**	**3.72**	**3.41**	**3.18**	**3.02**	**2.88**	**2.78**	**2.70**
60	4.00	3.15	2.76	2.52	2.37	2.25	2.17	2.10	2.04	1.99
	7.08	**4.98**	**4.13**	**3.65**	**3.34**	**3.12**	**2.95**	**2.82**	**2.72**	**2.63**
70	3.98	3.13	2.74	2.50	2.35	2.23	2.14	2.07	2.01	1.97
	7.01	**4.92**	**4.08**	**3.60**	**3.29**	**3.07**	**2.91**	**2.77**	**2.67**	**2.59**
80	3.96	3.11	2.72	2.48	2.33	2.21	2.12	2.05	1.99	1.95
	6.96	**4.88**	**4.04**	**3.56**	**3.25**	**3.04**	**2.87**	**2.74**	**2.64**	**2.55**
100	3.94	3.09	2.70	2.46	2.30	2.19	2.10	2.03	1.97	1.92
	6.90	**4.82**	**3.98**	**3.51**	**3.20**	**2.99**	**2.82**	**2.69**	**2.59**	**2.51**
125	3.92	3.07	2.68	2.44	2.29	2.17	2.08	2.01	1.95	1.90
	6.84	**4.78**	**3.94**	**3.47**	**3.17**	**2.95**	**2.79**	**2.65**	**2.56**	**2.47**
150	3.91	3.06	2.67	2.43	2.27	2.16	2.07	2.00	1.94	1.89
	6.81	**4.75**	**3.91**	**3.44**	**3.14**	**2.92**	**2.76**	**2.62**	**2.53**	**2.44**

(continued)

TABLE A.19 (*Continued*)

Within-Group df	1	2	3	4	5	6	7	8	9	10
200	3.89	3.04	2.65	2.41	2.26	2.14	2.05	1.98	1.92	1.87
	6.76	**4.71**	**3.88**	**3.41**	**3.11**	**2.90**	**2.73**	**2.60**	**2.50**	**2.41**
400	3.86	3.02	2.62	2.39	2.23	2.12	2.03	1.96	1.90	1.85
	6.70	**4.66**	**3.83**	**3.36**	**3.06**	**2.85**	**2.69**	**2.55**	**2.46**	**2.37**
1000	3.85	3.00	2.61	2.38	2.22	2.10	2.02	1.95	1.89	1.84
	6.66	**4.62**	**3.80**	**3.34**	**3.04**	**2.82**	**2.66**	**2.53**	**2.42**	**2.34**

Source: Compiled by authors.

TABLE A.20 **Distribution of Studentized Range Statistic for .05 and .01 Levels of Significance**

This table contains critical values to be used with the Newman–Keuls procedure. Across the top of the table are numbers of means being compared, ranging from 2 to 15. Down the left-hand side of the table are within-group degrees of freedom taken directly from the ANOVA Summary Table. If the exact degrees of freedom cannot be found, then choose the smaller *df*. If within-group *df* are 38, for example, choose 30 instead of 40 to obtain *q* values in the body of the table. Light-faced type defines .05 *q* values, while bold-faced type defines .01 *q* values. These *q* values will be used in the Table of Ordered Means created for making comparisons between sample means. Instructions are provided in the discussion of the Table of Ordered Means in the text for using these *q* values in statistical decision making.

						Means								
df	2	3	4	5	6	7	8	9	10	11	12	13	14	15
10	3.15	3.88	4.33	4.65	4.91	5.12	5.30	5.46	5.60	5.82	5.83	5.93	6.05	6.11
	4.48	**5.27**	**5.77**	**6.14**	**6.43**	**6.67**	**6.87**	**7.05**	**7.21**	**7.36**	**7.48**	**7.60**	**7.71**	**7.81**
12	3.08	3.07	4.20	4.51	4.75	4.95	5.92	5.27	5.40	5.51	5.62	5.71	5.80	5.88
	4.32	**5.04**	**5.50**	**5.84**	**6.10**	**6.32**	**6.51**	**6.67**	**6.81**	**6.94**	**7.06**	**7.17**	**7.26**	**7.36**
14	3.03	3.70	4.11	4.41	4.64	4.83	4.99	5.13	5.25	5.36	5.46	5.55	6.64	6.72
	4.21	**4.89**	**5.32**	**5.63**	**5.88**	**6.08**	**6.26**	**6.41**	**6.54**	**6.66**	**6.77**	**6.87**	**6.96**	**7.05**
16	3.00	3.65	4.05	4.33	4.56	4.74	4.90	5.03	5.15	5.26	5.35	5.44	5.52	5.39
	4.13	**4.78**	**5.19**	**5.49**	**5.72**	**5.92**	**6.08**	**6.22**	**6.35**	**6.46**	**6.56**	**6.66**	**6.74**	**6.82**
18	2.97	3.61	4.00	4.28	4.49	4.67	4.82	4.96	5.07	5.17	5.27	5.35	5.43	5.50
	4.07	**4.70**	**5.09**	**5.38**	**5.60**	**5.79**	**5.94**	**6.08**	**6.20**	**6.31**	**6.41**	**6.50**	**6.58**	**6.65**
20	2.95	3.58	3.96	4.23	4.45	4.62	4.77	4.90	5.01	5.11	5.20	5.28	5.36	5.43
	4.02	**4.64**	**5.02**	**5.29**	**5.51**	**5.69**	**5.84**	**5.97**	**6.09**	**6.19**	**6.29**	**6.37**	**6.45**	**6.52**
30	2.89	3.49	3.84	4.10	4.30	4.46	4.60	4.72	4.83	4.92	5.00	5.08	5.15	5.21
	3.89	**4.45**	**4.80**	**5.05**	**5.24**	**5.40**	**5.54**	**5.56**	**5.76**	**5.85**	**5.93**	**6.01**	**6.08**	**6.14**

(continued)

TABLE A.20 (*Continued*)

df	2	3	4	5	6	7	8	9	10	11	12	13	14	15
40	2.86	3.44	3.79	4.04	4.21	4.39	4.52	4.63	4.74	4.82	4.91	4.98	5.05	5.11
	3.82	**4.37**	**4.70**	**4.93**	**5.11**	**5.27**	**5.39**	**5.50**	**5.60**	**5.69**	**5.77**	**5.84**	**5.90**	**5.96**
60	2.83	3.40	3.74	3.98	4.16	4.31	4.44	4.55	4.65	4.73	4.81	4.88	4.94	5.00
	3.70	**4.20**	**4.50**	**4.71**	**4.87**	**5.01**	**5.12**	**5.21**	**5.30**	**5.38**	**5.44**	**5.51**	**5.56**	**5.61**
120	2.77	3.31	3.63	3.86	4.03	4.17	4.29	4.39	4.47	4.55	4.62	4.68	4.74	4.80
	3.64	**4.12**	**4.40**	**4.60**	**4.76**	**4.88**	**4.99**	**5.08**	**5.16**	**5.23**	**5.29**	**5.23**	**5.40**	**5.40**

Source: Compiled by authors.

TABLE A.21 **Distribution of the F_{max} Statistic for the Hartley F_{max} Test for Homogeneity of Variance**

This table contains critical values of F_{max} for the .05 and .01 levels of significance. Across the top of the table is k, the number of variances being compared, ranging from 2 to 10. Down the left-hand side of the table are df, where df are determined by $N-1$ where N is any given sample size if all sample sizes are equal. If sample sizes being compared are unequal, then the largest sample size should be used. If the exact df cannot be found, choose the larger df for entering the table. For example, if you have $df = 58$, choose $df = 60$, not 30, for entering the table and selecting the F_{max} critical value. Critical values of F_{max} are shown in light-faced type, while bold-faced type indicates .01 critical values of F_{max}. Any observed F_{max} that equals or exceeds the critical value of F_{max} shown means that homogeneity of variance does not exist.

df	k = number of variances								
	2	3	4	5	6	7	8	9	10
4	9.60	15.5	20.6	25.2	29.5	33.6	37.5	41.4	44.6
	23.2	**37.0**	**49.0**	**59.0**	**69.0**	**79.0**	**89.0**	**97.0**	**106.0**
5	7.15	10.8	13.7	16.3	18.7	20.8	22.9	24.7	26.5
	14.9	**22.0**	**28.0**	**33.0**	**38.0**	**42.0**	**46.0**	**50.0**	**54.0**
6	5.8	8.4	10.4	12.1	13.7	15.0	16.3	17.5	18.6
	11.1	**15.5**	**19.1**	**22.0**	**25.0**	**27.0**	**30.0**	**32.0**	**34.0**
7	5.0	6.9	8.4	9.7	10.8	11.8	12.7	13.5	14.3
	8.9	**12.1**	**14.5**	**16.5**	**18.4**	**20.0**	**22.0**	**23.0**	**24.0**
8	4.4	6.0	7.2	8.1	9.0	9.7	10.5	11.1	11.7
	7.5	**9.9**	**11.7**	**13.2**	**14.5**	**15.8**	**16.9**	**17.9**	**18.9**
9	4.0	5.3	6.3	7.1	7.8	8.4	9.0	9.5	9.9
	6.5	**8.5**	**9.9**	**11.1**	**12.1**	**13.1**	**13.9**	**14.7**	**15.3**
10	3.7	4.9	5.7	6.3	6.9	7.4	7.9	8.3	8.7
	5.9	**7.4**	**8.6**	**9.6**	**10.4**	**11.1**	**11.8**	**12.4**	**12.9**
12	3.3	4.2	4.8	5.3	5.7	6.1	6.4	6.7	7.0
	4.9	**6.1**	**6.9**	**7.6**	**8.2**	**8.7**	**9.1**	**9.5**	**9.9**

(*continued*)

TABLE A.21 (*Continued*)

df				k = number of variances					
15	2.9	3.4	4.0	4.4	4.7	5.0	5.2	5.4	5.6
	4.1	**4.9**	**5.5**	**6.0**	**6.4**	**6.7**	**7.1**	**7.3**	**7.5**
20	2.5	3.0	3.3	3.5	3.8	3.9	4.1	4.2	4.4
	3.3	**3.8**	**4.3**	**4.6**	**4.9**	**5.1**	**5.3**	**5.5**	**5.6**
30	2.1	2.4	2.6	2.8	2.9	3.0	3.1	3.2	3.3
	2.6	**3.0**	**3.3**	**3.4**	**3.6**	**3.7**	**3.8**	**3.9**	**4.0**
60	1.7	1.9	2.0	2.0	2.1	2.2	2.2	2.3	2.3
	2.0	**2.2**	**2.3**	**2.4**	**2.4**	**2.5**	**2.5**	**2.6**	**2.6**

Source: Compiled by authors.

TABLE A.22 Cochran's Test for Homogeneity of Variance, C

Across the top of the table are k = the number of variances, ranging from 2 to 9. Down the left-hand side are two columns, one for df, where $df = N - 1$ and where N is any sample size where sample sizes are equal. If sample sizes are unequal, then the largest of the sample sizes should be used. In the second column are probabilities for the .05 and .01 levels of significance. For any given k and df and probability level, critical values of C are given in the body of the table. Any observed C which *equals or exceeds* the critical value of C shown in the table means that homogeneity of variance does not exist. Only observed C values *smaller than* the critical C values shown indicate homogeneity of variance for any given df, k, and significance level. If the df lies between two df values, such as $df = 10$, use the larger of the two df points, or 16 instead of 9, in order to determine the critical value of C. This is a conservative choice and strengthens the case for homogeneity of variance if it exists under the circumstances of this test application.

df	Level of Significance	k = the number of variances							
		2	3	4	5	6	7	8	9
1	.05	.998	.967	.907	.841	.781	.727	.680	.639
	.01	.999	.993	.968	.928	.883	.838	.795	.754
2	.05	.975	.871	.768	.684	.616	.561	.516	.478
	.01	.995	.942	.864	.789	.722	.664	.615	.573
3	.05	.933	.798	.684	.591	.532	.480	.438	.403
	.01	.979	.883	.781	.696	.626	.569	.521	.481
4	.05	.906	.746	.629	.544	.480	.431	.391	.358
	.01	.959	.834	.721	.633	.564	.508	.463	.435
5	.05	.877	.707	.590	.507	.445	.397	.360	.329
	.01	.937	.793	.676	.588	.520	.466	.427	.387
6	.05	.853	.677	.560	.478	.318	.373	.336	.307
	.01	.917	.761	.641	.533	.487	.435	.393	.359
7	.05	.833	.653	.537	.456	.398	.354	.319	.290
	.01	.899	.734	.613	.526	.461	.411	.370	.338

(continued)

TABLE A.22 (*Continued*)

df	Level of Significance	2	3	4	5	6	7	8	9
8	.05	.816	.633	.518	.439	.387	.338	.304	.277
	.01	.882	.711	.590	.504	.440	.391	.352	.321
9	.05	.801	.617	.507	.424	.368	.326	.293	.266
	.01	.867	.691	.570	.485	.423	.375	.337	.307
16	.05	.734	.547	.437	.364	.314	.276	.246	.227
	.01	.795	.606	.488	.409	.353	.311	.278	.251
36	.05	.660	.475	.372	.307	.261	.227	.202	.182
	.01	.707	.515	.406	.335	.286	.249	.221	.199
144	.05	.581	.403	.309	.251	.212	.183	.162	.145
	.01	.606	.423	.325	.264	.223	.193	.170	.152

Source: Compiled by authors.

TABLE A.23 Cumulative Binomial Probabilities, .5

This table is used for interpreting Sign Test results when the sample size ranges from 5 to 25. Down the left-hand side are the total number of pluses and minuses, summing to the total N. Across the top of the table is m, which equals the sign (− or +) which occurs less frequently. The body of the table contains one-tailed exact probabilities where N and m intersect. For two-tailed, nondirectional interpretations, double the probabilities shown. Whenever Ns greater than 25 are examined, a Z test for significance can be used. This Z test is shown at the bottom of this table and the resulting Z can be interpreted as any other Z value, with one-tailed critical values of Z being 1.64 and 1.96 for .05 and .01 levels of significance, and two-tailed critical values of 2.33 and 2.58 for .05 and .01 levels of significance.

N	m	0	1	2	3	4	5	6	7	8	9	10	11	12	13	14	15
5		0.031	0.188	0.5	0.812	0.969											
6		0.016	0.109	0.344	0.656	0.891	0.984										
7		0.008	0.062	0.227	0.5	0.773	0.938	0.992									
8		0.004	0.035	0.145	0.363	0.637	0.855	0.965	0.996								
9		0.002	0.02	0.09	0.254	0.5	0.746	0.91	0.98	0.998							
10		0.001	0.011	0.055	0.172	0.377	0.623	0.828	0.945	0.989	0.999						
11			0.006	0.033	0.113	0.274	0.5	0.726	0.887	0.967	0.994						
12			0.003	0.019	0.073	0.194	0.387	0.613	0.806	0.927	0.981	0.997					
13			0.002	0.011	0.046	0.133	0.291	0.5	0.709	0.867	0.954	0.989	0.998				
14			0.001	0.006	0.029	0.090	0.212	0.395	0.605	0.788	0.910	0.971	0.994	0.999			
15				0.004	0.018	0.059	0.151	0.304	0.5	0.696	0.849	0.941	0.982	0.996			
16				0.002	0.011	0.038	0.105	0.227	0.402	0.598	0.773	0.895	0.962	0.989	0.998		
17				0.001	0.006	0.025	0.072	0.166	0.315	0.5	0.685	0.834	0.928	0.975	0.994	0.999	
18				0.001	0.004	0.015	0.048	0.119	0.24	0.407	0.593	0.76	0.881	0.952	0.985	0.996	0.99
19					0.002	0.01	0.032	0.084	0.18	0.324	0.5	0.676	0.82	0.916	0.968	0.99	0.998
20					0.001	0.006	0.021	0.058	0.132	0.252	0.412	0.588	0.748	0.868	0.942	0.979	0.994
21					0.001	0.004	0.013	0.039	0.095	0.192	0.332	0.5	0.668	0.808	0.905	0.961	0.987
22						0.002	0.008	0.026	0.067	0.143	0.262	0.416	0.584	0.738	0.857	0.933	0.974
23						0.001	0.005	0.017	0.047	0.105	0.202	0.339	0.5	0.661	0.798	0.895	0.953
24						0.001	0.003	0.011	0.032	0.076	0.154	0.271	0.419	0.581	0.729	0.846	0.924
25							0.002	0.007	0.022	0.054	0.115	0.212	0.345	500	0.655	0.788	0.885

Where $N > 25$, $Z = \dfrac{2m - N}{\sqrt{N}}$

Source: Compiled by authors.

TABLE A.24 Critical Values of ΣT in the Wilcoxon Matched Pairs-Signed Ranks Test

Critical values of ΣT are shown for Ns, the pairs of scores, ranging from 6 to 50. Where your N intersects in the body of the table with the level of significance you have chosen, your observed ΣT must be *equal to or smaller than* the critical ΣT value shown in order to be statistically significant at that level. Any larger ΣT value means that the groups do not differ at the level of significance indicated. When the pairs of scores exceeds 50, this table cannot be used. A Z test of significance can be applied, which is shown at the bottom of this table. The resulting Z value can be interpreted for one-tailed and two-tailed levels of significance, where .05 critical values of Z are 1.64 and 1.96 respectively, and 2.33 and 2.58 are two-tailed critical values respectively for two-tailed applications.

	One-tailed level of significance	.025	.01	.005
N	**Two-tailed level of significance**	**.05**	**.02**	**.01**
6		0		
7		2	0	
8		4	2	0
9		6	3	2
10		8	5	3
11		11	7	5
12		14	10	7
13		17	13	10
14		21	16	13
15		25	20	16
16		30	24	19
17		35	28	23
18		40	33	28
19		46	38	32
20		52	43	37
21		59	49	43
22		66	56	49
23		73	62	55
24		81	69	61
25		90	77	68
26		98	85	76
27		107	93	84
28		117	102	92
29		127	111	100
30		137	120	109
31		148	130	118
32		159	141	128
33		171	151	138
34		183	162	149
35		195	174	160
36		208	186	171
37		222	198	183
38		235	211	195

(continued)

TABLE A.24 (*Continued*)

N		.025	.01	.005
	One-tailed level of significance	.025	.01	.005
	Two-tailed level of significance	.05	.02	.01
39		250	224	208
40		264	238	221
41		279	252	234
42		295	267	248
43		311	281	262
44		327	297	277
45		344	313	292
46		361	329	307
47		379	345	323
48		397	362	339
49		415	380	398
50		434	398	373

$$\text{Where } N > 50, \ Z = \frac{\Sigma T - \dfrac{N(N + 1)}{4}}{\sqrt{\dfrac{N(N + 1)(2N + 1)}{24}}}$$

In the formula, 4 and 24 are constants.
Source: Compiled by authors.

TABLE A.25 Tetrachoric *r*, r_{tet} Values Equivalent to Values of *ad/bc* in 2 × 2 Tables

Applicable to 2 × 2 tables only, this table contains values of *ad/bc*, where *a*, *b*, *c*, and *d* are the cells in the table. Utilizing these values and applying the r_{tet} formula found in the chapter discussion of r_{tet}, locate your observed *ad/bc* value from the formula in the body of the table. The equivalent r_{tet} value is adjacent to it. This r_{tet} value is considered the equivalent of the Pearson *r* for 2 × 2 tabular formats, although r_{tet} does not have a PRE interpretation.

r_{tet}	ad/bc	r_{tet}	ad/bc
.00	0.–1.00	.51	4.07–4.20
.01	1.01–1.03	.52	4.21–4.34
.02	1.04–1.06	.53	4.35–4.49
.03	1.07–1.08	.54	4.50–4.66
.04	1.09–1.11	.55	4.67–4.82
.05	1.12–1.14	.56	4.83–4.99
.06	1.15–1.17	.57	5.00–5.18
.07	1.18–1.20	.58	5.19–5.38
.08	1.21–1.23	.59	5.39–5.59
.09	1.24–1.27	.60	5.60–5.80

(continued)

TABLE A.25 *(Continued)*

r_{tet}	ad/bc	r_{tet}	ad/bc
.10	1.28–1.30	.61	5.81–6.03
.11	1.31–1.33	.62	6.04–6.28
.12	1.34–1.37	.63	6.29–6.54
.13	1.38–1.40	.64	6.55–6.81
.14	1.41–1.44	.65	6.82–7.10
.15	1.45–1.48	.66	7.11–7.42
.16	1.49–1.52	.67	7.43–7.75
.17	1.53–1.56	.68	7.76–8.11
.18	1.57–1.60	.69	8.12–8.49
.19	1.61–1.64	.70	8.50–8.90
.20	1.65–1.69	.71	8.91–9.35
.21	1.70–1.73	.72	9.36–9.82
.22	1.74–1.78	.73	9.83–10.33
.23	1.79–1.83	.74	10.34–10.90
.24	1.84–1.88	.75	10.91–11.51
.25	1.89–1.93	.76	11.52–12.16
.26	1.94–1.98	.77	12.17–12.89
.27	1.99–2.04	.78	12.90–13.70
.28	2.05–2.10	.79	13.71–14.58
.29	2.11–2.15	.80	14.59–15.57
.30	2.16–2.22	.81	15.58–16.65
.31	2.23–2.28	.82	16.66–17.88
.32	2.29–2.34	.83	17.89–19.28
.33	2.35–2.41	.84	19.29–20.85
.34	2.42–2.48	.85	20.86–22.68
.35	2.49–2.55	.86	22.69–24.76
.36	2.56–2.63	.87	24.77–27.22
.37	2.64–2.71	.88	27.23–30.09
.38	2.72–2.79	.89	30.10–33.60
.39	2.80–2.87	.90	33.61–37.79
.40	2.88–2.96	.91	37.80–43.06
.41	2.97–3.05	.92	43.07–49.83
.42	3.06–3.14	.93	49.84–58.79
.43	3.15–3.24	.94	58.80–70.95
.44	3.25–3.34	.95	70.96–89.01
.45	3.35–3.45	.96	89.02–117.54
.46	3.46–3.56	.97	117.55–169.67
.47	3.57–3.68	.98	169.68–293.12
.48	3.69–3.80	.99	293.13–923.97
.49	3.81–3.92	1.00	923.98–
.50	3.93–4.06		

Source: Compiled by authors.

TABLE A.26 Fisher Z Transformation for Values of r

Down the left-hand side of the table are various r values from .00 through .99. The second column contains values of Z_F that can be used in the formula for determining the significance of difference between two r values. Find the respective r values, their Z_F values, and insert these Z_F values into the formula at the bottom of this table. The resulting Z value is the observed Z value reflecting the significance of difference between two r values. The critical values of Z for .05 and .01 are 1.64 and 1.96 (one-tailed) and 2.33 and 2.58 (two-tailed) respectively. Any resulting Z value from use of this formula that *equals or exceeds* these Z critical values would be significant statistically at the level of significance chosen for this test.

r	Z_F	r	Z_F	r	Z_F	r	Z_F
.00	.0000	.26	.2661	.51	.5627	.76	.9962
.01	.0100	.27	.2769	.52	.5627	.77	1.0203
.02	.0200	.28	.2877	.53	.5901	.78	1.0454
.03	.0300	.29	.2986	.54	.6042	.79	1.0714
.04	.0400	.30	.3095	.55	.6184	.80	1.0986
.05	.0501	.31	.3206	.56	.6328	.81	1.1270
.06	.0601	.32	.3317	.57	.6475	.82	1.1568
.07	.0701	.33	.3428	.58	.6625	.83	1.1870
.08	.0802	.34	.3541	.59	.6777	.84	1.2212
.09	.0902	.35	.3654	.60	.6931	.85	1.2561
.10	.1003	.36	.3769	.61	.7089	.86	1.2934
.11	.1105	.37	.3884	.62	.7250	.87	1.3331
.12	.1206	.38	.4001	.63	.7414	.88	1.3758
.13	.1308	.39	.4118	.64	.7582	.89	1.4219
.14	.1409	.40	.4236	.65	.7753	.90	1.4722
.15	.1511	.41	.4356	.66	.7928	.91	1.5275
.16	.1614	.42	.4477	.67	.8107	.92	1.5890
.17	.1717	.43	.4599	.68	.8291	.93	1.6584
.18	.1820	.44	.4722	.69	.8480	.94	1.7380
.19	.1923	.45	.4847	.70	.8673	.95	1.8318
.20	.2027	.46	.4973	.71	.8872	.96	1.9459
.21	.2132	.47	.5101	.72	.9076	.97	2.0923
.22	.2237	.48	.5230	.73	.9287	.98	2.2976
.23	.2342	.49	.5361	.74	.9505	.99	2.6467
.24	.2448	.50	.5493	.75	.9730		
.25	.2554						

Z formula is:

$$Z = \frac{Z_{F1} - Z_{F2}}{S_{D_z}}$$

$$S_{D_z} = \sqrt{\frac{1}{(N_1 - 1)} + \frac{1}{(N_2 - 1)}}$$

where

N_1 = 1st sample size and N_2 = 2nd sample size

Source: Compiled by authors.

TABLE A.27 Critical Values of Gamma for .01 and .05 Levels of Significance, One- and Two-Tailed Tests

Values of gamma, γ, for both the .01 and .05 levels of significance for one- and two-tailed tests are provided for sample sizes (N) ranging from 4 to 40, with a t critical value provided for samples in excess of 40. The sample sizes are listed down the left-hand side of the table. Notice that beyond sample sizes of 40, critical values of gamma are the equivalent of Z critical values for .01 and .05 levels of significance since the t distribution approximates the normal curve with increasing sample size.

N	Two-tailed test		One-tailed test	
	.05	.01	.05	.01
4	—	1.00	—	
5	1.00	—	.80	1.00
6	.87	1.00	.73	.87
7	.71	.91	.62	.81
8	.64	.79	.57	.71
9	.56	.72	.50	.67
10	.51	.64	.47	.60
11	.49	.60	.42	.56
12	.46	.58	.39	.55
13	.44	.56	.36	.51
14	.41	.52	.33	.47
15	.39	.51	.32	.47
16	.38	.48	.31	.43
17	.37	.47	.29	.41
18	.35	.45	.29	.41
19	.33	.44	.29	.39
20	.33	.42	.27	.38
21	.31	.41	.27	.37
22	.31	.39	.26	.36
23	.30	.38	.26	.35
24	.29	.37	.25	.34
25	.29	.36	.24	.33
26	.28	.36	.24	.33
27	.27	.34	.23	.32
28	.27	.34	.23	.31
29	.26	.34	.22	.31
30	.26	.33	.22	.30
31	.25	.32	.21	.30
32	.25	.32	.21	.29

(*continued*)

TABLE A.27 (*Continued*)

N	.05	.01	.05	.01
33	.24	.31	.21	.29
34	.24	.31	.20	.28
35	.23	.30	.20	.28
36	.23	.30	.19	.27
37	.23	.30	.19	.27
38	.22	.29	.19	.27
39	.22	.29	.19	.26
40	.22	.29	.19	.26
> 40	.96	2.58	1.64	2.33

Source: Compiled by authors.

TABLE A.28 Standard Scores or Deviates and Coordinates Corresponding to Divisions of Normal Curve Area into a Larger Portion (A) and a Smaller Portion (C)

B Larger area	Z Scored score	f Ordinate	$\sqrt{BC}$	C Smaller area
.500	.0000	.3989	.5000	.500
.505	.0125	.3989	.5000	.495
.510	.0251	.3988	.4999	.490
.515	.0376	.3987	.4998	.485
.520	.0502	.3984	.4996	.480
.525	.0627	.3982	.4994	.475
.530	.0753	.3978	.4991	.470
.535	.0878	.3974	.4988	.465
.540	.1004	.3969	.4984	.460
.545	.1130	.3964	.4980	.455
.550	.1257	.3958	.4975	.450
.555	.1383	.3951	.4970	.445
.560	.1510	.3944	.4964	.440
.565	.1637	.3936	.4958	.435
.570	.1784	.3928	.4951	.430
.575	.1891	.3919	.4943	.425
.580	.2019	.3909	.4936	.420
.585	.2147	.3899	.4927	.415
.590	.2275	.3887	.4918	.410
.595	.2404	.3876	.4909	.405
.600	.2533	.3863	.4899	.400
.605	.2663	.3850	.4889	.395
.610	.2793	.3837	.4877	.390

(*continued*)

TABLE A.28 (*Continued*)

B Larger area	Z Scored score	f Ordinate	$\sqrt{BC}$	C Smaller area
.615	.2924	.3822	.4867	.385
.620	.3055	.3808	.4854	.380
.625	.3186	.3792	.4841	.375
.630	.3319	.3776	.4828	.370
.635	.3451	.3759	.4814	.365
.640	.3585	.3741	.4800	.360
.645	.3719	.3723	.4785	.355
.650	.3853	.3704	.4770	.350
.655	.3989	.3684	.4754	.345
.660	.4125	.3664	.4737	.340
.665	.4261	.3643	.4720	.335
.670	.4399	.3621	.4702	.330
.675	.4538	.3599	.4684	.325
.680	.4677	.3576	.4665	.320
.685	.4817	.3552	.4645	.315
.690	.4959	.3528	.4625	.310
.695	.5101	.3503	.4604	.305
.700	.5244	.3477	.4583	.300
.705	.5388	.3450	.4560	.295
.710	.5534	.3423	.4538	.290
.715	.5681	.3395	.4514	.295
.720	.5828	.3366	.4490	.280
.725	.5978	.3337	.4465	.275
.730	.6128	.3306	.4440	.270
.735	.6280	.3275	.4413	.265
.740	.6433	.3244	.4386	.260
.745	.6588	.3211	.4359	.255
.750	.6745	.3178	.4330	.250
.755	.6903	.3144	.4301	.245
.760	.7063	.3109	.4271	.240
.765	.7225	.3073	.4240	.235
.770	.7388	.3036	.4208	.230
.775	.7554	.2999	.4176	.225
.780	.7722	.2961	.4142	.220
.785	.7892	.2922	.4108	.215
.790	.8064	.2882	.4073	.210
.795	.8239	.2841	.4037	.205
.800	.8416	.2800	.4000	.200
.805	.8596	.2757	.3962	.195
.810	.8779	.2714	.3923	.190
.815	.8965	.2669	.3883	.185
.820	.9154	.2624	.3842	.180

(*continued*)

TABLE A.28 (*Continued*)

B Larger area	Z Scored score	f Ordinate	$\sqrt{BC}$	C Smaller area
.825	.9346	.2578	.3800	.175
.830	.9542	.2531	.3756	.170
.835	.9741	.2482	.3712	.165
.840	.9945	.2433	.3666	.160
.845	1.0152	.2383	.3619	.155
.850	1.0364	.2332	.3571	.150
.855	1.0581	.2279	.3521	.145
.860	1.0803	.2226	.3470	.140
.865	1.1031	.2171	.3417	.135
.870	1.1264	.2115	.3363	.130
.875	1.1503	.2059	.3307	.125
.880	1.1750	.2000	.3250	.120
.885	1.2004	.1941	.3190	.115
.890	1.2265	.1880	.3129	.110
.895	1.2536	.1818	.3065	.105
.900	1.2816	.1755	.3000	.100
.905	1.3106	.1690	.2932	.095
.910	1.3408	.1624	.2862	.090
.915	1.3722	.1556	.2789	.085
.920	1.4051	.1487	.2713	.080
.925	1.4395	.1416	.2634	.075
.930	1.4757	.1343	.2551	.070
.935	1.5141	.1268	.2465	.065
.940	1.5548	.1191	.2375	.060
.945	1.5982	.1112	.2280	.055
.950	1.6449	.1031	.2179	.050
.955	1.6954	.0948	.2073	.045
.960	1.7507	.0862	.1960	.040
.965	1.8119	.0773	.1838	.035
.970	1.8808	.0680	.1706	.030
.975	1.9600	.0584	.1561	.025
.980	2.0537	.0484	.1400	.020
.985	2.1701	.0379	.1226	.015
.990	2.326	.0267	.0995	.010
.995	2.5758	.0145	.0705	.005
.996	2.6521	.0118	.0631	.004
.997	2.7478	.0091	.0547	.003
.998	2.8782	.0063	.0447	.002
.999	3.0902	.0034	.0316	.001

Source: Compiled by authors.

TABLE A.29 Correction Factors for Pearson's C, the Coefficient of Contingency

Table Size	Correction	Table Size	Correction	Table Size	Correction
2 × 2	.707	3 × 9	.843	6 × 6	.913
2 × 3	.685	3 × 10	.846	6 × 7	.930
2 × 4	.730	4 × 4	.866	6 × 8	.936
2 × 5	.752	4 × 5	.863	6 × 9	.941
2 × 6	.765	4 × 6	.877	6 × 10	.945
2 × 7	.774	4 × 7	.888	7 × 7	.926
2 × 8	.779	4 × 8	.893	7 × 8	.947
2 × 9	.783	4 × 9	.898	7 × 9	.952
2 × 10	.786	4 × 10	.901	7 × 10	.955
3 × 3	.816	5 × 5	.894	8 × 8	.935
3 × 4	.786	5 × 6	.904	8 × 9	.957
3 × 5	.810	5 × 7	.915	8 × 10	.961
3 × 6	.824	5 × 8	.920	9 × 9	.943
3 × 7	.833	5 × 9	.925	9 × 10	.966
3 × 8	.838	5 × 10	.929	10 × 10	.949

Source: All correction factors for tables where $r \neq c$ have been determined by a procedure described in Charles C. Peters and Walter R. Van Voorhis, *Statistical Procedures and Their Mathematical Bases* (New York: McGraw-Hill, 1940) pp. 393–399, and Thomas C. McCormick, *Elementary Social Statistics* (New York: McGraw-Hill, 1941), pp. 207–208. Table compiled by authors.

TABLE A.30 Values of *r* for Different Levels of Significance

Degrees of freedom (*df*) are calculated as *N*–2 for using this table. These *df* are located down the left-hand column. Across the top of the table are levels of significance ranging from .1 to .001. If a *df* cannot be found, such as *df* = 88, or *df* = 99, then use the *smaller* of the two *df* values where the observed *df* occurs. Use 60 *df*, for instance, if you have *df* = 69. If your *df* exceeds 100, then use 100 *df*. Any observed value of *r* *equaling or exceeding* the value of *r* shown in the body of the table is statistically significant at the level of significance shown. A cautionary note is that as sample sizes increase, the statistical significance of *r*'s rapidly diminish. Thus, if a researcher has *df* = 400 and the level of significance met is .001, the *r* value may be statistically significant but it may mean little or nothing. The best interpretation of an *r* value is its predictive utility, or r^2. This value, r^2, is the amount of explained variation between the two variables. $1-r^2$ is the amount of *unexplained variation*. Thus, an observed *r* = .30 is statistically significant at the .01 level of significance with 80 *df*. But $r^2 = (.30)^2$ = .09. This means that *r* explains 9 percent of the variation between the two variables. $1-r^2$ = unexplained variation. 1–.09 = .91. This means that 91 percent of the variation between two variables is unexplained by their mutual predictability. Thus, there may be statistical significance, but it may have little or no predictive value.

df level of significance	.1	.05	.02	.01	.001
1	.99	.99	.99	.99	.99
2	.90	.95	.98	.99	.99
3	.81	.88	.93	.96	.99
4	.73	.81	.88	.92	.99

(continued)

TABLE A.30 (*Continued*)

df level of significance	.1	.05	.02	.01	.001
5	.67	.75	.83	.87	.95
6	.62	.71	79	.83	.92
7	.58	.67	.75	.78	.90
8	.55	.63	.72	.76	.87
9	.52	.60	.68	.73	.84
10	.48	.58	.66	.71	.72
11	.48	.55	.63	.68	.80
12	.46	.53	.61	.66	.78
13	.44	.51	.59	.64	.76
14	.43	.50	.57	.62	.74
15	.41	.48	.56	.61	.72
16	.40	.47	.54	.59	.71
17	.39	.46	.53	.58	.69
18	.38	.44	.52	.56	.68
19	.37	.43	.50	.55	.67
20	.36	.42	.49	.54	.65
25	.32	.38	.45	.49	.60
30	.30	.35	.41	.45	.55
35	.27	.32	.38	.42	.52
40	.26	.30	.36	.39	.49
45	.24	.29	.34	.37	.46
50	.23	.27	.32	.35	.44
60	.21	.25	.29	.32	.41
70	.19	.23	.27	.30	.38
80	.18	.22	.26	.28	.36
90	.17	.21	.24	.27	.34
100	.16	.19	.23	.25	.32

Source: Compiled by authors.

TABLE A.31 Critical Values of Spearman's Rho, ρ

This table contains critical values of Spearman's Rank Correlation Coefficient, ρ, for the .05 and .01 levels of significance, where sample size ranges from 4 to 30. Both one- and two-tailed test values are shown. If a particular sample size cannot be found, such as 29, use the smaller of the two sample sizes, 28 and 30, for determining the critical value of ρ. If the observed ρ value *equals or exceeds* the critical ρ values shown in the table, then the observed ρ value is significant at the level of significance shown. When the researcher has a sample size in excess of 30, this table cannot be used to determine the significance of ρ. A Z approximation can be computed as shown, whenever N exceeds 30 and these critical ρ values cannot be used.

N One-tailed test	.05	.01
Two-tailed test	.10	.02
4	1.00	—
5	.90	1.00
6	.83	.94
7	.71	.89
8	.64	.83
9	.60	.78
10	.56	.75
12	.51	.71
14	.46	.65
16	.43	.60
18	.40	.56
20	.38	.53
22	.36	.51
24	.34	.49
26	.33	.47
28	.32	.45
30	.31	.43

Where $N > 30$

$$Z = \frac{r_s}{\dfrac{1}{\sqrt{N-1}}}$$

N = the sample size; r_s = the observed ρ value

Both one- and two-tailed interpretations of Z may be made by consulting Table A.2, Areas of the Normal Curve.

Source: Compiled by authors.

APPENDIX B
Answers to Numerical Problems
at Chapter Ends

Any discrepancies in numerical results between manual calculations and *SPSS* software are usually attributable to rounding error and slightly different calculation methods. These are not especially important differences and may be disregarded, depending on the method you choose to generate correct answers. Some answers for particular statistical procedures are not available through the *SPSS* program, while other answers may be determined by inspection or manually much faster than with *SPSS* programming and the data editor. The first values below are answers that have been computed manually, while the second values have been computed through the *SPSS* software program.

Chapter 3

3.1.a. .156 (10/64)
   b. .272 (65/239)
   c. .664 (18 + 55/110)

3.2.a. 579.5, 574.5, 577
   b. 999.5, 1,999.5, 1,499.5
   c. .2355, .2385, .237
   d. 19.5, 14.5, 17
   e. 179.5, 159.5, 164.5

3.3.c. Interval upper limits: 629.5, 619.5, 609.5, 599.5, 589.5, 579.5, 569.5, 559.5, 549.5, 539.5, 529.5, 519.5, 509.5; interval lower limits: 619.5, 609.5, 599.5, 589.5, 579.5, 569.5, 559.5, 549.5, 539.5, 529.5, 519.5, 509.5, 499.5
   d. Interval midpoints: 624.5, 614.5, 604.5, 594.5, 584.5, 574.5, 564.5, 554.5, 544.5, 534.5, 524.5, 514.5, 504.5

3.4.a. .058
   b. 1.217
   c. There was a 182 percent increase in the population from 2000 to 2007.

3.5.a. 1:131
   b. 1:130
   c. Prison D; 1:67 (Prison A = 1:131; B = 1:168; C = 1:82)

Chapter 4

4.1.a. 40 (40 *SPSS*)
   b. 29.5 (29.5 *SPSS*)
   c. 13, 29 (determined by inspection)

4.2.a. 674.6 (674.6 *SPSS*)
   b. 673 (determined by inspection)
   c. 673 (673 *SPSS*)

4.3.a. Upper limit = 579.5; Lower limit = 574.5
   b. Upper limit = 1999.5; Lower limit = 999.5
   c. Upper limit = .2385; Lower limit = .2355

4.4.a. 33.1 (33.2 *SPSS*)
   b. 26.5, 38.5, 40.5 (determined by inspection)
   c. 34.5 (34.5 *SPSS*)

4.5.a. 825 (825 *SPSS*)
   b. 829, 838 (determined by inspection)
   c. 826 (826 *SPSS*)

4.6.a. 30.2 (30.2 *SPSS*)
   b. 29 (29 *SPSS*)
   c. 31 (determined by inspection)

4.7.a. 63.9
   b. The grand mean may be influenced, either upward or downward, depending on sample size fluctuations. If there is a large mean, 200, among several smaller means, and if the large mean is based on a small sample such as 10 compared with other sample sizes of 30, 40, and 50, and if these three other samples have smaller mean values, such as 75, 70, and 60, the grand mean will be much larger and make it appear that all samples have larger means than they actually have. Alternatively, if one large sample of 200 has a mean of 20, while six other sample means are 30 or higher but the sample sizes are small, ranging from 10 to 20, the grand mean will be reduced in magnitude so that it will appear much smaller. This will give the false impression that the means are generally smaller than 30 or higher. The grand mean is intended to portray the average mean value among k samples. Thus, depending on the circumstances, the grand mean may be a misleading figure depending on whether there are substantial fluctuations among samples according to their size. The best meaning of the grand mean is obtained whenever a given set of means is averaged where all sample sizes are equal.

Chapter 5

5.1.a. 85 percent
   b. 87 percent
   c. Group 2 is more heterogeneously distributed according to booking offense.

5.2.a. 21.3 (21.3 *SPSS*)
   b. 65 or 70 (65 *SPSS*)
   c. 442.3 (442.3 *SPSS*)

5.3.a. 11.6 (11.8 *SPSS*)
   b. 43 (determined by inspection); 42 (*SPSS*; not taking into account upper and lower limits of largest and smallest scores)

5.4.a. 37.9 (37.9 *SPSS*)
   b. 120, 130 (120 *SPSS*)

5.5.a. 19.6 (19.6 *SPSS*)
   b. 383 (383 *SPSS*)
   c. 67 (66 *SPSS*; not taking into account upper and lower limits of largest and smallest scores)

5.6. C.

5.7. D.

Chapter 6

6.1.a. .3770

b. .1293

c. .4980

d. .4868

e. .0753

f. .4772

6.2.a. 142

b. 82 or 83

c. 124 or 125

d. 100

6.3.a. .4946

b. .1574

c. .7620

d. .0691

6.4.a. .0179

b. .9987

c. .9974

d. .0013

6.5.a. .9066

b. .0262

c. .5714

6.6.a. .7062

b. .0385

c. .1137

d. .9586

6.7.a. 179

b. 121

c. 238

6.8.a. .1587

b. .9953

c. .8413

6.9.a. .9628

b. .0027

c. .0025

6.10.a. 2.33

b. 0.00

c. −5.83

d. 3.33

6.11.a. 42
    b. 237
    c. 153
    d. 10

6.12.a. 8,000
    b. 5,000
    c. 1,505
    d. 3,500

6.13.a. 288
    b. 394
    c. 350
    d. 150
    e. 181
    f. 531

6.14.a. 6.95
    b. −11.08
    c. Distribution 2 is more skewed, and to the left.

Chapter 7

7.1. D.

7.2. B.

7.3.a. 197.13–202.87
    b. 197.76–202.24
    c. 199.09–200.91

7.4. Summarize major differences between point and interval estimation.

7.5. All of them.

7.6.a. Has a mean equal to population μ.
    b. Is normal in form.
    c. High and low probability areas can be identified and hypotheses can be tested.

7.7. 200^{15}

7.8. 4.50

7.9. D.

7.10. A.

7.11. B.

7.12.a. 86.53–97.47
    b. 88.93–95.07
    c. 90.21–93.79

7.13.a. ±1.96
    b. ±2.33
    c. ±1.28
    d. ±3.28

Chapter 8

8.1.a. −.794
 b. ±2.101
 c. 18 *df*
 d. −1.10
 e. No significant difference between means.

8.2.a. −1.62
 b. ±2.617
 c. 160 *df*
 d. No significant mean difference, fail to reject H_o.

8.3.a. 4 *df*
 b. 25 *df*
 c. 29 *df*
 d. 3.857
 e. 2.76
 f. There is a significant difference between the sample means.

8.4.a. 644.49
 b. 31.20
 c. 4.50
 d. 2.33
 e. 12.8
 f. 2.91
 g. 5
 h. 93
 i. 98
 j. 800.49
 k. There is a significant difference between the means.
 l. Homogeneity of variance does not exist using the Hartley F_{max} test.

8.5.a. .83
 b. 4.16, 3.98, 3.74, 3.40, 2.83
 c. 3.45, 3.30, 3.10, 2.82, 2.34
 d. 12–16, 12–17, 12–19, 12–21, 14–17, 14–19, 14–21, 16–19, 16–21, 17–21

8.6.a. 10,693
 b. 522.7
 c. 4
 d. 134
 e. 138
 f. 12,884
 g. 6.55
 h. 2.44
 i. 5.49
 j. 2.04
 k. There is a significant difference between *k* sample means.
 l. Using the Hartley F_{max} test, homogeneity of variance doesn't exist.

8.7.a. 11.09

    b. 2.660

    c. 98

    d. There is a significant mean difference.

    e. 2.460

    f. There is a significant mean difference.

8.8.a. 87.1

    b. 40.1

    c. .460

    d. .437

    e. 4

    f. 16

    g. Homogeneity of variance doesn't exist at the .05 level.

8.9.a. 1.658

    b. 2.33

    c. 158

    d. Means do not differ.

8.10.a. 1

    b. 5

    c. 5

    d. 82

    e. 93

    f. 36.15

    g. 92.6

    h. 7.62

    i. 4.74

    j. 2.43

    k. 2.08

    l. 3.96 (1, 80 *df*)

    m. 2.33 (5, 80 *df*)

    n. 2.33 (5, 80 *df*)

    o. Main effect factor 1 is significant in that prison adjustment mean scores vary between the prisons; main effect factor 2 is significant, in that length of time served affects prison adjustment scores; interaction effects of type of prison and length of time served do not significantly impact prison adjustment scores.

Chapter 9

9.1.a. 11.28 (manual and *SPSS*)

    b. 6.635

    c. 1 *df*

    d. Reject null hypothesis; discretionary ability generally improved significantly from low to high ability.

9.2.a. 14.350 (*SPSS* and manual computation)

    b. 1 *df*

   c. 3.841

   d. Reject null hypothesis; close supervision yields high recidivism, while general supervision yields low recidivism.

9.3.a. 9.600 (*SPSS* and manual computation)

   b. 2 *df*

   c. 4.991

   d. Reject null hypothesis; there is a significant difference between the three treatment conditions; treatments 1 and 3 differ significantly; treatments 1–2 and treatments 2–3 do not differ significantly (this is through an application of Q test to two samples at a time through *SPSS* program.

9.4.a. 14.0 (*SPSS* and manual computation)

   b. 11.345

   c. Reject null hypothesis; this distribution of juvenile probation officers significantly differs according to their effectiveness.

9.5.a. 21.389 (*SPSS* and manual computation)

   b. 9.210

   c. 2 *df*

   d. Reject null hypothesis; there is a significant difference between what is observed and what is expected according to chance; higher professionalism, greater satisfactory reports; lower professionalism, and more unsatisfactory reports.

9.6.a. 4 *df*

   b. 18 *df*

   c. 7 *df*

   d. 16 *df*

   e. 4 *df*

9.7.a. 20.517

   b. 21.666

   c. 22.307

   d. 19.675

Chapter 10

10.1.a. Yes, the distribution of scores is different from what would be expected according to chance. Largest proportionate difference $= .262$, $P = .000$. Reject null hypothesis as there is no difference between the k categories. $Z = 3.306$.

   b. Yes. Chi-square could be applied to these data. A disadvantage is that some data would be lost, since the data would be treated as nominal and it is ordinal-level data.

10.2.a. The U observed $= 34$; the null hypothesis can be rejected at the .05 level (two-tailed); exact probability is .030; $Z = 2.176$; there is a difference in attitude scores between the two groups.

   b. Yes, the t test could be used, although the assumption of interval-level data would be violated. This is a conventional application of t, however. The t test for differences between means could be applied, with $(N_1 - 1) + (N_2 - 1)$ or $(11 - 1) + (13 - 1)$ or $10 + 12 = 22df$.

10.3.a. $k = 4$; $N = 9$; $df = k - 1 = 4 - 1 = 3$ df; the chi-square distribution is approximated with the Friedman test.

   b. The chi-square $= 20.517$, $P = .000$. The null hypothesis is rejected at the .05 level (two-tailed test). There is a difference between the k matched sets of scores.

   c. The Wilcoxon test for matched pairs could be applied as a two-sample probe. If the samples being compared are used as their own controls over k time periods, then the sign test could be used as the two-sample probe.

10.4.a. Observed H value $= 25.882$; critical H value (2 df, .05 level of significance, two-tailed test) $= 9.210$; $P = .000$. There is a significant difference between the k samples.

   b. No. Friedman test is for k-related samples, not k-independent samples.

   c. $df = 2$ ($k = 3$, $k - 1 = 2$ df)

   d. Chi-square distribution is approximated with $k - 1$ df.

   e. Mann-Whitney U test is most powerful two-sample probe for the Kruskal-Wallis H test; most powerful nonparametric test compared with the t test.

10.5.a. Fail to reject the null hypothesis as the groups differ; probability $= .052$; this probability level is close to .05, the chosen level of significance; the closeness of the result might be reported as $P > .05 < .06$ for reader information.

10.6.a. No, there was no significant change in officer scores from one time period to the next (.10 level of significance, two-tailed test; actual probability was .189). Summary results indicate 14 positive score changes from time 1 to time 2, 7 negative score changes and 1 tied score.

   b. No, the Mann-Whitney U test is inappropriate for these data. The data portray scores for related samples or a before-after scenario. The Mann-Whitney U test can only be applied to two independent samples. If it were to be applied here, it would violate a crucial assumption concerning the appropriateness of its application to a related-sample situation.

10.7.a. $P = .020$, significant at less than .05 (one-tailed test); there is a significant difference between the two groups.

   b. Yes, the runs test can be applied to any data where the Mann-Whitney U test can be applied. The Mann-Whitney U test is vastly superior to the runs test, however, since it takes into account the ranks in scores across the two samples investigated. Also, it is the most powerful nonparametric equivalent to the t test, while the runs test has power equal to about 75–80 percent in a similar comparison.

Chapter 11

11.1.a. $C = .34$

   b. C has no PRE interpretation. It is simply an index number. It also must be corrected with a correction factor in order to make it comparable with 1.00.

   c. $P = .000$

   d. Phi $= .36$; Cramer's $V = .36$

   e. Chi-square observed $= 28.78$

11.2.a. Gamma $= .43$; Kendall's tau $= .31$; according to gamma $= .43$, 43 percent of the variation in both variables is accounted for by their mutual predictability; tau is directly interpretable as a PRE measure; given a tau $= .31$, 31 percent of the variation in the two variables is accounted for by their mutual predictability; however, tau has a weakness applied to tied scores, which are prevalent in cross-tabulated data; as such, it is an unreliable measure of association, and we would defer to gamma for our accurate PRE interpretation.

   b. $P = .000$

11.3.a. $C = .37$; $\overline{C} = .48$; there is a moderately low association between supervision and offender recidivism.

   b. Chi-square observed $= 19.282$

   c. Phi $= .40$; Cramer's $V = .40$

11.4.a. Lambda $= .07$; symmetric and asymmetric values of lambda $= .07$; neither variable is the better predictor of the other.

   b. 7 percent of the association between the two variables is explained by their mutual predictability; 93 percent of their variation is unexplained.

   c. 4×3

11.5.a. $C = .27$; $\overline{C} = .35$; there is no PRE interpretation because C doesn't have one.

   b. Phi $= .28$; Cramer's $V = .28$; PRE for the phi coefficient is $\varphi^2 = (.28)^2 = .08$; therefore, 8 percent of the variation in the two variables is accounted for by their mutual predictability; Cramer's V has no PRE interpretation.

   c. Chi-square observed $= 10.51$

Chapter 12

12.1.a. Pearson $r = .24$

   b. $P = .46$; not significant

   c. Pearson rPRE $= (.24)^2 = .06$, meaning that 6 percent of the variation in the two variables has been accounted for by their mutual predictability; $1-6$ percent $= 94$ percent of the variation in the two variables has not been accounted for.

   d. rho $= .33$

   e. Spearman's rho PRE $= (.33)^2 = .11$

12.2.a. Spearman's rho $= .53$

   b. Pearson $r = .39$

12.3.a. Theta $= .33$

   b. PRE $= 33$ percent of the variation in the two variables has been accounted for by their mutual predictability.

12.3.b. 33 percent of the variation is explained.

   c. Moderately low association.

   d. The more the years on the job, the greater the job satisfaction.

12.4.a. Pearson $r = -.34$

   b. $P = .04$

   c. $(-.34)^2 = .12$

   d. Spearman's rho $= -.36$

   e. Interval level of measurement, randomness, homoscedasticity, bivariate normal distribution, and linearity.

12.5.a. Eta $= .16$
   b. Yes. Eta squared $=$ PRE, or $(.16)^2 = .02 =$ PRE. 2 percent of variation in two variables explained, and 1–2 percent $= 98$ percent unexplained.
   c. A low degree of association exists between the two variables; one might conclude that no relation exists between months to recidivism and inmate gender.

12.6.a. Spearman's rho $= .67$
   b. Yes. Rho squared or $(.67)^2 = .46$. 46 percent of the variation in the two variables has been explained by their mutual predictability. This is a significant amount of variation explained.
   c. Pearson $r = .68$

Chapter 13

13.1. .146, .088
13.2. .051, .062
13.2.a. .0026, .0038
   b. 0.26 percent and 0.38 percent of the variation, about 1/4 and 1/2 of a percent, very negligible explanatory power.
   c. They are similar.
   d. The variable for race.

13.3. .0298, .0115
13.3.a. .018, .0185
   b. .032 percent and .034 percent
   c. The variable for attorney type.
   d. The variable for race.

Chapter 14

14.1. The important statistics are the significance associated with the F statistic; the adjusted R^2, the significance associated with t, and the unstandardized and standardized effects.
14.1.a. Yes.
   b. Age, black.
   c. .012, 1.2 percent
   d. Race is the most important predictor.

14.2. No, all of the Tolerance statistics are close to 1, and all of the VIFs are below 4.

Chapter 15

15.1. The important statistics are the significance associated with chi-square, the Nagelkerke R^2, the significance associated with the Wald statistic, the unstandardized effects, and the odds ratios or EXP(B).
15.1.a. Yes, because the significance associated with the chi-square is below .05.
   b. Priors, gender, detention status, and the variable for trial.
   c. .34, which is 34 percent of the variance.
   d. Going to trial: 2.4 times more likely to go to prison as opposed to taking a plea bargain; the least is on offender's detention status, where the odds ratio is .685, or negligible.

15.2.a. 36.5 percent from the Nagelkerke R^2.

b. Positive relationship: age and gender; negative relationship: ever call the police and ever been victimized.

c. Older persons and females are more likely to be satisfied with the police, those who have called the police, and those who have been victimized are more likely to be less satisfied with the police. The variables with a significant influence are those whose significance level is below .05.

15.3.a. 35.6 percent

b. Age and gender have positive relationships; high school graduates; employment and marital status have negative relationships. None of the variables are positively related to being indifferent versus approve.

c. Those who are older and female are more likely to disapprove, high school graduates, those unemployed, and those married are all less likely to approve. Those older, those who are college graduates, and those unemployed are less likely to be indifferent. To determine significance, we looked at the asterisked variables.

d. Females are 2.43 times more likely to disapprove than males; and for those older, the odds ratio is 0.95, which means there is not much difference regarding age.

GLOSSARY

additivity The combined effect of multiple variables on the variance of a dependent variable.

alpha (α) error See *Level of Significance.*

analysis-of-variance summary table (ANOVA) A table summarizing the results of the F test for k-independent samples; contains df, mean squares, sums of squares, total sums of squares, and an observed F value.

applied significance See *Substantive Significance.*

area sampling plans See *Cluster Sampling Plans.*

array An arrangement of scores from low to high or high to low, usually observed for a given sample of persons.

association Any apparent relation between two or more variables, usually expressed numerically by a coefficient of association; establishing a relationship among variables and the first step toward demonstrating that causal relationships exist.

asymmetric PRE interpretation Type of proportional reduction in error interpretation where one variable accounts for a greater amount of variation in the other, depending upon whether it is used as an independent variable or a dependent one; both variables may be used as independent in relation to each other, and separate amounts of variation are accounted for in each variable as a result; some measures of association are symmetrical. See also *Symmetrical PRE Interpretation.*

asymptotic property of the normal distribution Feature of the normal distribution where the ends of the curve extend away from the center of the distribution toward each tail, approaching the baseline but never touching it; ends of tails extend toward infinity in both directions to the left and right.

attitudinal scales Any measuring instruments designed to measure our feelings or orientations toward something or someone; measures include Likert and Thurstone scaling, as well as several other scaling methods; usually variables measured by attitudinal scales are measured according to the ordinal level of measurement.

autocorrelation Phenomenon existing where errors for cases in close proximity with each other are correlated.

average deviation (AD) The average variation of scores around the mean of the distribution; all score departures from the mean are summed and divided by the number of scores to produce this value.

axes The horizontal and vertical ranges of scores which have been cross-tabulated in a figure; usually there is an X axis and a Y axis; association between variables may be observed by examining the intersection points of scores in the figure, known as a scatter plot.

axis A line, either horizontal or vertical, representing the range over which scores are distributed; usually depicted as an X axis and a Y axis, score values are plotted in a scatter plot which yields a pattern which can be interpreted.

bar graphs Any depiction of the frequencies of scores in different intervals with the use of horizontal or vertical bars; may also be used to portray the numbers of persons with particular characteristics with the use of bars representing numbers of persons with these characteristics or scores.

β coefficient Represents the unstandardized effects of independent variables in a regression model.

best-fitting line A theoretical line drawn through intersecting points of two variables in a scatter plot where the distance or variation of the line from all intersecting points has been minimized; also called the regression line.

Beta (β) error The probability of failing to reject a null hypothesis when it is false and ought to be rejected.

Beta weight Represents the standardized effect of independent variables in a regression model.

between-group variation Actual variation in scores between k samples; determined by a formula that can yield sums of squares and mean squares.

bimodal A frequency distribution of scores with two modes.

bivariate correlation matrix A table of Pearson rs that represents every variable correlated with every other variable.

bivariate normal distribution Two-variable association where both variables are assumed to be normally distributed; an assumption underlying the proper application of a Pearson r value.

Cameron and Trivedi test Procedure that discloses whether data are overdispersed.

causality Links variables together and predicts relationships; associates the concepts of cause and effect; the need to show association, time order, and nonspuriousness in order to substantiate some degree of causality.

cells Partitions in any $r \times c$ table, where data have been cross tabulated; data are frequencies occurring in particular cells representing where two variables intersect.

centiles Representations of points in a frequency distribution in 1 percent units.

chi-square test, χ^2 A nonparametric statistical technique that determines the goodness of fit between observed and expected frequencies, either in a cross tabulation or in some other data arrangement.

chi-square test for two independent samples A nonparametric statistical technique designed to determine the goodness of fit between two independent samples on some variable which has been cross tabulated into a $r \times c$ table.

chi-square test for k independent samples A nonparametric statistical technique, an extension of the chi-square test for two independent samples, designed to determine the goodness of fit between k independent samples which have been cross tabulated into a $r \times c$ table.

cluster sampling plans Methods for drawing samples from large geographical areas, where horizontal and vertical grids are drawn, and which result in multistage samples from which smaller geographical areas are delineated; subsequently a random sample of smaller geographical areas results in clusters of farms or homes being sampled; one of several probability sampling plans.

Cochran C test Procedure for determining homogeneity of variance between k samples; usually used in conjunction with applications of the F test for analysis of variance.

Cochran Q test A nonparametric, k-related sample, chi square–based procedure for determining the goodness of fit across k samples according to some variable measured according to a nominal scale.

coefficients of association Numerical expressions of the degree of correlation between two or more variables; usually calculated from a statistical formula designed to determine the degree of association between variables.

coefficient of determination Sometimes called the coefficient of multiple determination and denoted as R^2, numerical result yields the amount of variance explained in the dependent variable with all independent variables combined.

coefficient of multiple determination See *Coefficient of Determination*.

collinearity Occurs when an independent variable or group of independent variables is perfectly correlated with another independent variable or group of independent variables.

computer-determined draw The selection of sample elements from a population of them through a computer program.

confidence intervals Specified areas around an observed mean that has a likelihood of overlapping the population μ at some point; such intervals are constructed by using the standard error of the mean and a Z value from the normal curve table consistent with the probability level one wishes to use; such intervals are useful in numerous hypothesis tests.

confounding variables See *Rival Causal Factors.*

continuous variables Any quantities or phenomena which can be infinitely divided or that can assume an infinite number of subclassifications such as age, amount of education, and attitudes.

control variables Factors held constant in order to determine the independent effects of independent variables of interest to investigators.

correlation Any correspondence or association between two or more variables, usually numerically expressed and ranging from 0 or no association to ±1.00, or perfect positive or negative association.

Cox and Snell R^2 Alternative statistical procedure for the coefficient of multiple determination.

Cramer's V A chi square–based measure of association between two nominal-level variables; has no PRE interpretation; may achieve +1.00; can never be a negative number; to obtain a negative or inverse association interpretation, table must be inspected for the distributional pattern of frequencies in various cells; may be applied to tables of any $r \times c$ size.

critical regions Areas in the tails of sampling distributions, such as the sampling distribution of the mean, that contain low probabilities; these regions are so-named because observed statistical values that occur in these regions result in rejecting null hypotheses and supporting accompanying research hypotheses; also called regions of rejection.

cross tabulation Any tabular arrangement where two or more variables have been combined to create two or more columns each and where relationships between variables may be observed.

cumulative frequency distributions Any frequency distribution where the numbers of scores in intervals containing the smallest scores are added to the intervals containing the next larger scores until the interval containing the largest scores is reached; this number will equal the total number of frequencies found in all intervals.

curvilinear Any association between variables where variables are nonlinear and where one variable increases for a time and then decreases in value, while a second variable either increases consistently or decreases in relation to the first variable.

curvilinearity Any pattern of intersecting points in a scatter plot where two variables are nonlinear and the relation between them is curved; usually results from one variable increasing (or decreasing) for a time and then decreasing (or increasing) while a second variable continuously increases or decreases.

Data Editor Window in *SPSS* software program where data may be entered and viewed, usually in a data view or variable view.

data entry Process of entering data into a computer software program for purposes of analyzing the data by applying statistical tests and measures; transmitting data from one form to another, as in transforming information from a questionnaire to numerical form on a computer software program such as *SPSS* for data processing.

data set A compilation of information about a specific sample or population being studied, usually consisting of raw scores on a variety of variables, such as age, gender, type of crime, attitudes about different issues, and other descriptive information expressed in numerical form; program analyses with programs such as *SPSS* are conducted on such compilations or data sets, and valuable information about the sample or population is subsequently disclosed.

data view Particular mode for viewing information entered in the *SPSS* software program.

deciles Representations of scores in distributions in 10 percent units or segments.

decision rules Several standards established in advance of any statistical test and setting forth the criteria for determining whether hypotheses will be rejected or not rejected; includes level of significance, sampling distribution of a specified statistic, and a critical region defined by the significance level.

degree of association Amount of departure of a coefficient of association from 0 or no association;

usually $0-.25$ = no or low association; $.26-.50$ = moderately low association; $.51-.75$ = moderately high association; $.76-1.00$ = high association; association coefficients may be $\pm$ to reflect either negative or inverse association $(-)$ or positive or direct association $(+)$.

degrees of freedom (*df*) Defined differently for different statistical applications, in the general case, the number of values in a set which are free to vary; *df* are useful for analysis-of-variance summary tables, locating critical values in statistical tables; may be $k-1$, $(r-1)(c-1)$ in a cross tabulation, $N-1$, and so forth.

dependent variables Any quantities or phenomena that rely on the values of other variables for their own value; any variable that changes in value in response to a change in another variable or variables, typically referred to as independent variables.

descriptive statistics Any one of several statistical techniques that describes the properties of a sample, such as a sample mean or standard deviation; any numerical notation that represents sample characteristics.

deviant scores Outliers or scores markedly different from most of the other scores in a frequency distribution; existence of such scores often skews the distribution upward or downward, depending on the magnitude of these scores (i.e., very small or very large).

dichotomous variables Any descriptors that may be divisible into two discrete values, such as male/female, yes/no, prison/jail, or felony/misdemeanor.

direct association A positive association where two or more variables vary in the same direction together, either upward or downward. Also known as a positive association.

disarray Numerical data arranged in no particular order.

discrete variables Any quantities or phenomena that can only assume a limited number of categorical designations, or subclassifications, such as race, ethnicity, gender, political affiliation, or type of crime.

disproportionate stratified random sampling plans Methods for including elements in a sample where the elements included are disproportionate to their distribution in the population from which they are drawn.

distribution-free statistics Tests or procedures where the normal distribution is not assumed with the collected data and scores; such tests include all nonparametric statistical procedures and are alternatives to parametric tests where more stringent assumptions apply.

dummy variables Factors that are dichotomized or made binary by forcing them to assume either "0" or "1" values; by creating dummy variables, the influence of a non-interval-level independent variable on a dependent variable can be assessed.

elements Persons or things, usually in reference to samples drawn from populations.

equality of draw In random sampling, drawing population elements in such a way so that each person has the same chance of being drawn.

error-free association Relation between variables in any $r \times c$ table, where all frequencies accumulate or bunch up in the diagonal cells in a perfect distributional arrangement; for example, if all males should "agree" with a given view, they do; if all females should "disagree" with that same view, they do; there are no exceptions in error-free association, where some males disagree and some females agree.

error term Quantity added to a regression equation to account for error or variation.

eta, η, the correlation ratio A two-variable nonparametric measure of association, where one variable is measured according to the nominal level of measurement and the other is measured according to the interval level of measurement; η^2 is interpretable as a PRE measure.

expected frequencies In any cross tabulated $r \times c$ table, these frequencies are determined usually on the basis of the marginal totals; they yield what would be expected in various cells of a table according to chance; these frequencies are compared with actual or observed frequencies in a table; the discrepancy between observed and expected frequencies is evaluated, usually by a statistical procedure such as chi-square and goodness of fit is determined.

expected value The mean of the sampling distribution of a statistic.

expected value of the mean The mean of the sampling distribution of the mean.

explained variation Amount of fluctuation in one variable explained by another variable used as a predictor of it.

extreme scores Any score in a distribution that departs markedly from most other scores. See also *Outliers and Deviant Scores*.

first-order partial derivative Calculated by the equation dy/dx or $\Delta y/\Delta x$ which gives the rate of change in Y for a change in X.

fishbowl draw Using a fishbowl to draw slips of paper from as a means of obtaining a random sample of elements; all population elements are typically numbered and these numbers are placed on slips of paper placed in a fishbowl and then drawn randomly; method is outmoded and has been replaced by draws of elements through tables of random numbers of computer-determined draws.

Fisher Z approximation Test of significance of the difference between two observed Pearson r values; involves converting r values to Fisher Z values; tabled values of Fisher Zs can be used in determining the significance of difference between the two converted r values.

Fisher Z transformation See *Fisher Z Approximation*.

Fisher Z values Numerical representations of the significance of difference between two Pearson r values; the numerical result of the Fisher Z transformation or Fisher Z approximation.

frames of reference Any approaches or views toward research problems that are used to explain or account for these problems; a way of looking at a research problem and why it occurs and persists.

F ratio, F statistic Term in ANOVA summary table calculated by dividing the mean square for between groups by the within-group mean square, or MS_{bet}/MS_{within}; compares sample variances between two groups; used to determine whether an overall OLS regression model is statistically significant.

frequency distribution Any tally of values for raw scores in an orderly fashion; may include either ungrouped or grouped data.

frequency polygon A continuous line drawing made from a histogram where the highest and central points of intervals have been connected with lines; ends of distribution are anchored at midpoints of next lowest and next highest intervals where no frequencies occur, usually directly on the horizontal axis of the distribution.

Friedman two-way analysis of variance test A nonparametric chi square–based statistical procedure for determining the significance of difference between k related samples according to some ordinal-level variable.

F-test for analysis of variance k-sample test of significance to determine the difference between two or more (usually three or more) sample means where the interval level of measurement is assumed.

gamma distribution Used in negative binomial regression and introduces another error term into the equation.

Gauss-Markov theorem States that if the all of the assumptions of OLS regression are met, then OLS is the best linear unbiased estimator.

Goodman's and Kruskal's gamma, γ Measure of association between two ordinal-level variables; unrestricted by table size or N values; may achieve ± 1.00; interpreted as a symmetric PRE measure.

goodness of fit The similarity between whatever is observed to occur in any $r \times c$ table and what is expected according to chance, as evaluated by a statistical procedure such as chi-square.

goodness-of-fit tests Any statistical procedure, primarily chi-square, which determines the significance of difference between what is observed and what is expected according to chance; generally a tabular model exists with observed frequencies; expected frequencies are calculated and the result is a measure of how closely one's observations fit those that would otherwise be expected according to chance; the greater the discrepancy, the more significant the difference.

grand mean The average of two or more sample means.

graphs Any line drawings or figures depicting distributions of scores or characteristics of persons.

grouped data Arranging one's numerical information into orderly intervals of a size smaller or larger than 1; creating categories for placements of scores in some orderly fashion; usually applicable to sample sizes greater than 25.

growth rates Proportionate changes in some variable or quantity over time, such as some population or persons with specific characteristics, such as gender, race/ethnicity, political affiliation, and crime.

Hartley F_{max} test Procedure for determining whether homogeneity of variance exists among k samples.

heteroscedasticity Phenomenon occurring whenever the average variance of the errors about the regression line is not constant along the entire regression line.

histograms Bar-graph-like portrayals of frequencies in successive intervals; usually portrayed similar to a vertical bar graph.

homogeneity of variances Equal variances; this is an assumption underlying various statistical test applications, such as the F test for analysis of variance; it is assumed that homogeneity of variance or equal variances exists; can be tested by different measures.

homoscedasticity Arrangement of intersection points around a regression line where the ellipse is shaped like a football; one assumption underlying the proper application of a Pearson r value.

H test See *Kruskal-Wallis H Test*.

hypothesis Any statement, usually derived from theory, that can be tested through empirical research; a stated relation between variables or value of a population parameter; a tentative generalization that may become a factual statement over time and through repeated testing and verification.

hypothesis sets Pairs of hypotheses, usually research and null hypotheses, that are ideally set forth for the purpose of testing; a theoretical formulation of a pair of hypotheses, where rejecting one hypothesis, usually the null hypothesis, will result in support for the research hypothesis; also a failure to reject a null hypothesis results in a failure to support a research hypothesis.

independence of draw The feature of randomness which mandates that the selection of each element from the population for subsequent inclusion in a sample will not affect the chances of other elements or persons of being drawn.

independent samples Two or more samples that are drawn in a way so that they are mutually exclusive of one another; a single sample may be subdivided into several independent samples according to predetermined criteria; various statistical tests have been designed for two or more samples drawn in this fashion.

independent variables Any quantities that bring about changes in other variables when they change in value; variables are categorized according to whether they influence or are influenced by other variables.

index of qualitative variation (IQV) Mueller's and Schuessler's measure of attribute heterogeneity; useful for analyzing attribute heterogeneity for distributions of values measured according to a nominal scale.

influence Refers to outliers, those cases outside the distribution of the rest of the cases that may alter the results of logit regression output.

instability Condition existing where deviant or outlier scores are present and distort the meaning of computed values of central tendency or dispersion or variability.

interaction In statistics, refers to a change in one variable that has caused, or is associated with, a change in another variable.

interaction effects The influence of two or more independent variables on a dependent variable; an assessment of the degree to which the independent variables influence each other in this general relation.

interval estimation Process of determining an interval surrounding an observed mean where a given likelihood or probability exists that the population mean occurs within this interval; on the sampling distribution of the mean, for example, an observed sample mean may have an interval created around it with a specified probability of overlapping the population μ; this interval is called a confidence interval, since a particular probability of including μ within this interval is expressed.

interval level of measurement Property of a scale that renders equal distances between different values; minimum level needed for certain arithmetic operations, such as computations of means and standard deviations; the same distance exists between a "5" and "10" as exists between a "25" and a "30."

interval midpoints The precise points in intervals that divide intervals in a frequency distribution into two equal parts; adding half the interval size to the lower limit of the interval (e.g., 750–754 has midpoint of 752; 10–19 has midpoint of 14.5, and so on).

intervals Numerical categories of different sizes for placing raw scores in some organized fashion.

interval size The magnitude of an interval where raw scores of particular sizes are found.

Jaspen's *M*, the coefficient of multiserial correlation Two-variable measure of association, where one variable is measured according to an ordinal scale and the other variable is measured according to an interval scale; interpretable as a symmetric PRE measure.

Kendall's coefficient of concordance, *W* Nonparametric measure of association for determining the degree of agreement between k ordinal-level variables; does not have a PRE interpretation.

Kendall's tau, τ Two ordinal-variable measure of association for data in any $r \times c$ size; values of tau may be $\pm$; has only a symmetric PRE interpretation.

k-sample tests of significance Any procedure for determining the significance of difference between two or more groups, usually three or more, since specific two-sample tests of significance exist for this purpose.

Kolmogorov–Smirnov single-sample test Nonparametric statistical procedure that determines the significance of the proportionate difference in a distribution of frequencies for a single sample throughout k categories, where the data are measured according to an ordinal scale.

Kolmogorov–Smirnov two-sample test A nonparametric statistical procedure that determines the significance of the proportionate difference between two distributions of persons according to k categories; it is assumed that the two samples are independent and the variable under investigation is measured according to an ordinal scale.

Kruskal-Wallis *H* test Nonparametric statistical procedure for determining the significance of difference between k independent samples according to a variable measured at the ordinal level; considered an extension of the Mann-Whitney U test, although the H test is interpreted as a chi-square value and thus is chi square-based.

kurtosis Curve peakedness; distributions may be flat-appearing or platykurtic; or abruptly pointed or leptokurtic; or bulging or mesokurtic; normal distributions have no substantial kurtosis.

lambda, λ, Guttman's coefficient of predictability One of the best measures of association between two variables measured according to a nominal scale; used for tables of any size; no sample size restrictions; has both symmetric and asymmetric PRE interpretation; yields only positive values, although interpretation of direction of relation may be determined by inspecting distribution of table frequencies.

latent variables Factors that are not directly measured but can be estimated in the model from those variables that do have direct effects.

leptokurtosis Condition in a distribution where scores accumulate closely near the center of the distribution resulting in a very peaked curve.

level of measurement Refers to the nature of measurement that underlies particular variables and how they are classified or numerically represented; depending upon how variables are conceptualized, they may be measured according to the nominal, ordinal, interval, or ratio level of measurement.

level of significance Probability established for the purpose of making a hypothesis test; also known as Type I error and alpha (α) error, probability of rejecting a null hypothesis when it is true and should not be rejected; this probability is established and set by the investigator; conventional rules for establishing such levels of significance are usually followed.

Likert scaling Method of measuring attitudes using graduated weights ranging from "Strongly Agree" to "Strongly Disagree"; yields scores measurable according to the ordinal level of measurement; sometimes called cumulative ratings scale.

linear A straight-line relationship between two variables.

linearity Condition existing of a straight-line relationship between two variables in a scatter plot where two variables have been cross tabulated; a major assumption underlying multiple regression is that the relationship between two variables is a straight line.

linear regression Technique that can calculate the straight line in a scatter plot of data points.

logistic regression Correlational technique that can be used for dependent variables that are dichotomous.

logit coefficient Measure of the log of the odds of a change in y for a change in x.

lower limits of intervals The theoretical points in intervals in frequency distributions where the bottom of the interval is reached and where the lowest numbers occur in the interval (e.g., 750–754 has lower limit of 749.5; 10–19 has lower limit of 9.5, and so on).

main effects Direct effects of independent variables on a dependent variable, usually in a two-way analysis of variance test.

Mann-Whitney *U* test Nonparametric statistical procedure considered the most powerful in relation to the parametric *t* test for assessing the significance of difference between two independent samples on a variable measured according to an ordinal scale.

maximum likelihood estimation Technique used in logistic regression where the program estimates what the coefficients are, examines how close its estimated model has come to reality, and then recalculates the model until the likelihood of getting a group of coefficients with the same proportion of 0s and 1s that are in the data is maximized.

McNemar test for significance of change A nonparametric chi square–based statistical technique that determines the goodness of fit between before-after scores according to nominal scale; a related-sample test used for persons used as their own controls in a before-after experiment.

mean, $\overline{X}$ Average value in a distribution of raw scores; computed by summing the scores and dividing by the total number of scores.

mean of means, $\overline{X}_T$ Grand mean, or the overall average of two or more sample means.

mean squares (*MS*) Sums of squares for between and within groups divided by *df* for between and within groups.

measures of association Any statistical procedure that discloses the amount of correlation between two or more variables; usually, though not always, coefficients of association may vary between 0 or no association to ±1.00, or perfect positive or negative association.

measures of central tendency One of several types of characteristics of a distribution of sample scores that depict the centrality of the distribution or the points around which scores in the distribution tend to focus; examples might be the mode, median, and mean.

measures of dispersion or variability Any one of several types of characteristics of a distribution of sample scores that depict how scores in a distribution are spread around some central point; examples might be the range and standard deviation.

median, *Mdn* Measure of central tendency that defines a point that divides a distribution of scores into two equal parts.

mesokurtosis Condition in a distribution where scores are scattered throughout the distribution so as to produce a bulging effect if a graph is drawn to depict the distribution; larger numbers of scores are found in various intervals far away from the mean of the distribution and produce this effect.

mode, *Mo* Measure of central tendency depicting the most frequently occurring score in data in ungrouped form, or the midpoint of the interval containing the most scores in a frequency distribution of raw scores.

multicollinearity Collinearity between more than two variables.

multimodal A distribution with more than one mode.

multinomial logit Logistic regression technique for use with nominal-level dependent variables.

multivariate statistical analyses Allow researchers to be able to account for a number of causally related factors and determine the separate independent effects of each variable as well as the combined effects of all variables together.

multistage sampling plans See *Cluster Sampling Plans*.

Nagelkerke R^2 Alternate form of the coefficient of multiple determination.

nature of association Usually observed in a scatter plot of intersecting points, refers to the distributional pattern of intersecting points between variables *X* and *Y*, where both variables have been cross tabulated.

negative association A relationship between variables where one variable increases (or decreases), while the other variable decreases (or increases).

negative binomial regression Correlation technique for use if your data are overdispersed.

Newman–Keuls procedure A post hoc test for determining the significance of difference between *k* sample means, where two means at a time are compared; usually all sample means are portrayed in a table of ordered means; critical values are determined which are used to evaluate all mean differences.

nominal level of measurement Lowest level of measurement, where variable subcategories are defined in a discrete sense; no category is considered higher or lower than any other category; example might be gender, whose subclasses may be "male" and "female."

nonlinear Any relationship between variables which is not a straight-line association; a curvilinear relation would be nonlinear.

nonparametric tests Any one of several statistical procedures used in hypothesis testing and decision making where normality is not assumed, where smaller sample sizes (less than 100) are involved, and where the level of measurement is either nominal or ordinal.

nonprobability sampling plans Methods for drawing samples of persons from populations of them where no attempt is made to randomize the selection of elements; such samples have limited generalizability as a result.

nonspuriousness Addresses ensuring that no other variable could be responsible for the relationship between two variables.

normal distribution Also known as the standard normal distribution, unit normal distribution, and bell-shaped curve, a theoretically derived distribution with several constant and important properties; mean, mode, and median occur at center of distribution; has asymptotic property where ends of distribution taper off in opposite directions toward the baseline of the horizontal axis and never reach it; all area under the curve is equal to 1.000, and different portions of curve area are equal to portions of 1.000; used in statistical inference work; an assumption underlying every parametric statistical test and measure of association; perfectly symmetrical; parameters are a mean = 0, standard deviation = 1.

normality Having a distributional shape similar to the normal distribution.

normalize To convert raw scores to fit the parameters of the normal distribution, with a $\mu = 0$ and a $\Sigma = 1$. See also *Standardization, Standardize*.

notation systems Symbolic expressions selected to stand for different phenomena studied, such as the mean or average, the sum of scores, standard deviation, or range.

null hypotheses Statements derived from research hypotheses that are subsequently tested in criminological or social science research; statements are usually contradictions of research hypotheses, but they are carefully worded so that their rejection leads to the support of a specific research hypothesis whose truthfulness has been explained and predicted by a theory.

observed frequencies In any cross-tabulated $r \times c$ table, observed frequencies are the actual frequencies in the various cells of the table.

Occam's Razor Addresses parsimony and is the principle developed by William of Ockham; states that the simplest model is the best one.

odds ratio Statistic given as a part of logistic regression output denoted by Exp(B) and which determines how many times more likely it is that the value on the dependent variable will be "1," given the value of the independent variable.

ogive curve Line drawn for a cumulative frequency distribution showing the growing accumulation of the smallest scores to the largest scores in a frequency distribution.

one-tailed test Any test of significance involving a directional prediction.

ordered logit Also referred to as ordinal logit regression, is a technique similar to binary logistic regression except that it is for use with dependent variables that have more than one outcome and that are of an ordinal nature.

ordinal level of measurement Scale property which enables researchers to state that numerical scores representing some measured phenomenon are rankable relative to one another; ordinality refers to rankable data, such as rank-ordering scores; such a measurement level assumes that equal distances between scores do not exist; thus the difference between a "1" and a "2" is different from the difference between a "20" and a "21"; scores on such scales are closely associated with attitudinal measurement, including the use of Likert and Thurstone scales.

ordinary least squares regression Technique used for dependent variables that are measured at the interval level; it finds the best-fitting line in data values with two or more variables in such a way as to provide for any value of x the best corresponding value of y.

outliers Deviant scores in a distribution of scores; raw scores that are markedly different from most of the other scores; such scores often cause distortions in the central tendency and dispersion of scores in any distribution where they occur.

paired-samples t test A procedure similar to the t test for determining the significance of difference between two means, except that the means for the paired-sample test are related and not independent.

parametric tests Any procedure where normality is assumed, where the interval level of measurement is achieved, and which are applied to larger sample sizes of 100 or more.

parameters Characteristics of a population of persons, such as their average age, years of education, racial/ethnic distribution, and gender.

parsimony Explaining the most with the least; choosing between the simpler of two models.

part correlation Sometimes called semi-partial correlation, is the foundation for multiple regression; the separate effect of an independent variable on the dependent variable, controlling for the other independent variables.

partial correlation Refers to the relationship between two variables less the correlation or overlap from both; the effect of an independent variable on the dependent variable less the overlap only.

path analysis An expansion of regression; assesses the effects of relationships between variables in a causal model.

Pearson product-moment correlation coefficient, r Best-known parametric measure of association between two interval-level variables; assumes homoscedasticity, linearity, randomness, bivariate normal distribution, and interval-level variables; has a symmetric PRE interpretation; used in many advanced multivariate techniques; r^2 is the measure of PRE.

Pearson's C, the coefficient of contingency A basic measure of association between two nominal-level variables; may be computed for tables of any $r \times c$ size; an index number that cannot achieve ± 1.00 without a correction factor being used; not interpretable as a PRE measure; computed directly from a knowledge of N and chi-square.

percentages Proportion of a given number of persons with particular attributes or scores in relation to the total number of persons in a sample multiplied by 100.

personal computers (PCs) Any electronic device, portable or stationary, that is capable of data processing and information retrieval; typically uses a processing system such as Windows XP or Windows 2000, or some other more advanced technology; may be used for storing data, running software programs, and accessing the Internet for information retrieval and general data searches.

phi coefficient, φ Measure of association between two nominal-level variables arranged into a 2×2 tabular format; φ^2 is interpretable as a symmetric PRE measure; may generate $\pm$ correlational values.

pie chart Any circular graph, named such because it resembles a pie, where data are divided into pie-shaped segments; pie segments usually represent portions of circle area, with the sum equalling 1.00 or 100 percent.

platykurtosis Flat-appearing distribution where scores are distributed sparsely around the central point and larger portions of scores are found in the tails of the distribution compared with more bell-shaped or normal-appearing distributions.

point estimates Predicted values of some parameter, such as the population mean, μ, usually based on previous information.

point estimation Process of predicting the value of a population parameter and comparing this predicted value with an observed sample statistic that represents it; usually based on prior information known about population and values one is estimating.

Poisson regression Correlational technique used for count data.

population All persons identified in a universe about which one seeks information; for example, all corrections officers in Louisiana, all federal court judges, all probation officers in Illinois.

post hoc tests Any procedure for probing for significant differences among specific pairs of means following an overall significant difference has been found by the application of the F test for k sample means; the Newman–Keuls procedure is a post hoc procedure.

positive association A relationship between two or more variables, where the magnitude of each variable moves in the same direction, upward or downward, compared with one or more other variables. Also known as a direct association.

postmortem tests See *Post hoc Tests.*

power The ability of a statistical test to reject false null hypotheses; test power is measured by $1-\beta$ error.

PRE See *Proportional Reduction in Error.*

predicted probabilities Formula is $P = e^{a+bx}/1 + e^{a+bx}$, which will give the effect on the dependent variable of a particular value on the independent variable; these probabilities should be calculated for meaningful values of x, and is a more practical and more easily understandable as the effect of an x on y.

predictive utility Refers to the ability of an explanation of an event to explain its occurrence with a high level of accuracy.

probabilities Actual likelihoods associated with different event occurrences; likelihood expectations that whatever is observed is not due to chance but rather to some independent variable whose connection with an event has been explained and predicted by a theory.

probability sampling plans Any one of several sampling plans where the elements have been drawn in such a way so that each person drawn from the population has an equal and an independent chance of being drawn.

probability theory General theoretical principles governing statistical decision making where laws of probability apply and where estimates can be given probabilities for their subsequent occurrence.

proportionate stratified random sampling plans Sampling methods which are considered probability sampling plans and where controls are introduced to govern the proportionate representation of elements in the sample to the same degree as their proportionate representation in the population.

proportional odds assumption Test that determines whether the slopes of the various categories are equal, in essence it makes a determination of whether the proportional odds are different; tests the null hypothesis that there is no difference in the proportions of the odds, or the slopes.

proportional reduction in error (PRE) Amount of variation in one variable accounted for by using another variable as a predictor of it.

proportions Parts of an entire sample of persons expressed as a portion of 1.00, usually .30, .46, .82, and so forth; computed by dividing a part of the sum of scores and/or by the total number of scores and/or persons.

qualitative research Data-gathering and analyses of information based on observation, interviewing, or analysis of written documents; nonstatistical data analyses and investigations.

quantitative research Statistically driven studies, usually survey or questionnaire information, that have been converted into numerical form for various testing and analysis purposes; heavily numerical data easily amenable to quantitative methods, including statistical tests, measures of association, and other data manipulation and control.

quartiles 25 percent points in a distribution of scores, where distributions are divided into 25 percent units or segments.

r × c table A cross tabulation representing a certain number of rows (*r*) and columns (*c*).

randomness The selection of elements or persons from a population of them for inclusion in a sample where each person has an equal and an independent chance of being drawn.

random samples Smaller numbers of persons drawn from a population in such a way so that each person has an equal and an independent chance of being included.

range The distance over which 100 percent of all scores in a distribution are spread.

rates Ratios that express change in some variable, usually over some time interval, such as a day, month, or year; may be proportionate expressions at a given point in time, such as population growth rates; usually expressed according to a given standard, such as 100,000, 10,000, and so on. See also *Growth Rates*.

ratio level of measurement Highest measurement level, where scores on a scale of them have an absolute zero.

ratios Comparisons of two numbers, such as the numbers of prison correctional officers to inmates; usually expressed as 1:10, 1:2, and so on.

raw scores Any numerical indicators, usually derived from scales designed to measure attitudes and other attributes, that reflect the degree to which someone possesses that attribute or characteristic; sometimes scores are categorical and refer to discrete variable categorizations.

regions of rejection See *Critical Regions*.

regression line A theoretical line drawn through the intersecting points of two correlated variables in a scatter plot; this is also known as the best-fitting line, and it is based on the least amount of variation or distance of each intersecting point on variables *X* and *Y* from the line itself, hence the best-fitting line.

rejection regions See *Critical Regions*.

related samples Two or more samples that have either been matched according to several salient characteristics or where persons have been used as their own controls over *k* time periods; specific statistical tests and procedures are designed for these types of samples.

relationship Any correlation between two or more variables, usually expressed as a numerical value ranging from 0 or no association to ±1.00, perfect positive or negative association.

research Any investigative activity designed to provide answers to questions about events of importance to us; in criminology and criminal justice, investigations may be conducted into why there are high recidivism rates among probationers and parolees, or why there is juvenile delinquency; any question in need of an answer is a researchable question.

research findings Any results from a survey or study, numerical, recorded observations, verbal reports, or other output that may be used for various purposes, such as testing theories or hypotheses drawn from them.

research hypotheses Statements of uncertainty derived from theory which are subsequently tested through social science research; any statement deductively derived from a theory and which is capable of being tested by gathering and analyzing relevant data.

research problems Any question about events, criminological or otherwise, in need of an explanation; any questions capable of being investigated through scientific inquiry.

residuals The differences between the actual Ys and the predicted Ys from the regression.

rival causal factors Any factors, other than the independent variable under investigation, that may be responsible for the change in the dependent variable.

robust Property of a statistical test where the test yields observed values under conditions of assumption violations similar to values yielded if those assumptions were not violated.

robustness The ability of a statistical test to render similar numerical results even under conditions where certain assumptions have been violated and the test is applied in data analysis anyway; under certain conditions, some of the assumptions of statistical analyses may be violated with no serious repercussions as to numerical outcomes.

Roncek's semi-standardized coefficient (B_R) Calculates a semi-standardized coefficient for a logit equation, and multiplies the b-coefficient by its standard deviation, which will yield the proportional effect on y for a standard deviation change in x.

run In the Wald-Wolfowitz runs test, a single group of scores from the same sample that are immediately adjacent to one another when arranged into an array of them from low to high or high to low.

Runs test See the *Wald-Wolfowitz Runs Test*.

sample A part of the population of persons about whom we seek information; a smaller part of a population which is considered representative of it; a group of persons with characteristics that are generalizable to the population from which it was drawn.

sample size The magnitude of one's sample; the number of persons selected for inclusion in one's sample and which is drawn from a larger population of elements.

sampling distribution of a statistic All possible values a statistic may assume when computed for all possible samples of a specified size, n, drawn from a specified population, N; a theoretical distribution where sampling with replacement is used to generate all possible statistics for samples of a specified size drawn from a specified population.

sampling plans Any one of several different methods of drawing samples of persons from populations of them; may include probability and nonprobability sampling plans.

sampling with replacement Obtaining sample elements from a fixed number of population elements where each element is replaced in the population once drawn; therefore, it is possible to draw the same person two or more times as a theoretical possibility for inclusion in a subsequent sample; this sampling method is used for all statistical procedures treated in this book.

sampling without replacement Obtaining sample elements from a fixed number of population elements, where the drawn elements cannot be drawn more than once.

Sandler A test Procedure for determining the significance of difference between two related samples, where the data are measured according to an interval scale; the related-sample counterpart to the t test for differences between means.

scaling Any method of converting opinions and ideas into measurable properties that express how strongly persons feel toward ideas or things or other persons; scaling methods include Likert and Thurstone scales.

scatter plot A figure representing the intersectional points between two variables; intersecting points are dots which have particular distributional shapes and can be depicted by a line running through them as either linear or nonlinear.

Scheffé procedure Test for determining where significant differences between pairs of sample means occur following an overall significant application of the F test for analysis of variance.

scientific method A way of knowing or discovering truths about phenomena and their occurrence, usually through objectivity and reasoning; incorporates cumulative information about given events; a theoretical foundation; restriction of study to empirical events; and nonethical views toward why events occur.

semi-partial correlation See *Part Correlation*.

sign test Nonparametric statistical test of significance of difference between two related samples for a variable measured according to an ordinal scale; test is usually applied in before-after experimental scenarios for a sample where elements are used as their own controls.

simple random sampling plans One of several types of sampling plans where sample elements are drawn in a way where each element has an equal and an independent chance of being included.

skewness Distribution shape where scores accumulate in one end of the distribution or the other; may be positive or negative skewness; positive skewness is indicated where the scores accumulate in the left tail of the curve, and negative skewness involves score accumulations in the right tail of the curve; the normal distribution has no skewness.

slope The slant of a line drawn through intersecting points in a scatter plot, which usually charts the relation between two variables, X and Y. The lower the slope, the less the association.

Somers' d_{yx} Measure of association between two ordinal-level variables unrestricted to table size; has both an asymmetric and a symmetric

PRE interpretation; superior to various versions of Kendall's tau.

Spearman's rho, ρ A nonparametric measure of association between two interval-level variables; sometimes called the rank-order correlation coefficient, this measure has a symmetric PRE interpretation; it does not hold up well under conditions where numerous tied ranks exist between variables correlated.

specification error Refers to whether the correct equation that accounts for changes in the dependent variable is being utilized.

stability Condition in a distribution of scores where central tendency values or measures of dispersion reliably accurately reflect the points around which scores focus and the nature of this distribution pattern.

standard deviation The square root of the variance; the variance is average of the sum of the squared deviation scores about the mean; in general usage, the standard deviation is the most stable measure of variability and is used frequently in statistical inference; it has a constant interpretation from one sample to the next, concerning the number of scores encompassed between the mean and one or more standard deviations from the mean.

standard error of the difference between means The denominator term in the formula to determine the significance of difference between two observed sample means; a significant difference between means may mean the population means of which the sample means or estimates also differ; standard error values decrease as sample sizes increase.

standard errors of statistics Standard deviations of sampling distributions of statistics.

standard error of the mean The standard deviation of the sampling distribution of the mean.

standard error of the sampling distribution The standard deviation of the sampling distribution of a statistic.

standard error of the treatment means Standard error term used in the Newman–Keuls procedure for identifying critical values for assessing pairs of means and their statistical significance.

standard error terms Any standard deviation of any sampling distribution of any statistic.

standardize To normalize a distribution of scores, usually to fit the parameters of the normal distribution, with a mean = 0 and a standard deviation = 1. See *Standardization*.

standardization Normalizing a distribution of raw scores; establishing a common distribution by which scores from different distributions of raw scores may be compared; typically means converting raw scores to fit the parameters of the normal distribution, with a mean = 0 and a standard deviation = 1.

standardized effects Usually denoted by the Greek symbol for beta (β), and allows comparison of the magnitude of effects of the independent variables because it is not calculated according to how the independent variables have been measured. These standardized values are computed by converting the raw data to Z scores and will allow rank-ordering of variables in order of importance of influence on the dependent variable.

standard normal distribution See *Normal Distribution*.

standard scores Values, also known as Z scores, which represent different points along the horizontal axis of the unit normal distribution and cut off fixed proportions of curve area; these areas have been determined and are tabled; raw scores which have been converted to a standard form, usually conforming to a distribution with a mean = 0 and a standard deviation = 1; other standards besides 0 and 1 may be used as alternatives to these parameters for a more general meaning of this term.

statistical evidence Numerical results that can be used to verify theories that explain and predict relationships between variables or to confirm or refute hypotheses tested.

statistical hypothesis Symbolic expression of either a research hypothesis or null hypothesis or both; usually contains the symbols that are a part of a statistical formula used in determining a particular result or outcome; statements about the real world that are symbolically expressed and capable of being tested.

statistical inference The process of making estimates about the value of population parameters based on an examination of their sample statistic counterparts.

Statistical Package for the Social Sciences (*SPSS*) Software program capable of analyzing large data sets and performing complex procedures very rapidly; contains numerous statistical procedures for graphic presentation and statistical analyses and decision making; marketed by SPSS, Inc., in Chicago.

statistical significance The probabilistic importance of a hypothesis test, which is usually evaluated by comparing observed with critical values of various statistics; the probability that any observed difference did not occur according to chance but rather to one or more independent variables that have been logically linked to an event's occurrence.

statistical significance of an association The statistical test conducted to determine the significance of an observed correlation coefficient; each coefficient observed differs from 0 or no association, and this difference can be assessed in terms of its statistical significance; *SPSS* software produces significance levels for all observed correlation coefficients, and manual methods exist for determining the significance of an association as well; there is a difference between statistical significance and whether the correlation is strong, however; much depends on the sample size investigated; the larger the sample size, the smaller the error term, and the greater the statistical significance of an observed coefficient of association.

statistical symbols Any symbolic notation used to represent sample characteristics or formula components.

statistics General body of methods and procedures used to assemble, describe, and infer facts from numerical data; numerical, graphic, and tabular descriptions of collected data; characteristics of a sample taken from a population.

strength of an association The amount of correlation observed between two or more variables; may range from 0 or no association to ±1.00, or perfect positive or negative association.

structural equation modeling (SEM). Technique for testing causal models of the relationships between variables.

subclasses Any category on a variable, such as "male" or "female" on the gender variable, or "Hispanic," "Caucasian," or "African-American" on the race variable.

substantive significance The practical implications stemming from hypothesis tests and their relevance for solving practical problems; such significance has policy implications and is the basis for interventions and treatments designed to bring about desired and predictable effects in any sample studied.

sums of squares (*SS*) Term in an analysis-of-variance summary table reflecting the amount of variation between and among scores in *k* samples.

symmetric PRE interpretation Meaning given to an association coefficient reflecting its ability to yield a mutual prediction interpretation about the relation between two variables; some amount of variation among two variables is accounted for by their mutual predictability; some measures of association only yield asymmetric interpretations, while others yield asymmetric PRE interpretations. See also *Asymmetric PRE Interpretation*.

table of ordered means A summary table showing a horizontal and vertical array of sample means from lowest to highest; used with the Newman–Keuls procedure for determining the significance of difference between all pairs of sample means following an overall significant *F* value in the analysis of variance *F* test.

table of random numbers A massive array of numbers from which random samples are selected; numbers are not presented in any particular order, and they may consist of numerous pages; samples drawn in a systematic way from such a table are considered random samples.

tail One end or the other of a distribution; may refer to the normal distribution or to a distribution of raw scores; a tail is one end of the distribution, either to the far left or far right from the mean of it.

tails of the distribution Both areas at the far left and right of the mean of a distribution of scores; the extreme regions of the normal distribution; also called areas of low probability, critical regions, and/or regions of rejection.

tests of significance Any one of many statistical procedures designed to yield values that have probabilistic interpretations for hypothesis testing; such tests are used for testing null and research hypotheses; any type of statistical procedure used to make a decision about the truthfulness of a null or research hypothesis.

tests of significance of difference between two and *k* samples Any statistical test designed to determine the probability that two or more samples significantly differ at some probability level on a measured characteristic.

tests of significance of measures of association Any statistical test designed to determine the probability that an observed coefficient of association differs significantly from no association or zero.

tests of significance of point estimation Usually Z or t tests that yield a probability that a predicted parameter, such as μ, is accurate by comparing μ with an observed sample mean; the magnitude of difference between the observed mean and hypothesized μ is evaluated by a standard error term, and the resulting statistical value is interpreted in a probabilistic context.

theoretical significance It is theory-driven and implies that our findings are generalizable to other samples. Whenever we conclude that a finding has theoretical significance, this means that it contributes to our understanding of interrelationships between variables.

theory Integrated body of assumptions, propositions, and definitions arranged in such a way so as to explain and predict relationships between two or more variables.

Thurstone scaling Elaborate scaling technique based on the use of judges who assign items weights based on their believed intensity to reflect whatever trait or characteristic is being measured; through averaging weights, overall weights are assigned different items, which are then chosen by respondents; further averaging of weights of limited number of selected items gives a raw score, purportedly yielding an equal-appearing interval scale; realistically, this scale yields at best data measurable according to an ordinal scale; Likert and Thurstone scales are similar in the representation of one's feelings or attitudes toward different issues measured.

time order Examines variables to assess any changes between independent and dependent variables; an important step since in order to infer cause, the independent variable must be shown to either precede the dependent variable in time or change before the dependent variable changes.

tolerance Test of collinearity in the regression model; explains how much of the variance of an independent variable is not dependent on other independent variables; value ranges from 0 to 1, and the closer the value is to 1, the more independence the variable has; a value close to 0 indicates the presence of multicollinearity.

trend analysis The examination of data over time, usually to discover patterns or trends in data fluctuations between different time intervals, such as days, months, or years.

trend data See *Trend Information.*

trend information Any data arranged to depict changes in some variable over time, such as the number of executions in the United States by year.

trimodal A frequency distribution of scores with three modes.

***t* test** Procedure for determining the difference between two sample means or between an estimated μ value and an observed sample $\overline{X}$.

***t* test for differences between means** Procedure for determining whether two sample means differ from one another at some level of significance; inference is made that if the sample means differ, then the population means they represent also differ.

Type I error The probability of rejecting a null hypothesis when it is true and should not be rejected. See also *Level of Significance.*

Type II error (β error) The probability of failing to reject a null hypothesis when it is false and ought to be rejected.

2×2 table Any cross tabulation where there are two rows and two columns.

two-tailed test Any test of significance where no direction of difference is predicted.

two-way analysis-of-variance test A statistical procedure for determining the influence of two independent variables acting upon a dependent variable.

unbiased estimate Any statistic that has a sampling distribution whose mean is equal to the population parameter the statistic is intended to estimate; for example, the sample $\overline{X}$ is an estimate of the population μ because the sampling distribution of the mean has a mean, μ, equal to the population mean, μ; statistics lacking this feature cannot be considered unbiased estimates of their respective population parameters.

unexplained variation Amount of fluctuation in one variable that is not accounted for when another variable is used as a predictor of it; for the Pearson r, for example, R_2 is the amount of variation explained through the mutual predictability of the two variables measured, whereas $1-R_2$ is the amount of unexplained variation between the two variables.

ungrouped data Any distribution of raw scores, usually 25 or fewer, which have been unordered or ordered; no attempt is made to classify these raw scores into categories.

unimodal A frequency distribution of scores with a single mode.

unique variance The contribution of an independent variable on the dependent variable that is not shared with any other variable.

unit normal distribution See *Normal Distribution.*

unstandardized effect Usually referred to as a b-coefficient, gives the metric effect of an independent variable on the dependent variable in a regression; has many valuable qualities, such as minimizing the sum of squared errors, adjusting the scale of the independent variable to the scale of the dependent variable, converting the units of the independent variable into the units of the dependent variable, and explaining how the value of the dependent variable will change with an increase or decrease in the independent variable.

upper limits of intervals Theoretical points in intervals in a frequency distribution where the top of the interval is reached and where the largest numbers occur in the interval (e.g., 750–754 has upper limit of 754.5; 10–19 has upper limit of 19.5, and so on).

U test See *Mann-Whitney* U *Test.*

variables Any quantities or phenomena that can assume more than one value; may be dependent or independent, discrete or continuous (e.g., type of crime, recidivism rate, job satisfaction, gender, political affiliation, race/ethnicity).

variable view Particular mode for observing data that has been entered into the *SPSS* software program.

variance The mean of the sum of the squared deviation scores about the mean; if the absolute deviation scores about the mean are squared and summed, this sum is divided by *N* to yield the variance.

variance inflation factor scores (VIF) A statistical diagnostic test for collinearity in the regression model.

Wald statistic Test used in a logistic regression model to determine whether an independent variable has a significant effect on a dependent variable.

Wald-Wolfowitz runs test A nonparametric statistical procedure designed to determine whether two independent samples come from the same population according to their distribution on an ordinal-level variable; scores from both samples are placed in an array from low to high or high to low and scores from the same group are combined to create a run; the greater the number of runs, the less likely the two samples are different statistically.

weight In grand mean or mean of means computations, multiply each sample mean by the sample size, whenever sample sizes differ when averaging two or more sample means; weights may also refer to values given to responses on Likert or Thurstone scales to indicate the degree to which one agree or disagree with statements presented; also individual item weights purportedly measure the intensity with which certain attitudes exist.

Wilcoxon matched pairs-signed ranks test A nonparametric statistical test designed to determine the significance of difference between two related samples, usually between *N* matched pairs of subjects, for a variable measured according to an interval scale; has both small-sample and large-sample applications and numerical results may approximate a *Z* value which can be easily interpreted for its significance.

Wilcoxon's theta, the coefficient of differentiation, θ A two-variable nonparametric measure of association where one variable is measured according to a nominal scale and the other variable is measured according to an ordinal scale; may assume ±values; the absolute value of theta is interpreted as a symmetric PRE value.

within-group variation Amount of variation of scores in each sample from the mean of the sample; term in an analysis-of-variance summary table resulting in a sums of squares value and a mean squares value.

Yates' correction for continuity An adjustment measure that reduces the magnitude of the discrepancy between whatever is observed and what is expected according to chance in a chi-square test for two independent samples; only applicable to 2×2 tabular cases; size reduction is .5 of a difference between each observed and expected cell frequency.

Z scores Standard scores; points along the horizontal axis of the normal distribution that cut off fixed proportions of curve area; scores converted from a raw score distribution to a standard form with a mean = 0 and a standard deviation = 1.

Z test Procedure to determine the significance of difference between two sample means or between a hypothesized population mean, μ, and an observed sample mean, $\overline{X}$.

NAME INDEX

SUBJECT INDEX